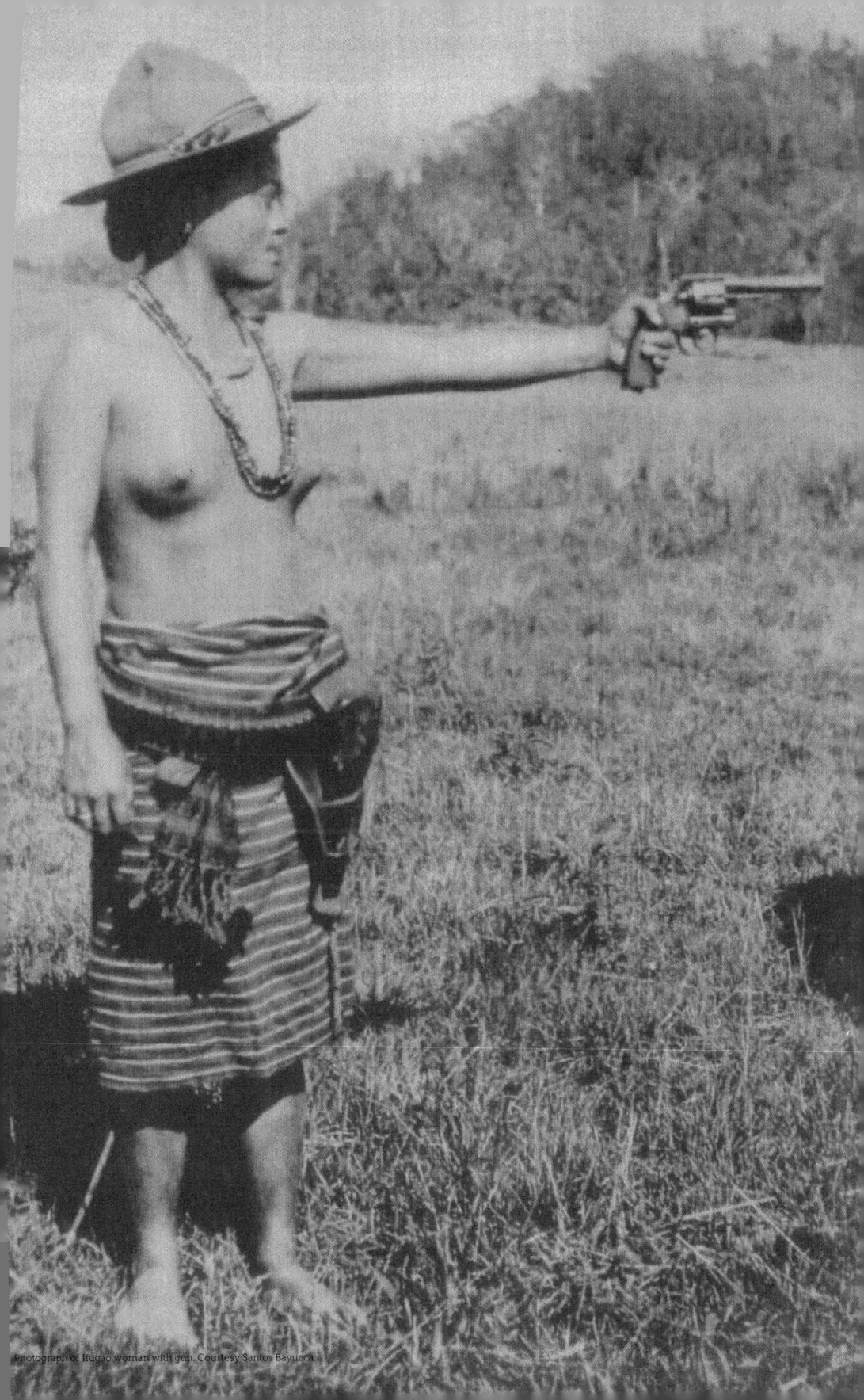
Photograph of Ifugao woman with gun. Courtesy Santos Bayucca.

TIW-TIWONG

An Uncyclopedia to Life, Living, and Art in Baguio, the Cordilleras, and Beyond

Baguio Kunst Book Publishing
Partners for Indigenous Knowledge Philippines
AX(iS) Art Project
Singapore Biennale 2013

Publishers

Baguio Kunst Book Publishing
5/F VJV Azotea Building, 108 Session Road, Baguio City, Philippines
baguiokunst@gmail.com

&

Partners for Indigineous Knowledge Philippines
54 Evangelista Street, Leonila Hill, Baguio City, Philippines
pikp.org

© 2022 AX(iS) Art Project
© 2022 Individual contributors

All artworks are © the artists unless otherwise stated.

All rights reserved. Apart from any fair dealing of the purposes of private study, research, criticism, or review, no part of this publication may be reproduced, stored in a retrieval system, or transmitted in any form or by any means, electronic, mechanical, photocopying, recording, or otherwise, without prior written consent from the Publishers.

The Publishers do not warrant or assume any legal responsibilities for the publication's contents. All opinions expressed in this book are of the authors and do not necessarily reflect those of Baguio Kunst Book Publishing or Partners for Indigineous Knowledge Philippines.

All reasonable efforts have been made to contact the rightful copyright owners. The Publishers would be grateful to hear from any copyright owner who is not acknowledged here and will undertake to rectify any errors or omissions in any subsequent reprints of the publication.

Printed and bound in China

Cover + Inside front cover
A Chronicle of the Land and People of the Cordilleras (triptych), Kawayan De Guia, mixed media, 267 x 801 x 14 cm, 2018.
Courtesy Kawayan De Guia.

Inside back cover
Dreamhouses, Kawayan De Guia, wall paper, 2009.
Courtesy Kawayan De Guia.

National Library of the Philippines
Cataloguing-in-Publication entry

Tiw-tiwong: an uncyclopedia to life, living, and art in Baguio, the Cordilleras, and beyond/edited by Kawayan de Guia [and five others].—Baguio City: Baguio Kunst Publishing, [2022], c2022.
368 p. ; 23.5 x 16 cm

ISBN: 978-621-96739-0-7 (hb/bp)

1. Baguio (Philippines) – History. 2. Cordillera Administrative Region (Philippines) – History. 3. Baguio (Philippines) – Social life and customs. 4. Cordillera Administrative Region (Philippines) – Social life and customs. 5. Baguio (Philippines) – Description and travel. 6. Cordillera Administrative Region (Philippines) – Description and travel. 7. Arts – Philippines – Baguio City. 8. Arts – Philippines – Cordillera Administrative Region I. De Guia, Kawayan. II. Cajigan, Rocky. III. Cariño, Allan. IV. Toh, Joyce. V. Perez, Padmapani. VI. Cimatu, Frank. VII. Title.

959.91122   DS689.B2   2022   P220220209

Baguio Kunst Book Publishing is an independent publishing group focused on producing and publishing art books primarily about the Cordillera Region. It is an offshoot platform of the Axis Art Project, a non-profit artist collective that programs events including festivals and community collaborations, that study access to contemporary art in communities in the Cordillera Region.

BKBP's inaugural book project is Tiw-tiwong: An Uncyclopedia to Life, Living, and Art in Baguio, the Cordilleras, and Beyond, a byproduct of the exhibition Tiw-tiwong: The Odds to Unends that was presented at the Singapore Biennale in 2013.

Partners for Indigineous Knowledge Philippines is a learning network of organizations and individuals in the Cordillera and the Philippines with initiatives promoting and strengthening indigenous knowledge. The PIKP network includes researchers, writers, educators, artists and advocates doing documentation and promotion of indigenous knowledge and stories shared.

PIKP also works in partnership with other indigenous peoples knowledge organizations, in the Philippines and internationally, for recognition and revitalization of indigenous knowledge systems and communication of the necessity, diversity and contemporary relevance of that knowledge.

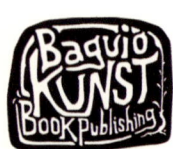 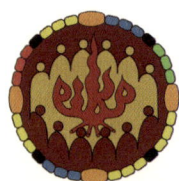 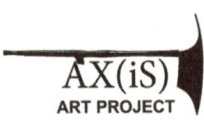 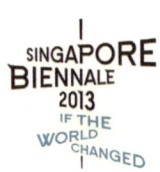 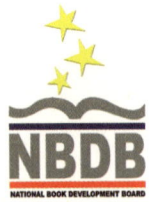

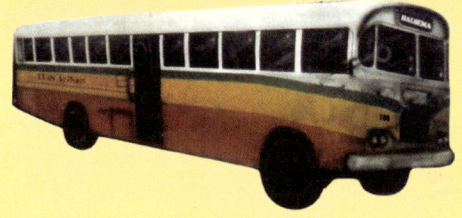

Editors
Kawayan de Guia
Rocky Acofo Cajigan
Allan Lumbaya Cariño
Joyce Toh
Padmapani Perez
Frank Cimatu

Editorial Assistants
Gail Vicente
Mariah Reodica
Solana Perez

Contributors
Adelaida Lim	(AML)
Armi Millare	(AOM)
Allan Lumbaya Cariño	(ALC)
Butch Guerrero	(JBG)
Celestina Arvisu	(CAA)
Charisse Acquisio	(CCA)
Chavy Romawac	(CVR)
Chris Mongalini	(CPM)
Deidre Mckay	(DM)
Delfin Tolentino	(DLT)
Demetrio del Rosario	(DLD)
Dumay Solinggay	(DOS)
Feliz Perez	(FLP)
Frank Cimatu	(FYC)
Gawani Domogo-Gaongen	(GAD)
Grace Subido	(GTS)
Hector Kawig	(HZK)
Janice Bagawi-Cabahit	(JBC)
Jason Taguyungon	(JT)
Jen Sabado	(JST)
John Nassr	(JN)
Joyce Toh	(JTH)
Jude Baggo	(JB)
Katrin de Guia	(KatDG)
Kawayan de Guia	(KDG)
Kelly Ramos	(KVR)
Kervin Calabias	(KC)
Kidlat Tahimik	(KT)
Krip Yuson	(KY)
Lilledeshan Bose	(LB)
Louie Stuart	(LS)
March Fianza	(MF)
Mark Walther	(MW)
Martin Masadao	(MM)
Napoleon Paris	(NEP)
Padmapani Perez	(PLP)
Penelope Domogo	(PAD)
Rachel Pitlongay	(RLP)
Rica Aquino	(RA)
Rica Concepcion	(RC)
Richard Kinnud	(RHK)
Rocky Acofo Cajigan	(RAC)
Roland Rabang	(RR)
Ruel Bimuyag	(RBB)
Sacha Weygan-Jasmin	(SKW)
Sue Llamado	(SOD)
Tad Ermitaño	(TE)
Tommy Hafalla	(TDH)

Layout and Graphics
Rocky Acofo Cajigan
Kawayan de Guia
Clang Sison
Arnel Agawin
Gari Buenavista
Faith Erasmo

Ilustrators
Illustrated Alphabets: Willy Magtibay
Abbie SJ Lara
Arnel Agawin
Benjie Mallari
Bong Sanchez
Boy Garovillo
Carlo Eustaquio
Jason Domling
Joyce Toh
JV Romawac
Kalipay de Guia
Kawayan de Guia
Leonard Aguinaldo
Louie Cordero
Mark Tandoyog
Matilda Glass
Rene Aquitania
Robert Langenegger
Roberto Villanueva
Rocky Acofo Cajigan
Shant Verdun
Sirk Deuda

Photographs/Film or Video Stills
Andy Zapata
Angel Velasco Shaw
Arnold Baladad
Ashley Jude
At Maculangan
AV and DSM Maricel Cating
Ed de Guia
Egay Navarro
Emmanuel Santos
Erlyn Alcantara
Ernesto Enrique
Faith Erasmo
Frank Callaghan
Gari Buenavista
Joyce Toh
Kawayan de Guia
Kidlat de Guia
Kidlat Tahimik
Kimberly dela Cruz
Leonida Dumsang
Mia Fokno
Midori Yamamura
Miko Lim
Nona Garcia
Ompong Tan
Roland Rabang
Roberto Yñiguez
Rica Concepcion
Shallah Montero
Tommy Hafalla
Tony Birch
Virginia de Guia
Wig Tysmans

Artists
Angel Velasco Shaw
Art Lozano
BenCab
Bumboo Villanueva
Carlo Villafuerte
Cenon Rivera
Chris Atiwon
Chris Mero
Clemente Delim
Demetrio del Rosario
Emmanuel Santos
Fang-od
Gaston Damag
Ged Alangui
Gemma Mallillin
Ifugao Woodcarvers
Iñong Geslani
Irene Bawer Bimuyag
Isabel and Alfredo Aquilizan
Jaime de Guzman
Jason "Dehon" Taguyongon
Jed Escueta
Joey Cobcobo
Jordan Mang-osan
Juan Franco Sabado
Kabunyan de Guia
Katipunan Artists
Kawayan de Guia
Kidlat de Guia
Kidlat Tahimik
Kigao Rosimo
Lady Alberto
Leonard Aguinaldo
Marion Codeo
Mark Tandoyog
Mark Zero
Marta Lovina
Mighty Bhutens, The
MM YU
Nona Garcia
Oliver Abuan
Pandy Aviado
Perry Mamaril
Pio Abad
Randy Gawwi Bulayo
Rene Aquitania
Rishab Tibon
RJ Fernandez
Roberto Villanueva
Rocky Acofo Cajigan
Roland Bay-an
Ruel Bimuyag
Santiago Bose
Santos Bayucca
Shant Verdun
Sonny Yñiguez
Sultan Mang-osan
Tioan Medrano
Tommy Hafalla
Victor Oteyza
Vincent Navarro
Willy Magtibay

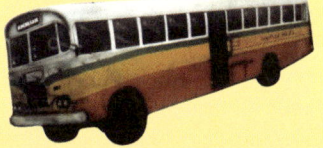

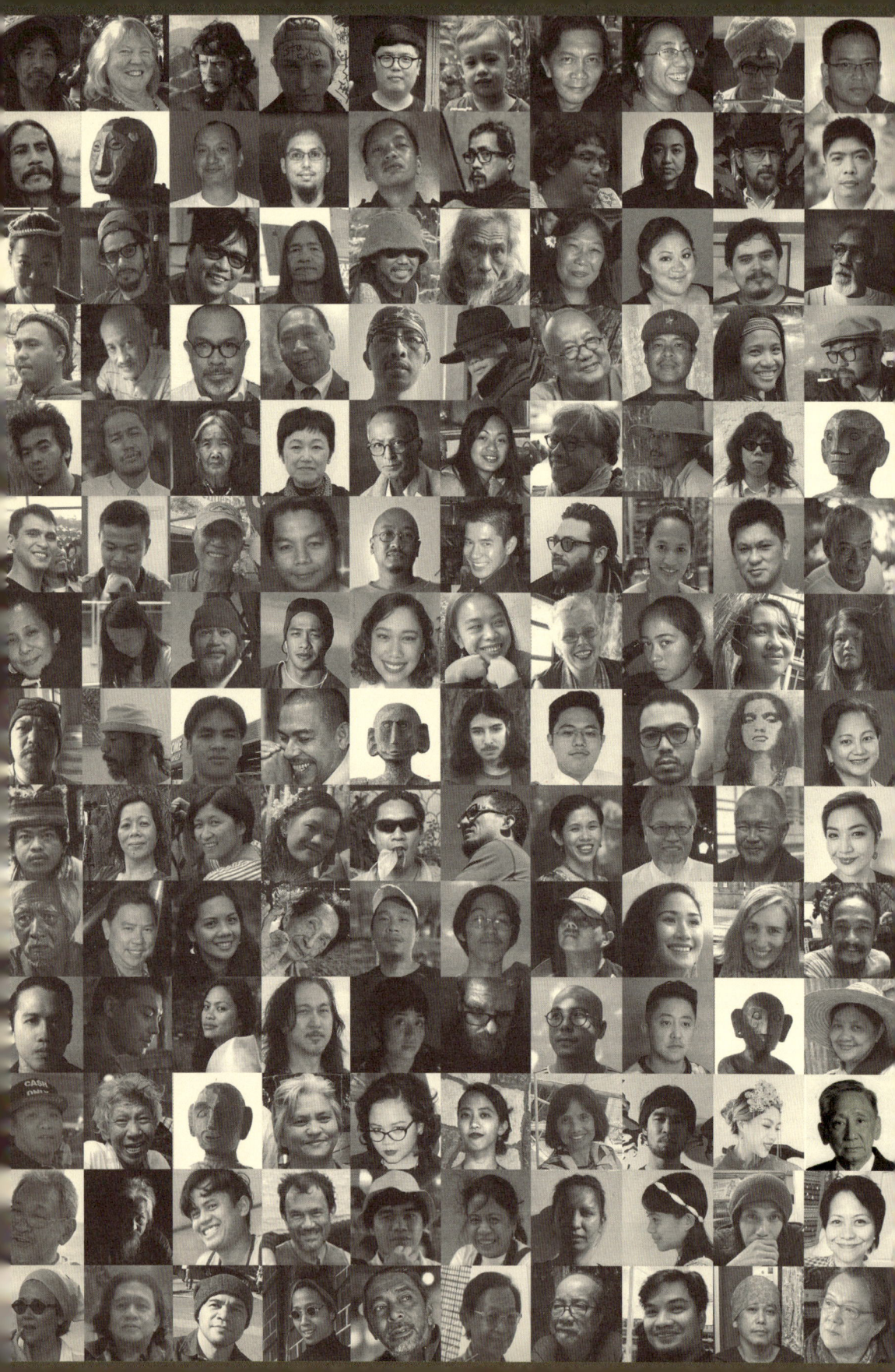

Contents

9	How to Use this Book	
11	Preface	
13	Introduction	
18	Parts of an Entry	

Featured Writings [ ]

*This list of featured writing is comprised of significant longer entries and essays. Of note, they include a number of pieces of writing responding to the works and themes of artists/projects that were featured in the Singapore Biennale 2013. For each of those artists/projects, a comment on their work is included from Kawayan de Guia, one of the 27 curators of the Biennale, in addition to a **longer essay** opening out the contexts of their work in relation to Cordillera culture.*

25	Anthropology, Questioned	Padmapani Perez
29	Architecture: Defining Cordillera Vernacular Architecture	Dumay Solinggay
37	Baguio Arts Guild, the History of	Sue LLamado
39	Baguio Arts Guild: The Future of Curating a Complicated History	Kelly Ramos
41	Baguio Arts Guild: In the Spirit of Kapwa	Katrin de Guia
46	Baguio Ghost Stories	Frank Cimatu
	BOSE, SANTIAGO:	
64	Reconciling and Resisting in the Post-Colonial Cordillera: How Santiago Bose Transmuted Baguio's Cultural Landscape into an Artistic Revolt	Lilledeshan Bose
68	The Ghost in the Studio	Kawayan de Guia
	BUL-UL:	
72	Bul-ul	Delfin Tolentino
76	Binulol	Kawayan de Guia
80	Calendar	Frank Cimatu
89	Country Music: Top Ten Country Songs in the Cordillera	Hector Kawig
	COWBOY:	
94	Mark Zero and the Benguet Cowboy	Grace Subido
97	The Diamond in the Rough Trade: Mark Zero for the Records	Kawayan de Guia
101	Dangwa: How to Sleep in a Dangwa Bus	Arnel Agawin
	DOG-EATING:	
110	Dog Eat Dog: A Fair World	Rocky Acofo Cajigan
114	Howl of the Underdog: The Katipunan Dog Meat Museum	Kawayan de Guia
	ETHNOGRAPHIC MAPPING:	
122	Ethno-ethos	Padmapani Perez
128	The Inside-outer	Kawayan de Guia
133	Folk Music: Folksingers	March Fianza
134	Food: On a Quest for Cordillera Cuisine	Chavy Romawac
	GONG:	
144	Notes on Gangsa (The First Gongmaker)	Tad Ermitaño/ Rica Concepcion
147	The Last Gongmaker	Kawayan de Guia
148	On Shaman Wars	Krip Yuson
158	Haselma Hijinks	Joyce Toh
	INDI-GENIUS:	
172	Romancing D' Ifugao Bahag	Kidlat Tahimik
177	Memories of Overdevelopment: A 33-year Film-in-Progress	Kawayan de Guia

195	Literature: Searching for Contemporary Cordillera Literature	Rachel Pitlongay
209	Mosaic: The Baguio City Mosaic	Grace Subido
216	Music: Cordillera Soundscapes	Rica Aquino
217	Music: What is Cordillera Music?	Dumay Solinggay
232	Paper: Cogon grass paper	Louie Stuart
234	Papermaking	Leonard Aguinaldo
239	Pink Ponies	Feliz Perez

PLAY:
244	Rene Aquitania at Play	Katrin de Guia
248	Shoeless Gentleman	Kawayan de Guia
249	Rene Aquitania: Walking Still	Rocky Acofo Cajigan
266	Stargazing: The Best Way to Observe Stars	John Nassr
267	Swardspeak	Kervin Calabias

SALT TRADE:
268	Weaving Cultures, Dissolving Boundaries	Dumay Solinggay
272	The Vibrant Colors of Silence	Kawayan de Guia

SOUND:
274	The Speed of Shant	Armi Olbes Millare
277	Shant Wants to be Alone	Kawayan de Guia

TATTOO:
288	Fathoming Fang-od, Tattoo Artist	Roland Rabang / Padmapani Perez
292	Hand-tapped Taboo	Kawayan de Guia

UKAY-UKAY:
296	Ukay-ukay	Martin Masadao
300	Colossal Imprints	Kawayan de Guia

309	Weaving: The Way of Weavers	Adelaida Lim
315	Woodcarving: Carving and other tools	Jason "Dehon" Taguyongon

WAITING SHEDS:
316	Waiting for Waiting Sheds	Gawani Domogo-Gaongen
319	The Mighty Bhutens	Kawayan de Guia

329	Topic Lists and Category Notes
338	References
342	Filmography

345	Afterword: Reflecting on the AXE: A Brief History of the AX(iS) Art Project

352	Appendix A: Text/Caption for the AX(iS) Exhibition at the Singapore Biennale 2013
356	Appendix B: Markets of Resistance 2014
358	Appendix C: Kabilbiligan (Re-imagined): The Restoration and Re-imagination of Santiago Bose's Mural
360	Appendix D: Forgotten Modernism
362	Appendix E: "Save the Baguio Market" Exhibition

How to Use this Book:

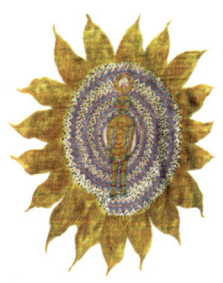

Use this book like a compass.
Know that it will get you lost.

As an Uncyclopedia, this book is a collection of stories, morsels of history, a treasury of images, and an assortment of facts that its many proponents, contributors and midwives wanted to share with you, or deemed interesting and important enough to show you. So pick an entry. Any entry. Then go and find where and how it might exist in the far reaches of the Cordillera region, in the nooks and crannies of its boomtowns and cities, or in the minds and hearts of its people.

The entries in this Uncyclopedia are arranged in alphabetical order. A topic guide has been included at the back of the book to help you plan a route through the expansive culturescapes contained in these pages. Most of the entries will suggest your next stop or other topics for you to look up. You might find yourself led from the softness of a woman's body to a mountain in a valley and back again.

This book is actually a time machine. You could get yourself thrown from a certain 20th century exhibit in Missouri, further back in time to an ancient ritual and then forward again to a videoke bar in contemporary Baguio. Due to the nature of quantum timelines and the parallel realities contained in this book, we are sorry that we cannot guarantee your return to your present or presence.

The pages of this book are best read in random order. That's because this book is a lot like real life. Real life is deceptively messy, sometimes unfathomable, and no matter how much you may want closure, there will always be loose ends. But as the wise ones say, there are no accidents and sometimes – illumination, epiphany! Ah! There is no 'whole' story, no straight-edged logic. This book is made up of hundreds of voices speaking of hundreds of memories – memories passed down from one mouth to several ears and from generation to generation, memories printed in previous books, memories of colonial impositions, memories of indigenous victories, memories that are true, memories that are imagined, memories that are sweet and precious, memories that could use a grain of salt or more. Many entries note their contributor but many others do not - being given informally or anonymously. Here you will read and hear the voices of the elders, the voices of colonialists, the voices of scholars, the voices of contemporary revisionists, the voices of romantics, the voices of critics, the voices of youth and the voices of artists. There is no one Voice of Authority here, no One Truth. It's complicated, that way.

Use this book as a guide to a frontier – for the Cordillera is still a frontier, in many ways. It's where wild, as-yet-unimagined things can happen, where anything is possible including the revitalization of old rituals and the invention of new traditions. It is a frontier too for art and intellect; pushing the boundaries of the way we see and know our world, and changing what it means to be 'cultured.'

Avoid the complications of an orgy and read this book instead. If you can imagine, Art, Politics, History, Ancient Tradition and Pop Culture make rather strange bedfellows. But here they are, getting naked and cavorting between the covers of this book. Shed your mental blinkers, throw your clothes off and jump right in!

Go on an art walk without moving your feet. This Uncyclopedia includes 13 major articles that tie up with the 2013 Singapore Biennale, featuring the work of participating artists. In these articles the artists are doorways – their work, windows – drawing your gaze to particular aspects of life in the Cordillera, inviting you to step in. Each article is accompanied by curator's notes, in which Kawayan de Guia tells the stories behind the artists and their projects.

If a rabid dog growls at you in the dark alleys of Lakandula and Katipunan, throw this book at it.

When parking or stalled on the steep inclines of the Halsema, use this book as a kalso (usually a rock, or a hefty piece of wood used as a wheel-block for added support and to keep the vehicle from rolling down of its own accord).

Use this book as a pillow when attempting to sleep on a typically bumpy Cordilleran bus ride. Let it take the hammering for your lolling head.

Shake this book at dull, inanimate friends and objects.

Use this book like the North Star.
Perhaps it will point you home. PLP.

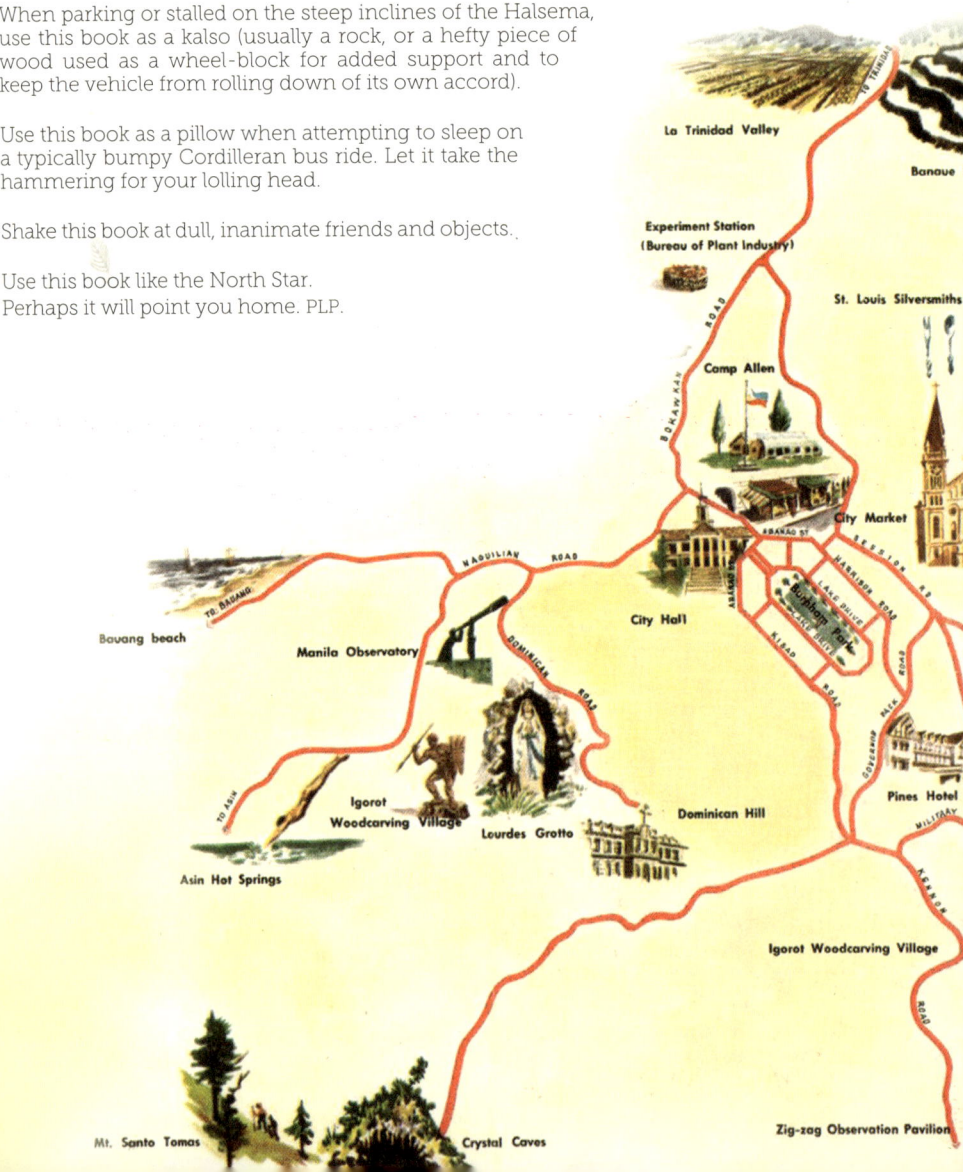

Preface

The vast histories of the Cordilleras and its indigenous peoples are located across different sites. Some have been inscribed in part in scholarly pages, yet they also thrive in the oral lore of village elders clinging to and regenerating what remains of 'living in the mountains as an indigenous.' These elders tell oral histories to upcoming generations that are transitioning or have transitioned from those oral traditions to online culture. Like the expanding roads and trails of the mountains, histories are collaged on top of each other. Through the lens and lives of a community of creatives, this book peeks through the matrices of histories untold, retold, over-told, appropriated, decorated, and left in the limestone cracks of forgotten footpaths.

As traditions melt into the archives of academic 'isms' and contemporary Igorots traverse parallel lives of being in the city and in the rice fields, or vice versa, until the order of identity-origin is a game of chicken-and-egg, the histories of the mountains scatter further from linear form. The convergence of diverse indigenous communities and migrants in the streets, universities, and cafes of Baguio City leads to a colorful diffusion of historicity. Here, writers and artists newly negotiate timeworn anthropological findings about the trails and knowledges of the indigenous north as part of their own lives and their own inheritances. In these streets, creatives are transformed into culture-makers even by unassuming gestures of documentation and interaction with indigeneity in their art-making. They muse and hack both at the policing of documentary texts by the academe and the co-opted performance of culture by a tourism industry run by capital.

In these streets, this book found its beginnings. Firstly it was in the casual confluence of artists that founded an organization called AX(iS) Art Project, intended to create more discourse and experience around *"art access for all."* AX(iS) Art Project started as an arts festival in Baguio City in 2011, and then became a travelling arts caravan along the Halsema Highway from Baguio City to Bontoc, Mountain Province in 2012, then another caravan in 2013 but extending to Hapao, Ifugao for the Singapore Biennale in 2013 (when the book began to take shape), and then partnered with Markets of Resistance in 2014 (See Appendices A and B).

At the onset of developing material in early 2013, writing organizations Ubbog Cordillera Writers and Baguio Writers Group provided the traction needed in the creation of the first texts on the 13 major art activities AX(iS) Art Project exhibited at the Singapore Biennale 2013. These projects included painting and installing artworks on 36 waiting sheds along the Halsema Highway, over 80 woodcarvers creating bu-luls in their own images, and the creation of a dog museum that refocused the discourse on dog-eating from animal rights to colonization. The rest of the text was guided by the need to write an 'uncyclopedic' response to correcting revisionist and wrongfully presented texts, interesting details about the Cordilleras, and contemporary life in the mountains. A flood of contributions came from artists, writers, cultural workers, activists, and locals of the Cordilleras and elsewhere. The editorial team's approach was to wait for the project to grow organically, allowing the communality to take over the process. The rest isn't history.

The few years following 2013 were characterized by stringent production work as the weight of the voices represented required a visual direction that meant poring over thousands and thousands of images and compositions. The editorial team would soon rediscover that the book could write itself to the end. RAC.

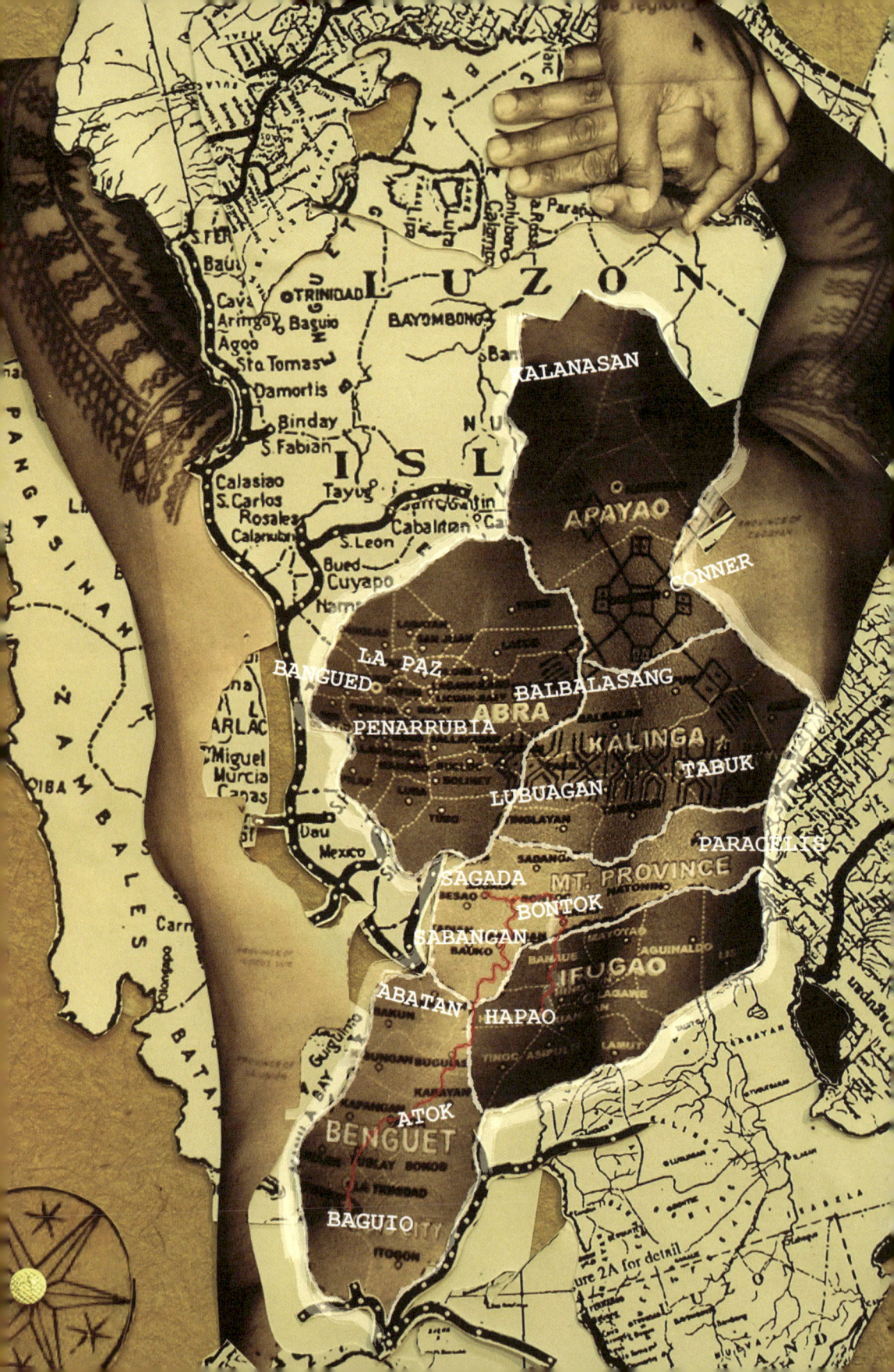

Introduction

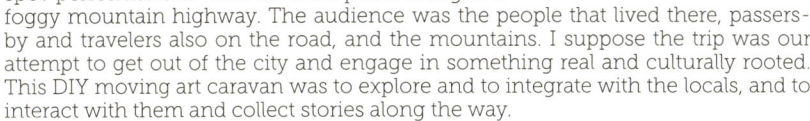

It has been several years now since the AX(iS) Art Project took a Dangwa bus ride up Halsema Highway into the hinterlands of the Cordillera. During the week-long trip, a motley crew of 50 artists created outdoor installations and held film showings, concerts and on-the-spot performances. This all took place along the foggy mountain highway. The audience was the people that lived there, passers-by and travelers also on the road, and the mountains. I suppose the trip was our attempt to get out of the city and engage in something real and culturally rooted. This DIY moving art caravan was to explore and to integrate with the locals, and to interact with them and collect stories along the way.

We didn't know it then, but that bumpy ride – AX(iS) to the End of the World – became the template for a show presented at the Singapore Biennale in 2013.

When I found myself at the negotiating table with the Singapore Art Museum (SAM) discussing bringing AX(iS) to their city, the thing I kept returning to was the worry that the exhibition could easily be misrepresented as a Cordilleran showcase like that of the infamous 1904 Saint Louis Exposition in the US. Once again the 'exotic' world of the Cordillera was going to be shipped away for display to an audience so far from its core. As part of addressing that, I struck a deal with the SAM, the consideration of which I am very thankful for, that they would help us produce a book that would focus on some of that wider context and would allow Cordilleran artists and writers to describe their world more fully.

Our objective for this book was to illuminate the broad range of knowledge that hid underneath the surface of Baguio art and would show its core muse – the indigenous culture of the Cordilleras. Artists are often misunderstood and can get caught between society's different frameworks – whether it is the social norms of different cultures, or the rigid theories of the academe, or the standard life paths laid out for people to follow. We wanted to show that artists serve as bridges between different worlds. They are like ambassadors that translate or encrypt cultural codes and can bind and bring about understanding between different parts of society. Artists may not follow structured diagrams and often intentionally break conventions but they have a vital role to play.

We decided to call this book an 'uncyclopedia' to reflect some of that attitude. We wanted to show the diversity of information and perspectives we draw from within our community. What we gathered comes from a wide array of sources and people: glimpses of the earliest recorded impressions of Spanish conquistadors; to forgotten anthropological books; to remembered myths and legends that were handed down orally from community 'dap-ays.' I think of someone like the great culture-bearer, photographer, and storyteller Tommy Hafalla who, in spite of not being a Sagada native, after decades of integrating himself with the community, now sits alongside Lakay Pulat in keeping the stories and prayers of the Sagada dap-ay alive.

Those stories and lives are things we cherish and celebrate in this book and give praise to all the beings like Tommy, Kidlat and Lopez Nauyac that have devoted themselves to stories and myths that otherwise might have been forgotten.

Many books have been written about the Cordillera but too many are also misleading, outdated, overly academic, or so specific that it is hard to form a more holistic picture. In this book we didn't want to present ourselves as experts on the field but rather people living it. We wanted to show the correlations between aspects of our lives and the subjects, objects, and history surrounding us. So, we have heavily stressed the living parts of ancient traditions and the hybrid ways people live them. That way, we hope, our picture will be approachable and not be exclusive in who can find value in it.

We dedicate our work to the Cordilleran people. It would not have seen print without the input of countless artists, activists, writers, thinkers, village folk and others who all shared in the goal of testifying about their own lives, stories, and experiences of this place.

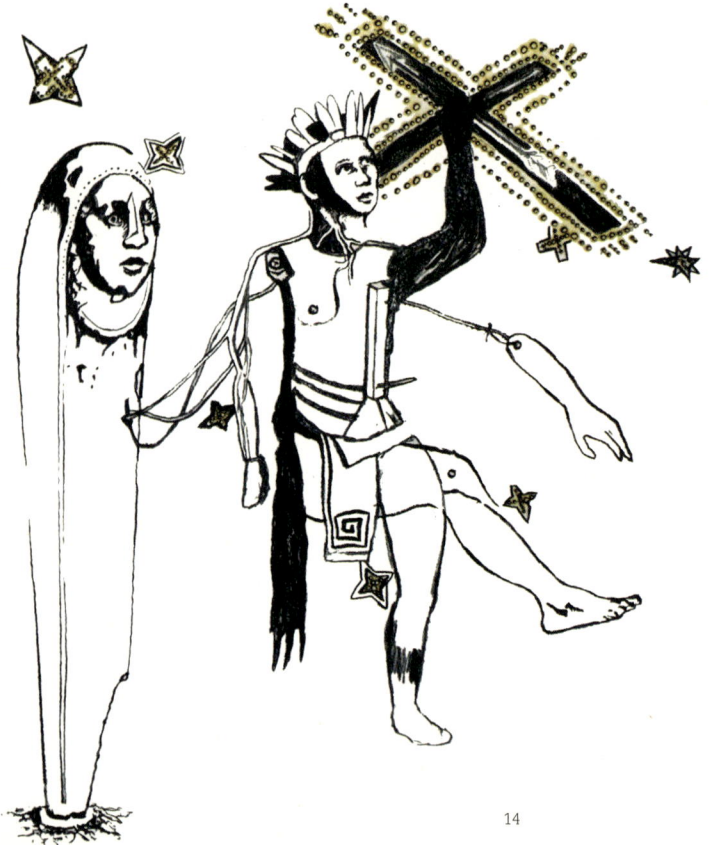

One thing I think is important in this age of great change is that those stories don't die and that the ways of our ancestors are passed on to future generations. This book is inspired by the idea of 'Tiw-tiwong,' an Ifugao term for 'a spirit that has gone astray but is destined to come home.'

Oh Apo Kabunyan! May you guide the great spirit of our times that has gotten drunk on material things, money and progress! May you guide and enlighten it on the narrow trails back to the village and, in our darkest hour, illuminate the path on which a more meaningful way of living is carved out, one with respect for the great mountains, skies and waters of the Cordillera. KDG

If the World Changed. Such was the title of the Singapore Biennale 2013, and indeed, it was a proposition, a puzzle and a paradox that reverberated on several levels as the biennale unfolded.

In conceptualising the Singapore Biennale 2013 (SB2013), the curators wanted to grapple with and understand the Southeast Asian region and its art, in ways that went beyond the customary means of curating exhibitions that take place within a museum. Singapore Art Museum (SAM) focuses on the contemporary art of Southeast Asia, and as the organiser of SB2013, we wanted to explore new ways of thinking about the region.

Several curators from the region were invited, many of whom were artists as well. In total, there were 27 curators, with four based in the Philippines, including Charlie Co (Bacolod), Abraham Garcia Jr. (Mindanao) and Claro Ramirez (Manila). Kawayan de Guia, who is based in Baguio, was however extremely reluctant to take on the role. I travelled up to meet with him, and one late night, he simply asked, "What do you want from me? What do you want from us?"

Posed as a question, it was really a dare – and I did not have an answer. Consequently, Kawayan invited me to join the road trip he was organising, *AX(iS): To the End of the World* in 2012. To begin to grasp what Baguio and the Cordilleras are, was to traverse the terrain and feel the land and life of the mountains and its peoples – complex, complicated, contradictory, and beautifully so.

Yet even though we travelled to the 'End of the World' on the Halsema Highway, getting the Cordilleras to Singapore was another challenge altogether. How were we to 'take' and present Baguio and the Cordilleran mountains in a city-state like Singapore, in a manner that retained its spirit and made sense to an urban audience? There was a danger that shorn of its locale and roots, it would appear as exotic spectacle – the possibility that 86 bul-lus would look at odds and jarring in a contemporary art museum space haunted us. Other risks reared, such as how a presentation on dog-eating culture might offend the sensibilities of animal rights activists.

In the end, Kawayan became the bridge that brought Baguio and the mountains into our museum, and I bridged from our Little Red Dot of a city. If there were worries that the audience could not make sense of the project, *AX(iS): The Odds to Unends*, we got an answer when visitors said they could feel the spirit of the place within those gallery walls. And those bul-luls? They all looked quite at home.

And far from an 'end', even as it ended, the exhibition in SB2013 became the seed for another beginning: that of this book. This book is the culmination of the tireless efforts of many – Kawayan, Rocky, Padma, Frank – and several other collaborators and contributors. For myself, it has been a sheer joy and privilege to have participated in this project and publication, and to help realise it to fruition. I am grateful and touched by the generosity of spirit and sharing of all the immense knowledge, and to feel the deep love that Baguio and the mountains engenders.

At the time of writing, we are approaching the Singapore Biennale 2019. Yet holding the proof of this book, it is AX(iS), Baguio and the Cordilleras instantly, all over again: it is Shant standing stones upright along Chico river; it is the smell of chicken poop fertilizer in the bracing mountain air; it is the rhythms of a drum circle in the wee hours of the night; it is the smoky saltiness of etag that Chavy has cooked into the rice; it is curling up into odd, twisted shapes to sleep on the Dangwa bus; it is Kawayan picking up folks again in Betty, his truck; it is warming up to mystery bodies in the tent each freezing night – it is 35°C in Singapore and I'm shivering in the mountains once more.

Both Kawayan and I didn't quite know the route when we started on SB2013, and so we teased and tested out steps at each turn. Along the way, I had to unlearn much, to learn more.

I went up the mountains, and came down a different person – a world had changed for me. JT.

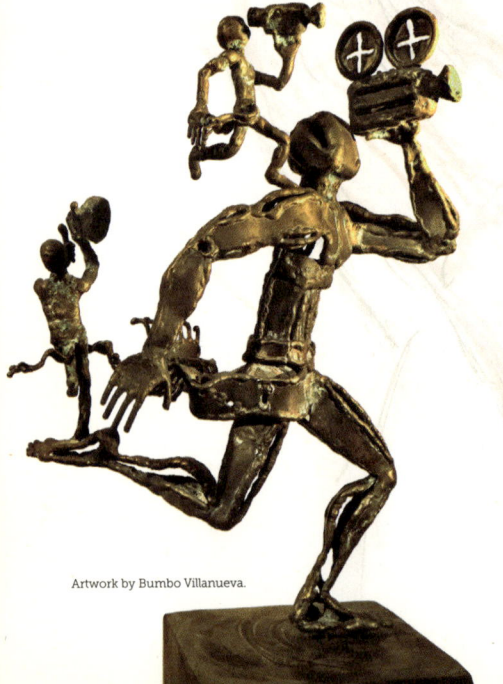

Artwork by Bumbo Villanueva.

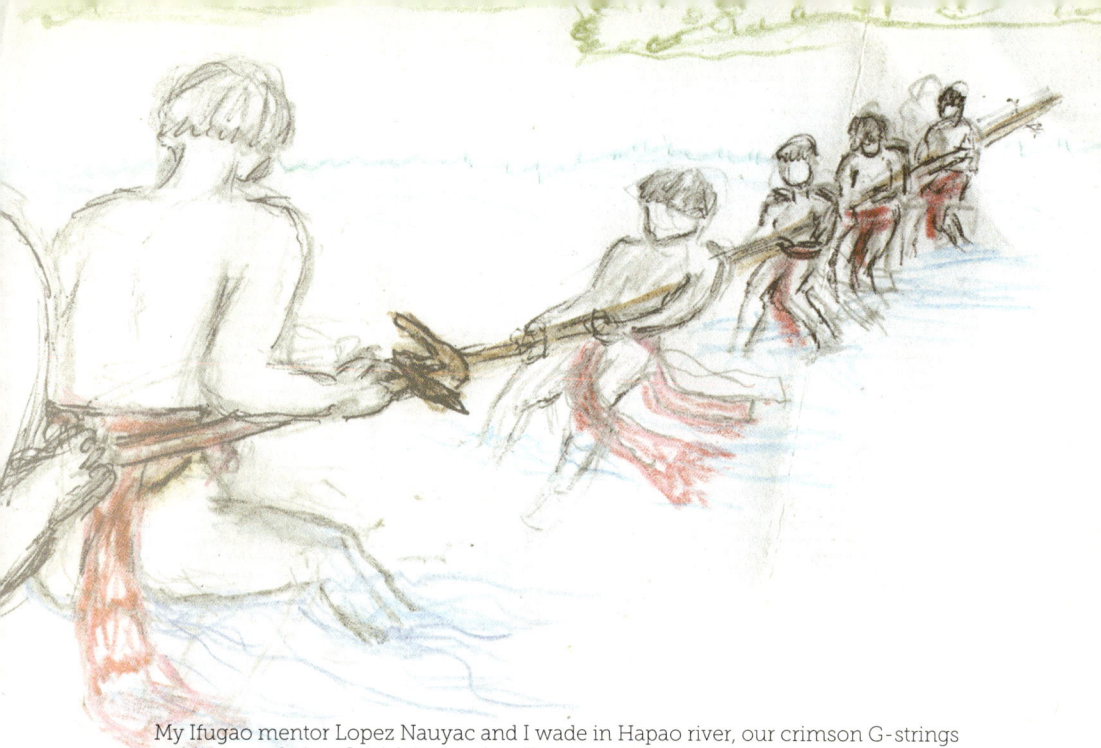

My Ifugao mentor Lopez Nauyac and I wade in Hapao river, our crimson G-strings swirling gently in a fluvial dance. Apo Kabunyan! Thanks for those auspicious rains last week, giving us the gentle currents that now host the Pun-nok tug-of-war games.

Its more fun – Pun-nok, our post-harvest thanksgiving... We're all children, splashing happiness – as we tug fiercely for victory. Our wet and wild laughter drowns the roar of the river – re-convening the oneness-with-nature of our forefathers.

Wow! 17 years since Na-uyac's revival of this Ifugao ritual in 1998. UNESCO just declared our indigenous water olympics as an Intangible Cultural Heritage in its world preservation list. Adiwo!

Salamat! Apo Kabunyan for letting this Uncyclopedia see print – opening overlooked archives that dramatize why our ancestral cultures must never become jurassic in the shadow of a gobbling global greed;

Ay Apo Kabunyan! Bless this artistic effort that dares to bookbind crisp glimpses into our pre-colonial worldviews – reflected in orally-transmitted legends, in the dog-eating memories of the Saint Louis Expo balikbayans, in the Bag-lish bar-talk of bartok millenials, in Benguet fashionistas sporting cowboy-boots. And yes, in the naughty man-in-the-barrel mocking our macho colonizers;

Let the Nauyac's hybrid-English, re-launch into orbit the dignity and genius of the indigenous – reverberating in his cosmic mispronunciations: "To our indi-genius culture – a toast of Baya rice wine!! May it survive beyond our grandkids." Adiwo!!!!

Yet another toast of baya! – that the untrivial trivia clustered in these pages lives on – to be digested by the great-grandchildren of our grandkids. Adiwo!!!

Sugod mga Kapatid! Pa-tungo sa LIWANAG ng Indio-Genius natin!

Kidlat Tahimik

National Artist from the Cordilleras
Green-Card holder (for green terraces of Hapao)
Kultur Warrior

Parts of an Entry

ENTRY TITLE   LANGUAGE OF ORIGIN   THE SAME WORD IN ANOTHER LANGUAGE

DEFINITION 1

Ab-abiik *(KAN)* also **Linawa** *(IFU)*, **Ali'chugwa** *(KAL)*, **Leng-ag** *(BON)*. (1) The soul that is conceived at the same time as the body and lives after death. It is always with you but can sometimes travel without you. Every living thing has an ab-abiik. TDH.

DEFINITION 2

MAIN BODY OF ENTRY

INITIALS OF CONTRIBUTOR

(2) The ab-abiik is the immaterial but animate part of you; it is like a soul but more at home in the world of the spirits. You must call to it before leaving a place, especially one you've visited for the first time. You should call yours and those of your companions, especially those of children. Say, *"Maykan, maykan [insert name], awan ti mabatbati."* If you forget to call it when you go home, it might enjoy playing with other souls, and you could feel restless until it comes back to you. Children whose ab-abiik have been left behind are not themselves until the ab-abiik comes back. They become irritable, cranky, and even sickly and nothing can soothe them. As remedy, you must bring the child back to the place you last visited and call to her ab-abiik. If they are too ill to travel, bring the clothes they were wearing while there. Wave the clothes around the place while calling out, *"Maykan, maykan; awan ti mabatbati,"* and the child will soon be alright. JBC.

MAIN BODY OF ENTRY

INITIALS OF CONTRIBUTOR

See also: Ayag; Ayak; Hidit; Kaduduwa; Padpadaya; Pasang; Pattaliat; Ulliyan.

RELATED ENTRIES

Language/
Language Place/People of Origin Abbreviations

BON	Bontok
FIL	Filipino
GAD	Gaddang
IBA	Ibaloi
IFU	Ifugao
IKA	Ikalahan
ILO	Iloko
ILN	Ilongot
ISN	Isneg
KAL	Kalinga
KYA	Kalanguya
SPA	Spanish
ITN	Itneg (exonym Tingguian or Tinguian)
ITW	Itawit
Lit.	Literally

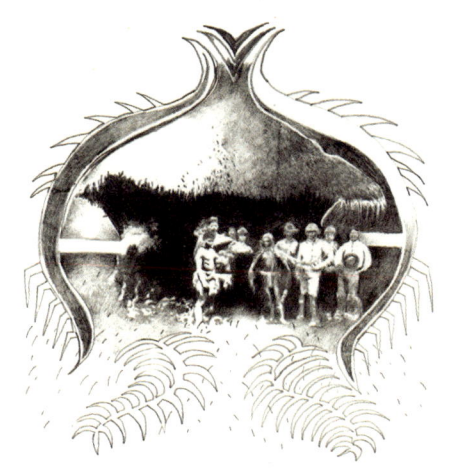

Ab-abiik *(KAN)* also **Linawa** *(IFU)*, **Ali'chugwa** *(KAL)*, **Leng-ag** *(BON)*. (1) The soul that is conceived at the same time as the body and lives after death. It is always with you but can sometimes travel without you. Every living thing has an ab-abiik. TDH.
(2) The ab-abiik is the immaterial but animate part of you; it is like a soul but more at home in the world of the spirits. You must call to it before leaving a place, especially one you've visited for the first time. You should call yours and those of your companions, especially those of children. Say, *"Maykan, maykan [insert name], awan ti mabatbati."* If you forget to call it when you go home, it might enjoy playing with other souls, and you could feel restless until it comes back to you. Children whose ab-abiik have been left behind are not themselves until the ab-abiik comes back. They become irritable, cranky, and even sickly and nothing can soothe them. As remedy, you must bring the child back to the place you last visited and call to her ab-abiik. If they are too ill to travel, bring the clothes they were wearing while there. Wave the clothes around the place while calling out, *"Maykan, maykan; awan ti mabatbati,"* and the child will soon be alright. JBC.
See also: Ayag; Ayak; Hidit; Kaduduwa; Padpadaya; Pasang; Pattaliat; Tiw-tiwong; Ulliyan.

Ab-abo *(ISN)*. Dust that covers locusts.

Aban *(KAN)* also **Uban** or **Eban.** Cloth sheet or blanket used to carry a baby. With the baby held close to the body, one end is draped over the caregiver's shoulder and the other end is passed under the caregiver's other arm. The ends are then knotted together to secure the baby to the carrier's body. Alternatively, the aban can be tied in front when one prefers to carry the baby safely on one's back. To ubba is to carry with an aban. JBC.

Abang ni keshel *(IBA)*. Lit. Wrestling with the pigs. This is a featured highlight of a peshit. Each participating village releases one pig into a fenced arena. All pigs, including one extra pig, must be black. Representatives from each village wrestle and try to capture them. Others may come and assist in tying. The pigs are all killed by owik on the main ground of the feast and then moved to areas designated for each village where they are butchered and cooked. The extra pig is taken to the host. After dancing and eating, each village distributes watwat from the pig they caught and the shares of meat are brought to people back home who weren't able to attend the peshit. (Ballard et al. 2011, 20) SKW.
See also: Bingit; Owik; Peshit; Watwat.

Abeb *(KAN)*. The May bug (cockchafer in Europe). It is important in Sagada, Mountain Province because its presence or appearance signals the time for certain rituals. TDH.

Abeggan *(KAN)*. Collective residence for unmarried girls that is usually the house of a widow. Men from the dap-ay often come to woo their chosen muse at the abeggan. DOS.
See also: Bale; Dap-ay.

Abig *(KAN)*. *"Superstitious belief (i.e. not part of the main religious dogma or ritual requirements). Men-abig or abigen means to refuse on such grounds. Ma-amma-abig means being careful in observing superstition."* (Scott, 2011, p. 148).

Abistong *(KAN)* also **Piwpiw** *(KAN)*, **Olifew** *(KAL)*, **Olibew** *(KAN/KAL)*, **Bikkong** *(IFU)*. (1) Cordilleran mouth-harp. Usually made of bamboo, it has a tongue or reed in the middle that is about two inches long. The length depends on the mouth of the maker who makes his lips the model for the instrument. The abistong is often played while on the way to the fields, to make one's presence felt. The sound produced is like a gushing wind that can be blown and heard from a distance. DOS.
(2) *(IFU)* The lover's harp. A flat thin metal plaque which can vibrate when held on the lips and and struck with one hand. In the evenings, the Ifugao boys would use the bihong to whisper their melodious sweet nothings. FYC.
See also: Dew-dew-as; Gangsa; Kuliteng; Music.

Abkil *(BON)*. Armlet made of boar's teeth held together by a woven rattan band. In Kankanaey, a wild boar tusk is known as sawing. DLD.
See also: Tangkil.

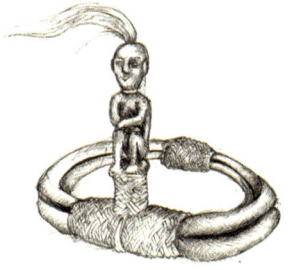

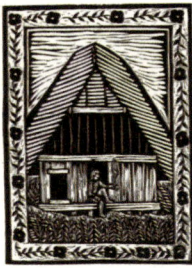

Abong *(KAN)* also **Ab-afong** *(BON).*
(1) Small house.
(2) The title of a charming and award-winning movie by Japanese Koji Imaizumi. The story revolves around Lamot, a Japanese-Filipino also known as Hapon (played by Joel Torre) from Lubong Norte (Northern World, a fictitious place but set in Hapao, Ifugao), who is a jeepney driver in Baguio. His wife went abroad and Lamot was left to take care of their three children in Lubong Norte. In the end, the mother returns but it is Lamot's turn to go to Japan to work. FYC.
See also: Allang; Bale; Banaue: Stairway to the Sky; Big Bird Cage; Igorota; Irisan (the movie); Kung Mangarap Ka't Magising; Vacacionista.

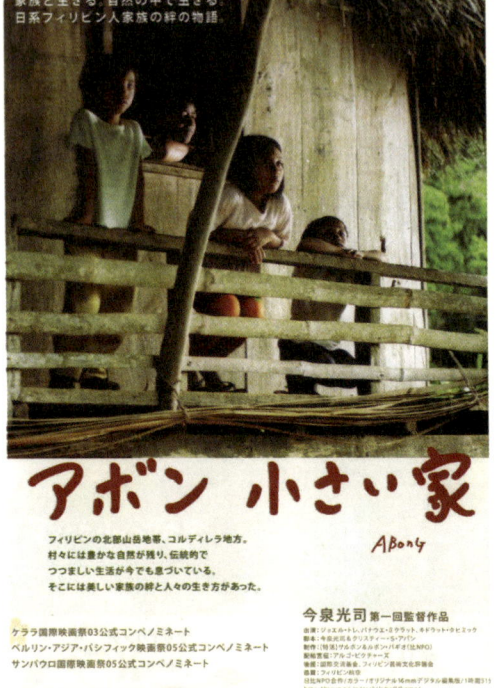

Poster of the movie *Abong*, 2002. Courtesy Koji Imaizumi.

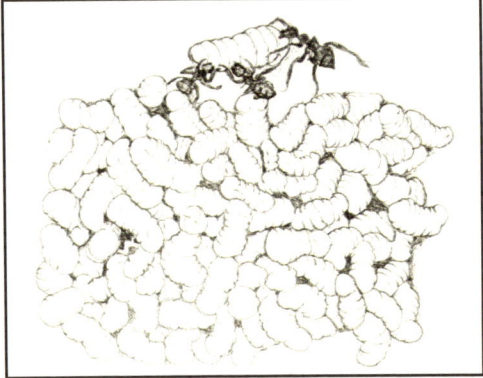

Abu-os *(ILO/ITN).* Red ants' eggs; considered a delicacy. The eggs are sautéed with garlic or cooked in adobo, especially in Abra. Red ants usually thrive in trees like sua (pomelo), longboy (black plum), and guyabano (soursop). Abu-os hunters go to the forest with their sibbul, a reed long enough to reach the nest of the ants hanging from the twigs. When the nest is successfully harvested, it is placed in a basket or bucket and left alone for an hour to let the mature ants escape. The eggs and larvae are then gathered into containers ready to be sold or cooked. First time eaters of the delicacy may experience heart palpitations, shortness of breath, and itchiness on the skin. DOS.
See also: Babate; Niyek.

Abungol *(ISN).* A traditional delicacy of river crabs wrapped in banana leaves combined with grated coconut and left to ferment for two days. When it is ready, it is cooked in a pot with salt and chili to taste. Salt is added with care because too much salt makes this mixture undesirably bitter. When cooked, the dish can keep for up to a week. The dry fermented mixture is usually added like seasoning to leaves, gabi (taro) stems and river shells. GAD.
See also: Aw-aw; Bakkay; Safeng.

Adivay *(IBA).* (1) Fellowship, communion, visiting for consolation, shared grief, or reunion.
(2) The name for the pan-Benguet festival that began in the early 21st century and is held annually in La Trinidad.

Adoyon *(IBA)* also **Obowan.** System of mutual and reciprocal work. A farm family obtains manpower by asking for help from their neighbors to work together on a project, such as planting or harvesting. In return, the farm family is obliged to reciprocate with similar work for their neighbors. Such work may take the form of repairing irrigation canals or building a house. (Ballard et al. 2011, 24) SKW.
See also: Baddang; Ob-obbo; Tambo; Tinawon; To-ned.

Afable, Cecile. (1918 – 2012). Many will remember her as "Auntie Cecile," and the mention of her name would call up phrases such as: stalwart leader, fearless doyenne of local media, grand dame of writers. She was also mischievous, trailblazing, a firebrand, and a Baguio witch. But, above all things, she was a matriarch of Baguio as a teacher and a writer. She and her siblings Sinai and Oseo Cariño Hamada founded the Baguio Midland Courier shortly after World War II. Her column, "In and Out of Baguio" ran from 1946 until her death in June 2012. Legend has it that she grew up reading Shakespeare on the back of a carabao. In her later years her already formidable presence was accented with her love

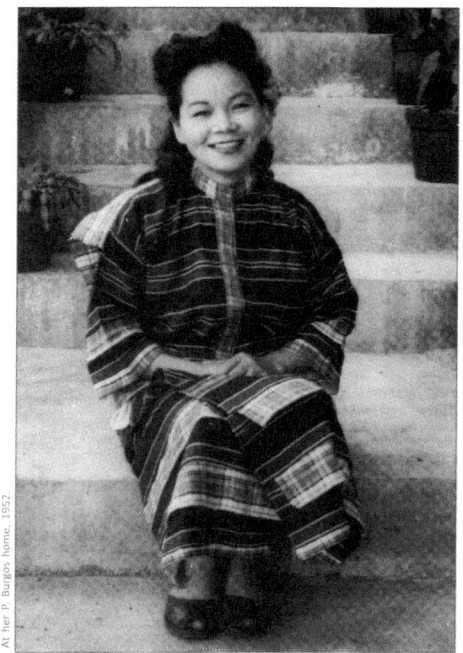

Portrait of *Cecile Afable* in her P. Burgos home, 1952. Courtesy the Afable Family.

of fancy hats, bright colored dresses, stiletto heels and fishnet stockings. At cañaos everyone knew to make sure that as an Ibaloy elder she be served whisky and choice pieces of demshang.
See also: Ato Bookshop and Gallery; Three Witches.

Affrom *(KAL)*. Lit. *"Guess what it is?"* Start of a traditional Kalinga riddle.
See also: Ala.

AFRTN. *"The radio station AFRTN [Armed Forces Radio and Television Network] introduced me to rock and roll when I first heard the Beatles.*

It was necessary to visit the recreational facility in those days. To be seen playing golf or drinking an expensive drink in the U.S. facility was a measure of class and success.

Before my high school graduation, my romance with Camp John Hay came to an abrupt end. My friends and I were harassed and verbally abused by American MP's and guard dogs for having our car fog lights on as we approached the sentry post. This occasion indelibly brought home the fact that to the Americans, we were outsiders, we didn't count.

That no matter how many American appliances we owned, or how well we could mimic the songs broadcast from American airwaves or how closely we mimicked the postures and phrases of the Americans who used our town to keep the effects of living in the Philippines at bay, we would only be little brown interlopers who would never be anything more than second-class." (Bose, Baguio Graffiti).
See also: DZWT; Hay, John Milton; John Hay, Camp; Kung Mangarap Ka't Magising; Nikimalika; Pre-white; Squaw Men; Thomasites; Tribes.

Ag-aghom *(BON)*. Series of activities for thanksgiving done after the rice harvest, usually in September-October. In Guinaang, Bontoc, a designated household would make tufu and pinikpikan and invite relatives to eat supper there. The tufu is served as rice, although regular rice is also available for those who prefer it. The next day, another family acts as the host and serves the same menu. PAD.
See also: Pinikpikan; Tufu.

Agakong *(KAN)*. Small yellow flower that is included in rituals such as the daw-es. TDH.
See also: Daw-es.

Agay-o *(KAN)* also **Adsulit** *(BON)*. Lit. Long time ago. In Kankanaey, the term is especially used in chanting. DOS.
See also: Sinan-adom.

Agba *(IFU)*. Magic stick used for the purpose of determining the cause of an illness, or the answering of other difficult questions. The stick is believed to grow longer when it desires to make an affirmation. It is similar to the magic stick of the mall security guards. FYC.

Agbaxan *(ISN)*. That part of the waist around which the wanes is wound.
See also: Wanes.

Aggabau *(GAD)*. Lit. Onlooker-from-Above. The chief of the ghost-deities who lives in the clouds

Aginaya, Panginomnomatn ki *(IFU)*. Lit. In Memory of Aginaya. A long time ago in Ifugao, there was a very industrious woman named Aginaya. She had many children and grandchildren who were as industrious as her. Every day the men built terraces so the women could plant rice. When not planting rice, they planted camote.

When their rice and their camote were all planted they all had to wait. But, since they did not like passing their time for nothing, they carved wood into bululs: human-like figures into which sicknesses are sent during healing rituals. They also carved kitchen utensils.

One day a visitor from the lowlands came to exchange his salt for some highland rice. He saw the kitchen utensils and was amazed. He thought they would be good to trade in the lowlands. *"Agaramid kayo ti adu ta kayat ti Instik! [Make more as I'm sure the Chinese would love them]."*

True to the Ilocano man's word, people not only got interested in the Ifugao's kitchen utensils but also in their bulul. Even white men asked for the old bululs. They wondered how these white men could be so interested with what they threw their sicknesses into. But, since there was good trade, Aginaya's family went on carving. Even their neighbors and neighboring communitites were carving for the Ilocanos and the white men.

When Aginaya grew old and sickly she dreamt that her head was covered with many trees. Her hair had become trees of different kinds. She was also becoming bald. The trees were disappearing right off her very head.

In the morning Aginaya couldn't stop thinking about her dream. She told her husband and her husband invited some elders. The elders said they needed to butcher three chickens and pray to the gods. They took chickens from Aginaya's farm and prayed. During their ritual the gods came down from the skyworld and told them that they were losing their trees. *"If you do not plant, you too will perish,"* said Kabigat, the god of lightning.

"Yes, I thought of that." said Aginaya in a low voice. The elders talked among themselves and decided that they should teach their children and their grandchildren's children to plant many trees. They had to do this so that their trees would not perish. If there weren't enough trees there would be nothing to hold the water that fed their rice fields. If their rice fields dried out there would be no rice to harvest. If there were to be no rice, there would be nothing to eat and everybody would go hungry.

From then on the people decided to plant trees as much as possible. Even now, Aginaya's descendants continue their great great grandmother's advocacy for planting trees. DOS.
See also: Ampasit; Bul-ul; Camote; Doligen ed Kabunian, Si; Madmad; Pumapa-ot; Three Orphans of Sagada, The; Tree Cutting.

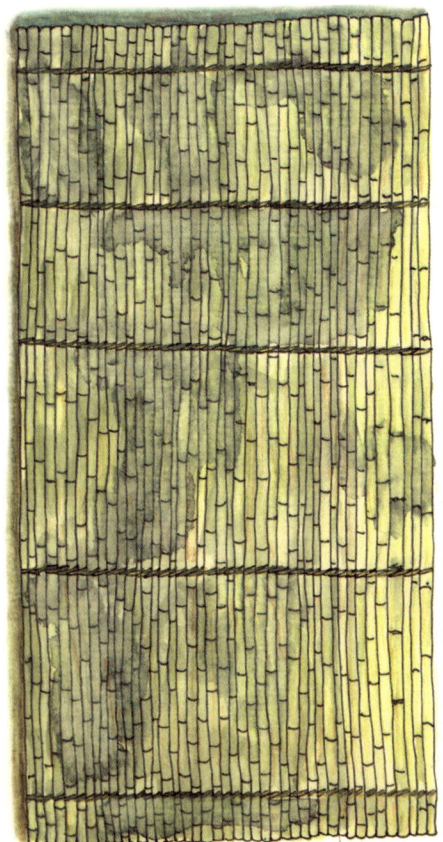

Agkufangfang *(BON)*. White camote. Other Bontoc terms regarding camote are Faangan (camote patch), Kinafa (roasted camote), Lokmog (boiled camote), Patokhi or Sosog (red camote), Tokhi (raw camote) and Finaliling (camote bed).
See also: Camote; Faliling.

Agpay *(IBA)*. A mat of runo or bunch of these sticks spread on the ground upon which ritual animals are butchered and offered for the spirits.
See also: Bangkilay; Runo.

Agrix. In the late 1970s, Agrix was a business conglomerate headed by fertilizer manufacturer Sofronio Blando. It was involved in movies and real estate. Then, a few years later, Agrix was revealed to be the first large-scale pyramid scam in the country. Its legacy in Baguio City is the Agrix Building at the corner of Magsaysay Ave. and Bokawkan Rd. The building is now one of the strongest enduring bastions of country-and-western music in the city. Bar fights are frequent there; that's why the police decided to locate their substation a few meters from Agrix. FYC.
See also: Batawa.

Agudong id Manitong *(KAN/BON)*. Lit. Snails in Manitong. A children's song. Sung to the tune of the American song "Pearly Shells," this song is about agudung (edible snails) in Manitong (a place in Sagada) that kudong (crawl) towards a pusong (pool of water). These river snails are pumaypaytok (leaping) to Bontoc (a place downstream). The song is one of the first songs a Kankanaey or Bontoc child learns. It is a no-fail performance when the child is asked by parents, relatives or visitors to sing a song for the adults' entertainment. GAD.
See also: Atubang; Bisukol; Falokag; Golden Kuhol; Ketan; Lisdeg.

Ahu *(KAL/KAN)* also **Asu** *(ILO)*. Dog. Your seeing-eye dog for supernatural beings. Kabunian's loyal friend.
See also: Kabunian; Kimat.

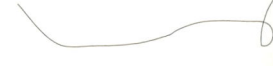

Akipur *(KAL)*. Beaded headdress for women.
See also: Apang; Bayoyok; Duwao; Kulatod; Panglao.

Ala *(KAL)*. Eyes. Answer to the riddle: *"Affrom, Fartog kon Tomchon iffon china kotton [Affrom, There is no distance my Thompson gun cannot reach]."*
See also: Affrom.

Alan *(ITN)*. Deformed spirits with wings, their toes pointing backward. They take a drop of menstrual blood, miscarried fetuses, and afterbirth to raise children of their own. Alan-alan is the Kalinga term for spirits of enemies killed by warriors. FYC.
See also: Bengao; Darupaypay; Ibwa; Nginin; Paniaw; Pasang; Tinguian Spirits.

Alingasiu *(BON)* also **Angep** *(ILO/KAN)*. Fog.

Alipatpat *(ISN)* also **Kikitap** *(KAL)*, **Kulintaba** *(KAN)*, **Kemkemti** *(KAN)*, **Kulkuldiyat** *(KAN)*. Firefly or glowworm.

Aliwan *(KAN/BON)*. The painful contraction of the uterus just after childbirth, to release blood clots and the placenta. It can even be more painful than labor pains. PAD.
See also: Etab.

Allang *(BON)* also **Alang** *(ISN)*, **Agamang** *(KAN/KAL)*, **Kallangan** *(KAN)*. Rice granary. Different from the traditional residential hut. It is a smaller structure built near the house or in clusters at the borders of communities and near the rice fields. In earlier times owning an allang filled with stored rice meant food security.

Now that commercial rice is available and houses are large enough to store sacks of rice inside, the allang is a rarity, though it can still be seen in some areas of Mountain Province and Kalinga. GAD.
See also: Abong, Architecture, Bale.

Amazing Grace. This popular song written by an English enslaver is a staple in Catholic and Anglican Cordilleran funerals. It is taboo to openly sing this song in public except at funerals.
See also: Badio; Batawa; Baya-o; Cherwasay; Cowboy; Dujung; Lover's Moon; Nan Layad Nan Likhatan; Waynasdi.

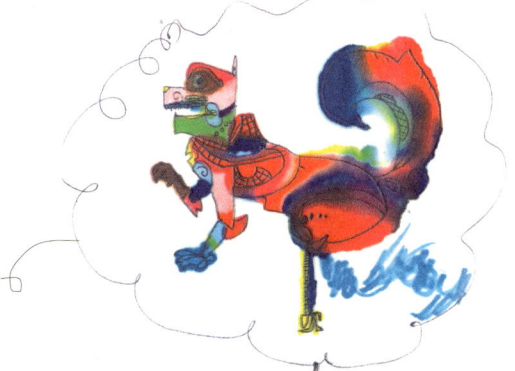

Ambaboy *(KAN)*. Name of the pinading, the serpent that guards the sacred tree of Demang, Sagada, Mountain Province.
See also: Demang; Papattay; Tree Cutting; Tuling.

Ambit, Ambot, Amboy. The most common nicknames of children in Benguet. When you meet a boy you don't know, it is safe to call him Ambot or if a girl, Ambit. It is a Cordilleran practice for parents to give nicknames to their children after the name of their dead ancestors based on what the child looks like or his or her characteristics. For those parents who can't decide, they could call their child Ambit or Ambot in the meantime. Amboy became a popular alternative for Ambot as it also means "American boy." HZK.
See also: Salabao.

Ambiyongan *(IBA)*. Greenish type of beetle.

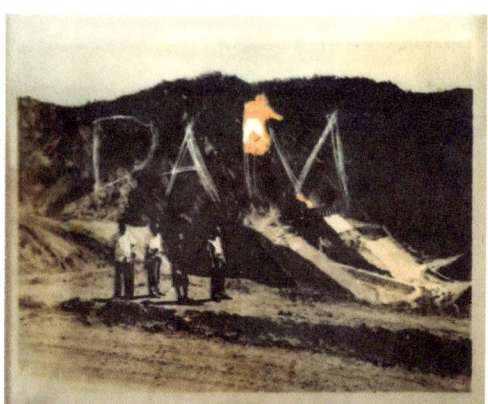

Photograph of the *Ambuklao Dam*, c. 1950s. Courtesy Virginia de Guia.

Ambuklao Dam. *"This latest addition to the wonderland beyond Baguio can be reached from the city down a 36-kilometer scenic highway. Now known as the Philippines' largest hydroelectric project, Ambuklao Dam promises to be one of the most attractive resorts in the Orient when its tourist possibilities shall have been fully exploited. Binga hydroelectric project, the second largest in the Philippines, is now under construction."* (Baguio City Police Department 1959).

It never became the tourist spot it wanted to be. Siltation choked Ambuklao and Binga and billions of pesos were used and wasted to make them operational. San Roque Dam downriver is now the biggest hydroelectric dam in Southeast Asia. Ibaloi families were displaced by the construction of Ambuklao and San Roque. FYC.
See also: Chico.

Ames *(KAN)* also **Emes** *(BON/KAN)*. Lit. Bath. **Men-ames** *(KAN)* or **Men-emes** or **Ummes** *(BON)*. Lit. To bathe. Before the introduction of pipes to houses, this was done either in the stream, river or outside of the house. Before the introduction of soap, one would use the igod to remove dirt and dead skins cells. Ames is also normally used to refer to cleansing when going to a water source during a ritual. Then, everyone washes away the bad luck of the year. Whenever this is done, the people say, *"Let it flow to the lowlands."* PAD/TDH.

See also: Igod.

Amkis *(KAN)*. Similar to a habanero or scotch bonnet chili. Also known as bituka (intestines) because of its shape. When you are drinking gin in Benguet and they say their appetizer is bituka, they don't mean intestines but the orange amkis. FYC.

See also: Mandesangat; Sichot.

Amolo *(KAN)*. A ritual performed before a marriage between persons who trace their roots to separate villages or hometowns. TDH.

See also: Kaon ya Teteg; Ngilin.

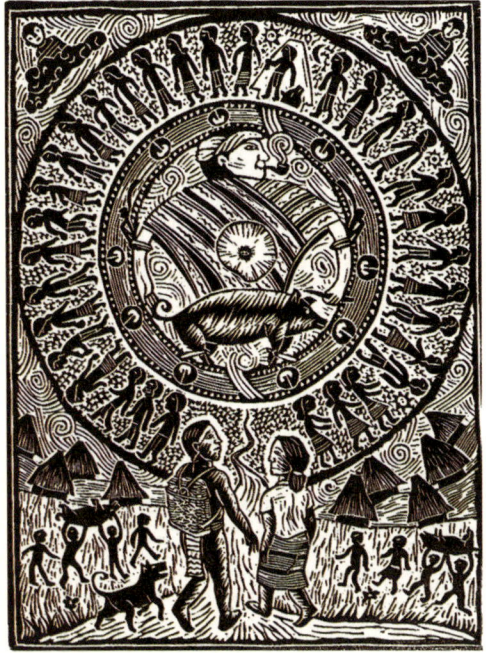

Artwork by Leonard Aguinaldo, 2013.

Ampasit *(IBA)* also **Temengaw** *(KAN)*, **Timmungao** *(KAN)*. Spirit owner or nature spirit. Ampasit are traditionally believed to inhabit forests, caves, cliffs, rocks and deep pools. They are said to administer the places and things they own. Thus, a madmad prayer is required to ask their permission before cutting a tree, cultivating a new field, or constructing a small-scale mine. If not appeased they are said to cause sore eyes, back pains, or skin diseases. Fear of ampasit has been credited as a key factor in the preservation of communal forests over centuries. (Ballard, 2011, 38) SKW.

(2) A malevolent spirit usually residing in springs, rivers, trees and hills. A Cordilleran child is always advised not to pee on or near springs since a temengaw is surely residing there. A man who suffers from penis enlargement or a woman who has vaginal itchiness may be natemengaw, punished by the temengaw for peeing near a spring. DOS.

See also: Darupaypay; Ibwa; Lapat; Madmad; Nginin; Paniaw; Samfu; Tinguian Spirits; Tree Cutting.

Aneb *(ITN)*. A necklace given to a child to keep evil spirits in tow. Some include a miniature shield or a bow and arrow. FYC.

See also: Paniaw.

Angelus. At exactly 6pm, the siren of the Baguio City Hall wails for a full minute. In the past, wherever you were, you had to stay motionless until the siren stopped. The Angelus practice stopped when the siren, which was also used to tell people what typhoon signal the city had, was destroyed in the late 1970s. When the siren was fixed ten years later, it was still sounded daily but the Angelus was no longer followed. Judge Del Claravall, then a councilor in the late 1990s, thought of bringing back the practice of the Angelus but the other councilors were not into it. FYC.

Anginaman *(ISN)*. A love amulet popular in courtship songs.

See also: Iwaxan.

Anglit *(ISN)*. The smell of burning hair. Maybe you are wearing Eau de Pinicpican, you got electrocuted or you are just having one of those extreme bad-hair days. FYC.

See also: Pinikpikan.

Anido *(KAN/BON/ILO)*. Bonfire.

Animbanan *(KAL)*. Lit. Church. *"Where heroes go to die and get imprisoned by malignant spirits."*

Anina! *(KAN/BON)*. An expression for pain or excruciating pain. One would say *"Anina! Mansasakit sugat ko [Anina! My wound is very painful!]"* NEP.

Anito. *"Belief in the anito is not, however, confined alone in the mountain peoples of Northern Luzon. There is probably not a single person in the Philippines that does not now cherish, or that has not at some time in its history cherished, a belief in the anito. Even the Negritos near Floridablanca, Pampanga, who are not Malayan, believe in the anito, but they probably acquired it from the*

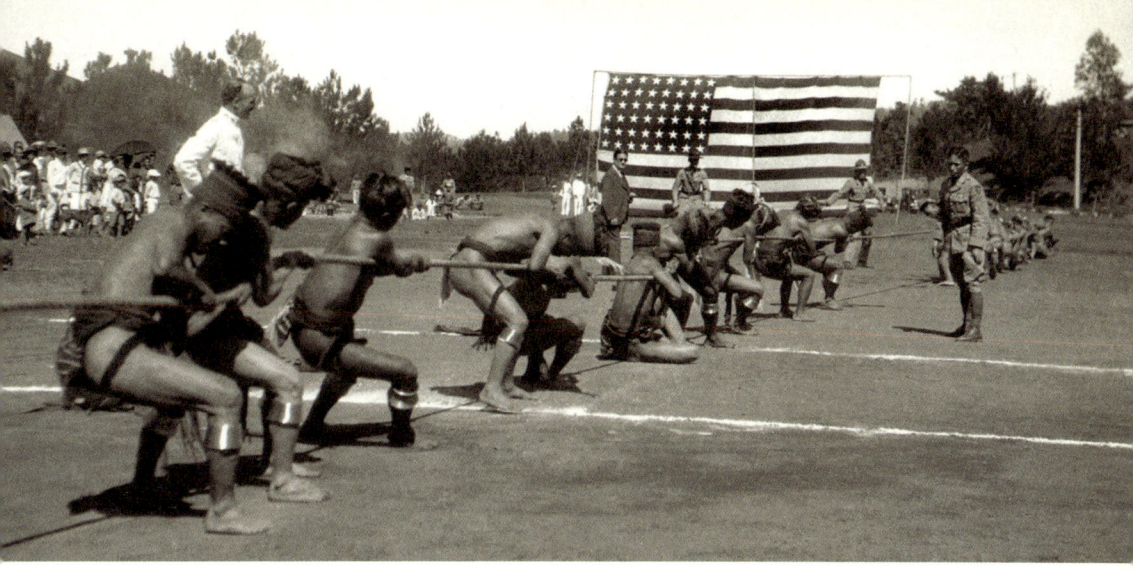

Photograph of Igorots playing tug o'war during the annual cañao. Photograph by Robert Larimore Pendleton. Courtesy University of Wisconsin.

Malayan people with whom they came in contact.

Loarca in his Relacion wrote: 'They said that the Batala (the Tagalog deity) had many agents under him, whom he sent to this world to produce, on behalf of men, what is yielded here. These beings were called anitos, and each anito had a special office. When the natives were asked why the sacrifices were offered to the anito, and not to the Bathala, they answered that the Bathala was a great lord, and no one could speak to him.

He lived in the sky; but the anito, who was of such a nature that he came down here to talk with men, was to the Bathala a minister, and interceded for them. In some places, and especially in the mountain districts, when the father, mother, or other relative dies, the people unite in making a small wooden idol, and preserve it.

Accordingly there is a house which contains one hundred or two hundred of these idols. There images are called anitos; for they say that when people die, they go to serve the Bathala.

Therefore they make sacrifices to these anitos, offering them food, wine, and gold ornaments; and request them to be intercessors for them before the Bathala, whom they regard as God." (Robertson 1914, 472).

Annual Headhunter's Fund. Money from the Philippine Commission in the 1900s for the holding of the annual cañao with participants (some of them enemies of the other tribes) from all over the region coming to meet American officers. During these cañaos, American sports like tug o'war, running with an American flag and baseball were played in the hope that their fervor for head-taking would be used up and the practice forgotten. Prizes in the sports included pigs, cloths, tools, blankets and even magnifying glasses. It was started in 1906 in Bontoc and the annual cañaos were later held in Lubuagan, Kiangan and other main towns. In 1910 in Bontoc where they held the biggest cañaos for Americans, there were 365 gongs played simultaneously. FYC. See also: AFRTN; Cañao; Pre-white; Squaw men; Tribes; White Elephant.

Antatadul *(IFU).* A large green caterpillar.

Anthropology, Questioned

The best way to question anthropology is to question anthropologists.

Trust me, I'm an anthropologist. It is not uncommon to hear indigenous leaders say, "We have been misunderstood and misrepresented by anthropologists."

Much has been said of how anthropologists impose their power and voices of authority over the people that we write about in our ethnographies. I can't help but wonder how many anthropologists would readily admit that – despite the authoritative voice on paper and in conferences – they had their egos smashed with the full force of their own powerlessness and insignificance while in the field?

The truth is, much of what goes into an ethically-produced ethnography is dependent on what a society, a village, or an organization will allow. Anthropologists are fully aware that we would get nowhere if the societies we study did not wish to have us around. As one anthropologist has put it, *"ethnographers end up studying whatever their hosts want to talk about"* (Metcalf 2002, 35). While there is certainly an imbalance of power in fieldwork, the scales alternately tip both ways; sometimes in favor of the researcher, sometimes in favor of the researched.

Between the claims of anthropologists and the accusations levelled against them by researched peoples is a gulf of misunderstanding. I don't think it would be useful to write yet another hifalutin, academic critique on the serious misdeeds and misinterpretations of anthropologists, or on the misleading blanket statements and revisionist tendencies of well-meaning informants and indigenous elites. Many such papers have been written and the healthy debates and damaging accusations go on and on and on.

Instead, what I have to offer is my initial attempt at creating a Research Tool for Researched People.

This "tool" is a list of questions that people may try asking anthropologists – or for that matter, any researchers that come to them. The act of questioning in itself may make some people feel uneasy, but that's not necessarily a bad thing. It would be a good thing for researchers to get used to being questioned. It would be a good thing for the researched to become skilled at asking questions, and to demand satisfactory answers. This Research Tool is not a weapon of antagonism or interrogation. It is a tool that I hope will lead to deeper, more meaningful dialogues between researchers and the researched. It is a tool that I hope will enable both the researched and the researcher to arrive at a better understanding of the impacts of research, academic or otherwise.

A Research Tool for Researched People:

Ask your anthropologist (or any researcher for that matter)

Feel free to add or remove questions and develop the Research Tool for Researched People so that it suits your own situation.

Entry Phase Questions

When the researcher first arrives, people are usually curious about this person. Below are some questions that are usually asked:

When were you born?

Who are your parents?

Where were you born?

Where were your parents born?

Where do you live?

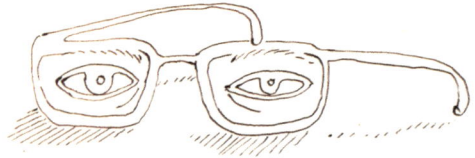

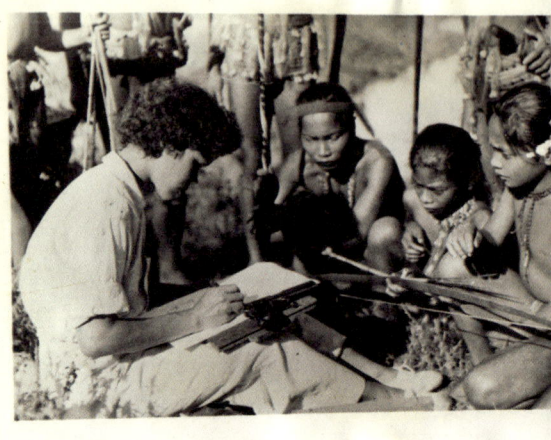

Photograph of the magazine illustrator **Margaret Renner** doing research in 1979. Photograph by Aleko E. Lilius from World Wide Photos. Courtesy AV Cating Family Collection

Are you a student? Are you working?

Why have you come here? Or, why did you choose us and our place?

In addition, you could also ask your researcher to tell you more about his/her study.

If research is new to you: Could you explain "research"? Explain your profession.

If you have had previous experience of research: How is your research similar to, or different from, other studies that have been conducted here with us?

Some general questions about the specific research project:

What is your research question, or what do you want to learn about while you are here? Why is that important to you? Why should it matter to us?

Would you be willing to answer the same kinds of questions that you ask us?

What will we gain from having you here?

What will you gain from being here and doing this study?

What skills do you have that might be of some use to us?

Will there be any practical consequences and/or benefits from your research?

Everyone has the right to refuse to be interviewed, just as everyone has the right to share his/her knowledge and opinions if he/she wishes to do so. Ask your researcher:

What are the risks and benefits for me, if I participate in your research or agree to be interviewed?

If there are risks involved, what measures will you take to protect me, my identity, or my family and my community from possible harm?

(A word of caution: Not all research projects will be able to afford to give the community money and/or practical benefits. And not all research is good research, and could in fact be damaging. It is important for individuals and communities to understand fully the possible implications of any research. This understanding is the responsibility of both the researcher and the researched.)

Mid-point Questions

Over time, you will get to know the researcher better and you will form your own opinions about them as a person, and as a professional or scholar. Some of you might become key informants or even good friends with them. At this point, you could ask them:

What have you learned so far?

Has anything changed in the way you see things, from when you first arrived here?

When you are done, are you going to make your research results available to us, in a format and/or language that we can understand?

Illustration by Carlo Eustaquio.

(You could also try asking your researcher questions that are similar to what they have been asking in your community.)

Exit Phase Questions

The work of a researcher is far from over when they return home or go back to school or the office. After they have left the community, it is time for the researcher to review the information that was given to them while in the community, and to analyze and write about what they have learned from their time with you. Before the researcher goes, you can ask:

What are you going to say about us, in classrooms, in conferences, in papers, in books, in films?

Who will listen to you? Who will read/hear about us from you?

What do you think the impact of your words and our story will be on the people that listen to you?

How do you think people will see us, if they read or hear your words about us?

If and when your work about us spreads to different people and places, what will the impact of that be on us?

Are you able to create a truthful account without compromising our dignity?

If we were to read your work about us, how do you think we would feel about it?

Do you have any plans to come back here?

Some researchers are able to keep in touch after they have gone back to where they came from. Some are able to return for visits as friends, as supporters in a cause that means a lot to your community, or for further studies. Some of them you will never see or hear from again. This is not always what the researcher prefers, but could be due to his/her personal circumstances, or in some extreme instances, it may be according to the wishes of the community. Whether or not you would like to see or hear from a particular researcher again, that is up to you, the researcher, and the kinds of meaningful words, acts and ideas you are able to exchange with each other. Peace. PLP.

Anuka *(KAN)* also **An-a** *(BON)*. In Mountain Province, whenever they run out of words or forget the term, they say, *"anuka."* One would say *"Anapem din anuka ta men-uto ta. [Look for the anuka so that we can cook]."* HZK.

Apag *(KAN)*. Carved wooden container that contains the first tapuy drawn from a just-opened jar which is then offered to the unseen spirits. The apag is also passed around for those participating in a ritual to partake of the tapuy. TDH.
See also: Basi; Bayas; Fuas; Iwa; Pitik.

Apang *(KAN)* also **Benge** *(KAN)*, **Appong** *(BON)*, **Apang** *(ITN)*. A headband made from beads or snake vertebra for women to hold their hair in place. It also provides protection from lightning and from headaches and is used throughout Mountain Province. TDH.
See also: Akipur; Cloth Dyes; Bayoyok; Duwao; Fukas; Kimat; Kulatod; Ong-ong; Panglao; Tsuli; Xaranait.

Apo Annu. Once languishing for years in a cabinet at the National Museum, the mummy of Apo Annu was finally brought to a cave in Natubleng, Buguias in April 1999. The mummy's past was legendary. He was said to be the child of a mythical hunter in Natubleng named Tugaka who chanced upon a big deer. The deer suddenly became a woman asking for help, Tugaka fell in love with her and she begot Annu. Annu (or Anno) became a great warrior as well and was mummified when he died.

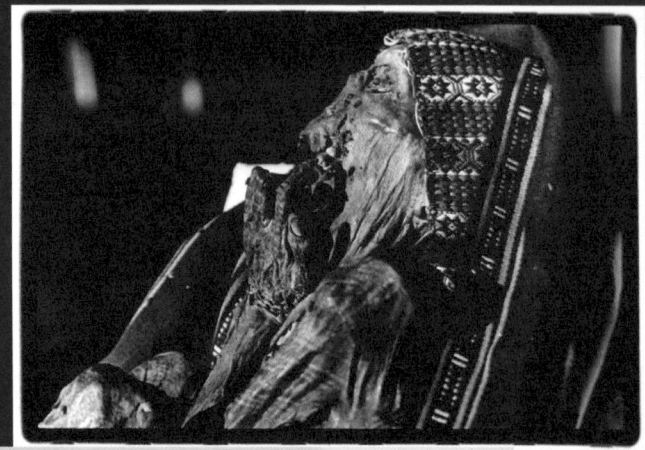

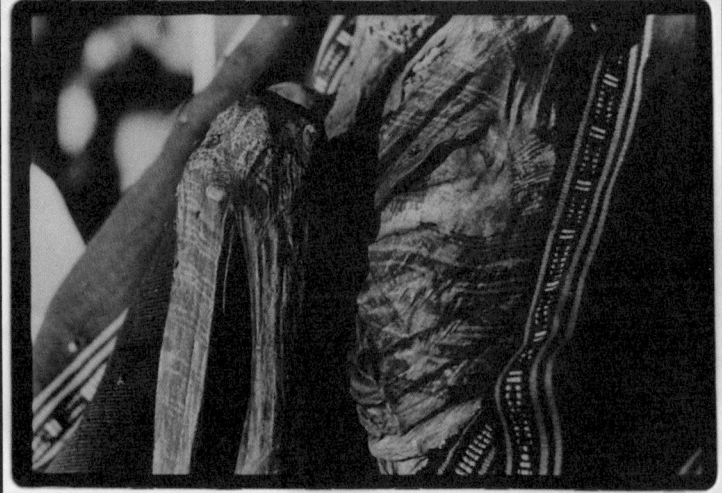

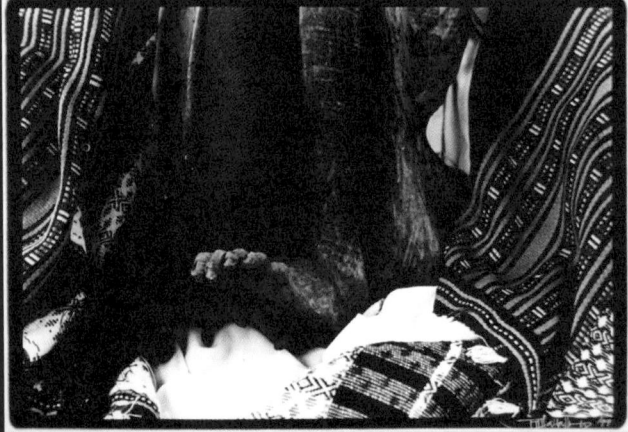

A pastor stole him from his hometown in 1918. In the 1950s, his mummified remains became a feature in a circus sideshow in the Philippines and the US. He was brought to the National Museum in 1989. A well-preserved and well-tattooed mummy, it was brought to Acmi Nabalicong after much fanfare. Apo Annu was deified into a god of rain after the whole of Baguio and Benguet experienced a very heavy downpour upon his return. FYC.

Photographs of *Apo Annu*, 1997. Photographs by Tommy Hafalla.

Apolaqui *(IBA)*. The god of war and safe travel.
See also: Iddaya; Kabunian; Kimat.

Apoy *(BON/KAN)*. [1] A series of activities in Bontoc to mark the start of the planting season (usually in the summer months) and to invoke the blessings from the Almighty for a good harvest. All households cook tufu. On the day of cho-or (rest day), some people are tasked to bring tufu along with cooked chicken and/or etag to children and relatives. This serves to strengthen family ties. PAD.
[2] Ritual connected to apoy (fire) such as cleaning the fields, or during All Soul's Day when people light bonfires on top of their relatives' graves (man-aapoy). TDH.
See also: Banuwat; Pes-ay; Tufu.

Apugay *(ISN)*. Traditional name for a tall but shy woman. Still in use, this name is given to females who are observed to have the same characteristics as the original ancestor who was first named Apugay. GAD.
See also: Ambit, Ambot, Amboy; Salabao.

Architecture:
Defining Cordillera Vernacular Architecture

Vernacular Architecture is one among the many facets of contemporary architecture. It describes buildings that are fashioned using introduced architectural techniques influenced by traditional architecture, or the other way around. Implicit to the term "vernacular" is the notion of building as an organic process, involving the society as a whole (Correa 1998).

To shed light on the technical process of this art and its hopes, Dumay Solinggay (DOS) undertook three interviews: with the seasoned architect and urban planner, Joseph "Jody" Alabanza (JA); with an experienced Ifugao hut builder, Santos Bayucca (SB); and a key contemporary practitioner not only in Cordillera architecture but also Philippine architecture, Bong Sanchez also known as Bong ti Baguio (BB).

Interview with Jody Alabanza

JA: Ok, now, perhaps the question that you will ask is, *"Is there a Cordillera architecture?"* First and foremost, let us define architecture. Architecture is the cultural manifestations on the physical, man-made aspects of an environment which have certain function in the living conditions of the people.

Climate strongly affected the architecture in the Cordilleras. For instance the thatched roof that goes that way (conical) is very common because of the heavy rains that needs to flow fast otherwise the rainwater accumulates and it could seep into the building.

In Cordillera architecture, there is a Kalinga architecture. There is a Bontoc architecture. There is an Ifugao architecture, and the issue is, is there a Baguio architecture?

Let's start up from the North. You will notice that Apayao architecture is influenced by lowland architecture coming from the Ilocos and Cagayan region. One of the distinctions of their architecture is the presence of stilts. Why do they have stilts? The space below is for animals.

On the other hand, the Bontoc architecture is on the ground. Around their houses are also a lot of available stones owing to being near a river, the Chico river.

If you go to Ifugao, their houses are raised from the ground and they even have detachable ladders. There is a space down the stairs where they put their pots and whatever. So the Ifugao architecture to me is strongly influenced by their rice culture because they need space for agricultural implements. It is also the climate that determined the long conical roof.

The Benguet house did not really generate a style because Benguet is affected by lowland influences. Although it is possible that their roofs are steeper because of the rains.

The Kalinga house is a little bit longer, it goes horizontal. So that's more or less the prominent feature of their architecture because it's the whole family that lives there.

> "...each area appears to have its own distinct type of a house, from the complex timber structures of the Apayao rainforests to the roof-heavy pine cubicles perched among the Ifugao terraces like gigantic mushrooms on four legs, from the soot-shiny darkness of Bontoc interiors to the split-bamboo floors of Kalinga that can be rolled up and carried down to the river to wash. (Scott 1962, 186)."

DOS: What do you think of modern architecture seen among buildings erected in Baguio and around the region?

JA: You define modern as something influenced by lowland architecture, and by the Americans or the Spaniards. Take note also of the very strong influence of Christian missionaries.

Modern architecture played more significance in the architectural design of the convents and buildings of religious orders.

When I teach architectural subjects, I often tell my students, *"even if you are coming out with architecture that is functional in nature, in other words, evolving architecture for functional uses like churches, residences, and so on, try to reflect*

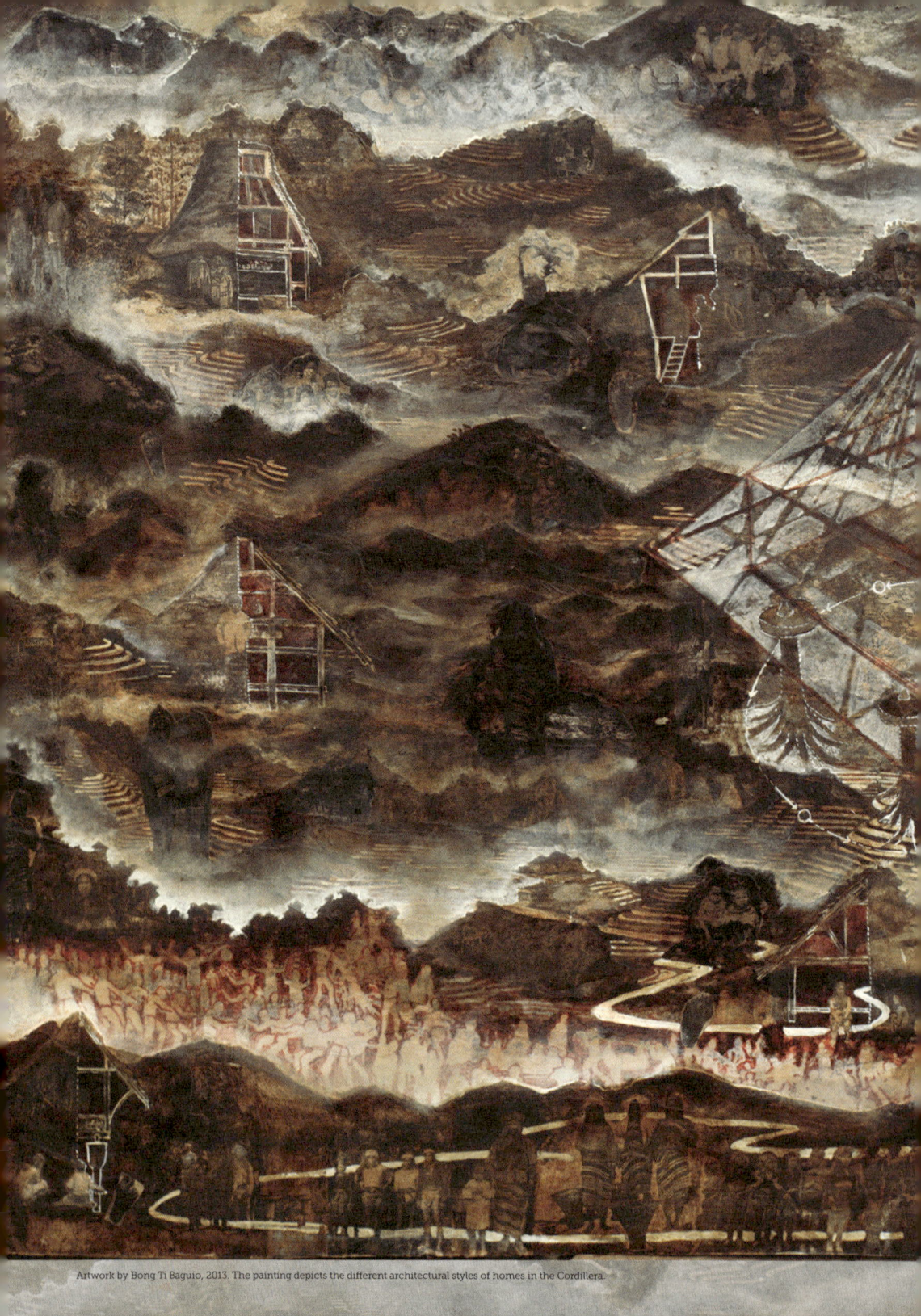
Artwork by Bong Ti Baguio, 2013. The painting depicts the different architectural styles of homes in the Cordillera.

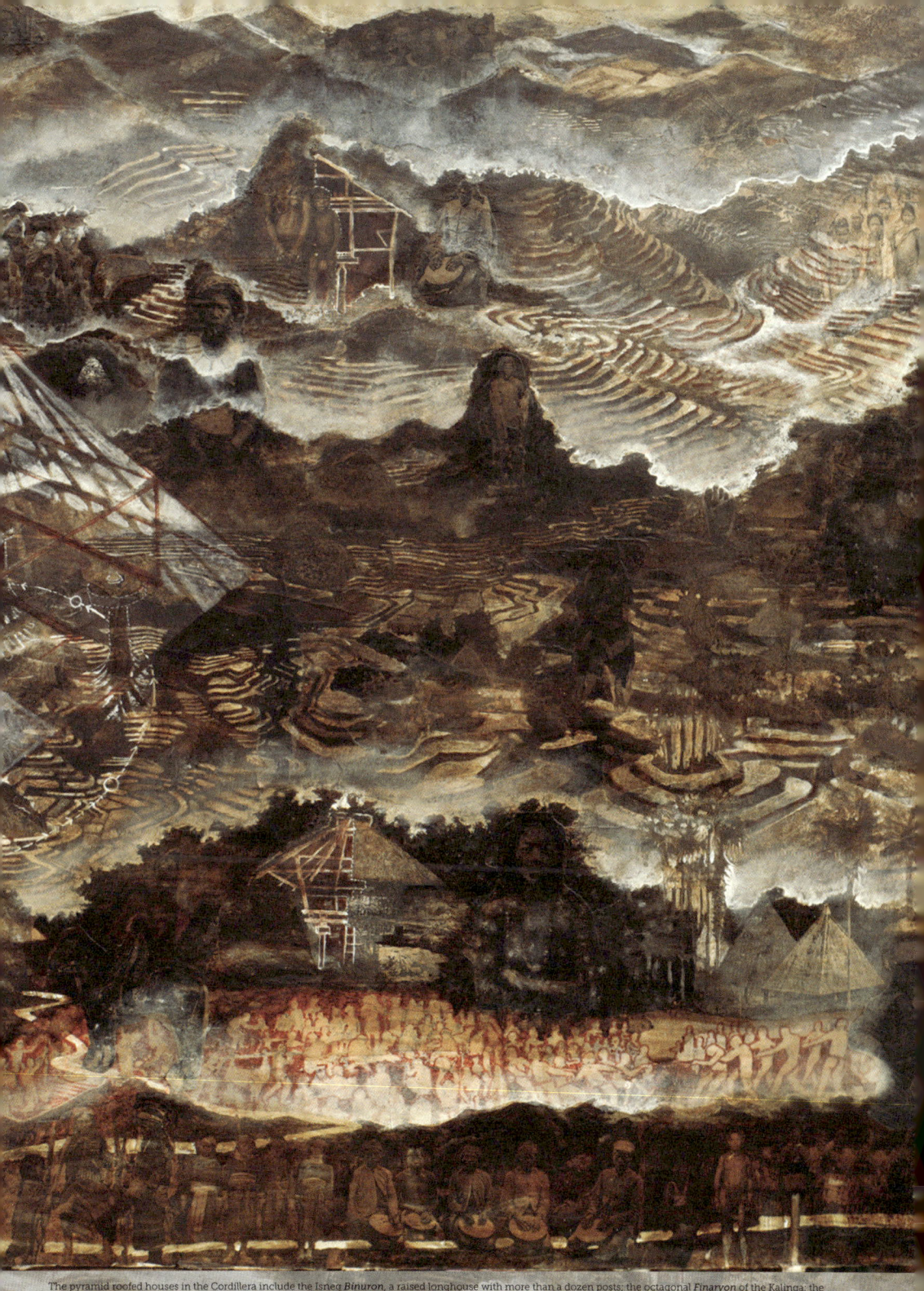

The pyramid roofed houses in the Cordillera include the Isneg *Binuron*, a raised longhouse with more than a dozen posts; the octagonal *Finaryon* of the Kalinga; the squareish *Fayu* of the Bontok that has a second floor granary; and, the raised Ifugao *Bale* that is known for the wooden cylinders attached to the top part of its posts that guards the house from field rats.

the architecture of the Cordilleras."

But now, I don't know. Look at the buildings we have here, 'modern?' Oh bullshit! (laughs)...

That's the tendency of young architects. They copy the architecture of Makati whose environment is entirely different from ours – culturally, and in terms of climate, and also the building materials. But still, I notice the kind of buildings being erected – and these architects, they don't think. That is my frustration.

DOS: Do you have hopes that Cordillera Architecture will have its own place again soon?

JA:Yes, I hope so. Although if you look at the buildings now, to them siguro it is more functional. Developers are more concerned about how to build it without thinking of the aesthetics, the culture, or the types of buildings that we should develop in the Cordilleras.

DOS: How should it be developed?

JA: The way to do it is through education. A very strong influence would be on the education of our architects or engineers.

DOS: Should there be a curriculum or subject developed?

JA: I would think so. There should be a subject on local architecture. Oh, we should develop our own! The shapes of our traditional buildings are ok — reflect the Bontoc! Get elements from Bontoc architecture! If we can develop our own architecture, it would be so nice. We're losing that sense of being proud of our architecture.

DOS: You mean to say, there really are no courses on folk or traditional architecture?

JA: None eh. I don't think so. I'll tell them that they should at least have one subject on native architecture especially Cordillera architecture. Saint Louis, UC (University of the Cordilleras, and UB (University of Baguio) – I'll talk to the heads of the architecture departments to require the students to try to reflect native architecture and not just copy from Manila and Makati or the U.S. I'll tell them to help develop a Cordillera architecture.

Interview with Santos Bayucca

DOS: Which part of the hut do you put the rice harvest?

SB: On the topmost floor, the balan. The ground floor which is out in the open is where people weave and do rituals. They do the cooking at the second floor so that the smoke goes directly to the rice storage at the third floor. The third floor, which looks like an attic, is made of runo (reed sticks) so the smoke easily goes up. If the rice harvest can't be contained in the storage, they make another hut. This is also where they put the bulul, the jars, and the gongs.

All of the parts of the Ifugao hut are detachable – the ladder, the posts, the beams. I asked the old ones once why, and it is so that the house can be moved. The roof is designed very steep for wind proofing. I have not heard of a house being carried away by a typhoon for a long time.

All of the parts have a name. The rat guards on the posts are called libong. The first beam is kuling, the second is mundilig, the center is gawaan. The mundilig and gawaan holds all the planks of the second floor. And there's another beam that holds all the wall-planks. There are no nails so if you raise this last beam called the buklog, the wall will collapse.

The last beam is for the attic, it also holds the second post. And below the beam is called the huklob. There are also four posts for the attic which is held by the smallest beam called the binulan, which is designed with a carving.

"Square in floor plan, it [the Ifugao hut] is elevated to about shoulder height by four posts (tukud), around which are fitted cylindrical wooden rat-guards (halipan), carrying two transverse girders (kuling) which support three floor joists into which the floor-boards (dotal) are fitted and wall boards (gaon and pamadingan) and studs (bagad) are mortised. It is typical of the exactness of Ifugao construction that the three floor joists are designed by different terms indicative of their purpose" the center one is the gawaan, "center", and the outer two are mundilig, a verb meaning the patting motion made with opposed hands to pack something together. The four studs, placed at the corner of the house, are mortised of their upper end into four tie-beams of purlins (wanan) which form a square to carry much of the weight of the roof as well as a central cross-beam (pumpitolan) on which stand two queenposts (taknang). These queenposts terminate in a small square (ambubuman) which supports the upper ends of the rafters (bughol), the roof being a true pyramid in form with four trianglar sides and thus rising into an apex without any ridgepole. The wall-boards are rabbeted into a transverse beam (huklub) at waist- or chest-height, at which point a shelf (patie) is fitted between them and the roof, whose eaves descend as low as the level of the floor. Above the tie-beams a reed floor or platform is often fitted to make an attic-like storage (palan) for unthreshed rice. Wooden panels close doorways on two opposite sides of the house, and entrance is gained by means of a ladder which is removed at night.. (Scott 1962, 188)."

There are two types of Ifugao huts. One is the Hungduan-Banaue-Hingyon, and the Mayoyao. The former is what I described above. The Mayoyao house has very short walls. The flooring extends to the sides of the roof. The Mayoyao house is also wider.

The roof of the Mayoyao house is so low you can't even see the walls and it does not have a libong. The posts are made of tree stumps but with roots. This, I heard, prevents earthquake damages.

The Mayoyaos like using narra tree for their houses. In Hungduan, we also use hardwood.

DOS: Why narra?

SB: If not narra, the people will accuse the builder of being binabai (effeminate).

DOS: Do you know anyone who innovates from the traditional architecture of the Ifugao hut?

SB: A few. On the way to Ifugao there are these two huts that have concrete posts. I made one in my village where I used the windows from the old houses in Vigan. The walls are also made of bamboo.

DOS: As a hut builder, do you get clients outside Ifugao?

SB: Yes, a lot. In Manila, we built one at the National Museum, also at Nayong Pilipino and in some private spaces. We also built one in Vigan.

There are those who build the huts in Ifugao and then they sell outside. There's this young builder in Hungduan who was able to sell huts in Baguio, Cebu, and even abroad.

DOS: Are there still a lot of Ifugao who know the architectural knowledge of building the hut?

SB: Mayoyao is faring ok. They always have the hut near their concrete house unlike in Banaue, Hingyon, and Hungduan. However, most of the huts now have iron roofing because the cogon roof rots in five to seven years' time. Everyone is using gas range burners for cooking so there's no more smoke that cures the roof.

Not a lot of young people know about it. When they come to the city, they learn other influences and prefer a concrete house over the hut. That's why I think in 10 to 20 years, Banaue would be called the "house terraces." Grabe, they set up ziplines from the highway to the rice fields so they can transport concrete materials.

I'm sure the only tourist spot that would remain in the future will be Sagada – because no one would build a house inside the cave (laughs).

DOS: Would you know if they're teaching the architecture of the hut in the IP education program of the K to 12 curriculum?

SB: I haven't heard of such but they should teach it in the carpentry classes for high school students.

The Ifugao architecture is a perfect architecture, because once a mistake is done in any of the parts, the house turns askew – the balance is uneven. There's no use of nails so everything relies on a perfect balance. Carpentry students should learn about 'balance' before anything else.

Interview with Bong ti Baguio

DOS: When did you decide to become an architect?

BB: I used to draw a lot when I was young. And my mother said once, *"When you grow up, you will become an architect."*

Back in high school, things changed – I wanted to become a priest. I applied at a seminary but I was not accepted. I thought of enrolling in fine arts but the nun I used to work for at the convent advised that I should just take up architecture because paintings are things just mounted on walls anyways. Architecture is the mother of all arts – paintings, artifacts, and artworks.

DOS: Who are your influences?

BB: In college, I looked into famous Filipino architects and Bobby Mañosa's works appealed to me. He utilized organic and indigenous materials. Now, I'm looking into Gaudi's works and his process. He does everything hands on. He casted cadavers for the Sagrada Familia.

In the Cordilleras, often it's only the Ifugao architecture getting credit. Napintas gayam ti Bauko. I also like Sagada architecture.

DOS: Your designs are obviously unique from other buildings because you pattern them from traditional Cordilleran architecture. How is your process?

BB: Before I work on a project, I share stories with the client. Initially, I am not after the design but the chemistry between us and the community around us. For example in Sagada, why did Gawani's house come out that way? Nag-ping-pong kami idiay, we shared ideas and came out with a modern kubo.

I look at the person, at the environment and then I think of something that could magnet people. That's what I want to project. That's why I don't call my work a project but rather a projection.

What matters most is not the design but the relationship you create with your work, your client, and workmates. I always tell my kakadwa (workmates/comrades) that we are not building 'a' house, we are building 'our' house.

I did a site analysis in Ambasing (Sagada). That would be the future Sagada lane, na-virus diay Poblacion gaminen ya. Let's try not to overdevelop that remaining part. I have another projection near Gawani's house which is a piano type apex house. I did a lot of schematical drawings for that design until it got approved. I don't use AutoCAD because I'd rather feel the flow of the design in my body. I value creating images with my raw imagination and the labor of my hands.

Most of the roofs that we see around are similar so I wanted to make another version. The piano type apex came out from my site analysis in the area. It's always raining there. The different levels of the roofs create different tones when the raindrops hit. Try to listen to it from the inside and it would project different rhythms depending on which side of the house you are.

This year all of my projects are bubong (roofs) so these are all Bong bubong projects. Tatay (Kidlat Tahimik) also asked me to help him with the roof of Cinematheque (at Ililikha, Assumption Road). Mayat diay collaboration mi ken Tatay. He suggested a lot of designs, he had many ideas and I asked him if he wants a 'wave'. That's when the ball stopped rolling on so many drawings, we already hit the point with the wave roof.

With Gawani's house, I named the roof 'Puli ni Asia' because I adopted a style that's all over Polynesia. In the nighttime, when the interior of the house is illuminated, you can see the letter D from the outside that stands for Domogo. On the other side, there is a pointed apex that looks like an A which stands for Aquino. My sister's house in Aurora Hill is modeled from the Brazilian V-roof. Her name is Margaret so I designed an M apex plus A which stands for her husband's name, Arlan.

When I started doing Gawani's house, I heard many comments like, *"A scientist is building a house."* After the house was finished, I heard someone say again, *"So when is the spaceship flying, astronaut?"*

DOS: What are your challenges?

BB: My batch-mates in college who are already in Dubai or Abu Dhabi often tell me, *"Pards, agsubli ka ti college"*. I don't have a license.

Artwork by Kawayan De Guia, 2008.

Sometimes I get tired mentally, and also physically because I travel from Baguio to Sagada then back again. I wish I could clone myself.

DOS: You're in demand.

BB: But I'm not doing it as a contractor. I'm doing my job as a laborer. Sometimes 'contractor' can be misspelled as 'corruptor.' For me it matters less if I get paid, as long as I execute my design and I know it's worthy of the name 'architecture' I'm happy with that. That's why I'm really thankful for my kakadwa who help me build the houses because my drawings would mean nothing if no one helps me materialize them. DOS.

Asbayat *(IBA).* Refrain or chorus to a lead bah'diw (chant).

Asin, Republic of. According to the late journalist Peppot Ilagan in his column for the defunct Baguio Gold Ore, revolutionaries and military officers, artists and journalists of Baguio declared the Asin Hot Springs as a weekend peace zone during the Martial Law era where anybody could bathe in the sulphurous water in peace. Outside of the 'Republic of Asin,' it was back to the cops-and-robbers life again. FYC.

See also: Peace zone; Vochong.

Asocena *(FIL).* A dog dish, usually eaten as a pulutan (finger food companion to liquor). Asocena has a long history but was again popularized during the release of Carlos Siguion-Reyes' *Azucena* (2000), a graphic film that uses dog-eating as a symbolism for acts of incest and violence. The term is often mistakenly thought to be the ritual dog meat of the Cordilleras; so much so that it has shaken people's perception on ritual dog-eating, like in the 1904 St Louis Fair in the US, where dog-eating Igorots were put on display.

However, the matter of word misattribution is clear to many Igorots who, for more than 300 years, were able to defend themselves from Spanish colonization. Being anti-Spaniards, it would be a wonder if Igorots used the word

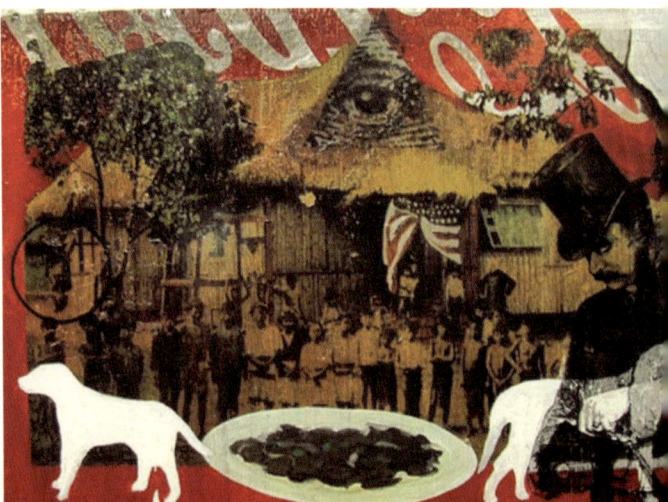

'asocena,' that derives from the Filipino word 'aso' meaning dog and 'cena' which is Spanish for dinner.
See also: Dog-eating; Niyek.

Ating-nganganu *(BON)*. A very venomous centipede.
See also: Tattoo.

Ato Bookshop and Gallery. Ato was one of the earliest bookshops in Baguio City. Cecile Afable opened the shop in the mid-1960s. It was located on the ground floor of the Insular Life Building on Session Road. Mrs. Afable carried a wide selection of Filipiniana. There was a weaving loom at one side of the store and every day, two weavers would come to do their work in the shop. The Ato also sold prison art. The shop closed after the military raided it and confiscated all of the books during the dictatorship of then-President Ferdinand Marcos. PLP.
See also: Afable, Cecile; Dap-ay; Three Witches.

Attifungalin *(BON)*. Rainbow.

Atubang *(KAN)*. Basket used by women for snails which they collect in the fields. TDH.
See also: Agudong id Manitong; Bisukol; Falokag; Golden Kuhol; Ket-an; Lisdeg.

Au-auni *(KAN/BON/KAL)*. Lit. By and by. In a moment. In a minute.

Aw-aw *(KAN)*. A variation of the tengba or safeng in Tadian, Mountain Province. Like tengba, it is naturally fermented rice and salt, but without the crabs. PAD.
See also: Abungol; Bakkay; Safeng.

Awanen *(ILO)*. "No more or gone. When this word is shouted by a miner when an American boss has just left a working place, he is calling those who are hiding somewhere to come out." (Chamber of Mines of the Philippines, 1939, p. 199).

Ayag *(KAN)*. (1) To call.
(2) It mostly refers to the ay-ayag, the ritual to call back a person's wandering or lost ab-abiik. TDH.
See also: Ab-abiik; Ayak; Padpadaya; Pasang; Pattaliat.

Ayak *(IFU)*. The ayak (soul-stealing) is a series of religious ceremonies wherein the sorcerer calls to a feast the ancestral spirits of some man whose death he desires to encompass, together with many maleficent spirits and deities, and bribes them to bring to him, incarnated as a blue-bottle fly, a dragon fly, or a bee, the soul of the man whose death he desires. When one of the insects mentioned comes to drink of the rice wine in front of the sorcerer, it is imprisoned and put into a bamboo joint tightly corked. The enemy, being thus deprived of his soul, will die. (Barton, 1946).
See also: Ab-abiik; Alan; Bengao; Hidit; Nginin; Padpadaya; Paniaw; Pasang; Pattaliat; Tiw-tiwong; Ulliyan.

Aye *(IFU)* also **Ayek**. (1) Expression of appreciation if the accent is on the first syllable but an expression of exasperation if accent is on the second syllable. PAD.
(2) *(BON)* Sigh of dismay or relief.

Ayot *(KAN/BON)*. Sexual desire. Ayutan means sexually licentious or profligate.

Ayum *(IFU)*. Amulet used to charm women.

Ayut *(KAL)*. To pierce the ears.

Ayuyang *(KAN)*. (1) Meeting place.
(2) A now-defunct folk bar in Baguio that was located beside the bus terminal on Governor Pack road at the Baden-Powell Inn. It used to be a favorite among artists and musicians because of its artsy-fartsy ambience. It closed in 2012. DOS.
See also: Bontoc Café; Fireplace.

Ayyew *(BON/KAN)*. An Igorot value for conserving and caring for anything, any place or anybody of value; zero waste. *"Ayyew nan mula, adi yo gatinan. [Loosely: Take care not to step on those plants. They are precious]." "Piditen yo nan kamogay tay ayyew. Men-aga. [Pick up all grains of rice dropped from the table or they will cry. Don't waste them]."* It is the value that has preserved the environment and has sustained Igorots for generations on seemingly scarce resources. PAD.
See also: Iuya; Lapat.

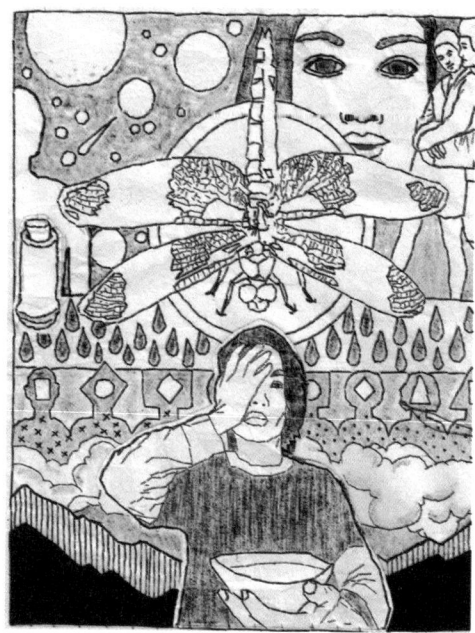

Artwork by Carlo Villafuerte, 2013.

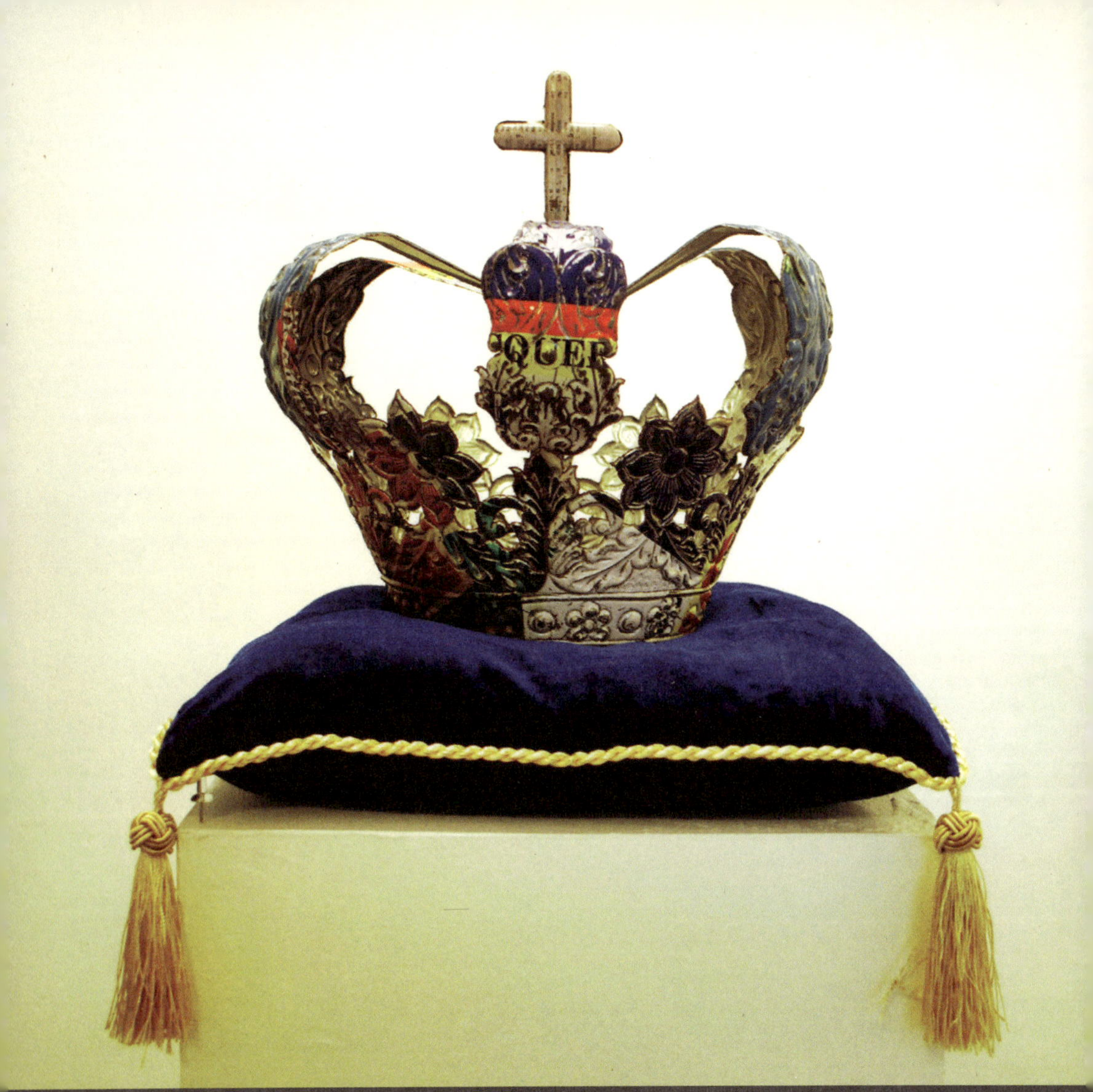

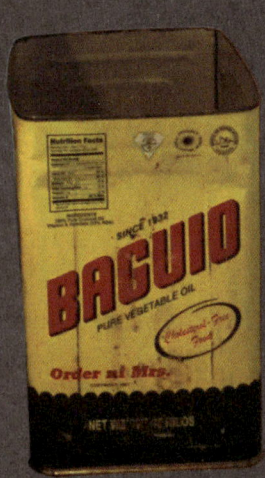
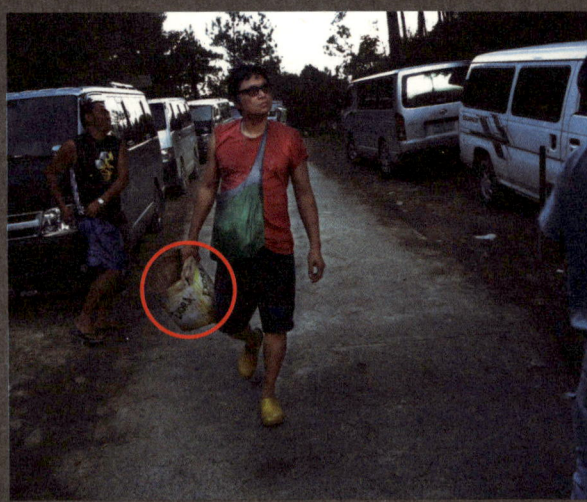

Everyone Wants to Be a Queen, Alfredo and Isabel Aquilizan, 2012. Courtesy The Drawing Room.
Photograph of the artist Alfredo Aquilizan in Sagada during the AX(iS) Art Project: To The End of the World, 2012.

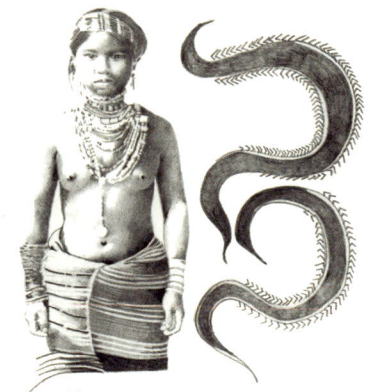

Baak *(KAL).* [1] Infertile.
[2] *(BON)* old person.
[3] *(KAN)* old person, widow, or widower.

Babate *(KAN).* Wood larvae eaten as a delicacy. These larvae of moth, also called Wichetty grub, are roasted over the fire and said to be high in protein and fat. A gourmet once said that the larva *"tastes like nut-flavored scrambled eggs and mild mozzarella, wrapped in a filo dough pastry."* DLD.
See also: Abu-os.

Baddang *(IFU)* also **Badang** *(KAN).* A group of people hired to help in harvest.
See also: Adoyon; Kamal; Ob-obbo; Tambo; Tinawon; To-ned.

Baddarong! *(IBA).* Expression of anger or frustration. A lesser oath is 'Bantiwel!'

Bading *(KAN)* also **Biding, Buding.** Rice birds that ravish the ricefields. Locals string the film of Betamax or VHS tape like nets over their rice fields to shoo away the birds. The glaring of light reflected from the tape works better than a scarecrow. FYC.
See also: Faked; Pasok; Vakla.

Badio *(IBA).* You have to be mournfully drunk to sing the badio – but not too drunk to think, as it is a song extemporaneously sung to give advice, pacify someone or narrate an anecdote. It has to have a catchy end so that the choir audience can sing the last line as a refrain. FYC.
See also: Amazing Grace; Baya-o; Cherwasay; Dujung.

Baggat Udan *(ISN).* Hail.
See also: Duyayu; Little Alaska.

Baggha-an *(IBA).* Slave or servant.

Bagong *(KAN).* *"The spirit of the beheaded person; howls in the night which, of course, cannot be understood because of it being headless."* (Scott 2011, 149).
See also: Baguio Ghost Stories; Carangat; Pinten.

Baguio Amusement Committee. Body organized by Gov. Cameron Forbes in 1914 to ensure that Baguio would have regular and year-round cultural and social events. FYC

Baguio Arts Guild,
The History of
(From "In the BAG"*)

It wasn't easy for a group of artists to put together an arts festival of a national standard on a shoestring budget without even an office or staff. But that is what the Baguio Arts Guild (BAG) did in 1989 when they launched the first Baguio Arts Festival. In the next four years between 1989 and 1993, the BAG found a home in the deserted basement of the Baguio Convention Center, which they converted into the Baguio Arts Center. When the devastating earthquake hit Baguio City in 1990, the artists in the Guild helped to staff a soup kitchen and donated art works to be sold at an auction (*Artquake*) in one of Manila's premier museums. They also offered art workshops for children whose families were left homeless and camping in Baguio City's central park, Burnham Park. Needless to say, the title of the second Baguio Arts Festival (1990), Art and the Environment, was in direct response to this environmental disaster that rocked the Baguio community.

During the fourth Baguio Arts Festival in 1993, I sat around a table at Café by the Ruins in Baguio City with artists from the Visayas and Mindanao in the Philippines, and others from Indonesia, Sri Lanka, and Japan, all of whom were participating artists. One of the artists expressed how inspiring it was to see the accomplishments of the BAG and to know that it was really possible to create and implement an artist-run festival of international standards. And to think that the Baguio Arts Festivals represented only a fraction of the work accomplished by the artists and supporters of the

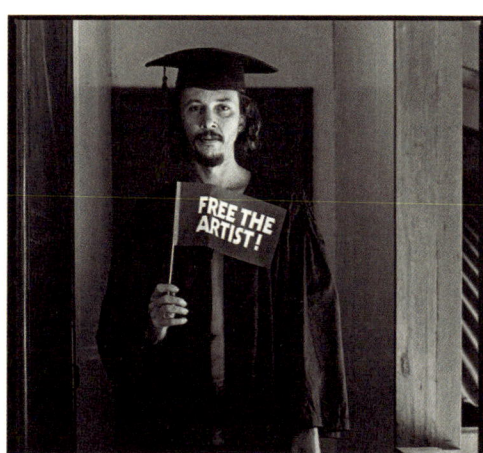

Portrait of the artist Pepito Bosch. Photograph by Wig Tysmans.

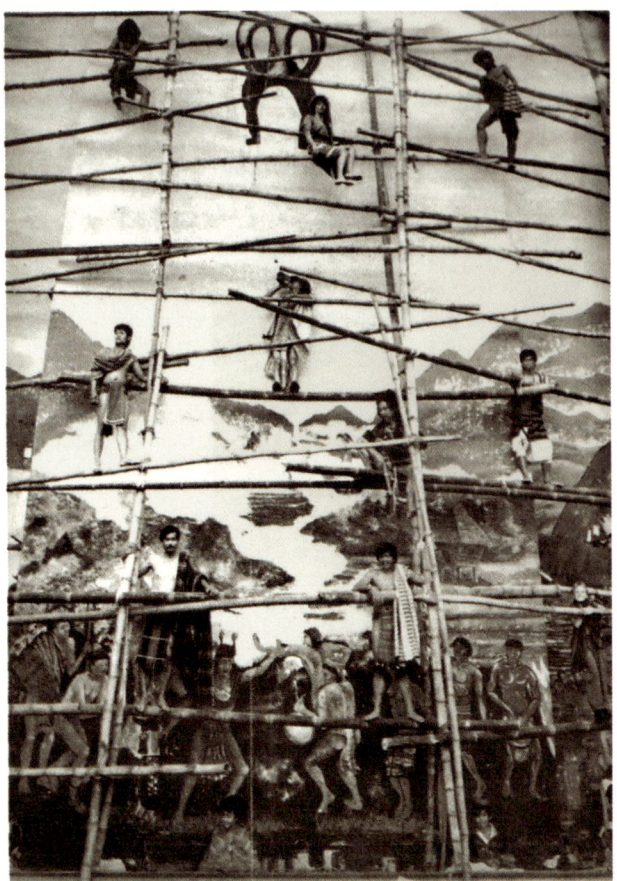

Photograph of the founders of the *Baguio Arts Guild* painting the mural 'Pax Cordillera' in 1988. Courtesy Baguio Arts Guild.

BAG! As one can imagine, there is a lot more to this story of how a small group of artists banded together and became not only an integral part of their immediate community but an inspiration to artists and arts organizations around the world.

Baguio City has long been seen as an educational and cultural hub of the Cordillera mountains in the Northern Philippines. Following the ousting of dictator Ferdinand Marcos and the end of martial law (1986), many Filipinos who had left the Philippines to escape the tyranny of martial law, returned. Among them were some of the founding members of the BAG. The confluence of cultures that has always given Baguio City its unique flavor, proved to be a source of inspiration for some of these artists. By 1987, the timing and the setting were ripe for the birth of the BAG. The small group of artists that came together to form the BAG quickly attracted young people from the Baguio community who were drawn to be artists but hadn't had the opportunity to study art in a formal setting. Through their association and collaboration with the founding members of the BAG, these young people not only began to embrace their creative potential and realize lives as artists, but also helped to integrate the BAG into the larger Baguio community. In this sense the Baguio Arts Guild was a true guild.

Community collaboration and process became signatures of the Guild's style. There are many examples of this in the BAG's early history but the most poignant is probably the earthquake atang (offering). As his piece for the third Baguio Arts Festival in 1991, Roberto Villanueva, one of the BAG's founding members, drew from an aspect of traditional Filipino culture and conceptualized the creation of spirit boats which, on the hour that the earthquake struck Baguio, were released in Burnham Lake at the heart of Baguio City. In the early morning of the designated day, people began gathering around the dap-ay of Café by the Ruins, turning beeswax into candles, constructing boats from bamboo and grass reeds, decorating them with prayers and objects of significance. When completed, the spirit boats were paraded through the city en route to Burnham Park. Candles were placed in coconut shells and strung on the back of boats and at 4PM, the boats were set free, floating through the mist on Burnham Lake. The following day, in the early morning, members of the Guild gathered the boats and brought them to the beach, an hour's drive down the mountains from Baguio. Here, they were released into the ocean. Though the concept was Roberto's, the implementation and output became the community's. There was not a tangible, finished artwork but the process and creative experience would stay in the minds of the participants long after the boats drifted away into the setting sun.

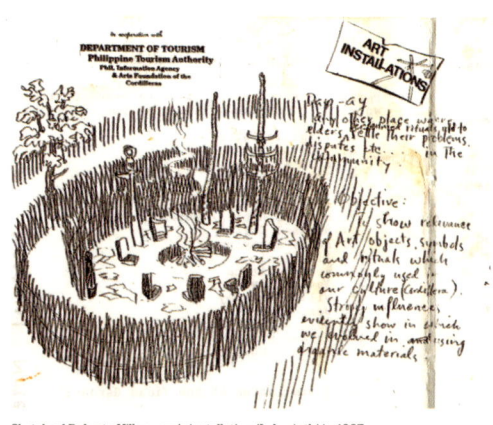

Sketch of Roberto Villanueva's installation 'Labyrinth' in 1987.

It would be erroneous and misleading to say that there was never dissension among the Guild's membership. Of course, there was: should the Guild use its limited material resources to reach out towards international collaboration or should it focus on the local, identifying and showcasing pockets of creativity within its community? This question was an ongoing debate among the Guild leadership. When one of the Guild's founding members was distressed at the direction the Guild was taking and was considering resigning, I remember thinking, *"It is time. All together we created something truly amazing, and like a child, it is time to let it go, to let the energy move in new directions, to leave a legacy of creative potential."* And that is what happened! SOD.

See also: Bose, Santiago.

* *"In the BAG" was the title of the Guild's newsletter.*

Baguio Arts Guild:
The Future of Curating a Complicated History

A story behind "The Baguio Arts Guild: 25 Years of Art for the Community, an exhibition of photos and mementos".

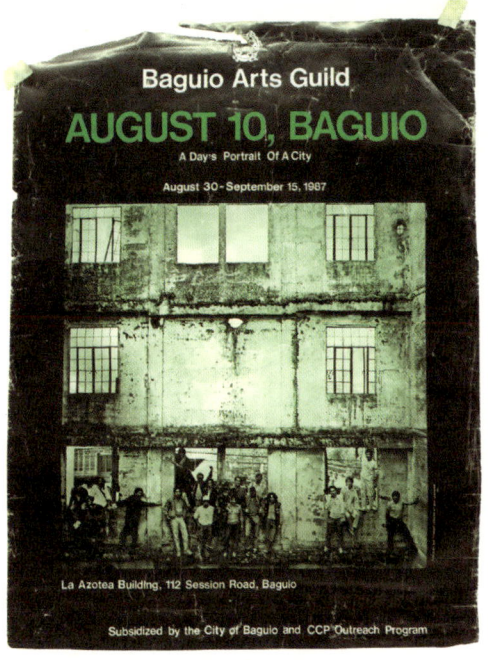

Poster of 'A Day's Portrait of a City,' 1987. Courtesy Baguio Arts Guild.

Prelude

In 1998, the City of Baguio graciously provided a space for its artists through the efforts of Baguio Arts Guild (BAG) founder Santiago Bose. The promised art space was a dilapidated greenhouse situated within the Botanical Gardens on the outskirts of the city.

This was after the BAG had to depart from its old sprawling venue in the basement of the Convention Center – the site of the popular and well-attended international art festivals and events hosted by the group since the early 90s which brought pride to the country and earned the city the name of 'Artist's Capital of the Philippines.'

After 15 years of occupying this space which we named The Greenhouse Effect Gallery; after improvements were made through sweat and tears, and funding from art patrons and sponsors; and after successfully creating an accessible center for culture dedicated to the community, the powers-that-be suddenly decided that they needed the space back and the artists had 45 days to vacate the premises.

Exhibition Concept

The crisis, although minor in the bigger scheme of things, was bound to shake people from complacency.

It was a problem of space: of ownership. We believed that we might need the help of the older, more well-known and influential members of the group but it also dawned on us that we might not get it. The greats who had first come together to form the Guild had left it long ago, leaving in their wake stardust and a faint smell of gunpowder.

In order to make a strong appeal to keep the space, we went through the Guild's old files. We went looking through dusty boxes forgotten in dark corners of attic spaces for mementos of the greatness that the Baguio Arts Guild once had. Aside from enough material for the planned Powerpoint to present to the powers-that-be, we found material that was good enough for a show. That is how the 'photos and mementos' exhibition was conceptualized.

Gathering the Material

One problem we faced was that these files consisted of nothing more than paperwork, really. They were a hodgepodge collection that hinted at a golden era of creative expression: old installation art concepts submitted to the Guild for one or the other of its many international art festivals; newspaper clippings from national and local broadsheets; different versions of the group's mission/vision/goals; rough, hand-drawn and silkscreened posters in the days before Photoshop; attendance sheets of BAG gatherings through the years; certificates and awards; brochures; minutes of meetings.

This time capsule of dusty old boxes allowed us to peer into the murky depths of both the past and

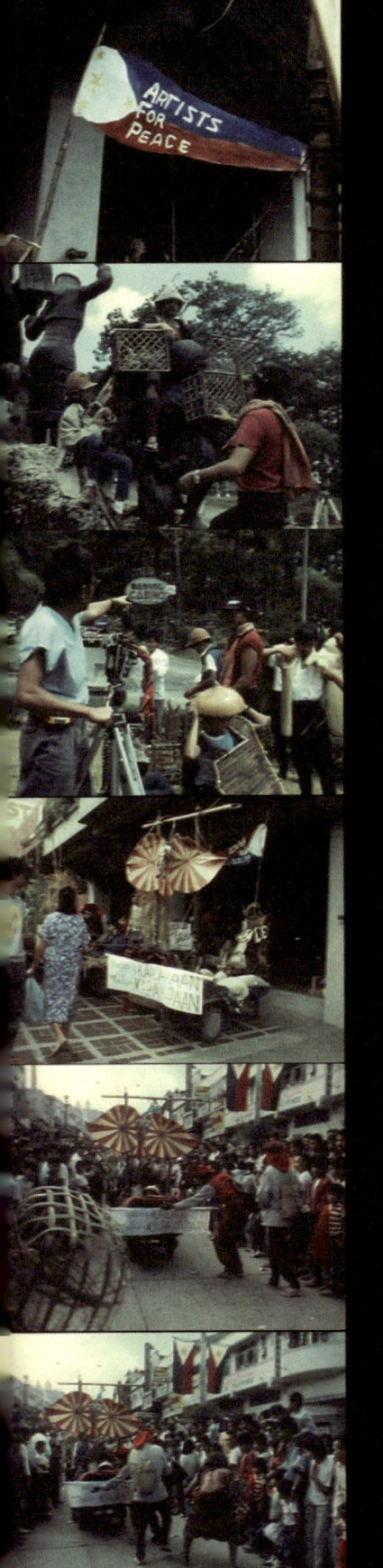

the possible future. Being the oldest art group in the Philippines, we were actually rifling through mementos of the grandmother of all art groups, which brought us to an intriguing question, *"Should art organizations which sprouted up around the country after 1987 expect a similar fate?"*

Photographs were missing from the files. We had no images to show one of the richest artistic periods in the life of the Guild. How ironic. Here had been history in the making, great art being made, and no photos! To make a successful show of this, a quest for old photographs was launched.

We learned that a boxful of photos which used to stand here in the gallery stockroom had made its way back to the family of the group's founder. We learned that, unlike today with its digitized files, some old members did have pictures but they were under piles of family photographs and hard to dig up in so short a time. We learned that most members did not have the luxury of point-and-shoot cameras as they went about their art activities in that time period. Luckily, a treasure trove of photographs surfaced – given by the artists who actually built the clay walls of the Greenhouse Effect Gallery. A few members who had the foresight to scan and upload their photos granted us the permission to use them. One or two more precious photographs from that golden age were also unearthed, and that was that. We had our show.

Bringing It All Together

Working with what we had, the exhibition opened on July 28, 2013 at the Guild's soon-to-be closed down gallery space. In the middle wall, visible as you enter, was a large image of the BAG logo printed on tarp juxtaposed with text from what we had collected from the files: a short history of its beginnings; a list of the original members, then a comprehensive list of all the members throughout the years; contributions to the community; awards and achievements; the objectives of the group; and a quote from founder-visionary Santiago Bose, who said:

> *"We struggled to change society, which is difficult and dangerous, and we also sought to preserve communal aspects of life.*
>
> *I too am haunted by visions of hardship, poverty, disenfranchisement of the primitive tribes, but between outbursts of violence and exploitation are also tenderness, selflessness and a sense of community. These will always remain unspoken and unrecognized unless we make art or music that will help to transform society."*

Film captures of Kidlat Tahimik's 'Why is Yellow the Middle of the Rainbow,' 1980-1993. Courtesy Kidlat Tahimik.

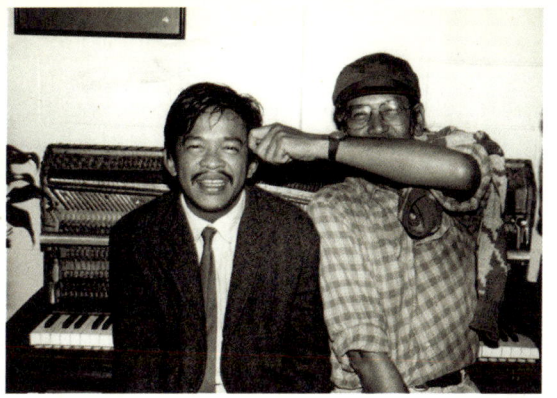
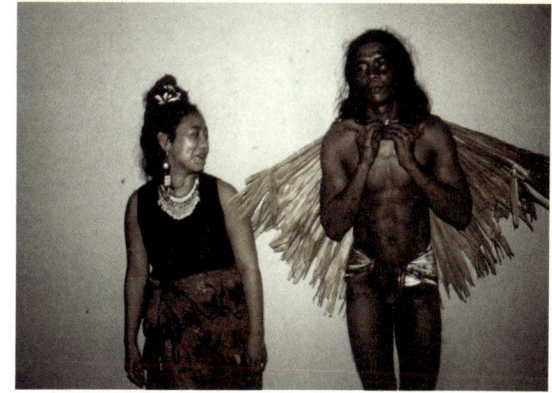
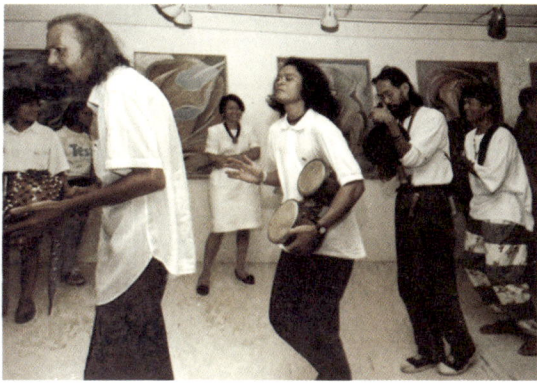
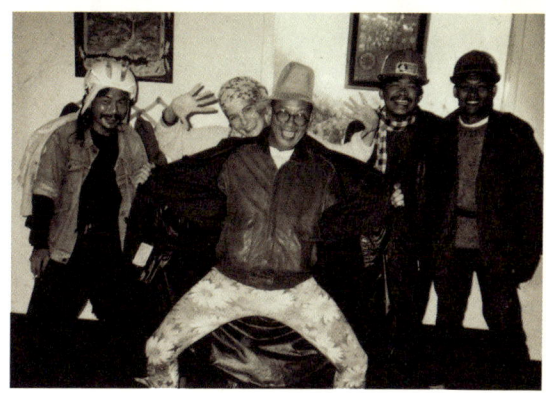

Photographs of some of the founders of the *Baguio Arts Guild*. Photographs by Angel Velasco Shaw.

The Exhibition of Photos and Mementos

If you had entered the gallery, you would have paused to take in the middle wall with the history of the BAG laid out in text. Slowly now, you might have taken in the visual offering. From the right side of the gallery going forward: a timeline of photographs, starting with a collection of art festival posters organized by the Guild since 1987; then photos of the founders in action; art activities around Baguio during that period such as installation art at the Baguio Convention Center grounds and various community projects; then photos of the alternative building process and materials using compacted clay and runo sticks to build the gallery walls; more community projects; an awarding ceremony at the Cultural Center of the Philippines; and present-day summer workshops for children.

On the adjacent wall to the tarp of BAG history you might have perused, in bulletin board format, a wide collection of proposals for installation art concepts: rough sketches on bond paper, some colored and some in black-and-white. Some of them were actually executed, and some were not. On the other side of the wall you might have read news clippings and the other odds and ends: attendance sheets with members' signatures (sparking imaginings of groupings and connections and the cultural landscape of the era), a secretary's notes of the meetings tell us the concerns and plans and assigned responsibilities of the time, more bric-a-brac.

And It's a Wrap!

This exhibit was a look into the past. But the past is over. Whatever wounds that era sustained, we bury them now in the face of the present. Their wars are not our wars. Their sins are not our sins. Whatever was created was created. It is now a part of Cordillera art history. I would go so far as to say that it has rightfully earned its place in Philippine art history. The current crop of artists might not burn as bright, but they are here. They are creating art. And there is always the future to look forward to. Egress is over. On to the next show! KVR.

Baguio Arts Guild:
In the Spirit of Kapwa

In the aftermath of EDSA I, and its celebration of indigenous Filipino cultural heritage, a fireball appeared on the social horizon of this cool northern town: The Baguio Arts Guild was born in 1987. Listed as the founding members were: Dr. David Baradas, Santiago Bose, BenCab, Yñong Geslani, Kidlat Tahimik, and Roberto Villanueva. Santiago Bose was the first president, followed by David Baradas, BenCab, Kidlat Tahimik, Willy Magtibay and others. Among the original members of the Guild were young maverick

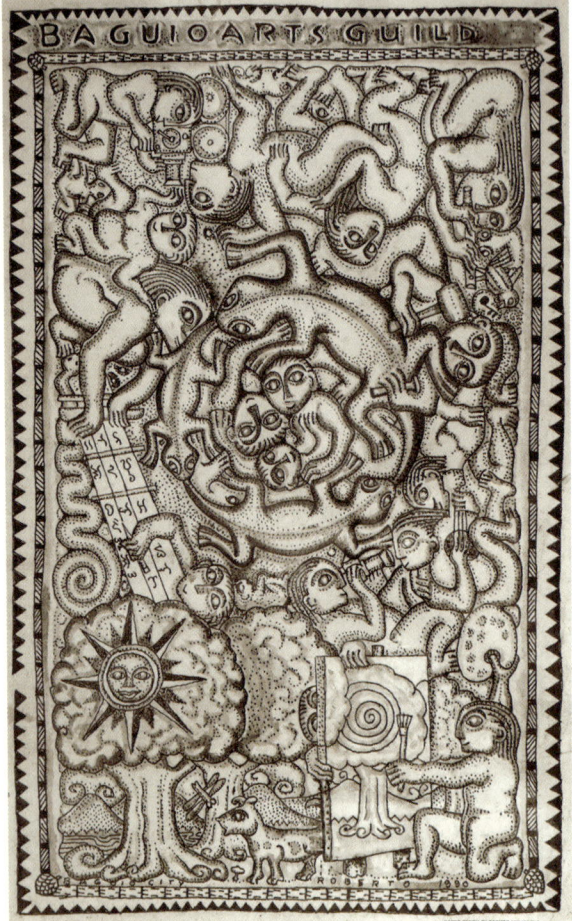

Artwork by Roberto Villanueva, 1990.

Rene Aquitania and his friend Perry Mamaril; and Baguio old timers Willy Magtibay, Wig Tysmans, Ompong Tan, Arturo Tibaldo (A.K.A. Artibal), and Tommy Hafalla; mirgrants Briccio Santos, Peter Pinder and Katrin de Guia; and the Cordillerans Rhona Carantes, Jocelyn Banasan, Vins Villareal, and Shay Tamayo (among other Baguio artists).

Next, a group of traveling troubadours (musicians/performers/craftsmen) arrived from Bacolod. Gerry Baguio, Boy Garrovillo, Tito Martinez and Shant Verdun wore colorful garbs, had handmade drums, and played the two-stringed guitars of the lumads. The "Bacolod boys" joined the Guild and regular music jams were "in". Street performances happened. Eventually, a new Filipino World Music Group – the Pinikpikan Band – came to be, with Grace Nono as lead singer.

The Guild attracted regular artistic collaborators. From the NCR there was Myra Beltran, the choreographer, who founded her Dance Forum Company M.B. as an outcry for artistic freedom in a Western dominated domain. Egay Navarro and Rica Concepcion filmed most of Roberto Villanueva's shamanic performance-installations. Angel Shaw from New York was a regular guest at the Guild. The ballet enfant terrible Enrico Labayen danced on bamboo poles under Baguio's sky.

The unique thing about the Guild was that its members bonded across artistic domains. Visual artists Santi Bose, BenCab and Willy Magtibay joined filmmakers Briccio Santos, Jocelyn Banasan, Arturo Tibaldo and Kidlat Tahimik, who worked with photographers Boy Yniguez, Wig Tysmans and Mannix Santos. Performance artists Rene Aquitania, Gerry Baguio, Vins Villareal and Sonny Balangan collaborated with musicians Boy Garrovillo, Tito Martinez and Shant Verdun. So did installation artist Roberto Villanueva, Ged Alangui, Clemente Delim and others. In the spirit of Kapwa, everybody helped everyone.

The thing that bonded all these artists together, across ethnicity and educational or social backgrounds, was a pro-Filipino Kapwa orientation that drew inspiration from the ancestral Filipino cultural heritage. To most of the Guild artists, the community was more important than individual fame. "ART FOR ALL" was their slogan and, together, they sought ways to create art that made sense for the people; art that was relevant for the time.

Such was the mood that birthed the Baguio Arts Festivals. The first of these happenings was called *Kalat-Kalat*. The venue was the soccer field of Burnham Park. A handful of scattered installations, assembled from found materials, dotted the space. At night, as opening ceremony, torchbearers on horses connected the individual works by lighting fires or candles around each. Percussions dramatized the moment. Grace Nono chanted the Salidumay in the light of the rising full moon, on the only available microphone.

Kalat-Kalat started a string of no-budget art events in Baguio that were organized by the Guild. Everyone in the community could join. Even after the BAG caught the attention of sponsors, the Kapwa spirit prevailed. After some time, the Guild became a buzzword in Manila and the Baguio Arts Festivals turned international – especially during the presidential terms of Santiago Bose.

The so called "first generation" of the BAG artists were those who already had names in the international art community: The mixed media artist Santi Bose, the painter BenCab, and the filmmaker Kidlat Tahimik. Soon, the ceremonial

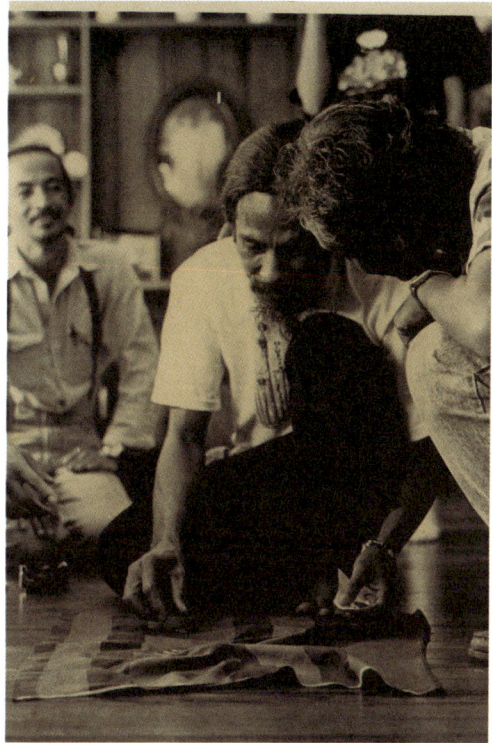 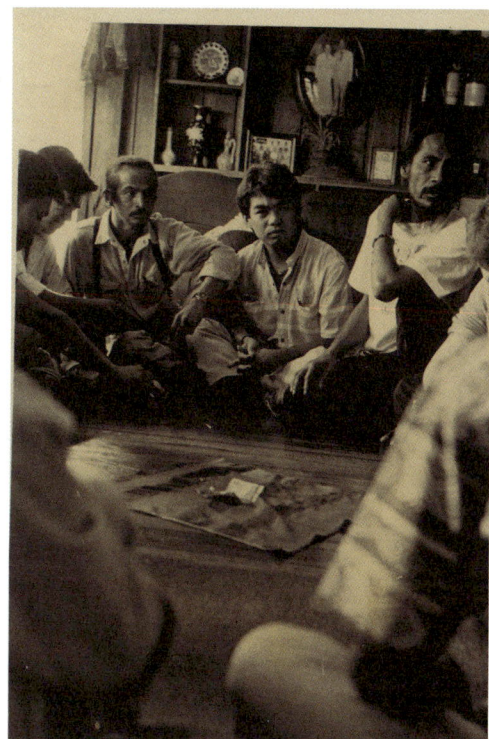

Photographs from one of the monthly Baguio Arts Guild meetings. Photographs by Ernesto Enrique.

artist Roberto Villanueva, the painter Willy Magtibay, and heritage photographer Tommy Hafalla, followed. And then, there was the "second generation" of the BAG artists who made it to fame: the painter/performer John Frank Sabado, the painter/print maker Leonard Aguinaldo, the solar painter Jordan Mangosan, painter/installation artist Ged Alangui and Kigao Rosimo, as well as, painter Roger "Rishab" Tibon. With these painters, the core group of the Tamawan Artists Group was born – hatched, headed and nurtured by the National Artist BenCab.

However, the BAG was never really about name and fame. It was not about competing and the like. It was about fun, relevance and creation. It was about making statements. It was about the love for art and the responsibility of being an artist. Truly Pinoy in spirit, it was Kapwa-based art.

The 'third generation' of artists who maintain this Kapwa art spirit of the Guild are the grown-up children of the Baguio Arts Guild founders and their friends. Among them are Roberto Villanueva's nephew Bumbo Villanueva; the writers Jenny Cariño and Padma Lim Perez with daughter Solana; Chavi Romawac, the drummer of Session Road Band who turned culinary chef; and photographer/filmmaker Kidlat de Guia, visual artist Kawayan de Guia, and mosaic artist Kabunyan de Guia. Installation artist and fashion designer Laydeh Alberto, junk-art artists Rommel Pidazo and Carlo Villafuerte, the Cordilleran talents Randy Bulayo, Ruel Bimuyag, Rocky Cajigan, Mark Tandoyog, Bong Sanchez, Paulo Sunggay, Jason Taguyongon, and others.

This 'third wave' of Baguio artists imbibed the culture-bearing art of their elders but moved it further along, spiced it up with graffiti, techno, and urban pop elements. *Copy Right,* a mixed media show at the Print Gallery by Kawayan de Guia (one of the energizers of the 'third generation') attests to this. KatDG

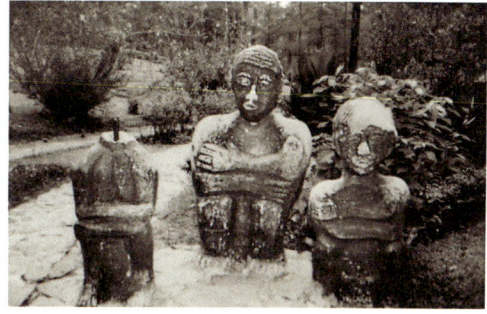

Photograph of sculptures at the *Botanical Garden*
Photograph by Kawayan de Guia.

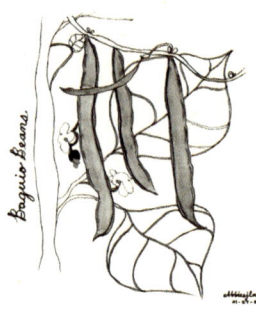
Baguio Beans

Baguio Bean. Also known as snap bean, green bean and French bean (although the French bean being sold in Baguio is the fine bean, which is thinner and crispier).

What is thought as the 'native' name of Baguio Bean which is 'lubyas' is actually the Arabic name for 'bean.' FYC.

See also: Buguias Patatas; Sayote; Zucchini.

Baguio Boy. Term used for men who were born and raised in Baguio, to distinguish them from migrants. Curiously, the term "Baguio girl" is rarely used.

Baguio Cathedral. On All Soul's Day, 1907, Fr. Seraphim Devesse was one of eight CICM priests to start their religious mission in the Philippines. Weeks later, Fr. Devesse arrived in Baguio and in 1908, he built the St. Patrick Church along Session Road. He also built another church in Campo Filipino, which later became the St. Vincent Church. Fr. Devesse was succeeded in 1913 by Rev. Fr. Florimund Carlu who then built the Baguio Cathedral over the St. Patrick Church in 1920. It was finished 16 years later. Towards the end of World War II, thousands of residents sought refuge there hoping to be spared from the carpet bombing of the Americans (who ironically built the city decades before). A Filipino spy, however, transmitted wrong information that Japanese soldiers were among those inside the cathedral and so American planes bombed it and thousands died there. They were interred in the catacomb below the altar. Fr. Carlu remained in the Cathedral until he died in 1950. The only other time that the Cathedral was closed for more than a week was after the July 1990 earthquake. FYC.

See also: Gingined.

Baguio Cine. The first movie houses in Baguio came around 1923 with the Garden Theater and the Baguio Cine, which was later renamed the Alhamar and later Alhamar-Chainus, in honor of Elizabeth Chainus Guirey, the first Benguet Carnival Queen. The movies shown then were all silent films and both movie houses had their resident pianists accompanying the movies. In the 1930s the Baguio Theater and Pines Theater were also built. After the war, Session Theater and Plaza Theater were built. FYC.

See also: Baguio (the movie); Guirey, Chainus; New Baguio Theater; Pines Theater; Plaza Theater.

Baguio Convention Center. In 1978, President Ferdinand Marcos hastened the construction of the Baguio Convention Center done in the style of neo-Cordilleran architecture so that the city could host the World Chess Championship between Anatoly Karpov of Russia and émigré Viktor Korchnoi, who defected from Russia to Switzerland. The series, the second longest in history, was also the most bizarre, with charges of hypnotism (from a parapsychologist in team Karpov), possible assassination (from an Ananda Marga couple named Didi & Dada in Team Korchnoi), and an unexpected blueberry yoghurt seen as a coded message for Karpov. The chairs were also X-rayed to be extra sure. Karpov raced to a 5-2 lead but by the 31st game, the series was leveled at 5-5. Karpov won the last game to clinch the title. BCC was later used as a venue for other important international chess tournaments. By 1988 to the early 2000s, it became the venue for the Baguio International Arts Festival. FYC.

See also: Baguio Arts Guild, The Future of; Baguio Arts Guild, The History of.

Baguio Distillery. Chuan Suy Coy and Kee Koy opened the Baguio Distillery in Pico, La Trinidad before World War II to manufacture home brewed local wines and liquor. (Cheng & Bersamira 1997, 138-137).

Baguio Express. In 1931, it meant a train going from Tutuban in Manila to Damortis, La Union, then being driven up to Baguio by Benguet Auto Lines. First class fares included sleeper and dining cars with chauffeured automobile service worth a grandiose PHP14.33 at the time. FYC.

See also: Benguet Auto Lines.

Baguio General Hospital School of Nursing. Founded in 1923, this was the first college in Baguio and the Cordillera region.

Baguio (Geological Story). *"Viewed in a geological time frame, the 1,500 meter high Baguio plateau is a transitory phenomenon soon destined to be washed into the Western Philippine Sea. On the south, the Bued canyon cuts a kilometer deep gorge whose rocky, almost vertical sides are constantly undermined by the swiftly flowing Bued River. To the northeast and north, the Asin/Galiano and Trinidad rivers drop almost precipitously, while on the east, streams race toward the Agno gorge far below. Raging torrents in the summer rainy season, the rivers later dwindle to mere trickles."* (Leith 1938, 15-18).

Baguio Gold. [1] Mining company founded in 1903 by American Neils Petersen after he was brought to the area near Tuba by overzealous Igorots. Petersen went broke and was taken over by mining tycoon Judge Haussman who incorporated it in 1930. The company was devastated by World War II and was later rehabilitated. It became a gold mine on paper as the Baguio Gold Holdings Corporation. In 2007, it became the PAL Holdings Inc. under billionaire Lucio Tan. FYC.

[2] A strain dominantly of C. sativa said to have a spicy and even floral aroma. Provides

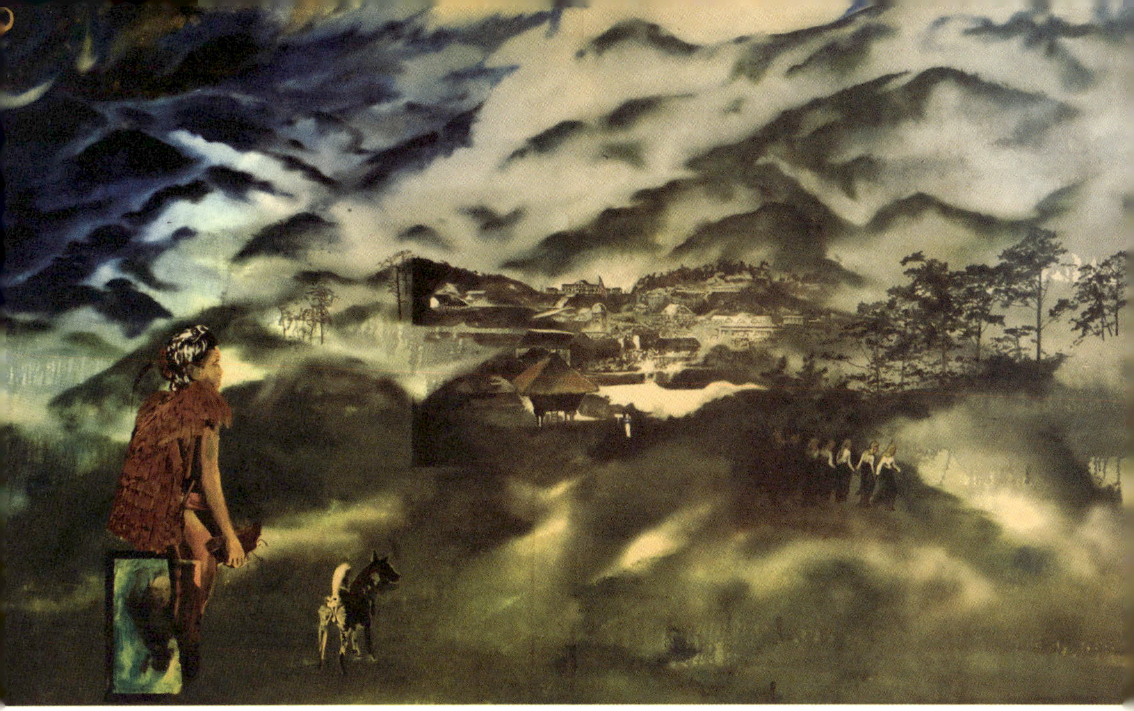

Artwork by Kawayan de Guia, 2001.

intense closed-eye visuals and composes active imagineering. May be too potent for hash.
See also: Tonglo.

Baguio Newspapers before WWII. The Baguio News was the first newspaper in Baguio, started during the summer of 1911. The Baguio Banner was the first weekly managed by Baguio residents, started right after World War II. In November 1930, The Manila Bulletin started publishing a weekly supplement known as Baguio Bulletin. FYC.

Baguio Oil. In 1932, the Cheng Ban Yek family, which had a large grocery store in the Binondo area in Manila, established the first locally-owned cooking oil factory in the country and decided to call it the International Oil Factory (IOF). To make their brand of coconut-based cooking oil more cosmopolitan, they decided to name it after the summer capital of the country. They also took the most picturesque part of Kennon Road to go with their brand illustration. The IOF, however, overlooked the fact that coconut oil solidifies in cooler climate so the use of cans (which in Manila are just punctured to let the oil pour) made it impractical in Baguio. However, the large cylindrical cans of Baguio Oil would be used by Igorot women in the 1970s and 80s to haul water in hard-to-reach areas like the top floors of commercial buildings along Session Road and the tight corridors of the city market. Baguio Oil's earlier slogan *"Para sa Kalusugan ng Buong Mag Anak [For the Health of the Whole Family],"* was in reference to the health benefits of lauric acid. Its later slogan *"Ang Order ni Misis [Wife's Order],"* was seen as an indirect reference to Imelda Marcos during the Martial Law years.

Interestingly, IOF's *"Lion Margarine"* came before the Lion's Head at Kennon Road. And because the illustration came before the sculpting of the Lion's Head, this huge sculpture is not visible in Baguio Oil's Kennon Road. IOF later came out with Baguio Corn Oil and Baguio Canola Oil. FYC.
See also: Kennon Lion; Kennon Road.

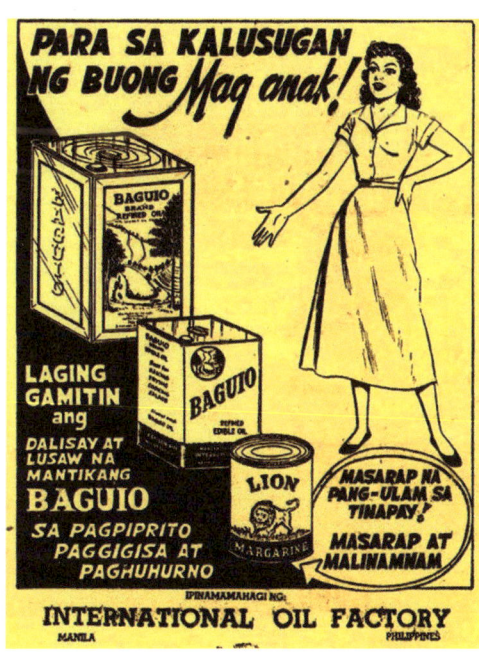

Illustration of the International Oil Factory's famous coconut-based cooking oil brands with their popular slogan *"Para sa Kalusugan ng Buong Mag-anak."* Still the country's #1.

Baguio Ghost Stories

Someone once said that true love is like a psychic experience: everybody loves to tell stories about ghosts, but only a few have actually encountered them. So if Baguio has earned the title 'Honeymoon Capital of the Philippines,' you can put it down partly on all those ghost sightings. Not only do they provoke enough shivers to make getting close to someone inevitable, but even Baguio residents find that recounting their favorite ghost stories goes perfectly with a romantic bonfire or a candlelit dinner. And if honeymoons are occasioned by a bride in white, so too does Baguio have its White Lady of Loakan Road, with all the elements of the classic ghost story: A nearby cemetery with neatly lined-up white crosses, a blanket of fog, a grove of pine trees, and a solitary tree right in the middle of the road. That tree was cut down several years ago, but on some rainy nights, people traveling there swear that it comes back to life like one of J.R.R. Tolkien's Ents, those tall humanoid trees.

Baguio-based writer Nonnette Bennett wrote a prequel to the White Lady of Loakan for the series of monologues in *Baguio Stories*. Bennett's monologue was of the carnival queen Chainus Guirey waiting for her father to fetch her after the carnival at Burnham Park, unaware that she had passed on and had become the White Lady. *"That's the essence of ghosts. They are all waiting,"* said Bennett.

That also defines the ghostly couple at Quezon Hill, she added. *"They are old people waiting on a bench outside a house in that area. From a vantage point of Baguio, they are also waiting for someone to pick them up."* The ghosts of Baguio are different from those in other places in the country. There are no aswangs (ghouls) terrorizing the city residents or even the horse-like tikbalang smoking marijuana atop a pine tree. The Spanish collective unconscious is not so apparent in Baguio, so there are no stories of headless priests or tiyanak, which are said to be babies who died before they were baptized.

Bennett said ghosts are not really as frightening as their cinema counterparts would have us believe. *"They are pleasant to look at. They walk normally but you'd discern that they are ghosts only when you realize that you did not see their feet,"* she said. You become aware of their presence, Bennett said, when your head seems to swell. Others get the shivers, their hairs bristle, they feel a sudden gust of cold air or they get this feeling that they are being watched. Add the fog and the pine trees that are part of Baguio, and you have the perfect setting for a ghost story.

A traumatic experience for Baguio, as it was for the rest of the country, was World War II. The Baguio Cathedral compound, for one, was bombed by Americans at the end of the war. Hundreds perished there, and ghost stories have thrived since. Ogilby Hall, the oldest wooden building in the city, was turned into a Japanese infirmary during the war. And there are still Japanese tunnels at the Baguio Botanical Garden and nearby areas where children and treasure hunters are reported to have heard groans and utterances in Nihongo. Students of Brent School in Baguio also talk of seeing Japanese soldiers marching about at night. *"Want to hear a ghost story?"* asked Brent deputy head Ursula Daoey. *"We can talk for hours."*

A scary, and possibly ghost-inducing event in Baguio was the July 16, 1990 earthquake. The Spirit Questors Baguio identified Nevada Square, the University of Baguio parking lot (the site of the former FRB Hotel), and the Hyatt Terraces grounds on South Drive as paranormal tourist spots. In the first séance by the Spirit Questors at the Hyatt Terraces grounds shortly after the 1990 earthquake, one of the first spirits that channelled did not belong to any of those who died in the quake, but was that of an Igorot warrior guarding the place. Some sources claim that he lives in one of the trees still standing there.

Igorots are very spiritual. Anito is a term used for the spirit of the dead, and in Ifugao it means an evil spirit that causes sickness by detaining wandering souls. Among the Igorots, there's also the familiar term annong (to sacrifice) or naanannongan (to be made ill by a ghost). One particular spirit is the bagong or binagong, which is the spirit of a headless person. There's also ambaboy or the spirit inhabiting the sacred trees or pinad-ing or patpatayan.

It is important to note that most Baguio ghost stories are tied to trees, like the White Lady of Loakan and the Warrior of Hyatt, because they are said to return to the cycle of nature and spirituality: you cut the trees and the spirits leave.

It is said around these parts that when evil, in the form of natural calamities, comes and people become ghosts, they hope to inhabit a tree to stop them from wandering. But, if another person comes and cuts down the tree, then the cycle repeats itself. The restless soul finds another tree to inhabit until it too is cut down. The cycle never ends, which also explains why a bonfire of pine logs and the sound of wind whistling through pine needles are essential while listening to Baguio's ghost stories. FYC.

See also: Ambaboy; Anido; Anito; Bagong; Gingined; Guirey, Chainus; Loakan Road White Lady; Naanannongan; Papattay.

Opposite page: Photograph of Banaue houses by Frank Callaghan, 2012. Courtesy Frank Callaghan.

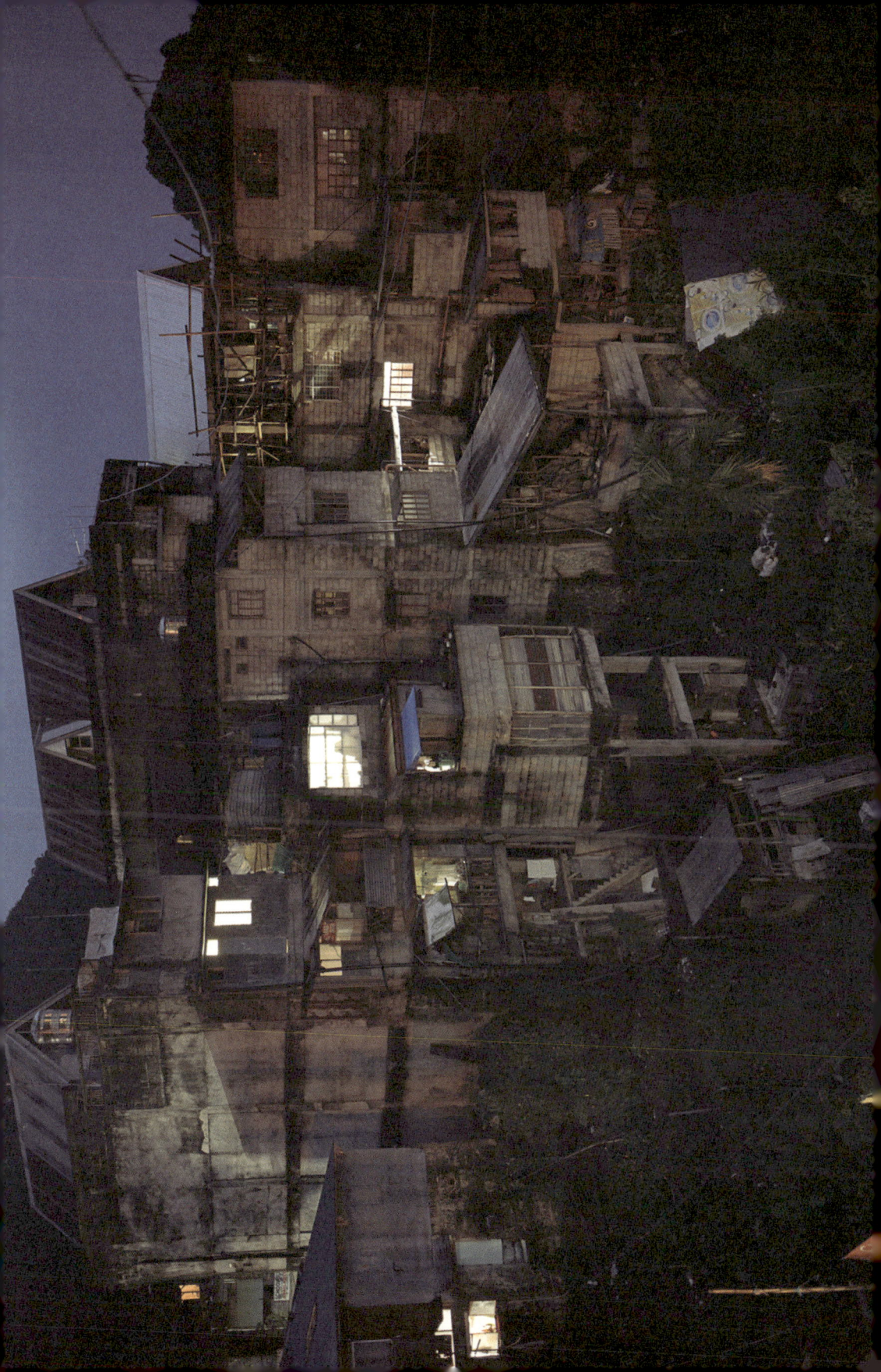

Baguio [the movie]. In October 1950, an ad in the Baguio Midland Courier sought native talents as leading man and woman, villain and villainess for a movie with *"the glorious setting of Baguio and Mountain Province"* and simultaneous world premieres in Baguio, Manila and Hollywood. It would be directed by Tor Villano, a famous movie director. Selection was not done by audition, but through ticket-selling. Those who sold the most tickets would get the parts. By December, the search became feverish. Among those who joined were Alfredo Iamen, Mina Ruiz, Catherine Carantes, Josephine Adaro, Terry Aquino, Nick Sali and Joven Villanueva. In the end, it was Sali and Aquino that became the leading actors while the villains were Mary Pecley and Pol Bastawang. Sadly, the search was a fraud and there was really no Baguio movie. FYC.

See also: Abong; Baguio Cine; Banaue: Stairway to the Sky; Cielo, Marky; Igorota: The Legend of the Tree of Life; Irisan (the movie); Kung Mangarap Ka't Magising; Vacacionista.

Baguio, The Naming of. *"Turning in the first place to the old Spanish records treating of the country around Baguio, we are struck by the absence in them of that city's name so familiar to us at present. We thus look for it in vain in Quirante's report on his expedition to the gold-mines in and around 'Antamog' in 1624, although he seems to have visited all that neighborhood. The name Baguio, spelled phonetically, presents itself as the Inibaloy term bagyu which denotes, in this as well as in the Ifugaw dialect, that submerged slimy water plant with floating leaves that is known to botany as Potamogeton, and to the Tagalog as lumot. Old inhabitants assured me that this was the name given formerly to the watery bottom of the Kisad valley between Baguio and Trinidad, tho none of them could tell how it had come to apply to the locality now so designated. For Baguio, as the term generally current in the Philippines for 'typhoon', the Ibaloys have the word puok. As will appear further on, Baguio bore in olden times the name Kafagway [Ilk. kapaway, stem paway, grassy clearing] which alludes to the center of the Baguio basin, a piece of prairie that was more conspicuous before the creek Minak meandering thru it was expanded into the present Burnham Park Lake. As a matter of fact, all topographic designations used by the natives go very much into detail, covering often but a few hectares of land, and, with the frequent desertions by the Ibaloys of their settlements – as often as not a silent protest against outside interference – also the names of their former dwelling-places and adjoining useful grounds fall into oblivion. The oldest extant Spanish records, now, that treat in detail cultural developments in and around the area at present, constituting the jurisdiction of Baguio, are accounts of certain missionary endeavors carried on there by Augustinian friars around the year 1755."* (Scheerer 1975, 176)

See also: Burnham Lake; Burnham Park; Gateway to Wonderland; White Elephant.

Baka-baka. Childhood insects in Baguio have repeating names like budo-budo (hairy caterpillars which sometimes hang on silvery strings in the morning and can cause inflammation and extreme itchiness when touched), lawa-lawa (spiders which are captured and kept in matchboxes and then made to battle on a broomstick), kadang-kadang (Daddy Longlegs, which sadistic children play with by yanking their legs only to laugh as the legs move frantically without the bodies), and baka-baka (member of the Butrespid beetles) that have a hard black exoskeleton. Baka-baka live on the bark of pine trees, and pinch your lips when you try to kiss them. FYC.

See also: Yayas.

Bakget *(KAN)* also **Wakes** *(BON)*. [1] Wrap-around belt used by Kankanaey and Bontoc women to hold their gaboy, or tapis. The bakget can be up to three yards long and is worn somewhat like the Japanese obi. At both ends of the bakget are fringes that are then tied together. One of the discriminatory utterances towards the highlanders is *"Igorots have tails."* This phrase might have come from the loincloth that men use, and the women's bagket. Both appear like tails to some outsiders. DOS.

[2] Wide woven cotton belt (sometimes of synthetic threads) used to hold the tapis in place. A special one without tassels is for a newly-delivered mother. This belt is wound tightly around the lower abdomen to hold the body in its proper alignment after giving birth, holding the uterus to avoid a sagging or protruding belly. It also helps to relieve aliwan. It also strengthens the back while working and carrying a load. It is supposed to be worn just after childbirth until the next pregnancy. Bontoc women traditionally use it all throughout their lives, giving them slim waists. PAD.

See also: Aliwan; Igorot Tail; Tapis; Weaving; Wanes.

Bakkat *(ISN)*. An animal killed in a trap.

Bakkay *(KAN)*. Naturally-fermented corn kernels mostly made in Bauko, Mountain Province; very sour and could be added to any vegetable, usually gabi (taro). PAD.

See also: Abungol; Aw-aw; Safeng.

Balbalasang. People who think that Balbalasang, a village in Balbalan, Kalinga is a village of balasang (girls in *ILO*) should think twice because it means, 'place where the balasang tree grows.' Balbalasang is an old Kalinga village that was visited by foreign anthropologists and photographers such as Hans Meyer, Alexander Schadenberg and Fay Cooper Cole. In 1925, it became one of the mission points of Episcopalian missionaries and St. Paul's Memorial High School was opened there. FYC.

Balballo *(KAN)* also **Bagbaxo** *(ISN)*, **Fab-al-lu** *(BON)*. Handsome young man.
See also: Gannawa.

Bale *(IFU)*. It is the general term for house. Baletau means 'our house,' Balemi means 'our house' excluding the listener, and baleyu means 'your house.' Abong is a small house. Strictly speaking, for purposes of defining the social status of people in earlier times, bale would include only the structure now labeled as the Ifugao native house.

The Ifugao native house follows a more or less uniform pattern although the designs might vary. It is elevated by four posts, the height usually more than a foot above the average height of a man (so that would be approximately six and a half feet). The four posts are made from the lower trunk (usually including the upper part of the roots) of mature trees. The posts are arranged to form a square approximately six to eight feet apart from each other. Each of the main posts stand on a smoothened boulder. The upper part of every post is chopped to accommodate a disk from a wider trunk that forms a ring around the post. This is called the lidi, which, aside from its aesthetic purpose also serves as protection from rats and other pests that might climb the house. Two kuling (shafts) usually made of sturdy wood requiring the whole trunk of a tree, are chiseled and dovetailed to the front posts and the hind posts. Two mundilig (joists) connect the kuling. A gawa'an (center joist) is also held in place. Fitted to stand on the mundilig are the bagat (columns), the posts on the four corners. Resting on the bagat are the wanan (rafters). Floors are fixed in between the mundilig and the gawa'an while walls (wooden or made of bamboo) are clipped by the mundilig and the wanan. The panto (door) is usually positioned perpendicular to the gawa'an. The wanan serves as the platform of the roof's wooden framework which is pyramidical in shape and composed of several parts: the bilid, the kaho and the binollan which are all bound at the middle by what is called the puhuhan. The roofing is usually made of cogon and fastened by bamboo splits.

After all these are assembled, you are left with a one-room structure measuring about 80 to 100 square feet. The assemblage also includes cupboards. The place in between the wanan and the roofing accommodates a patye for storing household things such as dining utensils on one side, beddings on another, and clothes. The pyramidical roofing also shelters palah (cupboards or storage area for the rice harvest). These cupboards would also accommodate other valuables such as the bulul, and small wine jars.

The Ifugaos also have the pinadel, referring to big houses made from concrete, wood and iron. The pinadel does not follow the uniform pattern of the traditional house.

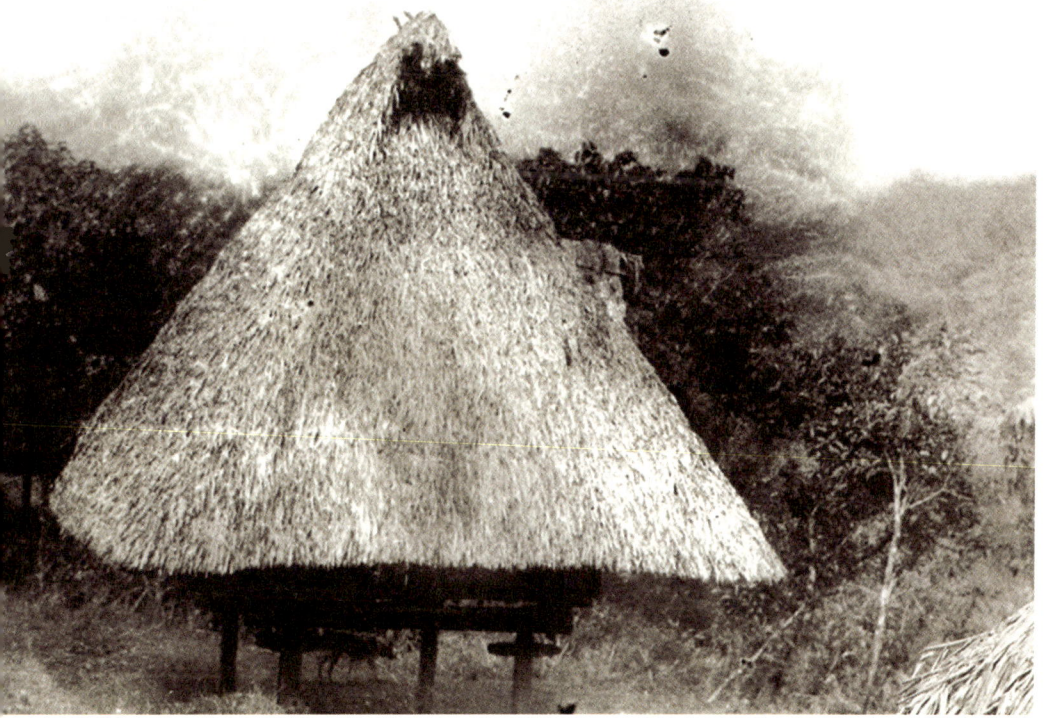

Photograph of the *bale* or *abong*, 2006. Photograph by Kawayan de Guia.

There are distinct terms for houses used for special purposes in Ifugao. One is the agamang (not to be confused with the Kankanaey agamang), the sleeping quarters for adolescents and unmarried adults. There are separate agamang for males and females. A village could have several agamang. These are informally organized, and the occupants do not pay rent. Usually, these are the houses of widows, widowers, or unmarried adults. Sometimes a bawo (literally, an empty house, but referring to houses that are left behind by its owners who may have moved to another place or house) can also be used as an agamang. Courtships often happen in the agamang for women.

Another bale of special purpose is the alang. It is solely for the purpose of storing the rice harvest. It is usually resorted to when the rice field is too far from the residence of the owner and the harvest is substantial. RHK.

See also: Abong; Allang; Architecture.

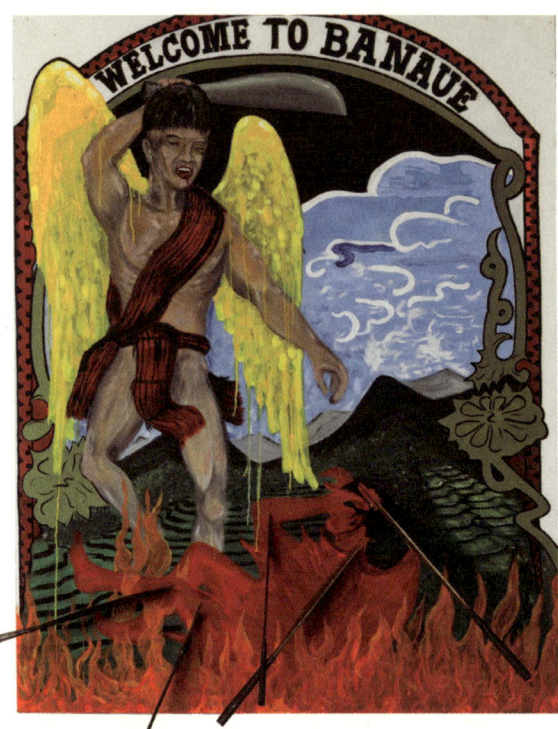

Artwork by Gaston Damag, 2016. Photograph by At Maculangan.

Balikawkaw *(IFU).* Ring around the moon.
See also: Beska; Lennek; Moon Craters; Seddag; Teke.

Baliw *(ISN).* A kind of divination practiced by a dorarakit attending to a sick person.
See also: Dorarakit.

Baliw-a *(KAN).* Water troughs made of stone, often in the shape of birds, snails and other animals. Mostly found in Sagada, they were said to have been made by Japanese masons and carpenters who migrated to that town in the 1920s. FYC.
See also: Horse-watering trough.

Balkah *(IKA).* Planting of tiger grass at the sides of vegetable terraces to prevent soil erosion and maintain soil fertility by using the mulch. FYC.

Balweg brothers. How exciting or unnerving it must have been as guest of the Balweg family at dinner, especially in the late-1980s. One of them was a healer, another a professor in La Trinidad who once ran under the Kilusang Bagong Lipunan (KBL) party of then-president Marcos, while another was a New People's Army (NPA) commander. Who would lead the prayers? Conrado Balweg is the most famous of these brothers. Conrado became a Society of the Divine Word (SVD) priest at the late age of 37 in 1971, at the onset of martial law, and subscribed to the teachings of liberation theology. He was a priest in Sallapadan, Abra when the Marcos regime introduced the Cellophil project in the province. In solidarity with the Itneg people, Fr. Balweg joined the underground army in 1979 and became 'Ka Ambo.' In 1987, he defected from the New People's Army (NPA) and took with him the elite Lumbaya company, which he headed. He then renamed the company the Cordillera People's Liberation Army (CPLA) that gained members from all over the region. His brother, Jovencio, a barangay secretary of Maligcong town and mass leader joined the NPA at the same time as Conrado. He, however, stayed with the NPA and 'Ka Rudy' eventually rose through the ranks, becoming the top cadre in Abra. It is said that it was Jovencio who ordered the killing of Conrado Balweg on Dec. 31, 1999 when he finally returned to their hometown in Bangilo, Abra. Ka Rudy was captured in 2009 and was released two years later. Eldest brother Bienvenido Balweg retired as a professor of the Benguet State University and remained loyal to the KBL. Their other brother, Crispin, was a timmawidan who could detect diseases and prescribe herbs to counter them. He was empowered by their Buanao village's spirit idol known as Sangasang, which is embodied in the stone monuments found at the entrance to the village. FYC.

See also: Cellophil; Chico; Dulag; Macli-ing; Mambunong; Peace Zone; Vochong.

Banan *(ISN).* To sneeze. When a group of Isneg is about to leave for a journey or a hunt and one of them sneezes, he or she will proceed while the rest will have to postpone because if they proceed, they will be drowned or wounded. FYC.

See also: Fungais; Okat!

Banaue Breakfast. "The so-called Banaue Breakfast is enjoyed every morning by the President and [his] family during his stay in this rancheria. It is tasty, light and digestible, cheap and easy to prepare. It consists of milk and coffee, fried camote, and five to seven millimeters' thick of butter. It is named thus by the President." (Ocampo 2008).

Banaue: Stairway to the Sky. The great film director Gerry de Leon's final film tells about the story of how the Banaue rice terraces were made and how headhunting came to be. Anthropologists will hem and haw about whether the rice terraces could be carved out of the mountains after only a few years, but Filipino film fans in 1975 (the movie was first shown in April 1975) would remember this as the movie where Nora Aunor, as Banaue, fell in love (in and out of the movie) with Christopher de Leon as Sadek. The film contains a controversial olog (a kind of courtship house) scene as well as a tribal war scene between the Ifugaos and the Kalingas (led by Ronaldo Valdez as the warrior Aruk), where Banaue's father's head is taken by Aruk. Banaue took her father's head back by going to Kalinga and charming Aruk but when she failed to return to Kalinga as promised, another war was waged ending with the deadly battle between Sadek and Aruk. Needless to say, the movie won a slew of awards even if most of the shots were taken in the Baguio Botanical Garden. FYC.

See also: Abong; Baguio (the movie); Big Bird Cage; Botanical Garden; Igorota: The Legend of the Tree of Life; Irisan (the movie); Kung Mangarap Ka't Magising; Vacacionista.

Banaue Vespa. Wooden scooters constructed by Banaue residents. The famous downhill road of Banaue, Poblacion is conducive for scooters and luges. There were only a few crude scooters a few years ago, but when the Gotad festival was started, wooden scooter races were introduced. Riders started wearing loincloths and the wooden scooters became more elaborate, with jaguars or dragons on their crashbars. Even the stories fed to the media became more elaborate. There were claims that they race to settle boundary disputes and the like. Some use the scooter to deliver water or LPG tanks. FYC.

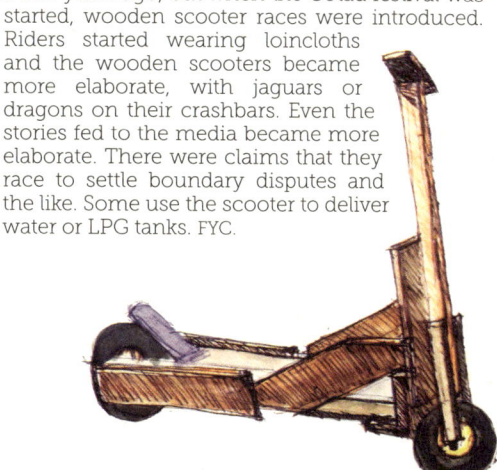

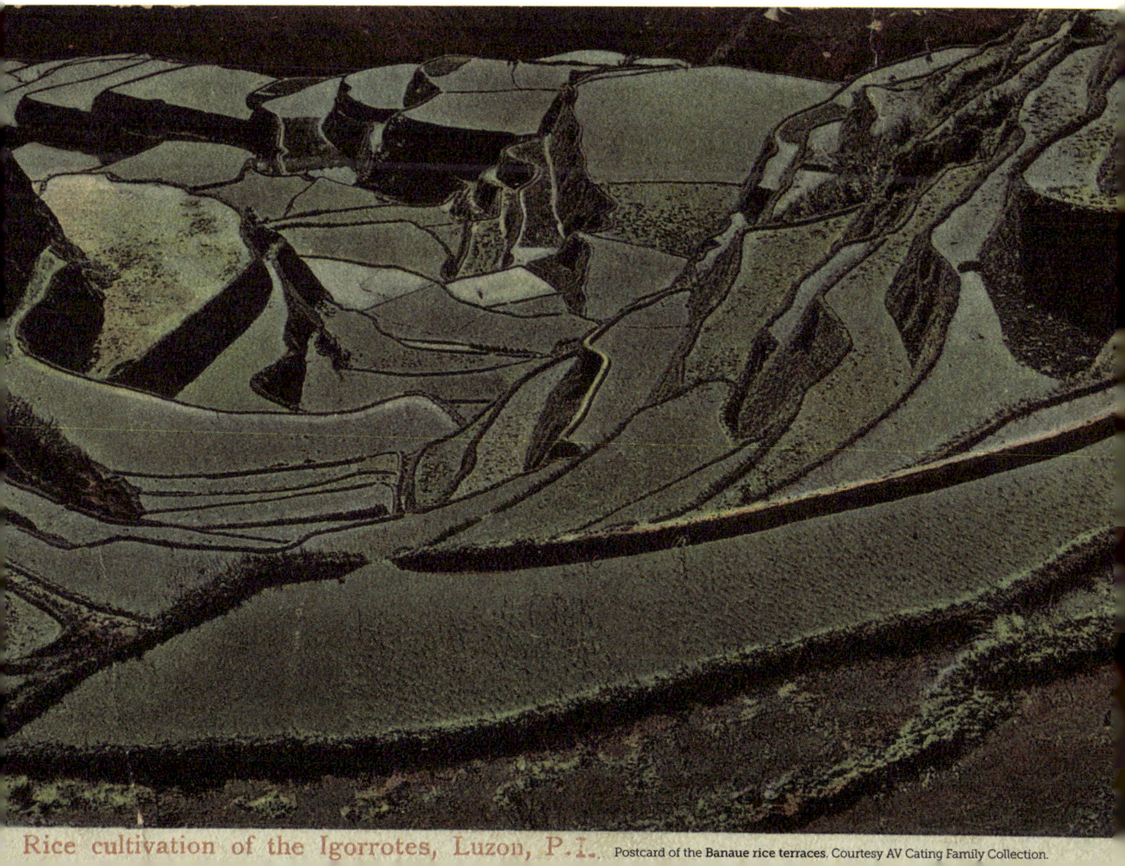

Rice cultivation of the Igorrotes, Luzon, P.I. Postcard of the Banaue rice terraces. Courtesy AV Cating Family Collection.

Bangan *(KAN)*. The wife of the lightning god, Gatan.

In the heavens, Gatan was watching over Bangan and her mother. He took pity on the two women who were living together without a male companion. So, one night he went down to earth and descended into the yard of Bangan. The door of the hut was closed so he was not able to enter. He instead made himself smaller so he could enter the small door of the beki (a chicken house) and stayed there for the night. In the morning he was invited to the house and he proposed to Bangan who accepted him. Bangan gave birth to two demi-gods, Kabigat and Longayban. DOS.
See also: Aginaya, Panginomnoman ki; Headhunting (the tale); Longayban.

Bangbangbang Bangued! This is how residents of the capital town of Bangued, Abra would jokingly refer to their hometown. The town is known as a hotbed for assasinations from politicking during election season. DOS.

Bang-gor *(IFU)*. Necklace.
See also: Apang.

Bangibang *(IFU)*. Wooden clanger used in rituals.

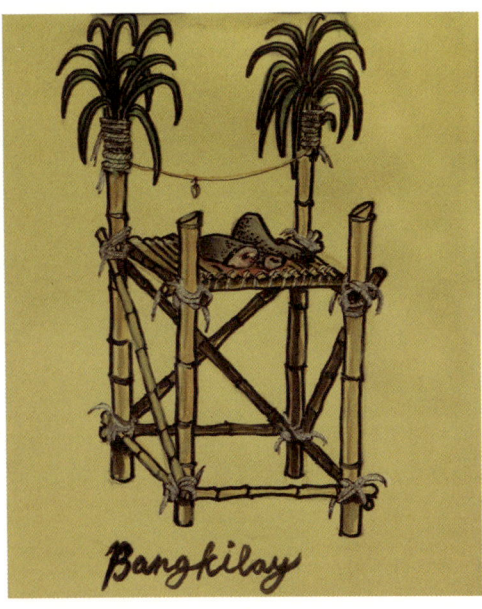

Bangkilay *(IBA)*. A raised platform of runo and saplings upon which ritual offerings are served and presented.
See also: Agpay; Runo.

Bangon *(KAN)*. During the begnas, the men go to a sacred place and keep vigil through the night. At the crack of dawn, they make noises to wake up the birds. This is the bangon. This is done to look for omens from the birds. TDH.
See also: Bedbed; Begnas; Ichaw; Ikik; Iyag; Labeg; Sabusab.

Bangonan *(ISN)*. Amaranthaceous herb with speckled leaves of different colors that shamans wear like hairbands. It is also the first to be planted during the planting of tobacco.

Banig *(KAN)*. [1] *"A ghostly apparition that so frightens one he cannot move, hence nabanig: rooted to the spot."* (Scott 2011, 149).
[2] *(KAL)*. *"A terrifying spirit that throws stones at travelers in the dark."* Scott (ibid).
[3] *(IFU)*. *"A death-portending phantom."* Scott (ibid.).
See also: Alan; Bagong; Carangat; Darupaypay; Ibwa; Nginin; Tinguian Spirits.

Banuwat *(KAN)*. Fire-starter used in rituals connected to Apoy, made up of a bundle of dried rice straw tightly tied together. TDH.
See also: Apoy.

Barako *(FIL)*. [1] Colloquial for wild and apparent machismo.
[2] *(FIL/ILO)*. Refers to coffee of the lowland Liberica or Robusta varieties. In the Cordilleras, it means any brewed black coffee that's not straight out of a sachet poured into hot water. Mountain people prefer to percolate their coffee. In Bontoc's old market, you can ask for half a cup or a full cup of strong coffee or say *"dilyut."* Barako is best ordered at first brew, 6:30 in the morning in the old market. Order a hotcake sidekick called sadkik. Your choices are: plain, with butter, with condensed milk, or a batter mix with chocnut candy.
See also: Sadkik.

Barangal *(KAN)*. A men's hand-woven scarf made with intricate beadwork worn in Eastern Mountain Province. TDH.

Baruti *(ILO/KAN/IBA)*. From the inside of a house, these are the exposed horizontal frames of a wall which are used for putting stuff on, like moma, hats, wallets and kitchen utensils, much as you would with a shelf. HZK.
See also: Abong; Bale.

Basi. *"The only intoxicating drink made and used by this people is the fermented juice of the sugar-cane, known as basi. The juice when extracted from the cane is boiled with water for four or five hours. It is placed in a large jar together with cinnamon bark, and is tightly covered over with leaves. Fermentation begins almost at once, but for a month the drink is raw and little prized. In three or four months, it becomes quite mellow and pleasant to the taste. Jars are sometimes stored away to be opened only for some important event,*

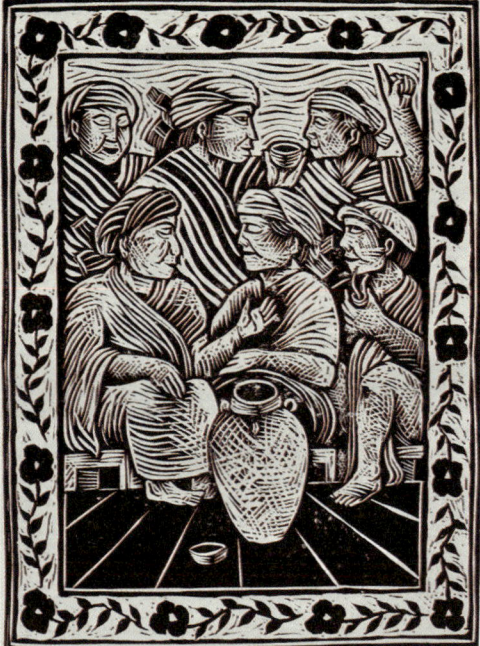

Artwork by Leonard Aguinaldo, 2013.

such as a marriage festival or the celebration of a great ceremony. At such a time a very definite procedure is followed. The most honored guest is invited to do the serving. He removes the covering, dips into the liquor, and pours a little on the sides of the jar, and then a few drops on the ground as an offering to the spirits. A coconut shell cup is then dipped out, and is carried to the lakay or some other old man. Before he drinks, he raises the cup to the level of his face, and, beginning at his right, offers it to each person in the circle. The one saluted makes a gesture away from his body with his right hand, the palm upturned. When all have refused the cup, the man drinks, often he stops to sing the daleng, an improvised song in which he compliments his host, bespeaks the welfare of his family, or praises the other members of the gathering. One after another the guests are served, but always according to age and importance, the women and young people being left to the last. The liquor is quite intoxicating, two or three drinks being sufficient to put the company in a jovial mood. It often happens that one or more will become gloriously drunk, but, as a rule, they are not quarrelsome, and there seems to be no unpleasant after-effects." (Cole (1922) 2004).
See also: Bayas; Fuas; Iwa; Pitik.

Bata-ey (KAN). Bridge to the unseen, or to the heavens.

Batakagan (KAN). Brightest star.
See also: Tokwifi.

Batang (KAN). Young pine trees.
This sometimes confuses listeners when a Kankanaey broadcaster would say in Filipino, *"May mga batang nahulog sa daan"* and it is misconstrued as, *"There are some children who fell on the road,"* rather than young pine trees falling because of landslides. FYC.
See also: Fatang; Landslide; Talang; Tree Cutting.

Batawa (KAN). [1] It refers to the physical world.
[2] Love song popularized by Juanito Cadangen. In the song, the singer laments that the girl he's yearning for preferred a *"rich man's son"* over him. Its popularity can be attributed not only to its universal theme of unrequited love, but also to its novelty. When it was released, the radio waves were then permeated by English and Tagalog songs. This Kankanaey song endeared itself to the listeners more than the other pop songs at the time. JBC.
See also: Agrix; Cowboy; Lover's Moon; Waynasdi.

Baya-o (KAN). When someone is dead, everyone is given a chance to share a summary of the life of the dead person. It can be a funny or serious story and is usually told with the cadence of a chant. TDH.
See also: Amazing Grace; Badio; Cherwasay; Dujung.

Bayas. (KAN). [1] Sugarcane wine.
[2] *"Wedding, especially one's initial wedding ceremony. Menbayas means to perform the Bayas, i.e., marry and set up housekeeping. Babayas means the wedding season, occurring three times a year. Bomayas, binmayas: the marrying or married couples."* (Scott 2011, 149).
See also: Basi; Iwa; Kaon ya Teteg; Libek; Ngilin; Pitik.

Bayoyok (KAN). A headdress made of a woven circular cap with two groups of feathers, and worn by men, especially during rituals. It signifies that the wearer has passed through the steps and trials of life. If a man's bayoyok has two groups of feathers, his wife is still alive. If he's wearing a bayoyok with only one group of feathers, he is a widower. In Bontoc, the cap is studded with long rooster feathers if the male is fab-allu. It is adorned with less feathers if he is married, and no feathers if he is old. TDH/RAC.
See also: Akipur; Apang; Balballo; Basi; Duwao; Kulatod; Panglao.

Bedbed (KAN). Red turban worn during begnas or during weddings or any time they invoke spirits, so the spirits will not bother the wearer. If you meet a group of old men wearing bedbed, you must not speak or disturb them. You must move away from their path and avert your gaze for your own safety from the unseen spirits around them. TDH.
See also: Begnas; Bangon; Sabusab.

Bees of Tinoc. *"There are six kinds of bees found in Tinoc. First is the Linawan which is yellow in color. Its beehives are yellow-brown in color. These beehives are usually found on caves and in trees with holes. These bees produce all season but produce best during summer. Putyukan are bees that are light yellow in color. Their beehives are found on slanting trees. Kammihnit are small bees that are white. Babbayong are bees with black wings. Lukutan are black bees and they position their beehives hanging on trees. And the last is the Inalit. These bees have red wings with black bodies. Usually, their beehives hang on rocks."* (Baggo 2013).

Begnas *(KAN).* The rituals of begnas originated from warfare, to protect Sagada, Mountain Province from war, from the busu or busol (enemy or headtakers). As times changed the begnas evolved so that it became a ritual for the welfare of the community. Now it is connected to the agricultural cycles of Sagada. TDH.
See also: Bangon; Bedbed; Busol; Headhunter's Drink; Headhunting dance; Headhunting requirement; Headhunting (the tale); Iyag; Sabusab; Sidey; Tambo; Tuling; Tupig.

Belbelting *(IBA).* also **Babelting**. Cricket.

Bengao *(IBA).* An aromatic herb whose stems and roots are dried and worn to ward off evil spirits.
See also: Alan; Ampasit; Banig; Carangat; Darupaypay; Dila anito; Ibwa; Nginin; Paniaw; Pasang; Tinguian Spirits.

Benguet Auto Lines. The government-owned bus company (acquired in 1930 by Manila Railway Corporation, later known as Philippine National Railways), which serviced Baguio and the mining areas as well as Manila and Laoag. The old terminal at Marcoville in Baguio is still referred to by old-timers as BAL or PNR.
See also: Baguio Express.

Beska *(KAN).* First-quarter moon. Cordillerans believe that the first quarter moon is a good time to plant and wean animals. DOS.
See also: Balikawkaw; Lennek; Moon Craters; Teke.

Bessang Pass, The Battle of. The most successful military operation mounted by the Filipino guerrillas against the Japanese Imperial Army in Northern Luzon during WWII. About 120 infantry of the United States Armed Forces in the Philippines-Northern Luzon (USAFIP-NL) that mostly consisted of poorly-armed Igorots, fought in a hand-to-hand combat against the Japanese army in Bessang Pass, Cervantes, Ilocos Sur. The guerila finally triumphed on June 14, 1945. DOS.

Bet-bet *(KAN).* also **Puta**. The killing of a carabao before a wedding. TDH.
See also: Cañao; Kaon ya Teteg.

Betnek *(IBA).* Short and squat.

Big Bird Cage. The ultimate in Blaxpoitation and prison films! Captive Women! Young Girls in Chains! Brutalized! Barbarized! Savaged! This 1972 B-movie written and directed by Jack Hill features Blaxpoitation superstars Pam Grier, Anita Ford and Candice Roman together with favorite

---

The Benguet Lily

By Luther Parker

If you should ask the Benguet lily, "Whither goes the trail?"
Just watch its pointing finger that signs to hill and dale,
Along the knife-like ridges that the Igorotes love.
To far, upstanding mountains with their gleaming clouds above.

Then ask where goes the butterfly with iridescent wing.
And watch the upturned finger point to where the wild shrubs fling
Their flower-decked branches 'gainst the blue from parapets on high,
And thus your answer silently, "There goes the butterfly."

Go ask the modest Benguet Lily, "Whither goes the spray,
That, rainbow-tinted, decks the fail throughout the summer day?"
"It answers to the earth's strong call through yearning to be free
And laughing, leaps through ferny dells towards the clamorous sea."
You may ask the Benguet Lily, "Whither goes the breeze,
That plays among the branches of the balsam laden trees?"
It signs toward the valley where the cool, sweet breezes blow
To carry life and vigor to the swooning plains below.

Then ask the silent Benguet lily, "Whither goes the soul,
When this short life has run its course and you have reached the goal?"
The patient finger points to earth beneath the brooding skies,
Where waits reincarnation when another Spring-time flies.

(Parker 1919, 18).

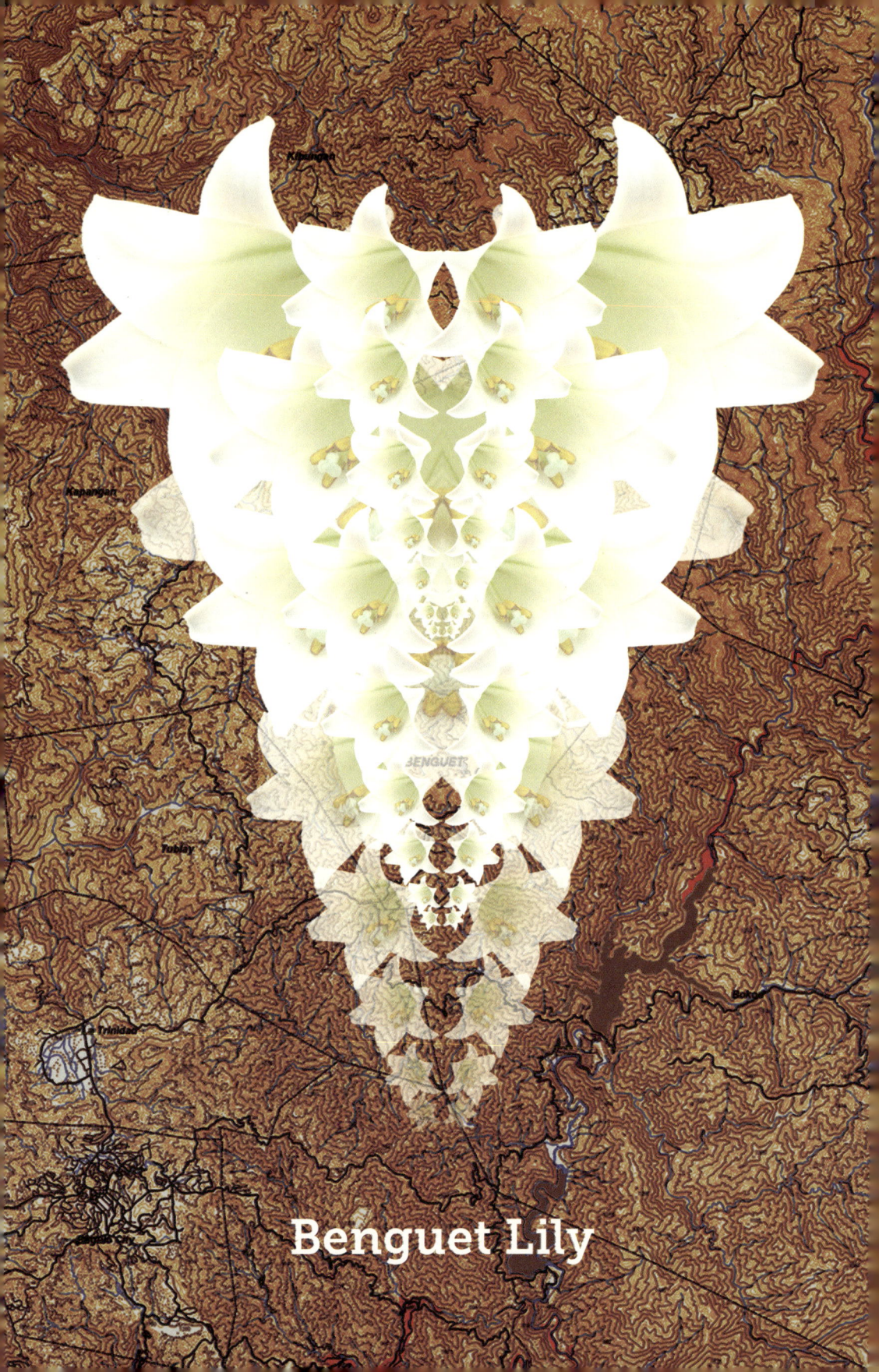

Filipino villain Romy Diaz at the Banaue Rice Terraces. If only for the kitsch value, watch the mud wrestling on the payew (rice field), and the inferno that was the big bird cage, where only two of the prisoners survive. FYC.

See also: Abong; Baguio (the movie); Banaue: Stairway to the Sky; Igorota: The Legend of the Tree of Life; Irisan (the movie); Kung Mangarap Ka't Magising; Vacacionista.

Bikutkut *(IFU).* The hunch of old people.

Bimtak *(ILO).* "Burst or explode; rubber hose which breaks or the explosion of the powder with primers." (Chamber of Mines of the Philippines 1939, 199).

Binaod *(KAN).* A steamed rice cake made in Sagada. It can be plain or filled with etag or salted pork intestines and wrapped in sayote leaf or woven sugarcane leaves. It is especially made for community rituals like begnas and family rituals like the installation of the roof in a new house. Women of the village usually prepare binaod in their homes and bring those to the dap-ay that is hosting the begnas, or to a new house being built. PAD.

See also: Begnas; Dap-ay; Etag; Food; Sayote.

Bingit *(KAN/BON)* also **Kua.** A piece of pork (approximately a kilo) given to the elders or relatives during celebrations where pigs are

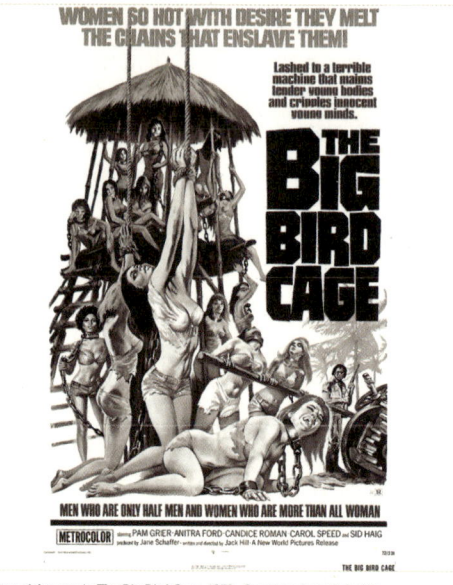

Poster of the movie *The Big Bird Cage*, 1972. Courtesy Joseph Smith.

butchered, such as at weddings, house blessings, healing rituals, funerals, requiems. PAD.

See also: Patpatok; Uka; Watwat.

Binokbok *(IFU).* A ceremony performed three days after a burial. The soul of

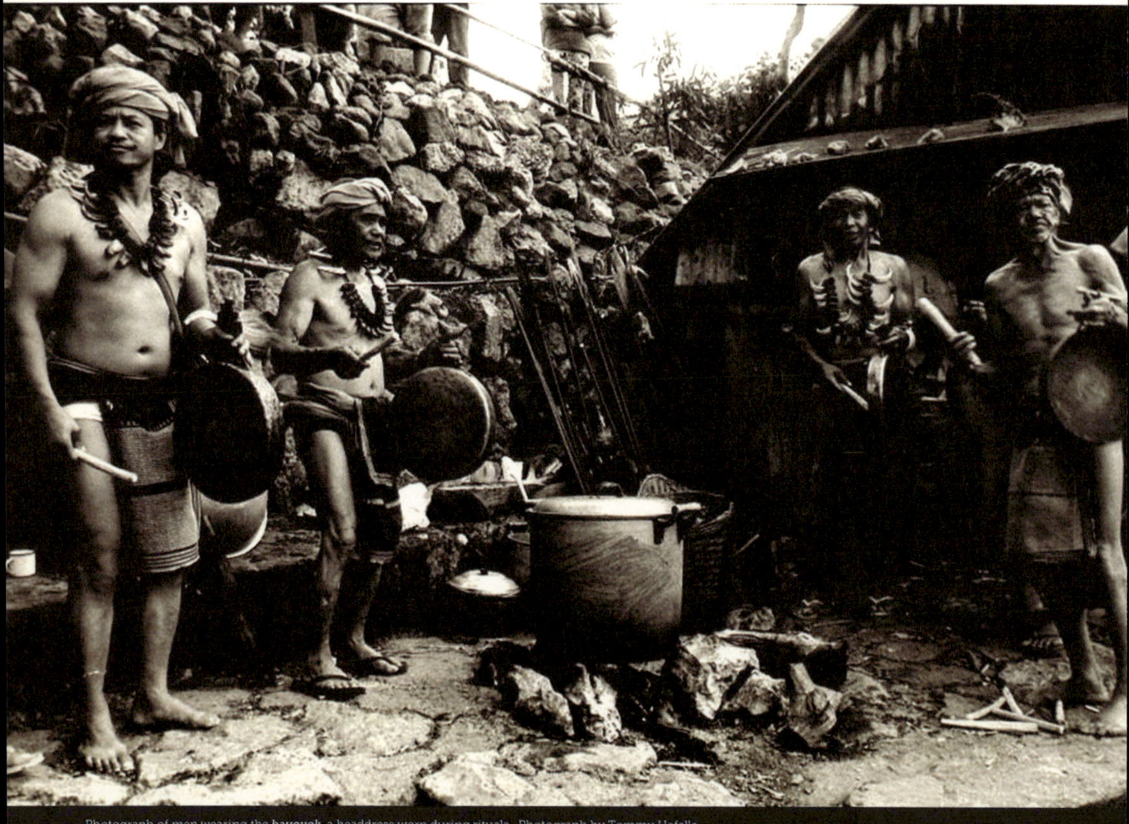

Photograph of men wearing the *bayoyok*, a headdress worn during rituals. Photograph by Tommy Hafalla.

the deceased is brought back to the village and interviewed. (Barton 2012).

Bisukol *(KAN/BON/ILO)* also **Binga** *(KAN)*. Snail with a black hard shell, found on riverbanks or rice paddies. PAD.
See also: Agudong id Manitong; Atubang; Falokag; Golden Kuhol; Ket-an; Lisdeg.

Bitog *(IFU)*. Silver necklace.
See also: Padang.

Bitoto *(KAN)*. A woven basket for bringing cooked rice when working in the fields. TDH.

"Blue Seal" Yosi Quotas. The special privilege of buying limited PX (imported) goodies like tax-free Blue Seal cigarettes, liquor, and chocolates. Holders of Camp John Hay (CJH) passes in the 1950s could get a daily quota of two packs, one quart Bourbon, and two Hershey bars. The CJH passes were issued by Victor de Guia, a one-man screening committee, appointed by the base commander. The still-unclaimed passes allowed de Guia to pick up PX quotas of absentee holders. This resulted in a closetful of imported filter cigarettes (filter-tips were a new thing in the 1960s). The overstocks never entered the black market. They remained un-smoked only to gather mold during Baguio's rainy seasons (except for the few packs snitched by his teenage son and shared with his high school gang mates). KT.
See also: AFRTN; John Hay, Camp.

Boko *(KAN)*. Flour made from thinly-sliced camote that is then sun-dried. Once dried, it can be stored for months. It can be pounded to a powder, mixed with a little water, and made into balls then wrapped in leaves of sugarcane or banana. These are steamed or boiled. PAD.
See also: Camote; Intum; Kineykhey; Sinalupsop.

Bongtot *(KAN)*. A children's game where a child holding a crooked grass or stem will shout among playmates, *"Let us see who farted [Bongtot]!"* and then twirl the grass to see who it points to.
See also: Butubutu-ukiuki; Kalu-os; Play.

Bontoc Bar. A bar that had a cozy dance-floor and live combo music in the Pines Hotel (the only five-star hotel in Baguio in the 1950s). Tim Tesoro at the keyboards and Poping de Guia on the trumpets. KT.
See also: Bontoc Café; Fireplace.

Bontoc Boogie also **Fogfokhi** *(BON)*, **Bogibogi** *(BON)*. Taken from boogie-woogie. *"This dance consists of a ring of young men crouched or seated on the ground, striking a very fast beat on the gongs, which are held and struck in the same manner as for the falliwes (dancing in circles). One young man and one young lady take to the 'floor', and begin their dance. It consists mainly of a variety of foot movements, for which the man leads and the lady follows, facing each other across the 'floor', and gradually rotating round it. This progresses to the stage when the dancers hold hands and repeat their steps around the circle, sometimes the man looping under his partner's arm, the lady then looping under his. A third stage occurs when the young man places his hands on his partner's hips and follows her around the circle in a repeat of the original steps."* (Reid 2009).
See also: Challichog; Salip; Tadek.

Bontoc Café. Not for the intelligentsia and habitues of the Bontoc Bar. Located on Carantes Street, parallel to Session Road, this is where you got your half-half. In its waning years in the mid-90s, a mere glance at the next table would have merited you more than a piercing gaze. FYC.
See also: Ayuyang; Bontoc Bar; Fireplace; Folk Music.

Bontoc Disco. *"Each rancheria possesses a few (cañao) places with two or three dead trees with pointed branches, upon these trees the (hunted) heads are spitted, and dancing takes place around the trees."* (Schadenberg 1975, 147).
See also: Cañao.

Bontoc Elections. In the mid-1920s, the first informal elections were held in Benguet and parts of Bontoc. At the prescribed hour on Election Day, voters were convened on one side of the plaza while the candidates for municipal presidents were seated some distance away from each other. When the signal was given, the voters would cross the plaza and surround their choice. The one with the most fans, won. This was called Fotos Linlinya. Later on, it would evolve into Fotos Kinnolor where the candidates would sit lined in front of the voting booth bearing a color to their name. Colored paper squares were used as ballots. The person with the most squares won. FYC/GAD.

Bontoc Eulogy. A 1996 mockumentary by Marlon Fuentes, very popular on the Asian-American Film Studies circuit. It tells about the narrator's ancestors: Emiliano, a Filipino soldier who died during the Philippine American War, and Markod, a Bontoc warrior who became a member of the Igorot delegation to the 1904 St. Louis Fair. Historical film footage is interspersed with a faux-recording of Markod's impressions of the fair. FYC.
See also: Dog-eating.

Bontoc Kiss. *"Igorot do not kiss or have other formal physical expression to show affection between friends or relatives. Mothers do not kiss their babies even. The Igorot has no formal or common expression of thankfulness. Whatever gratitude he feels must be taken for granted, as he never expresses it in words."* (Jenks 2005).
See also: Iya-iyaman; Namwaw.

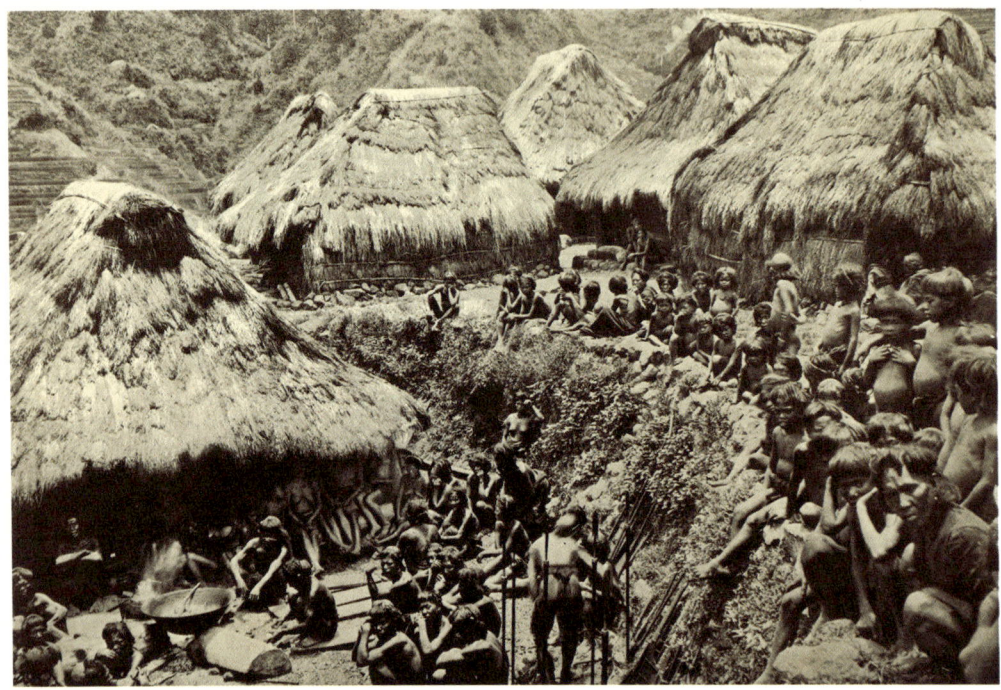

Photograph of a Bontoc village. Courtesy AV Cating Family Collection.

Bontoc Studio. Shichisaburo Yamane became a government photographer for Mountain Province in 1926, taking photos mostly of American officials. In 1928, he opened the Bontoc Studio, the first photographic studio in the highlands. Many of the unacknowledged photos in the Mountain Province at that time were said to be his. Bontoc Studio burned down in 1945 during the American bombing of Bontoc. FYC.

Boom boom chack chack man. Name given by Santi Bose to the blind percussionist at the overpass beside Sunshine Mart in Baguio City, who used a brown gasoline container and maracas as instruments. FYC.

Bosesero. *"A boss who talks too much."* (Chamber of Mines of the Philippines 1939, 199).

Botanical Garden. *"The latest of tourist attractions in this City is the Baguio Zoological and Botanical Gardens. It is located at Forbes Park and is accessible via the Leonard Wood Road. It is adjoining Teachers' Camp. It was originally conceived on March 12, 1951 but it is the present City Administration which brought this plan into realization. It is stocked with animals and different birds all of which are donated. The pet deer of the late President Magsaysay is kept here. Deer, monkeys, eagles, different kinds of other animals, including a bear, and birds inhabit the zoo."* (Baguio City Police Department 1959). Magsaysay's deer is no longer there and neither are the rest of the animals. Its name was changed to 'Imelda's Park' (and then it was renamed as the Botanical Garden when the Marcos era ended) and Cordillera houses were built there. The Baguio Arts Guild (BAG) built their gallery there but when the BAG founders left the group, what was left of the BAG remained in the area. In 2009, the park was renamed the Centennial Park to mark the anniversary of the city.

See also: Baguio Arts Guild, The History of; Baguio Arts Guild, The Future of.

Brent School. In 1902, on a ship headed to the Philippines, conversations between then Governor-General William H. Taft and Charles H. Brent (the newly elected Episcopal Bishop of the Philippines) would lead to a discussion about the need for a boarding school for the sons of civil servants, military and businessmen residing in the Philippines, especially those in the outlying provinces. Taft, as the 'biggest booster' of Baguio, felt it was the ideal location to open a boarding school. But it was not until 1908 that, with funds donated by William Cameron Forbes and his cousin Henry S. Forbes, land was purchased for the school. W.C. Forbes assigned the Insular Architect, A.E. Parsons, to draft designs for the school building and Warwick Greene (Forbes personal secretary and assistant to the Director of Public Works) to oversee the construction. In February 1909, work began on the first building erected on the Baguio Campus: the rectory for

Rev. Robb White (who ran the Easter School which opened in 1906). Construction for the main school building began a few months later (named in 1923 after the first headmaster, Reverend Remsen Ogilby).

The November 1, 1909 opening of the school was delayed for several months by a typhoon on October 19 that flooded the plains and washed out bridges between Manila and Baguio (23 inches of rain in 10 hours recorded at the Jesuit Observatory in Baguio). So the first classes (consisting of 8 students) of Bishop Brent's Baguio Boys School were held in November of 1909 at the YMCA in Manila. Two months later, on January 5, 1910, the first classes held on the Baguio campus commenced.

Always small (as compared to the much larger American School in Manila), as the city grew, so the Baguio Boys School grew. In 1925, enrollment was increased with the construction of Hamilton Hall, the girls dormitory, allowing the institution (which was subsequently renamed in honor of its founder) to became a co-educational boarding school. In the late-1930s, Brent School admitted Filipinos and in 1938 recorded its first Filipino graduate ("salutatorian" in a class of 10 students).

During WWII the school was closed (December 1941) when it was used for a short time as the assembly point for foreign civilians (including Chinese nuns from the convent) to be interned by the Japanese and then as a Hospital and Officers Residence for the Japanese Imperial Army. The school was re-opened in November of 1947 by Reverend Arthur Richardson, who had held the pre-war position of Headmaster and had been interned along with his family during the war.

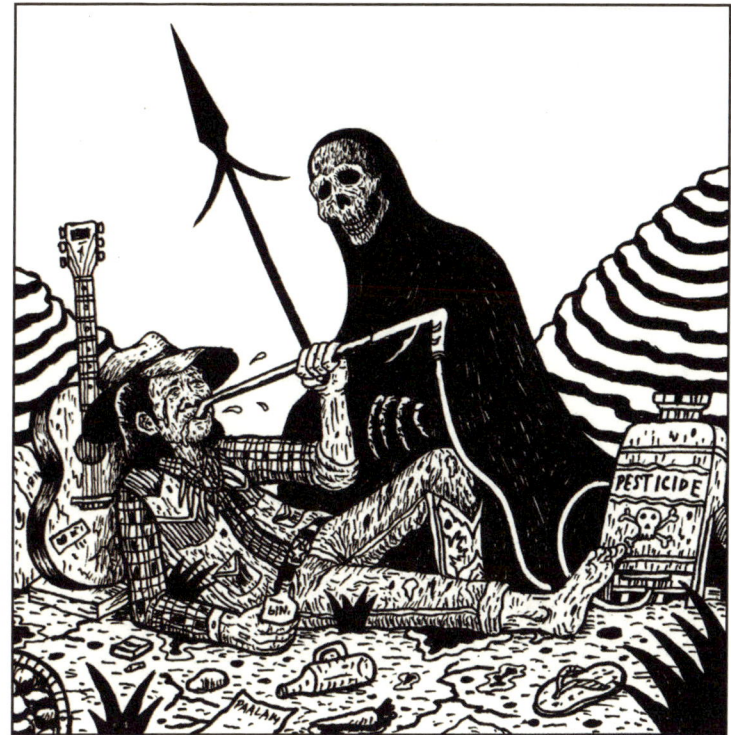
Artwork by Louie Cordero, 2017.

Over the decades Brent School has managed to survive recessions, numerous typhoons, the carpet bombing of Baguio, earthquakes, and the closing of the US bases, adapting and re-inventing itself while striving to maintain the high standards set by Bishop Brent and its first Headmaster Reverend Ogilby. MW.

Buaya *(FIL/KAL/ILO/KAN)*. Once upon a time, there was a pond filled with crocodiles. Then the pond dried up and the crocodiles left but the name of this village in Kalinga stayed. Contrary to popular perceptions, the Philippine crocodile is not ferocious and will not attack unprovoked. FYC.

Buaya Economic Classes *(KAL)*. These classes are used in most Cordillera languages: Kadagdagu or Pusi (pitiful), Kadangyan (wealthy) and the Nangginaw-an (in between people or the middle class).
See also: Hagabi; Immuya-uy; Kudo; Pes-ay.

Buguias Cocktail. Death by suicide, especially among the young, far exceeds the country's

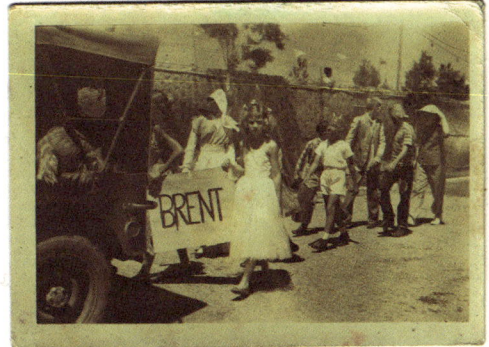
Photograph of *Brent School* parade in Baguio, circa 1940s. Courtesy Virginia de Guia.

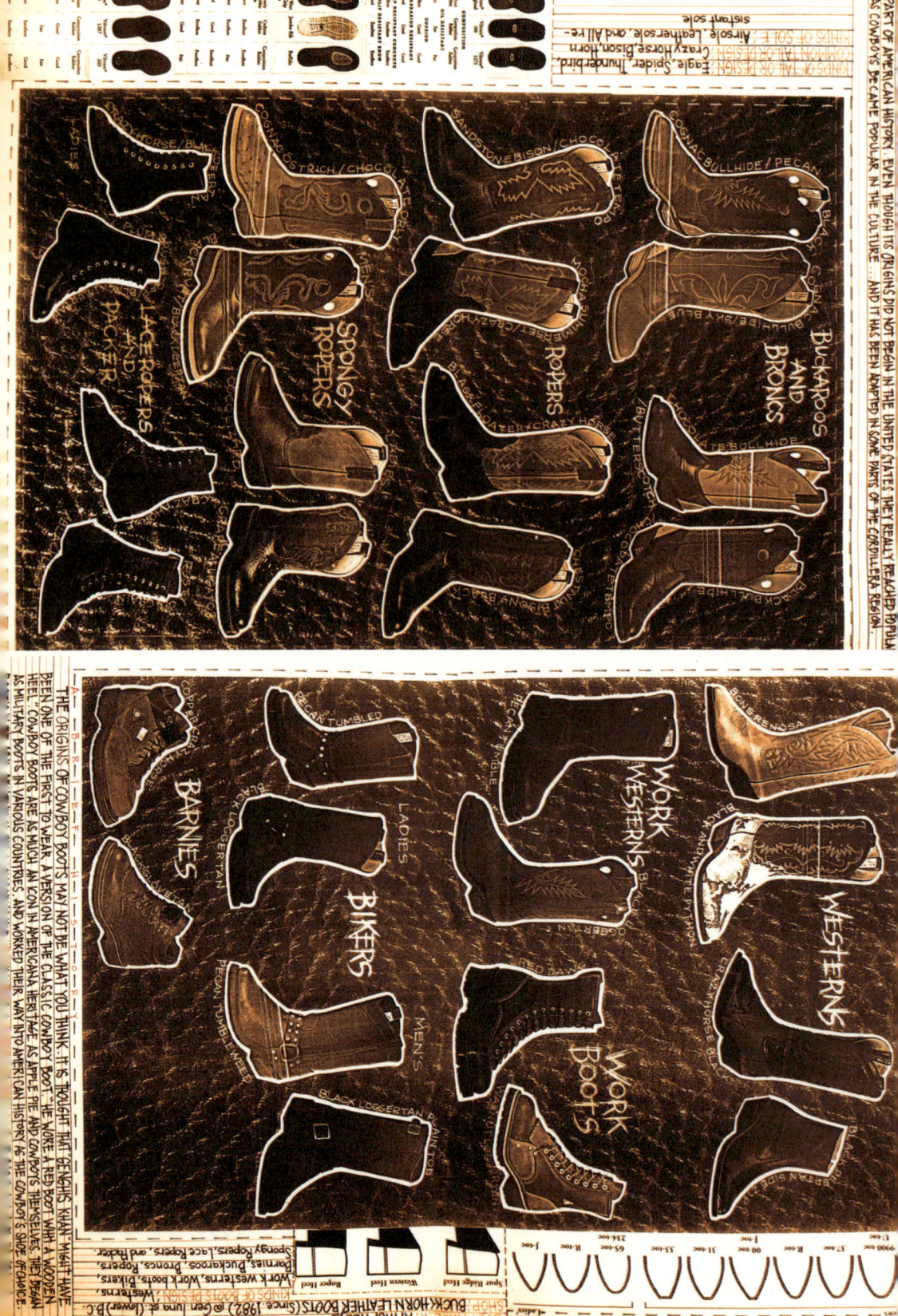

average in the towns of Kibungan, Buguias, and Atok in Benguet. Among the reasons given are boredom, drunkenness, country music and the availability of pesticides as a means of killing oneself. One particular herbicide is being eyed as the popular choice of suicide victims here. So the choice is instant death by pesticide or a longer suicide by using and being exposed to the pesticides of these farming areas. FYC.

See also: Buguias Soil; Cowboy; Kalabog-kalabog-Buguias-patatas!.

Buguias Patatas. Introduced (together with cabbage) by the Spaniards in the Cordilleras from either as early as the 1600s or as late as the administration of Benguet Gov. Blas de Banos in the 19th century. Chinese and Japanese gardeners who came during the building of Kennon Road further enhanced potato and cabbage production in Benguet. According to the Philippine American Commission in 1909, about 4,000 baskets of potatoes were sold annually in Baguio by 1908. (Lewis 1992) FYC.

See also: Baguio Bean; Buguias Cocktail; Kalabog-kalabog-Buguias-patatas!; Kennon Road; Korta; Loo; Num-a; Sayote; Zucchini.

Buguias Soil. In Buguias, the soil is classified as Laboy (heavy loam found in flat areas, good for the uma or agricultural patch of land), Komog (weathered dioritic rock, infertile), Lagan (mountain sand, sterile and infertile), Tapo (alluvial silt, fertile), Oplit (clay soil), or Liang (red clay soil, very low fertility).

See also: Kalabog-kalabog-Buguias-patatas!; Loo.

Bukatot *(KAL)*. A long net or fish trap specifically used for catching river eel. TDH.

Bulayaw *(KAL)* also **Bulalakaw** *(FIL)*. A fiery flying creature, orb or perhaps a meteor that can foretell the death of a loved one or lead one astray when followed. FYC.

Bulbulagaw *(ILO)*. Joke-teller.

Bungbung. To use dynamite explosives when blasting rocks in mine tunnels or mountain slopes to create or widen roads. DOS.

Bungol *(IFU)*. Jewel, specifically, ancient agate beads.

See also: Apang; Dalanasip; Fukas; Ong-ong.

Bungot *(IFU)*. Ferocity. The nearest approach in the Ifugao language perhaps to 'bravery.' The Ifugao's ideal of bravery seems to be an aggressive and relentless, boastful, angry assertiveness. Mahui, a synonym, has the sense of relentless boldness. (Barton 2012).

Bungkaka also **Balingbing** *(KAN/IBA)*. Bamboo tube cut so that there are two thin vibrating strips at the end that are then hit with the palm of the hand to create a vibrating sound to drive away bad spirits (especially at night in the fields).

Bureau of Non Christian Tribes. Established by the Philippine Commission in October 1901 with anthropologist David P. Barrows at the helm. This put Barrows in charge of the majority of Filipinos at that time, as there were four times more non-Christians than Christians. It was upon the holding of the census in 1903 that Barrows used the term *"Igorotte"* as the general classification for this *"whole body of primitive Malayan tribes of Northern Luzon."* FYC.

See also: Cayat; Enmity between the Igorots and Christians, The Beginning of; Episcopalianism; Ethnographic Mapping; Igorot; Kain; Kayan; Remontados; Tribes; Zubieta, Ramon.

Burnham Lake. A swamp turned into the centerpiece of Burnham Park. From the Burnham Plan, Mayor Eusebius Halsema in the 1920s took out the racetrack around the lake and installed a fountain with multicolored lights. He also built an auditorium for the grandstand that survived even the 1990 earthquake. The auditorium became the city's community hall and, on some summer nights, an orchestra would play for the people in the park.

See also: Baguio, The Naming of; Burnham Park; Gingined; Halsema Highway; Leonard Wood Road.

Burnham Park. After spending a few days in the Philippines, including Baguio, the great American architect and urban planner Daniel Burnham, in October 1905, submitted the "Report on the Proposed Plan of the City of Baguio Province of Benguet, P.I." It was a challenge for him to design the *"future community"* of Baguio because of its hilly terrain so he used his urban plan of Washington D.C. as his template. Because Baguio was conceived as a sanitarium, he developed a plan

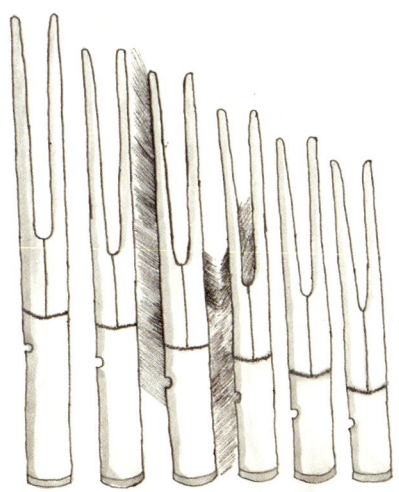

Illustration by Jason Domling.

Opposite page: Collage by Sirk Deuda.

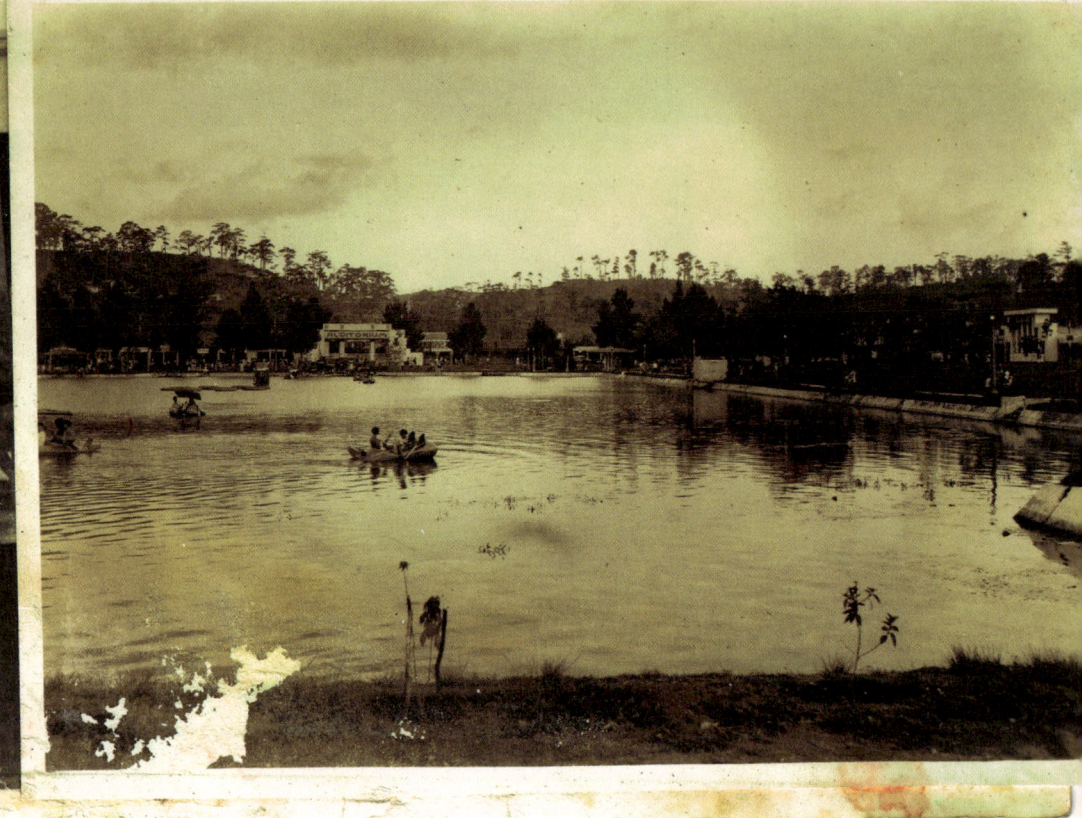

Photograph of *Burnham Lake*, circa 1940s. Courtesy Virginia De Guia.

where all the houses would receive direct sunlight from all directions so they were not to be placed in North-South or East-West configurations. So Baguio, in a way, was planned for both power (vis-a-vis Washington D.C.) and recuperation. Using his Axis plan, Burnham created Baguio's civic core with two building clusters on the opposite sides of the valley: on one side is the cluster of buildings for local government and the other for the national government, as Baguio became the Summer Capital of the Philippines. In the middle was a park, later known as Burnham Park that, in hindsight, looks like a mall. As David Brody wrote in *Visualizing American Empire: Orientalism and Imperialism in the Philippines*: "The location of this green space is in keeping with the esplanade, as marked on Burnham's original plans for the summer capital. The park has a small pond at its center, and regimented rows of grass and sidewalks accentuate the small-scale, "City Beautiful" – influenced design of this heavily used public space." The geometric road pattern around Burnham Park was laid down to complete the Axis. (Brody, 2010, 161) FYC.

See also: Baguio, The Naming of; Burnham Lake; Rainforest.

Busad di kaiw *(KAN)*. Lit. Heart of a tree.
See also: Tree Cutting.

Busil *(ISN)*. Clitoris.
See also: Mt. Clitoris.

Busol *(IBA)* also **Buhul** *(IFU)*. [1] Headhunter. Buhul in Ifugao means 'enemy of a village' or 'even a person of another village during wartime.' [2] Busol watershed in Baguio. Political heads often fell for allowing squatting there. FYC.
See also: Begnas; Headhunter's Drink; Headhunting dance; Headhunting requirement; Headhunting (the tale).

Butigi *(KAL)*. Growing stones similar to the trovants in Romania. These stones 'grow' after the rain. In Kalinga, growing stones are found near the river as they grow while soaked in water. Kalinga peoples use them as tombstones. It is also a practice to place a pot of rice under the butigi tombstone as it is believed that the dead need food when travelling to the otherworld. HZK.
See also: Ufo.

Butong *(IFU)*. Drunk but still somewhat in control of drunkenness while heading into belligerence.
See also: Liwliwot; Nafutengak.

Butu *(KAL)*. [1] The term is perhaps derived from the Spanish 'voto' for vow or oath. A major provision in the bodong where a killer has to kill one of his relatives to make it even with the warring tribe. This was the first step towards peace negotiations.

Opposite page: Artwork by Willy Magtibay.

(2) *(ILO).* Penis.
See also: Butubutu-Ukiuki; Vochong.

Butubutu-Ukiuki *(ILO).* Lit. Penispenis-vaginavagina. It is a way of determining the gender of a stem of a wild grass. Kids bet on the stem's gender as a guessing game. The stem is the sturdy part of a wild grass as it produces its flower. The stem is uprooted from the ground and cleaned by cutting away the roots and the flower part. Two children would split the stem from both ends and extend the cut until half way. The stem is male if it forms the shape of an N and female if shaped like a diamond. HZK.
See also: Bongtot; Butu; Kalu-os; Play; Qua.

Buwaw *(KAN).* Lit. Shout. Manbuwaw means to drive away bading, or rice birds. The shooing sound is a prolonged shouting as in: *"Eeeeeyyyyyy!!!!"* DOS.
See also: Bading.

Buwaya *(KAN/KAL/FIL/ILO).* Lit. Crocodile. Among the Kankanaey, there is a ritually significant necklace called a buwaya, usually adorned with boar's teeth and at least one crocodile's tooth. Only men who have gone through the hardships of life or who are known to have lived a full life are entitled to wear the buwaya during rituals. TDH.
See also: Tangkil; Three Orphans of Sagada, The.

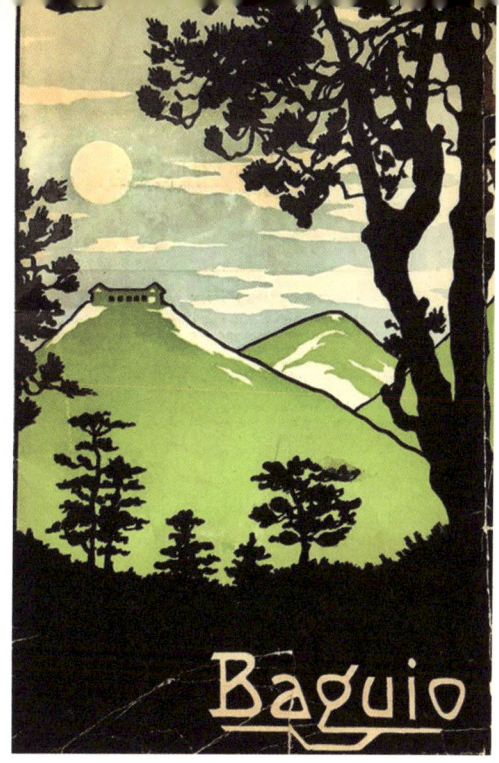

Poster of Baguio. Courtesy AV Cating Family Collection.

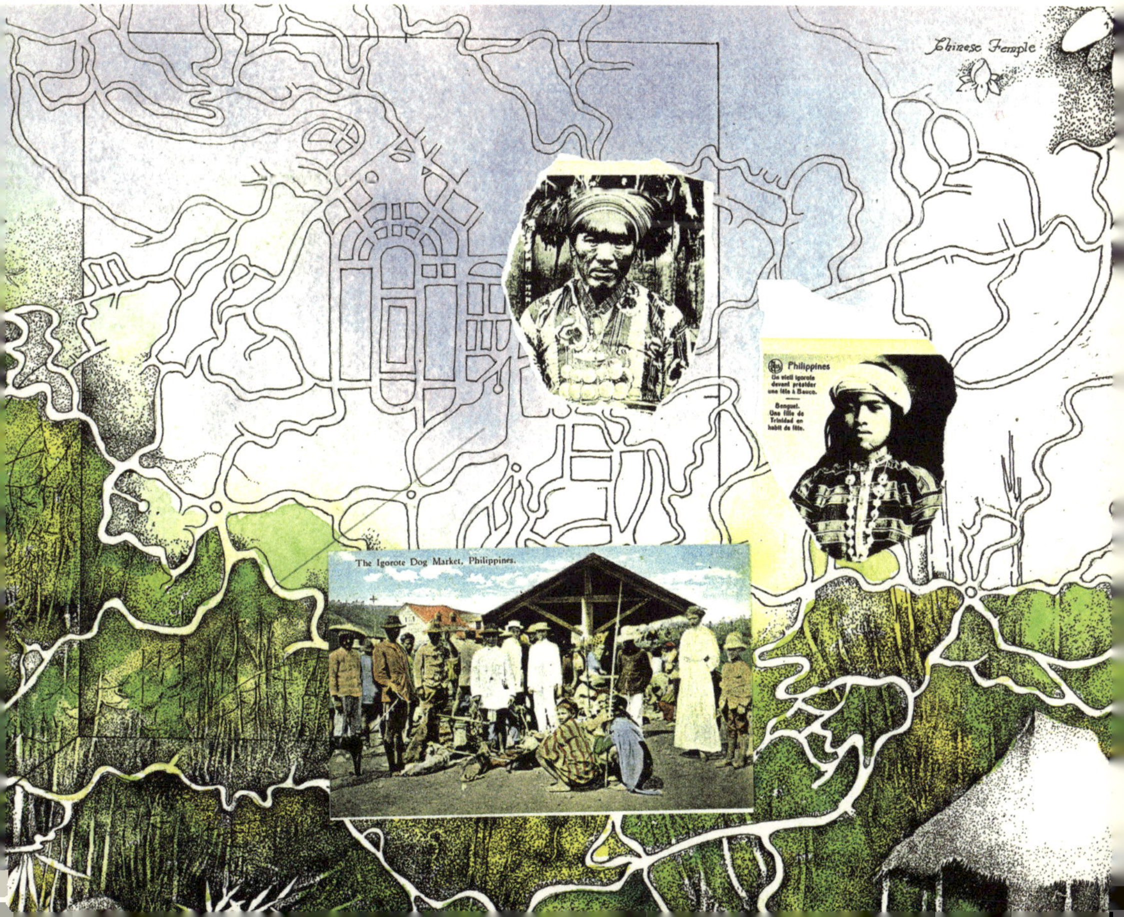

Reconciling and Resisting in the Post-Colonial Cordillera: How Santiago Bose Transmuted Baguio's Cultural Landscape into an Artistic Revolt

Like many Filipinos, Bose was shaped by the cliche that best describes the Philippine colonial experience under Spain and then the United States of America: *"Three hundred years in a convent, fifty years in Hollywood."*

As a child growing up in Baguio City, he built his identity upon layers of influence that contradicted yet co-existed with one another.

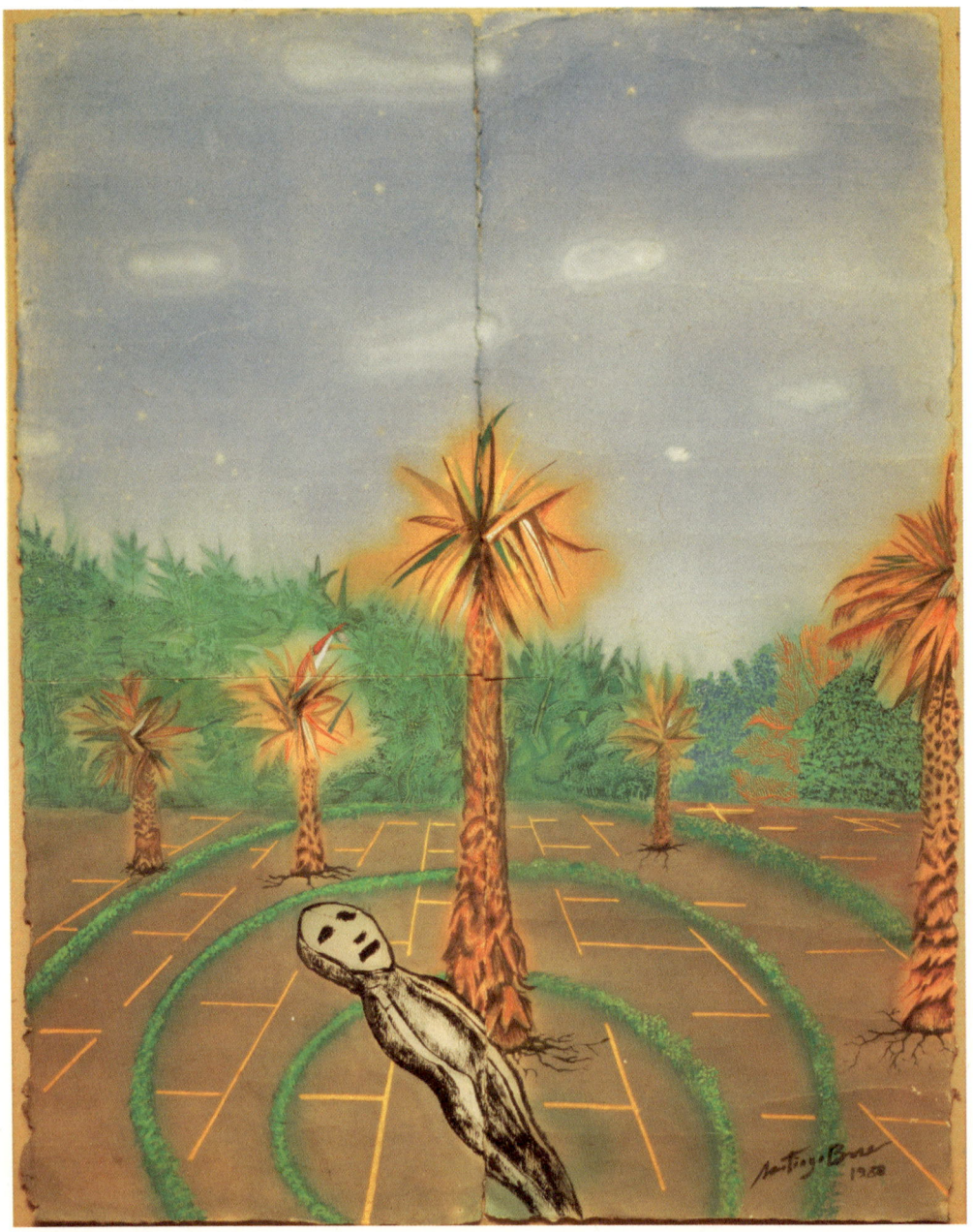

Artwork by Santiago Bose, 1988.

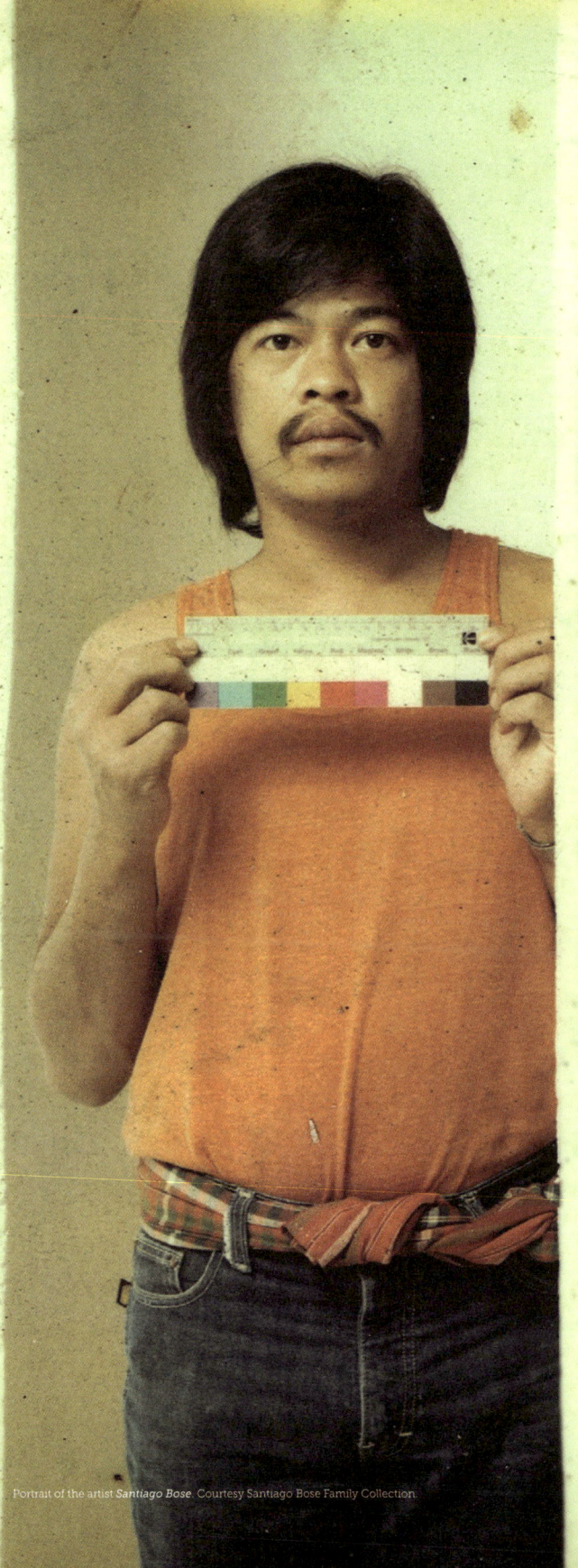

Portrait of the artist *Santiago Bose*. Courtesy Santiago Bose Family Collection.

BOSE, SANTIAGO

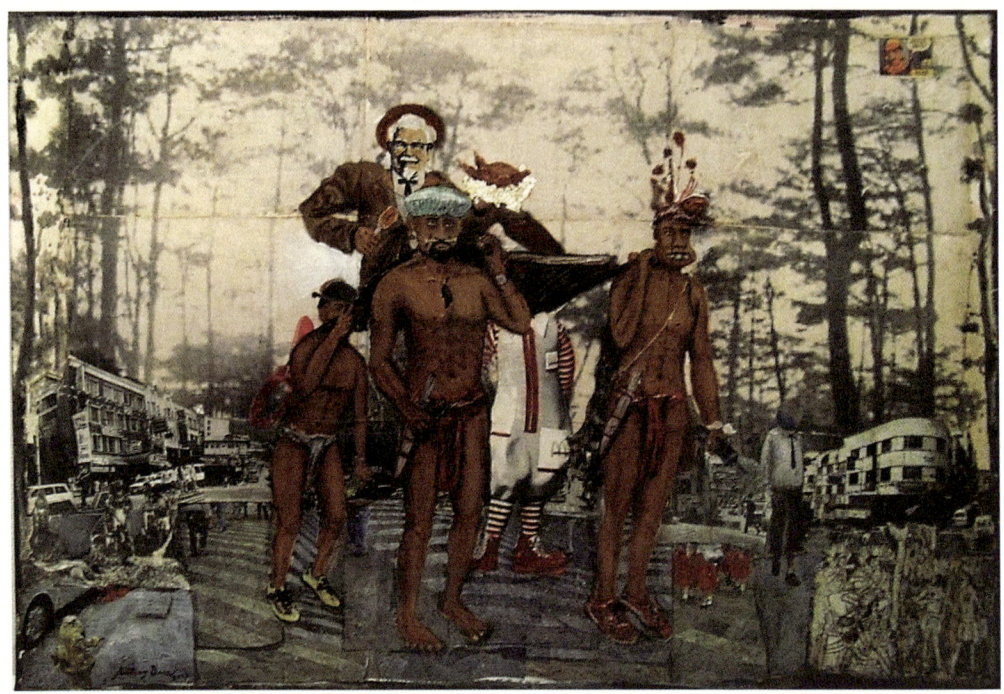

Carnivores of Session Road, Santiago Bose, mixed media, 122x183 cm, c. 1990s.

Raised in a middle-class Ilocano household, Bose's mother owned a stall at the market and his father was a traffic policeman. They were deeply religious, and Bose served as a sacristan at St. Vincent Church, and attended St. Louis University in his grade school and high school years. And yet, at the same time, pagan rituals were supported by his family; a rich uncle regularly visited faith healers when he was sick, and magical symbols of anting-anting (amulets or charms imbued with spells, believed to have special protective powers) were treated with respect and veneration.

In Baguio, mint chocolate chip ice cream was as widely available as cheeseburgers and apple pie. Like many other Baguio citizens, Bose was more comfortable speaking English – which was taught in school with more proficiency than Tagalog. His first art teacher was an American. Bose loved the Beatles, the Monkees and the Rolling Stones. It's probable that his beloved Mad magazines helped develop his caustic sense of humor. Bose often wielded this sense of humor in his work, such as when he was pretending to be a Showman/Shaman in a performance about faith healers, or exploring visual irony by showing a Filipina at the 1904 World Fair in St. Louis standing on top of a pink penis tip in his painting *Pinay's Curtain Call*. He was also a hoot in real life, criticizing other artists to their face by asking philosophical inanities such as, *"Is it art, or is it fart?"*

But while Bose's pop-cultural tastes were American, a result of the proximity of Camp John Hay, an R&R spot for U.S. servicemen in the Cordilleras, Bose knew the value and beauty of folk art, through wood carvings and other indigenous knick knacks from indigenous carvers that his mother sold in her market stall.

In some ways, his close proximity to these colonial presences made it easier for Bose to question and be critical of both the foreign paradigm and home.

For example, for most lowlanders, Western culture was filtered only through what came on the big screen, TV and radio. For Baguio folk, the allure of all things PX was ever-present, with Camp John Hay tantalizingly within reach. As a high schooler, Bose, was harassed by Camp John Hay sentries. To be made to feel like an outsider in the city he was born and raised in, within his country's borders, was the first realization he had that, *"No matter how many American appliances we owned, nor how well we could mimic the songs broadcast from American airwaves, nor how closely we mimicked the postures and phrases of the Americans, we would only be little brown interlopers who would never be anything more than second-class."* (Bose 2002, 265).

In a way, that feeling of being marginalized, of being 'othered,' also inspired him to seek out his artistic identity. That he was educated in the University of the Philippines in the 1960s and 1970s – a time of great social upheaval both nationally and worldwide – fostered a need to reconcile the cultural clashes he grew up with.

His time spent in Manila, and a longer stint in New York, opened Bose's eyes to a deeper understanding of Philippine nationalism. It also exposed him to the *"marginalization we experienced as a nation [and that] which each of us had experienced personally."* (Bose 2002, 265). Distance and time away from Baguio helped hone his art practice, and it was through this practice that Bose was able to sort out these contradictory experiences and emotions. He was always actively trying to reconcile the differences between what he was taught, what he was, and what he should take at face value.

Bose's art practice burgeoned into a strong resolve to resist commonly held standards, beliefs and practice. He brought the marginalized to the forefront of his work, both through process and product – and this was wrought out of both necessity and philosophy.

His resistance of the accepted, Western, standards of fine art gave a sense of total freedom for Bose. Although he was trained as a fine artist at the university, he refused to accept that only expensive paints were a legitimate medium. Bose used materials and techniques that were available at low cost, creating mixed-media assemblages using everything from his daughters' drawings to lahar when Mt. Pinatubo exploded, making work that was both accessible, recognizable and current for many Filipinos.

This also freed Bose to bring to focus ethnic methods of art making that were not traditionally accepted in fine art, such as solar painting (i.e., using a magnifying glass to burn images onto handmade paper). Most importantly, this rejection of the Western canon helped Bose find his voice as an artist whose practice was in the Third World. *"To make art,"* he said, *"you need nothing but your own imagination."*

This philosophy was a great tool in his community building efforts and this is another way by which Bose contributed significantly to the Cordillera region. As the first president of the Baguio Arts Guild, Bose – alongside co-founders Roberto Villanueva, BenCab, Kidlat Tahimik and others – was integral to exposing Baguio residents to art. By removing the conversation of art from the hallowed ground of museums, galleries and art magazines and taking it to the sidewalks of Session Road, Burnham Park and the Baguio Convention Center, Bose's leadership in the Baguio Arts Guild had a higher purpose. It was a way through which a group of like-minded artists could educate the city they loved so much through living, breathing, art practices that had not been seen in Baguio before.

He became an example for young artists of the Cordillera who did not have his fine art training, or could not afford to get it. He taught them that you did not necessarily need fancy oil paint or canvas to create; instead, using indigenous materials could be seen as a way of reclaiming power, and the standards of art, for Baguio artists. Bose taught now-renowned Jordan Mang-osan how to solar paint. Sculptor Perry Mamaril was another apprentice.

Whether he was challenging the artistic status quo by using indigenous materials, taking on symbols of colonialism by painting distorted visions of Mickey Mouse and Kentucky Fried Chicken or recreating our history by painting anting-antings over historical photos, Bose never stopped questioning commonly held truths. *"My art is a means by which I can gradually work towards reinstating the importance of indigenous traditions in establishing a contemporary world view, and in developing contemporary cultural symbols."* (Bose 2002, 267).

As visual artist Pat Hoffie, professor at the Queensland College of Art, Griffith University said:

"The extent to which Santiago Bose's art has influenced the development of contemporary art in the Philippines has yet to be fully fathomed. His introduction of indigenous materials, his mining of Filipino iconography, his re-writing of Filipino history, his commitment to indigenous forms and practices, his bringing together of new media – such as performance, video and installation – with older forms such as rituals, festival paraphernalia and altarpieces – have made a rich and deep contribution to contemporary art practice not only in the Philippines but also abroad. And along with art practice there is the legacy of his writings, his presence, his long years of commitment to communities in his home town of Baguio and to other elsewheres where he set down roots. Santi's work wove past histories into the present, and then on into probable and improbable futures. In the face of what often looked like insurmountable odds, he always continued to make art that breathed with the potential for new imaginings." (Hoffie, 2003, 4).

In his art practice, Bose explored Baguio and the Cordilleras. By using its landscape as a medium, its materials to create his work, and its people to communicate a common identity, Bose empowered a generation of Baguio artists and residents. Within that process, he left a legacy of over 5,000 prints, drawings, installations and paintings created in a period of 30 years, which defined and portrayed the Filipino psyche through a Baguio boy's eyes. LB.

See also: AFRTN; Baguio Arts Guild, The Future of; Baguio Arts Guild, The History of.

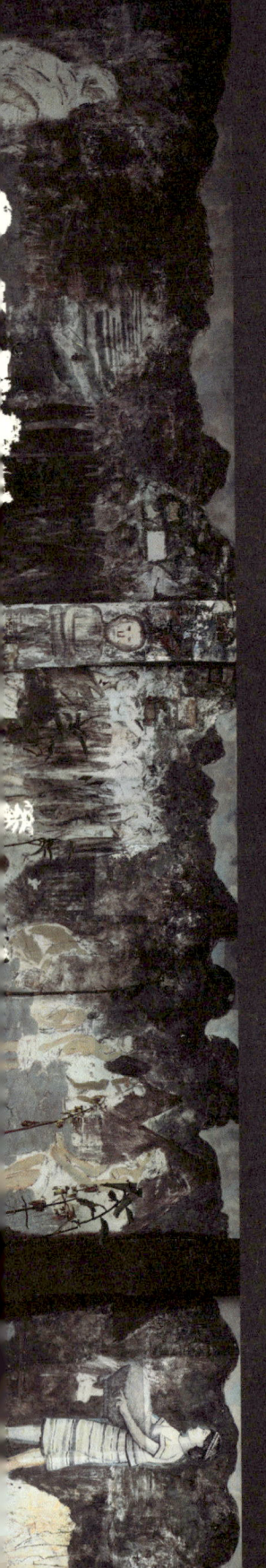

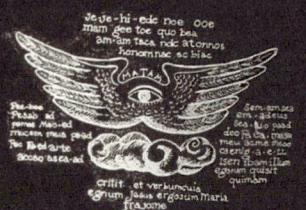

The Ghost in the Studio

In the early 1900s, the Americans arrived with candy in one hand and a camera in the other – held out like the crosses and swords used earlier by the Spanish to lure the inhabitants of the impenetrable Cordilleran mountains into submission. Until then, the highlands and its free-air-conditioning climate were in a particular stasis that nobody had been able to disrupt, despite the lack of salt and matches as paramount necessities and much-wanted trading items.

Much to our dismay, with one swift political move later known as McKinley's 'Benevolent Assimilation' (or assassination?), this Ibaloy terrain where 'primitive savages' roamed, was turned into a testing ground for a race towards a cultural makeover, as if such was badly needed. The heart of the Philippines, our Baguio, suddenly became a 'Little America' with the crafty use of Protestant Missionary teachers, called the Thomasites, propagating an education that howled *"Educate and Christianize them Filipinos!"* To this day, it echoes from the walls of Baguio's Teacher's Camp, where thousands of Filipino teachers from all over the Philippines went to learn how to speak proper English and learn Christian moral values – as if we didn't have our own.

This is the Baguio where Santiago Bose witnessed the clash of the old and the new culture, a world torn apart between extremes. In this city, he had begun to subtly infuse his beliefs into his artistic creation via the different mediums he made use of. Instead of the typical oil painting techniques he had learned in school, he turned to soil or solar painting – with, of course, a tiny swipe at fine-art, with his impish charismatic wit, the kind that does not easily wilt, like the mountain grass he so enjoyed.

Often hanging out at his studio to play chess and listen to his stories and jokes, I discovered the complexities of attraction: there was always something new every time I looked at his work, they were never tiresome and never grew old, they grew on me. Particularly, his paintings that had spawned one of my first shows – a dare I had taken from Rene Aquitania. Santi was the uncle I never had, literally a 'Tito Santi.' He was never patronizing over how young we were or how old he was. Of course, this never fooled anyone. He was a driving force, and would give me a run down of the consequences in certain things I had only begun to take interest in, whatever they were.

Little did I know that seven years after Santi's death, when I was in search of a bigger working space, I would find myself in his studio, working with "him". I enjoyed toying with the idea of being possessed by him as I created my work in his old creative spot which is today the Santiago Bose Foundation, something that he had always wanted to have, a place to house his works. Presently, it is still a mixing plate of artistic energies in the form of informal residencies, which the family hopes to organize and concretize into a formal program in the course of the coming years.

For the Singapore Biennale 2013, I had wanted to highlight the artist's mural in Sagada. I was intoxicated with the idea of the complete restoration of this mural, as it kick-started Santi's career in 1976. Unfortunately, this plan did not come to materialization, and perhaps that was what the artist would have wanted. And, as I write this, the music recorder in the corner of the studio turns on by itself and sings:

Sagada Mural, 1977. Photograph by RJ Fernandez.
Artwork by Santiago Bose from the *Anting-Anting Series*, 1998

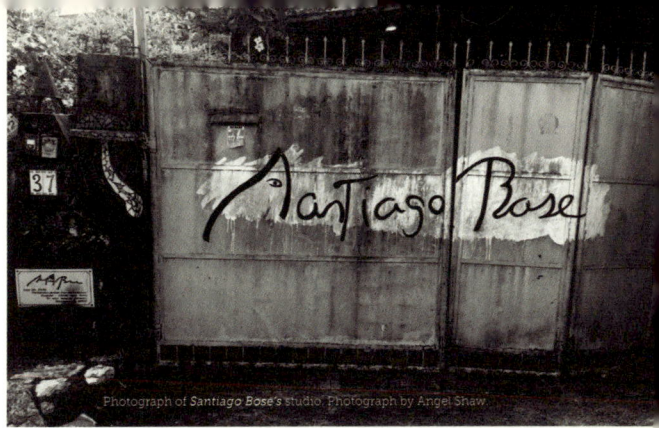

Photograph of *Santiago Bose's* studio. Photograph by Angel Shaw.

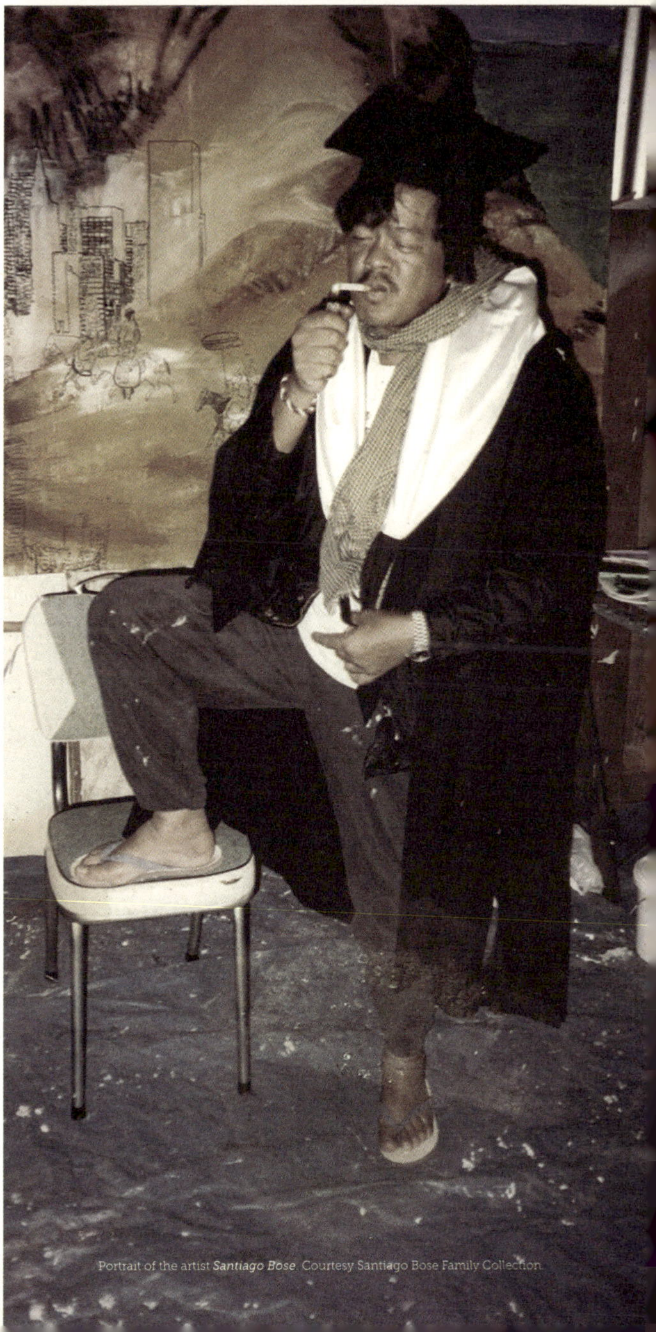

⬛⬛⬛⬛⬛⬛ Blues
⬛⬛⬛⬛ lost in ⬛⬛
⬛⬛ your gravity
⬛⬛⬛⬛⬛⬛⬛⬛⬛
⬛⬛⬛⬛⬛⬛⬛
⬛⬛⬛⬛⬛⬛⬛⬛
⬛⬛ you see Saint ⬛
I ⬛⬛ move
My fingers ⬛⬛⬛⬛ knot
⬛⬛⬛⬛⬛⬛ the strength
⬛⬛ get up and take another shot
⬛⬛ my ⬛⬛ friend
⬛⬛⬛⬛⬛⬛⬛⬛⬛
⬛⬛⬛⬛⬛⬛⬛⬛
⬛⬛⬛⬛⬛⬛⬛⬛
⬛⬛he invites you up ⬛⬛⬛
⬛⬛⬛⬛⬛ kind
And careful
⬛⬛he takes your voice
And leaves you howling at ⬛⬛
⬛⬛⬛⬛⬛ Project Hill
You must pick up ⬛
⬛⬛⬛⬛⬛⬛ the ⬛⬛⬛⬛⬛ claim
⬛⬛ look ⬛⬛⬛⬛
⬛⬛⬛⬛ back to
⬛⬛ the
⬛⬛ man
⬛⬛ the author ⬛⬛
⬛⬛⬛⬛⬛⬛⬛ and boast
⬛⬛⬛⬛⬛⬛ the sergeant ⬛⬛
⬛⬛⬛⬛⬛ Angel who
⬛⬛⬛⬛⬛⬛⬛⬛
⬛⬛ left ⬛⬛⬛⬛ a ghost
⬛⬛⬛⬛⬛⬛⬛⬛
⬛⬛ out on ⬛⬛
⬛⬛⬛⬛ the harder ⬛
⬛⬛⬛⬛⬛⬛ stand behind
⬛⬛ the game
⬛⬛ the joke
⬛⬛⬛⬛⬛⬛⬛⬛⬛
I do believe ⬛⬛⬛⬛
ALC

Bob Dylan

KDG

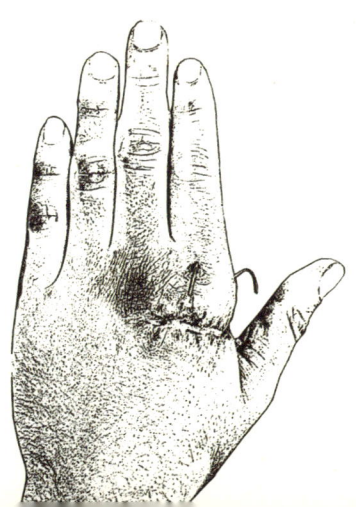

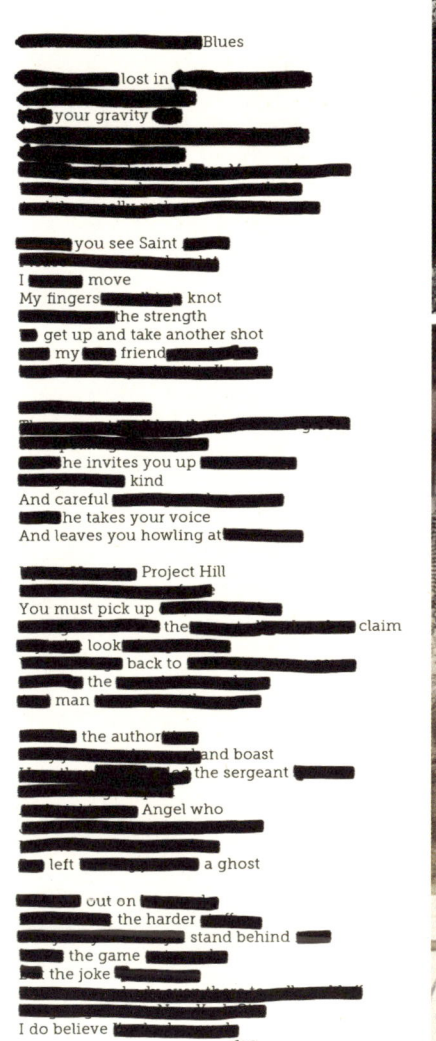

Portrait of the artist *Santiago Bose*. Courtesy Santiago Bose Family Collection.

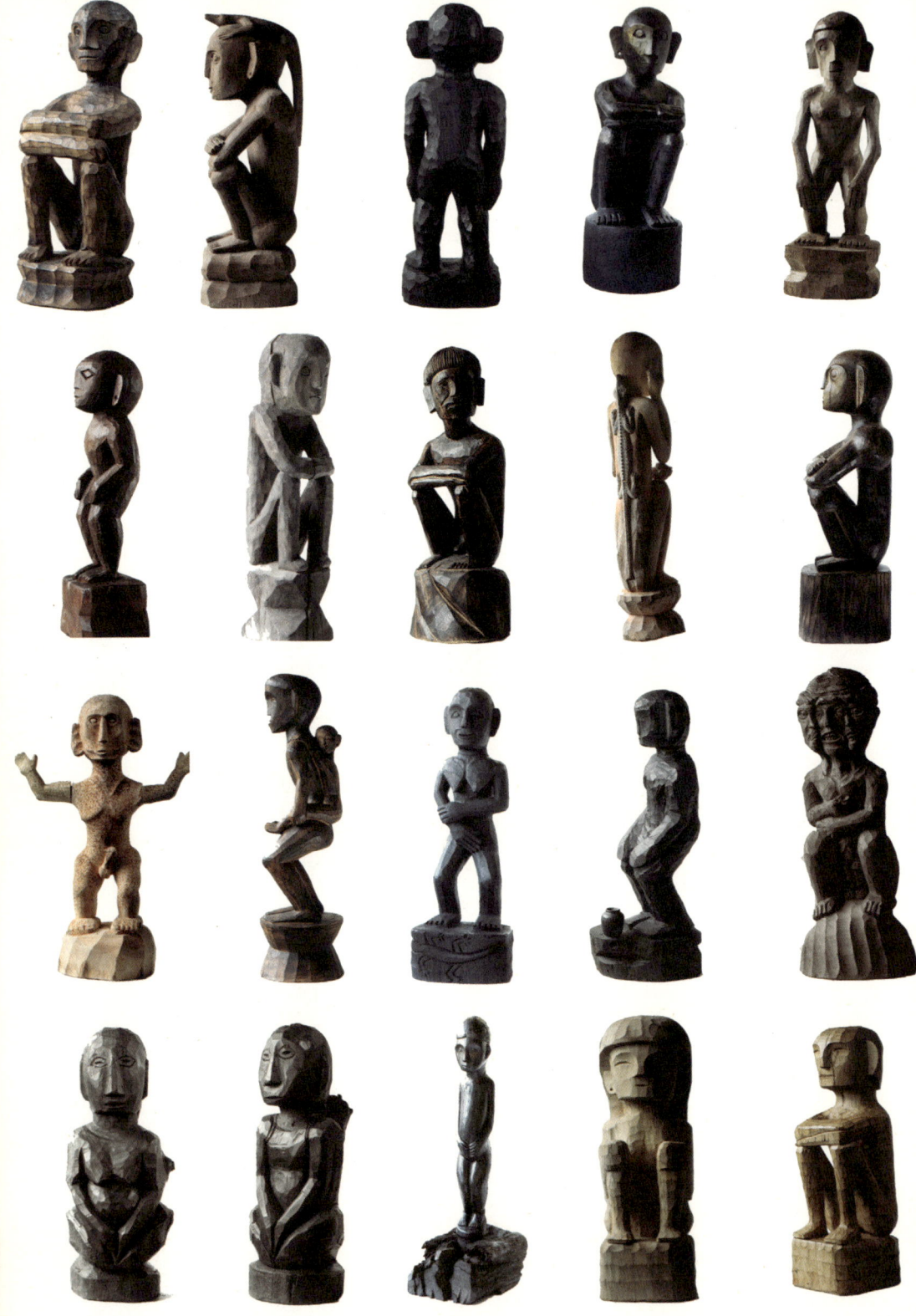

Photographs from the Binulol Project, Singapore Biennale, 2013. Photographs by Gary Buenavista and Faith Erasmo.

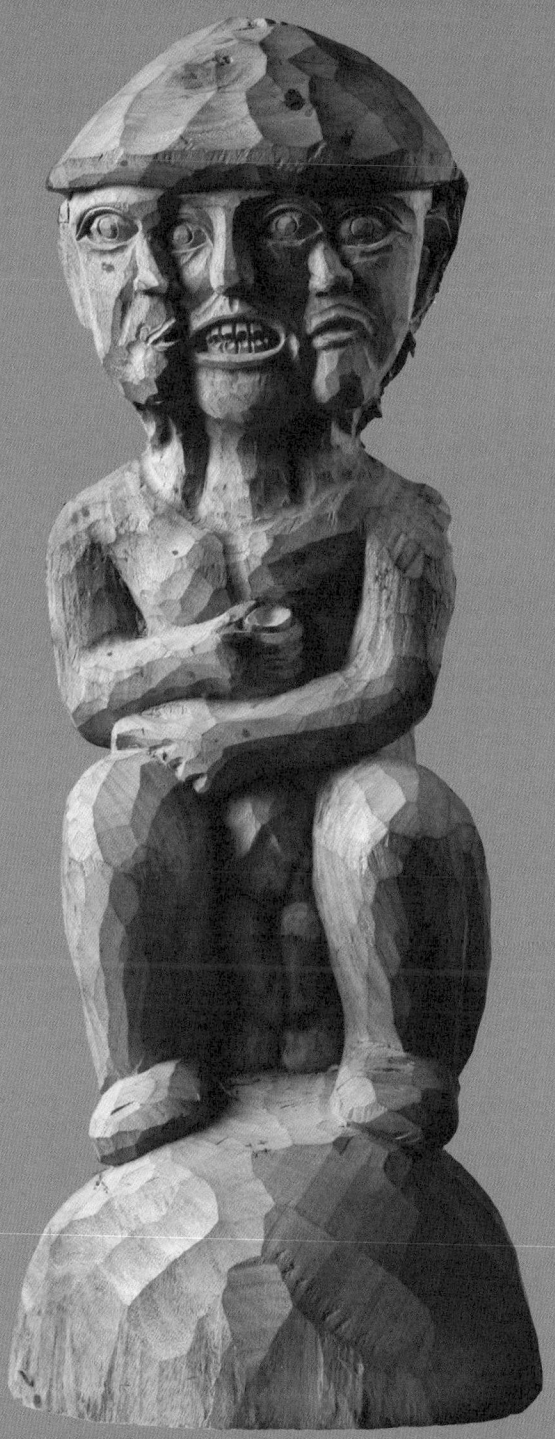

BUL-UL

Reproduction of a Santiago Bose print carved by Dehon Taguyungon. Photograph by Gary Buenavista.

Bul-ul

What is the most prominent design element in Cordillera culture today? We can cite three contenders. One is the lizard motif. Endowed with various meanings, from long life to good fortune, it can be seen in a wide range of objects, from wooden coffin lids to souvenir T-shirts. Another is the lingling-o, derived from ancient jade ornaments and regarded as a fertility symbol. It is now frequently seen in earrings or necklace pendants, in brass, silver or gold. But the most famous Cordillera icon is perhaps the Ifugao bul-ul.

The bul-ul is a free-standing wooden sculpture that is said to represent the Ifugao rice god. Bul-ul carvings always take a human form. As in the sculpture of many tribal or pre-industrial societies, the human form of the bul-ul is highly stylized. Body parts are not realistically rendered, and facial details are often merely implied.

The human figure of the bul-ul comes in two basic positions. There is the seated bul-ul with arms crossed over bended knees. In the standing bul-ul, the legs are slightly flexed. Within these basic forms, there could be variations in details, and even some embellishment – a tuft of hair on the head or shards of glass to represent the eyes. Today, people also speak of regional variations, calling attention to differences between bul-ul produced in the Banaue-Mayaoyao, Hungduan, Tinoc or Kiangan areas (Beyer 1981; Palencia 1998). The Kiangan bul-ul, for instance, is unique because of its removable outstretched arms.

Among the various ethnolinguistic groups in the Philippines, the Ifugao have probably the most complex religious system, with hundreds of gods and countless ritual practices. In his early studies of Ifugao culture, Barton (1946, 80-82) asserts that in the Ifugao pantheon, the bul-ul is a class of deities who are invoked to guard the rice fields and granaries and to ensure abundant harvest. The bul-ul spirit is thought to inhabit the wooden carvings after the images have been activated through an elaborate sequence of rites. The ritual series starts with a journey to the communal forest to obtain the wood that will be used in carving the bul-ul, and ends with a feast in which the carving is finally consecrated through a ritual officiated by the mumbaki (native priests).

Rice culture occupies a central position in traditional Ifugao society. Given this, it is easy to understand why bul-ul carvings figure prominently in the traditional life of the Ifugao. Appeals to the bul-ul deities are made through various ceremonial practices throughout the agricultural cycle, and bul-ul carvings are brought out of storage to take part even in rituals not strictly associated with rice production.

That the bul-ul is an image of the Ifugao rice god is a generally accepted explanation, but it is not the only one. In some accounts, it is said that the spirits of dead ancestors could also reside in the carvings. This is understandable in light of the traditional belief, widespread in the Cordillera, that it is not only the deities but also the ancestral spirits whose intervention in human affairs must be sought. Today, there are also claims that the bul-ul is not related to the Ifugao rice god and therefore has no role to play in rice agriculture. An interesting account comes from a carver, Santos Bayucca, born in Hapao but now working outside Ifugao, who has now and again returned to the province to rediscover his native culture. He contends that based on his talk with the elders and native priests, the bul-ul is used primarily in healing rites where it functions somewhat like a trash can where diseases are dumped. In these healing rituals, whatever it is that ails the sick is removed

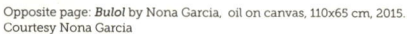

Opposite page: *Bulol* by Nona Garcia, oil on canvas, 110×65 cm, 2015. Courtesy Nona Garcia

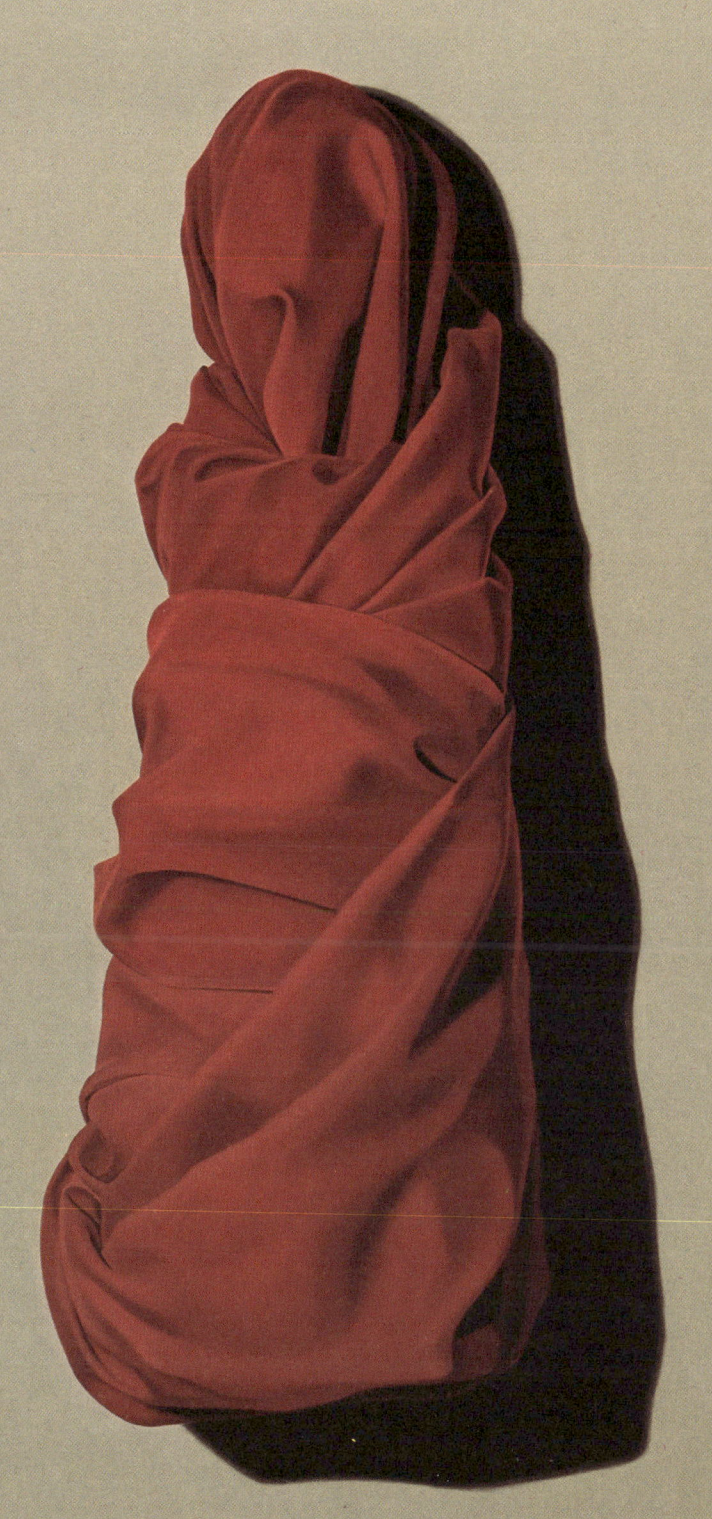

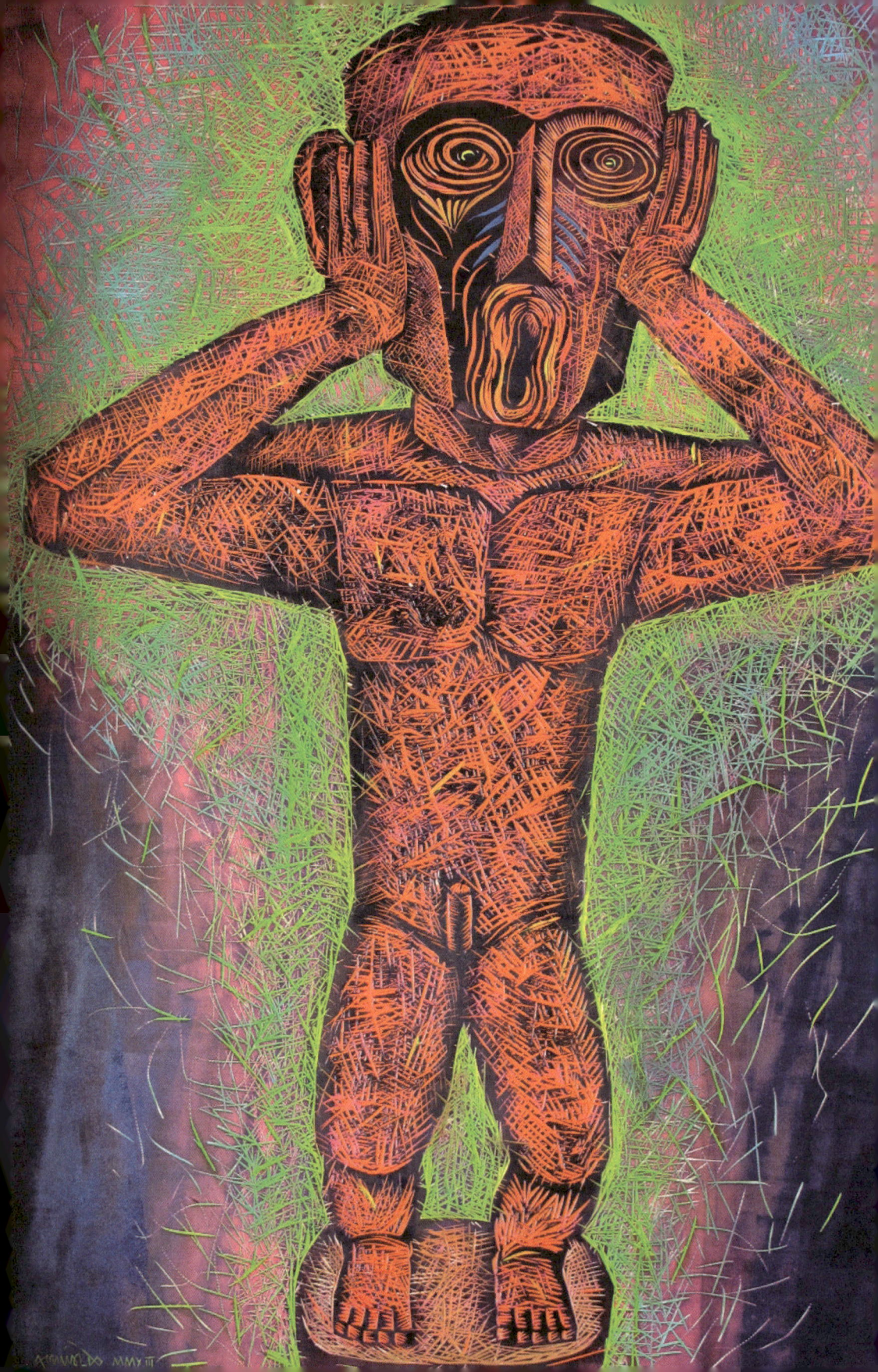

from the body and transferred to the bul-ul through the mediation of the mumbaki. Such an interpretation of the bul-ul seems to suggest that the meaning of some traditional objects is now being modified to accommodate the needs or requirements of changing times. Bayucca, in cooperation with AX(iS), has spearheaded the collecting of 86 bul-uls, to be exhibited with photographic portraits of their makers, in an assemblage that aims to shed light on the Ifugao artisan as artist.

Ifugao society is now rapidly modernizing. Influences coming from the outside, through education, mass media, and electronic technology, have deeply altered the society. Many aspects of traditional life are now being replaced by new social practices.

Today, it is said, only a few consecrated bul-ul pieces remain in Ifugao as ritual life weakens. And yet, Ifugao artisans continue to produce bul-ul by the hundreds, prompted by essentially different motives. Almost all of the carvings being done today are no longer meant for ritual use but for sale to tourists and collectors. Because they are no longer meant to fulfill any religious function, these carvings do not have to go through the required consecration rituals. As a result, they are disconnected from their original network of meanings.

This has led to mutations of the form. From a free-standing sculpture, the bul-ul has become a recurrent design element or decorative relief in various types of objects – bul-ul figures can now be found as ornamental details in commercial furniture (tables, benches, stools), home furnishings (wooden caddies, plant holders, vases, racks), and even in souvenir trinkets like pendants and key chains. The free-standing form, on the other hand, having become a staple of the trade in ethnic curiosities, has become an accent in the garden or an obligatory token of 'tribal chic' in interior design.

Despite these developments, the bul-ul continues to function as an ethnic marker, assuming a symbolic function within and outside Ifugao society. Although the Ifugao do not treat the commercial bul-ul with the kind of reverence given to the sacred, they nonetheless do not treat it as something unconnected or irrelevant to their society. Cut off from ritual connections, the secular bul-ul retains an expressive value that is tied up with the Ifugao people's sense of their own creativity. At the same time, it also articulates their contemporary self-perception as well as their abiding sense of their uniqueness. It is used to adorn public spaces where the projection of an ethnic spirit is considered desirable. The bul-ul form, as it appears in a stylized way on logos and seals and in new objects like decorative textiles, is

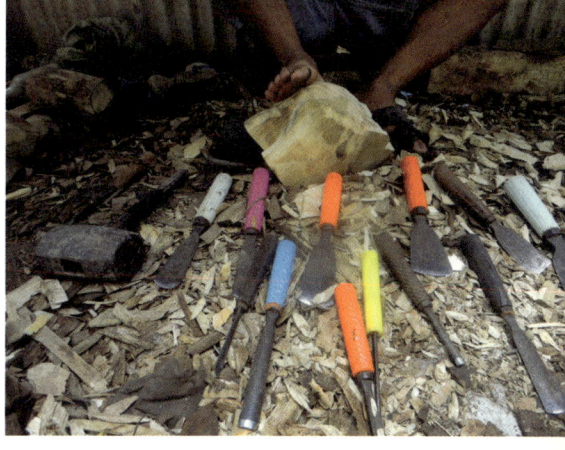

made to function as a sign of local identity.

In the 1960s, Filipino anthropologist Aurora Roxas-Lim went to Banaue to do a survey of *"Ifugao art."* Ifugao society at that time was already beginning to embrace the trappings of modern life. Because of its world-famous rice terraces, a tourist industry had developed and this, in turn, had led to the expansion of business enterprises run both by local people and by migrants from the lowlands. The changes wrought on Ifugao life by tourism and other forms of contact with outsiders were drastic. To these changes, Roxas-Lim (1973, 50) claimed, the Ifugao *"responded in a way that does not necessarily entail the erosion of Ifugao ethos."* Among the more significant findings of her research on Ifugao artistic perception are the categories used by the Ifugao in referring to objects considered to have some artistic value. Some of these categories imply that the Ifugao see the need to differentiate objects made to answer internal (and usually traditional) needs from objects fabricated for commercial purposes. They maintain, however, that both have a cultural value in their society.

The full significance of this finding is not completely explained in Roxas-Lim's (1973, 67) study, but when she wrote that the tourist trade not only *"provides more opportunity for the Ifugao artist to experiment and widen his technical skills"* but also to *"extend his perception of the world at a much faster rate than if he were to keep within the traditional norms,"* she introduced an important theme: that by the 1960s the Ifugao already knew that they were no longer confined to a social order defined exclusively by the agricultural cycle and its accompanying social practices. Like the world outside, their society had changed, and they now had to contend with its new requirements. Thus, the making of objects not associated with agrarian life signifies not only a new sphere of production but also a new way of re-shaping their identity as stipulated by new conditions within and without. DLT.

See also: Three Orphans of Sagada, The.

Opposite page: *Screaming Bulol #5*, Leonard Aguinaldo, handcolor carved rubber (ukir), 91x61 cm, 2012.

Binulol

The bulol (also spelled bul-ul or bulul). How do you start talking about the bulol when there is truly so much myth around the subject? The locals on one side of the mountain will tell you a different story altogether than those on the other side, and not only that, there are the so-called experts from the academe down through to the collectors. So how, or by who, will we understand it?

A few years ago, we had a great exhibition of pre-colonial art? objects? from the Philippines that were showcased at the Musee du Quai Branly in Paris. Wow! And the primary focus was showcasing the bulol. Imagine. This must have been the largest gathering of bulols ever to take place. Unfortunately, this was only for the eye and not for the spirits who were trapped behind glass cases. And the dress code was formal: coat and tie; red wine and not baya (rice wine). But that's how it's done here in the Philippines too, right? As my father puts it, coat and bahag (G-string)! But there was no sign of bahag at the Musee du Quai Branly. Oh yes...there was. A 'WOW Philippines' dance troop. But that's different... and I think that's when we stumble into the problem.

Once 'culture' is seen as commodified exotica, what better item to latch on to than the bulol?

It is one of the few pre-colonial figurative sculptures. Why is that?

Would there have been more figurative sculptures if the Spanish conquistadors, with the backing of the Catholic Church, had not gone on a witch-hunt and burned everything down to the ground? We are left clueless to our historic past. Is this the reason why we are so attracted to the bulol now? I'm sure the bulol would not be here today if The Cross had gone up to Mt. Pulag 300 years ago. Perhaps we would not be praying to Apo Kabunyan.

Lets try to understand him/her again, the bulol, and get this straight: a bulol is a representation of someone. If a bulol is carved by 'Kabigat' then the bulol is called a kinabigat. Because it was kabigat who carved it. Like any artwork today, it carries the name of the artist. Kabigat, or the artisan who created the bulol, also had to partake in the ritual and go on long fasts and what not. Many bulols were created for healing in which an artisan/carver had to create a representational figure of the sick or ill and then a baki or mumbaki, in partnership with the carver, would perform rituals, sometimes very long rituals, to transfer the sickness to the bulol.

Now let me ask you: would you like to display your used IV tubes and cancerous cysts in a jar in your living room? Well, only a few would. Many would either throw it away or bury it. For most Igorots, after the rituals are performed, the bulol finds its way to the rice granary where it is hidden from everyday life.

All of this changed when the first Americans in search of gold found their way up to the mountains and, by chance, had their eyes on the bulol. You can just imagine:

(American, seeing bulol in rice granary. Igorot, does not understand English.)

AM What is that?

IGT : rice..

AMN: Rice ?

IGT: god .

AMN: God?

IGT:god???

AMN : Ahhh Rice God!!!!

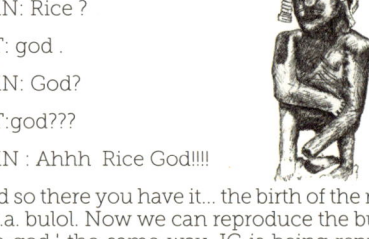

And so there you have it... the birth of the rice god! A.k.a. bulol. Now we can reproduce the bulol, 'the rice god,' the same way JC is being reproduced in every corner of the country without a care for our daily bread, so too the bulol and our daily rice. Of course, this reproduction of bulols only really started after the second world war, when Ifugao was bombed down to the ground by the 'Great Liberator': the American military machine. Unfortunately, Mt. Napulawan, which is located in Hungduan where the best carvers of the Cordillera are from, was the place where general

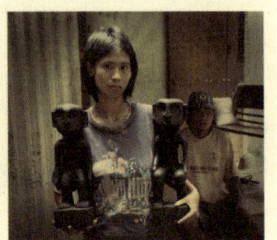
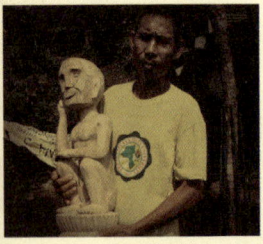
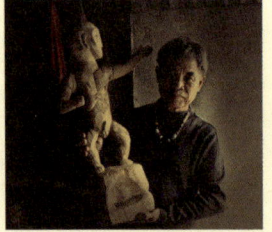

Photographs of carvers with their *bulul* from the Binulol Project, Singapore Biennale, 2013. Photographs by Gary Buenavista and Faith Erasmo.

Yamashita and the retreating Japanese soldiers of South-East Asia decided to take shelter.

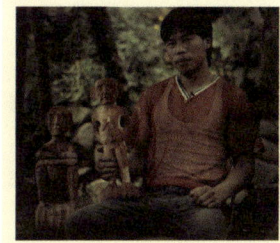 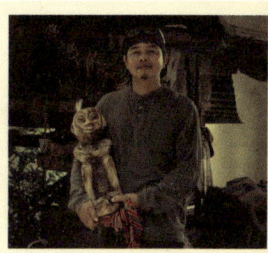

After the war, Ifugao and the great rice terraces, like the rest of the country, lay in ruins. Lopez Nauyak, an orphaned young boy, and his sister, decided to walk from Ifugao all the way to Asin, just six kilometers away from Baguio City, where they would be adopted by some relatives. Like Lopez, many Ifugao carvers migrated to Baguio after the war in search of greener pastures, and this is where wood and wood carving became commodities. Such was the case for our dear friend, the bulol.

Oh, my dear friend bulol, I grew up with you as my playmate. These dark, rustic figures were located in every corner of the house. I didn't know about statues as gods. As far as I was concerned, they were my friends. And, growing up in a house filled with Baguio artists that questioned Western art practice, the bulol became a symbol of the independent spirit of a living, and ancient, culture. The bulol was present in Tito Santi's paintings and Roberto's installations and, of course, with every screening of *Perfumed Nightmare* (1977). Kidlat Tahimik put together an installation of *"Cinema tonto"* where he used bulols staring into T.V monitors, their souls sucked out into that big void of desire. That, perhaps, is what it has become.

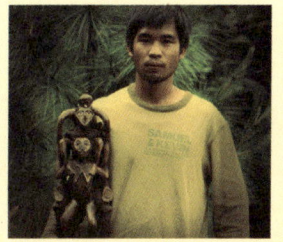 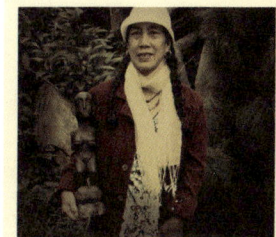

The bulol will perhaps be a reminder of something we never quite understood: a figure that represents something, or someone, we never met. It exists in a culture now losing its grip on the earth and its havens of the past, only to be rudely awakened to a material culture of the 21st century.

Having all this in mind for the Singapore Biennale 2013, we wanted to approach this project with great care and bring the bulol back to where it came from: a representation. Along with Santos Bayucca, who spear-headed the project entitled *Bi-nulol*, we went driving around the Cordillera – a span of 600km going to different wood carving communities. We asked each carver, *"If you were a bulol, what would you look like?"* And boy, did they vary. The oldest carver was around 90 years of age; the youngest was nine years old. We had a blind carver, Roherio, whose bulol had eyes and could see, and a man whose bulol had breasts because he insisted he was the one giving the milk to the family. There are female carvers too who participated in the project.

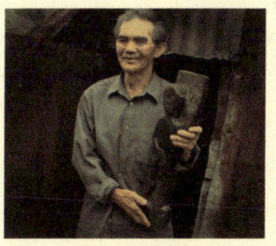 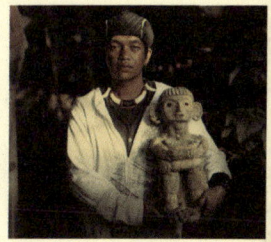

In the end, Santos had gathered 86 carvers from Tarlac to Isabela. I feel this particular project bound the exhibition together. Because, for one, it destroyed your instant notion of what contemporary art should look like, and reminded you that we are in South East Asia. We are igorots! We are not focusing on the exotic but rather we are looking at portraits of an inner space through an age-old practice.

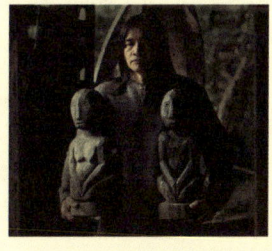 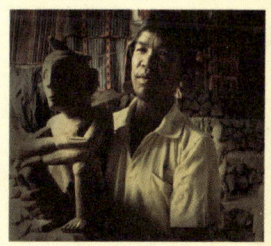

I hope that one day we will be able to publish the complete collection of binulols, as well as house them. But perhaps not behind glass boxes.

I'll tell my nephew who's name is Binulan, nick name Binu... BINU LOL Laugh out loud! KDG.

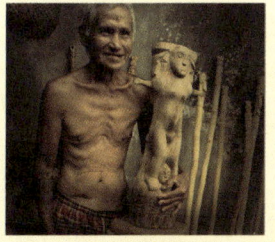 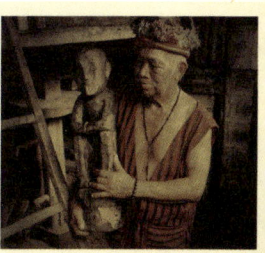

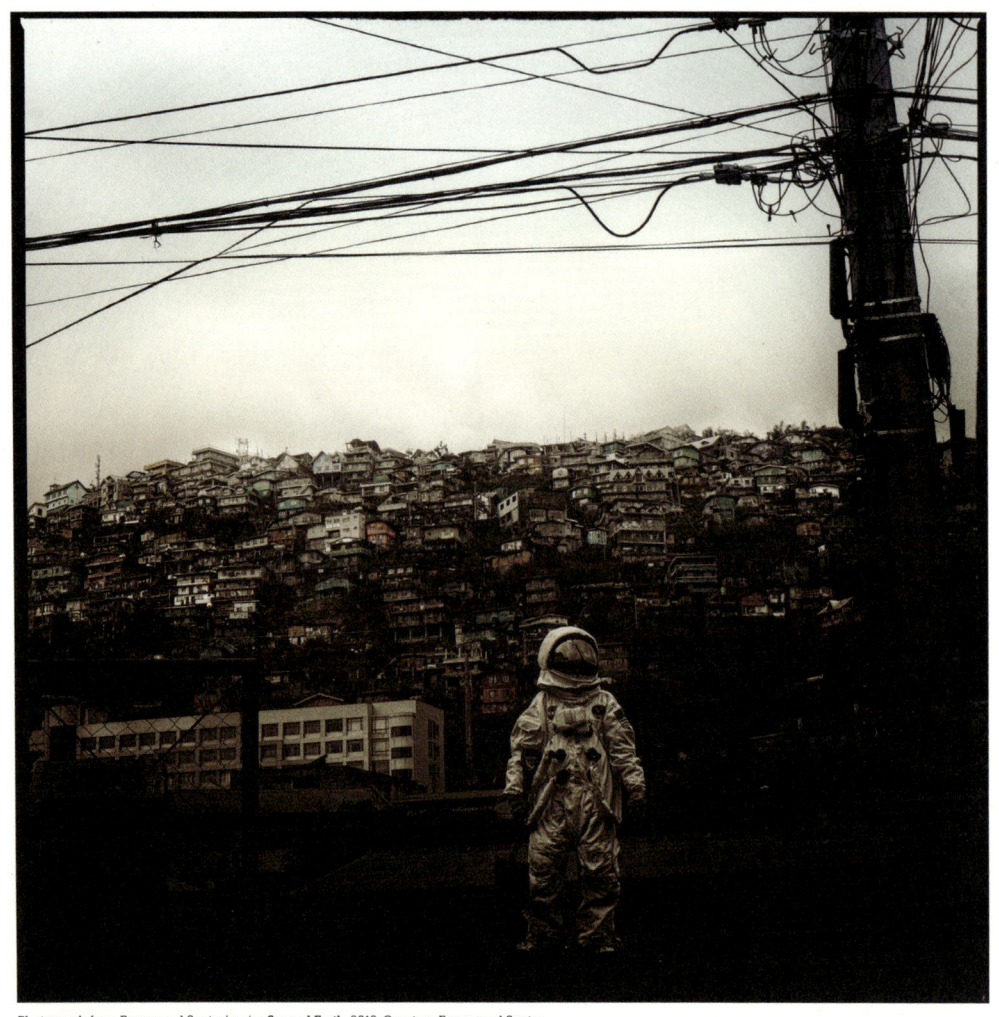

Photograph from Emmanuel Santos' series *Second Earth*, 2012. Courtesy Emmanuel Santos.

. . . AND IT SPEAKS ITSELF FROM NOTHING, OR PRIOR MISSED WORDS THROUGH MY HAND . PRETEND AT OWNERSHIP . AT FIRST I WAS AMUSED, THE HABITUAL AND FAMILIAR MESS OF YOU STILL STUCK FROM EARLY CHILDHOOD . BEING ASKED FOR OR NEEDED . THE HUSHED AIR SHIFTS THE BLANK OF MIST . THE SAME OLD ROOSTER CROWS ITS INCITEMENT . A CIRCLE OF LIGHT IN THE EAST SKY. BROKEN MORNING . ONE TONE PARTS . THE FOG STARTS SHOWING ROOFTOPS AND PLASTIC SHEETING . YOU TUNE UP . RAINBOW PAINT AND RUST . PIGS STEP ON THE GRATING OF A TRUCK . CAR FUMES AND MUSIC LEAK UP FROM THE STREET . THIS IS A CRY . A TASTELESS SLOGAN . A CALL TO PRAYER . BURNT FEATHERS SOUR AND THE SUGAR OF MEAT COMBINE IN THE WOODSMOKE . LEAD PAINTED CITY OF MEMORY REHEARSE YOURSELF INTO EXISTENCE YET AGAIN . REPEAT YOUR LINE . SOME THINGS ARE EVERGREEN YOU SAY SOME THINGS FADE WHITE . BOTH A FAMILY HOME AND MUNICIPAL BUILDS GO TO DYNASTIES OF TERMITES . BREATHE TO ME, MOVE ON THE WATER IN THE GUTTERS OVER BRICKDUST AND OLD TIMBERS IN THE RAIN . BAGUIO YOU SQUATTING, NATIVISED CONQUISTADOR, KARAOKE COWBOY, SKYLAND GOD . IMPROVISE YOUR GAGGLE OF HOLY NAMES . I SAW YOU APPROACH THROUGH THE PINES AND STUMBLE YOU VANISHED . THE GHOST OF CITY . I ASK YOU, HERE I SUMMON YOU . GHOST OF A CITY, DIRT ON YOUR FEET . HERE I SUMMON . BOW TO MY MOUTH SMELLING OF RESIN, OF SHIT, OF HAIRSPRAY, AND SUNFLOWERS CURLED TOWADS DEATH IN THE BLAZE OF THEIR SEASON . ASSUME YOUR RITUAL FORMS . CLAIM AND COUNTERCLAIM TURNS ON ITSELF GETS LOST TO DISTANCE . STILL I SUMMON YOU, GIVE YOU YOUR DUES, HALF MY BLOOD, MY NAME, WHICH YOU DESERVE . AND IN THE NIGHT I ALMOST CAUGHT THE WAY YOU CAME, LOST WHERE THE CITY SWALLOWED ITSELF IN THE HAZE OF BURNING HALOGEN . NOW THIS TIME APPEAR AS CLOSE AS EYESIGHT, AS TOOTH ENAMEL . RETURN ME COMPLETE, FAITHLESS, HUMAN TO MY OWN VOICE . YOU STICK TO MY SKIN . CRAWL FORWARD . FALL FAST TO MY TOUCH IS WHAT I ASK . THE WORLD TREMBLES . THE TREELINE FILTERS THE WIND TO NEAR STILLNESS. I LOSE MY STEADY HAND TOO SOON AND THINKING WHAT MORE TO SAY THERE'S NOTHING . NOTHING MORE . HERE I SUMMON I ASK ACCEPT . THIS IS MY WEAPONISED WHITE FLAG – ALC

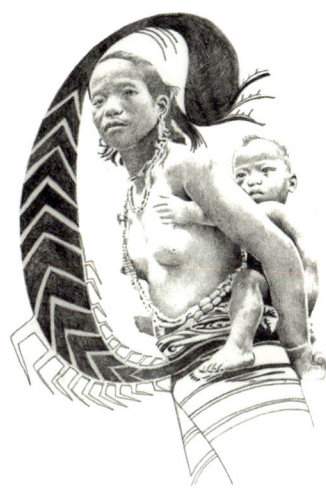

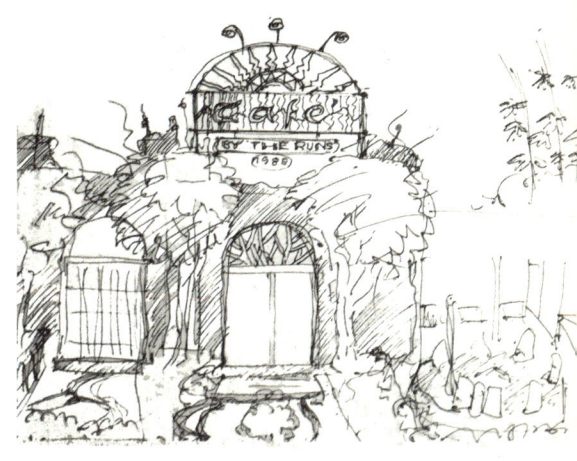

Illustration of *Café by the Ruins*, 1989. Illustration by Roberto Villanueva.

Cabbage King. Dr. Charles Cheng in his 1997 book, *The Ethnic Chinese in Baguio and in the Cordillera*, used the titles *"kings"* and *"queens"* to describe the most important Chinese in connection to a vegetable, flower or food: Tai Kien is the Cabbage King for developing a new cabbage variety; he is the father of Tai Pong, the Celery King; Mrs. Chow Wong Shy is the Puto-Kutsinta (rice cake) Queen; Puan Sing is the Lettuce King; Chan Kok Shiu is the Broccoli King; Yuyo Ong is the Vegetable King (although he should be the Potato King but that title was conferred to Robustiano Choy); Tai Ping is the Gladiola Queen while Ruben Kantala is the Rose King of Benguet. FYC. See also: Quan Nga Yen.

Caddies. *"Young Igorot boys from the mission schools caddied for us on the country club golf links. Naked from the waist down except for red G-strings, wearing short jackets of hand-woven fiber, and round skull caps, they were agile and picturesque figures. Should the same boy caddie for you frequently, he was likely to become extremely partisan. With suspicious regularity you would catch up with your dubious drive to find your ball enjoying a perfect lie."* (Ingersoll 1971, 71) FYC.

Café by the Ruins. A restaurant that started out from the ideas of a group of friends in Baguio who wanted a simple yet artistic space. It was to be for the Baguio people and everyone who wanted the modern and traditional Cordillera with a twist. Baguio friends, Christine Arvisu, Adelaida Lim, Su Llamado, Ba-boo Mondoñedo, Roberto Villianueva, Louie Llamado, Boy Yuchengco, and BenCab opened Café by the Ruins on March 20, 1988. It was built around the ruins of the home of the American Governor General of Benguet, Phelps Whitmarsh. During World War II, Phelps Whitmarsh's home was bombed and the ruins were all that was left. At first it was completely covered by blooming bougainvillea vines; today, those walls surround a warm, wooden interior boasting a cogon roof built after Cordilleran vernacular architecture. The Café holds monthly art exhibits featuring local artists. It hosts food workshops, poetry readings and musical performances. CAA.

Cah'sheman *(IBA)*. The day before yesterday.

Calapjao *(IBA)*. A rain cape made of dried palm leaves.

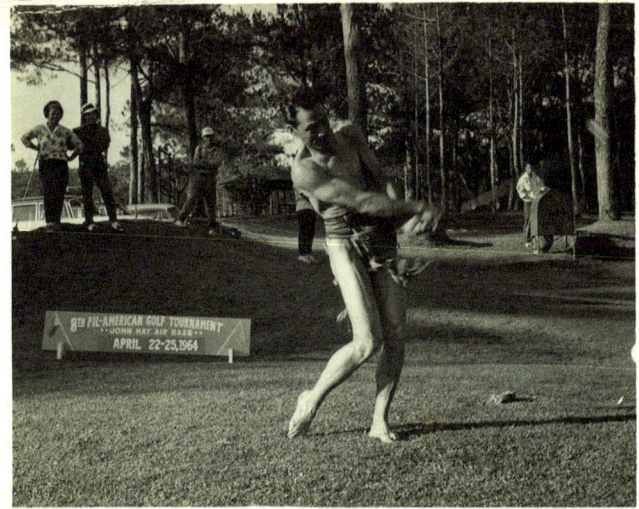

Photograph of Sabas C. Hafalla caddying, 1964. Courtesy Tommy Hafalla.

Calendar

What's is the shape of a year for the old Igorots? It depends on who you're asking. In the old Mountain Province, it meant the seasonal calendar which closely resembles the lunar calendar but is more down-to-earth.

According to the late historian William Henry Scott, the seasonal calendar is more determined not by looking at the moon but more by what's around you.

> "The seasonal year may be defined as a completion of a cycle of any number of seasons determined by non-astronomical observations of the environment – the coming of rain, the flowering of plants, the migration of birds, and so forth," Scott (1958, wrote in "Some Calendars of Northern Luzon."

Migratory birds that make their appearance at certain times of the year determine half of the 12 seasons in a traditional Mountain Province calendar. This includes the kiling bird whose cry means that the first rains have come. Other birds named for a season include the adog and bakakew. When the baby kiling bird cries "ki-ik," it means that it is time to sow and when the same bird develops its full-throated "kiling," it means it's time to transplant the same rice, Scott said (ibid.).

The old calendar is so tied up with these natural signs, as well as the rice cycle, that the term "year" perplexed the people.

> "Far from considering a month to be a fixed number of days, the old-time Igorot doesn't even know how many days there are in a month. This is also true of his native word for 'year,'" Scott said (ibid.).

> "'What is a year?' put to an old Igorot one at harvest time, brought the cryptic reply, 'Now.'" There are even some old farmers in Tetepan (a village in Sagada) during whose lifetimes a second crop has been introduced who allow that the years nowadays are much shorter than they used to be," he added (Scott 1958, 565).

> "Men do not reckon their own ages or know how many years ago a specific event happened, and mothers present their babies at clinics not knowing how many months old they are."

Until this day, the civil registry offices in the Cordillera are still swamped with requests from residents for non-existent birth records. I remember how hard it was for my former office to authenticate the birth records of the late journalist Isidoro Chammag as there were no records that he was born in Barlig, Mountain Province.

But there was indeed no need for accuracy then, not only because life went at its own pace, but also because the calendars were only for agricultural purposes. That is why, among the Ifugaos, the native breed of rice called 'tinawon' also means 'every year.' Introducing the second cropping into the traditional rice culture of the Cordilleras indeed disrupted their culture. Not only were non-traditional rice varieties introduced (they are rarely used for making rice wine) but the rituals became outmoded. When the rituals were forgotten, the beliefs embedded within them were also put aside.

Climate change also drastically altered the Cordillera seasons as we know them. The decimation of the birds, which used to signal the seasons, also abetted the end of the old way of keeping time. FYC.

See also: Beska; Lennek; Teke; Tinawon.

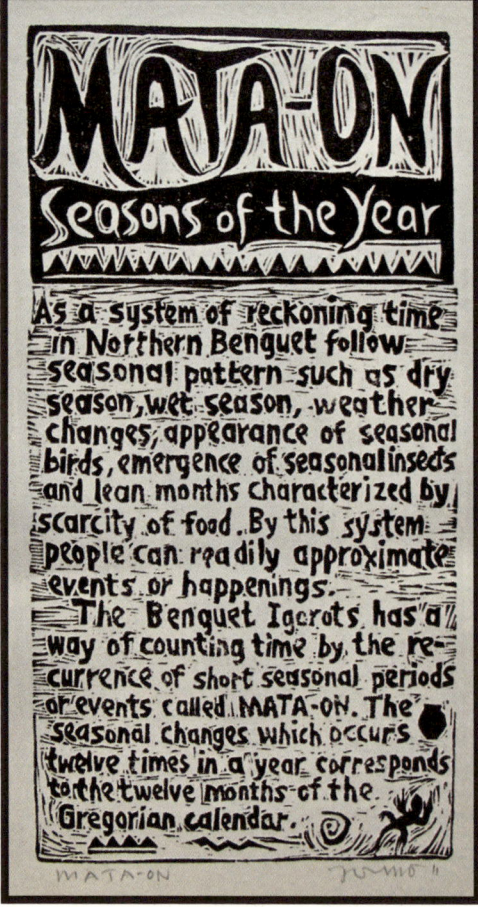

Rubbercut prints by Leonard Aguinaldo illustrating the different seasonal calendars in the Mountain Province, 1999-2013. Courtesy Leonard Aguinaldo.

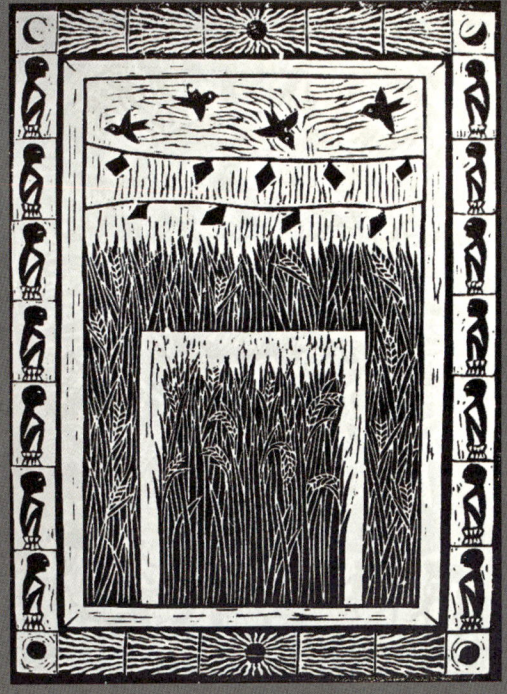
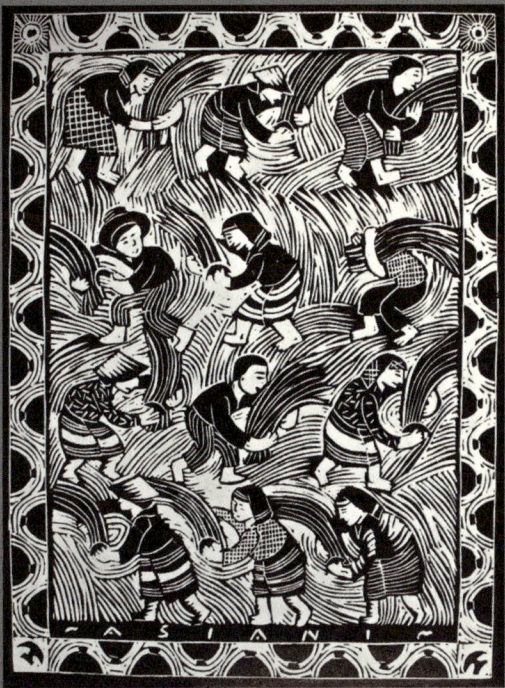
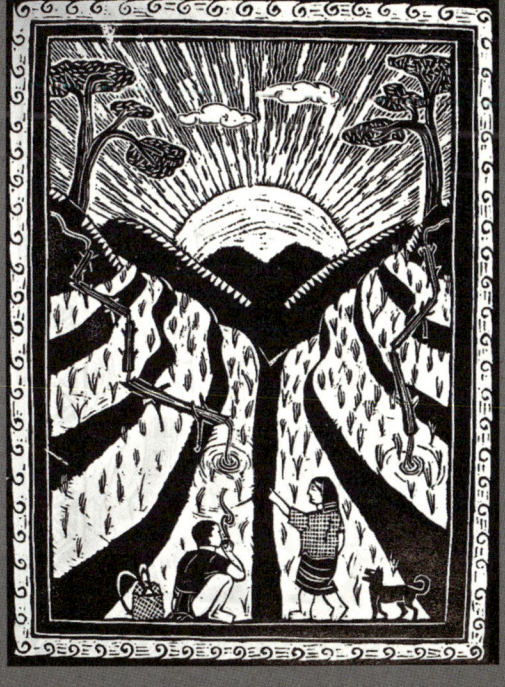
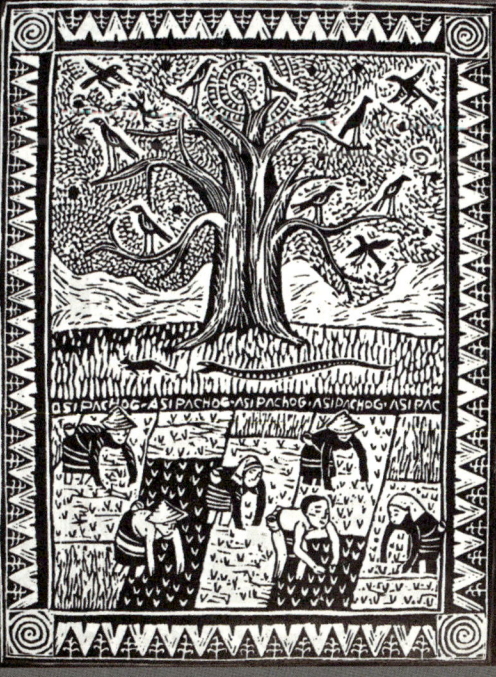

Camote *(FIL/ILO)*. Sweet potato. *"Go home and plant camote,"* an American teacher taunted her high school students in the 1930s, triggering the first nationwide student strike in the Philippines. But in the Cordillera, the students may just heed the call. In Mountain Province, Benguet, Ifugao and other Cordilleran provinces, camote planting is an art. It is referred to as the brown gold of the highlands, especially since it used to be the staple food of Igorots when the high yielding rice varieties had not yet been introduced to the communities. Camote is planted in swidden fields, in a slanted position so that the roots will be concentrated in the buried portion. The root crop can be harvested after three months while the leaves can be harvested almost every week. Camote is a favorite viand not only among Igorots but also among the lowland neighboring communities. In Ifugao, camote is harvested in a bamboo basket called the tayaban. The Ikalahans practice gengen and day-og (building of drainage ditches around the plots near the bottom of the slope to prevent waterlogging). In Bontoc, some camote plots are spiral shaped. The native varieties of camote in Bontoc are Sampido, Sisa, Bulla, Ponce, Bokboktot, Banawei, Bayahan, Gayyadik, Kalbo-oy, Kiangan, Pansil, Kontegan, Toklong, Tocano, Kuyapap, Kaasan, and Imelda. Dinamdam is the Kankanaey term for roasted camote. FYC/DOS.

See also: Agkufangfang; Boko; Buguias Patatas; Faliling; Gengen; Intum; Kineykhey; Mabukag; Sayote; Sinalupsop; Unsek.

Cañao *(IBA/KAN)*. Ritual festival. The cañao is a ritual festival for either dilus (death ritual) or peshit (thanksgiving ritual). It is hosted by a family and officiated by a mambunong especially in the ritual prayers and the butchering of animals. Community members share in an organically systematized way of preparing for the cañao – men would start butchering the ritual animals and women would start cooking food without the need for a manager ordering around who should do what. At the core of the cañao is the gathering of a community's people to rejuvenate its spirituality and bond through the sharing of food, conversation, dance, music, and prayer.

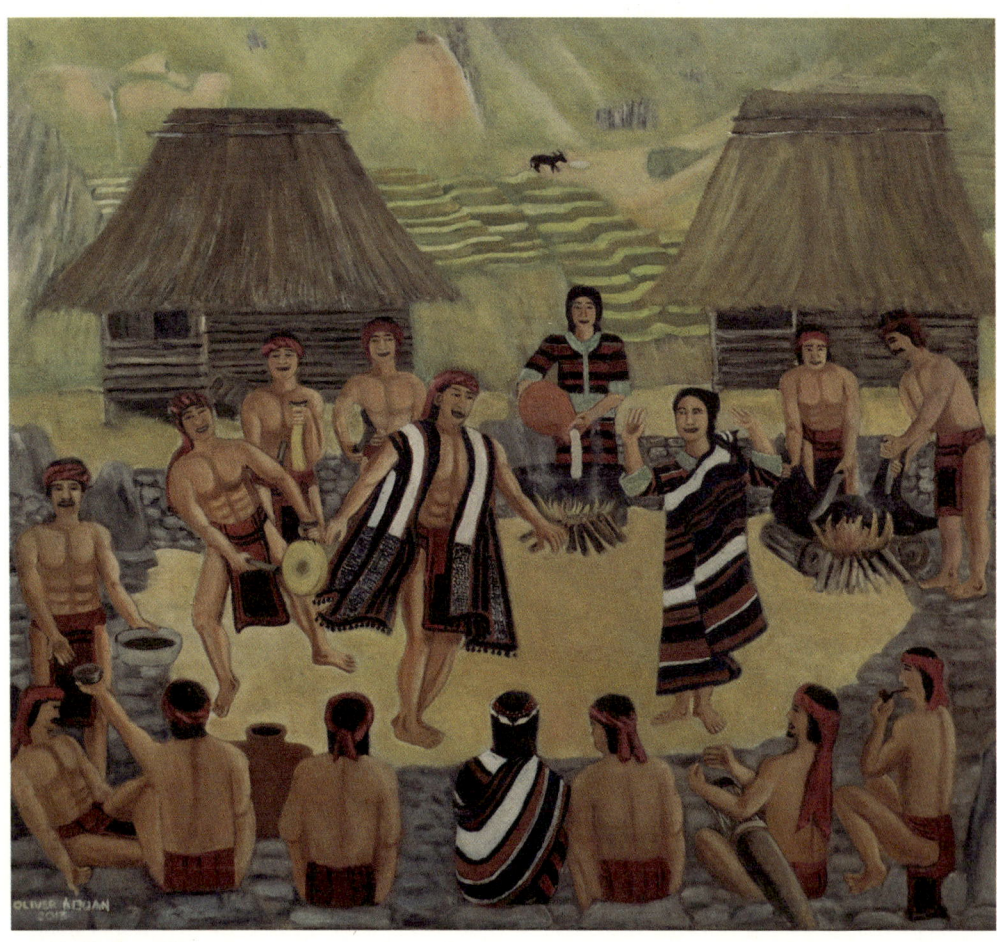

Artwork by Oliver Abuan, 2013.

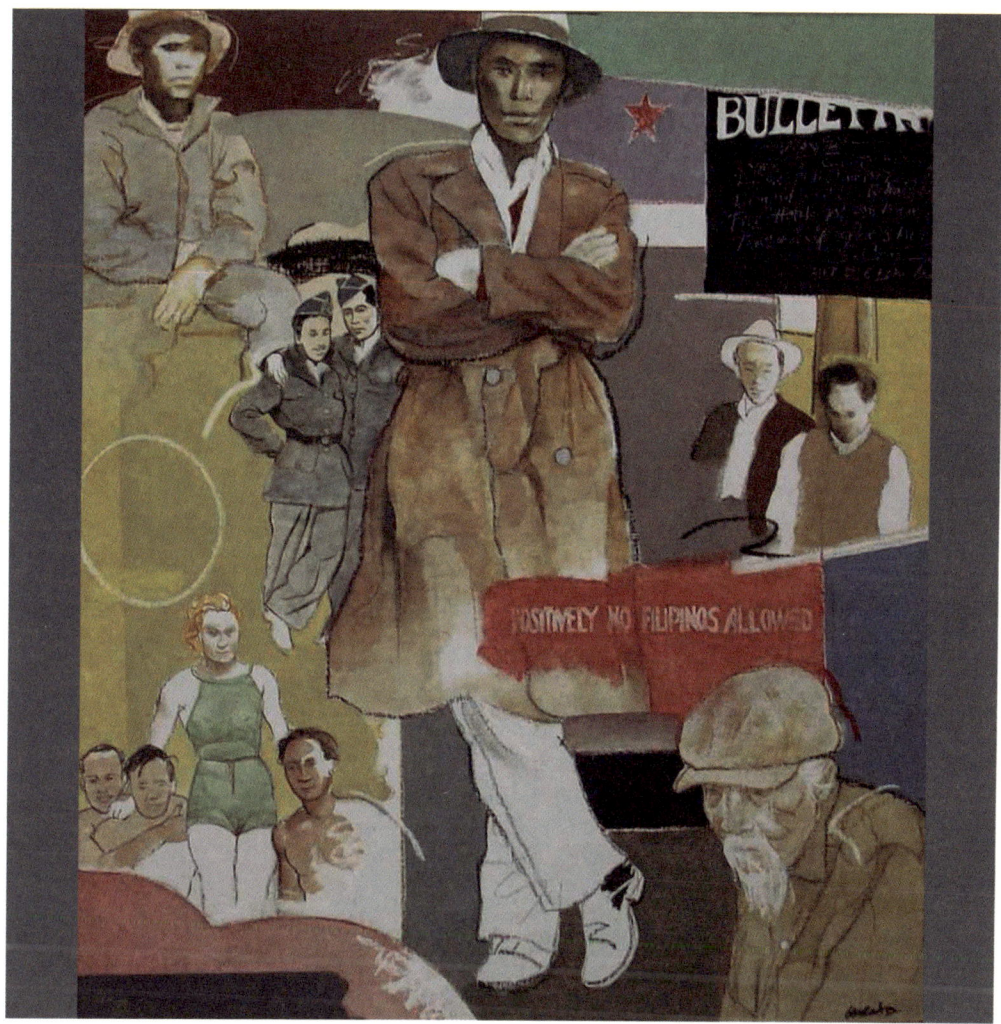

Artwork by BenCab, 1972.

Throughout history, it has been exploited over and over by colonizers, missionaries, tourism organizers, politicians, and propagandists since the nature of the cañao is to draw crowds.

See also: Dangtey; Entako Menlambak; Mambunong; Tivangdal; Peshit; Watwat.

Carangat *(GAD).* Thieves of human souls that can cause disease and even death. They live in balete and tamarind trees, big boulders and in the ground.

See also: Alan; Bagong; Banig; Baguio Ghost Stories; Darupaypay; Ibwa; Maingal; Nginin; Tinguian Spirits.

Cariño, Dr Jose. Son of Mateo and Bayosa Cariño, he studied at the Rush Medical School in Chicago and became the first Ibaloi doctor. After World War II, he became the first Ibaloi mayor of Baguio. FYC.

See also: Pitapit.

Carlos Bulosan's Failed Kodak Moment. *"My clothes began to wear out. I was sick from eating what the traders discarded. One day an American lady tourist asked me to undress before her camera, and gave me ten centavos for doing it. I had found a simple way to make a living. Whenever I saw a white person in the market with a camera, I made myself conspicuously ugly, hoping to earn ten centavos. But what interested the tourists more were the naked Igorot women and children. Sometimes they took pictures of the old men with G-strings. They were not interested in Christian Filipinos like me. They seemed to take a delight in photographing young Igorot girls with large breasts and robust mountain men whose genitals were nearly exposed, their G-strings bulging large and alive."* (Bulosan 2006, 67).

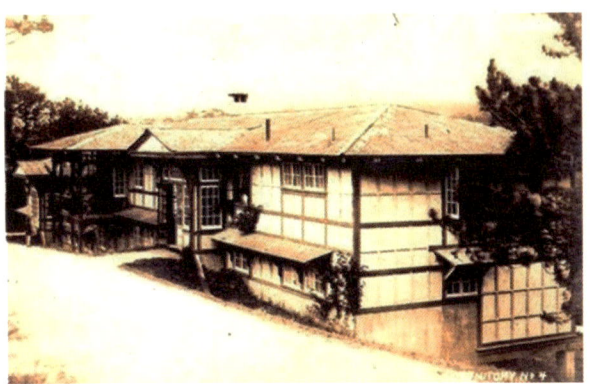

Photograph of *Casa Vallejo*, c. 1930s. Courtesy Erlyn Alcantara.

Casa Vallejo. Originally built in 1909, Casa Vallejo is one of the few remaining historical, pre-World War II structures in Baguio. It was formerly known as Dormitory 4, which housed employees of the Philippine Commission and the executive branch of the American administration whenever they came up for 'the season.' At the time, the building had sawali wall partitions. The exterior walls were a combination of wood and galvanized iron, as were most of the government buildings constructed in that period.

In 1916, 160 German Prisoners of War were billeted there. They helped to build the Baguio stone market.

In 1923, this building was leased to Salvador Vallejo, a Spaniard who came with the Spanish army at the turn of the century. He married in Baguio and never left. He opened Vallejo Hotel with some renovations that blended with the original Dormitory 4 structure.

During World War II, hundreds of foreign refugees stayed in Casa Vallejo. After the American carpet bombing of Baguio in 1945, Casa Vallejo and the Baguio Cathedral were among the few buildings that remained standing. Baguio City High School held its classes in the building in July 1945.

Afterwards, the Vallejo family resumed management of the hotel. Their descendants operated the hotel until 2000, during which time it became a hub for community meetings and international conferences in the city. After their lease ended, the property was administered by a government agency.

Developments and restorations thus far have remained faithful to the architecture of the early American period of Baguio's history. The building still features the grace and atmosphere of the original exterior. Wood is still its primary material.

The property has recently been titled in favor of an indigenous clan claiming Casa Vallejo as part of their ancestral land from pre-colonial times.

This has led to a dispute of jurisdiction between two government agencies and a case in the Supreme Court filed by the city government of Baguio. The situation has sparked a heated discussion on indigenous peoples' rights, the preservation of heritage, and the land use issues of Baguio City. In an ideal world, indigenous ownership, heritage, and urban development should not be opposed to each other. But the way the Casa Vallejo debate is going, it seems that people see each one as threats to the others. What will come out of this legal and very public mess? Will Casa Vallejo be preserved and respected as a landmark of Baguio's heritage? Or will it go the way of the rest of Baguio – down the drain of over-development? And whose version of the truth shall prevail? Casa Vallejo's past was, as local historian Erlyn Alcantara puts it, *"part of a much larger history."* Its future history remains uncertain. PLP.

See also: Baguio, the Naming of; Ethnographic Mapping; Season; White Elephant.

Casna *(IBA).* Blood from a ritual animal which is smeared on the foreheads of the family members sponsoring the ritual. FYC.

See also: Ethnographic Mapping.

Cavite also **Tuping, Riprap.** *"Men who built the rice terraces and supplied them with water understood very well how to build cavites, dry walls of carefully chosen stones. These held together without mortar even when they were as much as 15 meters high and 100 meters long. The drainage ditches the Igorots built to carry off the torrents of rain that fell during the typhoons were as true to grade as if surveyors had laid them out..."* (Halsema 1991, 214).

Cayat. A Baguio old-timer who, in January 1937, was charged with the unlawful possession of a bottle of gin and ordered to pay PHP50 or face imprisonment because of a 1907 Act banning all non-Christians from purchasing or possessing alcoholic beverages other than the local ones brewed in Cordillera villages. A group of young highlander lawyers led by Sinai Hamada defended Cayat up to the Supreme Court and won their appeal. Let's drink to Cayat and Sinai! FYC.

See also: Bureau of Non-Christian Tribes; Enmity between the Igorots and Christians, The Beginning of; Hamada, Sinai; Kain; Remontados.

Cellophil. Short for Cellophil Resources Corporation, the 200,000 hectare logging and paper-pulp concession that was awarded to Marcos crony Herminio Disini in 1973 and would have provided rayon and cigarette filters exported to Japan. It would have also denuded most of the Western Cordillera's forests had not the Tinguians and Kalingas protested the concession. It came to

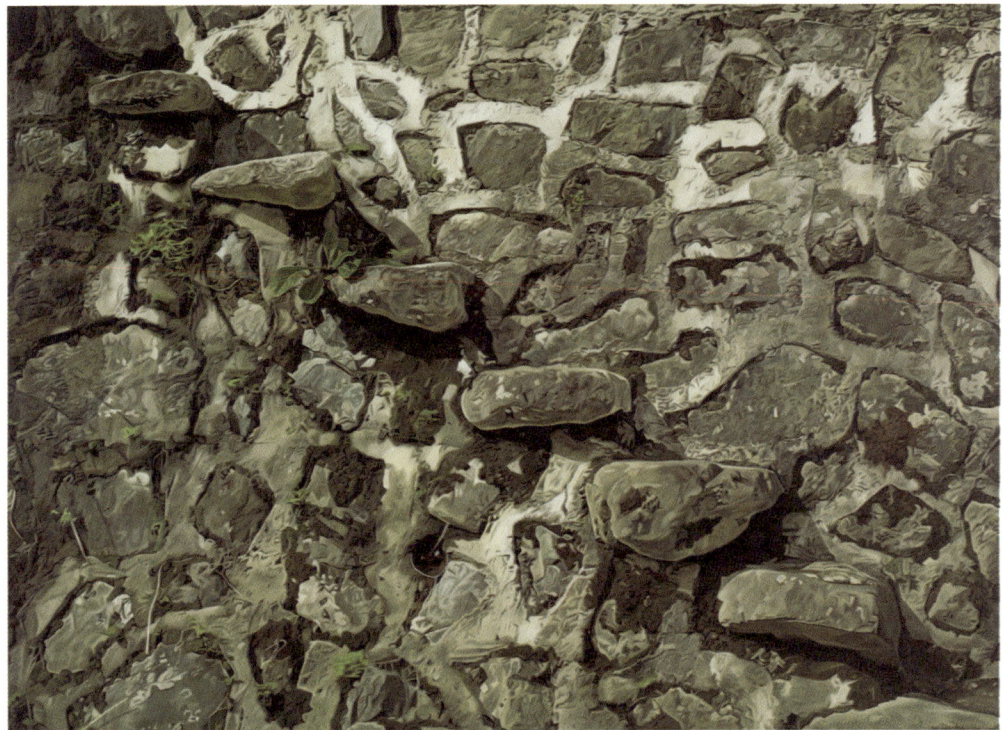

Ascend 2, Nona Garcia, oil on canvas, 152x213 cm, 2016. Courtesy Nona Garcia.

a point where some of the opposition (including from priests Fr. Cirilo and Bruno Ortega, Fr. Nilo Valerio, and Fr. Conrado Balweg) went underground to further their cause. The project was stopped and its former plant at Tayum, Abra remains a ghostly reminder of what could have been. FYC.
See also: Balweg brothers; Chico; Dulag; Macli-ing; Mt. Data; Peace zone; Vochong.

Cervantes. The town in Ilocos Sur known as 'the gateway to the Cordilleras.' It shares its northern boundary with Benguet and eastern boundary with Mountain Province. DOS.

Chakang *(IBA)*. A solid gold band fitted into the front teeth. *"Silence is golden,"* joked colonizer Dean Worcester, as the chakang would make it impossible for the Ibaloi women who wore them to speak.

Challichog *(KAL)*. A unique dance form nationally recognized, together with the Banga dance, as distinctively Kalinga. Originating from Lubuagan, Kalinga, Challichog is now popular with cultural performing groups all over the Cordillera. They almost always make this a representative part of their Kalinga repertoire. Unknown to many, Challichog was first performed in public during the peace pact of Lubuagan and Sumadel in the 1980s. Irene Bawer, who then danced with three of her friends, created this dance form inspired by manchelok (soil preparation in the rice fields). Manchelok involves the stomping of feet with hands clasped behind the back, which is characteristic of the Challichog dance form. RBB.
See also: Bontoc Boogie; Salip; Tadek.

Chanchanag *(KAL)*. Ritual for elders.

Chapai *(BON)*. The flat stones or boulders in the ato.
See also: Dap-ay.

Chaparral. A uniquely named bar in Baguio in the 1970s with a 'zing' to its name – so much so that it attracted Manila visitors. It was also the buzz-word in Baguio nightclubbing and the red-light-district bar scene. It was owned by Dr. Pay Seng before he became a born-again Christian. KT.
See also: La Casita; O-O.

Chapilang *(KAL)*. An object made of coconut shell, chicken feathers and the tail of a civet cat. It is used by a manchachawak during a healing ritual. In Kalinga, aside from the manchachawak, other households also carry the chapilang. When the manchachawak is consulted about a sickness, he or she would blow at the chapilang and the sick person would be healed. Chapilang can also be used to put a curse on someone. HZK.
See also: Mambunong.

Chayag *(KAL).* Red. Red lips are made by smearing on a dye from ground anatto seeds.

Cherwasay *(KAL).* Funeral song.
See also: Amazing Grace; Badio; Baya-o; Dujung.

Chicken dung. Essence d'Halsema Highway. Mostly delivered in sacks stacked on ten-wheelers from big Bulacan poultry farms. It goes to the vegetable gardens in Atok and Buguias. Shilan, La Trinidad was once a major depot for chicken-dung, earning the moniker: Shitland. DOS.
See also: Halsema Highway.

Chico. [1] Rio Chico de Cagayan, the 'river of life' of Kalinga. It is the tributary of the Cagayan River that also has its tributaries: the Bunog, Tanudan, Biga, Mabaca, Saltan and Pasil Rivers. Named so because its color is that of the chico fruit. FYC. [2] The Chico River Basin Development Project was started up during the Marcos era with funding from the World Bank to provide electricity to Luzon. The planned dam would have inundated most of the areas along the river's tributaries. It was strongly and successfully opposed by the indigenous peoples in Bontoc, Sadanga, and Kalinga. FYC/DOS.
See also: Balweg brothers; Cellophil; Dulag; Macli-ing; Mt. Data; Peace zone; Vochong.

Chinamwi *(BON).* "Ang-way of ato Somowan performs the chi-nam-wi ceremony once or twice each year during the cold and fog of the period Sama [land preparation in the agricultural cycle], when the people are standing in the water-filled sementeras turning the soil, frequently working entirely naked. Many times I have seen the people shake – arms, legs, jaw, and body– during those cold days, and admit that I was touched by the ceremony when I saw it. A hog is killed and each household gives Ang-way a manojo of palay. He pleads to Lumawig: "Tum-ke-ka ay li-fo-o ta-a-ye-o nan in sa-ma-mi." This prayer is: "No more cold and fog! Pity those working in the sementera!" (The pleading really translates as "No more fog, as ayyew are our just-plowed fields). (Jenks 2005).
See also: Ayyew; Tinawon; To-ned.

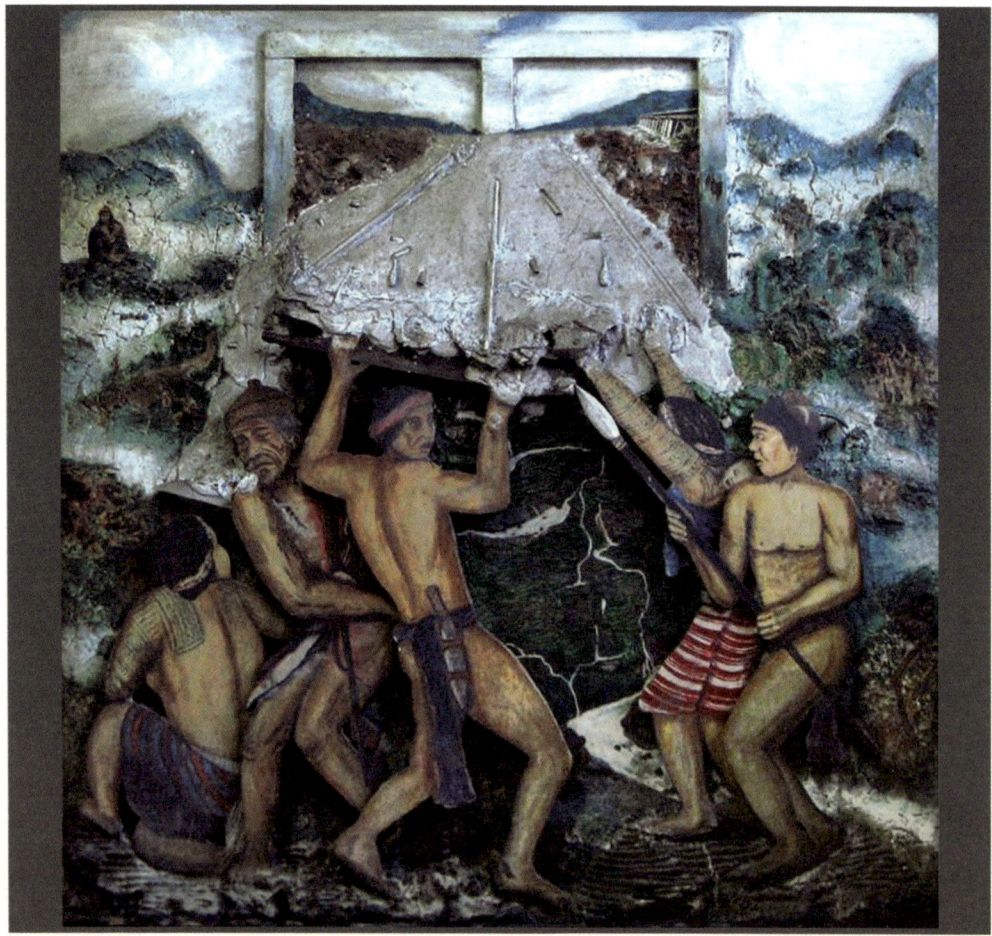

Bury My Soul in the Chico River, Santiago Bose, mixed media: cement, wood, metal, 124x122 cm, 1981. Courtesy National Gallery Singapore Collection.

Chinuyas *(KAL)* also **Dinuras, Pilawot.** A person without tattoos. Among men, it means he has not killed any enemy and so is excluded from various rituals. Among women, it means she is less nubile because she is not willing to endure pain and would rather endure loneliness. FYC.
See also: Tattoo.

Chokang *(BON).* A rain stick.

Chumanchil *(KAL).* A mountain in Tinglayan, Kalinga that has been repeatedly raided and torched by drug enforcement agencies because of the hectares of marijuana plants at the foot of the mountain. Some of the plants have been there for years and reach up to seven feet high and so have lost their potency. People wonder why the marijuana just keeps on growing despite the repeated raids. The reasons for the abundant growth include the presence of armed groups that protect the planters and the effect of police helicopter blades which inadvertently help propagate the seeds. Rumors have been spreading for years that a hashish factory is maintained on the slopes of Mt. Chumanchil. FYC.

Christine's Gallery. Once upon time, a Beetle burst into flames on Loakan Road. It was an ancient Volkswagon bug – a vintage car in those days – driven by Christine Arvisu. The accident, which was caused by faulty wiring, sparked the idea to open an art gallery to be called the Phoenix: something that arose from ashes.

This may seem far-fetched but that's how serendipity works, with loose connections and chance encounters. Christine, who was a friend to artists and other 'creatures,' went on to establish an exhibit space in her family home. It was an old Baguio house built in the style of what is now called 'green-and-white architecture,' next to the Café by the Ruins. Many of the currently recognized artists held shows there with Christine's encouragement. Notable among them were Leonard Aguinaldo, John Frank Sabado, and Willy Magtibay.

BenCab, a partner of Christine in the café enterprise, lent his famous name to the place, as well as Roberto Villanueva and Santiago Bose. Dr. David Baradas curated the shows which, aside from the usual paintings on walls, included experimental performances.

Yason Banal, early in his career as a conceptual artist, executed a number of acts like wrapping himself in food-grade plastic film, snoozing in a chest freezer dressed in a wedding gown, and conversing with the late Roberto Villanueva while having a blood transfusion.

Many amazing works and artists arose from Christine's Gallery, in that special time when our hearts were young and gay. AML

Cielo, Marky. Mark Angelo Cadaweng Cielo (May 12, 1988 - December 7, 2008). More popularly known as Marky Cielo, he was a television actor who rose to fame by winning the TV talent search *StarStruck* on March 12, 2006. He was of Kankanaey descent and lived part of his short life in Sinto, Bauko, Mountain Province. He studied Architecture at St. Louis University in Baguio City and was a member of the SLU Dance Troupe when he auditioned for *StarStruck*. It was his celebration of his ethnic identity coupled with his impressive dancing skills that gave him the edge over the other contestants. He appeared in the television shows Encantadia, Pag-ibig Hanggang Wakas, Bakekang, Asian Treasures, Boys Nxt Door, Zaido: Pulis Pangkalawakan, Sine Novela: Kaputol ng Isang Awit, Codename Asero, and LaLola. He also appeared in the movie *Till I Met You* with Robin Padilla and Regine Velasquez. He died suddenly in the morning of December 7, 2008. His death has been shrouded in mystery. JBG.

Cloth Dyes. *"Blue is ordinarily produced by placing the leaves and branches of the indigo plant, tayuni (Indigofera tinctoria) in water for a few days; then to boil them, together with a little lime. The thread is dipped in the liquid. Pink is secured by crushing lynga (Sesamum indicum L.) seeds and boiling them in water. Threads are placed in this for five nights, while during the day they are dried in the sun. The root of the apatot (Morinda citrifolia or umbellata) is next crushed, and water is added. The threads are now transferred to this liquid, and for ten days and nights are alternately soaked and sunned. A copper color results, but this soon changes to pink. It is said that the apatot alone produces a red dye. It is also claimed that the seeds of the apang (Bixa Orellana L.) and of a variety of rattan, when boiled, give a permanent red. A yellow dye is produced by boiling the leaves of the Tamarindus indica L. in water until a strong liquor is obtained. Bark head-bands are stained a purplish-red by applying a liquid secured through boiling kalyan (Diospyros cunalon D.C.) bark. For ceremonial purposes they are also colored yellow by applying the juice of the konig (Curcuma longa), but as this has a disagreeable odor, and the color is not permanent, it is not much used in every-day garments. Lemon juice is also applied to bark to give it a yellow hue. Fish nets are colored brown by dipping them into a dye made by crushing the katakot vine in water, or by staining with the juice of the taotawa (Jatropha curcas L.). The bamboo strips used in decorating basketry are blackened by holding them in the smoke of burning rice-straw. Black designs, such as appears in the ornamentation of lime holders and the like, are secured by rubbing oil and soot into incised lines, and then holding the object in the smoke of burning rice-straw."* (Cole (1922) 2004).

See also: Xamata.

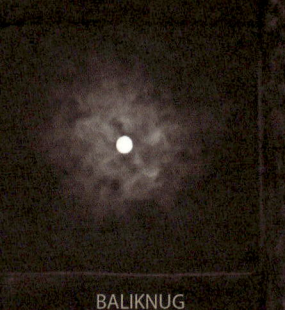

BALIKNUG
Clouds that surround the sun/moon

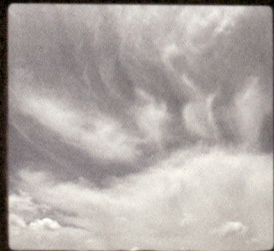

BUNABUN
Clouds that expand

HALIBUBU
Clouds that look like floating water plants

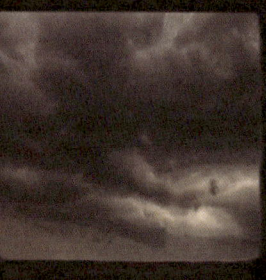

IMBUNONG
As if a shadow under a cloud

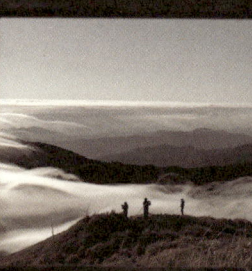

KULPUT
Clouds that scurry low

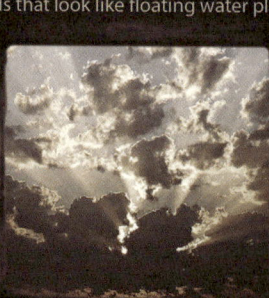

LIBBUWOG
Clouds that hide the sun

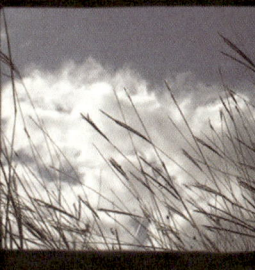

MAMULIYO
Clouds carried by gentle wind

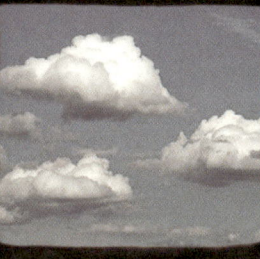

MANULUL
Clouds that exchange places

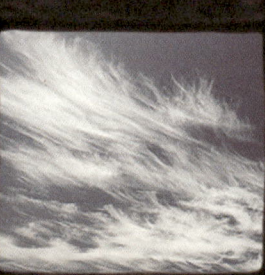

MAUGO
Light white feathery clouds

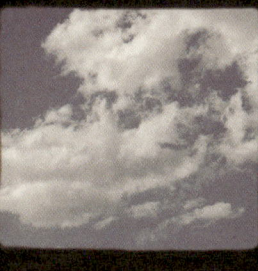

MOMPAIDU
Clouds that pass through each other

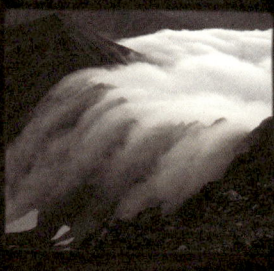

MON-ABUNAB
Clouds that hug the earth

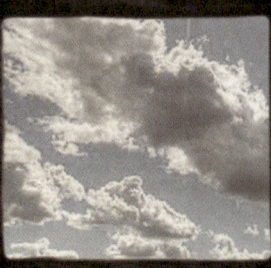

MONHANUBANGAL
Clouds that pass each other

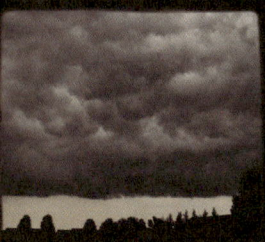

MUMBULYUN
Nimbustratos clouds

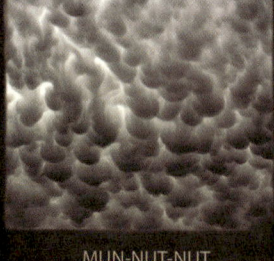

MUN-NUT-NUT
Clouds that drop down like seeds of cotton

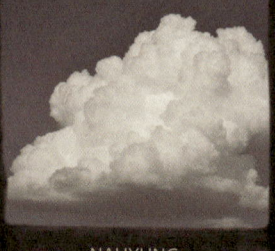

NAHYUNG
Cumulus clouds

Cloud Atlas

Roy Barton (1946, 40-41) compiled these Ifugao cloud terms:

Baliknug: Clouds that surround the sun/moon

Bunabun: Clouds that expand

Halibubu: Clouds that looks like floating water plants

Imbunong: As if a shadow under a cloud

Kulput: Clouds that scurry low

Libbuwog: Clouds that hide the sun

Mamuliyo: Clouds carried by gentle wind

Manulul: Clouds that exchange places; cross each other

Maugo: Light white feathery clouds

Mompaidu: Clouds that pass through each other

Mon-abunab: Clouds that hug the earth

Mon-ambayug: Clouds that appear to wear a hip bag

Monhanubangal: Clouds that pass each other

Mumbulyun: Nimbustratos clouds

Mun-nut-nut: Clouds that drop down like seeds of cotton

Nahyung: Cumulus clouds
See also: Finabdas.

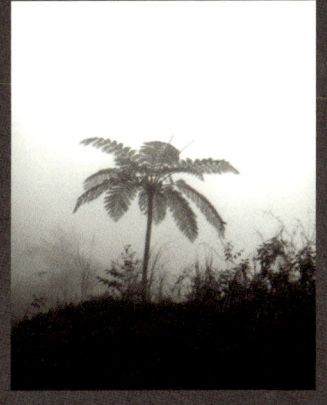

Images showing the different clouds with their respective Ifugao terms.

Company 1, 48th Infantry. The first American soldiers to set foot in Benguet in January 1900. The company was composed of African-American soldiers who mostly distributed candies to Kapangan children and befriended the people there, as they were there to engage the remnants of the Filipino revolutionary army who were already on the other side of the region. FYC.

Concrete Pine Tree. 'Grown' in the middle of Session Road in 1994, the now-defunct concrete pine tree was put up by Rep. Bernardo Vergara to promote the pine tree in Baguio City. The trunk and branches were made of concrete, and the needles, rusty steel. At its base one found the message *"Plant me and protect me."* They were also seen by many as a symbol of pork barrel spending (the Senate and Congress' Priority Development Assistance Fund that was constantly plundered by officials themselves) and so was 'cut down' due to popular demand during the term of Mayor Peter Rey Bautista. CPM.

Co-op *(KAN/BON).* Owl.
See also: Bading.

Country Music:
Top Ten Country Songs in the Cordillera

*When you hear twin fiddles and a steel guitar,
You're listening to the sound of the American heart.*

Armed with an accordion, an autoharp, a banjo, a bass, drums, a fiddle, a guitar, a harmonica, a mandolin, a piano, and a yodel, Country Music set out to conquer the Cordilleras, and it did so one song (or nine) at a time.

For over a century now, American Country Music has greatly influenced the Cordilleran's musical taste. Stories of love, life, and home are patched like leather stitched together to form a coat that Cordillerans love and are proud to wear. Cordillerans love to live simply, relaxed but not slack, where daily activities are repetitive like the country rhythm. They are never in a hurry, not like in the busy urban life.

Cowboys and Indians were arch-enemies at points in the history of the American West. Presently, in the Cordilleras, the Cowboy and the Igorot are friends. The white man who yodels and line dances can be friends with the mountain man who dances around with gongs. But, as is more often the case, the Igorot becomes the cowboy – the Igorot Cowboy.

Sing a song about the heartland, sing a song about my life

George Strait's "Heartland" (1993) tells us something about the Cordilleran culture. Life revolves around the land. Land is life itself. Cordilleran life seemed to mirror the introspective lyrics of this country song.

Country Music is timeless; contemporary pop songs die young: alive in the morning and dead before dusk. Today's Cordillerans seem to cherish their country songs as much as their traditional songs. Children today are musically diverse; they listen to contemporary music, they can still chant some traditional songs, and still listen to their dad's and even to their grandpa's music collection of country songs.

Hit songs are identified by their number of record sales, downloads, and by airplay. It's different when it comes to Country Music, here in the Cordilleras. It's about the number of people who make the music part of their lives. The musical competition was never stiff here. Country musicians don't have to sing with tight and sexy outfits on a flashy stage. That is not the Cordilleran's way either. Cordillerans just listen to the lyrics and melody of a song with their heart.

It is hard to decide on the top ten country songs of all time in the Cordillera. To be safe, it is better to consider ten of the most unforgettable songs in the Cordillera; songs that are surely revered and familiar to every person who grew up in the Cordilleras.

The list is long and there are singers that would surely be worthy of this list: Johnny Cash, Merle Haggard, George Jones, Hank Williams, Patsy Cline, Elvis Presley, Willie Nelson, Dolly Parton, Tammy Wynette, Charlie Pride, Bill Monroe, The Dixie Chicks, Brooks and Dunn, Carrie Underwood, Alison Krauss, and many more.

There'll be a load of compromisin'
on the road to my horizon.
But I'm gonna be where the lights
are shinin' on me.

The Cordilleran knows that life is tough but, in order to succeed, a person has to work hard. The Cordilleran attitude towards work is *"kinokoboy nga aramid"* [like the cowboy way]. Of course, the song that suits this attitude is about a Rhinestone Cowboy. The song became popular in 1975 and it was famous in the Philippines, beyond the Cordilleras. It was still popular in the 90s and in 1994 it was adapted by Fred Panopio using the same tune but different Tagalog lyrics and the title "Ang Kawawang Kowboy."

Most Cordillerans work with their hands: layman, farmer, and miner – all have to gamble before they turn a profit. Cordillerans are always equipped with intuition when it comes to investing their hard labor. Cordillerans never tired of Kenny Rogers' 1978 "The Gambler". You can hear the song played regularly if you hitch and chance upon an Elf truck along Halsema Highway.

A bottle of gin, 3PM Friday, Rocky Cajigan, acrylic on canvas, box construction, 2016. Photograph by Arnold Baladad.

*You got to know when to hold 'em, know when to fold 'em,
Know when to walk away and know when to run.
You never count your money when you're sittin' at the table.
There'll be time enough for countin' when the dealin's done.*

Garth Brooks' "The Dance," released in 1989, became an instant classic, hitting the airwaves all through the 90s. In the videoke bars, once the piano intro of the song starts, everyone sings the first line of the song together *"Looking back, on the memory of the dance we shared..."*

*And now I'm glad I didn't know
The way it all would end the way it all would go
Our lives are better left to chance I could have missed the pain
But I'd have had to miss the dance.*

The Cordillerans know that life is like a dance *"You learn as you go, sometimes you lead, sometimes you follow"* from "Life's a Dance," by John Michael Montgomery, 1992. You have to go with the rhythm and flow of the music, to take chances, and everything is still good even if all else fails.

Who wouldn't know the lyrics:

*I hear her voice, in the morning hour she calls me
The radio reminds me of my home far away
And drivin' down the road I get the feeling
That I should have been home yesterday, yesterday*

Despite the necessity of leaving home for many Cordillerans, the longing to go back is irresistible. The Cordilleran traveller will always be proud to tell you that their ili (town) is the most beautiful. John Denver's "Country Roads" released in 1971 is always played on the guitar during reunions, homecomings, gatherings, or even alone in a strange room outside the Cordilleras.

Country music, like any other music genre, is often about love. But, in country, it is sung simply, as in storytelling. The song "Don't Cry Joni" (1975) by Conway Twitty and Joni Lee dramatizes a simple love story that Cordillerans easily relate to.

*Joni, Joni please don't cry
you'll forget me by and by
you're just fifteen I'm twenty-two
and Joni I just can't wait for you
Jimmy, Jimmy please don't cry
you'll forget me by and by
it's been five years since you've been gone
Jimmy I married your best friend John*

Every time this song is played on a bus going to Sagada or Bontoc, you can hear everyone's (locals or tourists) 'sigh'. Sagada people translated this song into "Manang Cecilia ay eyon-a [Cecilia, our elder sister]" and turned it into a dirge for a beloved sister. Another song that was 'Sagadized' was "Tom Dooley" by Kingston Trio, which was turned into a Salidummay with the title "Gandoyan ay Kalalaydan [Beloved Sagada]."

Love songs are universal, especially if the rhythm and beat of the song is close to your heart. Country Music tends to be slow and that makes one's feelings of love sweeter or more painful. Randy Travis' 1987 hit single expresses how a Cordilleran loves. Listeners often react: *"Agasem ada pay 'amen' na!" [Whoa! It even adds an "amen]."*

*If you wonder how long I'll be faithful
I'll be happy to tell you again
I'm gonna love you
Forever and ever
Forever and ever, amen*

Four other songs (choice for 9th and 10th country song) that Cordillerans never fail to play during weddings are worth mentioning: Brian White's "God Gave Me You" (2010) and Shania Twain's "From This Moment" (1998) (both are played even in weddings in Manila), Lonestar's 1995 hit "Amazed "and George Strait's "I Cross My Heart" (1992).

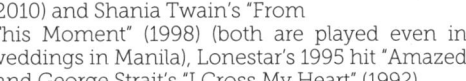

Keith Whitley's 1988 single "Don't Close Your Eyes" captivated even people who don't listen to Country Music. It reached the top of the charts on Pop radio stations during the 1990s. One could listen to this song in the 1990s on more or less 10 FM radio stations, during a scan of the frequencies.

*Don't close your eyes let it be me
Don't pretend it's him in some fantasy
Darling just once let yesterday go
You'll find more love than you'll ever know
Just hold me tight when you love me tonight
And don't close your eyes*

In a typical Cordillera family, when all the children have moved away to start their own families, couples reminisce about the triumphs and hardships they have had together as husband and wife. "Remember When" by Alan Jackson in 2001 is still being requested every day on 99.9, the only country music FM station in the Cordilleras. You can inevitably hear this song once or twice if you happen to spend a whole day in a 'wagwagan':

*Remember when we said when we turned gray
When the children grow up and move away
We won't be sad, we'll be glad
For all the life we've had
And we'll remember when.*HZK.

See also: Amazing Grace; Cowboy; Elf; Folk Music; Halsema; Ili; Music; Salidummay; Ukay-ukay.

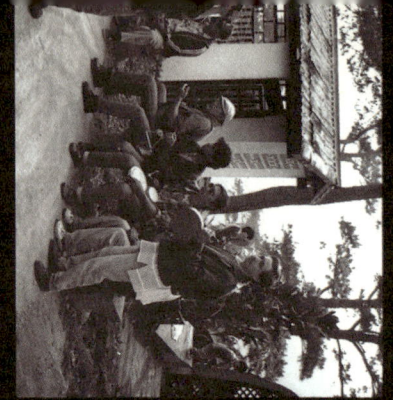
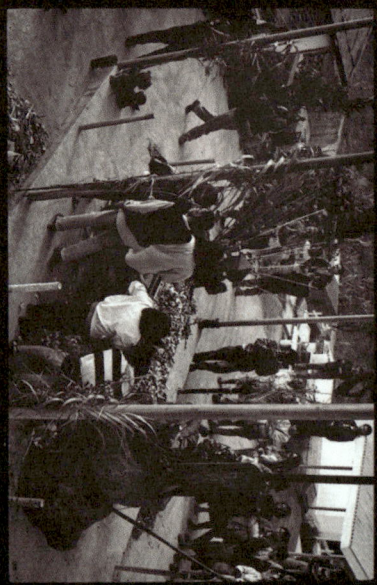
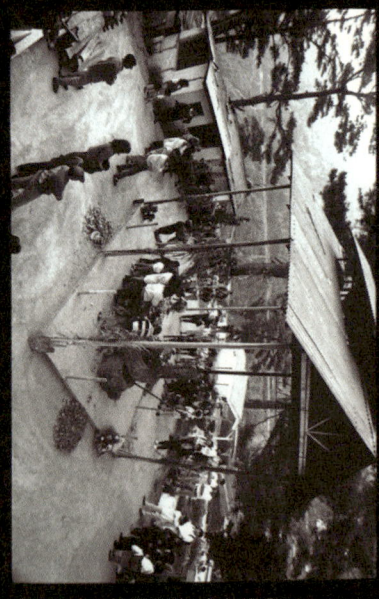

Cremation Shed. Before the high-technology crematorium days, this was a small cement platform in the Baguio cemetery. There, the few cremation believers (often ex-communicated by the Bishop) could say farewell to their beloved. An open fire, overnight, (two jeep-loads of pine wood under the body) would be the hot goodbye for the departed. Mostly they were Indian immigrants. Before the galvanized roof on top of the platform was demolished, the last remembered cremation was that of the extraordinary artist Roberto Villanueva. He was given a fiery, passionate farewell with Baguio artists dancing around the 13-hour blaze (complete with Igorot gongs). His cremation fire was jump-started with three baldes (cans) of Baguio Cooking Oil. KT.
See also: Baguio Oil; Gong.

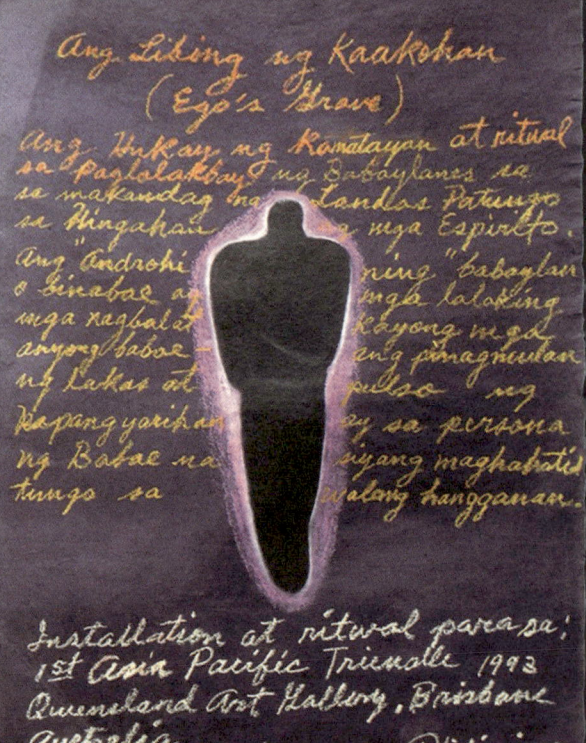

Contact prints of the *cremation shed* at the Baguio cemetery. Photograph by Kidlat de Guia.

Ang Libing ng Kaakohan (Ego's Grave) proposal, Roberto Villanueva, 1993. Courtesy Rica Concepcion.

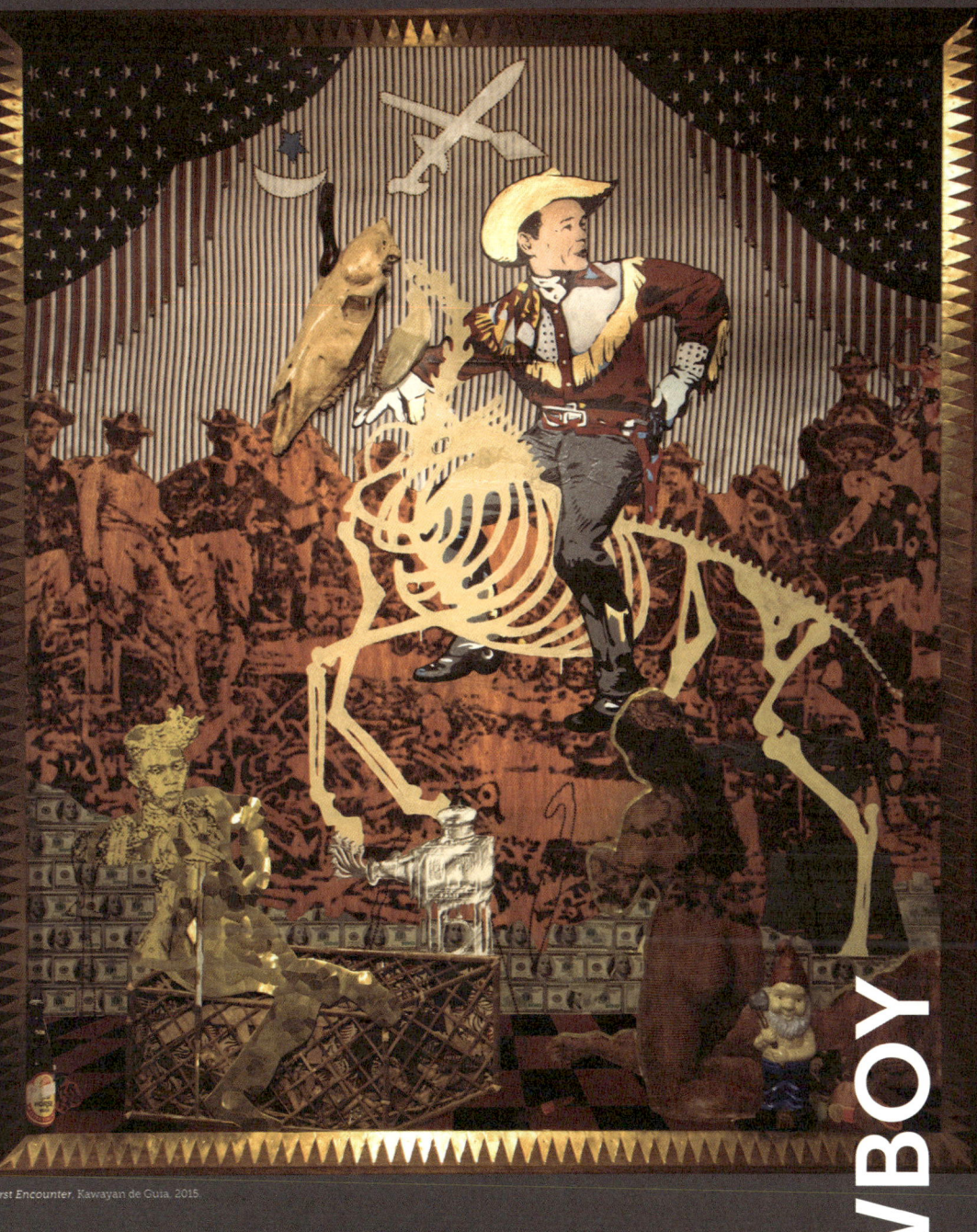

First Encounter, Kawayan de Guia, 2015.

COWBOY

Mark Zero and the Benguet Cowboy

Stetson hat, plaid shirt, fringed leather or denim jacket, cowboy boots: with riding crop in hand, or hanging from his belt at his side, he positions himself astride his horse and rides across mountain ranges where man and horse hold dominion. His boots and saddle were crafted at a local bootery, which offered a variety of choice in leather and design to suit his style. At the tavern, a country ditty plays. He casts aside the saloon's swinging doors, walks past the mechanical bull, and saunters to the dance floor to join a posse of similarly clad cowboys and cowgirls in line dancing. The music plays on and the singer begins the song. Despite the recognizably western music the words remain inaccessible to the western ear. The song's lyrics are in a local language – perhaps Ibaloy or Kankanaey. After all, this is not the cowboy John Wayne in a western film or a scene from the Texas Line Dance Jamboree. This is the Benguet 'Koboy' of the Northern Philippine Cordilleras who moves to the beat of his own distinctive, but lesser-known, permutation of western country music. It includes popular local artists such as Lourdes Fangki, the Kinnoboyan Band, and other winners of the country music singing contests regularly sponsored by the Mountain Province Broadcasting Corporation, a local radio station, who are collectively known as the Kinnoboyan Originals, Inc.

As a record collector, music enthusiast and sound archivist, Mark Joseph Young, a.k.a. DJ Mark Zero has long been in search of music of various genres and from different cultures. *"Some of these,"* he notes, *"have never had airplay on any radio station since they were released. Some were just meant to be played in jukeboxes and local gatherings, such as community dances."* His compilation of music, a good amount of which come in the form of vinyl record collectibles, ranges from the music of West Africa to Turkey; from Brazil to Ethiopia, as well as traditional, ethnic and popular Filipino music from the 1960s, 1970s and 1980s. More recently the move to relocate to Baguio City has opened up another area for Mark Zero's explorations in Philippine music history: the genre which has come to be known as the 'Cordillera Country Sound,' and the 'Benguet Koboy' culture with which it is associated.

Mark Zero is a disc jockey and sound designer with a mission – to bring the music & history of little-known or virtually unheard-of recording artists into the global arena and *"to be able to make music enthusiasts appreciate and, perhaps, have a glimpse into the complexities of evolutions and transformations of music."*

Armed with a turntable and some of his highland country music 'finds,' Mark Zero brings Cordillera highland country music to an even wider audience via the Singapore Biennale 2013. The title panel for his contribution to the exhibit consists of a collage of 40 different title covers, images and record labels gathered from research in the town of Abatan, Buguias, Benguet, which is a center for trade, culture and industry along the Halsema Highway. Album covers include lyric sheet inserts of songs translated from the local language, Kankanaey, to English.

Mark Zero's search for upland country music has brought him in contact with Cordillera country music performers. Among these, is Mario Asayco, a farmer from Abatan, Buguias whose involvement in the Cordillera country music industry began in the early 1970s. Mark adds: *"He was a member of The Harmonizers band, which played a unique style of country music boogie and ballads, and was later discovered by producer/composer Julio Tomas, owner of Tucocan Record Sales, a small, independent record production and distribution outfit in the Cordillera. The Harmonizers were the back-up band of many local country music artists."*

DJ Mark adds that record labels such as Highland records, Greenland Records and Abatan Records were instrumental in the documentation and distribution of Cordillera country music by artists such as Joel Tingbaoen, Morr Tadeo Pungayan (now a doctor of education and a well-known local linguist and newspaper columnist), Mario Asayco, Gener Pacheco, Rod Dangol, Cole Mendoza, Cris de Guzman and Artemio Lopez. Their brand of country music filled folk houses and country music taverns in and around Baguio City.

Abatan Records began in the early 1970s through

Fictional album cover of **Balitok**, Pine Tree Records, 2013. Courtesy Mark Young.

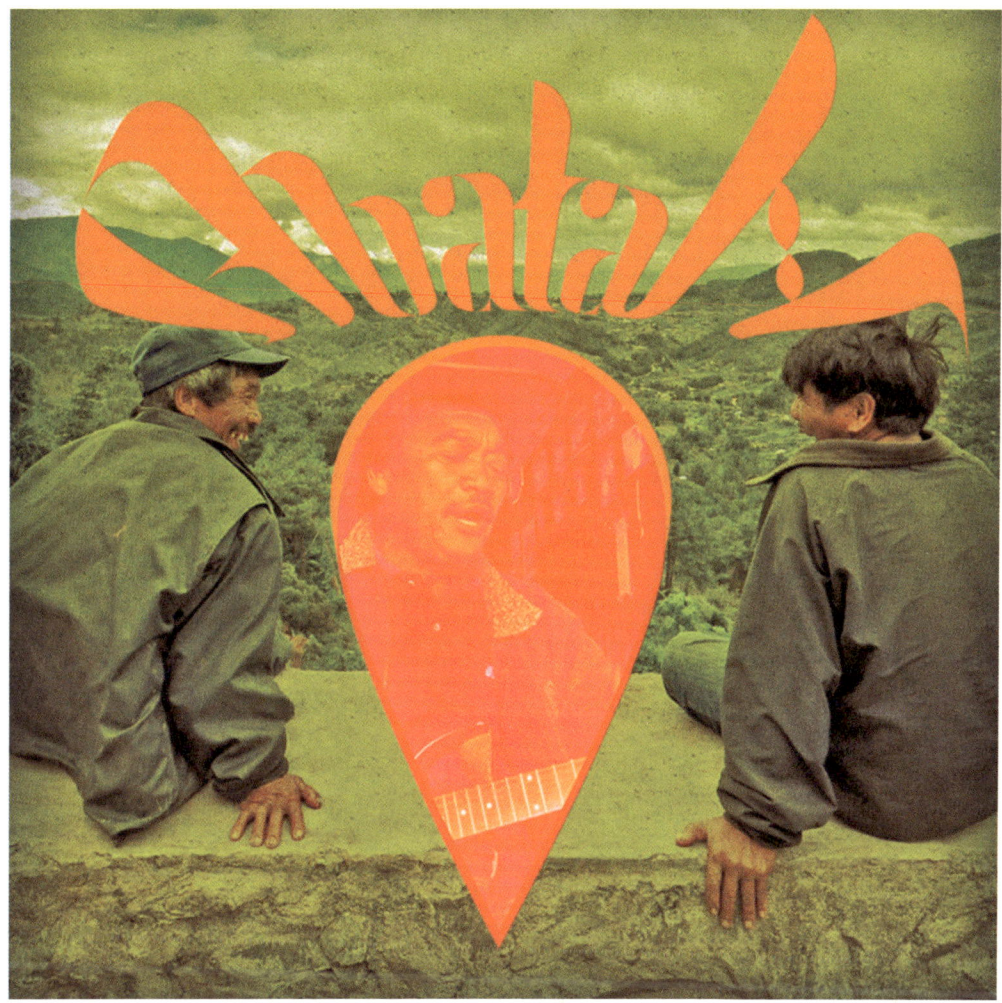

Fictional album cover of **Abatan Records**, 2013. Courtesy Mark Young.

the initiative of Elsie Gawidan Maliones, the company's owner. This highland country music production company began with recordings on vinyl and cassette tape of songs in Kankanaey and Ibaloy. Abatan recording, through Maliones, helped local country music talents travel to a sound studio in Manila to record and eventually get their music pressed on vinyl or reproduced on cassette tape for distribution. When Maliones' son-in-law, Marcons Dayaoen assumed management of the company, Abatan records put up its own recording studio. More recently, Abatan Records has brought Cordillera country music to a worldwide audience through the production of music videos uploaded to YouTube. As the genre's popularity continues to grow, and with an increased demand for this genre of local music from Cordillerans in the diaspora in communities all over Asia, the United States, Europe, and Canada, independent artists and local music production companies are confronted with the challenge of piracy of their original material. (Malanes 2013)

American Cowboy influence in the Cordilleras and the evolution of the local highland genre of country music can be traced to the ingress of the mining industry into the region.

Finin (2005) notes that the American mining engineers, or the Americans who held top positions in the mining companies established in the region during the American period, were more often than not from the American West, or if not, were previously engaged in mining, which was a principal industry there. They *"brought with them the imagery and material culture of the American West"* (170). Consequently, American and 'Spaghetti' Western films, and American country music gained much popularity among the locals.

It is very easy to dismiss the Benguet Koboy and

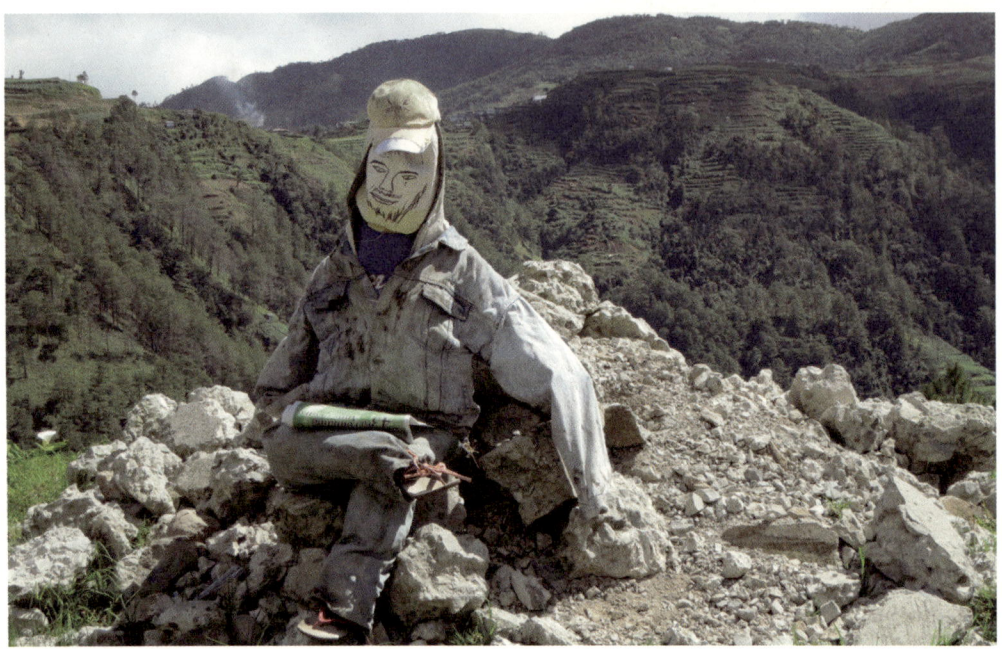

Photograph of *Benguet Cowboy*, 2012. Photograph by Kawayan de Guia.

Cordillera country music as media constructs and mere 'side effects' of exposure to western culture. However, studies have shown that this is not the case. There is definitely something more than 'colonial mentality' in these cultural formations.

Unlike its colonial predecessor, Spain, whose incursions into the region were met with fierce resistance, the Americans were relatively more successful. The Americans were soon to discover an indigenous 'cowboy culture' in the Cordilleras. Upon their arrival in the area of southern Benguet, the Americans found *"one huge 'Marlboro Country' with a head count in 1908 of 25,000 cattle, 2000 ponies, and 1000 colts. Centers of the cattle population were the basins of Kafagway and Puguis, the plateaus of Betdi and Chotken, the valleys of Loo, Pacso, Achaoay, Ambendi.... Sites of the dongba, or horse race, were Kafagway, Binga and Achaoay"* (Bagamaspad & Pawid 1985, 221). Historical records also reveal that although swidden farming, hunting, mining and the trade of gold from the rich stores of the precious metal nearby, were the primary industries in the area, cattle-raising was a flourishing industry in Benguet even prior to the coming of the Americans, encouraged in part by continuing trade relations with the lowlands (Tapang, 1985, 8). *"The main commerce between the highlands and the lowlands was always gold in one direction and livestock and manufactured goods in the other"* (Scott 1974, 183).

Today, Benguet cowboys and cowgirls have gained national renown. The Benguet State University's Highland Cowboys and Cowgirls (BSU-HCC) Rodeo Team, have consistently garnered awards in various events and have even emerged as overall champions at the Rodeo Masbateno, a cowboy festival held every April in Masbate Province in southeastern Luzon. *[see also Editor's Note- PLP]

With the introduction of western country music by the Americans and the ensuing surge in its popularity in the communities, local artists soon began to produce their own brand of country music. Early compositions appropriated popular western country tunes infused with lyrics in the local language, the first of which was an adaptation in the Ibaloy language of Hank William's "Blackboard of My Heart". (Fong, 2007, 111) Today, all-original Cordillera country music receives airplay on a local radio station, and CDs and videoke DVDs can be purchased from stalls in Hilltop, a section of the Baguio City market, as well as stores in the side streets around the city. Some artists also market their music by going door-to-door.

A study of Cordillera country music reveals the Benguet Koboy and Cordillera country music phenomenon as part and parcel of a continuing identity project. These songs, rather than being artifacts that simply reproduce western culture are functional self-representations. Western country music has been appropriated, revealing producers and consumers of these forms as aware of historical contingencies and actively engaged with the challenges they face in the contemporary world. Sights are set firmly toward the future. Cordillera popular music scholar Jimmy Balud Fong puts it quite succinctly. In "Batawa: Constructing Identity Through Country

Music in the Philippine Cordillera," he writes:

> Media representations of the Philippine indigenous people Igorot continue to exoticize and freeze them in an ideal, primitive past. This [research study] foregrounds certain cultural products now being produced by the Igorot using modern technology and media. In these self-conscious products, where they exercise agency, how are they representing themselves? In such songs where they use their own languages, they construct who they are and what they have become. Using mostly American folk, rock and country melodies, they tell stories of how they are making sense of their experiences in an unevenly globalizing, runaway world. (Fong 2007, 109)

Abatan Records, whose music Mark Zero has been collecting, is aptly named 'Abatan,' coming from the Kankanaey word 'abat,' meaning, 'to meet.' The Benguet Koboy and Cordillera Country Music are the curiously potent hybrids that have been forged at the crossroads of tradition and modernity. GTS.

(*EDITOR'S NOTE: Recently, Ibaloy cowboys revived the dongba and it is spreading across Benguet. The revival began in Dalupirip, Itogon, where cowboys and cowgirls from neighboring towns and Baguio City would make the trek on horseback to participate. Every year, Baguio City hosts a Pony Boys' Day, which includes events ranging from the heart-stopping pony races and steer wrestling, to the comical balloon-bursting, in which balloons are tied to the rear belt loops of the cowboys and cowgirls and they try to burst each others' balloons with rolled up newspapers – while on horseback. These gymkhanas usually end with an evening of country music and line dancing. -PLP)

See also: Country Music; Divang; Pink Ponies.

The Diamond in the Rough Trade: Mark Zero for the Records

It would be a pity to cage a DJ of Mark Zero's caliber to his fame in snooty lounges (where Manila's creme-de-la-creme seek his sounds). If I were to try to sum up the music mindset of Mark in a few words, I would always fall short. As a music diehard, his esoteric sensibilities don't end with his dedication alone.

I believe Mark is one of those people who get by through life fueled only by integrity of music and love for it, no less. You gotta see Mark playing underground gigs in remote towns of the Cordillera mountains. You gotta check-out his stern choices of 33 RPMs dug out from the sketchiest corners of flea markets. Without such ukay-ukay research, there would be no Jukebox Project – where I rehabilitated old rusting jukeboxes into Jeepney-bodied sound blasters.

For the Records is his collection of collaged Show Posters – an homage to the unsung musicians of a forgotten era. He is one of those unassuming musicologists who need no PhD – largely ignored in this fast-food age. Being a visual artist, I see in his posters, an impulsive, almost naïve, but deep concentration of genius.

I especially hold up a candle to his record-cover tribute to the myth that is now Abatan Records. I hold up a candle. The way that rag-tag company popularized Benguet country music in the age of 45 RPMs is mind-boggling. Can you imagine a vinyl-record pressing outfit in a small town in the Cordillera boondocks in the 1970s?

Abatan is a junction town on a ridge, leading to the richest gold mine in Asia. Here, after a hard day's work digging gold (for Lepanto Mines), tired miners would drink and listen to local bands. And suddenly there was a company to wax their songs for posterity.

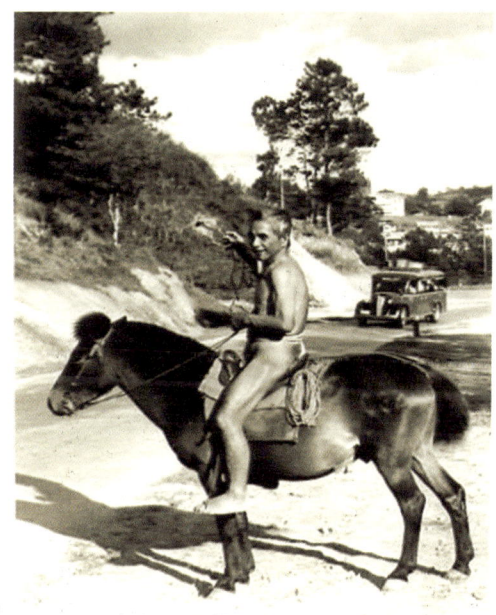

Photograph of *Benguet Cowboy*.

Abatan Records was a home to rural musicians – on the same frequency as Mark Zero. People that just loved music and 'doing' it. Mark's philosophy resonates with the rural recording company's interests, in resurrecting faceless gods and goddesses of the musical landscape – however remotely they might be found on the forsaken Halsema Highway. The poster show is a small way to share this man today (lest he only be appreciated decades from now). I don't want Mark Zero to become a myth, because I have read his 'book' and he has helped me write mine. KDG

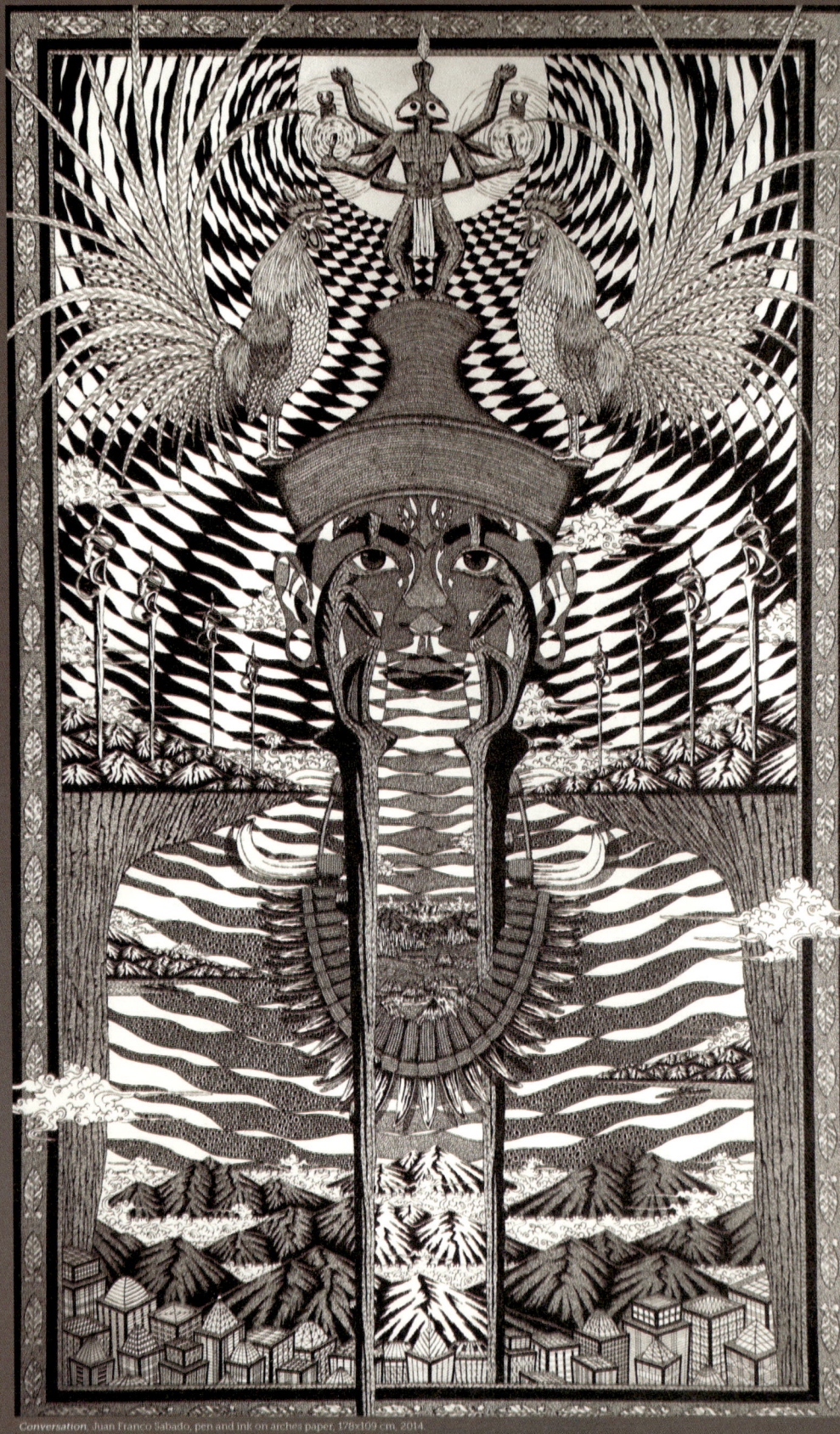

Conversation, Juan Franco Sabado, pen and ink on arches paper, 178x109 cm, 2014.

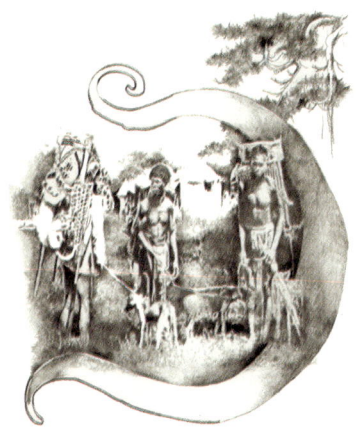

D&S Fine Food Store. Lina Ng was described by Dr. Charles Cheng as the first lady manager of Baguio City. A daughter of Baguio pioneer L.R. Leung, Lina studied at Jose Rizal College in Manila before taking over her father's Mountain Supply Store. After World War II, she opened the D&S Fine Foods Store beside Patria de Baguio, which sold the choicest groceries, dry goods and imported luxury foods outside of Camp John Hay. FYC.
See also: John Hay, Camp.

Dagdagas *(KAL/ILO)*. Any illicit sexual union or a lover – e.g. referring to a married man with a lover in another town, the lover is known as dagdagas (escorted). Also, unmarried Kalinga who have sexual relations without the intention to marry. FYC.
See also: Daladag; Luktap; Mandeki.

Daguio, Amador. Poet, fictionist, essayist, critic, and playwright. Daguio was born in Laoag, Ilocos Norte but grew up in Lubuagan, Kalinga, which was the milieu of most of his short stories. From Gemino Abad's critical essay on Daguio:

"One of ten honor graduates at U.P. in 1932, he returned to teach at his boyhood school in Lubuagan; in 1938, he taught at Zamboanga Normal School and later at Normal Leyte School in 1941 before the Second World War. During the Japanese Occupation, he joined the resistance and wrote poems in secret, later collected as Bataan Harvest. In 1952, he obtained his M.A. in English at Stanford University as a Fulbright scholar. His thesis was a study and translation of Hudhud hi Aliguyon (Ifugao Harvest Song). In 1973, six years after his death, Daguio was conferred the Republic Cultural Heritage Award." (Abad 2003) FYC.
See also: Hamada, Sinai; Hudhud; Moore, Lina Espina; Three Witches.

Dakitan *(IFU)*. The spot where a large river can be crossed.

Dakodak *(KAN)*. A major ritual in Sagada, celebrated every 20 years. It is one of the main rituals in addition to the dangtey. The purpose of the dakodak is to unite all the areas of Sagada. TDH.
See also: Dangtey.

Daladag *(KAL)*. Adultery. Historically it was the most frequent reason for murder according to the anthropologist Jules De Raedt. But, says De Raedt, adultery and headhunting were also the main sources of happiness and satisfaction. If you did not do them, you would be kicked around by the kaladings, or the souls of the dead, when you go to the skyworld. This was one reason given by the women who had affairs with other men. (De Raedt 1996).
See also: Dagdagas; Luktap; Mandeki.

Dalagadag *(IFU)*. In the Hudhud, it means late afternoon just before sunset.
See also: Hudhud.

Dalanasip *(KAL)*. Spanish or Venetian glass beads.
See also: Apang; Bungol; Ong-ong.

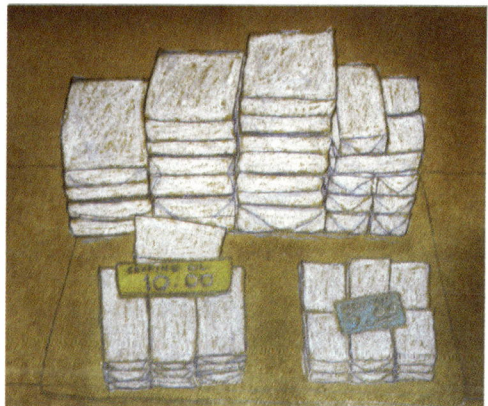

Daneb *(IBA)*. Lard, which in the Cordilleras is already congealed and sold in the market cubed and wrapped in clear wax paper or a plastic sheet. FYC.

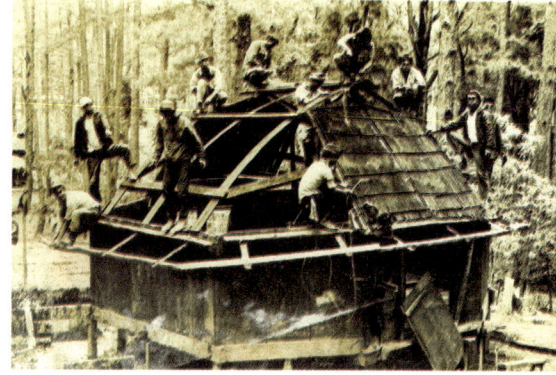

Photograph of men during **dang-ah** at the Baguio Botanical Garden, circa 1950s. Courtesy Virginia de Guia.

Dang-ah *(KYA)*. "When a person needs assistance in completing or quickening a difficult task such as carrying timber for a house from the pine forests, or even setting the foundation for building a new house, then this person can call for a dang-ah. In the dang-ah, the person's kailian gather together to assist in the task at hand. Usually, the size of the group and their collective labor makes it possible to complete the task in one day. Thus, the dang-ah is reserved for tasks that can be completed in a day by a large group of people working together. In exchange for the help, the person who called his/her kailian must feed the assembled laborers for the day with rice and meat, and also provide them with tapey, or rice beer.

Certain rules apply in the dang-ah. A person cannot respond to a call for dang-ah if he/she is not kailian. This is because without the relationship of kailian there is no obligation to reciprocate either the labor or the food. It is this principle of reciprocity that makes the dang-ah effective and the kailian a cohesive group. Also, individuals must not call for a dang-ah often, and take too much of other people's time from their own work or concerns. In fact, it is considered good practice to wait until one or two other kailian have called for dang-ah before considering to hold a second one in a year. If one is constantly absent from other people's dang-ah, social sanctions will come in the form of people refusing to attend the transgressor's dang-ah, and ultimately, the elders may ask such a delinquent kailian to shift his/her membership to one of the other cooperative groups existing in Tawangan. This shows that for the Kalanguya, social cohesion and the maintenance of good relations among community members is of utmost importance, and this is evident in the continuing practice of the dang-ah." (Perez 2010, 45-46).

See also: Ili; Inum'an; Kalanguya.

Dangas *(KAN)*. A form of labor mobilization based on the payment of meat and alcohol 'wages.'

Dangdangan *(ISN/KAN)*. To sit by the bonfire or to warm by the fire. DLD.

Dangtey *(KAN)*. ⁽¹⁾ A ritual feast performed every ten years as a periodic demonstration of village unity, the Dangtey ceremony is a composite of several rituals. Literally, 'dangtey' alludes to the foundation posts of a house – 'a part on which the frame rests.' Symbolically, it could mean the foundation of the community as a whole. Dangtey prayers invoke the intervention of guardian spirits and souls for community protection, good health and generous harvests. The souls of Sagada people – both the living and the dead – are called upon to return to their respective dap-ay as an act of solidarity. (Voss and Alcantara 2005, 45) GAD.

⁽²⁾ An Itogon cañao performed in a search for gold. A black boar is sacrificed and the mambunong, after invoking prayers for good luck and health, would sprinkle gold dust on the blood as it is added to the meat. The golden dinuguan (blood stew) is then served by the marikihbit (camote mine/pocket mine leader) to the guests. After the dangtey, the pocket miners are prohibited from carrying heavy loads, having any sexual contact or making loud noise or music for three days before they can enter the new mine. On the third day, the marikihbit must be the one to enter the tunnel first. FYC.

See also: Dap-ay; Mambunong; Pansejew; Saga-ok; Three orphans of Sagada, The; Tonglo.

Dangwa. Bado Dangwa was born May 5, 1905 and raised in Kapangan, Benguet. After graduating from the Trinidad Agricultural School, he was taught to drive the school's delivery truck, starting his fascination with motor vehicles. He started his bus business in the 1930s with three cars and PHP10.00 and by the outbreak of World War II, he already had 173 vehicles. He became a guerrilla leader and it is said that the Japanese soldiers were willing to pay a fortune for his head. He was able to revive his bus company after the war and 'Dangwa' became a generic term for any bus in the region. Its terminal in Sampaloc, Manila was also named Dangwa and is more known as the flower depot of the country's capital. FYC.

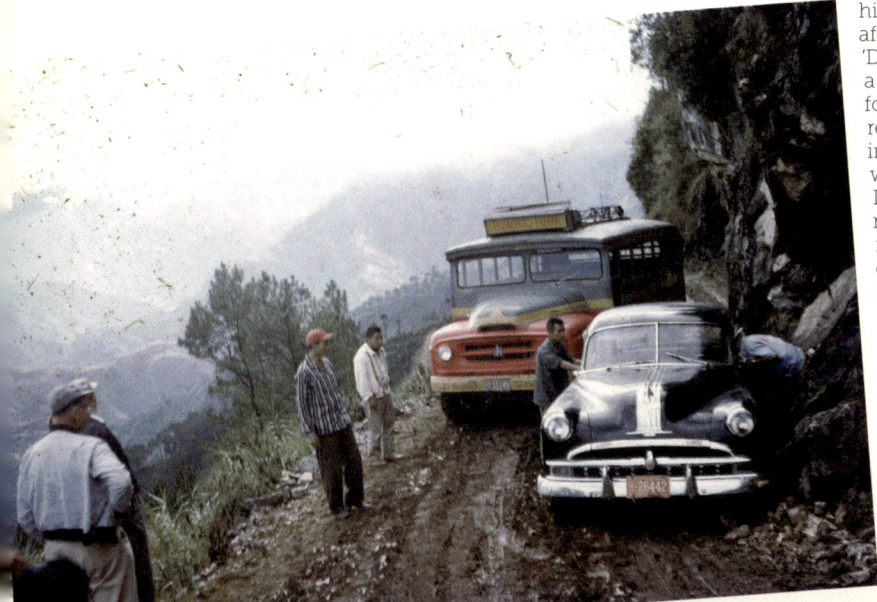

Photograph of the *Dangwa* bus traversing the Halsema Highway, c. 1960s. Photograph by Kevin Engle.

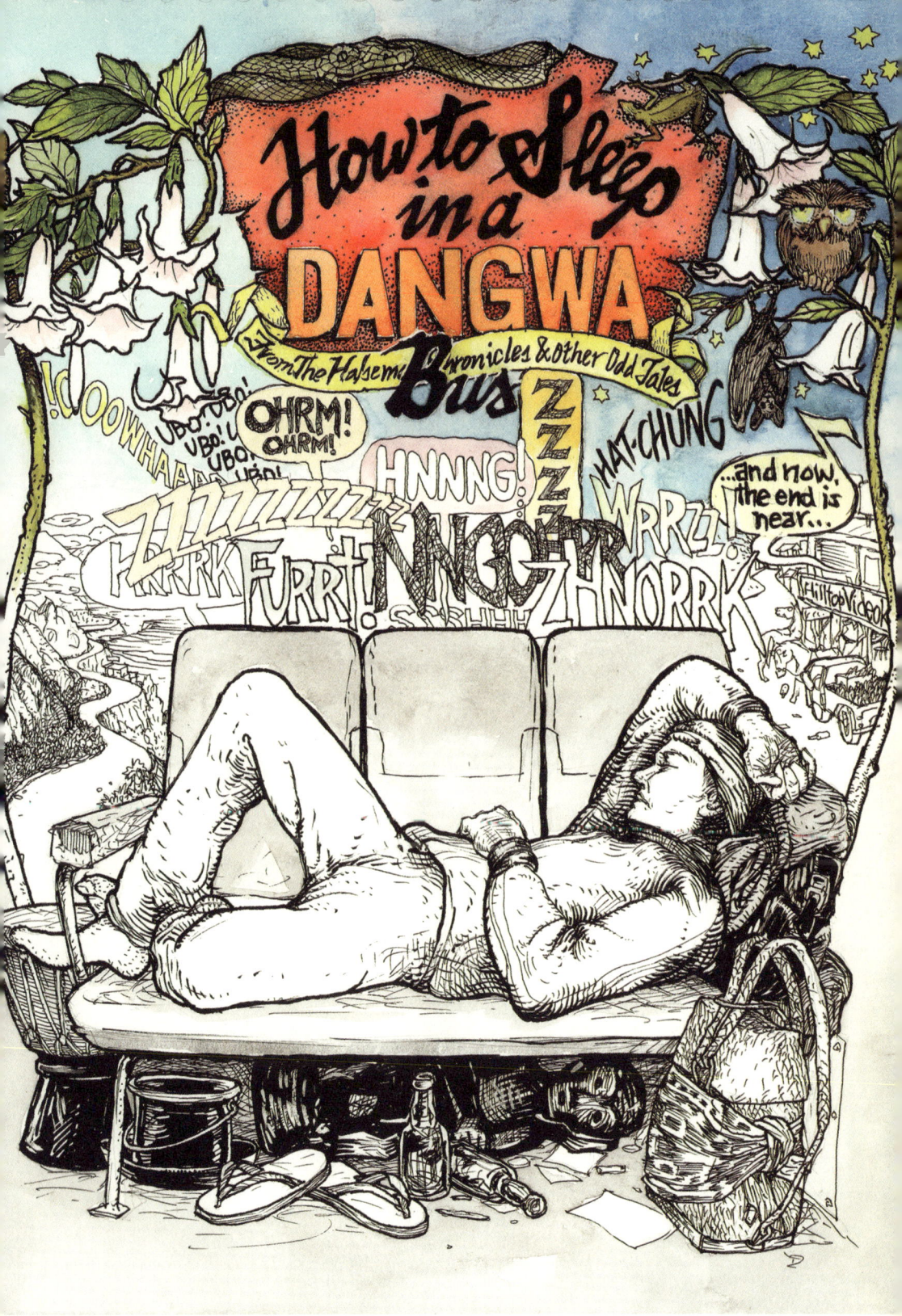

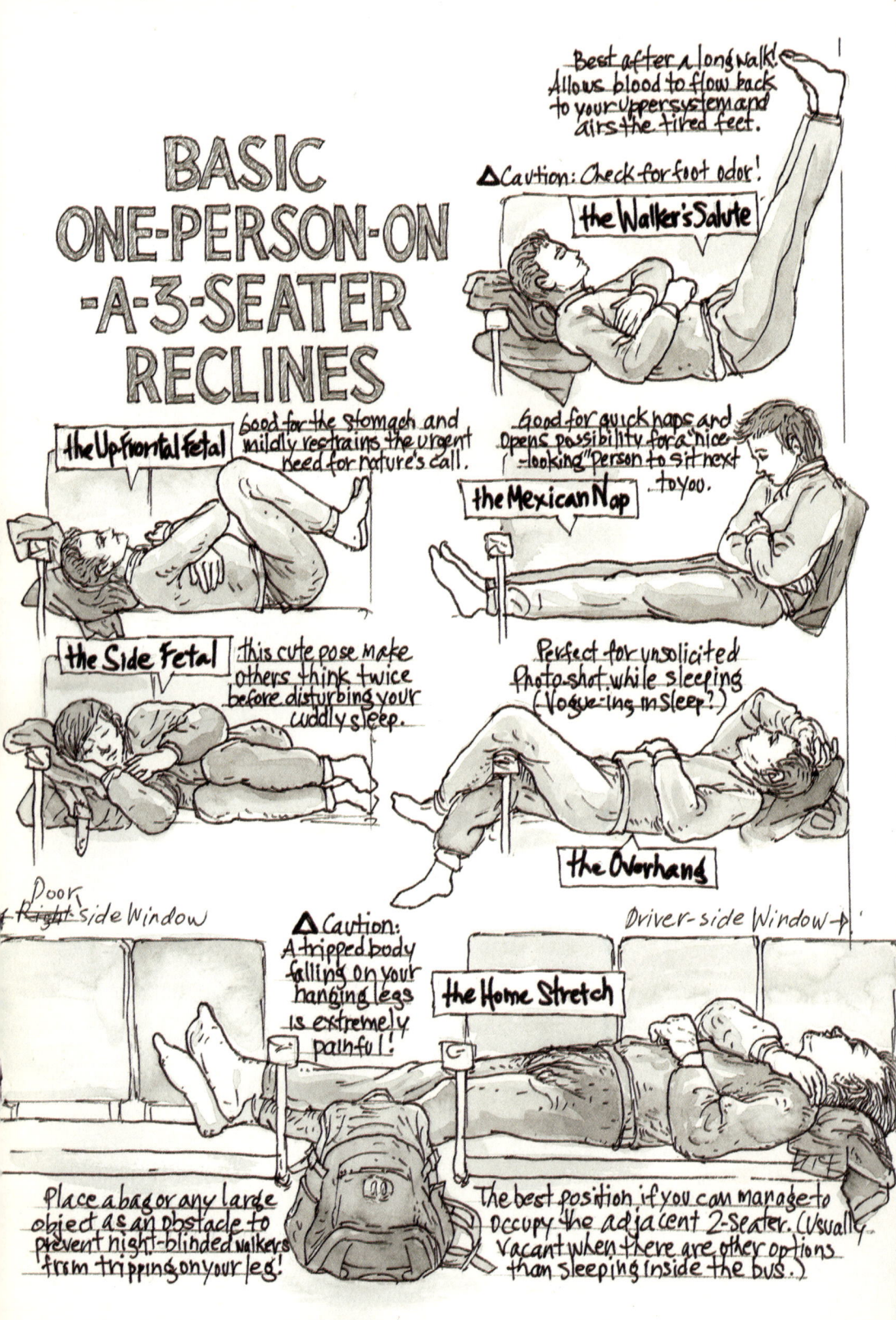

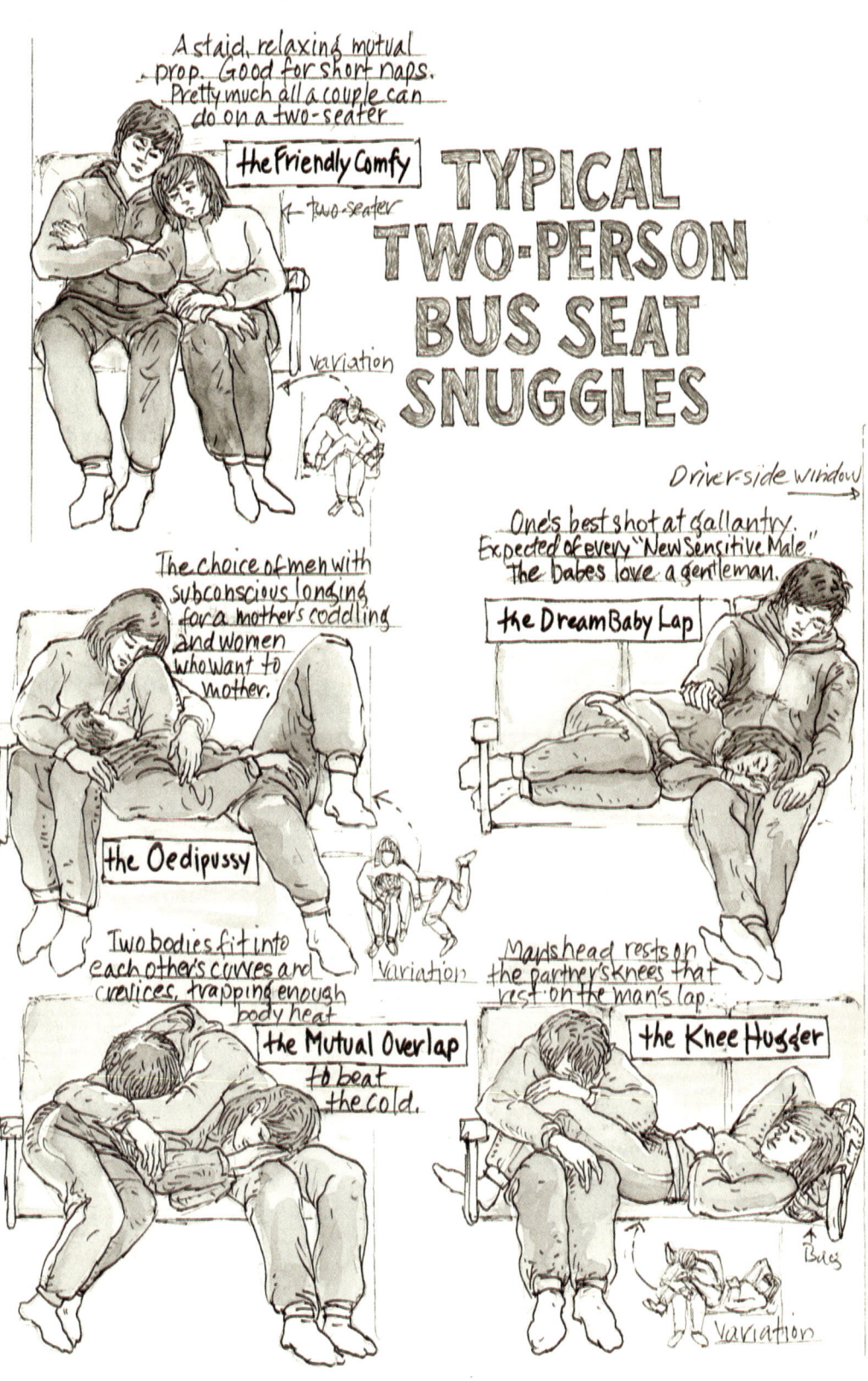

OTHER SLEEPING AIDS

Light Diffusers

Hats
Cowboy hats, fedoras, caps, visors, etc., any headwear than can be pulled down to the nose

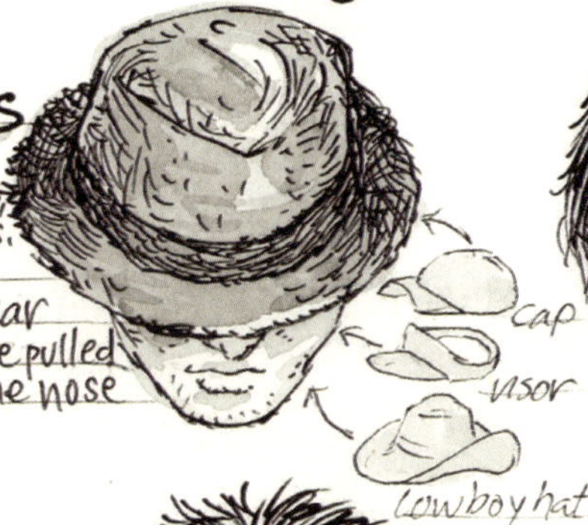

Cap
Visor
Cowboy hat

Wraparound Dark Glasses
Buy the cheapest available. When you break it during nightmares or stolen while you're dead asleep, you won't feel very bad.

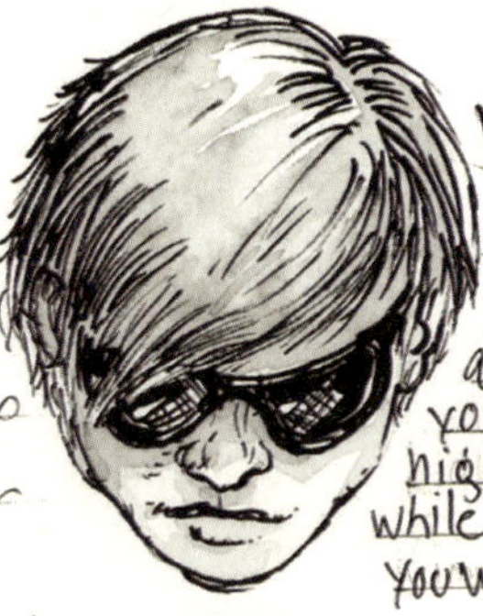

Scarf
Wraparound the eyes and ears, leaving just the nose and mouth for breathing.

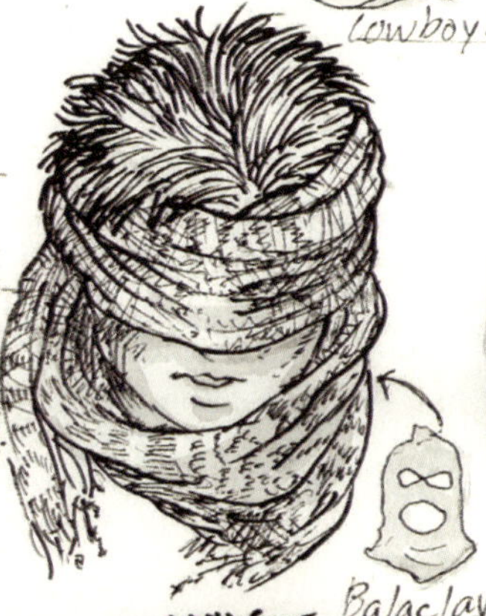

Balaclava

Rasta Hat
Also called beanies, tams, bonnets, etc. Dreadlocks have the advantage of pillowing the head and muffling the sound.

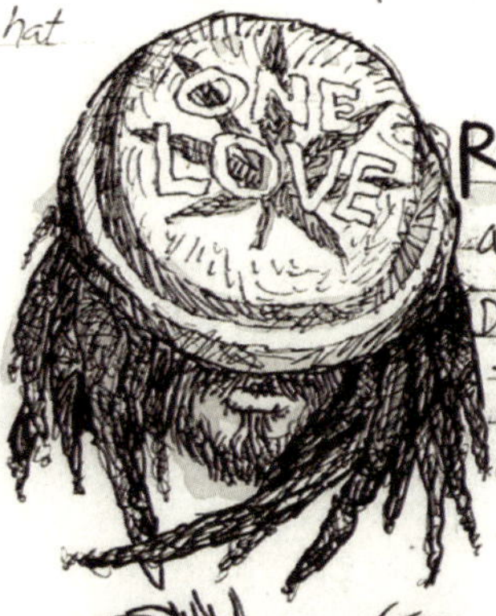

Petite Bra
Smaller sizes better. Good for wide and chubby face. Lace maybe too "boudoir," but then, to each his own fetish.

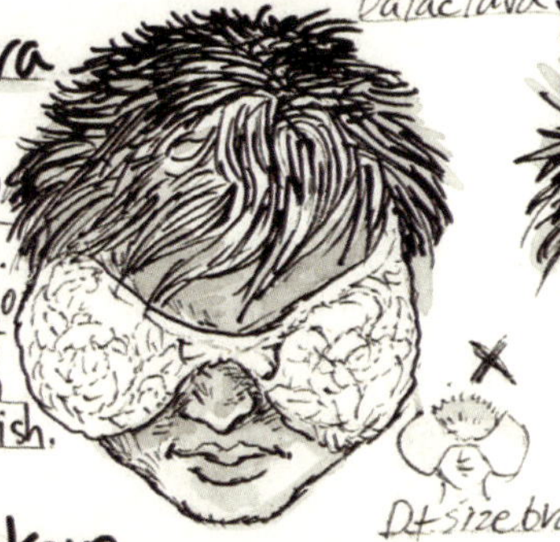

✗ Dt size bra

Underwear
Men's briefs, boxers, panties or trunks... Avoid thongs, crouchless, and the likes.

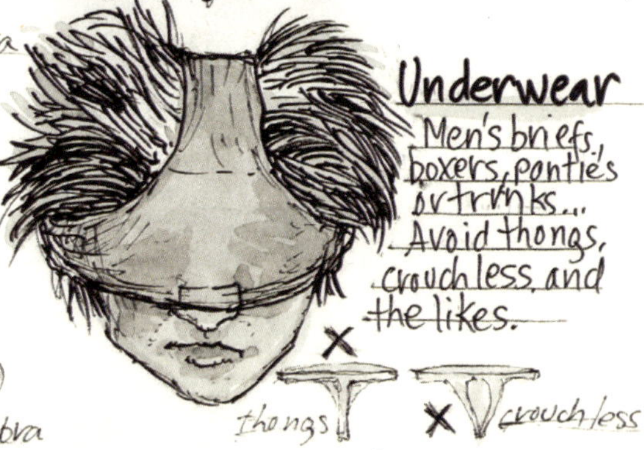

✗ Thongs ✗ Crouchless

Sound Blockers...
Sound off. Or... sound on, to drown out nearby noise like passing cars, barking dogs, karaoke or snoring sleepmate.

Swimmer's ear plug is the best noise stopper. In its absence, alternatives here will suffice.

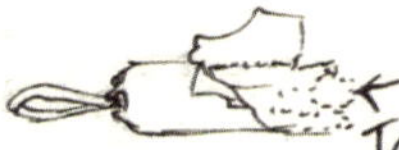

Make sure it is cut clean to size.

Tampon is a good source.

△ Chewing gum, marshmallows, soft candies, etc. should be avoided.

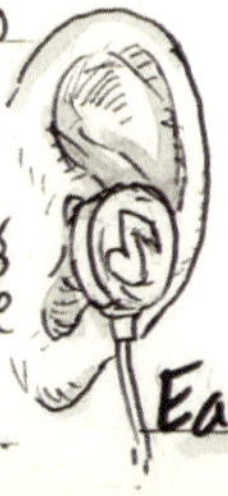

Earphone 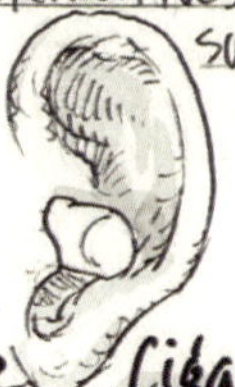 | **Cigarette filter tip** 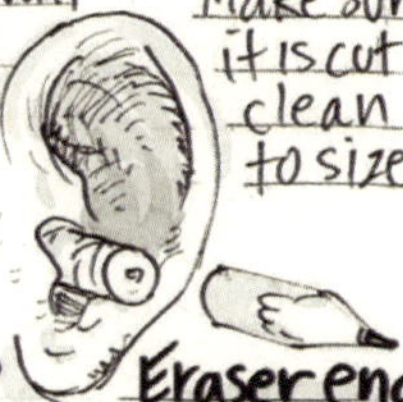 | **Eraser end of a pencil** 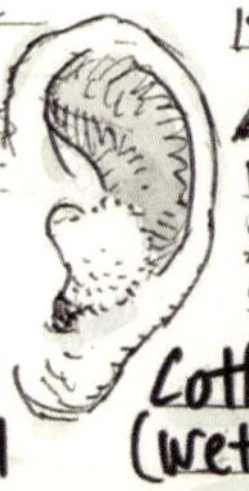 | **Cottonball (wet to shape)**

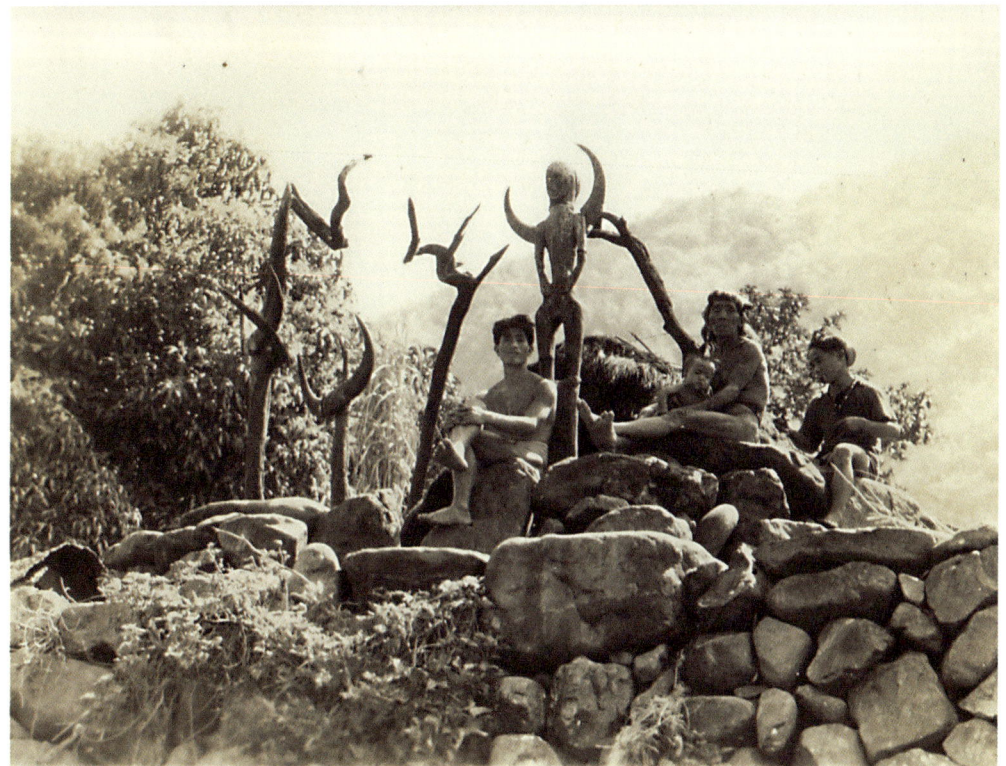

Photograph of a *dap-ay*, c. 1930s. Courtesy AV Cating Family Collection.

Dap-ay *(KAN)* also **Ato** *(BON),* **Ator** *(BON),* **Dinapdap** *(IFU).* The dap-ay is an elevated circle of stones with stone seats and backrests. This is where the elders and leaders come to meet; the figurative center around which community rituals revolve. In more traditional times, this was where the elders would educate the children with stories about their own heroes and ancestors. It was a public place where culture was generated, transmitted and kept alive. In Barlig, Mountain Province, the umu-ufok (elders and storytellers), would make sure that a fire was always burning, for the ator was the source of fire and light for all surrounding households, in much the same way that it was a source of knowledge, the center of government and culture (Arboleda 2007, 98). Arboleda (ibid.) noted that in Barlig, the significance of the ator seemed to be in decline due to changing social conditions and the death of the knowledgeable elders without replacements from the younger generation. In Sagada, Bontoc, and elsewhere however, the influence of the elders and the importance of the dap-ay remains vital, especially since community rituals continue to be held with wide participation. TDH.
See also: Chapai; Papattay.

Dark-hued New England Town Meeting. What independence will bring ideally to the Igorots. From the 1904 letter of US President Theodore Roosevelt to Rudyard Kipling: "In dealing with the Philippines, I have first [to deal with] the jack-fools who seriously think that any group of pirates and headhunters needs nothing but independence in order that they may be turned forthwith into a dark-hued New England town meeting." (Dyer 1980, 140) ΓYC.
See also: Headhunting (the tale); Igorot.

Darupaypay *(ISN).* A spirit that devours the unhusked rice before it reaches the granary.
See also: Alan; Ampasit; Banig; Bengao; Carangat; Ibwa; Nginin; Paniaw; Pasang; Tinguian Spirits.

Datil *(KAN).* Pathway made out of stone.

Daw-es *(KAN).* A cleansing ritual that is performed for a person who encounters a lot of misfortune or who has witnessed death. It is also performed for a person or persons who have seen a dead person. The sacrificial animal for a daw-es is usually a dog. TDH.
See also: Dog-eating.

Daya *(ILO)* also **Chaya** *(BON/KAN).* Skyworld.
See also: Ifugao.

Day-ag, Anselmo. An Ilongot born in 1935 in Bambang, Nueva Vizcaya, and who studied under famous sculptor Guillermo Tolentino when he took up Fine Arts at the University

of the Philippines. Already an award-winning sculptor even in his college days, Day-ag was commissioned to build the Kennon Lion, the Eagle Arch at the foot of Marcos Highway in Agoo, La Union, the Yamashita Shrine in Kiangan, Ifugao, the Hundred Islands Memorial in Pangasinan, and the Sunshine Park in Baguio. The Marcos Bust proved to be fatal for Day-ag. He designed the bust and was in the process of casting it when his car figured in a head-on collision at Baay, Pangasinan on September 20, 1980, a day before the anniversary of the signing of Martial Law. Day-ag was 46. FYC.
See also: Kennon Lion.

Dayapan *(ITN).* "According to tradition, the Tinguian were taught to plant and reap by a girl named Dayapán. This woman, who was an invalid, was one day bathing in the stream, when the great spirit Kabonīyan entered her body. He carried with him sugar-cane and unthreshed rice which he gave to the girl with explicit directions for its use. Likewise he taught her the details of the Sayang, the most important of the ceremonies. Dayapán followed instructions faithfully, and after the harvest and conclusion of the ceremony, she found herself to be completely cured. After that she taught others, and soon the Tinguian became prosperous farmers." (Cole (1922) 2004).

Dayasan *(KAN).* A long pan made of tin used for sluicing gold dust. DLD.
See also: Kaman gangi; Pansejew.

De Guzman, Jaime. Already a renowned painter in Manila and Mexico, Jaime and then-wife Ann, settled in Sagada, Mountain Province with their family in 1983. Ann was already a potter, and the De Guzmans would revive pottery there after discovering clay behind St. Mary's School. The De Guzmans built a kiln and trained some of the residents. They eventually left Sagada in 1988 and Jaime opened his pottery workshop in Quezon Province. He, however, regularly returned to Sagada and together with Archie Stapleton Jr. and David Fowler, ushered in the second coming of Sagada pottery.
See also: Sagada Ceramic Center.

De Guia, Virginia. (A.K.A. Gene Oteyza). A woman ahead of her times, Gene Oteyza descended in the mid-1930s from cool Baguio to the hotbed of activists in the University of the Philippines-Manila. The shy highlander 'promdi' became president of the UP Womens' Club, UP Tennis Champion, critically-acclaimed actress of the campus thespians, member of the Pi Kappa Pi honors society and headed the UP Law women's organization Portia Society and Sigma Delta Phi.

As brains-cum-beauty, she had the distinction of being the only person to defeat in debate, UP student Ferdinand Marcos (1939) and became a movie star opposite film heartthrob Rogelio dela Rosa in a movie called *Nagkaisang Landas* (1940).

Virginia de Guia was appointed the first woman city mayor by President Manuel Roxas effective July 4, 1946. As mayor, she led the rehabilitation of post-war Baguio. She organized the Baguio Carnival and expo, secured the city from the threat of the Hukbalahaps rebel movement, and successfully put Baguio on the tourism map internationally. Malacañang kept her as acting Mayor (when Mayor Jose Cariño was bedridden) but she quit politics upon the next elections as she saw the contradiction of poll spending and clean governance.

She would then organize Team Baguio, a non-government organization of concerned citizens that monitored City Hall's policies. She co-founded Alay sa Kalikasan to save Baguio's fragile environment. She joined forces with Leony San Agustin (former Baguio Museum Director) and Cecile Afable (former Baguio Midland Courier Editor) rallying Baguio's citizenry to oppose politicians' shady projects. The trio became know as 'Baguio's Three Witches.' As octogenarians, they led the fight against the controversial BGH flyover infrastructure project and

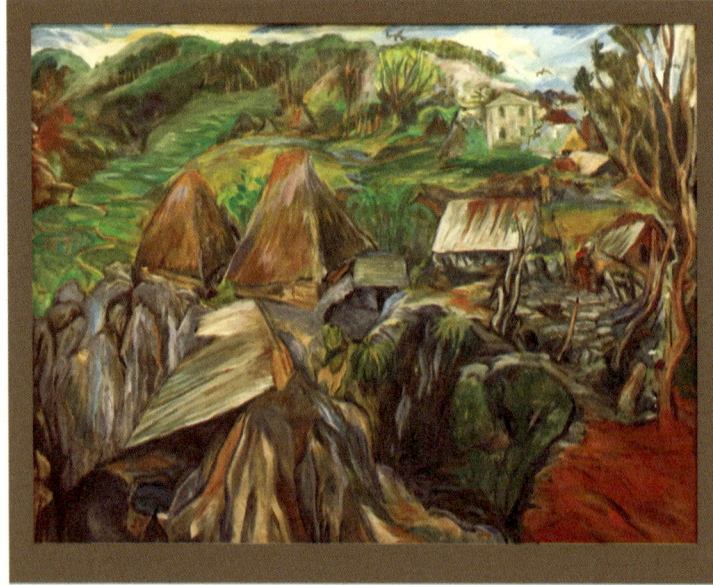

Artwork by Jaime de Guzman.

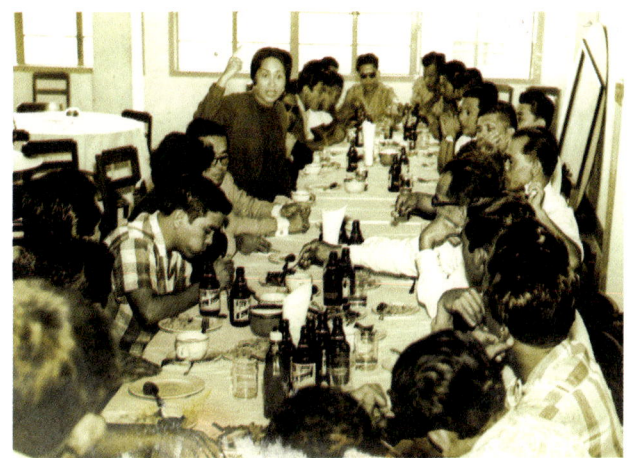
Photograph of *Virginia De Guia*, circa 1950s. Courtesy Virginia De Guia.

joined rallies against SM City Baguio Mall's cutting down of 182 pine trees for a parking complex. Tirelessly, they hounded (hexed?) the city council and Mayor to fulfill their duties (a mixture of fear and respect). Writing until she was in her 90s, she kept filling her Sunday column "Baguio ko, Mahal ko." Until her last breath, Gene was a faithful lover of Baguio. KT

Dekat *(KAN)*. In Sagada, the dekat is the public declaration of a couple's engagement. It is a big event in which two carabaos and six pigs must be ritually offered. Rough estimates say that about PHP400,000 is needed to complete the ritual. It is possible that this money could be earned back by the couple because, at the wedding, visitors drop money in a basket when they congratulate or greet the couple. This gift of cash, which can be of any amount, is called supon. TDH.
See also: Chomno; Duwaya.

Demetillo, Darnay. Demetillo, who died in 2012, is a founding member of Tahong Bundok, the first artists' group in Baguio. He joined what was then the University of the Philippines College Baguio in 1975 as a humanities instructor. He served as the college's artist-in-residence from 1978 until he retired in 2005. In the span of over 30 years as an artist, he had countless exhibits in Baguio. The growth and development of the fine arts program at UP Baguio owes much to the invaluable contributions of Demetillo. With him at the helm, the fine arts program grew from a three-year certificate program into a full-blown baccalaureate program. Under his tutelage, many students won awards and received citations in various prestigious art contests, such as the Shell, Petron, Philip Morris and Metrobank national art competitions, thus earning recognition, too, for UP Baguio's greenhorn of an art program on the little campus on the hill. As an artist Demetillo was wide ranging in his range of media and techniques with work encompassing painting, sculpture, printmaking and photography and which experimented with incorporating found objects or use of heat guns to alter the textural qualities of his materials. Through a keen discernment of the nature and qualities of different media and techniques, he was able to perfectly marry form and content. GTS.

Demshang *(KAN)*. To eat bits of meat while waiting for the main course in a cañao.
See also: Cañao.

Denas *(KAN/BON)*. Foot washing. Mendenas means to wash feet. In the past, pathways were muddy and to avoid dirtying the house or one's bed, everyone was supposed to mendenas (wash their feet) before entering the house. In cool areas like Besao, this was a minimum requirement for hygiene as taking a bath was not necessarily done on a daily basis. PAD.

Dentan *(KAN)*. Lit. To light or heat. It is a modern ritual done by farmers in Bauko and in other Kankanaey communities when their vegetables start withering for no apparent reason. A pinikpikan ritual is performed in the early morning at the garden plot. *"Ta sino kayo ay wada sina, ilaen yo ta tulungan yo koma dakami ay mangsolbar sinannay problema mi isnan mulmula mi ta wada iyat na ay gumabay [Whoever are present, help us solve our problems with these crops so they would grow],"* is the usual invocation to the spirits. FYC.
See also: Pinikpikan; Pinten.

De Vega, Juan Manuel. Dr. de Vega in his review of the Igorot miners in 1609 attested to their abstemiousness as they would get gold only according to what they intended to trade (mostly hogs, carabaos and rice from Pangasinan traders). *"They are people as void of covetousness as this; for they say that they have it there at hand for the times when they need it."* (De Vega 2005).

Dew-dew-as *(ISN)*. Bamboo pan-flute made of seven thin pieces of bamboo joined together with rattan weave.
See also: Abistong; Gangsa; Kuliteng; Music.

Digdiga *(KAL)*. Pride in one's work, strength or artistry.

Dila anito *(ISN)*. Lit. Spirit's tongue. Plant placed next to the entrance of an Isneg door to prevent anything evil from entering.
See also: Bengao; Purchos.

Dinak yat *(IFU)*. Talisman.

Dinet-aean *(KAN)*. A place with a pool of water in one of Sagada's cave systems near the mountains of Kanip-aw. An enchanted eel is said to inhabit its waters. A local farmer once caught here an eel the size of a man's thigh. He brought it home and placed it in a basin of water. During the night, the man dreamt that the eel he caught wore a pig as a pendant and was talking to him. The eel admonished the farmer and ordered that it be returned to Dinet-aean. When the farmer woke up in the morning, he found that one of his pigs had died. He quickly returned the eel to where he caught it. Those who later attempted setting up fishing lines in this same area returned home with their hooks broken. GAD.

Divag *(IBA)*. To be surprised.

Divang *(IBA)*. To check on animals which are out on the ranch or on pastureland.
See also: Koto ni Shontog.

Doligen ed Kabunyan, Si *(KAN)*. Lit. Doligen in Kabunyan. On a tall mountain in Bakun, Benguet, there lived a deity who fed every hungry passerby. Upon resting on the foot of that mountain, a passerby would automatically be fed by the deity, believed to be Kabunian himself (the mountain would eventually be named after him). Passersby would only hear the clattering of plates when they were served but no one could be seen preparing the food. The food was said to always be delicious. One day, Doligen passed by the mountain and was fed like many others before him. But, he made the mistake of gathering all the beautiful plates, and stuffing them inside his bag to bring them home. Kabunian got angry and slammed Doligen into a boulder so hard that he was permanently pinned to it. For some time, the boulder on Mt. Kabunyan bore Doligen's image with his legs forever parted, water flowing from his penis. Nowadays, his image on the stone is hardly seen but the spring continues to flow reminding people of the fate of Doligen whenever they drink from it.
See also: Aginaya, Panginomnoman ki; Mt. Pulag; Three orphans of Sagada, The.

Domoguing. The contrived act of bowing your head, especially during a protest rally in Baguio, with an 'I-cannot-do-anything' look. DOS.

Dorarakit *(ISN)*. A trance medium. They must always be female. She has the ability to be a ritual officiator, orator, healer and a channel between humans and the supernatural.
See also: I-langit; Mahimunu; Maingal; Mambunong; Manpapayad; Mansib-ok; Xaranait.

Duggong ti Intsik *(ILO)* Lit. Chinese snot; also **Sundot Kulangot** *(ILO)*. Lit. Snot Picking. This is kalamay, a delicacy made of ground glutinous rice, coconut milk, molasses or brown sugar. It is packed in shells of pitogo (sago palm) which are then sealed with red crepe paper and packed five a pod then tied and secured with bamboo sticks. A traditional souvenir at the Baguio market, the kalamay inside the balls is not the point, rather

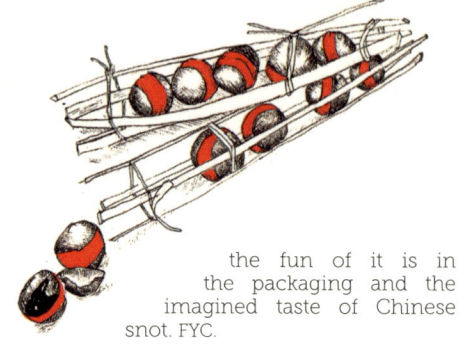

the fun of it is in the packaging and the imagined taste of Chinese snot. FYC.
See also: Man in the barrel; Penis ashtray.

Dujung *(IBA)*. An elegy sung in front of the dead usually sitting on a death chair. The virtues of the dead person are extolled and the last line repeated by the funereal crowd. FYC.
See also: Amazing Grace; Badio; Baya-o; Cherwasay; Sangadil.

Dulag, Macli-ing. A farmer, barangay captain, caminero and pangat who became the spokesperson of Bugnay, Kalinga against the planned Chico Hydroelectric Dam project. He later became the symbol of Igorot defiance against the Marcos dictatorship and development aggression. He was killed in April 24, 1980 by government soldiers. Cordillera Day is celebrated every April 24 in his honor. The official Cordillera Day, however, is celebrated on July 15. FYC.
See also: Balweg brothers; Cellophil; Chico; Pangat; Peace zone.

Duvilvil *(IBA)*. A handgun.

Duwao *(KAN)*. The duwao is a four-poled or four-feathered headdress worn by men. It signifies that all of the children of the wearer have married, settled down and have borne their own children. TDH.
See also: Akipur; Apang; Bayoyok; Kulatod; Panglao.

Duyayu *(KAL)*. Sleet.
See also: Baggat Udan; Little Alaska.

DZWT. Radio station established in 1966 by the Missionaries of the Immaculate Heart of Mary (CICM) with the mission to provide religious and educational programs for Benguet, Mountain Province, Ifugao, and Kalinga Apayao. To achieve this mission, it had to have high transmitting power and up to now, it has the widest reach among AM stations in the Cordilleras. By 1977, it started its own FM station. Playing mostly classical and pop music, it eventually turned to pop jazz in the late-1970s. By the 1980s, DZWT had all but gone country-western, thereby whetting the appetites of the Benguet cowboys. It remains the only country music network – probably in the whole country. FYC.
See also: AFRTN; Cowboy; Country Music; Sarsarita ni Uncle Pete.

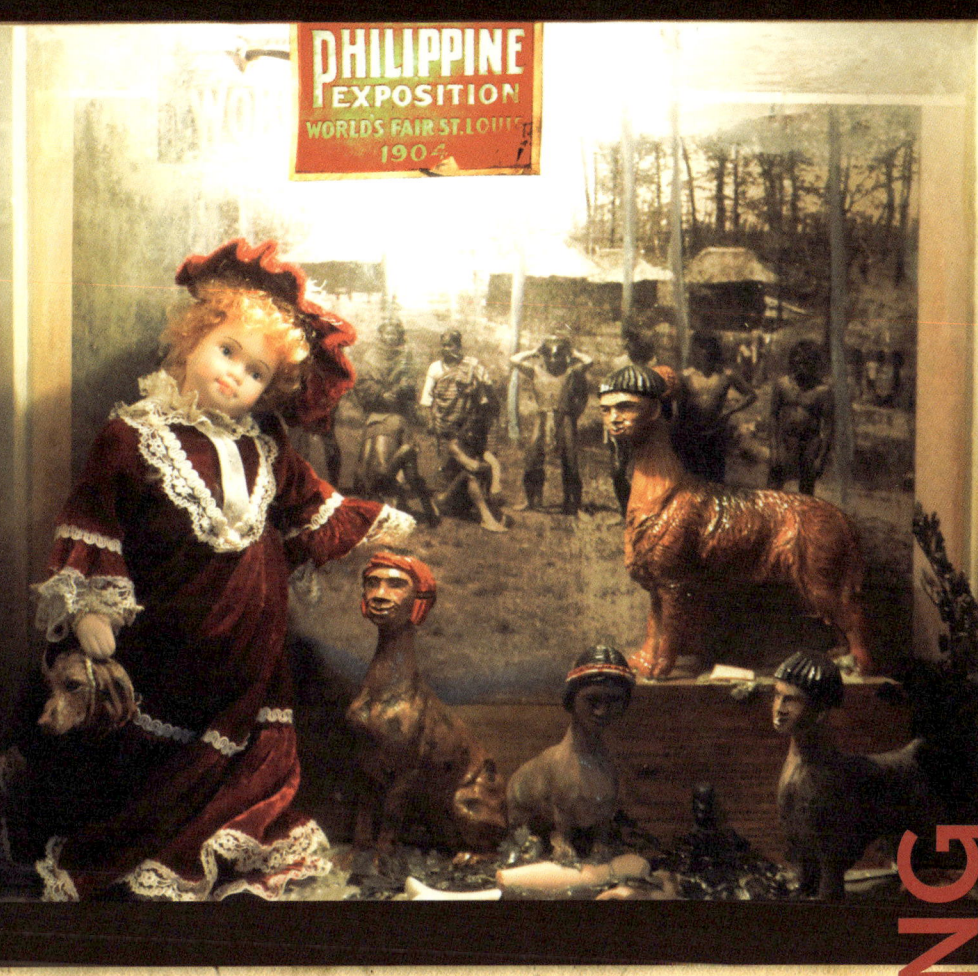

Top: Artwork by Rocky Cajigan, 2013.
Bottom: Back of postcard depicting a dog sacrifice before head hunting. Courtesy AV Cating Family Collection.

Dog Eat Dog: A Fair World

It was a bowl of adobo. The meat was cut into pieces with parts on sharp bones. It was darkened with soy souce, and the fragrant oil infused with garlic, ginger, and crisp scallions. This was my introduction to dog meat. We were living in a government compound in Bontoc, the capital of Mountain Province, where my father worked as an engineer. In that compound by the Chico River, domestic surplus was sometimes shared, from clothing to food. There was a hint of ritualized sharing, living on a mountain with very old traditions of being part of a village. But the way that dog meat was cooked, it could not have been from a ritual. If the meat had come from animal sacrifice, it would have been boiled and nothing else added. This bowl of meat dinner passed from a neigbor, over my head, to my father's hands. We ate pieces of the meat with steaming white polished rice. I was around ten. It was a dry baptism into the world of dog-eaters.

Paolo Sunggay, an artist, runs an eatery-slash-gallery that used to serve dog meat, in a district at the heart of Baguio City known for its row of carinderias specializing in dog meat. Self-taught as an abstract artist, he asks why everyone assumes the diverse Cordillera to be the same everywhere and all the time: exotic people emblemed by ubiquitous souvenir lizards and bululs, or a popular dog-eating culture.

It was when I started living in the city, often eating at his eatery, that I met Paolo. It came up a few times in laid-back evening conversations over cheap gin: the incoming storm of sweeping rules on humane food sourcing. The Animal Welfare Act fast becoming a matter of bitter debate in the Cordilleras.

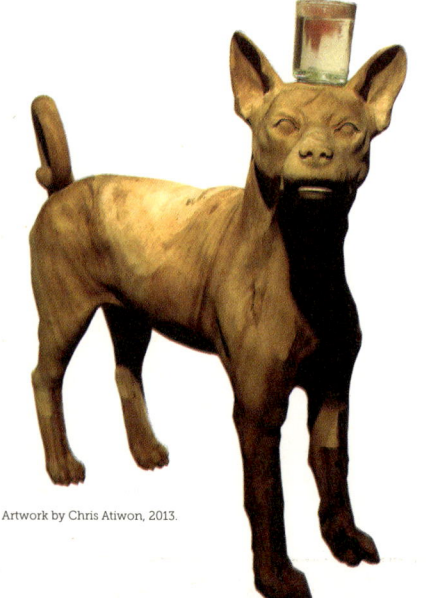

Artwork by Chris Atiwon, 2013.

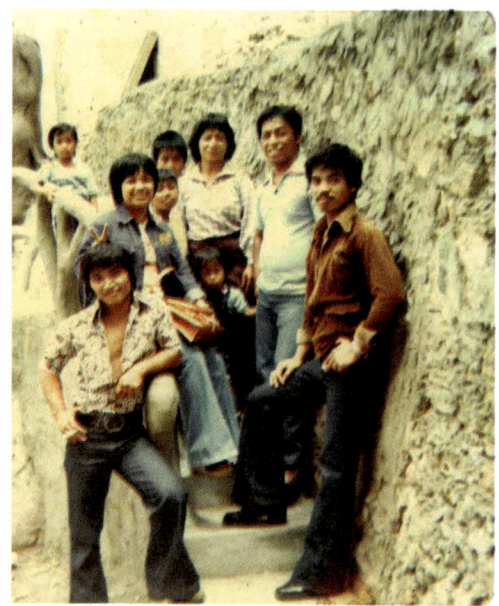

Photograph of the Sunggay family, c. early 1980s. Courtesy Sunggay Family.

Paolo's family has a dog on each floor of his four-story house. Like most animal welfare activists, he and his family take care of each of the dogs like family. I've always regarded his complex relationship with dogs-as-pets and dogs-as-food-business to be a constant reconsidering of the complex dialects of our human relationship with the canine species, or with the non-human world.

In his art and with his family, Paolo prefers an unpretentious way of viewing things. He simplifies speech and concepts to their basic form so that his ideas are bite-sized – digestible. His everyday is not in the restaurant kitchen but making silly jokes around the tables with his regulars. He took over the family-run eatery at the age of 24, inheriting it from his parents. It was his mother who built the business, a spritely woman with keen matriarchal management sensibilities, who built her life around the eatery business close to the Kalantiao Extension, also known as the Burned Area after the fire of 1978. She was a waitress and helper to a relative in the eatery business and she hopped from eatery to eatery until she settled in one whose owner got tired of the business and left it to her. She met her husband, a porter in the Dangwa bus station next to the Burned Area. The family would end up running a second floor space in one of the old buildings.

After a diploma in Industrial Engineering, Paolo got a job at a Subic assembly-line manufacturing Automated Teller Machines. Three days later, he quit. It was the food: served in sickly little portions. He missed the taste and abundance of mountain food piled on large plates. He also only wanted to work on his paintings instead. He returned to Baguio City, to that corner of his youth where streets were christened with the names of national heroes and revolutionaries. He took over Katipunan eatery, named after the late 19th century revolutionary movement against the Spanish colonization of the Philippines. Slowly, throughout a decade of running the eatery, he acquired another one in an adjoining building at street level, keeping the same name, Katipunan. He would marry his college sweetheart and start a family. He turned the Katipunan street eatery into an exhibition space for mountain folk who were always in and out of the area. When the Animal Welfare Act was passed and the Anti-Rabies campaign followed it, the sensible thing to do was to open the tables for talk about where the clash of moralities must be put to rest. Enraged welfare advocates who raided his eatery with the police in tow only left pitiful and violent slogans on the table, a mere act of force.

But it was a time when other debates were again becoming popular: cultural appropriation and transitioning indigeneities. It was a moment when the stage was being set yet again, monstrous and scheming, much like the human zoo at the 1904 St. Louis World's Fair. For people like Paolo Sunggay – an artist, businessman, dog-eater – they were being made to re-live this zoo.

The St. Louis World's Fair, also known as the Louisiana Purchase Exposition, *"was the grandest of all Fairs and the Philippine Exhibit took the honor of being the largest and most popular one at this Fair. It occupied 47 acres of land, had 100 buildings and was the most expensive to build at a cost of two million dollars."* (Pilapil 1994, 15).

Academic Virgilio Pilapil describes it further, *"The head-hunting, dog-eating Igorots were the greatest attraction at the Philippine Exhibit, not only because of their novelty, the scanty dressing of the males and their daily dancing to the tom-tom beats, but also because of their appetite for dog meat...."*

The 'savage' Igorots became a live billboard for an ignorant audience. The Igorots played along for the money, or what little they got after broken promises and the strangeness of foreign land. The irony was a circus. Dogs were killed to satisfy fantasies of exoticism, in butchering that was strictly beyond the realm of ritual, contrary to how it would have been done back home. The Igorots on display were caught in the unfolding of the American Dream and Industrialization.

The 1904 Fair was a political feast where *"the mandate of the Philippine Exposition had been made clear from the start. And so it was, that the racist bashing of the Filipino was institutionalized and Igorot ritual of dog-eating and its association with barbarity not corrected, but repeatedly reinforced, to great effect.."* (Castro, 2008, 78).

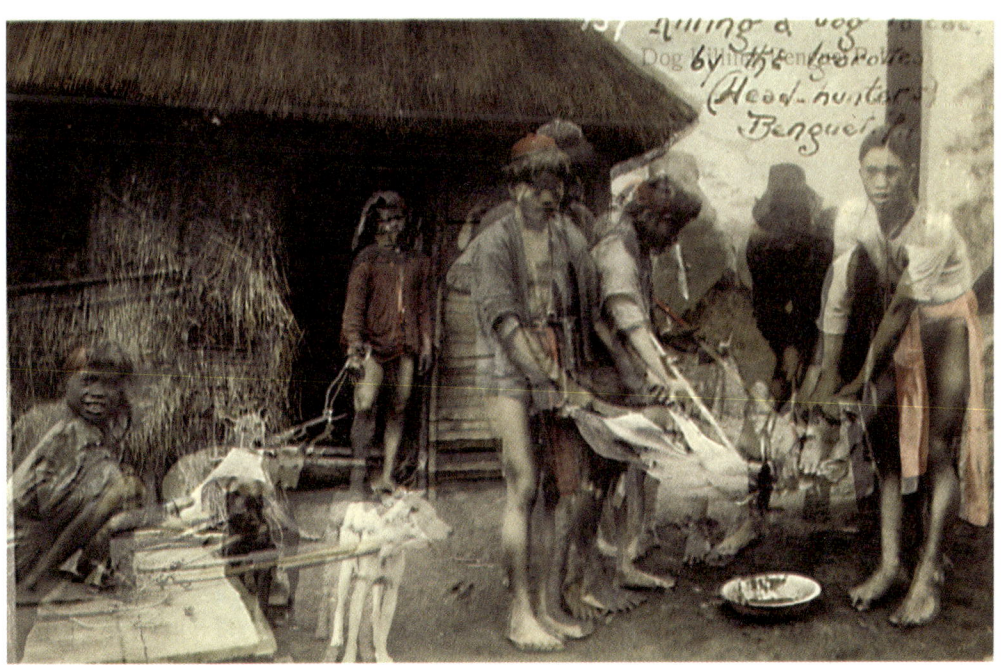

Photograph of a dog sacrifice. Courtesy of AV Cating Family Collection.

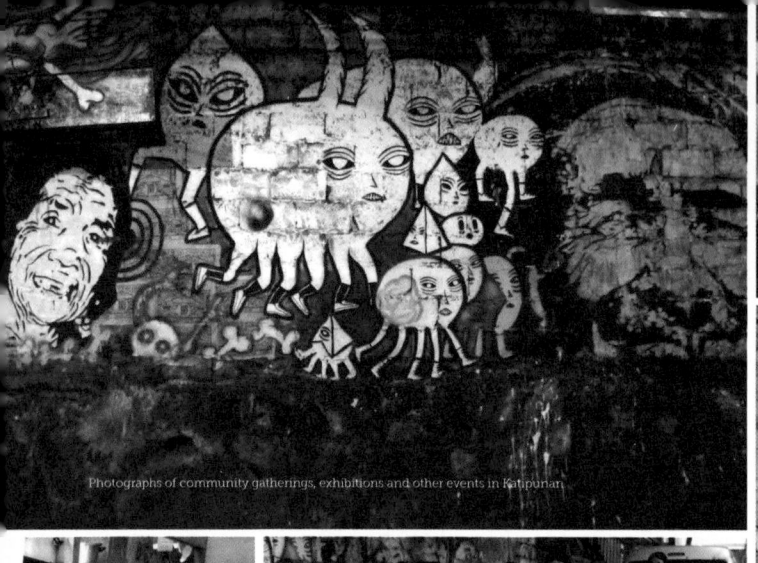
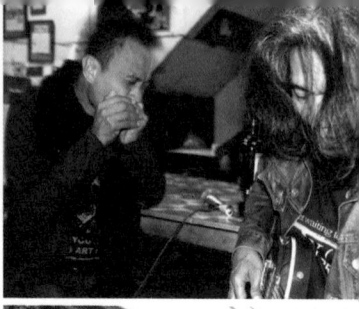
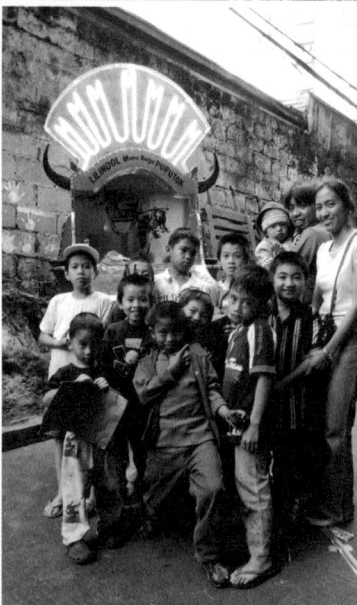

Photographs of community gatherings, exhibitions and other events in Katipunan

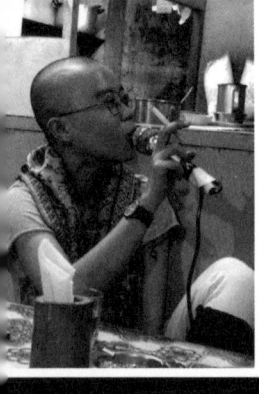
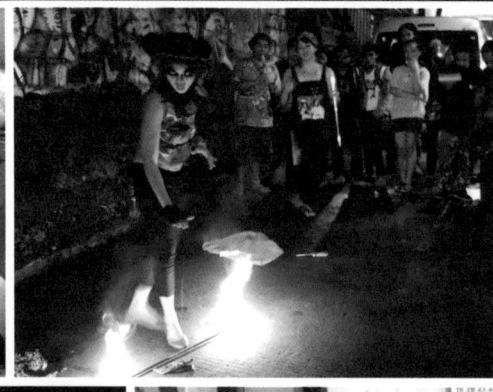
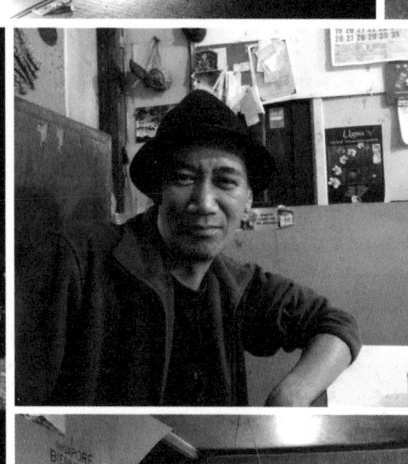
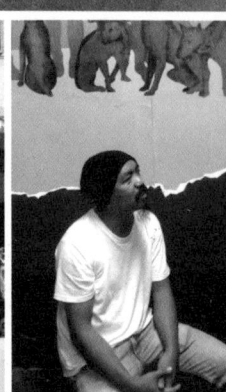
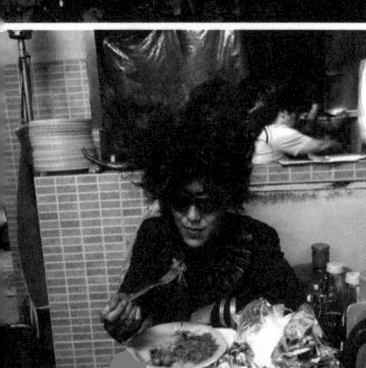
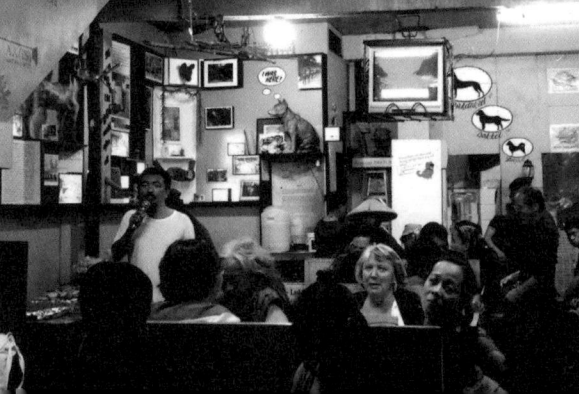

Back home in the Philippines, the spectacle would rewrite history for over a century in a series of images: the elite Filipinos fanning themselves, embarrassed that their 'cultured' and "educated" class had been misrepresented in the 1904 showcase; the swarm of anthropologists turning misled bouts of culture shock into a flood of regurgitated knowledges unfamiliar to their 'subjects'; and a good number of Igorots, determined to separate themselves from the dog-eating and head-taking culture, afraid of the 'savage' and 'pagan' label, sure that 'dog-eating' and 'head-taking' are cut from the same cloth. What is left of nurtured knowledge systems of an ancestry that lived close to the land always seemed to remain to be seen.

In the Igorot ethos, animals are butchered for prayer such as in the daw-es. But the ethos can evolve into a new culture of taste. It can become nostalgia for ritual, when dog meat is ordered from Paolo's eatery or one of the 50 or so eateries across Baguio City and in neighboring towns that serve dog meat. It often feels like a performance of history. I associate it with my father. In the first years of moving our family to the city, he had cooked the ritual chicken dish pinikpikan almost every month, much to the dread of his children who did not need to re-acquire the taste.

The conitnuing saga of cultural trauma is not lost to Paolo Sunggay, he regards anti-dog-eating prejudice as another form of culture bashing.

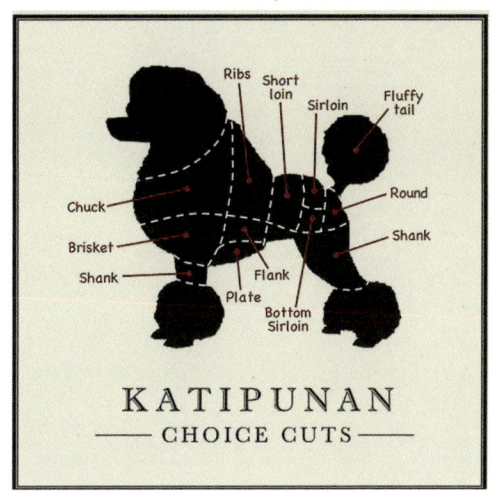

Illustration by Joyce Toh.

But an interesting irony in the bashing of the 'primitive' is the hotdog. Pilapil (1994) says that *"it was not until the St. Louis World's Fair that a sausage-on-a-bun was made up to be called the 'hot dog' for the first time. It is evident that sausages were known for a long time and were called by various names, but it was the St. Louis World's Fair that gave the name 'hot dog' to America."* Today, the hotdog, made from the carcass trimmings of large-scale industrial meat factories, is a cultural symbol, a staple in many a corner food-truck around the world, creating a new vision of 'food source' among a growing population of hungry consumers.

When the Animal Welfare Act was locally adopted, a compromise was set in a clause. It allows for ritual butchering of dogs if the involved indigenous elder informs the Bureau of Animal Industry. These rituals, called tomo by the Benguet Kan-kanaey, temmo by most of the Mountain Province Kan-kanaey, and sumang by the Bontok, are meant to drive away the evil spirits of enemies who died in battle. One of the varieties of the daw-es among the Kan-kanaey of Mt. Province is meant to cleanse a person of the evil constraints that might have provoked him to commit a crime. It may also be a ritual to cleanse a community following a natural disaster.

The Welfare Act definitively states the punishment for the maltreatment of animals and the trading thereof. The commercialization of dog meat had initially prompted an unwanted trade that triggered reactions from many groups, including Igorots themselves, who denounced dog-eating and denied that it had ever been part of ritual life. Animal welfare groups wanted to

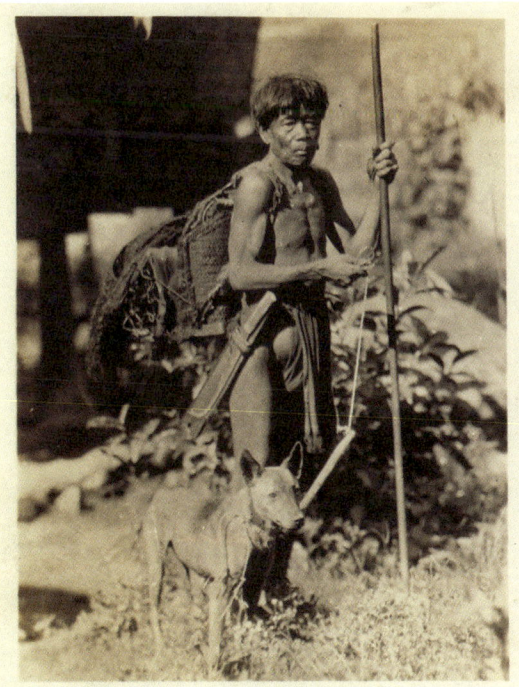

Photograph of Igorot man with dog, c. 1910s. Courtesy AV Cating Family Collection.

see people in prison to set the tone. But indigenous peoples themselves were barely consulted before the law was enacted. In indigenous practice, issues like these are discussed by a council of elders. For many who have never heard of it, it is a democratic response to criminalization and plain hate. This link to the pervasive branding against the "primitive," draws out the colonial vestiges of horrifying events like the atrocity that was the St. Louis World's Fair.

It was in response to this continuing debate that artists, with Paolo and the AX(iS) Art Project, turned Katipunan into a dog museum. Photographs of rituals and events at the 1904 Exposition are lit in boxes on the wall reminding people of this difficult history. The dog museum celebrates human and non-human bonds while at the same time, provokes questions about what and how we eat.

Part of the museum also looks at Paolo's family history: their fate along with the eateries and other family-owned shops hidden behind the city's fastfood mall culture. Paolo knows this. He

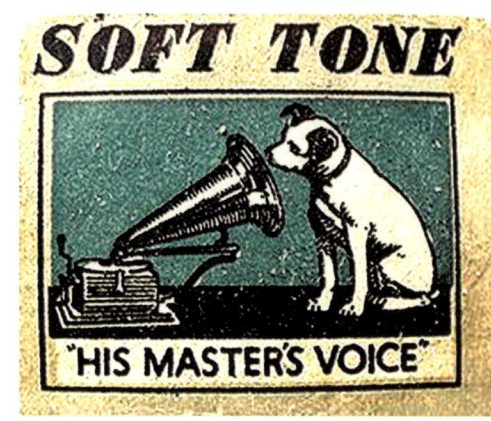

likes to sit quietly in his restaurant as he meditates over the museum walls, enveloped by the scent of that derelict side of the city. He waits until it is time for a katipunan. RAC.

See also: Worcester, Dean; Enmity between the Igorots and Christians, The Beginning of; Halsema Hijinks; Hunt, Truman; Jones, Isabela; Last No-Pant-On-Day.

Howl of the Underdog: The Katipunan Dog Meat Museum

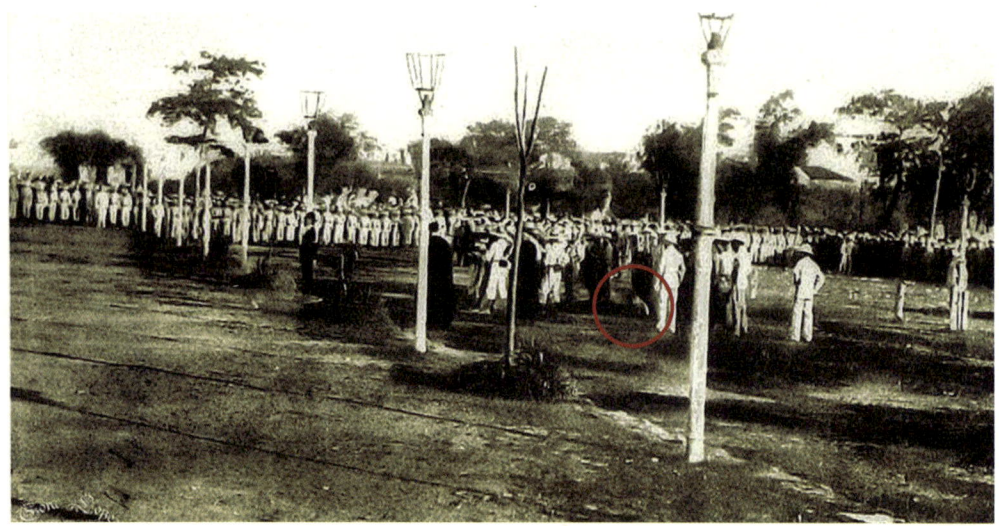

Photograph of a dog during Jose Rizal's execution, 1898.

This is NOT about dog meat. This is about the cultural sensitivities that surround dog meat, the law, and Katipunan. Everything in this hill-station town has been colonized: the way people dress, all the way to which god to pray to.

And now this! Our cultural palate! Our tongue! Our taste! A forced change with a bitter aftertaste!

Some may see dog meat as a gastronomic issue; others with animal rights filters. It is an age-old cultural practice and it hits a major vein down to

a ritualistic core. To partake in the killing of a black dog remains the highest form of animal sacrifice in the Cordilleras. Must we sacrifice all black dogs, just to revoke that congressional bill outlawing this practice? Let's trace where the legislation emanated.

Margaret Thatcher, a dog lover herself, and mother to four dachshunds applied the might of the British government on Third-World tuta-lawmakers to put pressure on local governments like Baguio to outlaw culinary 'barbaric acts!' (It is common knowledge that half of City Hall loves the delicacy). That post-colonial arm twisting trickled down to us, the Cordilleran local folk. Well, are we made of the same fiber as those that 'civilized' the world through swords and gunpowder?

Enter on stage the Katipunan eatery:

A hole – a howl – in the wall. One of the silent few doggy restaurants that don't advertise McDoggy. Situated at a back-alley of the Dangwa Bus station, literally the gateway to the mountains. The clients, mostly indigenous people: farmers who work the land, grow vegetables and harvest them for the stomachs of Manila; miners who dig out gold that they hardly profit from; or students who work their way up from the bottom only to find themselves losing a grasp of their roots.

It's the familiar taste of that hot broth that might just heat up your body and make you feel at home again. As for those fast-food-20 peso-21st-Century burgers, made from animals thrown into a giant chopping machine, often while the animals are still alive, that's less cruel? That's more civilized?

I've known Paolo Sunggay for at least 20 years now. And I've gotten to know his space, Katipunan, whose name alone means a lot to me. That age-old saga of the Filipino rebels in search for freedom is written all over the place. Ang mga Katipunero ay nagtipon-tipon... because it's the last place anyone would find you? That's what you think – until you find everyone else is there too. Does this mean that we've all been running away from the same sterile world? From colonial rule? From martial law? Or is it the pungent smell of urine in the alley outside? Is there that feeling of being underground just like the Katipuneros? Perhaps it's all of the above, and anyhow, I'm on my third beer and tonight's anthem is "With or Without You". It's blasting out of the karaoke and everyone's singing along to it! The only thing missing from this Katipunan are the bolos and the torches so we can burn the city down. Sugod mga kapatid!!! In the meantime, we belch out our frustrations.

It is this solidarity that I find here. The streets speak to you and a thousand stories unfold. That's only if you keep your ear open: the true voice of the gutter. You get tired of the usual crowd that goes to art openings, and you realize your audience is here. And they were here all along! You just didn't recognize them.

And so, as the story goes, a few of us, including Mark Tandoyog and Paolo, started organizing and bringing a whole array of art happenings to Katipunan and its dirty walls.

You never know when a show is pushing through. Submission of artwork at Katipunan means you are hanging the work as the show is opening. So perhaps that's exactly it, it isn't about the work, it isn't about how you hang the work; but perhaps it is the hanging of the work at that very moment that makes it a momentous event? That's a Katipunan opening.

Like the hanging of a Katipunero, a 'traitor' to the republic, the crowds gather to enjoy the spectacle of a public execution and the excitement of Death! DEATH, DEATH TO THE ARTIST!! Death to the young Artist! Death to the unborn artist! You, who have no part to play in society!! You, who have no role in this world!

And that's exactly why I come here. Because here, everyone is an artist, and here there are no artists with a capital 'A'. We are all just human beings one way or the other, just trying to get by, one day at a time.

Once, during our valentine special entitled "Total Eclipse of the Heart", Pepe Smith sang his very own "Ang Himig Natin" on the videoke. Everyone sang along and some shed tears. He got a score of 66...ouch! That must have been painful. Or, during the *More International Art Festival*, which was mocking the *Tam-Awan "International" Art Festival,"* with Frank Cimatu, Dumay and Allan Cariño's readings – unfortunately the sound system was so bad no one could understand a word they were saying. It didn't matter, no-one was listening anyway, but everyone felt the fire of those muffled words. In the end we all danced the night away to Caliph8's heavy esoteric beats! I have to confess, I don't know who got more kicks: us or the Katipunan regulars.

Many nights were spent this way – unpredictable, informal, and you never knew who or what would pop-up. The showing of Marlon Fuentes' *Bontoc Eulogy* along the alley was a sight to see. Watching about Igorots that had to perform the killing of dogs every day for thousands of American spectators during the St. Louis exposition of 1904. This was the American colonialist's way of showing the American public that the Filipinos were uneducated savages and were not ready for self-governance. A reason for the ongoing annexation of the Philippine Islands: to civilize and Christianize them Filipinos.

So what happened to the Katipunan? All killed. Just like our beloved stinky Katipunan. Paolo's restaurant was under fire. The raids intensified, backed by the media and foreign animal rights activists. This howl-in-the-wall had no choice but to stop serving dog meat or to close down. But not with out a fight! That was where the idea of creating a dog meat museum came from. It was our small way of getting things straight – a small reminder to never forget and never give up.

Mabuhay ang Katipunan! Mabuhay ang Rebulution! Mabuhay ka Inang Pilipinas!!! KDG.

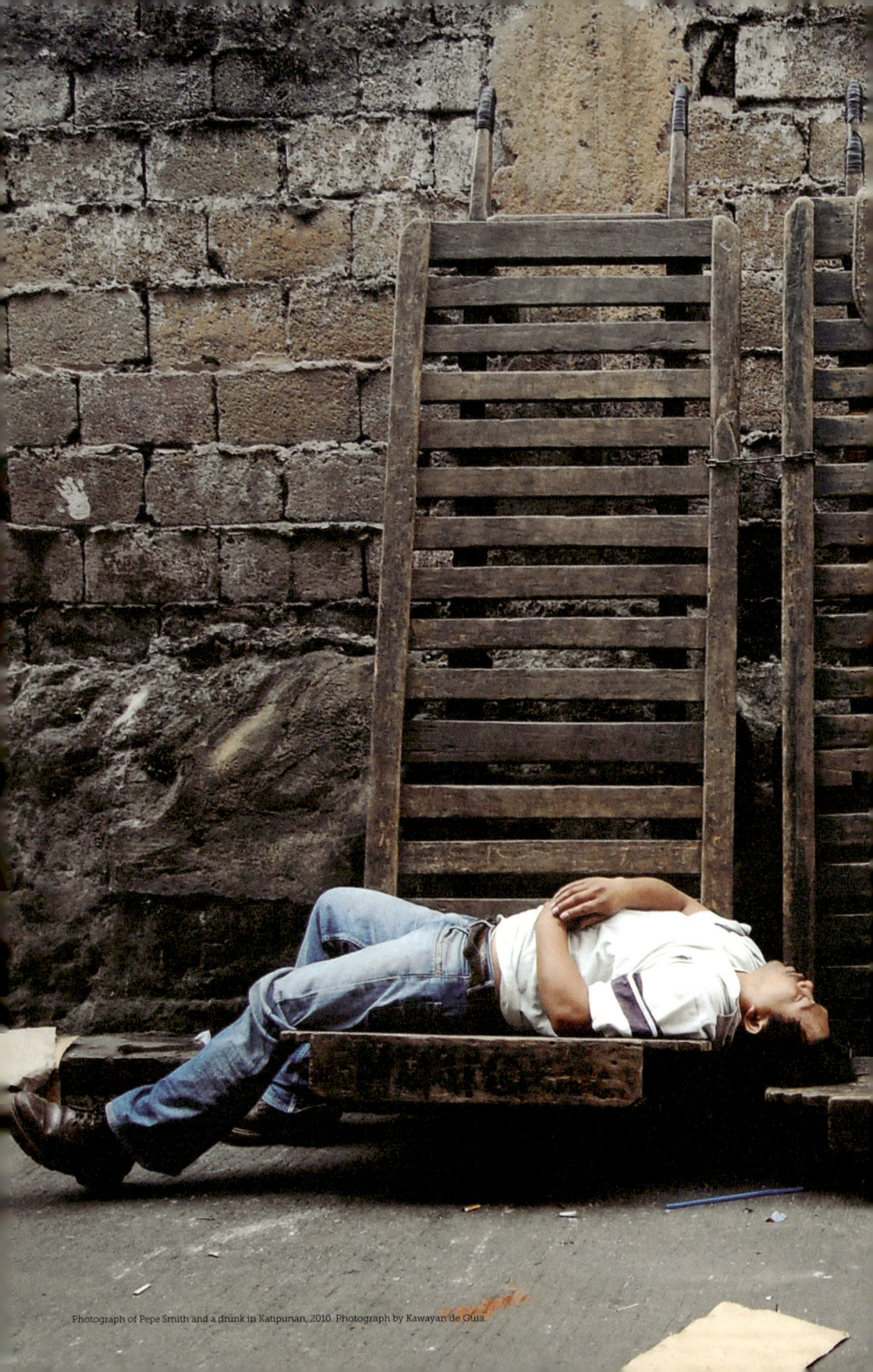

Photograph of Pepe Smith and a drunk in Katipunan, 2010. Photograph by Kawayan de Guia.

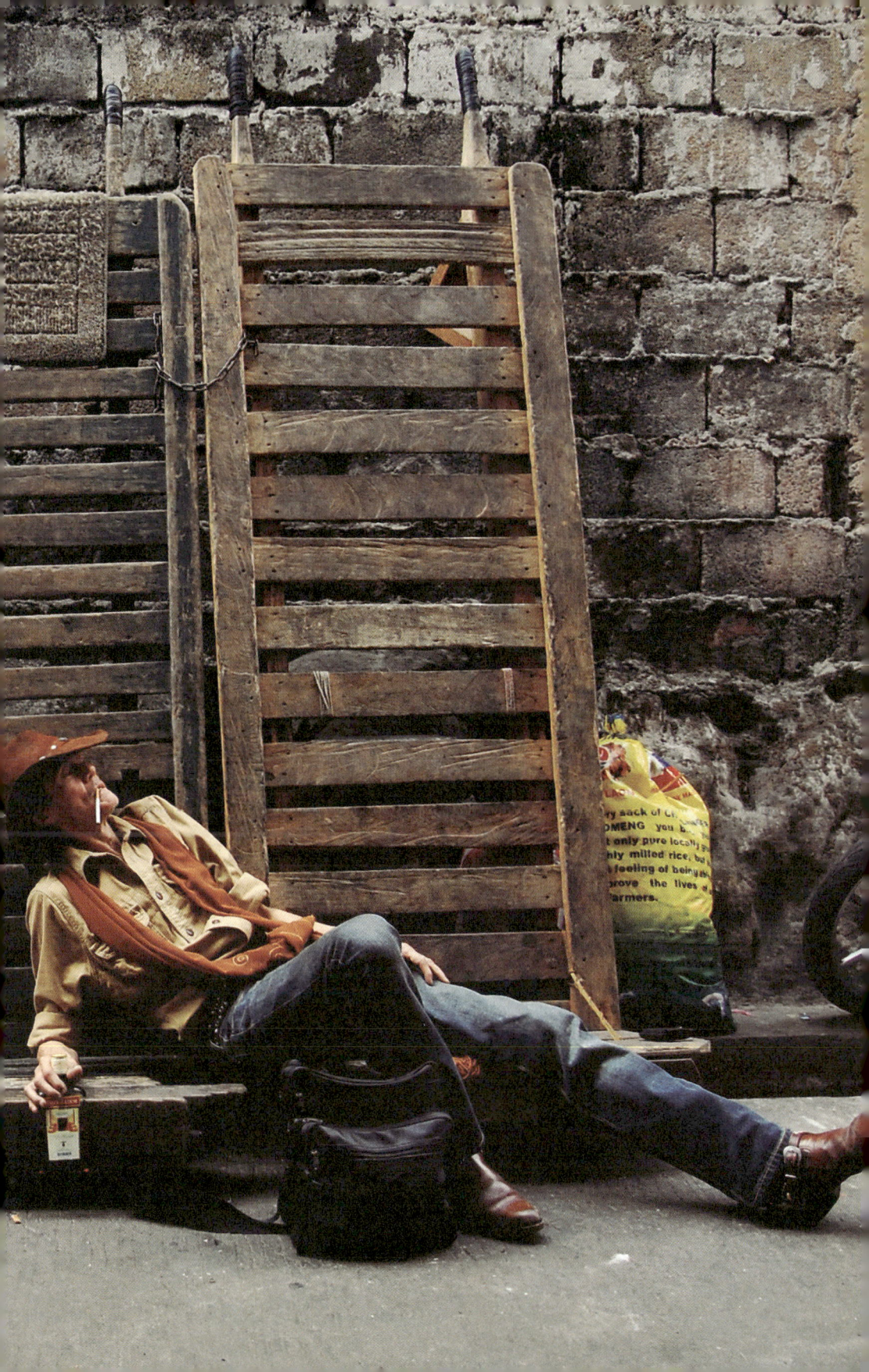

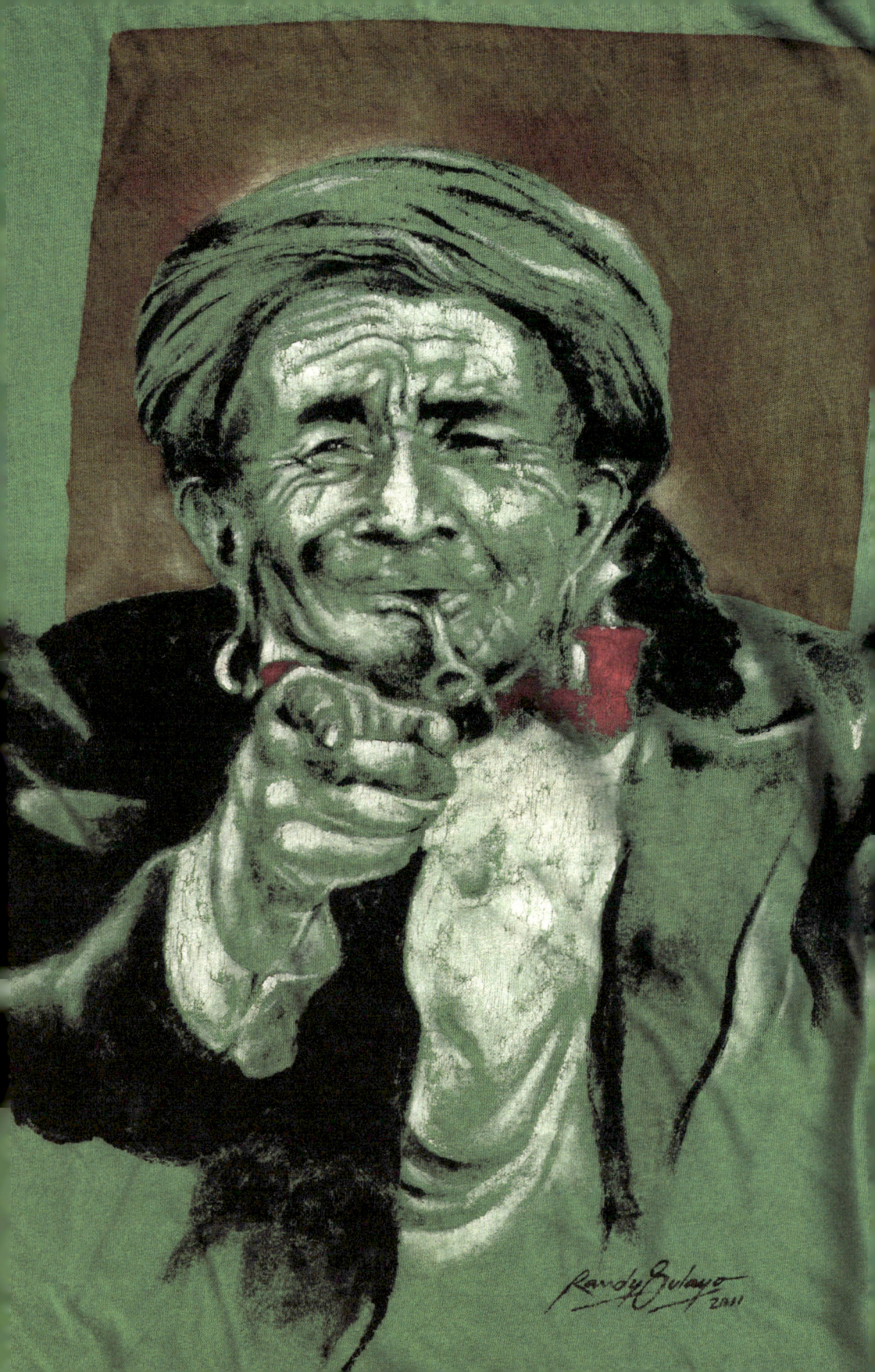

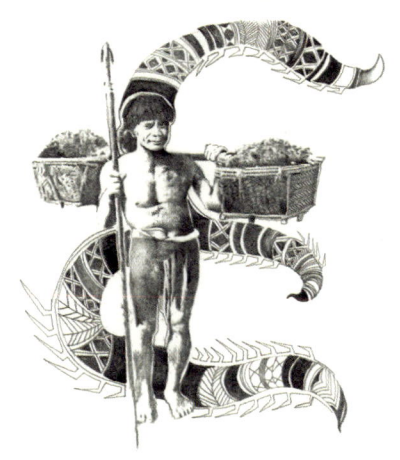

E *(KAN)* also **E-e** *(KAN)*, **Wen** *(ILO)*, **Arn** *(BON)*, **Aw** *(KAN)*, **Sha** *(KAN/BON)*, **Hya** *(KAN)*. E is the shortest 'yes' in the world. This Besao Kankanaey word – er letter – also serves as an affirmation. E-e, wen, arn, aw, mean yes and also serve as affirmation. Sha and hya are only used in affirmation. PAD.

Ear stretcher. *"Consists of two short pieces of bamboo forced apart and so held by two short crosspieces inserted between them. The bamboo ear stretcher is generally ornamented by straight incised lines. The plugs are not all considered decorative. Some are bunches of vegetable pith, others are wads of sugar-cane leaves. Some, however, are wooden plugs shaped quite like an ordinary large cork stopper of a bottle. The outer end is often ornamented by straight incised lines or with red seeds affixed with wax or with a small piece of a cheap glass mirror roughly inlaid. The long ear slit is not the end sought, because if the owner despairs of owning the coveted earring the stretchers and plugs are eventually removed and the slit contracts from an inch and one-half to a quarter of an inch or less in length. The long slit is desired because the people consider the effect more beautiful when the ring swings and dangles at the bottom of the pendant ear. The gold earring is the most coveted, but a few silver and many copper rings are worn in substitution for the gold."* (Jenks 2005).

Easter Weaving Room. Established in 1908, Easter Weaving Room (EWR) employs about 50 Cordillera weavers who produce bed covers, rugs, lamp shades, wall hangings, ladies' shoes, desk pads, pen holders, eyeglass cases, telephone pads, bookmarkers, vests, coats, jackets, hats, slippers, clog sandals, belts, neckties, skirts, blouses, mufflers, swaggers, stockings, hats, coaster napkins, and many more, using traditional looms. They weave patterns like colibangbang (butterfly), pagawa, cuabao (zigzag), tiktiko (diamond), kinen-ew (diamond and pestle), sinanbituin (starlight), bileg (triangle) and paracelis (stripes). EWR was established to give Igorot girls a chance to have a Home Economics class and earn on the side. Its original products were the wanes for the boys and tapis for the girls. The weavers were also taught to weave table runners and place mats for Americans. The EWR was bombed by the Americans during World War II but was revived in 1950. FYC.

See also: Cloth Dyes; Sagada Weaving; Tapis; Wanes; Weaving.

Ebgan *(KAN)*. A sleeping house for the young girls aged eight years and upwards.

See also: Dap-ay.

Edakdakian *(IBA)*. Lesbian.

See also: Vakla.

Edang *(IBA)*. Temporary separation between husband and wife for one reason or another.

See also: Es-eset.

Ejew *(IBA)*. To change one's mind about embarking on a trip.

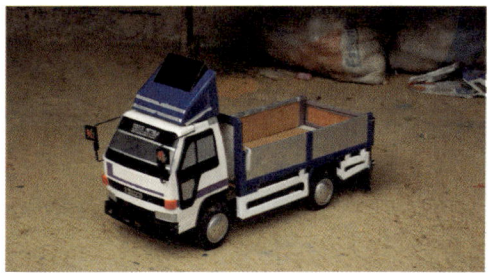

Photograph of a miniature Elf truck by Marion Codeo.

Elf. *"Ay waday Elf mo? [Do you have an Elf?]"* Daughters of Benguet farmers frequently ask their suitors this question. The Isuzu Elf (or similar medium-sized truck) is a status symbol among Benguet farmers and is sometimes preferred as a kind of dowry. DOS.

Elle't *(ISN)*. Strip of uncleared ground that is a natural boundary between two rice fields.

Emla *(KAL)*. Heroine of the Buaya epic called *Gasumbi*, an epic exclusively sung by women during the harvest season. She led an all-woman headhunt but was abandoned when they were nearing the enemy village. She managed to take an enemy's head and took the enemy's jewelry as well. (Coben 2009) FYC.

See also: Headhunting (the tale).

Engnga *(KAN)*. A newborn infant. After the infant has been baptized or ritually introduced to the spirit world, the child is then known as onga (Lit. child). The soul of the onga goes wherever the parents go even if physically the baby is at home and inside the house. For the well-being of the child the father would have to bring something back to the house, such as grains of rice if he came from the terraces or a sapling if he went to gather

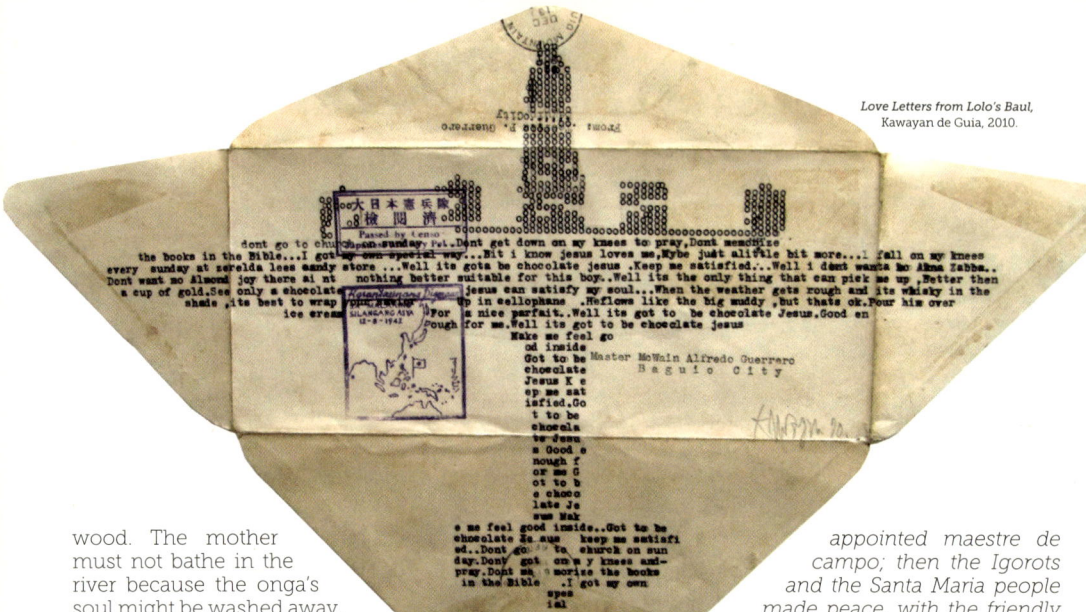

Love Letters from Lolo's Baul,
Kawayan de Guia, 2010.

wood. The mother must not bathe in the river because the onga's soul might be washed away. If the onga gets sick, it is taken to mean that the child's soul was left behind in the mountains so the parents bring the baby's blanket up to the mountain and call for the child to return home with them.

See also: Ab-abiik; Gobgobbao.

Enmity between the Igorots and Christians, The Beginning of. This story is retold by Robertson in his *"The Igorots of Lepanto"* and it is translated from Kankanaey: *"Langlangquiaon, Oaquing, Pasicat, Lobdoy, and Bocasi of the towns of Besao and Payeo, went down to the coast to find some work in the town of Santa Maria, Ilocos Sur. At the east of this town they met some hunters from Santa Maria, who were looking for a dog that had strayed from them. When they saw the Igorots they thought that the Igorots had stolen their dog, as it was known that Igorots eat dogs; the Christian persuaded the Igorots to follow them, telling the Igorots that one of them had some work for them to do; they went with the Christians, who had them that night to sleep inside of a strong bamboo fence; when they were sound asleep, the Christians killed everyone of them, with the exception of Bocasi, who succeeded in escaping. The Christians buried their bodies in the town of Santa Lucia. Upon Bocasi's return home, he told his townspeople what had happened to them. Thereupon the people of Besao and Payeo planned a head-hunting trip to Santa Maria; they started for that place, and when they reached the outskirts of the town they saw a young man carrying ears of corn on his head. They killed him and cut off his head, arms, and legs and returned home again, full of joy that they had avenged themselves for the cruelty of the Christians. From that time on, the Besao and Payeo people stopped going to Santa Maria until the time when Quiño went to Vigan and was appointed maestre de campo; then the Igorots and the Santa Maria people made peace, with the friendly help of the people from Santa Lucia."* (Robertson, 1914, p. 502-503).

See also: Bureau of Non Christian Tribes; Cayat; Dog-eating; Episcopalianism; Kain; Remontados; Salt Trade; Zubieta, Ramon.

Enoto *(IBA)*. Infested with lice.

Ensiluak *(BON)*. To commit suicide.

Entako Menlambak *(KAN)*. Lit. Let's go have a feast. A grand Cordillera festival organized in Baguio in 1992 featuring dances from all over the region. Then First Lady Ming Ramos attended. Cultural activists criticized it for *"prostituting the Cordillera culture."* Other pan-Cordillera festivals also criticized for *"grand commercialization"* were the *Grand Cañao* in 1981 and the *Highland Festival* in 1982. (Northern Dispatch, 1993) FYC.

See also: Cañao.

Episcopalianism. On October 11, 1902, the Episcopal Church (a.k.a. Anglican Church) in the US made the Philippines a missionary district and voted Charles H. Brent as the bishop and Rev. John Staunton and Walter Clapp as missionaries. Because Brent rejected the putting-an-altar-over-another-altar policy, he chose the Cordillera and Mindanao as the mission sites as well as the unchurched Chinese and Anglo-Saxons in Manila. In 1903, Staunton opened the Church of Resurrection in Baguio while Clapp lived with the Bontocs and eventually came up with the first Bontoc-English dictionary. Staunton later went to Sagada upon the invitation of Don Jaime Masferre, the father of famous photographer Eduardo. Staunton fell in love with Sagada and built the St. Mary the Virgin Church and then in 1909, opened St. Mary's School with Clara Mears as the first teacher. Later the St. Theodore's Hospital was built. Staunton's contributions to Sagada made the tourist town strictly Episcopalian. FYC.

See also: Brent School; Bureau of Non-Christian Tribes; Enmity between the Igorots and Christians, The Beginning of; Lumiang Burial Cave; Pitapit.

Es-eset *(KAN)*. Lit. To make good. A ritual performed for a husband and wife who have been reconciled by their families and elders after a quarrel that might have led to separation. A pig is offered to Kabunian and the ancestors and an appeal is made for material blessings for the family because they have promised to live a better life. NEP.

See also: Edang; Kabunian.

Etab *(KAN/BON)*. A kind of bean which is the ideal food for a newly-delivered mother to ensure sufficient breast milk, cleanse the uterus and body in general, and hasten the recovery of the mother. PAD.

See also: Aliwan; Bakget; Inaw; Kidlos; Kiya; Putting.

Etag *(BON/KAN)*. also **Itag** *(BON/KAN)*. Heavily salted, smoked pork. A traditional way of preserving meat. Pork is left hanging above the hearth where it is smoked. Once dried, it is stored in a loden or luchen (gourd basket) or rattan basket where it can keep for months. Some dry the meat under the sun after it is smoked but this won't keep long. It is important that raw sea salt is used for good results. Etag is an important ingredient in many Igorot rituals. Native dishes like tengba and pinikpikan incorporate etag. Before the commercialization of etag, villagers made sure there was always etag in the house. Traditionally, only a small piece of etag is added to the dish for flavoring. PAD.

See also: Food; Inasin; Intum; Pinuneg; Safeng.

Evin *(IBA)*. To make a round trip.

See also: Tiwtiwong.

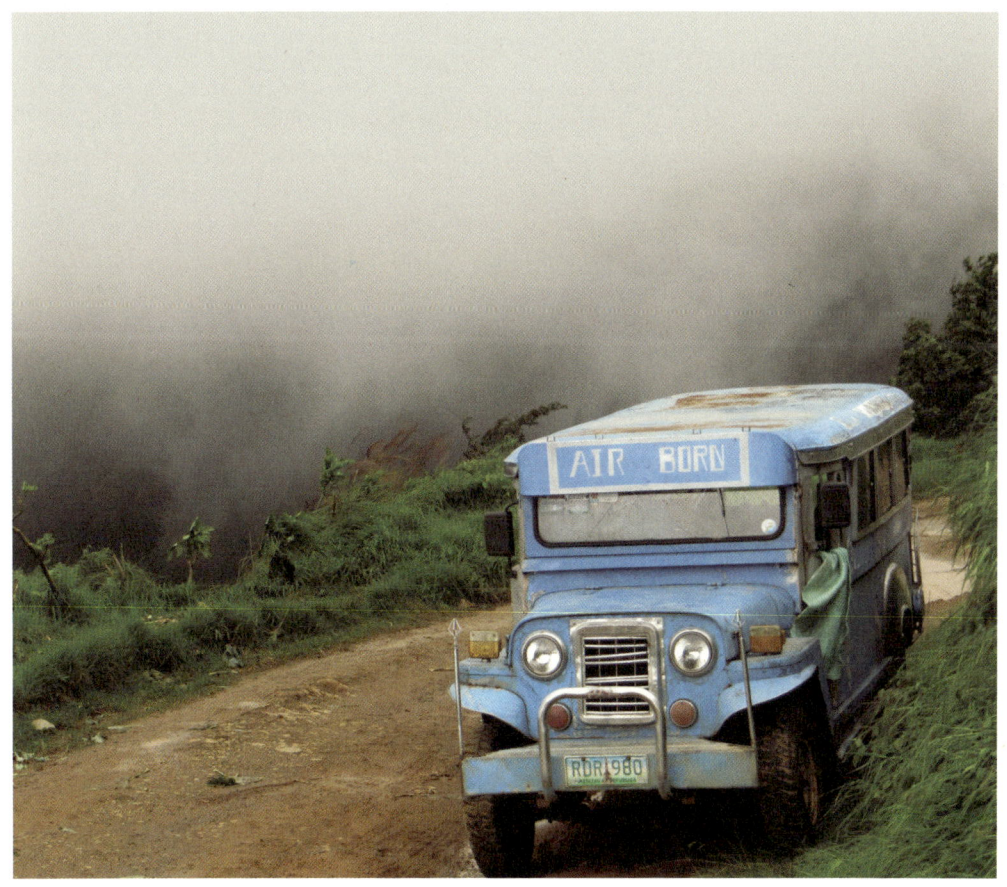

Photograph of a jeepney in *Mt. Santo Tomas*, Tuba, Benguet. Photograph by Kawayan de Guia, 2010.

Ethno-ethos

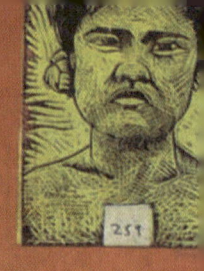
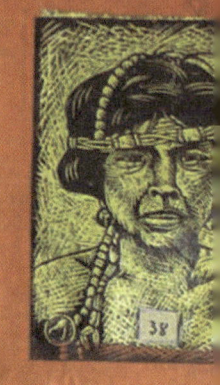

A Spanish friar's quill pen, an American commissioner's typewriter, a British traveler's fountain pen, a Filipino artist's brush. What do they have in common, apart from their being tools a person wields to turn fluid thoughts into fixed markings on paper? In the Gran Cordillera Central of the Philippines, these are some of the many implements by which four centuries of histories and movements of peoples have been set on paper.

Some of these records come out of the colonial ethnography of Spain and the United States of America, and clearly attempt to create orderly narratives out of a world that was, and still is in some ways, a fluid frontier. They tried to place neat boundaries between places and peoples, and saw sharp physical and social delineations where none mattered before. Categorization and boundary-making was part and parcel of the colonial project of subjugation.

Beginning in the 16th century, the first Spanish administrators and friars made a distinction between Spaniards and indios (today's Filipinos), and between indios dociles and indios feroces. They did not simply mean friends or foes, but *"the submissive and the unsubmissive, ...the good and the bad"* (Scott 1982, 40). In the late 18th century, Fr. Francisco Antolin wrote a lengthy manuscript in which he used the words "infieles Igorrotes", pagan Igorots, as a general term for the mountain peoples that had successfully resisted Spanish sovereignty since the crown first claimed the archipelago. (Scott 1988)

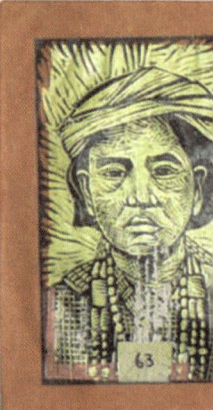

According to Scott, the term Igorot comes from the archaic Tagalog word, golot, which means mountain range. In Bontoc, Kankanay and Ibaloy, igolot means people of golot, or people of the mountain. *"The Spaniards first recorded the term during an expedition to the Baguio gold mines in 1576, and by the 18th century were spelling it igorrote"* (Scott 1988, xiii).

The Spaniards dispatched repeated expeditions in search of the mines, but they failed to yield gold, or to make Catholic, tribute-paying Spanish subjects of the mountain people. There were many punitive Spanish expeditions into the mountains across the centuries. Most were defeated.

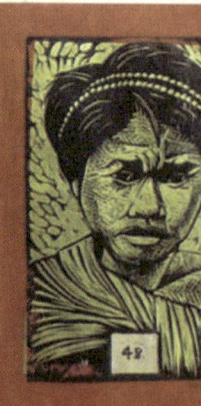

Specimens (series), Leonard Aguinaldo, rubber cut prints, 26x20 cm (each), 2007.

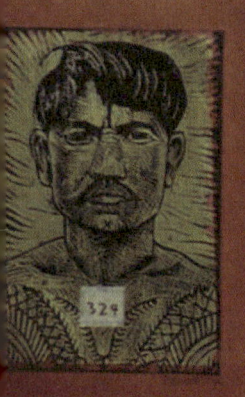
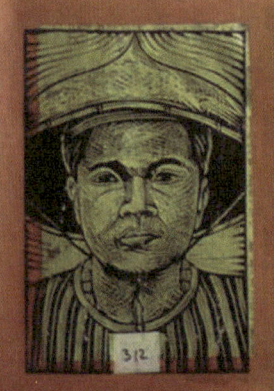
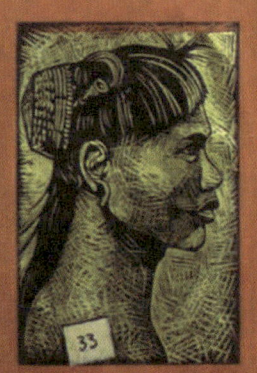
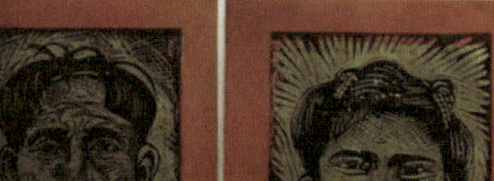
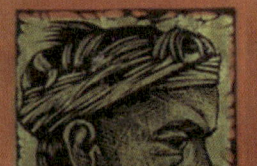
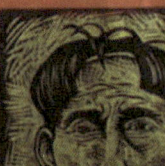

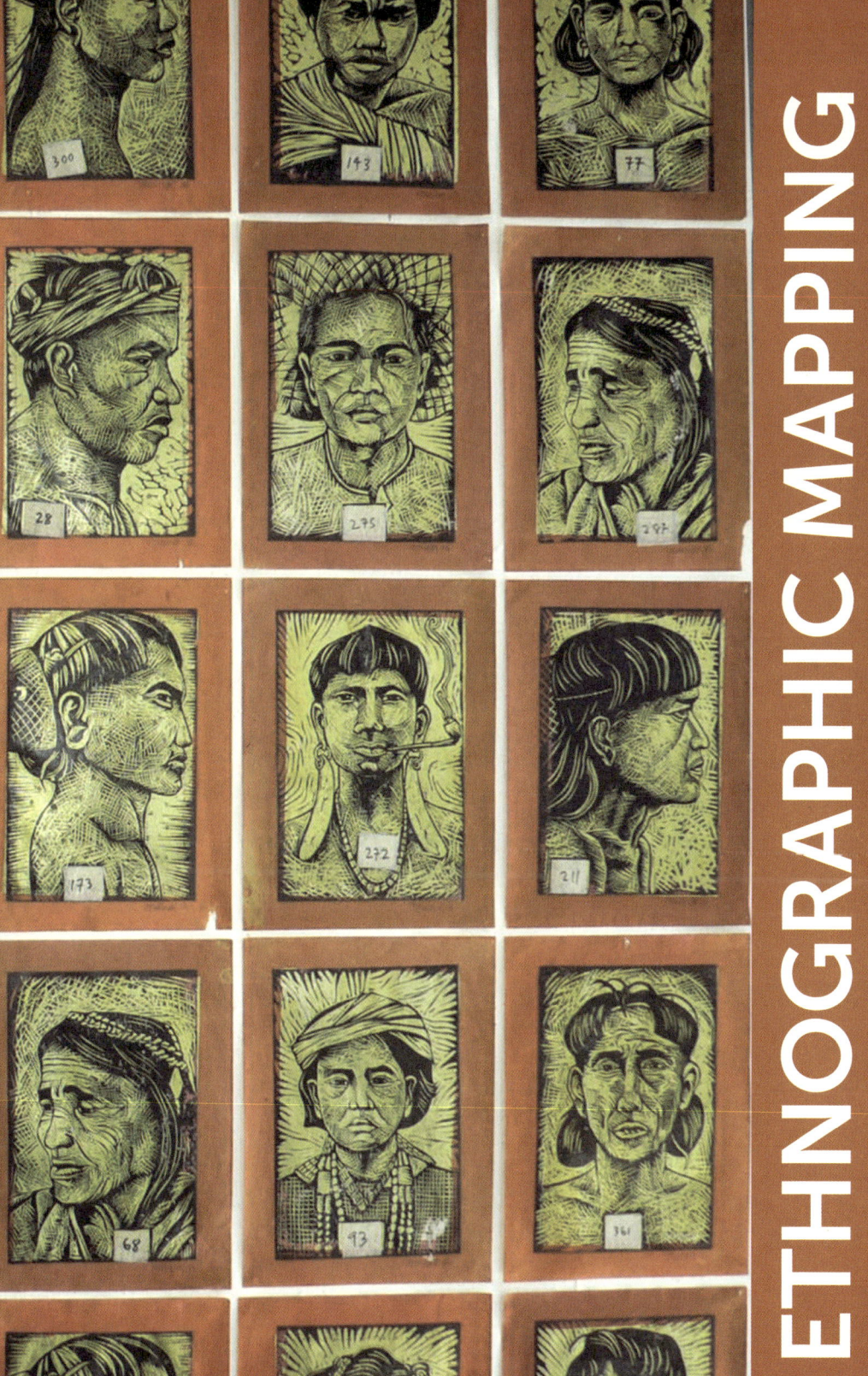

ETHNOGRAPHIC MAPPING

America's age of empire followed close on the heels of the Spanish colonial era. The establishment of the Mountain Province in 1908 put into place an American administrative grid that reflected *"a mode of thinking on the part of American colonial officials characterized by an affinity for packaging the Cordillera's complex historical and cultural realities into neatly compartmentalized bureaucratic structures, thereby allowing for placement of arbitrary social and political boundaries"* (Finin 2005, 14).

The seven sub-provinces of the Mountain Province were Apayao, Kalinga, Bontoc, Lepanto, Ifugao, Amburayan and Benguet. These sub-provinces corresponded to the ethnic boundaries created by Dean C. Worcester, member of the first and second Philippine Commission and Secretary of the Interior, in his attempts to *"scientifically"* classify the peoples of the Cordillera. (Fry, 1983). The sub province of Ifugao, which was created from the Spanish Nueva Vizcaya, was for the 'Ifugao tribe', Kalinga was created for the 'Kalinga tribes', Benguet was for the 'Benguet Igorots', and so on.

This system of classification was based on Worcester's personal perceptions of physical attributes and cultural practices related to war and dance (Finin 2005, 34), and not so much on language or cosmology. In their cataloguing of the "tribes" of the Mountain Province, the Americans classified groups according to evolutionary scales and racial wave migration theories that were current at the time. Today, these same ethnic labels are used by both outsiders and indigenous peoples themselves to refer to the several ethnolinguistic groups of each province.

People, whether they are government administrators, religious fundamentalists, or simple gardeners, make boundaries to separate themselves or to separate matter or certain objects from the rest of the environment. But boundaries are permeable. People create 'holes in fences,' and do things to re-connect what has been separated. Boundaries are places where people meet.

Ethnic identities are not created or maintained out of lack of contact between different societies. On the contrary, when people from different cultures get together, ethnic categories are kept distinct, and differences can sometimes be magnified rather than diminished.

Baguio City, envisioned by the Americans as a colonial hill station, was one such place where people came together, negotiated sameness, and asserted difference. In 1903 the Philippine Commission approved a resolution making *"the town of Baguio, in the province of Benguet, the summer capital of the Archipelago..."* (Reed, 1999, 88). Development plans were laid over the landscape and built over indigenous lands and histories, as though they never existed. (A pattern repeated all over the world.) But they were very much present. The area extending from the present City Hall to Burnham Park and its man-made lake once bore the Ibaloy name, Kafagway (Scheerer 1975, 176).

By the 1920s, Baguio would become quite culturally and socially diverse. Uplanders or Igorots came as traders and laborers, and later, they would come as students, government workers, or indigenous and political leaders. Lowlanders, Ilocanos, Manileño elites, Americans, Chinese, Japanese conducted business here, and tourists from neighboring Southeast Asian colonies came in increasing numbers.

It was to this bustling scene that the writer of "In the Land of the Headhunters" came in 1924. He quoted the following description of the Sunday market from a "local guide book": *"The up-to-date Filipino... mingles with the scantily dressed Benguets, Lepantos, Bontocs, Ifugaos, and occasionally Kalingas... In one corner sturdy natives of the hills will be buying the piece-de-resistance of a coming feast – a dog – which will probably have four or five days hiking over the mountain trails, carefully guarded by its purchasers, before its miserable existence is brought to an end. A little further down a fashionably dressed visitor will be buying curious; across the way, squatting on the ground, smoking a cigar a foot long, will be a native woman haggling over the price of rice or camotes; and next door one of the Baguio housewives will be buying locally-grown strawberries and cabbages; and so on without end"* (Cabrera 1991, 35).

"In the Land of the Headhunters" is an example of the kind of travel writing of its time, with the author (unfortunately his identity could not be found in the manuscript) casting himself as an intrepid explorer and candid observer of his new and exotic surroundings. He describes the locals thusly: *"These Igorot tribesmen fascinate me. They are dark brown in colour, with shapely limbs, but their faces are scarcely handsome – flat-featured, broad-nosed, eyes far apart, and lank black hair. The general aspect of these gentry is fierce and forbidding, as befits their head-hunting reputation..."* (Ibid 27).

National Artist BenCab, more popularly known as BenCab, found the original manuscript in a small antique shop in London in 1977. When Bencab began collecting antiques in the 1960s, his preference was for saintly figures, which many people were collecting at the time, along with Chinese ceramics and pottery. But when he saw sculptural pieces from Ifugao in a 1960's exhibition put up by the late William Beyer, son of anthropologist Otley Beyer, BenCab promptly *"abandoned the santos."* His interest in what he calls *"our original art"* grew while he lived in London from 1969 to 1985. There he was able to acquire rare Filipiniana, such as maps, prints and the abovementioned manuscript.

Unlike other collectors, BenCab usually chooses form and beauty over age. Most collectors will fork out money for a 300-year old, severely degenerated woodcarving, but BenCab will buy a newly made piece if it suits his personal aesthetic. What matters to BenCab is that the pieces he buys should have been at least used, once a part of somebody's life, perhaps part of a ritual, and thereby imbued with spirit and story.

"These are not just 'antiques'," BenCab posits emphatically. *"These are works of art too... (This) art is not studied or schooled, it really comes from the heart."*

BenCab's choices in collecting acknowledge and give value to recent innovations and the present-day creative talents of Cordilleran artists.

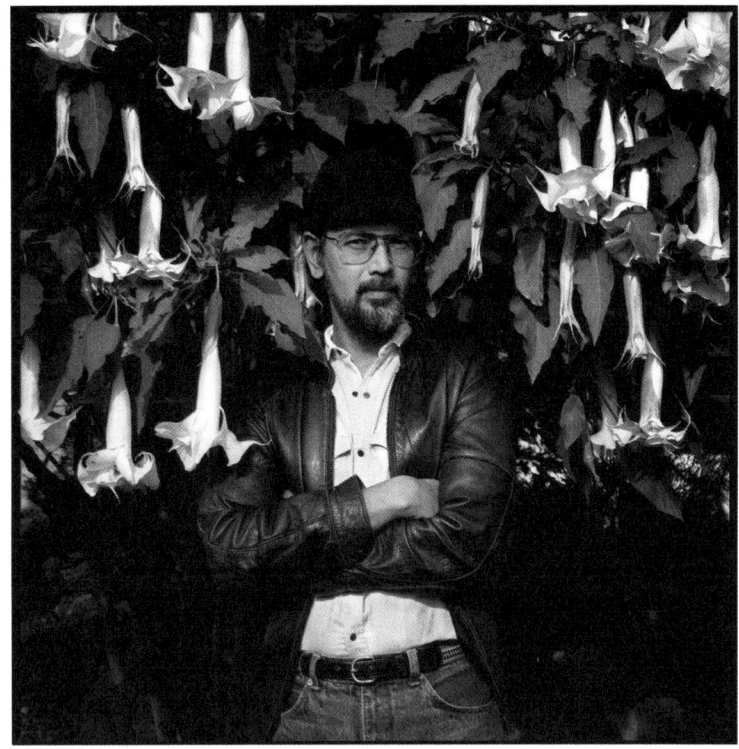

Portrait of national artist BenCab, 1984. Photograph by Wig Tysmans.

"I like transformation," he said.

In his work for the Singapore Biennale 2013 entitled, *I, Baguio*, BenCab depicts the transformation and diversity of Baguio in portraits of different individuals who are originally from here or who have come to this city from all over the Philippines and from other countries. But unlike those before him who describe the ethnic melting pot of Baguio with a colonialist's, ethnographer's or traveler's gaze, BenCab, a Baguio resident since 1986, is no stranger to the cultural landscape where he has built his museum. The museum houses his collection of bulul, tabayag or lime containers, baskets, jars, spears, shields, other Cordilleran objects, and modern Philippine art.

The day before BenCab officially opened his museum in 2009, he arranged for a traditional Ibaloy ritual for the blessing of the museum. Felipe Cornelio, a mambunong, or an Ibaloy ritual specialist, stood beside BenCab and chanted almost inaudibly, informing the spirits of the land that BenCab, who built his house upon this land, was making an offering to them and inviting them to join the feast. In the same breath he also called upon Jesus Christ to bless the sacrifice.

When the mambunong's assistants drove a wooden stake into the sacrificial black pig's heart, its cries pierced the heavens. The mambunong poured tapuy, or local rice brew into a glass, chanted over it quietly, and handed the glass to BenCab, motioning for him to empty it. At this very moment, gongs were heard from the street and a group of Ifugao settlers in their traditional regalia entered the museum grounds. These were elders from Hungduan and Kiangan who had settled in Asin, Tuba and were part of the woodcarving community that lived a few hundred meters from the museum. They were dismayed to see that the pig was slaughtered without them.

The Ibaloys and Ifugaos gathered around the pig and began to debate their ritual rights and rites.

"We came here to perform our ritual blessing for BenCab," said Erlinda Abaggue, one of the more vocal of the Ifugaos.

"But the Ibaloy spirits are dominant here," countered one of the Ibaloys. *"Anyway, we are all the same here. Ifugao, Ibaloy, Igorot, whatever. All the same!"*

Erlinda said with a smile, *"Yes, I-pugo or Ifugao means people, and yes we're all people here, but we must also do our rituals. These are not the same at all. We are still different from each other."*

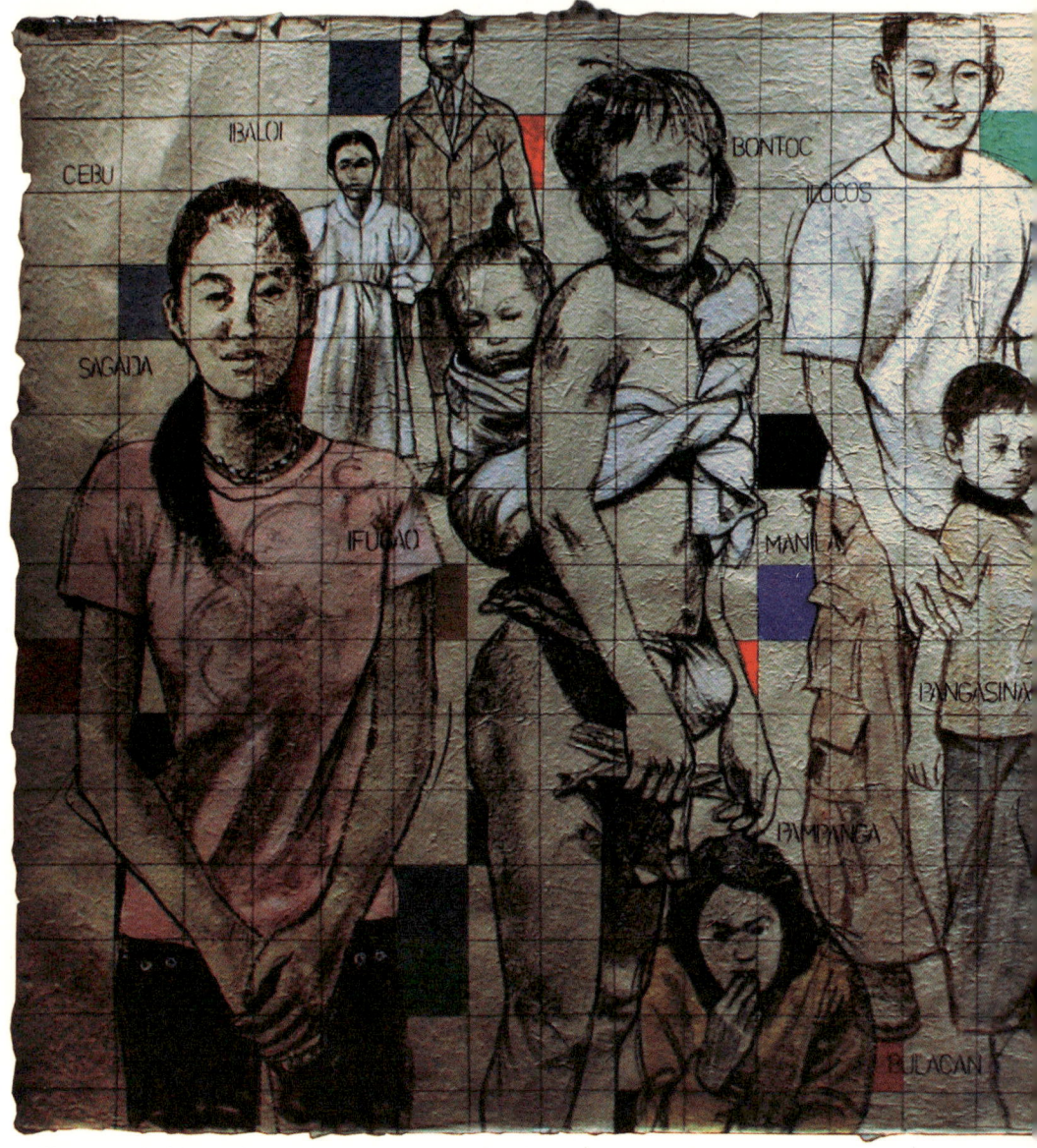

I, Baguio by Benedicto Cabrera, acrylic and pencil on handmade paper, 152x305 cm, 2013.

BenCab intervened and said to the Ifugaos in Filipino, *"We are all migrants here, you and I. It is right that the Ibaloys have the pig this time. But most of the pieces in my Cordilleran collection come from Ifugao, and now they are here in Asin, so if it is alright with you, will you bless them too?"*

This was considered problematic without a pig, but Erlinda agreed that they could chant, play their goings, dance, and offer baya. (Later, BenCab would decide that this should be done properly. He invited the members of the Asin-Ifugao community to return on Easter Sunday for a proper ritual with a pig and chickens.)

With every one placated, the mambunong picked up the liver with the bile sac attached, and explained the reading of the omens to BenCab. BenCab would be protected from bad luck, he would be wealthy, and his good fortune would stay with him.

Then the mambunong took a large wooden bowl filled with the pig's blood and briskly marked with blood the doorways and windows, and the frames, sides, or the walls of each painting in the museum, chanting to the spirits and Jesus all the while. The mambunong told BenCab to clean up after the ritual.

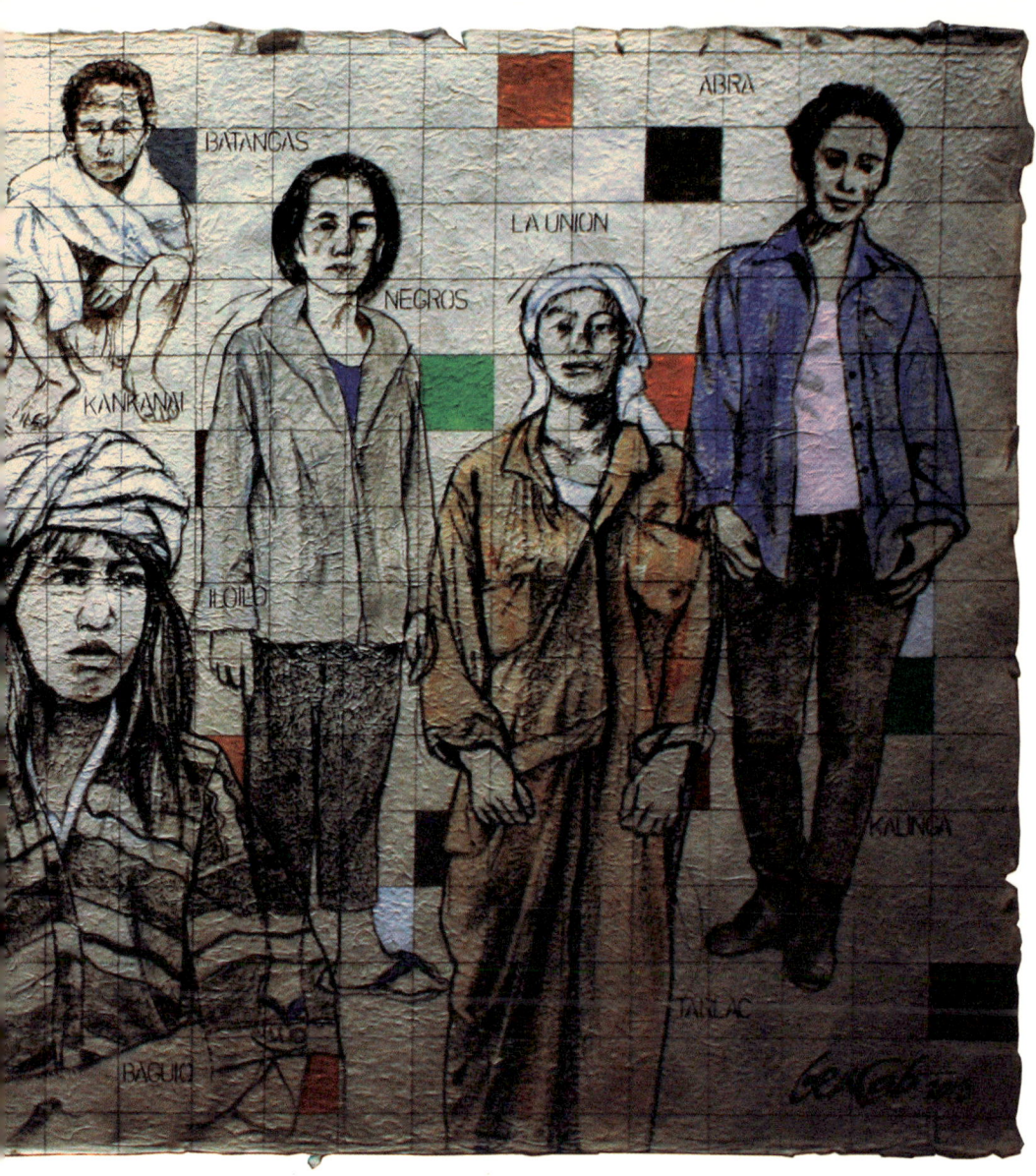

When they re-emerged the mambunong anointed BenCab's cheeks and head with pig's blood. Then, Romeo Buyagaw, mumbaki or Ifugao ritual specialist, cried out in a powerful voice whilst waving a bundle of purple dongla leaves at the museum. He called on the spirits to shower blessings on every person present, especially BenCab and his family. He called on the spirits to make the seeds planted by BenCab grow strong and bear fruit. He called on them to make the animals fed by BenCab multiply and be healthy. When he lowered the dongla leaves, the men struck the gongs loudly and in a graceful meandering line, the Ifugao men and women danced through the museum, pausing before the wall of towering bulul and in the Cordillera Gallery to chant and dance some more.

Afterwards, BenCab joined both the Ifugaos and then the Ibaloys in playing the gongs and dancing the traditional festive dances. Of his respect for the peoples of the Cordillera, National Artist BenCab said, *"I'm the one who's 'born-again.' I'm a born-again pagan."* PLP.

(Parts of this article are based on my previous piece, "Mambunongs, Mumbakis and National Artists." Philippine Daily Inquirer, January 27, 2009.)

See also: Annual Headhunter's Fund; Bureau of Non-Christian Tribes; Tattoo; Tribes; Worcester, Dean.

The Inside-outer

They say that for one to have a clear idea of the bigger picture you have to take a step back. Perhaps assume the position of not having encountered the picture at all – the outsider's point of view – to be naked of bias. In a culture like the Cordilleran culture, BenCab, best known to capture the perfect portrait, is that perfect eye – born a Pampagueño, one time a London immigrant, but now a Baguio boy at heart.

Ben is a perfectionist. A highly skilled, disciplined man, and with the price that comes with that, usually: a list of particulars to work to his standard and to get his agreement to join a project. For his art work he wanted this specific hand-made paper that Butch Perez had brought in from Kathmandu in 1997, which, uncannily, I had seen myself once upon a time, so I knew exactly what he was talking about. If I could find the paper it might be somewhat easier, or so I thought, to get him to join. Of course this was the half-eaten sandwich. An accomplishment to know what was required, but it wouldn't be easy finding something that had been lost for almost two decades.

I was this close to losing my mind, having learned that the paper had been missing for years. That paper was the only way to get Ben to start painting, and all-the-while the show was fast approaching. Time is always a pressure, but for this, my heart was beating right into my neck: no paper, no work! It brought me to belligerently bugging the hell out of poor Butch, who, with no further hope of finding that paper, had closed the door to his study, only to find it there! Standing this whole time behind that goddamn door. Eureka!

BenCab, who has been for decades, much-aware of his preferred practice in art, did not take long to fix on the intention of this work, which was to successfully take the viewer into using his, BenCab's, lens and to turn into an insider-while-being-the-outsider, looking at the 'natives' of Baguio. But who, today, are true Baguio natives? Due to countless migrations and back migrations, they are all mixed and changed. Clans and tribes and cultures from the highlands and the lowlands all intermarried. They intermingle. The whole city has become an entire planet on its own. In it live the most beautiful and colorful of people.

A vast variety of flora thrive too. Ben also dotes on his plants like a father would. His hands, that have crafted the masterpieces the world knows him for, also have green thumbs sticking out at their sides. He creates Bonsai and, lately, herbs and organic produce on the land surrounding his museum.

Ben, an 'outsider' to the culture of the Cordillera, has one of the largest collections of Cordilleran artifacts in the country housed in his museum of contemporary and indigenous art – the biggest of its kind in Baguio. He served as a purveyor for the beauty of Cordillera artifacts for most of us. Take for example his fondness for the little Tabayag (lime container). Nobody had taken a deeper interest in it until BenCab opened our eyes to its charm.

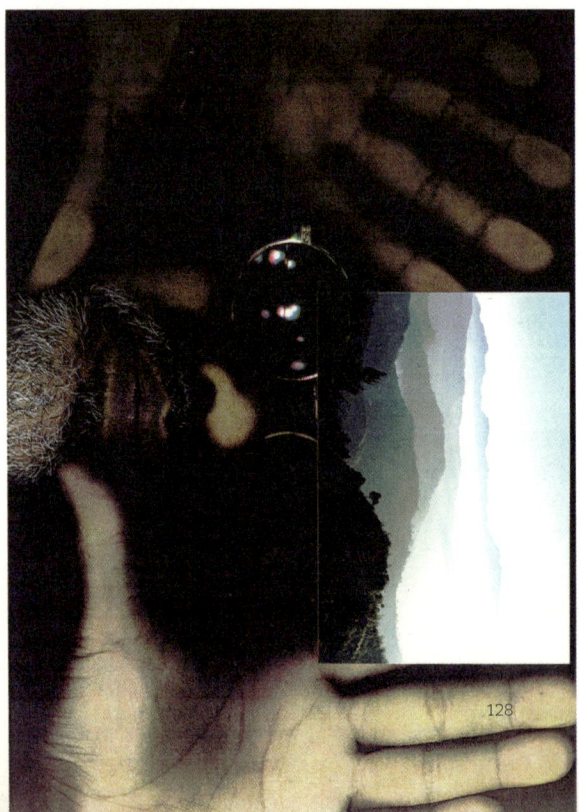

He is an architect, consistently at that, whichever spectrum of creation he chooses to decode. For a man of such skills, his interest and dedication never wanes. It only grows exponentially. Like the seeds he sows, his achievements are a forest that he has masterfully grown. An artist like this is only limited by the eye of his imagination. But what people don't see in this famous man is the person, who, like a Zen Master, chooses to remain simple, his feet firmly planted on the ground. From this position BenCab says: *"I am a National Artist, not an international one."* BenCab can see and draw beyond the typical interpretations of a sense of belonging. KDG

Scanned self-portrait by artist BenCab.

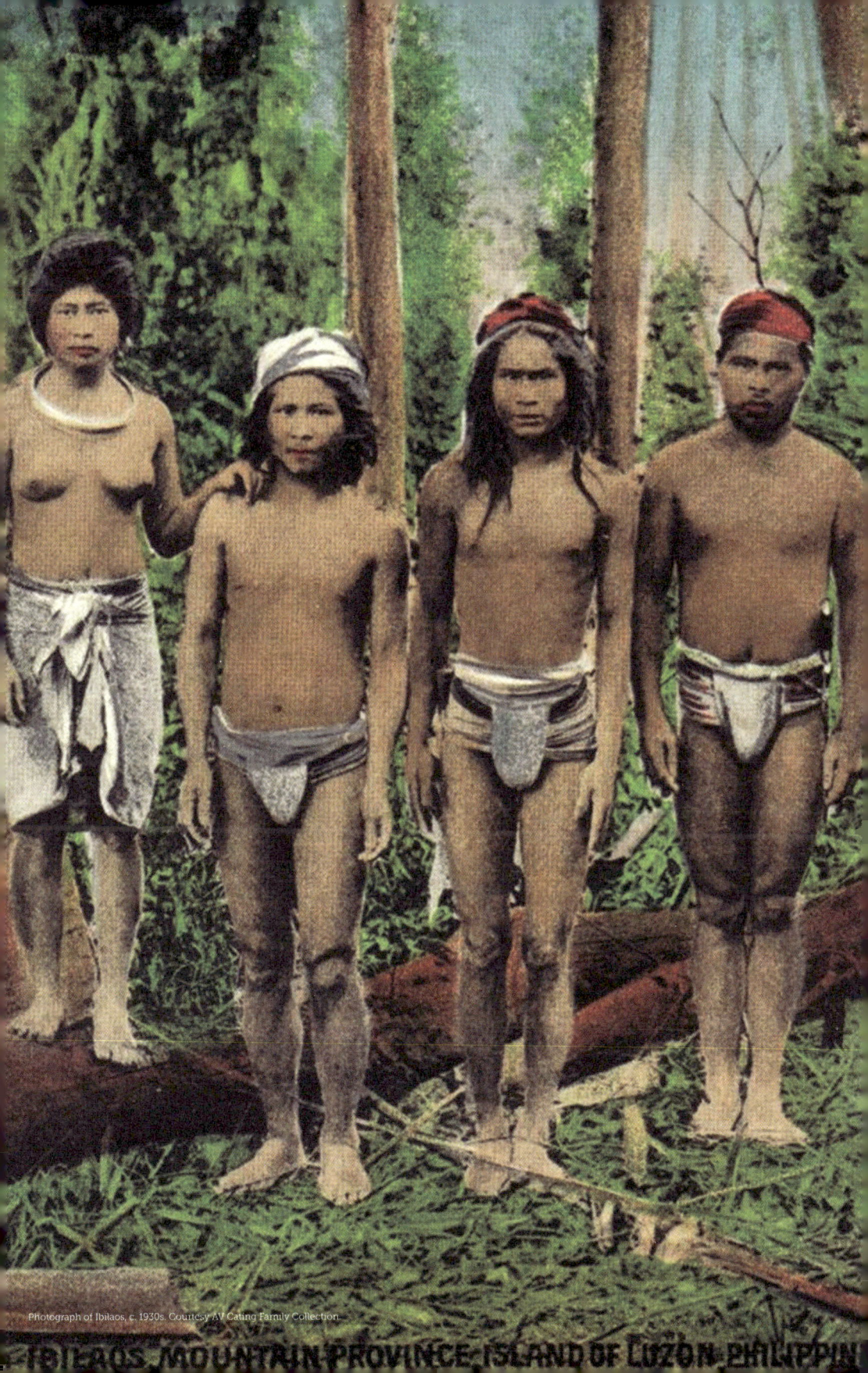

Photograph of Ibilaos, c. 1930s. Courtesy AV Cating Family Collection.

IBILAOS, MOUNTAIN PROVINCE, ISLAND OF LUZON, PHILIPPIN

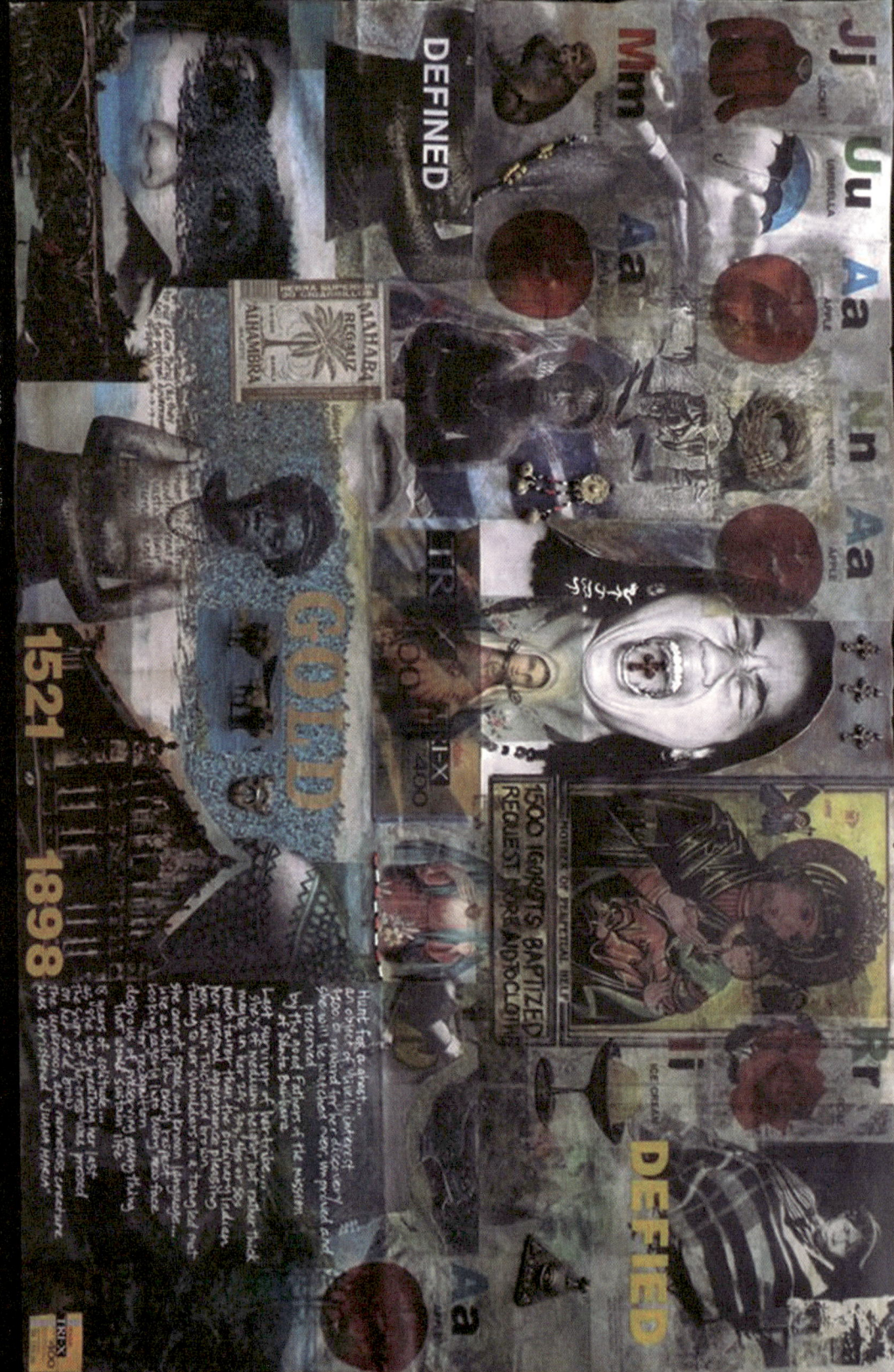

Connecting History in the Kodak Zone, Angel Shaw, mixed media, 61×91 cm, 1998. Courtesy Angel Shaw.

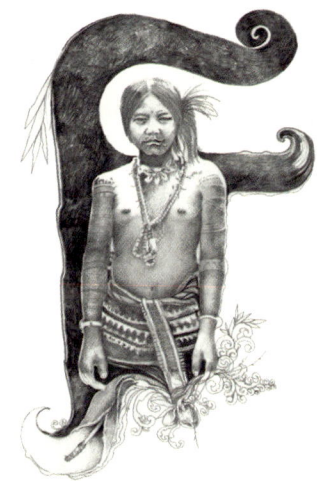

Fagfagto *(BON)* also **Bagbagto** *(BON/KAN)*.
(1) *"A man's rock fight between the men of Bontoc and Samoki. The battle is in the broad bed of the river between the two pueblos. The men go to the conflict armed with war shields, and they pelt each other with rocks as seriously as in actual war. There is a man now in Bontoc whose leg was broken in the conflict of 1901, and three of our four Igorot servant boys had scalp wounds received in lis-lis rock conflicts."* (Jenks 2005).
(2) *(KAN)*. In Sagada's bagbag-to, they use mud balls instead of rocks. TDH.

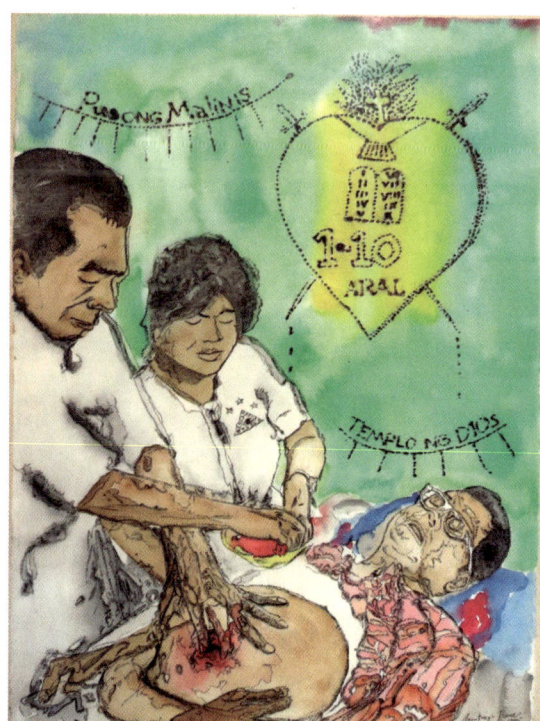

Artwork by Santiago Bose, 1995.

Faith Healing. Call them 'magicians of God,' 'medical charlatans' or 'psychic surgeons,' faith healers in Baguio contributed to the city's golden age of tourism in the 1970s and 1980s. During those decades, Loakan Airport was always full of Russians, Europeans, Americans and occasional Japanese wanting to be treated by these last-minute miracle workers. The taxi drivers were the best advertisers bringing passengers to the house of the faith healer that paid them for advertising. The most important faith healers in Baguio in those decades were Tony Agpaoa, Jun Labo, Placido Palitayan, Jose Segundo and Martin Caoili. Agpaoa later bought the Dominican Seminary on Dominican Hill and turned it into the Dominican Hotel. Jun Labo became the personal faith healer of President Ferdinand Marcos and was later elected as Baguio Mayor. From the 90s up to the present, the notable faith healers have been Johann Paquito, Laurence Cacteng, Mike Guinsadan, Joseph Calano and Alex Ampaguey. The Baguio Healing Circle was formed in 1994 to support the healers since they would often go abroad to heal clients. In 1995, the tourism department frowned upon the promotion of faith healers and so most faith healers decided to go to Europe, India, Russia, Australia and the US to do their healing. Most 'heal on the run' to evade authorities who sometimes accuse them of being quacks. Some, such as those who went to Poland, became captive workers of their promoters. Some patients continue to come to Baguio for 'miracle cures.' The most famous of the clients who came to Baguio was the late comedian Andy Kaufman who even included his meeting with Jun Labo at the end of his movie. It was the last laugh of the absurdist comedian but Labo pretended he had never had him as his patient. FYC.

Faked *(BON)*. Bamboo stripped and tied and stretched together across the rice bed to drive away the birds.
See also: Bading; Pasok.

Fakil *(BON)*. *"The Fa-kil' ceremony for rain occurs four times each year, on four succeeding days, and is performed by four different priests. The ceremony is simple. There is the usual ceremonial pig killing by the priest, and each night preceding the ceremony all the people cry: 'I-těng'-ao ta-ko nan fa-kīl' This is only an exclamation, meaning, 'Rest day! We observe the ceremony for rain!' I was informed that the priest has no separate oral petition or ceremony, though it is probable that he has."* (Jenks 2005).
See also: Manerwap; Tengngay.

Fakingol *(BON)*. Orchids.

Fakwit *(BON)* also **Bakwit** *(KAN)*. A corruption of the word 'evacuate.' (1) The period during World War II when all the main towns were evacuated. Some people lived in forests or caves where they cultivated patches of camote and other staples. They clothed themselves in pounded bark that was itchy but provided good camouflage. RAC.

(2) Evacuees in recent natural calamities like the 1990 earthquakes, strong typhoons, and landslides. HZK.
See also: Gingined; Landslide.

Faliling *(BON)*. The time to make camote beds.
See also: Agkufangfang; Camote.

Fallai *(BON)*. Black pigment (e.g. guava charcoal) used to color teeth.
See also: Cloth Dyes; Xamata.

Falokag *(BON)*. A leaf made into a funnel to hold snails.
See also: Agudong id Manitong; Atubang; Bisukol; Golden Kuhol; Ket-an; Lisdeg.

Fatang *(BON)*. A tall pine tree with few branches.
See also: Batang; Talang; Tree Cutting.

Feclat *(BON)*. Python or large snake. The traditional cinafay feclat (roasted python) includes stuffing the snake with palongpong (a Cordillera vine) to remove the slimy taste. It is cooked by roasting it chopped or whole.

Fikek *(BON)* also **Bio** *(IFU)*, **Whinuur** *(KAL)*. Goiters were already a common affliction known as fikek or fintokel among Cordillerans in ancient times. It was said that tattooing a cross hatch design over the goiter could check its growth. In the 1980s, iodized salt was introduced by the government to control goiter in the highlands. FYC.
See also: Salt Trade.

Finabdas *(BON)*. Red clouds at sunset.
See also: Cloud Atlas; Hinag; Libuo.

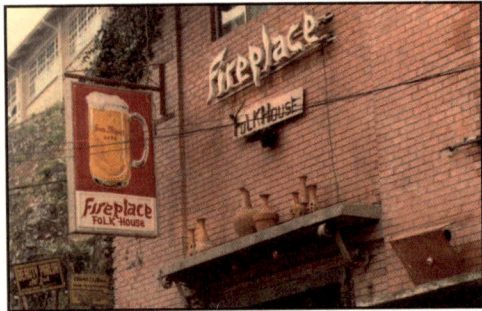

Photograph of *Fireplace* in the corner of Session and Assumption Roads, Baguio. Courtesy Frank Cimatu.

Fireplace. The birthplace of Baguio folksingers who sang better than Simon Garfunkel or John Denver (or any of their American counterparts). It was located at the corner of Session Road and Assumption Road and was the Mecca of folk singing in Baguio. Designed by Architect George Salvan, it was the coziest dating habitat: it had a big fireplace (you would sing above it) that was nostalgic for Manila vacationists, foreign backpackers and locals alike. It was a nightspot landmark where singing lawyers, jazz-playing optometrists and Benguet rockers sang American hits long after they became passé. And yes, not-a-few Baguio-boy folksingers sang their way into the lonely hearts of backpackers (who eventually got them spousal visas to the land of promise). From the 1970s to the 1980s, folk music was popular in Baguio and 'folkhouses' like The Fireplace, Gingerbreadman (later known as The Cuckoo's Nest), Tic-Tac-Toe, Cozy Nook, Harpo's, Music Box, Capriccio, and the Lone Star in Camp John Hay were all the rage. According to journalist-folksinger March Fianza, they were called folkhouses *"maybe because the performers sung a broad mixture of American folk music, folk-jazz, folk-country, folk-rock and other similar genres. Or maybe the nightspots were called folkhouses then because a majority of their regular crowd consisted of common people – students, professionals, government workers, farmers from nearby towns in Benguet Province, foreign and local tourists, US Peace Corps volunteers, and neighborhood drunks, of course."* KT/FYC.
See also: Ayuyang; Bontoc Bar; Cowboy; Folk Music.

Fire tree also **Caballero, Flame tree, Flamboyant tree.** Sp. Delonix regia. A large, deciduous tree with fern-like leaves and flowers that are large, showy, red, or red and yellow. It was introduced to the Philippines during the early Spanish period. When they blossomed, it was traditionally a signal for headtaking among the Ilongots. Newspapers near the area in the 1970s still published photos of the flowering fire trees as a warning for outsiders to leave Ilongot country. FYC.

Fischer, Bobby. The legendary American chess champion stayed in Baguio from 2000 to 2002 after the United States issued an arrest warrant against him for playing a USD5 million match series against Viktor Korchnoi in Yugoslavia in 1992. Fischer won but never set foot in his homeland again. Because Filipino Grandmaster and Baguio resident Eugene Torre was his friend, Fischer decided to stay in Baguio. While here, he was introduced by Torre to then 22-year-old Marilyn Young (aka Janice Ong) of Zamboanga and they had a daughter named Jinky Young who was born in Baguio (a DNA test in 2010, however, said that Fischer wasn't the father although the Youngs filed a protest). On September 11, 2001, right after the terrorist attacks in New York, Fischer went on air at the local Bombo Radyo and repeatedly applauded the acts and condemned the US and Israel. Chess players at Igorot Park remember that someone who looked like Fischer would watch over them, mumbling, but he never played. FYC.
See also: Baguio Convention Center.

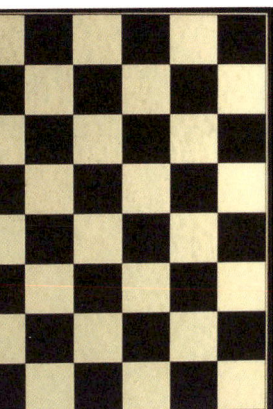

Excerpted from Bobby Fischer 9/11 Interview with Bombo Radyo Baguio

Mercado: We have on the line one of our friends we used to interview every now and then for the past several years, uh, I think for the past two years already. We have a chess grandmaster, the World Chess Champion Bobby Fischer. He's on the line right now and would like to give some thoughts of his own opinion, his global commentary on what happened at the World Trade Center just about a few hours ago, including attack of the White House and I think the Pentagon too, right? In fact, right now, Bobby, good day. It's evening right here.

Fischer: Yeah, how are you doing, Pablo? Yes, well, this is all wonderful news. It's time for the fucking US to get their heads kicked in. It's time to finish off the US once and for all.

Mercado: Of course, everybody knows how you... uh... how you...

Fischer: You know, I heard on the BBC a few months ago a very profound, but simple, statement. It really stunned me, I couldn't believe that guy was saying, you know, talking about some of the crimes of the US. You know, of the horrible behavior that the US is committing all over the world, and there the BBC guy just said it! I couldn't believe my ears! This just shows you that what goes around comes around, even for the United States. That is what has happened tonight. What goes around comes around, even for the United States.

Flat Earth. *"The earth, which is very flat, was made by the great spirit Kadaklan. He also made the sun and moon, which chase each other over and under the earth. Sometimes the moon almost catches the sun, but it always gets tired and gives up before it succeeds. The sun and moon are the lights of Kadaklan and so are the stones which are stars. The dog of Kadaklan is the lightning."* (Cole (1915) 2004).

See also: Kadaklan.

Flood, The Story of the. A story common to most if not all of the Cordillera that tells of the origin of current communities. As many versions of this story exist as there are storytellers (as though to make-up for the rarity of creation stories). Each community's tale starts with a Great Flood that blankets everything in water save a mountain peak or two. Generally, only a man and a woman (brother and sister in the Bontoc version) survive the flood, either both on the highest peak or separated on two peaks. Details vary on what they did, what they said to each other, and whether they liked each other instantly or not. Other versions include a dog that acts as messenger carrying a lit piece of firewood tied to its tail between the survivor on peak A and the other survivor on peak B. When the waters subside, man and woman (and dog, if present) descend from the peak/s, live together, and multiply. Today's people are their descendants. GAD.

Fogwah *(IFU).* Death anniversary.

Folk Music:
Baguio Folksingers

They still find time to play music together although many of them are successful in their selected fields. More than a dozen have migrated to the USA in search of better opportunities and protection in 'Uncle Sam's Arms' while the rest of the bunch preferred to be busy with their jobs in Baguio or elsewhere in the Philippines. Some of them remained in the music business and never stopped playing.

I am referring to the singers and musicians of the 1970s and 1980s who were the fixtures in the watering holes and restaurants-cum-liquor bars in Baguio City. These particular shops called 'folkhouses' were The Fireplace, Gingerbreadman which metamorphosed into The Cuckoo's Nest, Tic-Tac-Toe, Cozy Nook, Harpo's, Music Box, Cappriccio, and the Lone Star in Camp John Hay to name only a selection.

Ironically, singing, which they were best at and which they have been doing for four decades now, has made them the 'unsung heroes' of today. Their unity and bond became tighter while practicing for one of the first Baguio 'all-star cast' concert "May You Stay Forever Young," a song title borrowed from Bob Dylan, on December 10, 1977.

Many of Baguio's part-time folksingers in the 1970s sung their first song at The Fireplace or at The Gingerbreadman before scouting for extra singing slots in other folkhouses. The Fireplace and Gingerbreadman folkhouses practically served as training grounds for many folksingers in Baguio.

The Fireplace was where Filipino singer-composer-artist Tito Mina, now an expat in Germany, sang "Early Morning Rain" by Gordon Lightfoot, "Don't Think Twice, It's Alright" by Dylan and "You Can Close Your Eyes" by James Taylor, before he wrote his Filipino hit song "Ikaw Pa Rin."

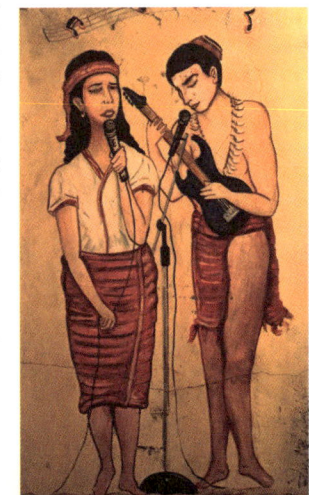

Photograph of a mural inside a bar in Baguio City. Photograph by Kawayan de Guia.

Singing as a part-time job went towards school fees for many of us. I know that because I was one who skipped late evening classes, once in a while, in order to play my sets. Bubut Olarte, a lawyer now for 30 years and a candidate in a past election, admitted that a big part of his law studies were supported by his singing.

Most of the singers at The Fireplace did not formally study music. But, their natural talents pulled them together such that the singing they did sounded so amazing a new duet or trio or quartet, could be formed right away during rehearsals.

'For-a-cause' concerts or benefit shows were familiar to the early singers of The Fireplace, Gingerbreadman or Cuckoo's Nest. As far as I can recall, we performed the first-ever benefit concerts in the Cordillera. In December 1977, the group that was once called the Baguio Musicians' Guild performed in Banawe, Kiangan and Lagawe in Ifugao; and at the Lepanto Mining Co. in the town of Mankayan, Benguet during the cold month of January 1978. These were replicated by another show at the University of the Philippines, Los Baños that benefited the Green Mountain Circle, an organization of students from the Cordillera Region.

Today, even while most of their time is occupied by work, the musicians and singers find themselves playing at benefit concerts for heart, kidney and cancer patients, or for any good cause. The reality is that the 'for-a-cause' musical event has already developed into a community effort. Just like the Baguio musicians who are scattered in the US, Canada, Europe and Asia, benefit concerts have come a long way. MF.

See also: Music; Cowboy; Country Music; Fireplace; Ayuyang; Bontoc Cafe.

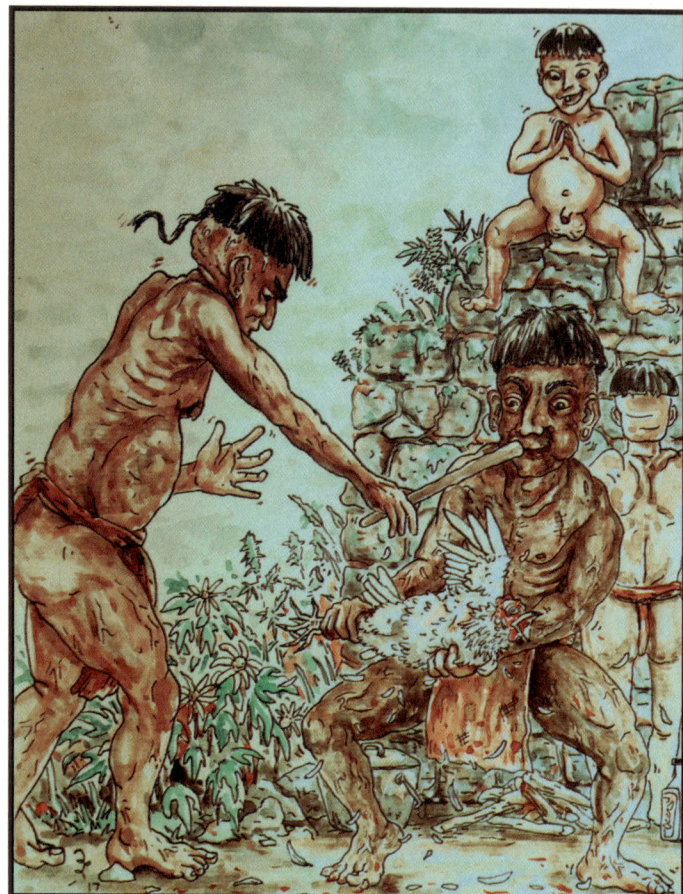
Pinikpikan, Robert Langenegger, watercolor and ink on paper, 27x21 cm, 2017.

Folu *(BON).* Giant bamboo found mostly in very wet areas.

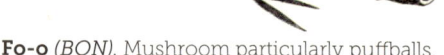

Fo-o *(BON).* Mushroom particularly puffballs.

Food:
On a Quest for Cordillera Cuisine

In the voyage that is my culinary career, I have been on several rewarding trips to the Cordillera mountain range. My simple task has usually been to cook for groups of fellow artists that travel to the mountains for workshops and interactions with the communities, or to participate in local festivities. With each trip, a vision unfolds and presents itself, clearly marking the path towards a goal: to explore indigenous culinary cultures and bring them into our home kitchens. This mission begins in my own kitchen.

Festive, community-centered, engaging, generous – that is how I would describe Cordillera cuisine based on my first-hand experience with communities here. The cultures of the Cordilleras are deeply rooted in the cultivation of rice and an intimate relationship with the environment through foraging and swidden agriculture. It is awe-inspiring the way in which these proud indigenous peoples uphold and preserve their culture and selectively block a total lowland cultural invasion. In this piece I share the little that I already know about key foods found and prepared in Cordilleran kitchens, terraces, gardens and forests: rice, watercress, mushrooms, root crops, and preserved meat.

All Rise for Cordillera Rice

Rice cultivation is a way of life – an art of living that indigenous peoples mastered since time immemorial. Numerous festive rituals have to do with the rice growing cycle, from the lukya rituals, which means 'opening,' marking the start of the planting season; to the kahiw rituals, where the rice cycle ends with thanksgiving for a bountiful harvest and for replenishment of rice granaries. Embedded within this cycle of living are simple yet bountiful practices of food preparation and consumption.

There are about 300 recorded rice species in the Cordilleras. In Ifugao, three broad terms for some of the varieties are : tinawon, unoy, and ulikan. The story of the tinawon rice speaks of the history of Ifugao rice. Liddum, a major god of Kabunyan (Skyworld), traded his aromatic large grain rice tinawon for fire with Wigan and his brother Kabigat,the son of Pudol (another ancestor of the Ifugao people). Wigan showed Liddum and the rest of the raw-eating Kabunyans how fire changed the taste of food (by the process we otherwise know as cooking).

Tangy Tangsuy

While tungsuy (watercress) is the oldest green vegetable known to man, not many Filipinos are familiar with its taste or appearance. This legendary cancer-fighter is not usually available in local markets below the cool climates of the North, and can only be stored fresh for a very short period of time. In the Cordillera, watercress grows wildly along and around the famously well-engineered irrigation systems of the mountain rice terraces. This semi-aquatic plant is botanically related to more common vegetables like mustard and radish. It has a peppery, tangy flavor that livens up salads and soups.

Watercress has been called a superfood and it would be nice to have it as a staple vegetable in every home kitchen. It can be used in any soupy poultry, pork, beef or fish dish. It can also be used in salads or in sandwiches. It can be served with omelet or quiche, or paired with fried protein.

Magic Mushrooms

There are quite a number of edible, wild mushrooms that grow freely in the low, moist temperatures of the region. Among these is the great bitbitli (fitfitli). These wild mushrooms are boiled prior to cooking to rid them of impurities. Like magic, they will slowly turn into a sharp shade of blue when sliced. This flavorful mushroom can be simply sautéed with garlic and onions.

Farmed Fibers and Homespun Starches

While mushrooms and watercress grow in the wild, there are other vegetables grown by farming on a household level. Eighty percent of Cordillerans are engaged in agricultural activity for both commercial production and subsistence. Cordilleran households always have the freshest ingredients ready for picking.

A Touch of Itag and Kiniing

While lowland kitchens are infiltrated by commercially available MSG-flavored enhancers like Knorr cubes or sachets like Maggi's Magic Sarap, folks in the Cordillera still use traditional, all-natural, home-cured itag (or etag). This is salted pork that is cured and aged underground in earthen jars, or hung and sundried in home kitchens.

Itag is bursting with good flavor and works best as a flavor-enhancer when dropped into soups and stews, or fried to a crisp and drizzled in small bits over non-sauce dishes and salads.

Kiniing is similar to itag but smoked. I call it Cordillera bacon. I use this indigenous ingredient the same way itag is used. It is also nice to use kiniing as one would use cured meats such as Prosciutto, Jamon Iberico, Salami and other hams and bacon. As a quick hunger-buster, I simply cut thin bacon-slices of kiniing to fry and eat with rice. CVR.

See also: Camote; Etag; Inasin; Intum; Pinuneg; Safeng; Sichot; Sinag-et; Sinaplak; Suwit.

Fuas *(BON)* also **Potong** *(ISN)*. Bamboo tube used as a pitcher for basi or tapuey. Potong is also used to store honey.

See also: Apag; Basi; Pitik; Taliwan.

Fukas *(BON/IFU)*. The large rectangular double spacers on Ifugao heirloom necklaces with duli (snake bones) or carnelian beads as the main strands. The fukas are made from white marble traded from the lowlands, which the Bontocs later cut and shaped as fukas. The last known Bontoc fukas cutter died in 1990. FYC.

See also: Apang; Bungol; Dalanasip; Ong-ong; Tsuli.

Fulifug *(BON)*. Pine cone.

Fungais *(KAL)*. A sneeze. It can be interpreted in many ways by the Kalinga. Sneezing before throwing a spear while hunting promises a sure hit. A person about to leave the house who sneezed would have to wait and postpone travelling. HZK.

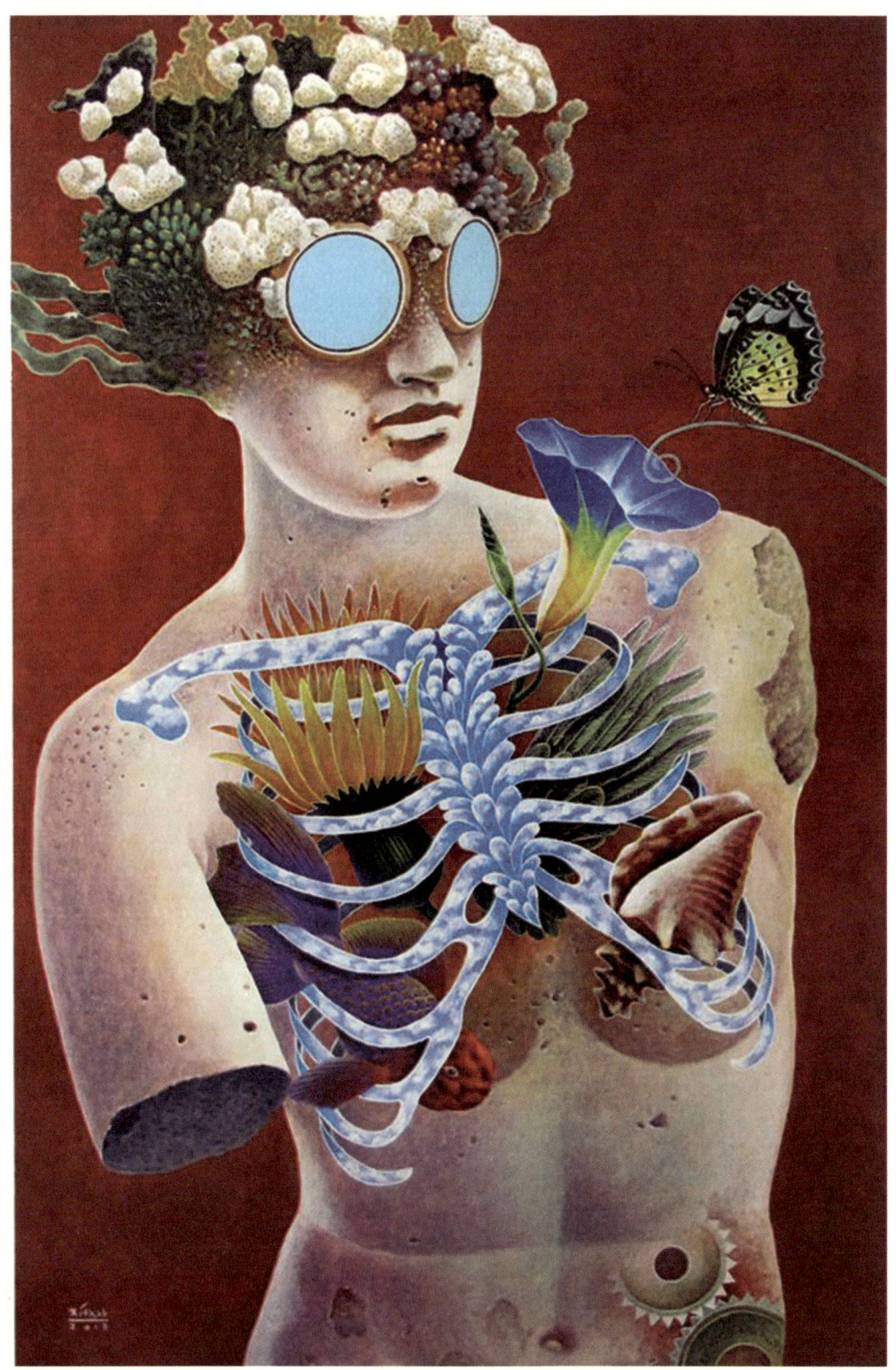

Venus, Rishab Tibon, acrylic on canvas, 91x61 cm, 2013.

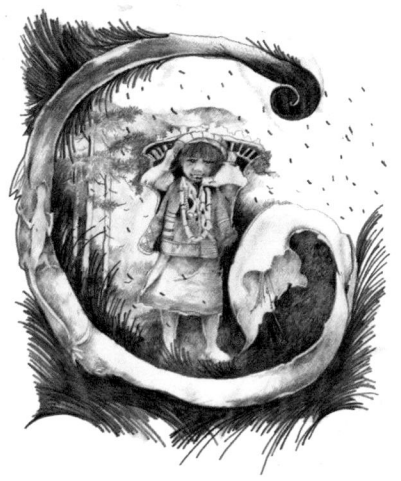

Gateway to Wonderland. Baguio City as referred to by Bontoc Deputy Gov. Samuel Kane in his 1931 travel guide. FYC.
See also: Baguio, The Naming of; White Elephant.

Gawis. Good or blessing. Sagada's St. Mary's School's motto is *"Adi tako bokodan di gawis [Let us not be selfish with our blessings]."* FYC.

Gayunan *(KAL)*.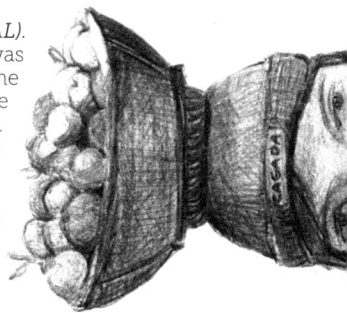
Orange. The fruit was introduced to the Cordilleras by the Spaniards via Kalinga. Balbalan was the prime source of oranges thus the popular 'Kalinga oranges' of the 1970s. In the 1990s, Balbalan councilors unsuccessfully tried to change their town's name (Balbalan refers to where they wash their head axes after headtaking) to Gayunan, the Kalinga term for oranges. Valencia orange cultivation was introduced to Sagada by the Abellas in the 1980s. Though greener than their Kalinga counterpart, Sagada oranges are larger and more luscious. They have since replaced the popularity of Kalinga oranges in the Baguio market so much so that even non-Sagada oranges coming mostly from China are now labeled as "Sagada oranges" not only in the Baguio City Market but even in Sagada. Table grapes, lychees, and apples, which are not produced commercially in Sagada, are also branded 'Sagada' at the Baguio market by itinerant vendors. FYC.
See also: Balbalasang; Persimmon.

Gagaban. An Igorot chieftain and the first Filipino to fly in an airplane. Gagaban rode with Lee Hammond, an American pilot, aboard a Red Devil biplane over Luneta Park on February 12, 1912 during the 1912 Manila Carnival. FYC.

Gaganayan *(IFU)*. The constellation of Orion used by the Ifugaos to time their planting season.

Gagaom *(IFU)*. Funeral shroud.

Galvey, Guillermo. Comandante General de Igorottes Guillermo Galvey came to La Trinidad, Benguet in 1829 and fell in love with the place. *"The soil was very well cultivated, with immense fields of sweet potatoes, gabe, and sugar cane, but I saw no paddy in this tract of land. All was well irrigated and fenced in by dividing lines of the earth after the manner of Spain, and provided with wells. The houses, which numbered some 500, were of broad pine boards but very dirty. It is in this valley that I have proposed to establish the capital of the district."* (Scheerer 1905). He named it La Trinidad after his wife, and then in the style of Spanish conquistadores of the past, burned and pillaged and decimated the land. He would make 44 more destructive expeditions to the Cordillera until his death ten years later. He was regarded as the greatest despoiler Spain had ever brought to the Cordilleras. Observers said that many years later, the scars made by Galvey, literally and mentally, were still there. FYC.
See also: Tonglo; Xandaro, Eduardo.

Gammal *(IFU)*. To make balls of your rice using your hands before you eat them.

Ganga *(KAL)*. Glow, as in glowing with health, wealth and political influence or literally from rubbing coconut oil on one's skin. FYC.

Gannawa *(KAL)*. A handsome gentleman and a brave warrior.

Gehhehhe *(IFU)*. In the Hudhud, when the soloist sings *"Gehhehheyandakami,"* she means "you are more alert than us" either because you woke up earlier or you did your task faster.
See also: Hudhud.

Gengen *(IKA)*. Using mulching and terracing to maintain soil nutrition.

Gingined *(ILO)*. Earthquake. The July 16, 1990 earthquake with a magnitude of 7.7 on the Richter scale caused deaths of more than 400 and thousands missing. The earthquake also shook the collective psyche of the people, particularly those in Baguio and Benguet. About 30 major buildings in the city collapsed and thousands more homes were destroyed. The city was isolated for a few days and it took the city three years to recover. People still mentally classify their lives pre-gingined and post-gingined.

From the *Catalogue of Violent and Destructive Earthquakes in the Philippines 1599 to 1909* by Miguel Saderra Masó (1910), the following were

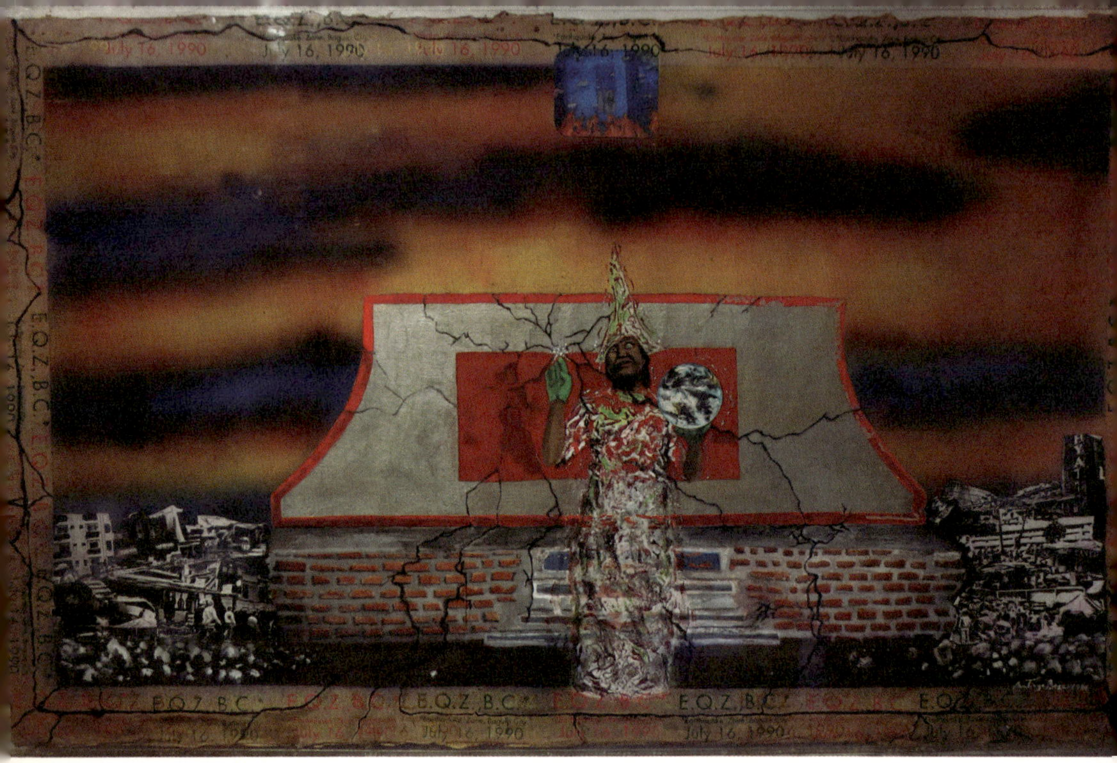

Artwork by Santiago Bose, 1990.

the destructive gingineds (earthquakes) that hit Cordillera:

"August 1627 – The historians mention it as one of the earthquakes which caused the greatest convulsions in Northern Luzon, especially in Ilocos Norte and Cagayan, but above all in the region of the Central Central Cordillera, Lepanto, and Bontoc. The data is somewhat vague. It is said that part of the northern Caraballo Mountains subsided.

January 4, 1641 – Destructive earthquake accompanied by great landslides in the mountains and eruptions of water and mud in the region of Northern Luzon which comprises the Provinces of the Ilocos, of Cagayan, and the Cordillera Central. All the historians of the Archipelago mention this cataclysm which occurred shortly after the almost simultaneous eruptions of Sanguir and Jolo.

September 9, 1862 – Ilocos Norte and Cagayan. The epicenter lay within the Central Cordillera. Did some damage to the church of Piddig and to other towns situated near the Cordillera.

September 10, 1873 – This earthquake was violent in Ilocos Norte, Ilocos Sur, and the Mountain Province. It was remarkable for its duration of nearly one minute. The resulting damage was negligible.

March 9, 1875 – Very violent earthquake in Abra and Mountain Province. Destroyed some houses and caused landslides on the mountain sides, ruining rice terraces. It was preceded by feeble shocks and followed by many repetitions until March 14.

February 10, 1883 – Very violent earthquake in Nueva Vizcaya and Benguet Provinces. It had been preceded by a strong shock four days earlier.

March 16, 1892 – Disastrous earthquake in the Provinces of Pangasinan, La Union, and Benguet. It created great havoc in the masonry of buildings such as churches, conventos, court-houses, and schools, besides a few private houses, of 30 of the principal towns within the meizoseismic area, produced great fissures and extensive subsidences in the alluvial plains, and many landslides in the

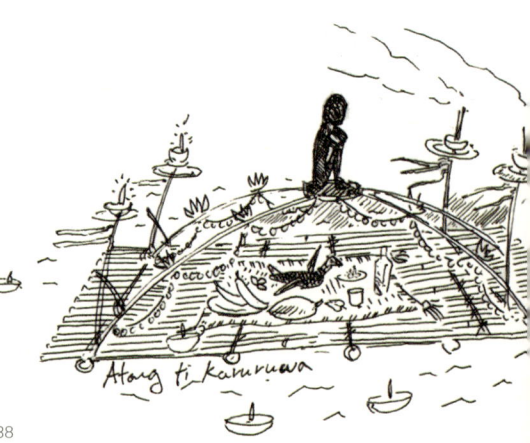

steep mountains of northern Pangasinan. Luckily, the falling buildings killed only one or two persons. Repetitions were frequent up to the end of the month; of these three occurring on the 17th and one each on the 26th and 28th, were of exceptional intensity.

January 18, 1897 – Very strong earthquake in Mountain Province and the Provinces of Isabela and Cagayan. Numerous aftershocks followed during the day.

October 2, 1904 – Very violent earthquake whose epicenter lay in the northern part of Mountain Province. Slight damage was done in several towns of Ilocos Norte and Cagayan, situated near the Central Cordillera.

May 25, 1907 – Very violent earthquake whose center was in the northern part of the Central Cordillera (Mountain Province). It did considerable damage in the Provinces of Ilocos Norte and Cagayan. The central part of the epicentral region, where the effects must have been more severe, is inhabited exclusively by wild tribes. No aftershocks have been recorded." FYC.

See also: Jegjeg; Landslide; Yumogyog ad Dalom.

Gipi *(KAN)*. "A prayer to 'blind' rats and ricebirds from seeking and eating ripening grain." (Scott 2011, 151).

Gisgisto *(KAN/BON)*. Head 'reflexology' using the fingernails and in a certain organized manner. Usually administered by young girls and boys to their mothers, aunties or any older woman. PAD.

Goat. (1) Not a ritual animal.

(2) During the Northern Luzon Athletic Association meets in the 1960s, the Cordillerans had a cheer which went, "Mountain Province, Mountain Province! We're not goats! We're Igorots!" The essence of the cheer was in the mocking of the Anglo-american pronunciation of Igorots as "Igoroats."

(3) Refers to the tail-ender of the graduating class of the Philippine Military Academy.

Gobgobbao *(KAN)*. (1) Done in Sagada and Besao, Mountain Province, this is a rite of thanksgiving done just after a baby's umbilical cord falls off. A chicken is butchered and the family gathers for lunch as witnessed to the naming of the baby. All immediate members of the family must be present for this occasion so if the husband needs to work elsewhere, he should not leave until the gobgobbao is done. PAD.

(2) also **Bagor** *(IFU)*. It is the naming ritual for a child. The child is introduced to the spirits, the deities, and to the cosmos. Normally, the child is named after an ancestor. TDH.

See also: Kammid; Linayaan.

God Stealer, The. National Artist for Literature F. Sionil Jose's most famous short story about Philip Latak, an Ifugao in Manila who accompanied American tourist Sam Cristie to Banaue to buy a bul-ul. Not finding anyone who would want to sell their bul-ul, Philip stole his grandfather's bul-ol and the latter died as a result. In the end Philip, in his G-string had to carve a new bul-ol. Philip and Sam obviously represent the Philippines and the US. This story also contributed to the misconception that the bul-uls are gods. (Jose 1968) FYC.

See also: Bul-ul.

Gojuman-nin no Isan. *The Legacy of the 500,000 (Gojuman-nin no Isan)*, 1963. A movie directed and starred in by Japanese actor and director, Toshiro Mifune in 1963 and the first Japanese film to be shot in the Philippines after World War II. Its title was *The Japanese Army's Hidden Treasure in the Philippines* but was released in Japan as *The Legacy of the 500,000*. It was Mifune's first film as a director and a producer (Mifune Productions). Akira Kurosawa edited the movie although his work was uncredited. It was shot entirely in Baguio. The film tells the story of a Japanese businessman who learns of a treasure of 10,000 gold coins left by the Japanese Army during the closing days of World War II. He contacts Matsuo (Mifune) who knows the location of the treasure. Refusing to cooperate, Matsuo is kidnapped by the businessman and, along with a group of treasure hunters, forcibly brought to the Philippines. They arrive in the Mountain Province where they end up fighting the Ifugao in the region. The movie ends tragically with the group failing to find the gold.

See also: Abong.

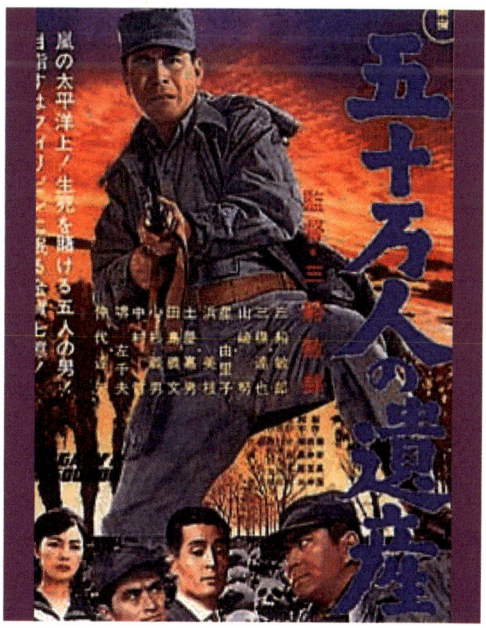

Poster of the movie *Gojuman-nin no isan*, 1963. Theatrical release poster.

Golden Buddha.

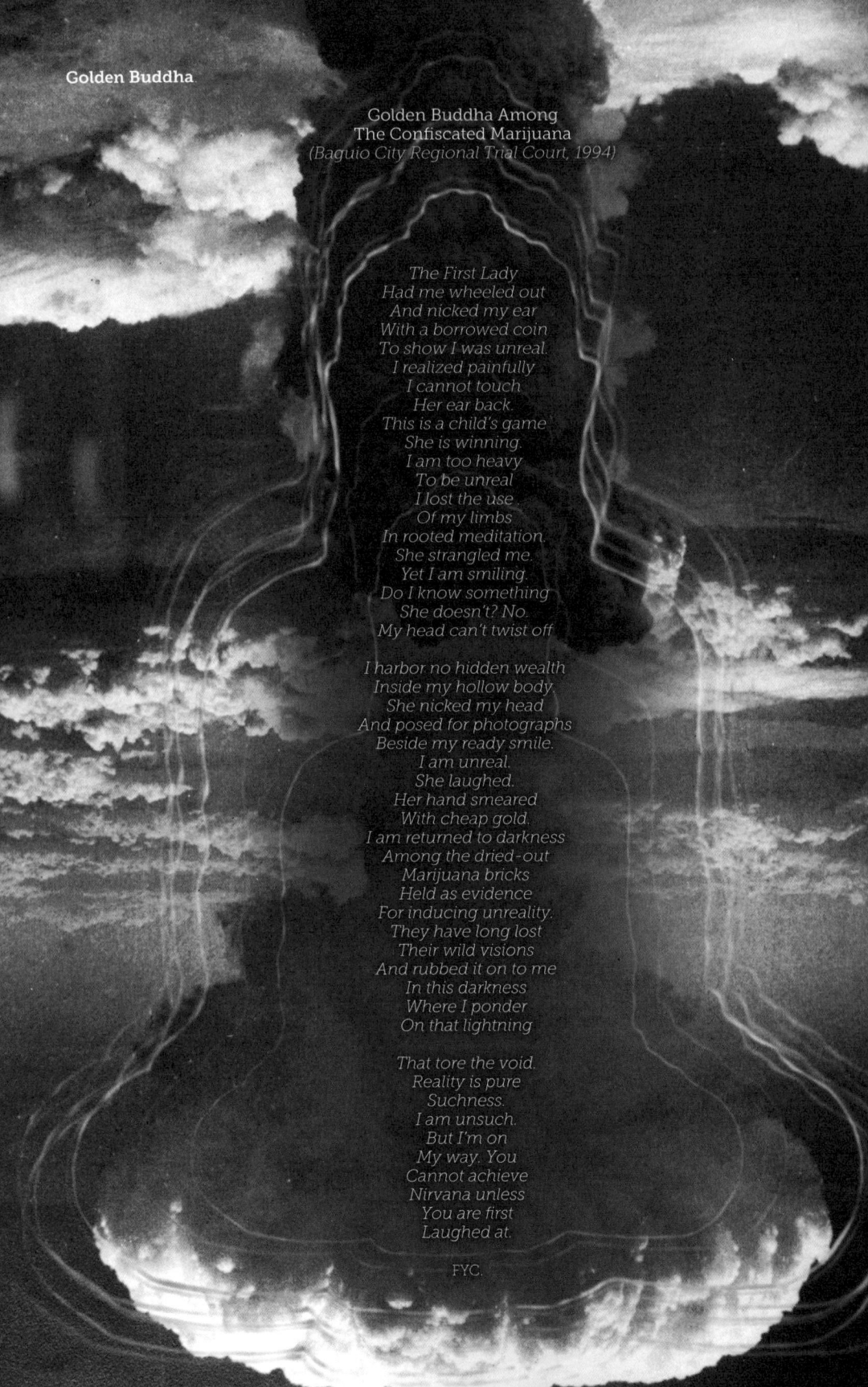

Golden Buddha Among
The Confiscated Marijuana
(Baguio City Regional Trial Court, 1994)

The First Lady
Had me wheeled out
And nicked my ear
With a borrowed coin
To show I was unreal.
I realized painfully
I cannot touch
Her ear back.
This is a child's game
She is winning.
I am too heavy
To be unreal.
I lost the use
Of my limbs
In rooted meditation.
She strangled me.
Yet I am smiling.
Do I know something
She doesn't? No.
My head can't twist off

I harbor no hidden wealth
Inside my hollow body.
She nicked my head
And posed for photographs
Beside my ready smile.
I am unreal.
She laughed.
Her hand smeared
With cheap gold.
I am returned to darkness
Among the dried-out
Marijuana bricks
Held as evidence
For inducing unreality.
They have long lost
Their wild visions
And rubbed it on to me
In this darkness
Where I ponder
On that lightning

That tore the void.
Reality is pure
Suchness.
I am unsuch.
But I'm on
My way. You
Cannot achieve
Nirvana unless
You are first
Laughed at.

FYC.

Gold Earrings. First, a model is made of the earring using beeswax then covered with clay used for pottery. A hole is left for the wax to escape when it is put on the fire. Gold is then put on top of the hole and the clay is put on the fire for about five minutes, until the gold melts and goes into the mold. The cast is cooled and then the clay is rubbed off. FYC.

Golden Kuhol. Snails introduced in the Philippines in the early 1980s by entrepreneurs hoping to make money exporting escargot snails to France. Hardy and fast-breeding, the golden kuhol *(Pomacea canaliculata)* was also envisioned as a protein supplement for the Filipinos. However, they became a major pest in the rice terraces of the Cordillera. FYC.
See also: Agudong id Manitong; Atubang; Bisukol; Falokag; Ket-an; Lisdeg.

Gongot *(IFU).* A small knife used to cut hair. A flat bamboo is set under the lock of hair before the gongot is used to chop your 'do. FYC.

Gotad *(IFU).* All-day drinking and dancing during the uyauy or balihong feast. It follows the holyat which is the night celebration. Nowadays, gotad is a government-sanctioned festival in some towns in Ifugao that leads up to a grand province-wide gotad. FYC.
See also: Ullalim.

Great Ifugao War. A near legendary event in the past often said to have taken place in the 14th Century (some say it could have been as late as the 18th Century), when about 4,000 invaders from the Burnay district went to the Cababuyan of the prosperous Bannawol and Pu'itan districts. The climax of the war was when the brothers Bitangnge and Pitagon from Matanglag village were able to kill Dago, the leader of the invaders. After that, the tide turned and the invaders were massacred after being pushed to a ravine. FYC
See also: Samiklay; Timicheg.

Guirey, Chainus. Born in 1902 in the mining village of Gumatdang, Itogon, Benguet as the eldest of ten children to Guirey, Gumatdang's rich man, and Flora Pacalso. Chainus was only 13 when she was selected as the Queen of the Benguet Carnival in Burnham Park, Baguio City. She was invited to the Manila Carnival and her gold and silver adornments were the talk of the town. After finishing her elementary at the Bua Public School in Itogon, she was asked to take up Education at the Philippine Normal School and then went on to St. Luke's Hospital to become a nurse. She contracted tuberculosis and died in 1920 when she was only 18. In 1930, J.J. Murphy opened a movie house near the Session Theater and called it the Alhamar-Chainus in memory of the Benguet Carnival Queen. Writer Nonnette Bennett in her monologue script for Baguio Stories suggested that Chainus is the White Lady of Loakan. FYC.
See also: Baguio Cine; Burnham Park; Loakan Road White Lady.

Gumassilang *(KAL).* To act like the White people. Probably from the word Kastila.

Gutti *(IFU).* Bad haircut. You were captured during a hunting raid and your head was about to be cut but then your headtaker, in a miraculous pang of compassion while holding you by the hair, decided to cut your hair instead and not your head. Then you were set free. FYC.
See also: Headhunting (the tale).

Gu-wab *(KAN).* Lit. Down. Down the valley. DLD.

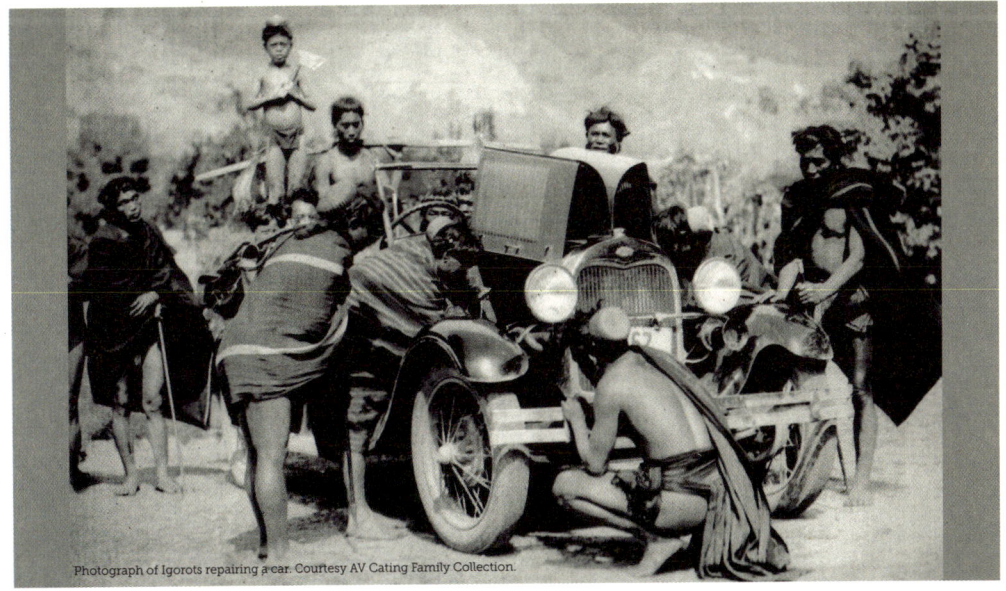
Photograph of Igorots repairing a car. Courtesy AV Cating Family Collection.

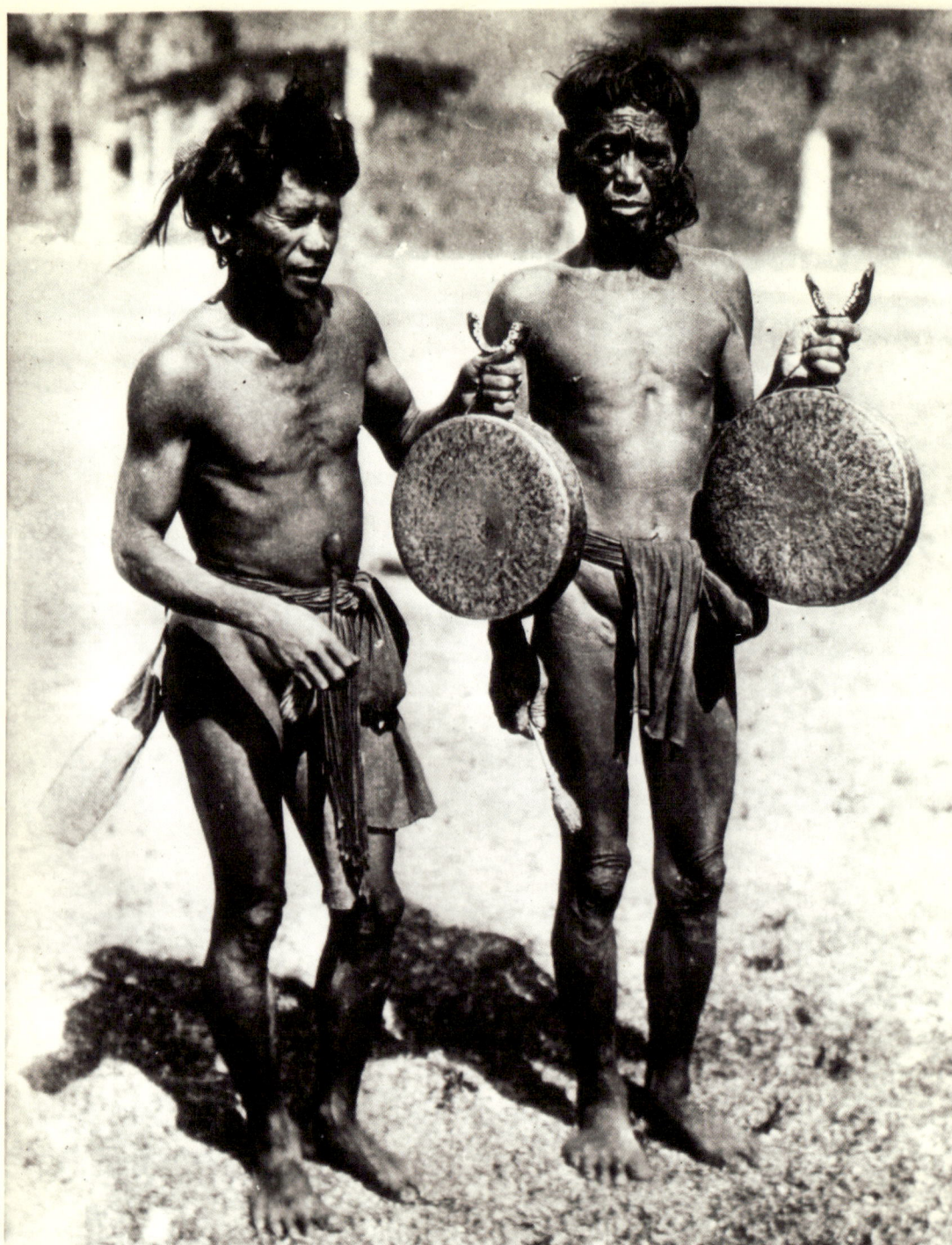

(NY5-FEB. 22) THEY DON'T NEED PANTS TO FIGHT--LOOKING LIKE TRULY PRIMITIVE WARRIORS, THE HEAD-HUNTING IGOROTS OF THE PHILIPPINES ARE SEEING ACTION WITH MACARTHUR'S TROOPS. IGOROTS RIDE THE TANKS, MACARTHUR REPORTS, DIRECTING TANK MOVEMENTS THROUGH HEAVY JUNGLE COUNTRY. ONE REPORT SAID IGOROT WARRIORS DIDN'T MIND WEARING UNIFORMS--IF THEY COULD LEAVE OFF THE PANTS.
(AP WIREPHOTO) (MS11615HO) 42

Photograph of Igorots with *gongs*, c. 1945. Courtesy Associated Press and AV Cating Family Collection.

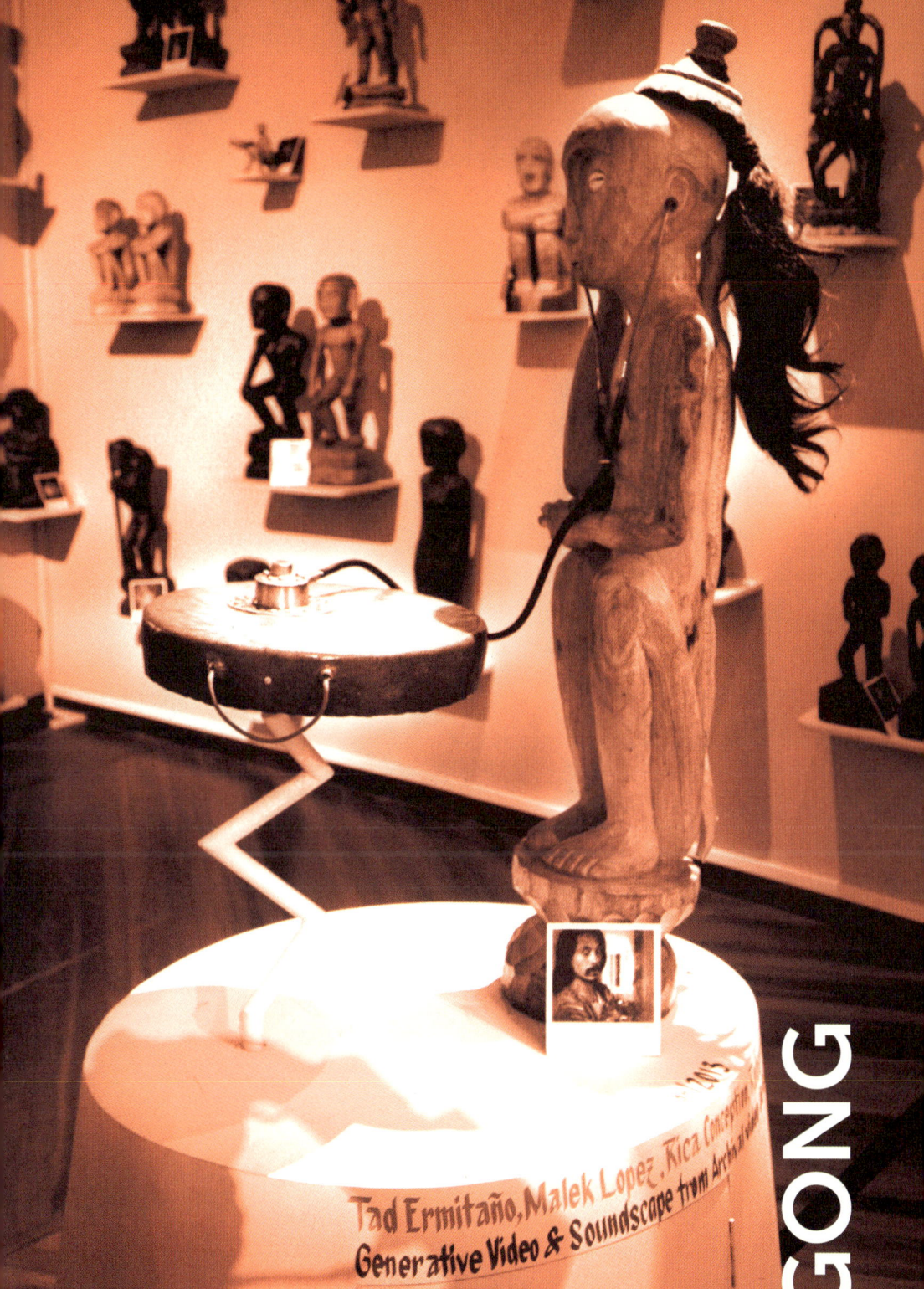

Exhibition photo of *Gangsa(The Last Gong Maker)*, Tad Ermitaño, Rica Concepcion, Malek Lopez, Singapore Biennale 2013
Courtesy Singapore Art Museum

Notes on GANGSA (The First Gongmaker)

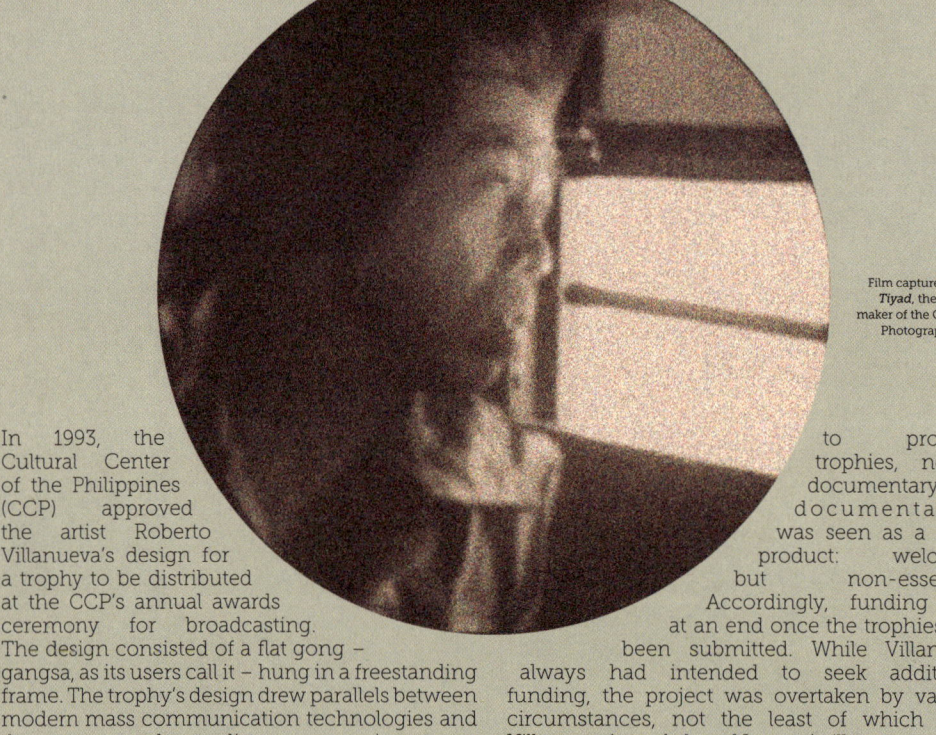

Film capture of *Cariño Tiyad*, the 'last' gong maker of the Cordilleras. Photograph by Egay Navarro.

In 1993, the Cultural Center of the Philippines (CCP) approved the artist Roberto Villanueva's design for a trophy to be distributed at the CCP's annual awards ceremony for broadcasting. The design consisted of a flat gong – gangsa, as its users call it – hung in a freestanding frame. The trophy's design drew parallels between modern mass communication technologies and the gangsa, whose distance-spanning tones have been used for thousands of years to knit communities together across the distances of the Philippines' Cordillera Region. The gangsa signals and commemorates. It is an indispensible component to Cordilleran rituals of birth, death, weddings, and harvest.

It was Villanueva's idea that the trophy's gong should not only be a genuine and playable musical instrument, but forged by Cariño Tiyad, an Ifugao blacksmith, and the last gong maker of the Cordilleras.

Villanueva put together a shifting crew of friends and volunteers (foremost of whom were the documentarists Egay Navarro and Rica Concepcion) to document the process of forging the gongs with a motley collection of Hi8 cameras. The accumulated footage was passed to Navarro and Concepcion, who were charged with the task of imposing structure on the chaos of material and (eventually) producing a documentary on Cariño Tiyad whose title would be *The Last Gongmaker*.

However, the CCP had given Villanueva a grant to produce trophies, not a documentary. The documentation was seen as a side-product: welcome, but non-essential. Accordingly, funding was at an end once the trophies had been submitted. While Villanueva always had intended to seek additional funding, the project was overtaken by various circumstances, not the least of which were Villanueva's and then Navarro's illnesses, which eventually resulted in Villanueva's death in 1995, Navarro's in 2013.

I have known Rica and Egay since the late-1980s when I became acquainted with them in the process of studying filmmaking at the Mowelfund Film Institute. While I still make the occasional film, I call myself a media artist these days; although I still work with sound and image, I consider my medium more to be the machines we process sound and image with. These days I make interactive pieces using computers, programs and electronics. I also often perform with the composer Malek Lopez, with whom I have been exploring the creative possibilities of networked computers for some years now. One of our more recent experiments involved chopping up Hulikotekan – an old film of mine – and writing programs that used its close-ups of household objects being struck, rubbed, and dropped – to generate interactive audiovisual music.

In early 2013, these circumstances combined with Egay's passing and condensed into the idea of applying the techniques Malek and

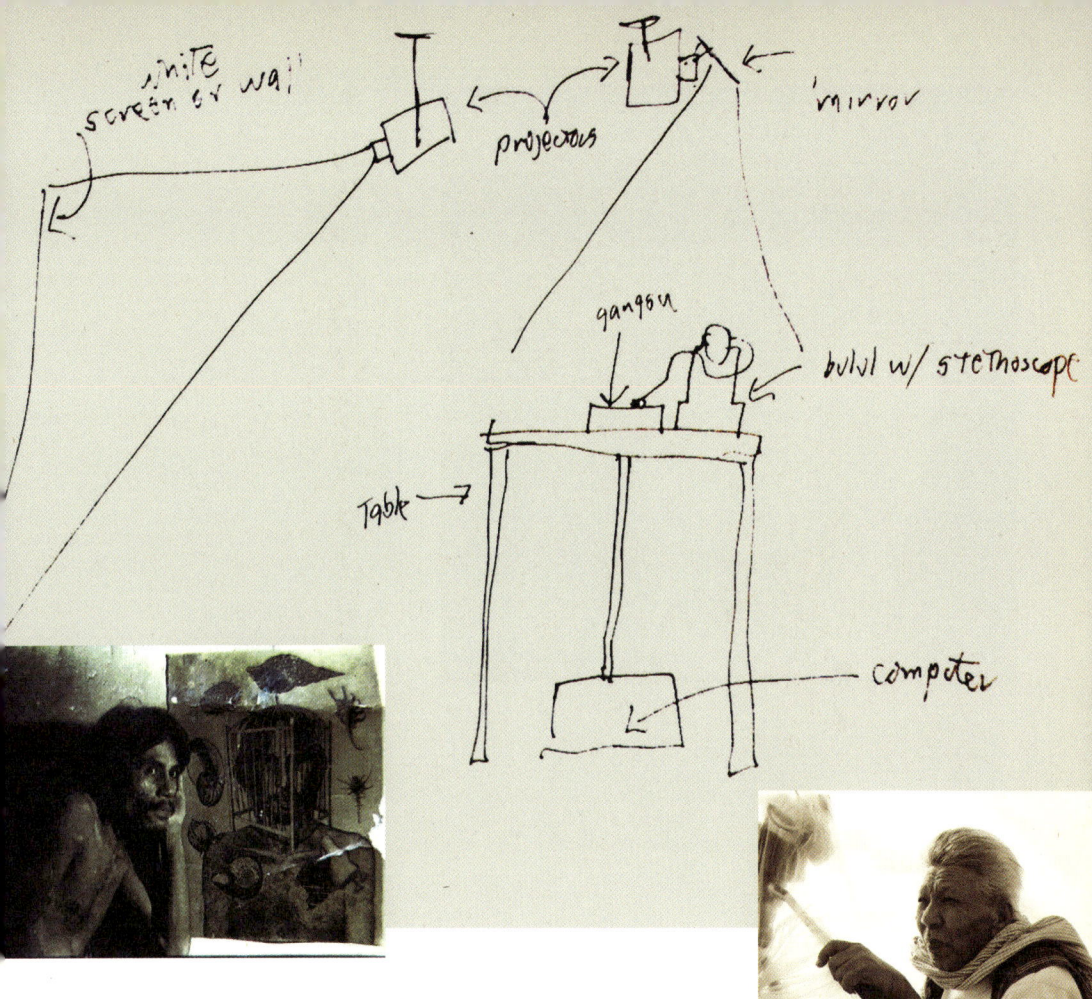

Top: Sketch of Tad Ermitano's installation.
Left: Self portrait of *Roberto Villanueva*.
Right: Photograph of *Egay Navarro*.

I had developed for the interactive version of Hulikotekan to the footage of Cariño the gongmaker. It emerged that there was a whole tapeful of footage covering the actual forging of a gong, filled with metallic noises perfect for the project.

Much time had passed, however, since Villanueva started his project. Many things had happened. Cariño himself had passed on. Tapes and notes had been lost or misplaced. Worst of all, Hi8 had become a near-obsolete format. The idea had almost come too late. Almost no one we knew owned a Hi8 camera, and the machines we were able to borrow had problems playing back the aging cassettes, some of which had grown so delicate that Rica thought they might not survive more than a single playback operation.

Fortunately, Rica found a company that was able to digitize the tapes, which, as she'd feared, became irreparably damaged in the process. Rica was admirably philosophical about it all, though she could only have viewed the process with mixed feelings. On the one hand, the footage is now in a form that can be accessed and archived.

Still, it couldn't have been easy to submit the tapes to a process that she knew would destroy them.

For Rica, the tapes and the footage must be inextricably linked to a time and a milieu. The tapes are sprinkled with shots of her friends, shots of her children, shots when she or Egay playfully turned the camera on one another. One tape documented the vigil that gathered around Villanueva at his deathbed. I think she felt the need to find some semblance of closure to the project, which had petered out without resulting in anything finished. Accordingly, she enlisted me and filmmaker Shallah Montero to assist her when she interviewed Joel Tiyad, Cariño's son, who had taken up his father's trade as gongmaker.

The Cordilleras are a shifting conglomeration of cultures and communities, where multiple dialects and/or languages often rule a single mountain. Villanueva was born a Tagalog speaker in the lowlands. Cariño's mother tongue was an

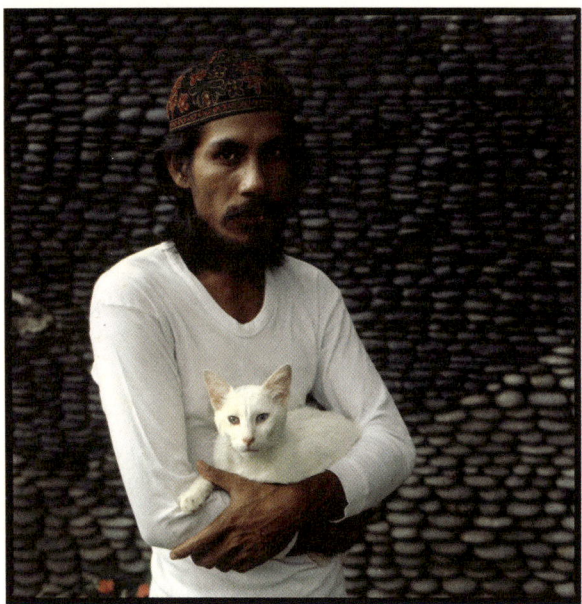

Portrait of *Roberto Villanueva* with his cat, 1982. Photograph by Wig Tysmans.

Ifugao language. While the two communicated in Ilocano, the process was never casual or smooth. Cariño was also a highly eccentric and moody person, who worked best after he had had a couple of drinks. All of these factors now appear to have impeded the communication of a critical fact: that while Cariño made gongs, he absolutely was NOT the last gongmaker.

Joel Tiyad is at home in Tagalog, the language of Manila, the Philippine capital. It is the Filipino language that Villanueva, Rica and Shallah and I grew up speaking. While Joel still feels most at home in barely tamed environments, one suspects he might be more comfortable in the city than his father was; a confident urbanity underlies his Ifugao reserve. It was from Joel that we learned that the technologies of gong-making had been lost long before his father was born. What he told us of his childhood paints his father as a true inventor, a technological obsessive in the vein of Thomas Edison, Howard Hughes, and James Dyson. Cariño was a man who began his journey by (unsuccessfully) trying to melt down a potful of peso coins and who constantly knocked on metal objects to explore their sonic potential. We found from his son that Cariño Tiyad had essentially reconstructed the technology from scratch. That he was in fact in a very real sense, not the last, but the first (perhaps one should say A first) gongmaker.

This image was, for Malek and me, the driving force behind the creation of *Gangsa*. While we would have admired an adept of an ancient smithing tradition, a guy who muddled his way to solutions by trial and error was a hacker – a figure we instantly recognized and identified with. Cariño, far from being a lonely and tragic remnant of a vanishing tradition, was revealed as an inspired, ebullient and half-crazed colleague, kindred to local hardware hackers like Lirio Salvador and Inconnu Ictu and the hundreds of nameless engineers improvising at their workbenches. Cariño had singlehandedly rolled back the forces of extinction. It was under this image of Cariño – an image freed from archeological reverence and spiky with accidental rock and roll tropes – Cariño drunk, longhaired, unkempt (and often bearing an uncanny resemblance to Steven Tyler) gleefully sledgehammering hot brass in torn jeans and a secondhand bathrobe – It was under this image that I evolved the conceit that gongs might carry memories of their making, and more importantly, of their maker. I thought of the gong as being a kind of robot, an artificial being whose body carried memories of the journey from matter to selfhood, memories that could be accessed by detectors, machines in the vein of CAT scanners, radar, microscopes, multitesters, and seismographs. Once this idea was in place, it seemed natural to think that the gong might remember its maker with gratitude and even religious awe.

So much of the discourse around the cultures of the Cordillera revolves around ideas of authenticity and indigenous pedigree. Discovering that an ostensibly ancient craft was instead a wholly contemporary act of practical engineering and the locus where a dead tradition had spontaneously regenerated itself is, I think, a revelation that none of us involved have fully digested.

For one thing, it occurs to me to wonder how many times this has happened before. It seems like it would be a remarkable coincidence if we managed to document (on videotape, no less!) the first instance that a technology was reinvented: How many times has fire been lost and found?

However, there is another issue that it touches on, and one that perhaps has more immediate relevance. The Philippines (or Manila, anyway) is haunted by a kind of cultural Cartesian anxiety, this longing for some kind of assurance that Filipino culture is not an unbearably light hodgepodge of importations, borrowings and imitations. This expresses itself periodically in movements to reject English or Spanish loan words in favor of Tagalog words; to preserve customs like 'mano,' a gesture of respect executed by touching one's forehead to the back of an elder's hand, and so on. It's an anxiety that haunts many postcolonial cultures and one that often expresses itself in a valorization of indigenous emblems. Frida

Kahlo's adoption of the dress of the Zapotec is a gesture that parallels Kidlat Tahimik/Eric de Guia's adoption of the bahag/Cordilleran G-string.

In that sense, I feel that Cariño's story is something like a corrective, a sign pointing to another view of the matter. These days I suspect that Villanueva's fascination with Cariño and the emblems of Cordillera culture had its roots in the cultural anxiety I mentioned earlier. It seems obvious however, that Cariño reinvented gongmaking out of a completely different impulse. It was a hot, dirty, and deadly serious journey made in an informational wilderness, and he took it on because he felt the lack of gongs to be a piercingly serious hole in the world. He was (as they say) just taking care of business. TE/RC.

See also: Abistong; Dew-dew-as; Hib-at; Jawbone; Kuliteng; Music; Tubbob.

The Last Gongmaker

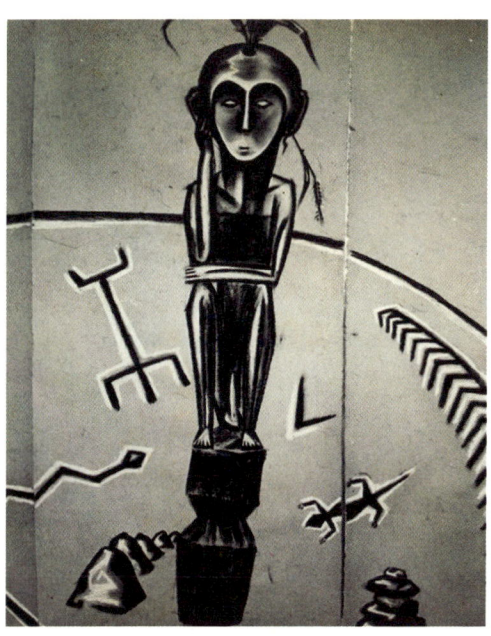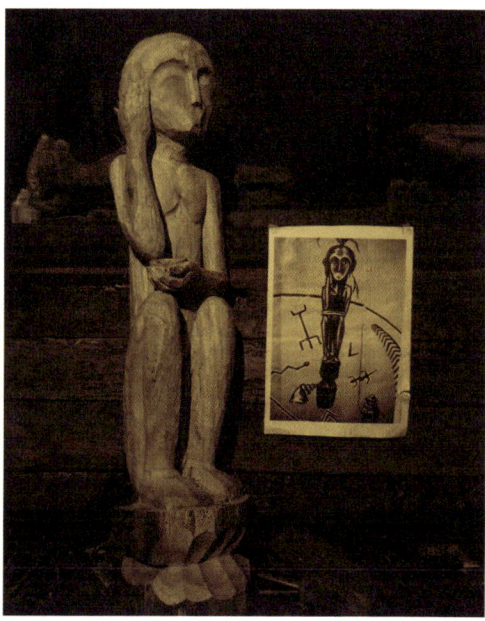

Right: Detail of an artwork by Roberto Villanueva, 1986.
Left: A reproduction of Roberto Villanueva's work carved by Apilis Mahiwo.

A project by Roberto Villanueva/Rica Concepcion & Egay Navarro/Tad Ermitaño & Malek Lopez

All this began after my second trip to Singapore, after stating that this project would be process – not product – oriented. I was not sure who and what was going to be presented for the Biennale. But on my last day of this trip, after an endless string of meetings, coming back to the Philippines and learning that Egay Navarro had passed away, it was during his wake that this project made itself known.

If I were to paint a picture of Roberto Villanueva, it would be one as ephemeral and mysterious as what he left behind when he went from this physical world and no artworks remained; only this presence that lingered: his art practice. It still plays a big role in what we know as Baguio art today.

The wake was a crazy time if there is any one way to put it. But it was also a time when friends atypically converged; and in those meetings some things surfaced, from the deepest of secrets to the most trivial of scenarios. During one of those long nights, Rica Concepcion, Egay's widowed partner jokingly said, *"Siguro, magkasama na sila ni Roberto and the barkada ngayon."* (I guess by now Egay and Roberto must be kicking it with the whole gang). And this 'joke' became more and more serious, such that that it led us to a series of stories which would later become one of our most important tales yet untold.

Egay, being a good friend of Roberto and having documented much of Roberto's life and work respectively, kept an archive of footage on his friend – ranging from 16mm, mini DV, Hi8, beta format and so on – and from one of these piles of hidden wealth surfaced *The Last Gong Maker*, a tale about Roberto's interaction with Cariño Tiyad, the alchemist of gong-making in the Cordilleras.

If there was one tangible item that always brought people together, it would be the gong, which was almost like Roberto Villanueva himself. Roberto brought us together: the members of the Baguio Arts Guild and the communities involved. He had that charisma that would lead artisans to interact with the artists, with no one getting left behind. He created these happenings that people just wanted to be a part of.

Along with the footage, was this one unassuming brass gong, but what do you do with just one gong? You can't just tie the footage together and project it on the gallery wall – this would not make Tito Roberto very happy. And then, just by chance, during a new media festival in Vietnam, I was introduced to the work of Tad Ermitaño and Malek Lopez – a month after stumbling upon the footage. That coincidence presented an opportunity to tackle my gong predicament.

So, now we had a gong, a ton of footage and these 'hi-tech sorcerers' who made computers talk with each other. All we had to do was to make the gong speak, make the story come out without explicitly giving it all away. And, through the wonders of technology, and perhaps the nod from Roberto himself, the project pulled through, exactly 20 years after it was born. KDG.

On *Shaman Wars*

The indie short film venture was titled *Shaman Wars*. It starred three of our friends as the macho protagonists battling over a go-go dancer in one of Baguio's infamous girlie bars of the time. Was it Nevada? Something like that. This was in 1981 or '82 or '83.

Our action stars were Eric de Guia (a.k.a. Kidlat Tahimik, the great grandfather of Philippine independent cinema himself!), Pepito Bosch the 'Ermita outlaw,' and the inscrutable Boy Yuchengco (Boyu).

Boy Yñiguez (Boyñi) served as the cinematographer, working with a 16mm Arriflex, if memory serves me right. I guess that's how Boyñi first earned his spurs that had him galloping away with cinematography honors in decades to come, including an award for Mike Alcazaren's *Puti*. (2012)

Soundman was Ruben Domingo, who later in that decade moved on to Hollywood. I last saw him in LA in 2000. He still had long, silky black hair that he often tossed away from his earplugs.

I was story consultant, faux direk, and propsman. I took care of Pepito's and Boyu's stashes of whatever. I also dispensed the necessary ablutions whenever I felt that they would do no damage to creative equilibrium.

Oh, and I also headed the crowd control crew, especially when we shot at that Nevada girlie bar.

The object of lust that sparked the shaman wars, I forget her name now, or her age. Either 19 or 20, if I'm not doddering along significantly. We asked her to act onstage, which was basically shimmying around to the music of Abba I think, while in a tasselled bikini top and bikini bottom, to be filmed. For the sake of art. And for more than just the usual table fee, of course.

And of course we also asked permission from the mama-sans and bouncers. We passed around a lot of Ginebra bilogs, even among the leering cowboys around the raucous tables, just so they kept their remarks on the clean side of Cordilleran appreciation.

We also shot our 'shamans' in various corners of that girlie bar, in various states of manly appreciation of the girl's gyrations. Kidlat was of course more naked than the girl, clad only in trad loincloth. He was the local shaman. Pepito was all in black, with a black hat, too. He was the Western shaman. Boyu was in his kung-fu outfit, as the celestial shaman.

We shot scenes at Wright Park and that gazebo with cement pillars, and I think also at the amphitheater in John Hay. Each protagonist displayed magical skills and tricks as they cavorted athletically amid the colonial architecture and greenery.

It was a lot of fun. A lot of laughs. One evening, I think we even took the girl to a cottage off the Country Club, fed her an elegant dinner and had her pose with us all reclining before the lit fireplace.

I'm not sure now if we still shot her, outside the Nevada club, that is. Maybe some close-ups. Or did we have her hold and lash out with a whip at Pepito, who in one vintage still I saw recently, appeared to be strapped horizontally before that same fireplace?

A pity I lost both the Betamax and VHS copies I had of that indie film that ran 15 minutes, I think. It won the Best Experimental Film award at the ECP (Experimental Cinema of the Philippines) contest later that year. Yes, *Shaman Wars* did. Thanks to its magnificent action and acting, its cinematography, its brisk editing (which might have been a collab among Boyñi, Ruben and me, and just about everyone else), the nubile pulchritude of the female star, and of course all of the metaphysical questions it provoked with the supernatural display of inherent spiritual prowess that had the stuntmen-actors typecast to begin with.

If anyone has a copy of *Shaman Wars*, I'd like to see it again, after being crazy all these years. It could be our only hope for sanity in these mundanely war-mongering times. KY.

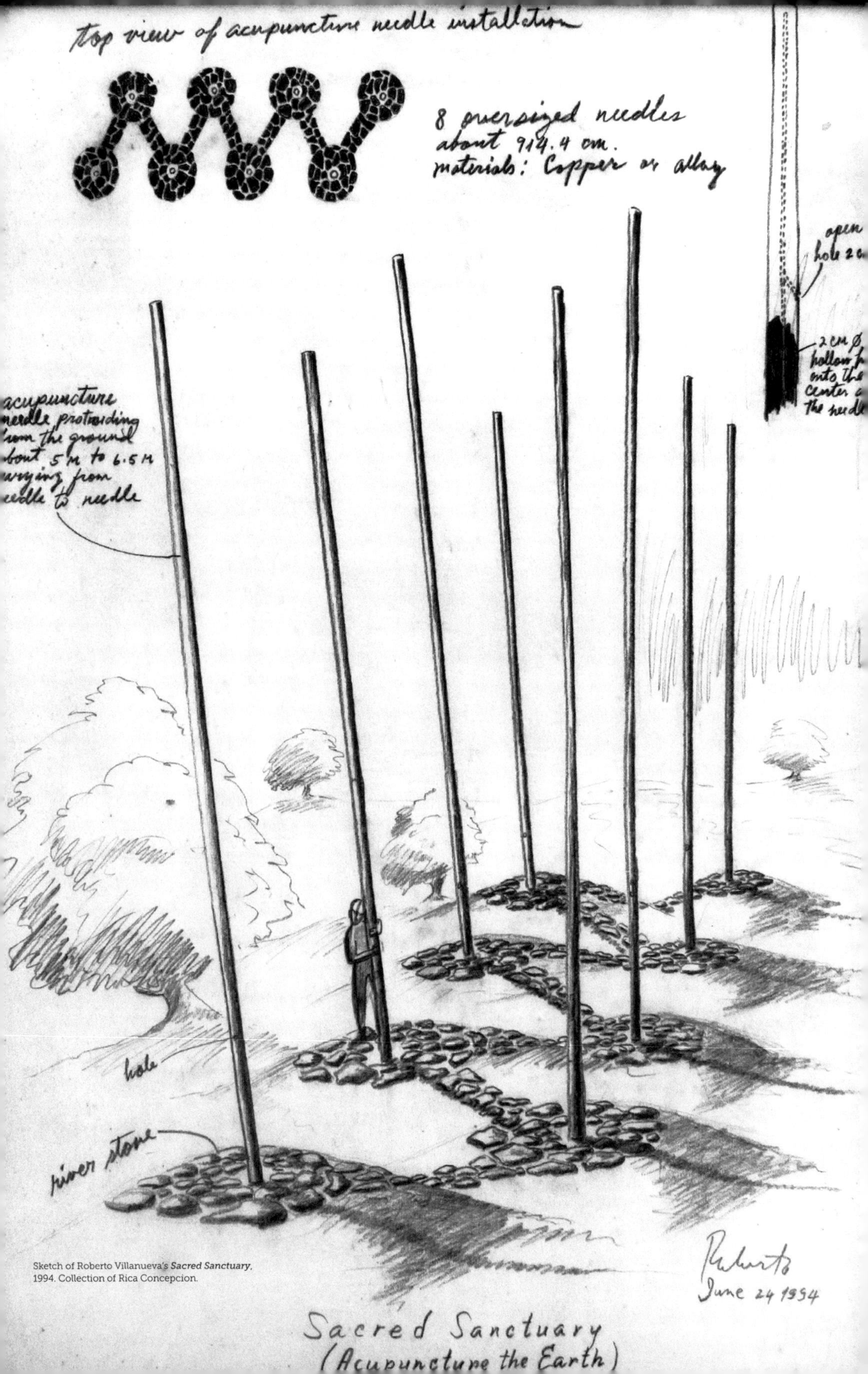

top view of acupuncture needle installation

8 oversized needles about 914.4 cm. materials: Copper or alloy

open hole 2 cm

2 cm ⌀ hollow [hole] onto the center [of] the needle

acupuncture needle protruding from the ground about .5 m to 6.5 m varying from needle to needle

hole

river stone

Roberto
June 24 1994

Sketch of Roberto Villanueva's *Sacred Sanctuary*, 1994. Collection of Rica Concepcion.

Sacred Sanctuary
(Acupuncture the Earth)

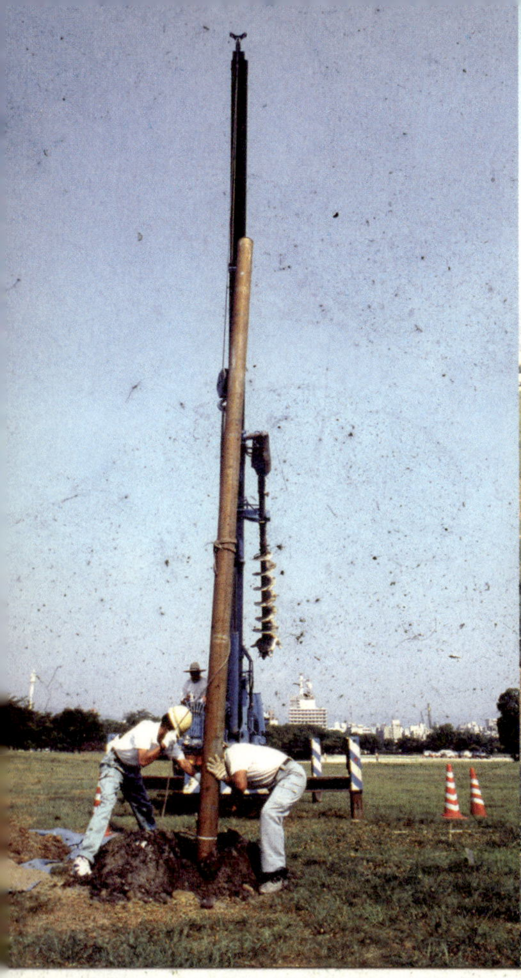

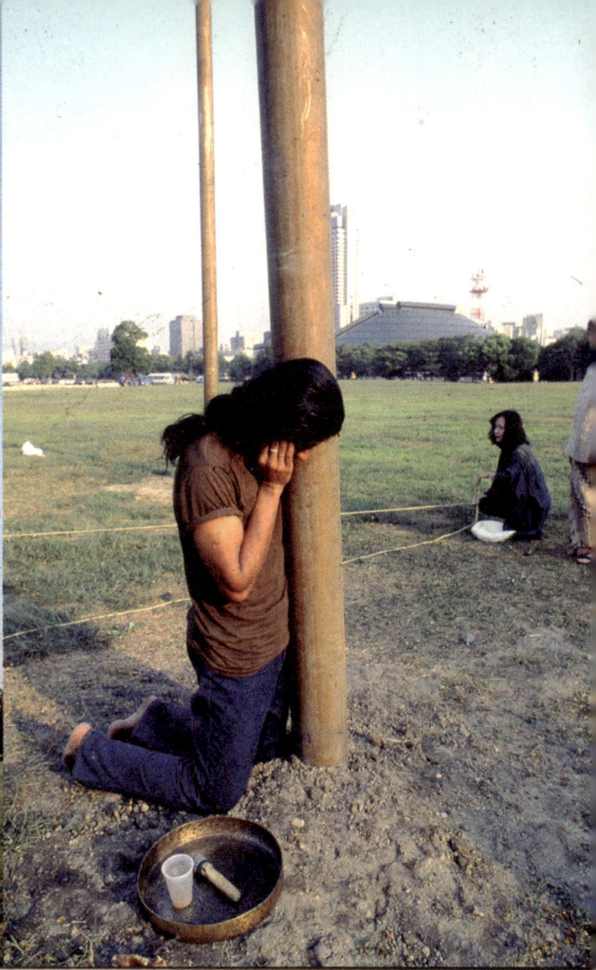

Photographs of the installation of "Sacred Sanctuary" during the "Hiroshima Art Document 1995" by friends and volunteers of *Roberto Villanueva* at the Hiroshima Peace Memorial Park. Courtesy Midori Yamamura.

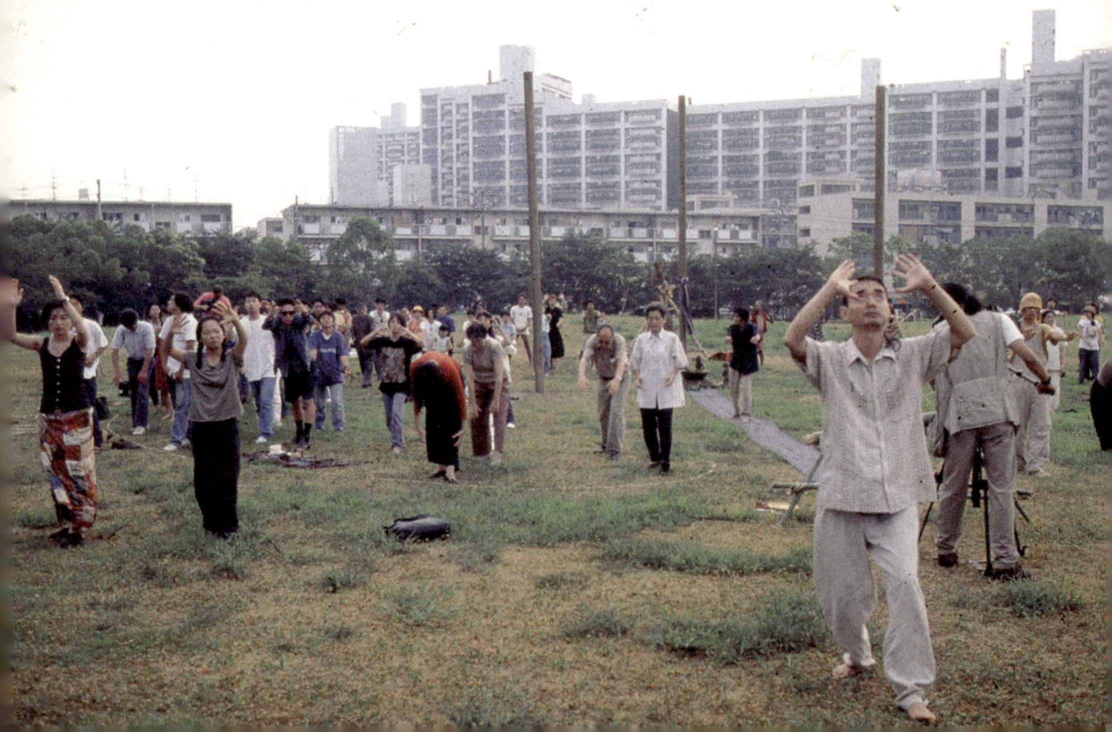

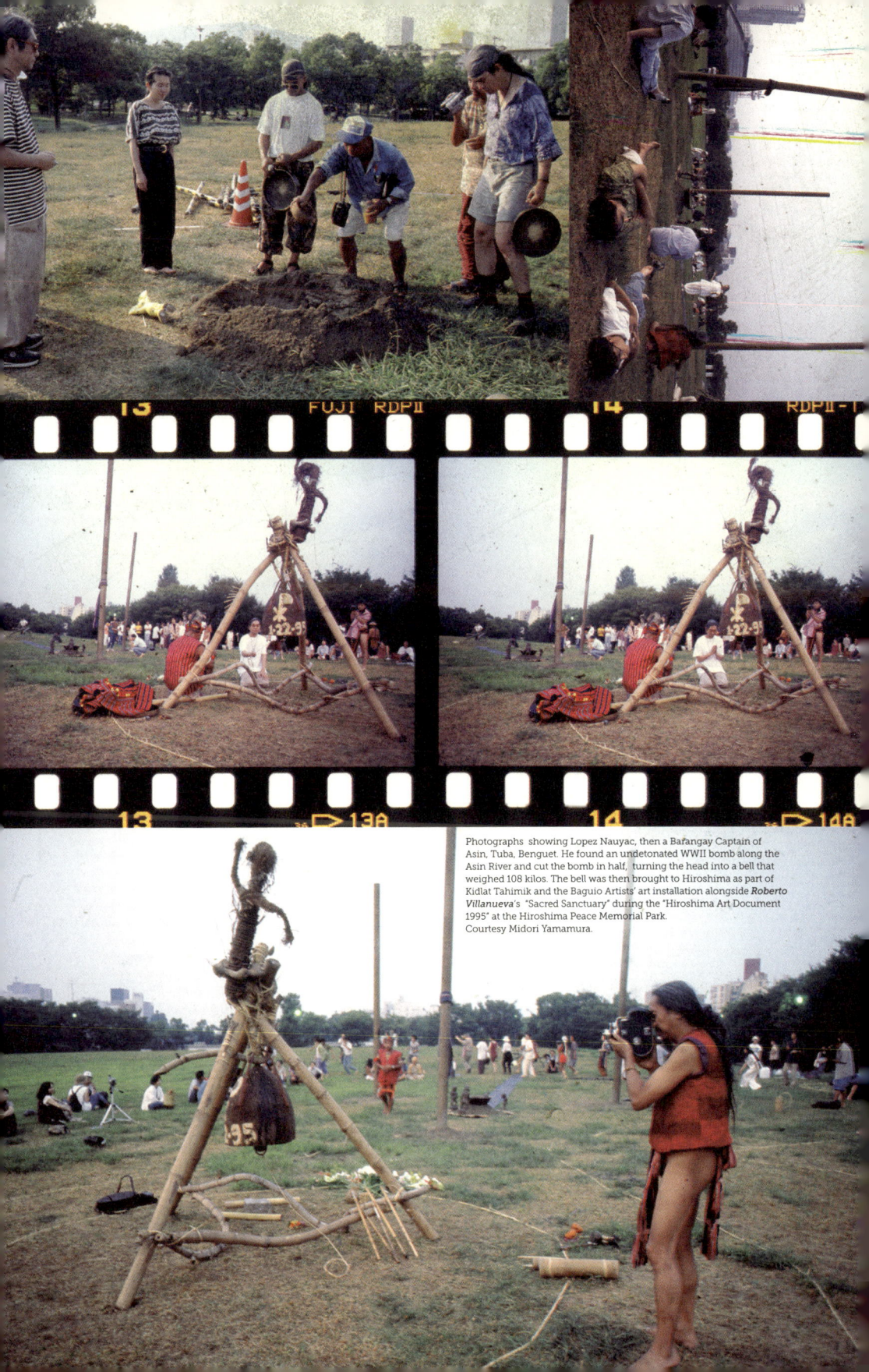

Photographs showing Lopez Nauyac, then a Barangay Captain of Asin, Tuba, Benguet. He found an undetonated WWII bomb along the Asin River and cut the bomb in half, turning the head into a bell that weighed 108 kilos. The bell was then brought to Hiroshima as part of Kidlat Tahimik and the Baguio Artists' art installation alongside *Roberto Villanueva*'s "Sacred Sanctuary" during the "Hiroshima Art Document 1995" at the Hiroshima Peace Memorial Park.
Courtesy Midori Yamamura.

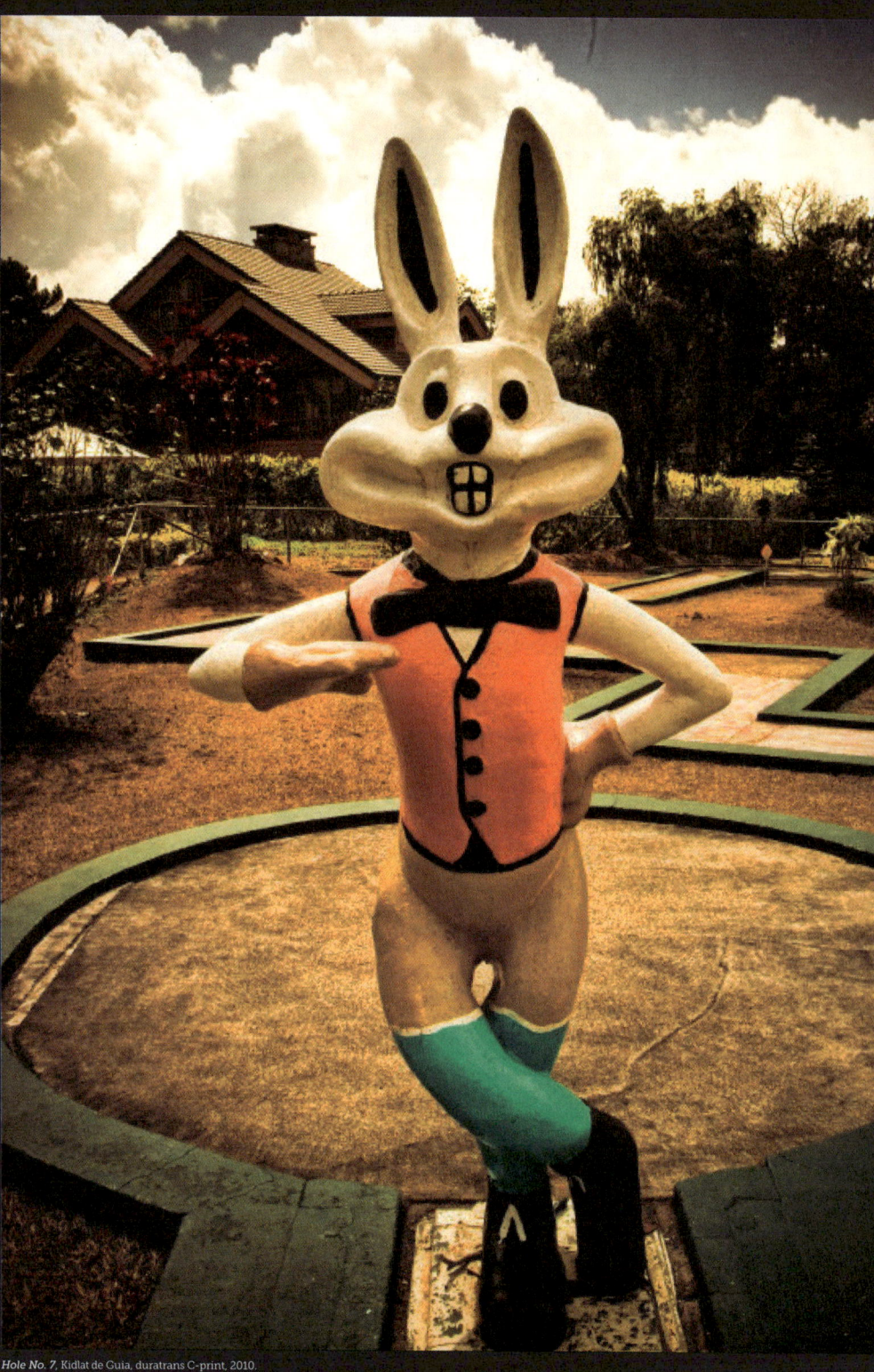
Hole No. 7, Kidlat de Guia, duratrans C-print, 2010.

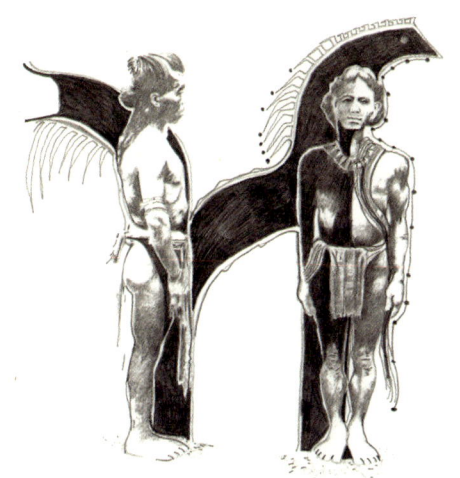

Hagabi *(IFU).* (1) *"A lounge cut out of a large tree trunk. It is the insignia of the upper class Ifugao.*

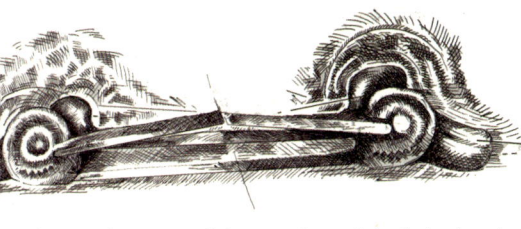

Its carving out of the trunk, and its bringing in from the forest, is an affair in which many villages participate, and is accompanied by pretentious ceremonies and feasts." (Barton 2012).

(2) Only tomonas are entitled to have one. Tomonas are the families that dictate the agricultural ritual cycle. A family becomes tomona when they own many of the rice paddies in the community. They have the power to call the bakis. Such a family will have performed all the rituals of the cycle of life, from conception to death. Tomona can also dictate when it is time for harvest to begin. TDH.
See also: Buaya Economic Classes; Immuya-uy; Pes-ay.

Haight's Place. Vegetable garden in Paoay Proper in Atok town. It was started by an American soldier in the 1900s named Guy Haight who went there to recover from tuberculosis. Haight married a native, built a house there, and cultivated 'American' vegetables and was soon supplying the Americans in Baguio. He also taught Atok villagers how to cultivate temperate vegetables. FYC.
See also: Hunt, Truman; Jones, Isabela; Moore, Lina Espina; Squaw Men.

Haking *(IFU).* One whose leg is shorter than the other.
See also: Yakingking.

Half-half. It depends on where you are. If you are in a honky-tonk bar, it means half gin and half water. In some bars near Baguio's Dangwa Station, you would be given two quatro cantos bottles: one is filled with agua and another with agua pataranta. If you are in a Chinese restaurant, it means pansit canton and pancit guisado. In some restaurants in Cervantes, Mankayan and Abatan, it means pancit and macaroni. In the 1980s in Naguilian Road, it would be half pork and half chicken, half pork and half dog, or half pig liver and half pork. Among the short-lived comedy bars (Baguio people don't want to be dissed before singing in karaoke), it is half Filipino and half Filipina. FYC/DOS.
See also: Bontoc Café.

Half-Way House. Previously the biggest earner at Camp John Hay. By day, it was the golfers' snack bar after Hole 9, before going to the second half of the 18-hole game. By night, it was a dance spot where you rocked to the Footnotes (combo of the Benjie Aquino brothers), or you could cha-cha to Romy Posadas' Latin Jazz. It was within walking distance of the main gate (near Military Circle) so barflies could roll down the hill to waiting taxis. KT.
See also: John Hay, Camp.

Halsema, Eusebius. The American, Eusebius James Halsema, born in New Bremen, Ohio, served as mayor of Baguio for 17 years (staggered from 1919 to 1941). During those years, Baguio's population rose by 600 percent to 25,000 and had the second largest Caucasian population

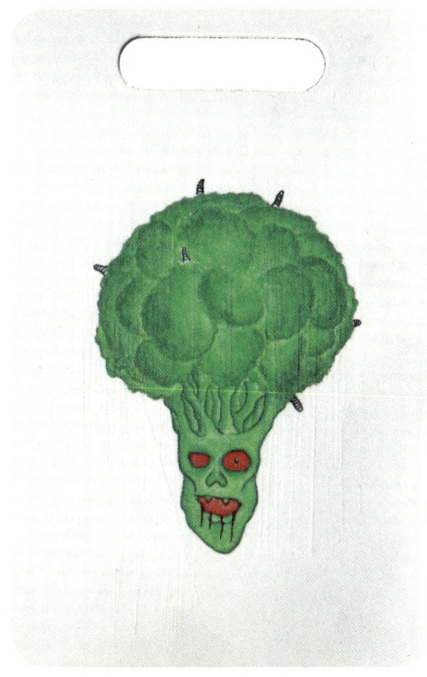

Artwork by Sirk Deuda from the *Angry Vegetables* series.

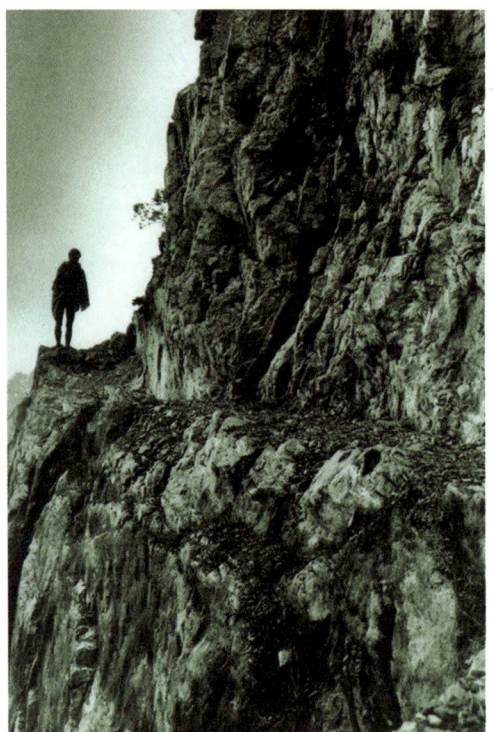

Photograph of an Igorot man on a mountain trail, c. 1920s.
Courtesy AV Cating Family Collection.

in the country (after Manila). An engineer, he built roads and schools for the city as well as the Halsema Highway. He also built the hydroelectric plants to supply power to Baguio, which are still operational today. His son, James Julius Halsema, grew up in Baguio and became editor of the weekly Baguio supplement of the Manila Daily Bulletin. Jim became an AP correspondent and wrote not only his father's biography but also *Bishop Brent's Baguio School*. (Halsema 1991) FYC.
See also: Halsema Highway.

Halsema Highway. The Halsema Highway, the highest Highway System in the country at 7,400 ft. above sea level at its maximum, was first built entirely by hand under the direction of American Engineer and former Baguio City Mayor Eusebius Julius Halsema. It is a 90-mile odyssey of mountain views, landslides, cliffs, clouds, and cold. It connects the two capital towns of Bontoc, Mountain Province and La Trinidad, Benguet. It was opened to minor traffic in the 1930s. Since then, tens of thousands of tons of vegetables and gold ore have passed along its length towards the cities. Mining clearly motivated the building of the Highway (among motives to penetrate the other resources of the mountains) during the American occupation of the country. The Halsema, wider and no longer one of the most dangerous highways in the world, is home to many 'waiting sheds' that are the waystations for both man and commodity between city and community. Thirty-six of these waiting sheds were mosaicked or painted over by AX(iS) Art Project in July and August of 2013. RAC.
See also: Burnham Lake; Chicken dung; Kennon Road; KM. 53; Leonard Wood Road; Masaflora; Sinipsip; Waiting Sheds.

Halud *(IFU)*. The blackening resin for the teeth. Makihalud (to offer halud) would later mean 'to court a girl' and even 'to court in order to gain sexual favor' by offering the pinewood or guava wood ash mixed with sugar cane juice to a girl. It attained a sexual meaning in an Abuwab tale. FYC.
See also: Fallai

Hamada, Sinai. Son of Josefa Carino and Reukitse Hamada. Sinai was one of the first Igorots to take and finish law at the University of the Philippines. He was also an editor of the UP Collegian and regarded as one of the best Filipino fiction writers in English in the 1930s. He later decided to concentrate on lawyering for his poor Igorot constituents and helped found the BIBKA (Benguet, Ifugao, Bontok, Kalinga, Apayao), and the Baguio Midland Courier, one of the biggest weeklies in the country. His short stories are still seen as key works in Cordillera literature. FYC.
See also: Daguio, Amador; Literature; Moore, Lina Espina; Three Witches.

Hangkuku *(IFU)*. Flaring of nostrils and deepening of breath as prelude to anger or rage. FYC.

Hay, John Milton. The US Secretary of State (1898 - 1905) who crafted the colonial policy of "Benevolent Assimilation" – the DNA of Filipinos' never-ending infatuation with the American way of life. Cultural warriors have playfully pointed to the policy as 'benevolent assassination' (or cultural genocide) after Washington DC got tired of the old American dictum: *"a good Injun is a dead Injun."* KT.
See also: Hunt, Truman; John Hay, Camp; Tribes; Worcester, Dean.

Headhunter's drink. According to anthropologist Fay-Cooper Cole (The Tinguian), victorious Tinguian headhunters drank the brains from the heads they chopped off. mixing it with baya. Sometimes the ear lobes and little fingers of the victim were added to the drink. (Cole (1922) 2004).
See also: Busol; Headhunting dance; Headhunting (the tale); Headhunting requirement; Iwa.

Headhunting dance. In Kalinga, only headhunters can dance with closed fists. Others could only dance with open palms, like the women. Headhunters could also dance with more than one woman during the sagang (the headhunting feast), unlike the non-headhunters who could only dance with one partner. FYC.
See also: Busol; Begnas; Headhunter's Drink;

Headhunting requirement;
Headhunting (the tale).

Headhunting requirement. In some communities, a man would have to kill two outsiders to qualify as a headhunter. Nowadays, even soldiers who have killed at least two men are considered headhunters. They are then given a kokolong tattoo on their hands and the kulkullipa if they killed more than two but less than ten men, and the dakag if they killed more than ten men. (De Raedt 1996). FYC.
See also: Begnas; Busol; Headhunter's Drink; Headhunting dance; Headhunting (the tale); Tattoo Designs and Descriptions.

Headhunting (the tale).
"The Moon, a woman called 'Ka-bi-gat,' was one day making a large copper cooking pot. The copper was soft and plastic like potter's clay. Ka-bi-gat held the heavy sagging pot on her knees and leaned the hardened rim against her naked breasts. As she squatted there – turning, patting, shaping, the huge vessel – a son of the man Chal-chal, the Sun, came to watch her. This is what he saw: The Moon dipped her paddle, called 'pip-i,' in the water, and rubbed it dripping over a smooth, rounded stone, an agate with ribbons of colors wound about in it. Then she stretched one long arm inside the pot as far as she could. 'Tub, tub, tub,' said the ribbons of colors as Ka-bi-gat pounded up against the molten copper with the stone in her extended hand. "Slip, slip, slip, slip," quickly answered pip-i, because the Moon was spanking back the many little rounded domes which the stone bulged forth on the outer surface of the vessel. Thus the huge bowl grew larger, more symmetrical, and smooth. Suddenly the Moon looked up and saw the boy intently watching the swelling pot and the rapid playing of the paddle. Instantly the Moon struck him, cutting off his head. Chal-chal was not there. He did not see it, but he knew Ka-bi-gat cut off his son's head by striking with her pip-i. He hastened to the spot, picked the lad up, and put his head where it belonged—and the boy was alive. Then the Sun said to the Moon: 'See, because you cut off my son's head, the people of the Earth are cutting off each other's heads, and will do so hereafter.' 'And it is so,' the story-tellers continue; 'they do cut off each other's heads.'" (Jenks 2005).
See also: Begnas; Busol; Headhunter's Drink; Gutti; Headhunting dance; Headhunting requirement; Kakala; Moon Craters; Tayangtang.

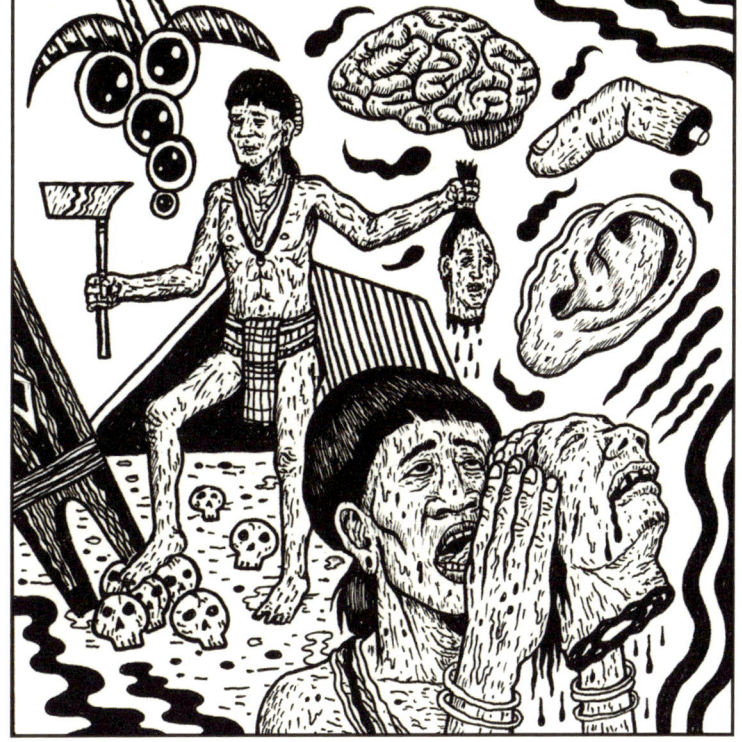

Headhunter's Cocktail, Louie Cordero, pen on paper, 2017.

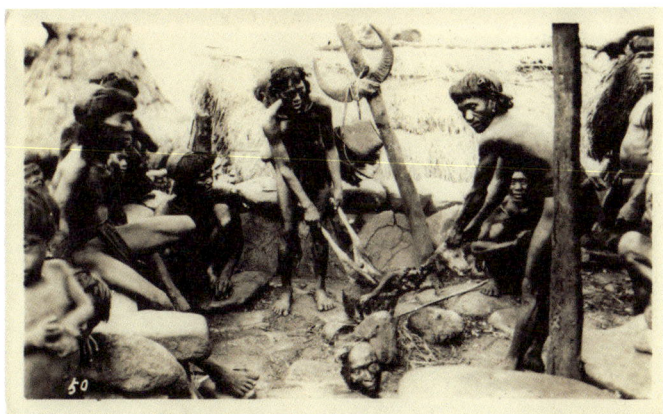

Photograph of Igorot men in a theatrical display of an act of head hunting, c. 1900s.
Courtesy AV Cating Family Collection.

Hegyat *(IFU)* also, **Segyat** *(BON/KAN)*, **Kugit** *(ILO)*. Penile circumcision. Hegyat is a necessary rite of passage among Cordillerans. The traditional circumcision is done by a medicine man who uses a sharp knife to cut the foreskin of the penis. Guava leaves are boiled to wash and clean the newly 'kugited' penis. HZK.

Hib-at *(IFU)*. Counterpoint in gong-beating or the gong used for counterpoint.
See also: Gong; Music; Tubbob.

Hidit *(IFU)*. *"Peace ceremony; peace deities; sickness inflicted by peace deities because of delayed peace ceremony."* (Barton, 1919).
See also: Padpadaya; Pasang; Pattaliat; Vochong.

Hihim *(IFU)* also **Sisim** *(ILO/BON/KAN)*. Galvanized Iron (GI) sheet used first by American miners and followed by Cordillerans who used the flat sheet as exterior walling because it traps heat inside the house. FYC.

Hikot *(IFU)*. Scabbard for an axe or knife.

Hinag *(IFU)*. Reddish rays at sunset.
See also: Finabdas.

Historical Trauma Response. A theory of intergenerational trauma experienced by indigenous peoples due to intense stress and no time to grieve or heal. Stressors are contact and colonialism, warfare, disease, forced removal, forced prohibition against language use and religious practices, compulsory boarding school, and ongoing discrimination and poverty. An example is how Ibaloys reacted to Galvey's attacks, deciding to live far away from each other. (Wesley-Esquimaux & Smolewski 2004)
See also: Galvey, Guillermo; Igorotism; Imperialist Nostalgia; Survivance.

Hogop *(IFU)*. House blessing.

Hole in the Wall. A narrow snack bar that previously existed on Session Road in Baguio City (near the present Star Café). It was run by a happy-go-lucky African-American woman named Maggie Smith (yes, like the actress). She was loud and boisterous but motherly to all. Her friendly daughter Frances served personalized burgers (long before the fastfood chain de-personalized burger making)!

Hopot ti Hoho *(IFU)*. Brassierre. Taken from the Ilocano *"Supot ti suso [bag for the breasts]"*. KT.

Horse-watering trough. Located in the middle of Abanao Street, this hidden landmark features two concrete horses stuck in time drinking from a mosquito-infested watering 'trough.' Erected by then-Mayor Jun Labo, this is a reminder of when horses were the main means of transportation and this area was where they tied and fed them. CPM.
See also: Cowboy; Faith Healing; Pink Ponies.

Hudhud *(IFU)*. Chanted by Ifugaos during harvesting and weeding of rice, funeral wakes and bogwa (bone washing) rituals. The epic could take three to four days to finish. Only women recite the more than 200 stories of 40 episodes each, in a language almost impossible to transcribe, full of wordplay, metaphors and repetitions. There is a munhaw-e (lead chanter) and something like a Greek chorus that instinctively knows when

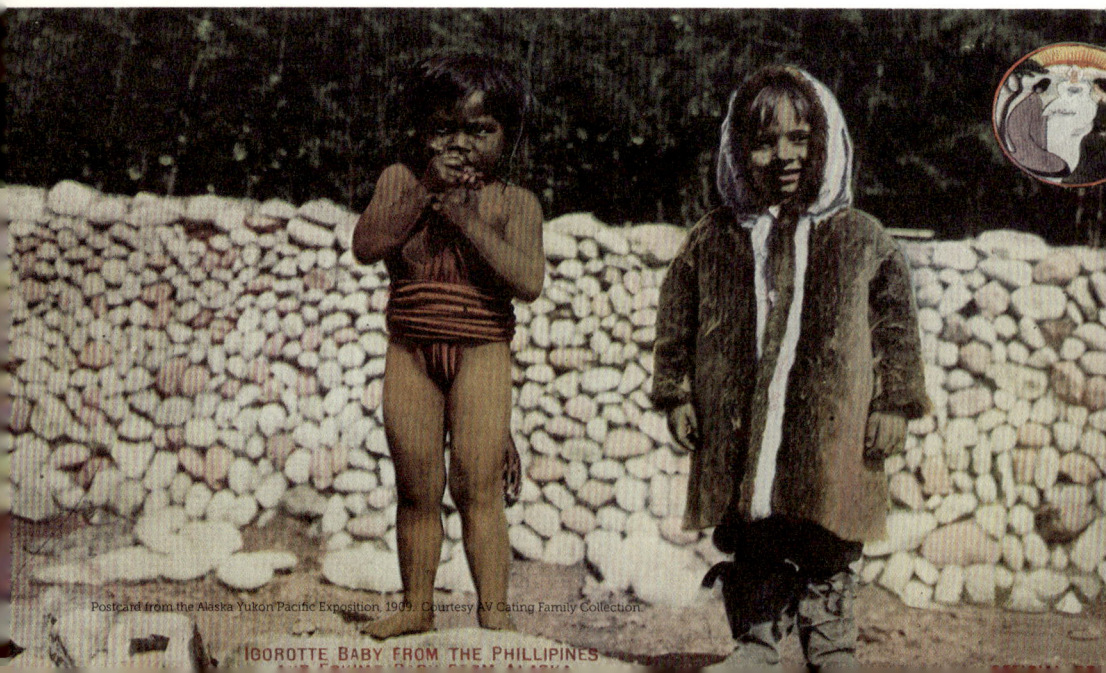

Postcard from the Alaska Yukon Pacific Exposition, 1909. Courtesy AV Cating Family Collection.

to chime in. The entry of Catholicism and mass media has led to a weakening of the tradition and the old women are hard up in finding younger substitutes. Together with the Alim, the Hudhud was chosen by the United Nations Educational, Scientific and Cultural Organization (UNESCO) to be included on the Intangible Cultural Heritage of Humanity List. FYC.

See also: Dalagadag; Gehhehhe; Humlun; Mampay; Salidummay; Ullalim.

Hukhuk *(IFU)*. To cover or hide something with one's hand.

Hulin *(IFU)*. In this ritual, a group of mumbaki will go to the muyong (the communal reserve forest above the agricultural land) to choose the right tree (normally narra) to cut a branch and assign an artisan to carve a bulul. This is not done in the commercial production of bululs. TDH.

See also: Bul-ul; Mambunong.

Humlun *(IFU)*. In the Hudhud, this is sung, *"Humlunanday mamadikit hi Aliguyun [they, the beautiful girls, arouse the feelings of Aliguyon],"* ergo, humlun means anything that arouses feelings or curiosity. (Nike Programme 2007-2010) FYC.

See also: Hudhud.

Hunger. Once upon a time, according to a story by the Tulgao people of Tinglayan, Kalinga, there was a farmer named Alangang who was so assiduous and indefatigable that even Kabunian was encouraged to till the neighboring uma or swidden. Because his new neighbor was God, Alangang worked doubly hard, even working on the sixth day which was taboo then. So Kabunian decided to put a huge tree in the middle of Alangang's uma. The farmer cut it and sap from the magical tree flowed over the uma and those of his kailian. And that is why the land of Tulgao is barren and the people are always hungry. FYC.

See also: Kabunian.

Hunt, Truman. A semi-surgeon during the Philippine-American War, a mining prospector in the Cordillera, lieutenant governor of Bontoc in 1903, and the impresario of the Suyoc delegation to the 1904 St. Louis Fair. He was more known as Giyad by his Kankanaey constituents. After the 1904 fair, Hunt went on with his own Igorot exhibitions, recruiting Bontocs to form an attraction at Coney Island and later touring America (Prentice 2014). Hunt, however, maltreated his wards, failed to pay them, and stole from them. In 1906, some of the Igorots filed suits against him for his theft. Hunt attempted to evade the authorities in a manhunt where he was followed by the US Government and Pinkerton detectives until he was brought to trial in Memphis, Tennessee. The all-white jury decided in favor of the Igorots and Hunt was sentenced to 18 months in the workhouse. Although the verdict was set aside by the judge and later declared a mistrial, Hunt languished for eight months in a Memphis jail. (Afable 2004) FYC .

See also: Dog-eating; Hay, John Milton; Jones, Isabela; MacArthur and the Igorot Soldiers; Nikimalika; Tribes; Worcester, Dean.

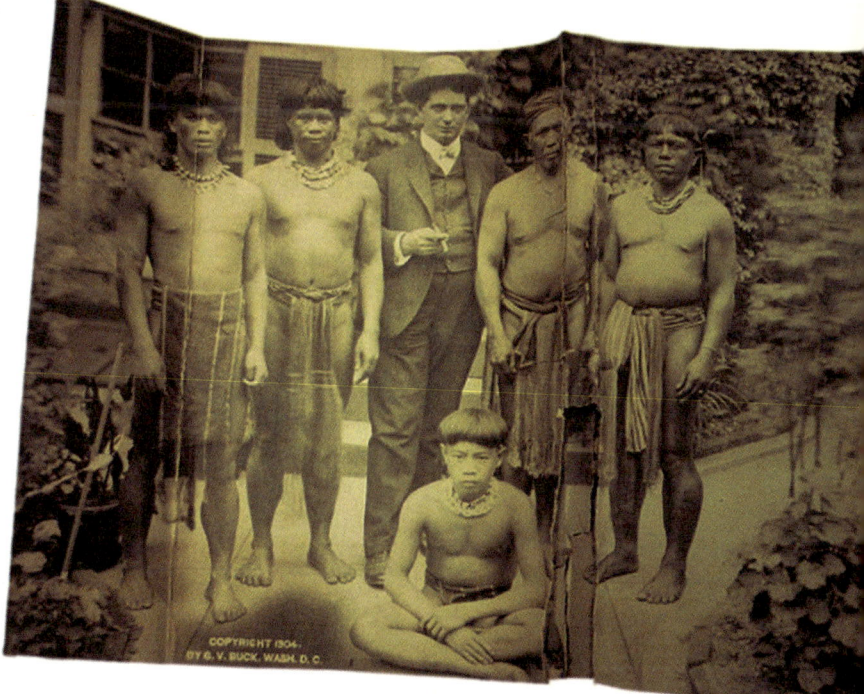

Photograph of *Truman Hunt* with Igorot men. Photograph from *The Lost Tribe of Coney Island*. Courtesy Claire Prentice Collection.

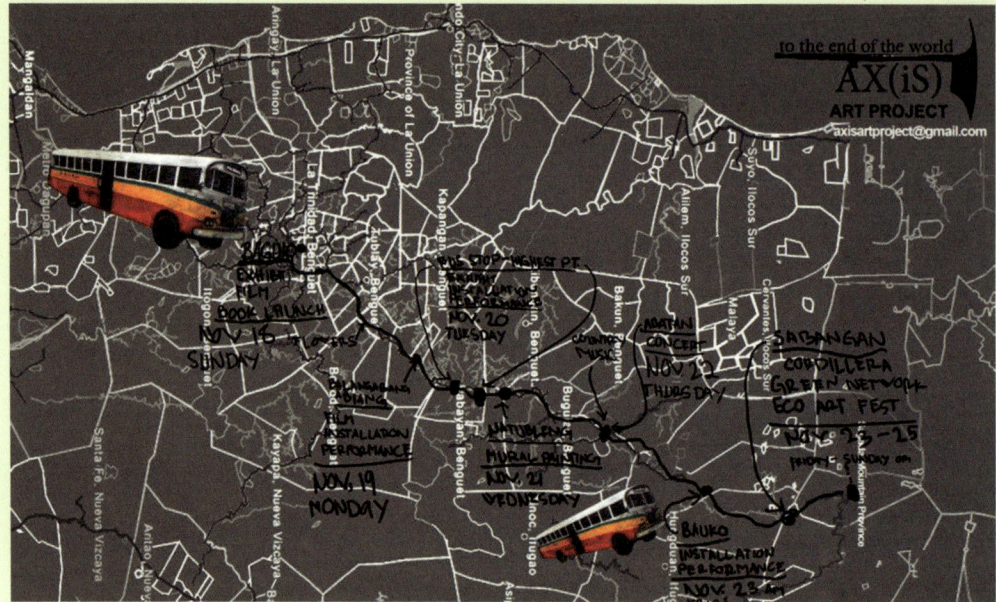

Invitation *To the End of the World*, 2013.

Halsema Hijinks

The words 'camping road trip' invariably strikes terror into the heart of many an urbanite contemporary art curator. Tossing 'mountain' and 'one of the world's most dangerous roads' into the mixture wasn't particularly reassuring either. And, when I asked my Philippine co-curator Kawayan de Guia for details about programme, route and accommodation, an interminable silence ensued. Then came the text message: *"bring sleeping bag."*

When Singapore Art Museum began the process of inviting co-curators from across Southeast Asia for the Singapore Biennale 2013, one of the aims was to reflect the art practices of practitioners located outside of the capital and metropolitan areas. For the Philippines, we eventually brought on four curators based in varied locales: Claro Ramirez Jr (Manila), Abraham Garcia (Mindanao), Charlie Co (Bacolod) and Kawayan de Guia (Baguio). All of them are also artist-curators, or as some might prefer to see it, artists who happen to curate or organise projects in their particular communities – or extended 'neighbourhood' as it were.

Since 2011, Kawayan de Guia has been the main driver for the AX(iS) Art Project, which in their words, *"is an art collective of region-based and metropolitan artists engaged in art projects that are guided by the principle 'Art Access for All': the belief that art is not exclusive and, hence, posited outside the confines of institutional norms. The declaration therefore entails the responsibility of artists to move art into the awareness of the local community and general public."*

In this case, it meant taking the project quite literally on the road: the 90-mile road known as the Halsema Highway. The ride was a hired cranky Dangwa bus, which, for several decades,

Photograph taken along Halsema Highway, 2012. Photograph by Kawayan de Guia.

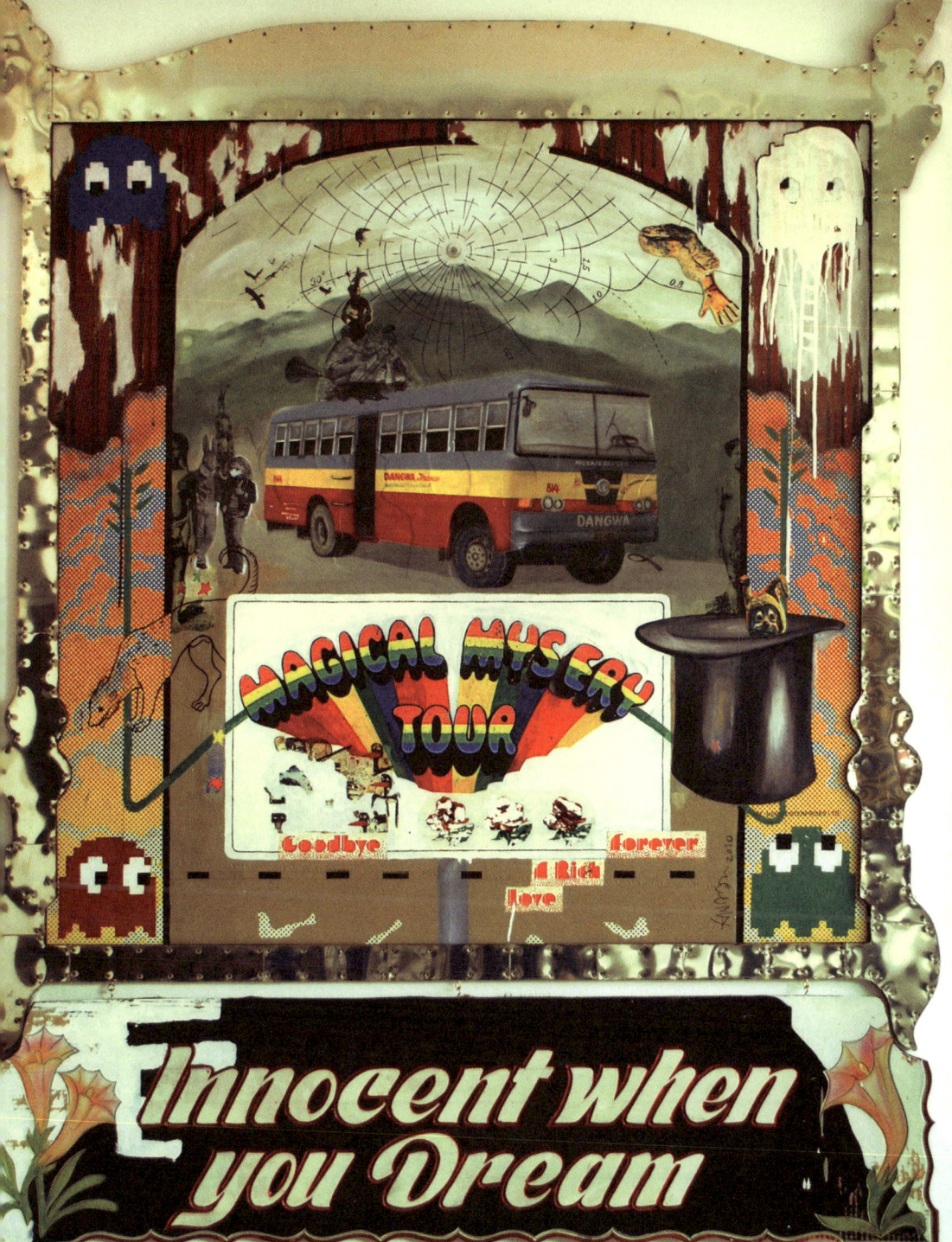

Innocent When You Dream, Kawayan de Guia, mixed media, 171x146 cm, 2010.

HALSEMA: AX(iS) ART PROJECT

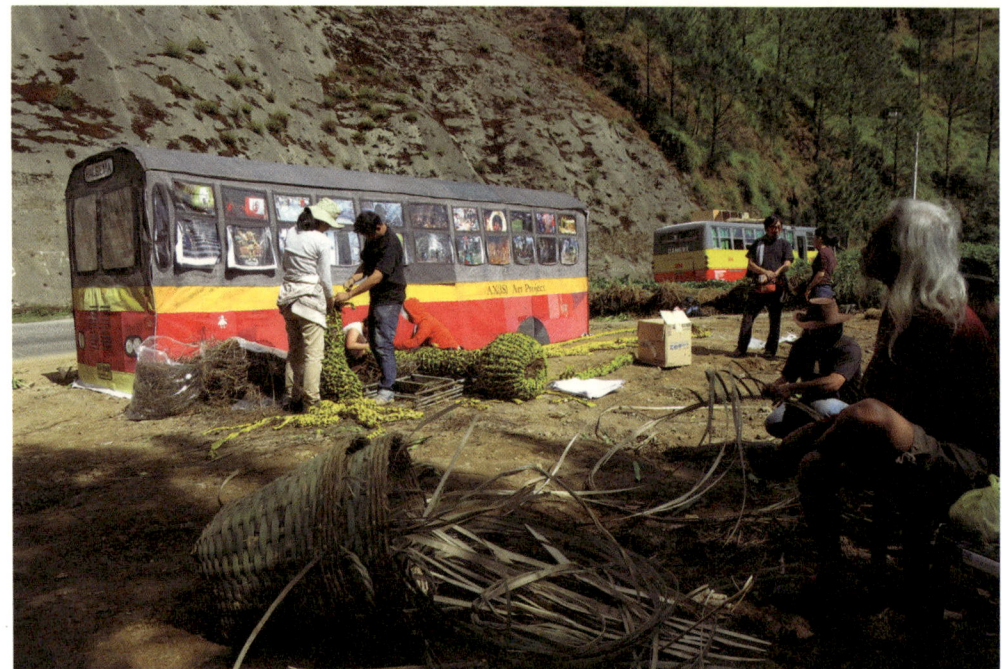

was the primary means of transport between Baguio and the hinterlands, with the unpaved Halsema as the main artery snaking through the mountains. Riffing off the iconic vehicle, Kawayan had made an AX(iS) 'tent' for an earlier exhibition in the form of the bus, and this canvas simulacrum would now double up as the trip's main accommodation.

With virtually no funding for AX(iS), and owing to other unpredictable elements, the schedule for the week-long journey was loose at best. Yet the rhythms of life in the Cordillera mountains have an order and pace of their own, things get done with its peculiar mode of economy, canny resourcefulness and speed – but it entailed letting go of expectations of the pre-programmed and scheduled 'efficiencies' that one is more accustomed to in city life.

Indeed, one of the objectives of AX(iS) is to shift the context and rattle the framework by which 'Art' and 'Artworld' are understood through a western paradigm that was imposed though the years of colonial rule and propagated in urban centres; and prompt a 're-cognition' that the categorical distinctions between art, craft, 'making', performance and ritual did not previously exist in indigenous practices, being part of a larger continuum in which material and spiritual worlds also cohabit. And more than co-exist, it is the opening of a space where sprits – old and new – come to party and play; it was a carnivalesque spirit that pervaded the journey and its travellers.

THE OPENER, 18 November 2012:

Apropos of any 'proper' art event, it began with an official launch event the evening before. The programme: a Japanese film about sustainable farming, spoken word and poetry readings, graffiti art and the launch of a literary journal by Ubbog, a group of young Cordilleran writers. The venue: Katipunan, a dog eatery – and by that, it is not the kind of café you bring Snowy, unless you love your dog... stir fried with spring onions. The audience: surprisingly vegetarian (much to the dismay of the restaurant's servers).

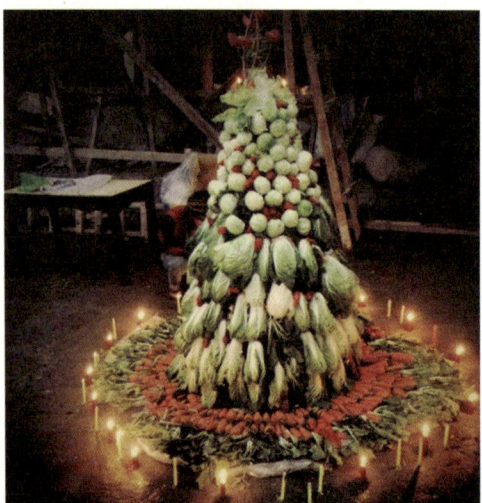

Photographs from AX(is) Art Project's community events and gatherings.

DAY 1:

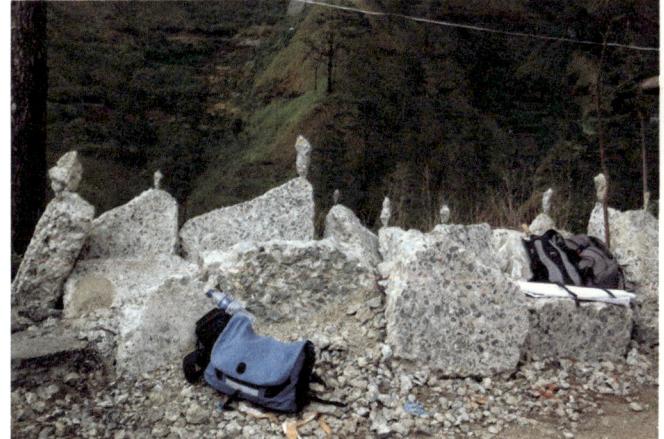
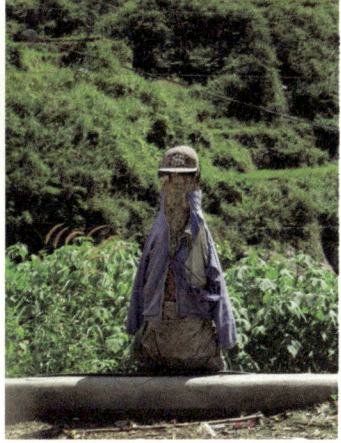

On the early morning of 19 November 2012, a motley crew of bleary-eyed artists, cultural advocates, writers, musicians, curators, chef and sous-chef boarded the bus. Armed with a toothbrush, a sense of humour and the willingness to forgo regular showers, we were off.

DAY 2: Highest Point

The next stop was close to the 'Highest Point' of the Halsema. At the diner by the bus terminal, the artist and academic Katrin de Guia, Shant and a few other artists constructed a christmas tree from vegetables commonly grown along the highway. Inside the bus diner, Kawayan set up a small exhibition that included the 'evil vegetables' by the artist Sirk. Comic in appearance, the drawings on small chopping boards offered a critique on the progressive poisoning of land because of agricultural practices, in particular the ever-increasing dependence on fertilizers that contaminate the soil.

DAY 3:

The camp stop on Day 3 can only be best described as a vegetable patch next to the highway. Despite the very imprecise location of said-vegetable patch, others were able to find us and joined the group. It included Eliode, a Swiss teacher and her friend, artist and filmmaker Kidlat Tahimik (not-so-fresh from a 36-hour journey from the United States), and Kawayan's 90-something grandmother, Virginia Oteyza de Guia. The

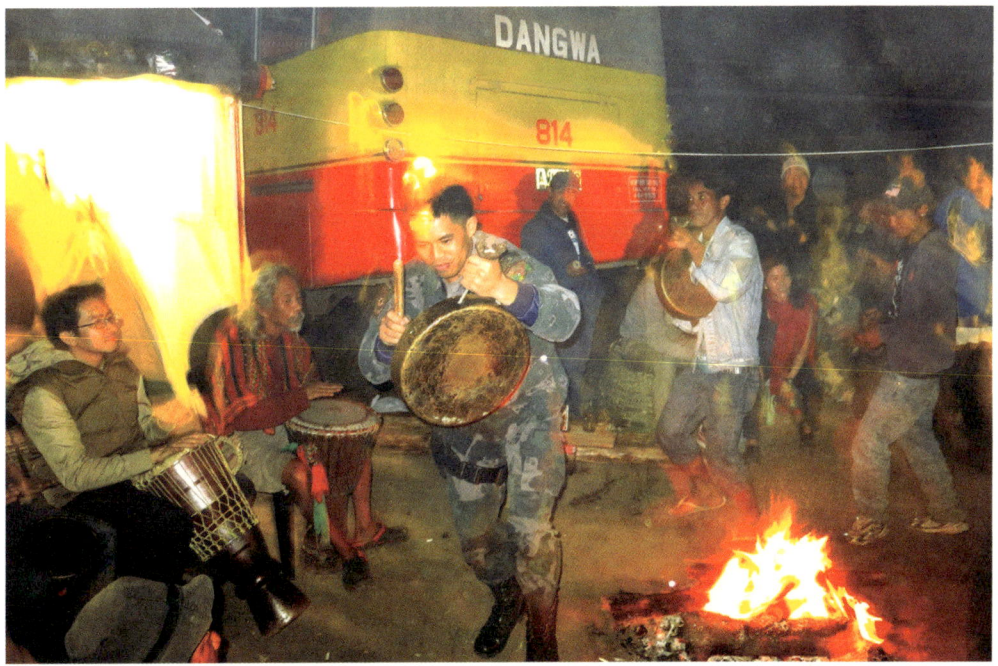

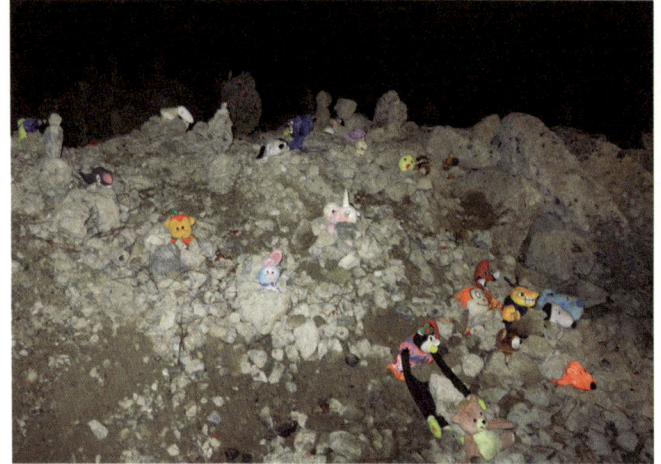
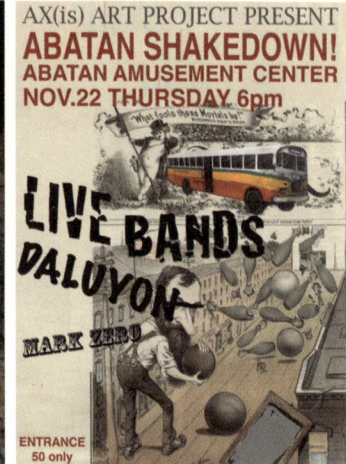

Photographs from AX(is) Art Project's community events and gatherings.

elegant matriarch – Baguio's first and only woman mayor – sat comfortably by the roadside, watching three of the crew install a particularly challenging work. Evidently born with the DNA of mountain goats, Pongz, Rocky and Santos scaled a near-vertical rock face in flip-flops with only a few ropes and sans official safety permits, and installed a 50m long 'snake' that had been woven from traffic hazard tape by a Japanese artist. As we watched, we realised the bracing mountain air was unexpectedly foul, and fowl was the reason. Every 20-minute interval brought a pungent gust of chicken dung as trucks transporting the cheap fertilizer barrelled up and down the highway; it was an olfactory experience that continued unabated throughout the entire night.

DAY 4&5:

Over the course of the next two days, other art events and performances continued, including film screenings, performances and a concert at the town of Abatan. The Dangwa-tent performed variously as a screening room, a make-shift gallery for an artwork installation, and much-needed shelter during the freezing nights. Close to the end of the trip, it decided it had worked hard enough and chose to fly. We returned from a day's trip to Sagada and discovered it at the bottom of a hill, crumpled amongst the vegetables after its spectacular leap for freedom.

Day 6, Final camp:

The trip ended in Sabangan, coinciding with a youth eco-festival organised by the Cordillera Green Network, and involved a number of Japanese artists. Away from the festival site, at the beginning of the Chico River, Shant began extensively standing several river stones, to the delight of the village children who either copied him or used the rocks for target practice. The scene of standing stones evoked one of Andy Goldsworthy's pieces, yet Shant did not regard or call it 'art' or a 'work.' He spoke of it as a continuation of a child's pastime, and so it did not bother him that some boys used it as a game. More importantly, other children who mimicked him began to get the feel for the stones; every intimate touch of the rock to find its centre established a direct connection with that single stone. At the end of the world, this was what mattered – the action, the doing – not its name and categorisation. Shant hoped to return to the village later to do a workshop with the children and carry out the monumental task along the long stretch of the river.

Out on the road, what also became apparent was the possibility of anything (and everything) to be transformed into a medium for art and 'making'. The most relevant and vital materials were not ones purchased from the art store but sourced, scavenged and salvaged directly from the immediately available – from farmed vegetables and wild callailies, to stones and chicken dung. The materials spoke of local conditions and site-specificity on an elemental level – and not merely by way of installation in a particular site. Admittedly not everything worked: Kawayan discovered chicken dung fertilizer possessed poor moulding qualities when he tried to sculpt a snowman.

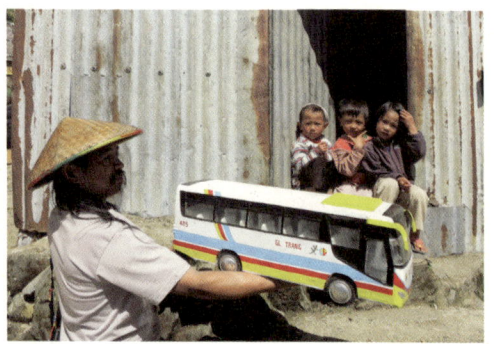

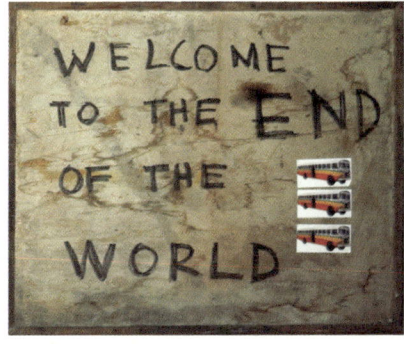

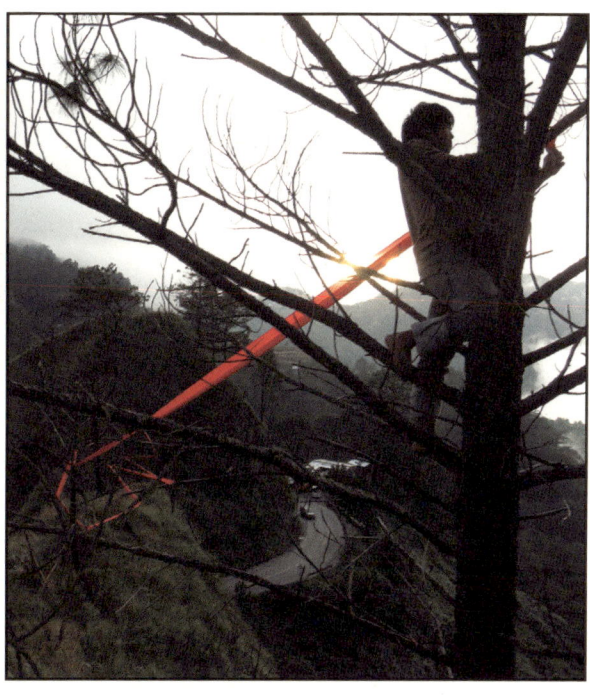

The trip in November 2012 has since become a trial run for what has become a more ambitious realisation of the Halsema project, for the Singapore Biennale 2013. At my last estimate, it now involves around 100 participants and is driven through some 14 sub-projects. Core to the project is the transference of knowledges and it will include the publication of the 'Uncyclopedia' book. The project with Singapore Biennale revisits some of the issues in the initial road trip and expands to include more topics, such as land use and rights, indigenous tattoos, the salt trade, the myth of General Yamashita's hidden gold hoard, and the perplexing popularity of country and western music in the mountains. Baguio-style, this party has gotten bigger, badder, better. Just remember to bring your toothbrush.
JTH

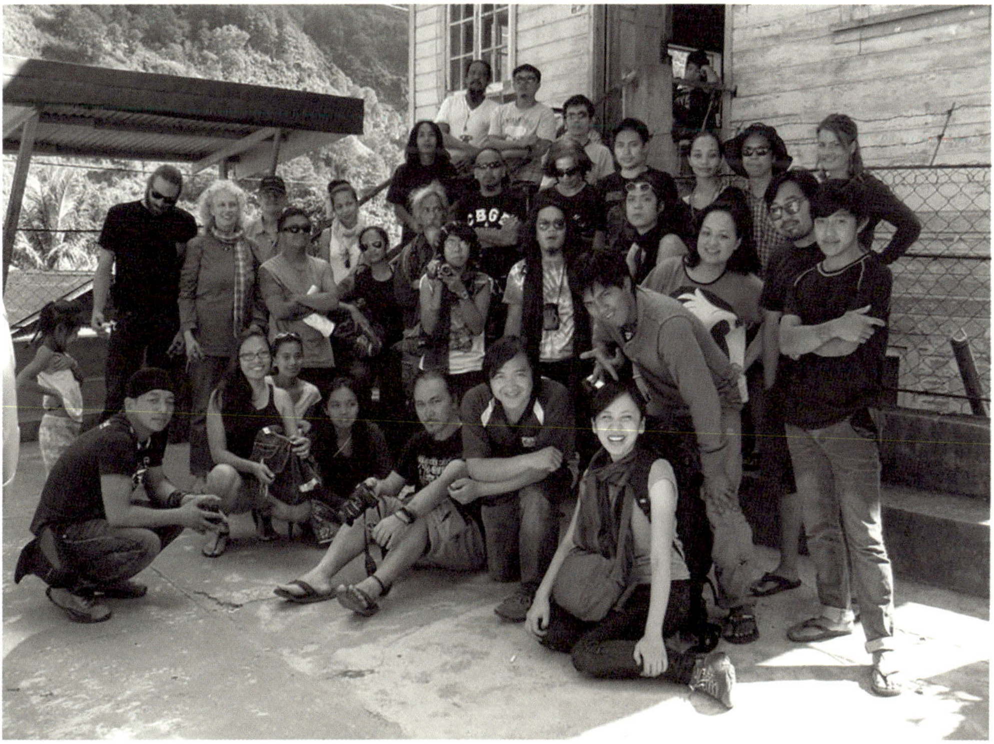

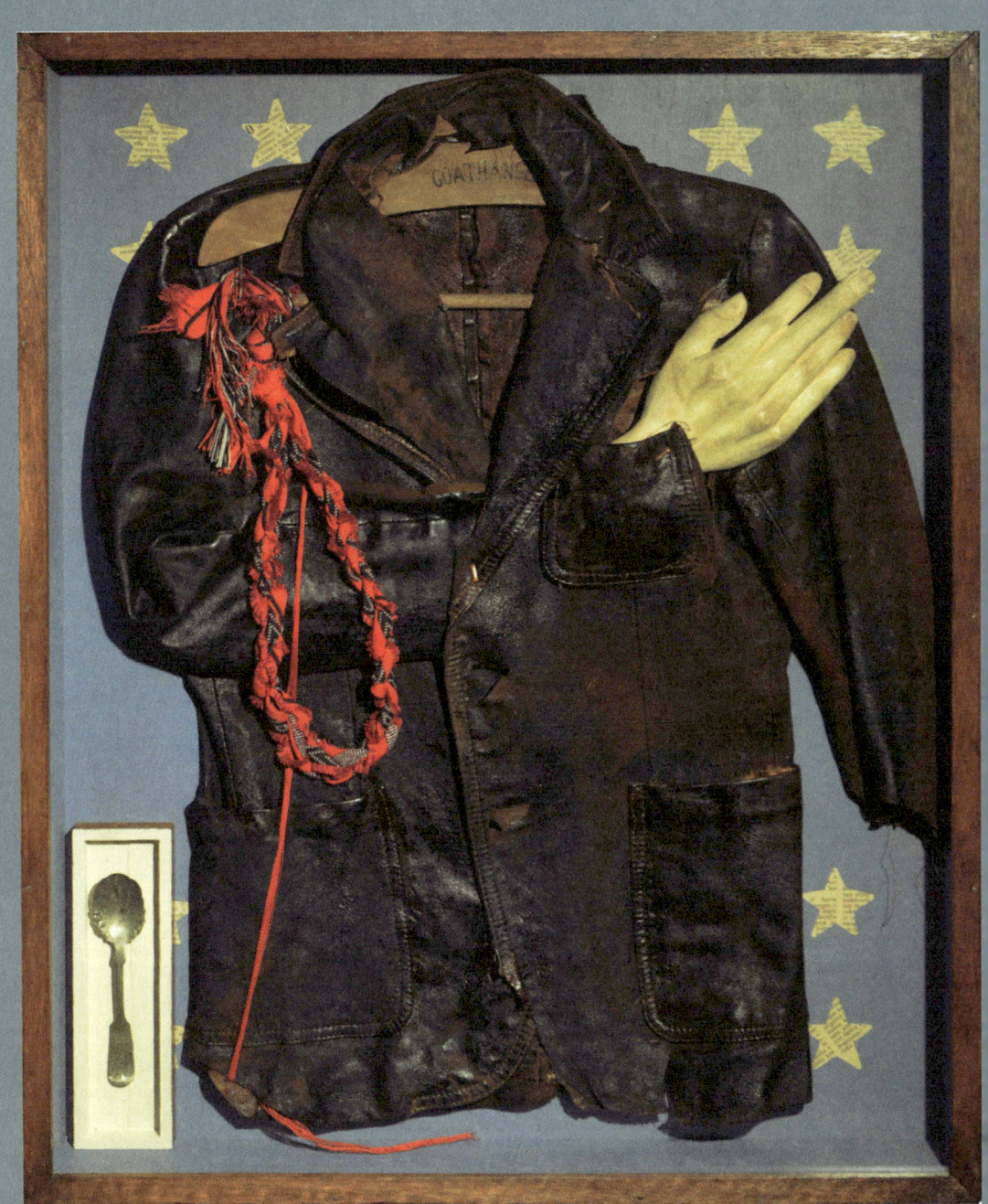

American Goathanger, Rocky Cajigan, box construction, 76x61 cm, 2015. Photograph by Arnold Baladad.

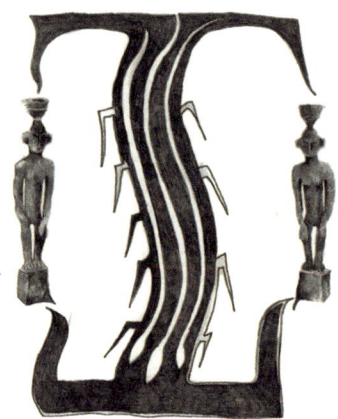

Ibbaw *(ISN)*. Small, slender, white clustered edible mushrooms.
See also: Kato; Tabayong.

Ibwa *(ITN)*. *"Ibwa is an evil spirit, who once mingled with the people in human form. Due to the thoughtless act of a mourner at a funeral, he became so addicted to the taste of human flesh, that it has since then been necessary to protect the corpse from him. He fears iron, and hence a piece of that metal is always laid on the grave. Holes are burned in each garment placed on the body to keep him from stealing them."* (Cole (1915) 2004).
See also: Alan; Ampasit; Banig; Bengao; Carangat; Darupaypay; Nginin; Paniaw; Pasang; Tinguian Spirits.

Ice. In 1969, Andy Cosalan co-authored a law establishing ice and cold storage plants in Baguio, La Union, Ilocos Sur, Benguet, Kalinga-Apayao, Bontoc, Pangasinan, Tarlac, Nueva Ecija and Zambales. *"Building ice plants would play a big role in transportation, preservation and distribution of food, fish, meat and vegetable products that can be distributed fresh to inland municipalities and stimulating commerce in these regions,"* he said. It also meant the introduction of ice cream, halo-halo and ice candies, especially in the Cordillera outside of Baguio. Baguio had already been selling ice and distilled water since 1909. FYC.
See also: Ice cream.

Ice cream. In one of the parties held by Dr. Hilary Clapp in Bontoc in 1932, ice cream was served. It came all the way from San Fernando, La Union. FYC.
See also: Ice; Pitapit.

Ichaw *(KAL)*. A small reddish black bird that is believed to be an omen bird. In Kalinga during hunting time, if the ichaw appears on the right of the hunter, the hunt will be fruitful. The hunt will be fruitless if it appears on the left. But, if the bird appears on the left and chirps three times, it is a good sign. HZK.
See also: Bangon; Ikik; Labeg; Mt. Polis; Sangbo.

Iddaya *(IFU)*. She is known to Ifugaos as a beautiful goddess famed for her industry and generosity. In January of 2012 the oldest pine tree in the city was killed by an over-zealous attempt to identify its age by boring into its core. The AX(iS) Art Project turned it into a totem. Ifugao

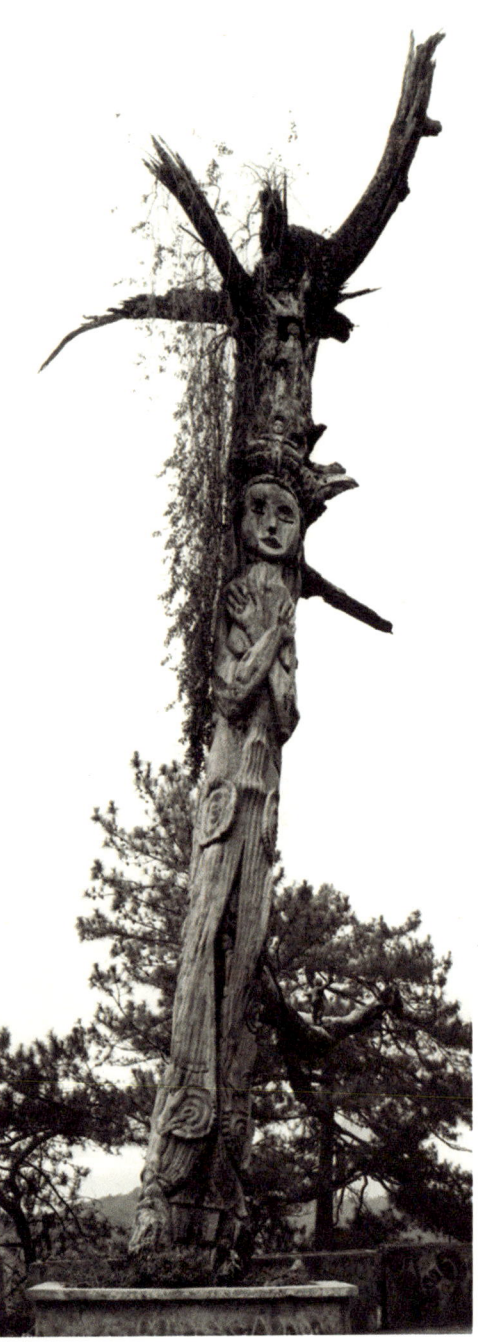

Photograph of the *Iddaya* totem created during the AX(iS) Art Project in 2012. Photograph by Tony Birch.

woodcarvers crafted the shape of a woman that was modelled after the goddess Iddaya. DOS.
See also: Inhabian; Longayban.

Idus *(KAN)*. Wooden spoon.

Ifugao. Mispronounced from Ipugaw or the People of Pugaw or Earth World. On the East is Lagud (Downstream); West is Daya (Upstream), Dalom (Underworld) and Kabunyan (Skyworld). These regions are filled with deities, spirits, ancestors, ghosts and demons. An Ifugao priest could name 1,000 of them. FYC.
See also: Kabunian.

Ifugao Marriage and Courtship Taboos.
"There are taboos relating to exogamy. In the presence of male and female kin that are of the degrees within which marriage is forbidden it is taboo: (a) to look fixedly at the woman's breasts or hips; (b) to speak of the dormitory of the unmarried; (c) to mention the love affairs of an unmarried couple except most guardedly; (d) to break wind; (e) to blackguard; (f) to play the bikong, lover's harp. Matters connected with sex must not be referred to unnecessarily; whenever it is necessary to refer to them, the most delicately veiled euphemisms must be used. Thus an unborn babe must be called 'the friend'; the placenta must be termed a 'blanket'; the short plank that constitutes the Ifugao's bed must be designated as a 'level'; even an egg must be referred to as a 'soft stone' or 'stone of the chickens.'" (Barton 2012).

Igadan *(ILO/KAN)*. [1] Grinding area for gold ore. [2] Tool seat for manual coconut grinding. DLD.

Igod *(BON/KAN)*. Stone used to remove dirt from the body during a bath. Men-igod means to use this stone in bathing. PAD.

Igorot. The collective term for the cultural identity of the Indigenous Peoples in the Cordilleras.

IGOROTAK According to Scott (1993), the etymology of the word comes from the Spanish golot or gulud meaning mountain, plus the prefix y-; thus ygolot or ygulud, meaning people of the mountain. Although the Kalingas, Ifugaos, and Apayaos prefer to be called by their own ethnic identity (some dislike the word because of its Spanish origins), many Kankanaeys, Bontocs, Ibalois and others enjoy being called Igorots.

In the past, the word Igorot was often used by lowlanders and foreigners in a derogatory way. For them, an Igorot was a filthy individual with bad manners who lives in the mountains. When their children got filthy playing outdoors, or behaved badly, they would sometimes scold them by screaming *"Igorot!!!"*

During the 90s, the use of the word Igorot became a trend due to the popularity of the Igorotak (I am Igorot) T-shirt. Even tourists became more interested in purchasing the Igorotak T-shirt instead of the souvenir shirts from Baguio City, Sagada and Banaue. DOS.
See also: Ethnographic Mapping; Igorotak T-shirt; Igorotism; Pow-wow: Dance of the Philippine Igorots; Rancherria de los Igorottes.

Igorot Advisory Council. A five-member advisory council set up in the 1920s, which would meet several times a year with the Baguio city council to resolve culture clashes between the Americans and the Igorots.

Igorot Tail. From *Human Tails – A Statement and a Correction* written by W.W. Keen (1926):

"The correction I wish to make is as follows: In my book 'I Believe in God and in Evolution,' I have included in the fourth edition a photograph of an Igorot with a tail, which I vouched for as I understood that it had been photographed by my own grandson, Mr. John Freeman. A few days ago within a few hours of each other, I received letters from Dr. Aleš Hrdlička, of the division of physical anthropology of the National Museum of the Smithsonian Institution, and Mrs. Ella F. Grove, who a year ago had been doing some work in the Philippines for the National Research Council. Both of these correspondents stated that the Bureau of Science in Manila had shown them the original of this photograph which showed that it was a fake photograph, the tail having been added to the original by a photographer, I suppose as a joke. On communicating with my grandson I find that I misinterpreted his letter and that he did not photograph this Igorot. My argument that human tails (of which I have shown that there are many undoubted instances) prove our animal ancestry is not in the least disproved by my having unfortunately used a photograph which further investigation has shown to be a fraud, for there are plenty of genuine tails." (359-360).
See also: Bakget; Igorot; Igorotism; Pow-wow; Wanes.

Igorota: The Legend of the Tree of Life. The trailer of this movie shows the country's most revered actress in the 1960s and 1970s, Charito Solis, baring her breasts in a river scene with dozens of non-Igorota women, witnessed by comedian Cachupoy and Ric Rodrigo in a Safari shirt. Then their eyes locked and shame came to Solis as Princess Maila and she put on her clothes and walked away as the camera zoomed out to reveal the Banaue Rice Terraces. Although the breast showing scenes were not shown in Philippine theaters, the movie, directed and written by Luis Nepomuceno, was an instant controversial hit in the Philippines in 1968. In the movie, Rodrigo as Albert would later marry Maila and they settled in Manila where her friends discriminated against her. They went back to

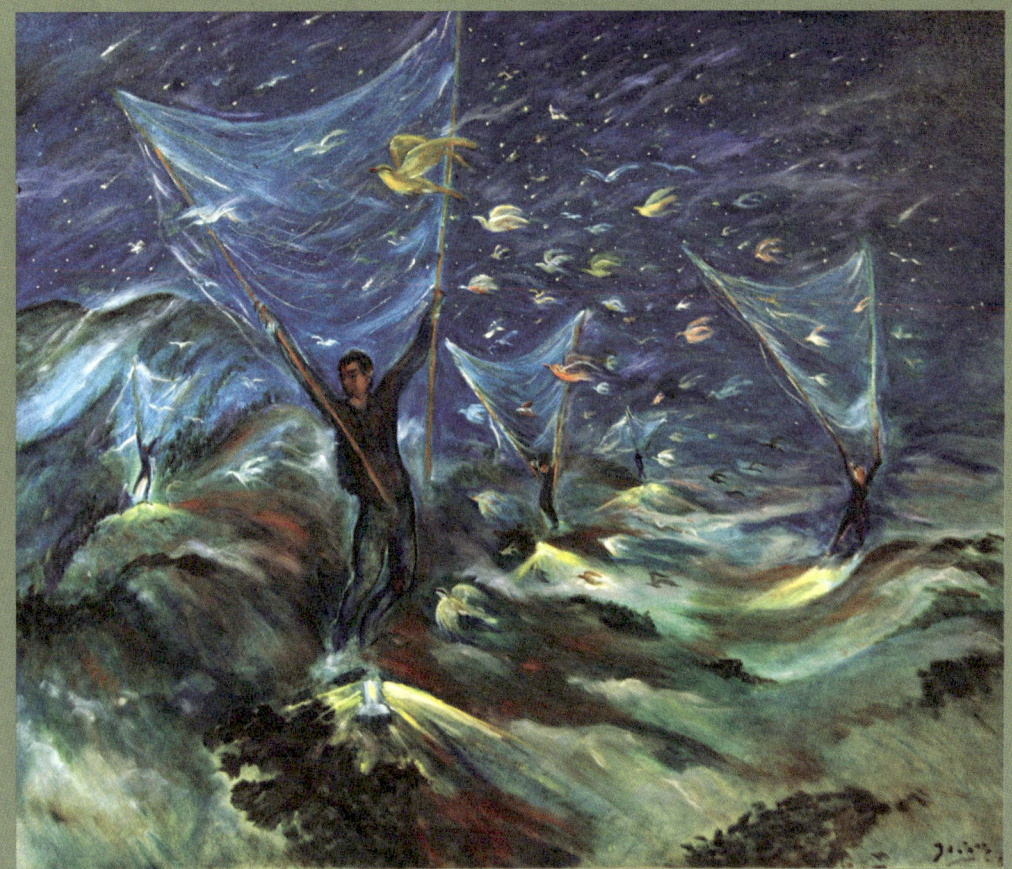

Mangkek, Jaime de Guzman, oil on canvas, 165x132 cm, c. 1990s.

the Cordillera and he got killed by an avenging headhunter. Solis won Asia's Best Actress Award for her role. FYC.

See also: Abong; Banaue: Stairway to the Sky; Big Bird Cage; Headhunting (the tale); Irisan (the movie); Kung Mangarap Ka't Magising; Mumbaki; Vacacionista.

Igorotak T-shirt. In 1997, Naduma Company decided to come out with a T-shirt printed with *"Igorotak"* using a splattered font. The T-shirt, usually black with the Igorotak stencilled white, became so successful that there sprung forth T-shirts proclaiming *"Ifontok," "Ifugao (already redundant if I-Ifugao)," "Y-Kalinga"* and even *"Ilocano-ak."* Actor Robin Padilla makes it a point to wear the Igorotak T-shirt whenever he comes home to Baguio. Another design, F.B.I. (Full Blooded Igorot), was not as successful because the Full Blooded Ilocano came first. FYC.

See also: Igorotism.

Igorotism. *"... [T]he advancement of highlanders' collective place in Philippine society as a people..."* (Finin 2005; 144).

See also: Historical Trauma Response; Igorot; Igorotak T-shirt; Pow-wow; Rancherria de los Igorottes; Survivance.

Igorot Worker's Welfare Association. Formed in February 1950 by 1,200 highland miners of Benguet Consolidated and Balatoc Mining. It was the first highland organization to use 'Igorot' in its name. FYC.

See also: Igorot.

Iho *(IFU).* Evil, bad. In Tagalog, it is a sign of respect as in the Spanish *"Ijo."*

Ikik *(KAN).* Bird catching. Mangkik means to catch birds. A popular traditional activity for men in Sagada that is also done in other Kankanaey areas like Sabangan, Besao and Bauko. Ikik season roughly covers the last week of August until the last week of November. During these rainy months, the elevated areas of Danum, Ampacao and Nabas-ang become villages of lights as bird catchers set up their traps at night. Bird catching is ideal during moonless nights and when it is dobdob (when the wind comes from the east). Ikik makes use of strong lamps that attract birds to a seped (net attached to two bamboo poles) held by the bird catcher. Before gas lamps became available, they made use of wood torches. Finds include local resident birds like tala (shrike)

and siteg (flower pecker), as well as migratory birds like pukaw (egret), balisoso (kingfisher), kuba (bittern), bagit (quail) and bakakew (cuckoo). People in earlier times caught birds as a protein supplement to the traditionally almost vegetarian diet. Stories of famed bird catchers tell of sacks full of birds caught in one night. Even now that chicken and pork are available commercially, this activity still enjoys popularity among the young people of Sagada who turn this night activity into an occasion for socialization, complete with food and drinks around a bonfire, and tents for overnight camping. The international outbreak of bird flu abated this activity temporarily. Environmental advocates have called for this activity to be converted into harmless bird watching. GAD.
See also: Mt. Polis.

Ilablab-ak *(KAN)*. When a child who trips is then told to stand up independently, the phrase *"Laton, ilablab-ak mo sa. [It's all right. You will grow from it.]"* is said to the child to ease the pain. DOS.

I-langit *(ISN)*. Sky spirits. When i-langit want to possess a ritual master, they use a bridge or ladder to come down to the earth.
See also: Dorarakit; Kabunian.

Ili *(KAN/BON/KAL)*. Town, nation, village, hamlet, borough, community, or motherland. According to Esteban Magannon in his 1984 essay, "Cognition of Time, Change and Social Identity: Kalinga History and Historical Consciousness," *"the 'ili' or 'hometown' is a 'second self' which is a permanent home of people as well as spirits embodying both the familial and religious affections and loyalty."* (Finin 2005, 301 n. 2) FYC.

Immuya-uy *(IFU)*. Refers to an individual or family who has been sharing their wealth and good fortune with the community. TDH.
See also: Buaya Economic Classes; Hagabi; Pes-ay.

Imok *(KAN)*. (1) To covet or lust for.
(2) To desire eagerly.
(3) To be greedy.

Imperialist Nostalgia. Described by Rosaldo (1993, 68) as *"a mood of nostalgia that makes racial domination appear innocent and pure."* He goes on to describe how *"imperialist nostalgia revolves around a paradox: A person kills somebody and then mourns the victim... [or] someone deliberately alters a life form and then regrets that things have not remained as they were... Imperialist nostalgia uses a pose of 'innocent yearning' both to capture peoples' imagination and to conceal its complicity with often brutal domination."* (ibid., 69-70).
See also: Historical Trauma Response; Survivance.

Inasin *(BON)*. Heavily salted pork allowed to soak in its own juices in a container, preferably a burnay (clay jar). After one week, it is taken out and hung in the sun or under a shade to air-dry. Once dried, it is stored in a gourd basket (luchen). PAD.
See also: Etag; Food; Pinuneg; Safeng; Suwit.

Inaw *(KAN/BON)*. Craving for sour food especially for pregnant women. This was not a problem in the past. Only a few experienced it and those who did just got pongpong from the mountains and ate them. PAD.
See also: Etab.

Inayan *(KAN)* also **Lawa** *(BON)*. Lit. Going against. It means to go against something, usually a customary law or a taboo. Elders may sometimes be heard scolding a young child who is misbehaving, *"Ay inayan!"* TDH.
See also: Kabalo; Mallawallawa; Ukas.

Ingat also **Talaksan.** Toothpick. As if in a cowboy film, one sits with a toothpick sticking out of one's mouth (the other end is chewed until it is frayed) even after a meal has been long finished. This is usually seen among men who just finished eating in Baguio restaurants like Jacks, Al's or Marosan's. JST.
See also: Shy Mango.

Inhabian *(IFU)*. The Goddess of Wind. A long time ago, Inhabian was pounding rice when a typhoon wind suddenly came and blew most of the rice away. She was pissed with the typhoon because she was left with little rice to cook. Then she went down under her hut and decided to do her weaving. She affixed the backstrap around her waist and called for the wind shouting, *"Now blow more if you can blow me away!"* Then a strong wind came that carried her away to a different place. After some years, she came back home and talked to her people, telling them that she bore many typhoon children in the place where the wind took her. She asked the people to make a pudung and place it visibly outside their huts whenever a typhoon was coming. If this pudung is seen by her children, they will not destroy the hut. Today, Ifugao huts are known to withstand the strongest typhoons. DOS.
See also: Iddaya; Longayban; Pudung; Purchos.

Top: Sculpture of *Inhabian* in the collection of Greg Sabado. Photograph by Gary Buenavista.
Opposite page: Installation of *Inhabian, the Ifugao Godess of the Wind and Marilyn Monroe* by Kidlat Tahimik, 2011. Photograph by Kawayan de Guia.

Ininop *(IFU)* also **Iitaw** *(KAN)*, **It-itaw** *(BON)*. Dream. Dreams often signal the need to hold a ritual in order to remember an ancestor or acknowledge the unseen.

Iniwitan *(KAN)*. The hind part of the wanes.
See also: Agbaxan; Igorot Tail; Wanes.

Inorngang *(KAL)*. A ritual performed after having a tattoo done. A pig is offered. The front toe of the pig is cut off, wrapped with a leaf and then this is rubbed on the tattoo so that it won't swell or get infected. TDH.
See also: Tattoo; Tattoo Designs and Descriptions.

Intum *(KAN)* also **Utum**. A traditional 'layered' dish in Lias, Barlig, Mountain Province. The bottom layer is made of runo leaves, gabi leaves on the next layer, then a layer of gabi stalks, then a layer of wild camote leaves, and topped with a few pieces of gadew (small river fish) and sprinkled with a little salt. The layers are in turn molded and wrapped with more layers of wide gabi (taro) leaves and then roasted over burning sticks or rice stalks that one finds along the riverbanks (no need for a pot or burner). One needs to make sure that the intum will not burn. PAD.
See also: Boko; Camote; Etag; Food: On a Quest for Cordillera Cuisine; Inasin; Kineykhey; Runo; Etag; Food; Pinuneg; Sinag-et; Sinaplak; Wading.

Inum'an *(KYA)*. "The inum'an or swidden fields of the Tawangan Kalanguya are, by all accounts, a testimony to the way of life of their ancestors. Tawangan elders remember a time when they often moved residence with their parents. According to the elders' accounts, this was because the Kalanguya were constantly in search of a place where their pigs could thrive. The health and growth of the pigs was a gauge of whether a place was suitable for living or not. The pigs roamed freely and were called in at feeding time. If the pigs were not doing well, they would leave a swidden and find a better area where another swidden could be started." (Perez 2010, 49). Although many Kalanguya families in Benguet are now involved in commercial vegetable gardening, the inum'an continues to serve as a valuable food safety net. *"Once a Kankanaey woman visiting in-laws and friends in Tawangan asked her hosts, 'Are you converting all your inum'an to gardens?.' Their answer was noncommittal. She urged them to keep their swidden fields, 'So that you will still have something to eat, even if you sometimes get bankrupt.'"* (ibid., 50).
See also: Camote; Dang-ah; Kalanguya.

Irisan. A 1960 film starring Rogelio dela Rosa and Lola Delgado and directed by Manuel Silos about the Irisan Lime Kiln in Benguet and the life of Felix Llorente, who revived the kiln after World War II. All that remains of the movie is a photo still displayed in the house of Llorente who died in 2003 at the age of 101. FYC.
See also: Abong; Banaue: Stairway to the Sky; Big Bird Cage; Igorota: The Legend of the Tree of Life; Kung Mangarap Ka't Magising; Vacacionista.

Ishemshem *(IBA)*. To keep something a secret.

Ishuh'dog *(IBA)*. To push or let something go through a hole or narrow opening like in threading a needle.

Is-is *(KAN)* also **Lagyet** *(BON)*. Drizzle.
See also: Menlemlem.

Itikmanokpato! *(ILO)*. Lit. Goosechickenduck! Shouted at the Hangar Market in Baguio City to mean, "Buy chicken, goose or duck." If you want pinikpikan, the feathers can be singed for free or for a small price, usually with a flamethrower. HZK.
See also: Pinikpikan.

Iuya *(KAN/BON)*. Lit. To give way. A Cordilleran value of sharing. A child is taught to let go or give way to his/her younger sibling. For example, during the meal of a family, the softer part of the chicken which is the leg often goes to the youngest. The older children are expected to

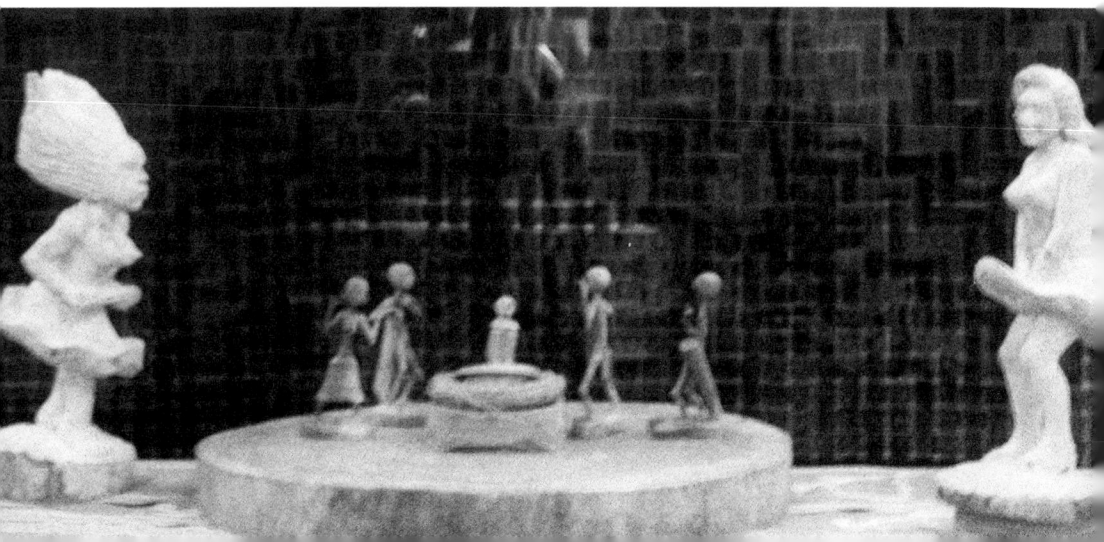

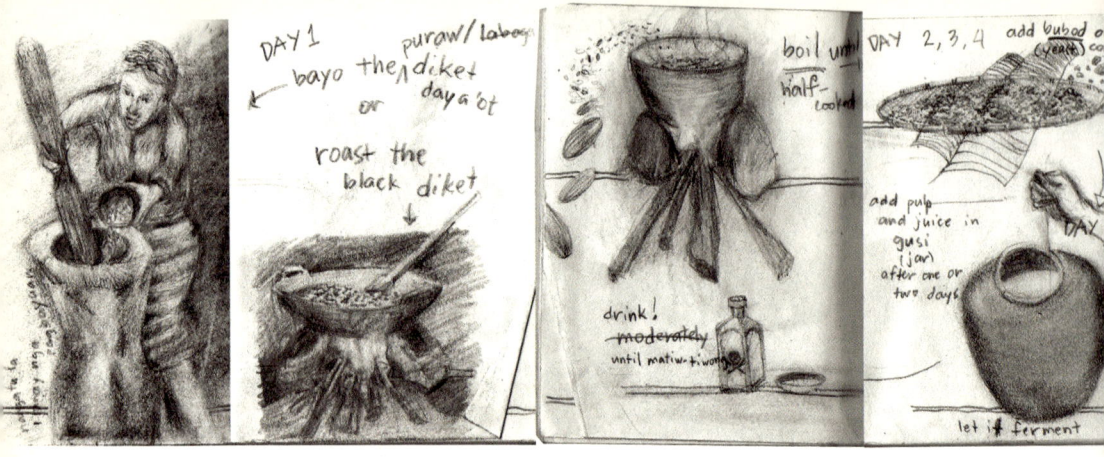

Illustration of the *Iwa* process. Illustration by Rocky Cajigan.

'iuya' the chicken leg – to give or share the favor instead of taking it. The term however does not necessarily apply to the value of sharing when uttered by elders. If used, it is to reprimand a disrespectful youngster and becomes an insult as the respect for elders should come as naturally as instinct. DOS.
See also: Ayyew.

Iwa *(IFU)*. The process of making baya (rice wine) which is the staple wine of the Cordilleras. It starts with the pounding of the daya'ot (glutinous rice). If the daya'ot is of the dark variety, it is first roasted and then boiled while the white variety is directly boiled. The rice is brought out half-cooked and spread over the ligawu (winnower). When it cools off, apul (yeast) is evenly mixed with it. The mixture is then wrapped with banana leaves that have been heated to kill microorganisms, and then set aside in a corner. After two to three days, it is pricked to let the tono (juice) come out which is then collected in a container for the next one or two days. The rice is then transferred to a jar, the tono re-mixed with it, and the whole thing is covered to ferment. Baya could be ready in about three days but the longer time it is left alone, the better.

Mun-iwa means to make the iwa or refers to the person making the iwa. RHK.
See also: Apag; Basi; Bayas; Fuas; Pitik.

I'waks. Also known as the Ygyuat, Dumanggi, Alegueses, Alagueses, Gumangi, Jumanggi, Jumanguis, Aua, Awa, Owa, O-ak, Alagot, Yumangi and Dagatan, the I'waks are found in Nueva Vizcaya, particularly Kayapa. Some of these peoples' bloodlines are also found in Caranglan, Nueva Ecija and Bokod, Benguet. Among the Spanish, they were known as the *"gabi [taro] eaters."* Their traditional houses were box-like wooden structures with cogon-thatched roofs and reed-matting walls. They also speak Ibaloi but remain distinct from them. FYC.
See also: Zambals.

Iwaxan *(ISN)*. The perfume spirit that enters the bottle of coconut oil often carried by Isneg lovers. FYC.
See also: Anginaman; Kalang; Landusan.

Iyag *(KAN)*. Lit. To shout. *"An omen-seeking, soul calling expedition to the mountainside the day before the Begnas festival begins."* (Scott 2011, 151).
See also: Bangon; Begnas; Sabusab.

Iya-iyaman. Iyaman is a word adopted from the Ilocano for 'Thank you.' Transcribed chants by early anthropologists of Igorot elders in rituals showed no words for 'thank you.' Ironically, Cordilleran rituals are meant for thanksgiving. The word Iyaman appeared in translations of biblical texts into Kankanaey. Now Iyaman is said to express gratefulness. To show sincerest 'thanks' in its superlative sense, the first two syllables are repeated to emphasize thankfulness: Iya-iyaman. It is the same thing with the Tagalog word 'salamat,' which when used in the mountains is said by repeating the first two syllables: sala-salamat. DOS.
See also: Bontoc Kiss; Namwaw; Pilpilak-Taltalak.

Iyu Myth *(KAL)*. According to Jules De Raedt (1993), in the Buaya version of the iyu myth (huge water snake), a town called Madodna-ao was decimated by the iyu except for two brothers. They found an iyu in the river, killed it and buried all the town treasures. They agreed to meet two years later on the same spot. But when they did meet, they could not recognize each other because of their tattoos (one went to Pasil while the other went to Pinukpuk) and the Pasil boy killed his Pinukpuk brother. In grief, he forgot about his town's treasures. Apparently there are other iyu myths in other Kalinga settlements to justify their migrations. The Buayas believe that the iyu still exists though and it is advisable not to gaze at your shadow on the river as the iyu will eat your reflection and you will die.
See also: Feclat; Labeg; Tsuli.

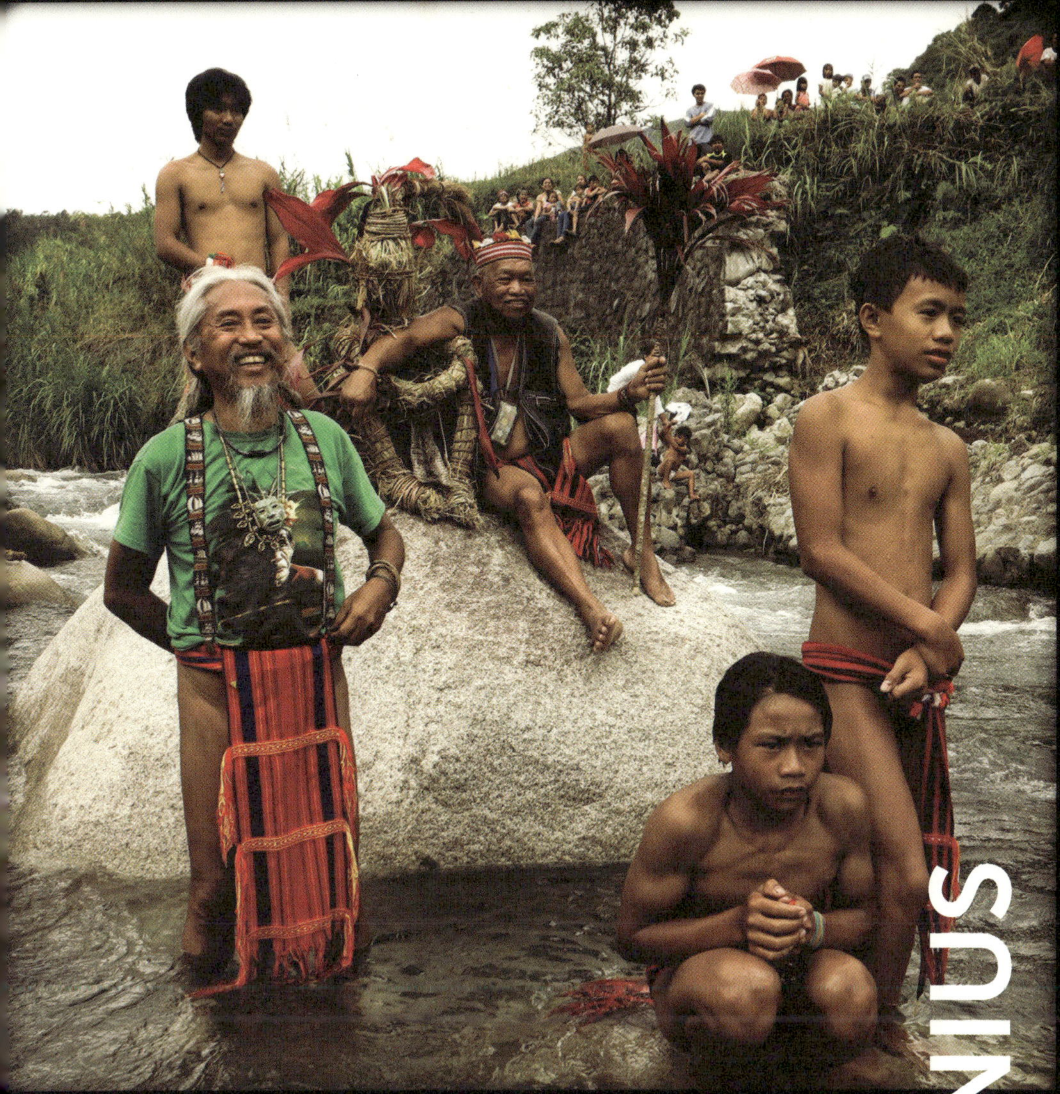

Photograph of Kidlat Tahimik at the Punnuk harvest ritual. Photograph by Kidlat De Guia.

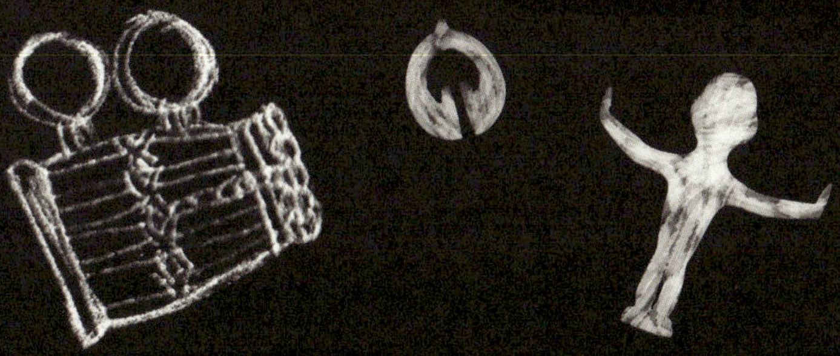

INDI-GENIUS

Romancing D' Ifugao Bahag

As a child in the 1950s, I saw on Session Road indigenous folk in coats and ties.

Wearing the 'tie' – their bahag, a.k.a loincloth or G-string – at waist-level (not at the neck), they were at home in their world. This hybrid adaptation had the warmth of a Yankee colonizer's jacket while enjoying the breezy comforts of pant-less splendor. Cool, man. Cool! Baguio's wannabe sophisticates (the 'educated' elite) looked down on the primitives. Such a pejorative point of view must have rubbed off on us, growing up in a hill station culture. Now, at age 70, after years of Romancing 'D Bahag, I see the Session Road strollers as hybrid walkers of Lopes Nauyac's balik-bahag (return to tribal) talk. Such re-framings of childhood kultur-discomforts regularly enter my film introspections.

Ifugao elder Lopes Nauyac would become my favorite quotable. Not for his declarations, but rather for his classic mispronunciation of 'indigenous' in his true-blue Ipugaw accent: *"We must preserve our fathers' indi-genius culture!"* More passionately, he lamented: *"How dare Manila-elite look down on our indi-genius practices?"*

Cosmically, he had coined a new word combining the 'genius' of the 'indigenous' into one word: indigenius. (Watch for it in the next Oxford English Dictionary). That indi-genius confidence we lost somehow in our wannabe American-Idol century. My university students got an overdose of that cosmic mispronunciation.

After a half-century of woodcarving for tourists in Baguio, he returned to his village Hapao, to resurrect the culture of Pinugo or ancestral forest watersheds. Even before quitting the city, he wore his G-string with knickerbocker knee-length socks (yellow!) complete with a gatsby cap and the latest Ray-Ban sunglasses (shades of MacArthur!). Whereas most Cordillerans were ashamed of their ancient ways (thanks to colonial missionaries), Nauyac donned his bahag naturally and stylishly.

To me, Nauyac is the poster boy of the Balik-Bahag apostolate. Check him out: He is articulate in English (strong moma accent); he is a devout

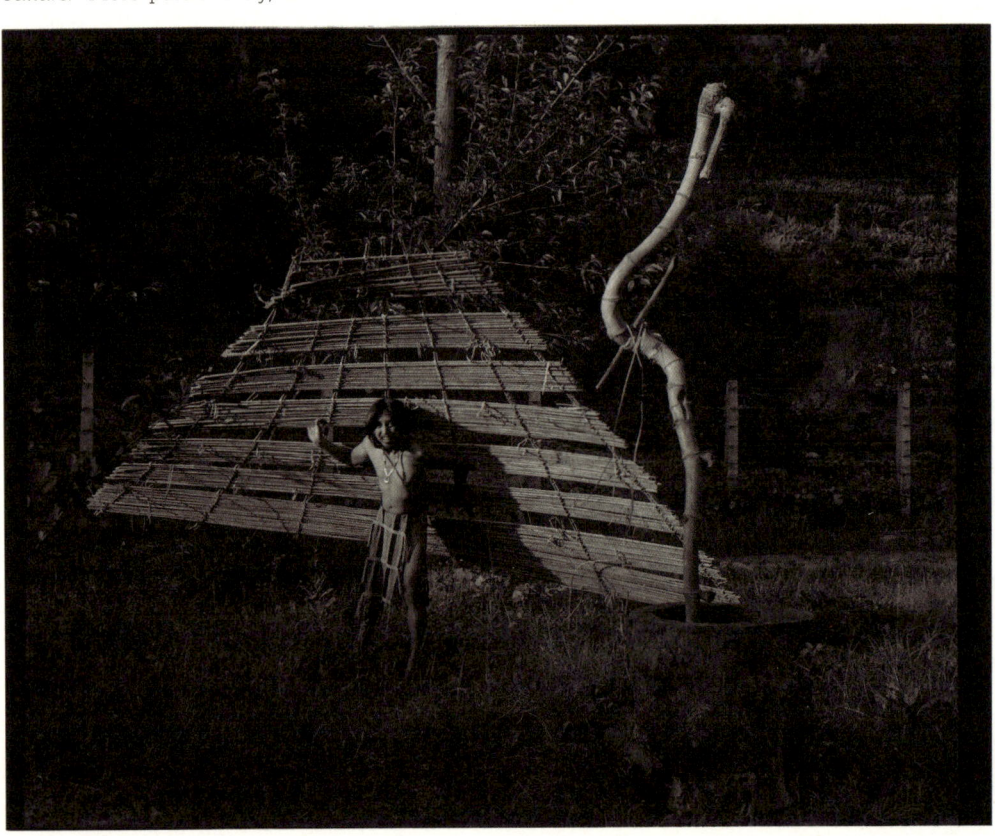

Portrait of Kidlat Tahimik in his *bahag*, 1982. Photograph by Boy Yniguez.

Catholic (singing hymns every 3AM between snoring sessions); as an indigenous PhD (sans diploma), he can spout the most philosophic Op. Cits and Loc. Cits. in his Ifugao accent.

All his west-meets-east behavior hints at an inner rootedness underlying his multicultural jeprox 1970s funky look. When he welcomed me to build my hut in Hapao, atop the rice terraces of his grandfather Kab-bigat, Nauyac's Ifugao-anchored cosmopolitanism would deepen the cultural texture of my film *Memories of Overdevelopment*, which is about Enrique de Malacca, Magellan's Filipino slave.

Whenever in Baguio, I shot kapa-kapa (without a script), creating montages that showed how the indigenous slave energized the master and determined the destiny of the first circumnavigation. Whenever in Hapao, I shot tribal holistic-ness endangered in our fastfood age.

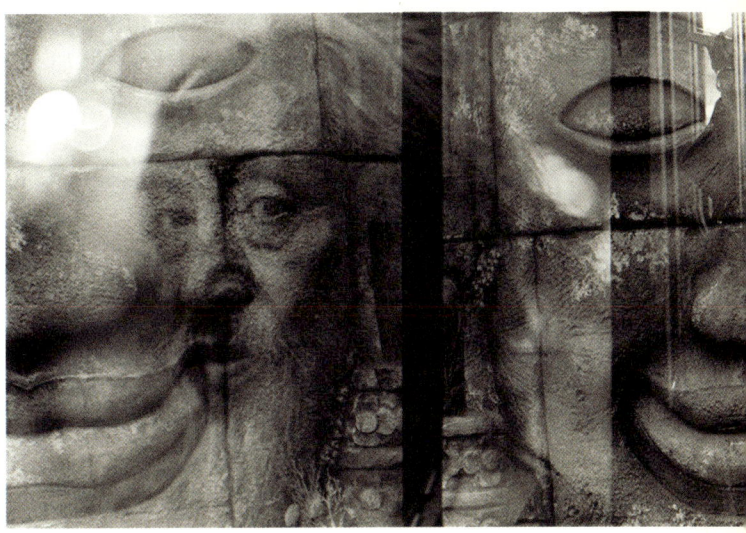

Portrait of Kidlat Tahimik, 2011. Photograph by Kawayan de Guia.

Three Film Clips: Anatomy of 33-Years of Shooting in Hapao – Sans Script

1980, First visit to Hapao. My son Kidlat, aged 5, trekked the steep terraces up to Patpat village (where I would later be adopted as part of the village) with Uncle Briccio's documentary crew. Exhausted, he ignores Nauyac's snoring and mine. Eight tired bodies huddled in the hut of mumbaki Kab-bigat.

At midnight, stealthy footsteps surround us – a patrol of NPA rebels checking if our visit had 'enemy vibes.' Nauyac is talking to them under the moon in his G-string. Between murmurs, the only words we make out were *"Apo Nauyac..."* The guerrillas courteously addressed the Ifugao elder. They left as gracefully as they had wandered in. Nauyac resettled beside us on the pine-plank floor. *"Okay. Alam nila [they know] you're artists – sympathetic to our indigenius culture."*

That brief negotiation with hard ideologues showing respect for an elder's wisdom, solidified my decision to cast Magellan's slave as an Ifugao survivor – the first man to circumnavigate the globe in a crimson bahag! I could swear I 'saw' that color waving in the Hapao full moon. We were lullabied by the mantra of a hundred thousand crickets. Sound was recorded on my open-reel Nagra recorder. I didn't dare run my Whrrrr-noisy 16mm shooter lest it spark a shootout a la Rambo!

After I moved into my hut in 1997, in the same place as that midnight encounter, my 16mm camera was slavishly churning (whrrr... whrrr...) capturing tribal life, landscapes, and shaman rituals, all framed obsessively by my infatuation with indigenous culture.

1997, A Moma lesson. We had just disassembled a nail-less ancestral hut at a dang-ah. The community convoyed pine floors, narra beams, runo roof-rafters from one mountain to the next. The ant-like procession snaked along terrace walls: muscled men with beams, women with truss poles, kids carrying sooty root platforms for drying rice bundles over the hearth. Down one slope, then across the river, then up the next slope, before we re-assembled the recycled "hardware." Hand-carved square-peg posts sitting in square holes in beams are so exact: a Lego-like precision. The sway of the resurrected hut is minimal.

Dog-meat is served to celebrate the bayanihan move, the community-powered effort. Lowlens ('Lorenz' pronounced with an Ifugao accent) is wrapping moma betelnut in a hapid leaf.

Whrrrr: Nauyac in G-String, adds a dash of apog (homemade lime pulverized from roasted shell) to spice up the chew-brew and yes, to redden the lips. He hands it to my 13-year-old son Kabunyan.

Whrrrr: I document this Oral Transmission Initiation of my bunso (youngest), to the joys of moma, bonding via betel quid sharing.

Kabu's lips got redder than Marilyn Monroe's iconic pout. Kabu was trying to decide if he enjoyed the indescribable taste. But he loved the hot flash on his nape. Surely he would come back to more tastebud-testing and to relive memories of the dang-ah house-move. He carried two bululs.

Whrrrr: Close-up of Kabu's red teeth chewing. Ngarr... ngarrr... ngarrrrr registers on Nagra tape.

2013, Bearded giant dancing. The closing of

Manila's last 16mm film lab forced me to embrace new technology: video. Video cams were silent, no WHRRR-ing. But they captured the synchronized sounds of Ifugao gongs, of pestles pounding rice in wooden mortars. They digitized the murmured prayers of the mumbaki and the gentle liw-liwa chanting of women harvesting.

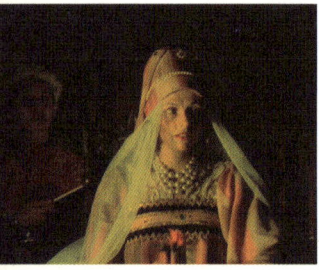

Movie still from *Memories of Overdevelopment*.

The community of Patpat, Hapao, is dancing to Ifugao wedding gongs, arms widespread like graceful eagles locked in a habagat wind. Nauyac leaves the prancing-as-one circle to invite my six-footer son into the ring. Kawayan is a filmable reincarnation of Magellan, with a full European beard from his Bavarian mother's ancestors. He spreads his wings, joining two dozen tranced "eagles" including myself, dancing and shooting with a camera.

Hapao folks are familiar with our father-son tandem – adopted into the community since 1997. Our out-of-town missteps provoke warm community laughter, registering above the drone of gongs. (Wow! Could be a soundtrack bonus to spice my closing sequence!)

As I video my urban kid dancing, spitting moma gracefully, I realize I captured a new at-homeness-in-the-world in him that is not unlike the hybrid Session Road strollers. This tells me a Magellan-in-jeans reincarnation can be edited into my indie film.

Alas, the 1980 moonlit crimson bahag was imprinted only in my memory. No film ASA was sensitive enough for moonlight. But the NPA sounds were captured by the Nagra. The 1997 betelnut red registered on 16mm celluloid. The 2013 festive son et lumiere ended as digitized bytes of ecstatic gongs synchronized with ecstatic faces.

Three clips of three sons contextualize the three-decade evolution of my romancing the Ifugao bahag – shooting Hapao life (technological obsolescence notwithstanding), my boys growing up, intimate with the rice cycle, while their father shoots more relaxed, in the-waist hugging bahag but minus the Ifugao romance.

Desperately Seeking the IndiGenius in Magellan's Slave

Nauyac's indigenius summed up the survivor talents of Magellan's slave, Enrique de Malacca. His tribal spirit let him roll with the kultur-punches of Renaissance Europe and survive winter shock too! Enrique's indigenius mindset must have spurred Magellan spiritually. Thus the vast Pacific was crossed, despite the odds.

In this cineaste's personal voyage, Nauyac became the lead role like Magellan was the star of Antonio Pigafetta's journals of the voyage. The more my 16mm Bolex captured Nauyac, the more I got hooked to his lakaran (literally, his walking the indigenius talk). Not advocating a return to the stone ages, Nauyac was simply asking, *"Are we Ifugaos dumping our rice-cycle lifestyle for their fastfood eat-n-run efficiencies? Are we dumping our ancestor's spirituality that once gave healthy brakes to our material needs? Must we shed our bahags to 'sophisticate' ourselves into our colonizers' fabricated needs: coat-n-tie, mall-n-buy, borrow-'til-I-die? And once 'civilized,' will we civilly raze our Pinugo forests to maximize profit?"* Profound questions long before Al Gore became the quotable green footnote.

In my early Hapao years, Nauyac was the convenient truth. It was sheer ecstasy to whrrrr-in on his nonstop seedling germination of tuh-werrs (sounds like whrrr), indigenous hardwood trees. His ancestral know-how of Pinugo watersheds flowed effortlessly – hardly needing any editing. Planting a million trees (without a cent of government aid) gave convenient visuals to inspire future green generations.

Even if he always complained he was 'poor' (by World Bank standards), he knew he was wealthy in his kultur bank vault. Filming/editing Nauyac up close converted me to his ancestral gospel – that we should treat forests,

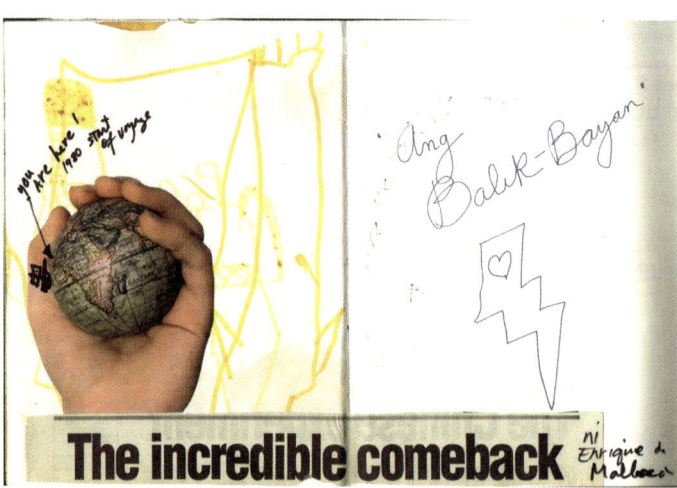

Doodle by Kidlat Tahimik.

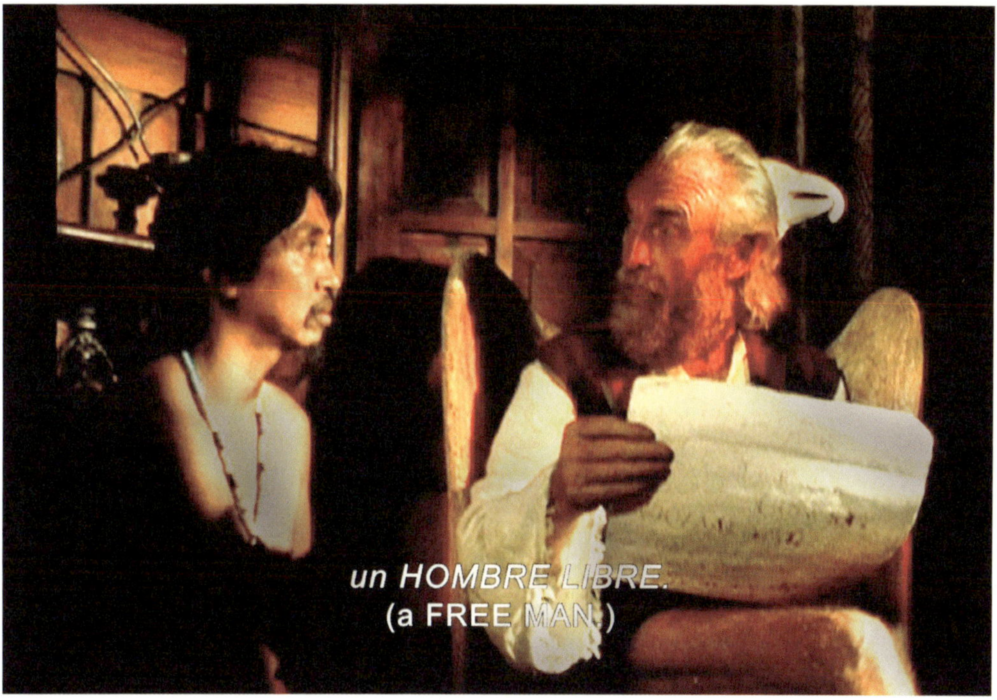

Movie stills from *Memories of Overdevelopment*.

rivers, and mountains like our fellow brethren: our kapwa gubat, kapwa ilog, kapwa bundok (fellow forest, fellow river, fellow mountain).

At the time, I didn't realize that Nauyac's harmony with nature was, in my scriptless film, fleshing out Enrique, the indi-genius survivor. Beyond the stereotypical slave, might he have been the spiritual master of the voyage?

Re-frame Nauyac: My non-armchair guru is the kultur-survivor, parrying total homogenization, and retaining his indi-genius jewels, just like Enrique survived total Europeanization as a medieval Overseas Filipino Worker experiencing Renaissance Europe. Enrique adopted the cold climate fashions, but his bahag culture esprit remained intact. During the torturous 90 days traversing the vast Pacific, the mutinous crew believed the edge of the world (a Niagara-like precipice) was inching slowly toward the galleons. Might Enrique's indi-genius confidence have kept the master steadfast on course?

Enter: Enrique, the spiritual master...

Besides film directing, I also happen to play the role of Enrique the slave. I must continually internalize the Hapao influence to act out the inner strengths of Enrique, the Ifugao. OMG! What is happening inside my own inner makeup?

Ethnic Docu vs. Village Home-Movies

Kidlat Tahimik was no ethnographic filmmaker. But video made life simpler for this backyard filmmaker, recording local concerns, registering rituals in dim shamans' huts. Video shooting was just as intense as those celluloid film days. But the user-friendliness of video-cams made it easier for the romance frame to recede.

After all, I was an adopted son – an accepted member of Patpat. I was the village-insider with a camera, living in my electricity-less hut, doing chores nonchalantly in my bahag. I was chatting with local folk on a first name basis, even if the Hapit language still eluded me.

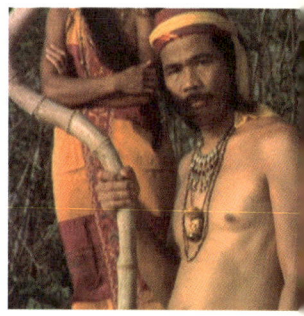

With video, my en-garde readiness to seize the moment (vocab of scene-hungry cineastes) would gradually give way to a more blasé observational shooting. Yes, I could listen to the ongoing story unfolding before my lens. I could dance, banter with rice-wine drunkards, soar with the shaman's trance, while shooting.

After I moved into my hut in 1997, my 16mm camera was slavishly churning (whrrr... whrrr...) capturing tribal life, landscapes, shaman rituals – framed obsessively by my infatuation with indigenous culture.

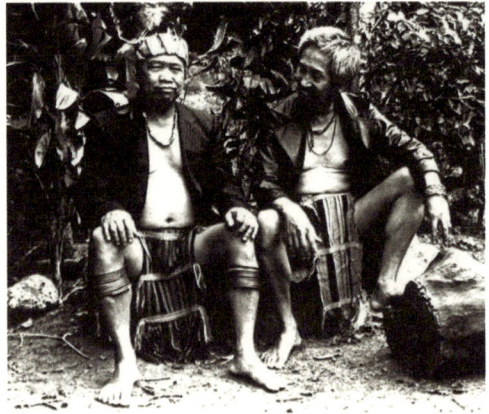

Photograph of Lopez Nauyac and Kidlat Tahimik, 1997. Photograph by Kidlat de Guia.

Once upon a time, my Bolex 16mm was aimed selectively at genuine G-stringed folk like Apo Tapo chanting, genealogies of the kadangyan elite; or shooting the funeral of Apo Hagitan, who refused to replace his G-String with jeans ('til death do us part). Today, whether dressed in backstrap-woven tribal garb or in ukay-ukay used clothes, the kultur-survivor story gets videoed quickly. Mas mabilis sa kidlat! (Quicker than lightning!)

No longer a star-struck cameraman stalking super-warriors, I snap shoot – everyday humans, living in normal villages, walking the normal talk. Sensei Nauyac grounded me to that 'normal' folk wisdom of Ifugao civilization, branded as backward by colonialists. Somehow, I have come to terms with the indigenius (sans 'd romance) and can sport that indigenous confidence outwardly in my bahag.

Today, I can go to any formal dress-code event, feeling more at-home than those in coat-n-ties. Yes, I wore my G-string as graduation speaker at the UP College of Music and at the Supreme Court hearing on the constitutionality of the Mining Law. Likewise, in my Ifugao garb, I joined the golden reunion of my fellow 1963 UP graduates and gave a lecture at the Harvard Film Archives.

And a crowning event: I received my 2012 Fukuoka Laureate award from the Crown Prince of Japan – in my bahag. Royalty deserved the most regally-dressed Pinoy!

Thanks to Nauyac's west-meets-east fashion-setter ways, I am better suited to be a man for all seasons (tropical wear wise). Bahagi na ng buhay ko ang bahag ko. (The bahag/loincloth is now part of my life.)

Postscript to a Sans-Script-Filmmaker's Three-Decade Diary

In August 2013, I scurried off to Hapao for a post-harvest ritual with my grandsons. (Yes, next-generation bahag immersions.) After a mumbaki's shamanic sacrifice for the gods' blessings, three villages surrounding Hapao River converged for a Punok traditional thanksgiving. Over 200 men and boys, clad in crimson G-strings, clenched long Hapid poles tugging and pulling to drag the other team into the river currents. Women teams have been added to the traditionally male tug-o-wars.

It's the 15th year since the Punok games were first revived in 1998 by Nauyac and I – after two decades of dormancy. Judging from the community's euphoria, Punok is here to stay. Rather than passively watching American basketball on the idiot box, Punok revival has become an annual physical contest. The balik-bahag movement is no longer an exclusive fraternity of Nauyac and his romantic disciple.

More than that, on the kultur-scoreboard, young boys at the Hapao 'Olympics' are wearing their bahags – without shame. The name of today's game: *"Yes, it's more fun in Bahag-kultur."*

The bahaging of 'D Ifugao kultur romance, my personal Enrique-zation, has come full circle.

Enter: Enrique de Hapao.

Lights! Camera! Chew moma... in your precious bahag! KT.

See also: Bale; Dangas; Dog-eating; Imperialist Nostalgia; Moma; Wanes.

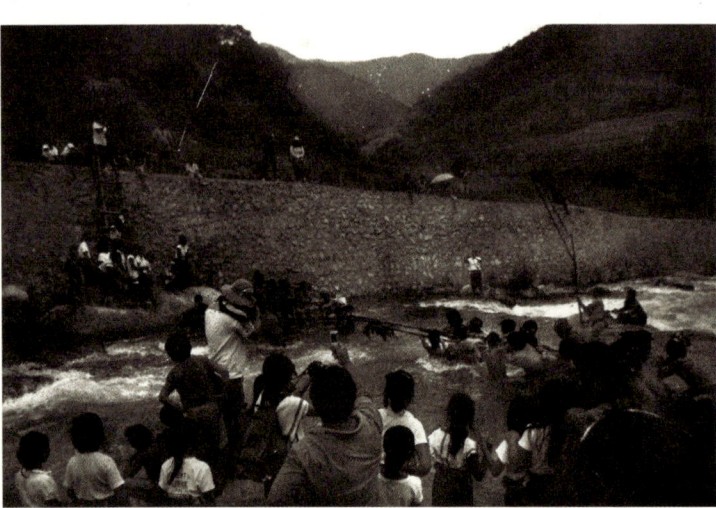

Photograph of the Punnuk festival, 2012. Photograph by Kawayan de Guia.

Memories of Overdevelopment: A 33-year Film-in-Progress

Doing this intimate piece is difficult. I am about to talk to the world about who my father is, to me. Yes, his son. I am one of the three reasons (my brothers are the other two) why his 33-year film is still in progress. His students, since 1980, know that *"Kidlat Tahimik is first a father and then a filmmaker – in that order!"* His words explain the never-ending film about Magellan's 'never-ending' voyage.

That Kidlat Tahimik (KT) often shelved the film in order to grow up with us, is fact. I should know. Best efforts, I am going to try to thicken that thin line of a tension between father and filmmaker, as I recall my one-third of a century with him:

Kidlat Tahimik always carries a camera with him. For the longest time, it was his 25-year old 16mm Bolex – in which many of his films were churned out – using expired film. Recently, he embraced videocams. But now, you see KT often brandishing his bamboo camera. (It's his visual metaphor for Filipino artists who frame our local stories – with our indigenous lenses.)

His life flow is just like his scriptless films – shooting intuitively with the cosmos as co-director. KT shoots with a 'Bathala Na' confidence, as he calls it – easily turning any film *"defect into effect,"* just as he churns out his life story, which becomes interchangeable with his film narrative. To be honest, this confuses even us who live with him. Our growing up days with him, we see on the screen. He framed us daily (ritually) in his Bolex 16mm camera viewfinder.

If you enter his room, you'll see how terrified he is of open spaces: piles of film cans, newspaper clippings, unread books, and memorabilia gathering mold. Then found objects, rocks picked from wherever, broken glasses, and debris from our burned home. Like sediments of time, they have amassed over the decades. If you dig deep enough, you will surely find jurassic cameras that don't run, cine fossils that have to be there probably because they evoke memories in him.

No one is allowed to touch his mess. If I am allowed to call his 'cave' a bedroom, I would be called a liar. On his bed is scattered debris and just a tiny spot for him to sleep; plus a pathway for him to walk to the closet or to the sink. A labyrinth, you'd take some time finding your way. But there is a way out. The same way KT, the unschooled filmmaker, takes his time to find a film ending.

I see his mess as one big altar. His organized chaos of a room. But you can bet, he knows where every single thing is. Just like he knows three dozen phone numbers by heart (because he refuses to

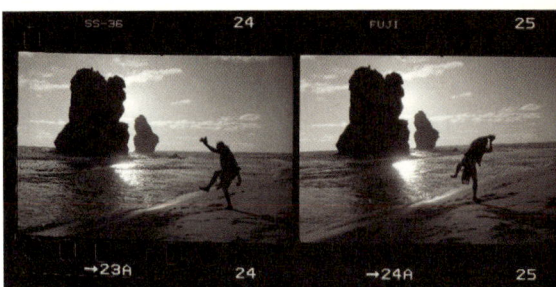

Contact print of Kidlat Tahimik dancing, 1993 . Photograph by Emmanuel Santos.

carry a cellphone). KT knows the relevant others will find him cosmically (usually through his sons' mobile phones).

KT is literally a war baby, 'crafted' by my grandparents after the Japanese attack on Pearl Harbor. Born nine and a half months later and in the anarchy of World War II, he turned out an intuitive eccentric whose existence is defined by learning all rules, only to be broken later. Big thanks to my German mother who, guiding KT thoroughly into creative freedom, opened his artistic eyes into Kapwa, our indigenous psychology, his adapted central perception today.

He likes to build, like his father who was an engineer by profession. Except that, intuitively, KT prefers to challenge the laws of gravity. Just like our crazy shaped home, re-building our burnt-to-the-ground house with no blueprints! You can tell that whenever a new room sprouts, there would be a cosmic story behind it. This is how he creates films: from footages collected impulsively, long before filmmaking was democratized by video. He threads those 'celluloid moments' together and then writes the 'script' long after his actors have delivered their lines, a literal post-script.

For a long time, we considered him to have given up on the Magellan's slave film. He often declared he would finish the film in his next lifetime. His original Magellan actor had died in 2001. The late George Steinberg, an Estonian forester with a beautiful bushy beard who was a greenthumb propagating seedlings in Baguio. Rumors say he was in hiding after being caught in a messy dispute with Nazis (or his beard was a disguise from hunters of ex-Gestapo fugitives).

When George's beard took the explorer's role, I was newly born. (Mind you, this film is only a year younger than me). Can you imagine how many times I've seen so many rough cuts? But when I watched *Memories of Overdevelopment (MOD)* earlier this year, I noticed something different in the opening credits: "A Film by Kidlat." All his films have "Tahimik" sitting comfortably next to his first name. In *MOD*, it was just Kidlat, which is also the name of my older brother Kidlat Sr. (a filmmaker in his own right). Did my father do this subliminally? Was my sibling Kidlat Sr. really destined to finish this film for our father/filmmaker?

This all changed in a cosmic detour in November 2012 during *AX(iS): To the End of the World,* our art caravan project along the Halsema Highway. Our 70-year old father/filmmaker (returning from a film tour in the USA) after flying 18 hours, plus a 6-hour bus ride to Baguio, decided to travel another three hours to document our nomadic art event. KT arrived exhausted in a Cordillera mountain village after a circumnavigation of the world. Much like the slave Enrique de Malacca did in a galleon only 500 years earlier. (See what I mean? That interchangeable film/life narrative? Which is real? Which is reel?)

The jetlagged father videoed me, the tired son, in the rickety bus. He framed a shaggy beard that seemed to have grown a harassed face on it. When he reviewed the footage: Wow a Magellan look-alike! He decided to cast me as the Portuguese explorer. In the film, my father himself, played the slave Enrique, portrayed as an Ifugao chance-passenger whose cosmic mind juggles interchangeable roles: he is the slave of Master Magellan and at the same time, might Enrique also be a spiritual master of the voyage? But the flashforward extended to this lifetime (shot in 2013), where I was conveniently reincarnated as his slave, seeking him, my mentor. This filmic twist (or is it karmic?) demonstrates the scriptless/open-ended way of KT, groping toward a film end 33 years later. This process is why I, as a curator for Singapore Biennale 2013 (SB2013), included *Memories of Overdevelopment, Redux.*

MOD had a meandering film history. In 1982, during the Imelda Marcos' Manila Film Festival, Werner Herzog was accused of stealing Kidlat Tahimik's idea of the voyage. The press played up Herzog's telex to a Manila starlet about auditioning for his new film *Magellan: the End of the Endless Voyage.* Later, Herzog assured my father the telex was just a ploy – to divert attention from his new *Green Ants* film. In 1983, the slave story came close to being co-produced by Zoetrope Studios. A snail mail letter, signed by Francis Ford Coppola, proposed to help finish the film. It never got to my father. This was before the era of emails! In 2012, Jeonju International Film Festival (JIFF) officials announced *MOD* as one of its grantees to finish the film. The Korean funding possibility fell through when politics replaced the original organizers. The new JIFF staff ignored the old grant awardees. So, the voyage was again adrift... eternally? Beyond recovery? But in 2013, cosmic impulses conspired (like my beard) so the circumnavigation would reach some sort of homeport – KT's "The End" is never absolute.

If I'm allowed to say it, the spirit of this independent filming of the endless voyage (during the Renaissance period) parallels the limitless optimism of the Indigenous slave. It's his indi-genius resignation to the cosmos – not unlike the crazy go-for-broke father/filmmaker meandering from 1979 to 2013. Like the 1521 slave, my father masterfully just flowed with the go, to complete his own journey.

As with many of his films, the never-ending cast and crew involved artists, friends, family, and foreign backpackers passing through. Many have gone on to the next life like Pepito Bosch who played Hieronymus Bosch, and George Steinberg who often urged my father, "Better finish the film before I die!" Other actors reincarnated in the 2013 sequences were Laida Lim as the Chinese merchant who sells the slave; Dave Barradas

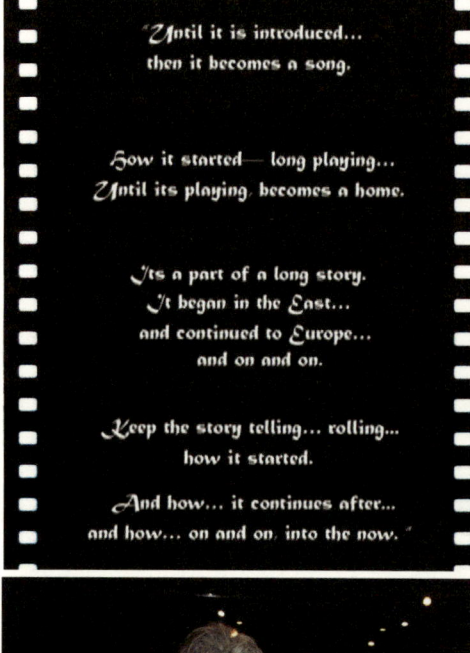

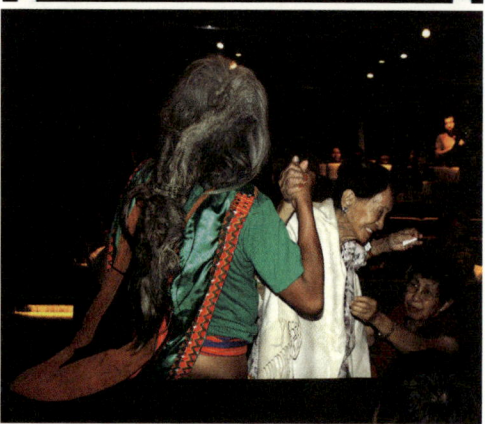

Photograph of Kidlat Tahimik and his mother Virginia de Guia during the premiere of *Memories of Overdevelopment* in Singapore, 2013.
Photograph by Joyce Toh.

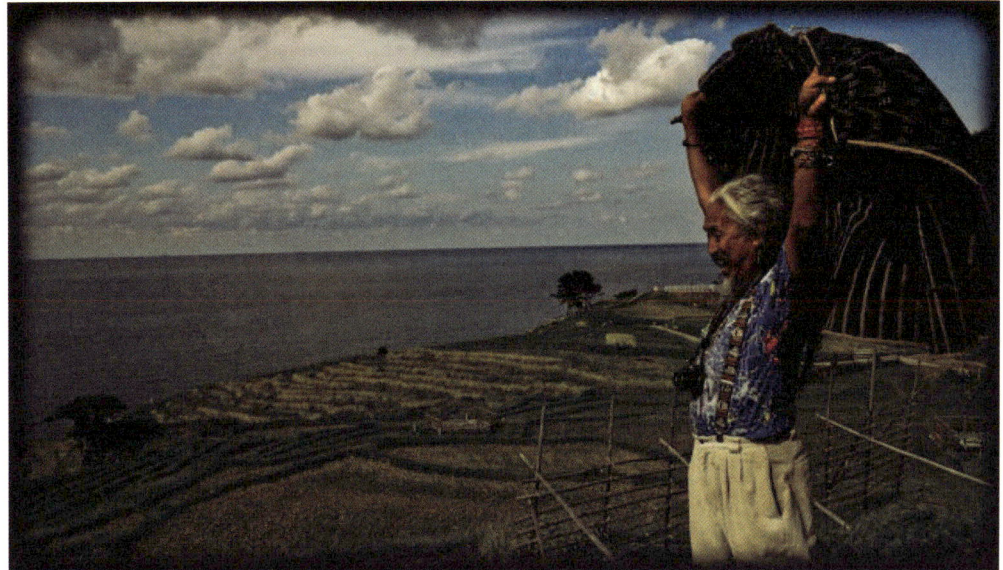

Photograph of Kidlat Tahimik, 2011. Photograph by Kidlat de Guia.

who masterfully acted LapuLapu, the slayer of Magellan; and Wig Tysmans as Antonio Pigafetta, who documented the slave's feat.

Recording on celluloid the talents and faces of 1980s Baguio artists in the 1980s, gives archive value, an extra reason to include *MOD* in SB2013. Off-camera talents included Boy Yniguez (cinematographer), Ed de Guia (sound), and painter Santi Bose (set design), the renegade Baguio team. My mother Katrin de Guia (besides playing Princess Isabelita), designed and sewed the costumes, funkily reinterpreting royal fashions in medieval paintings.

Me and my brothers (who played child cameo roles in the 1980s), were all re-cycled as medieval sailors. My youngest brother Kabunyan, who in 1985 played the mestizo bastard child of the slave, returned as a 2013 Pigafetta reincarnate.

Perhaps the making of a 33-year-old film can be likened to the impossible dream of Magellan and Enrique sailing the Pacific – 90 days, relentlessly in a time when the world was believed to be flat, never knowing when they would sail over the edge (The End?). The *MOD* story was in danger of being 'overdeveloped' owing to the time it took to tell such a story. But it's a tale. One that grows constantly and doesn't exactly end. (Watch out for more versions of voyage!)

This is Kidlat Tahimik's legacy as an artist – not just a filmmaker. He tells a story humorously, the way some cosmic accidents happen in life. The ones that only leave you laughing because there's nothing else left to do.

When you're so engrossed in what you do, you become the artwork. My father becomes the cosmic voyager. As the closing film-line goes, *"Follow the setting sun... and you will meet the rainbow's twin."* So, Kidlat Tahimik comes full circle. KDG.

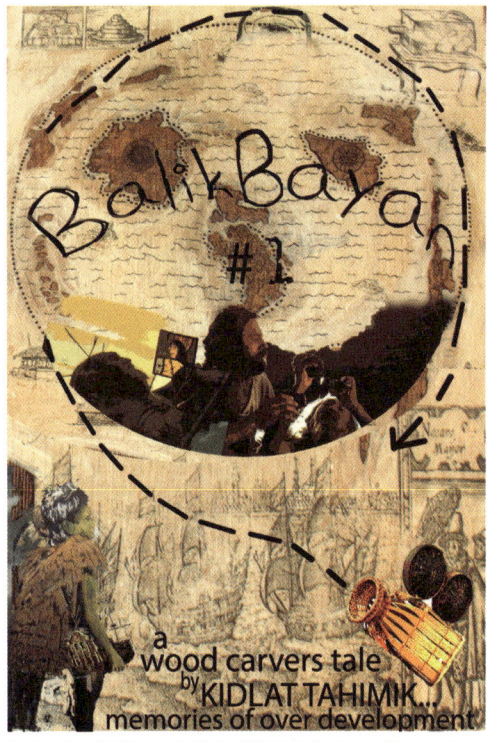

Movie poster of *Balikbayan #1* a film by Kidlat Tahimik. Courtesy Kabunyan de Guia.

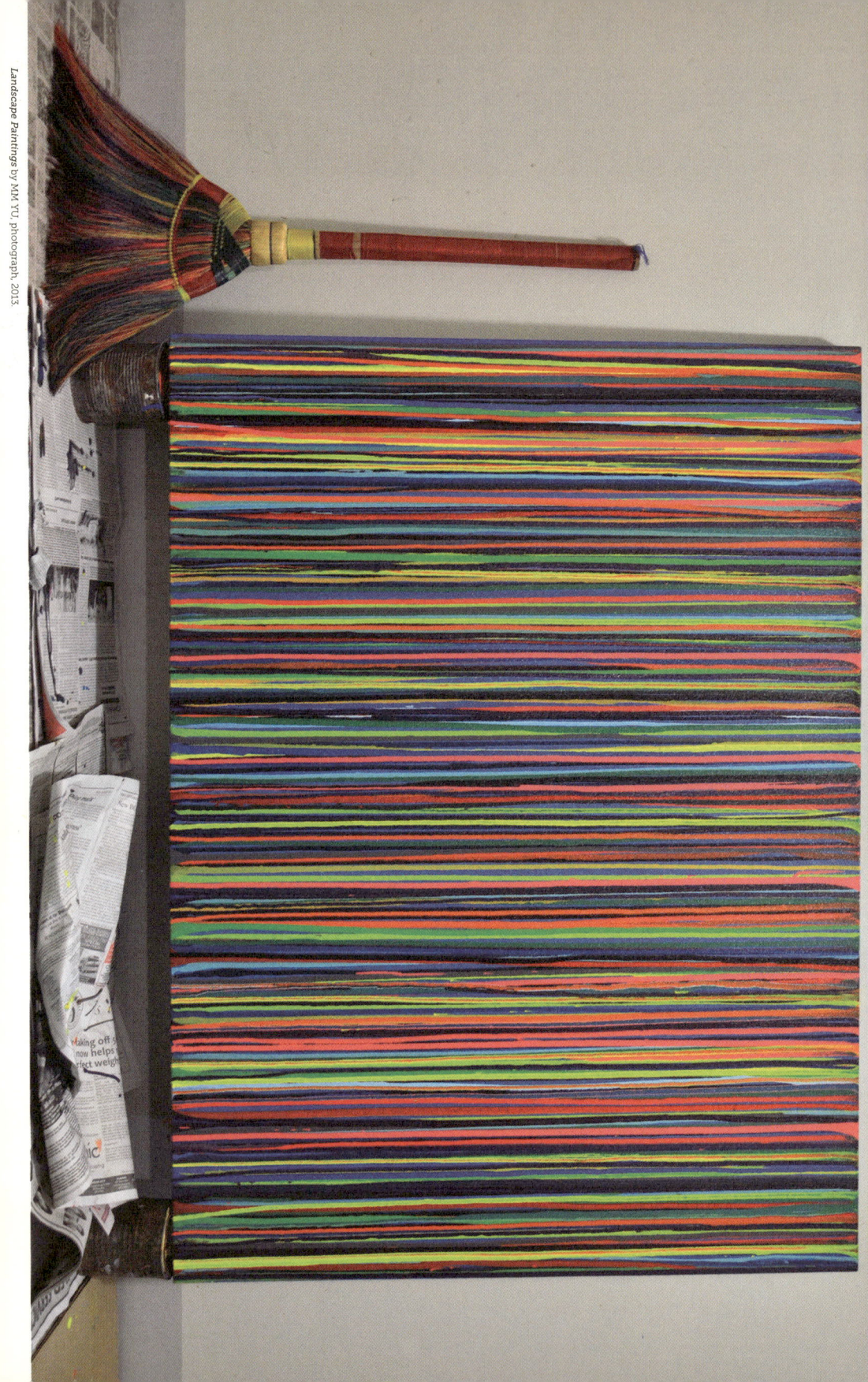

Landscape Paintings by MM YU, photograph, 2013

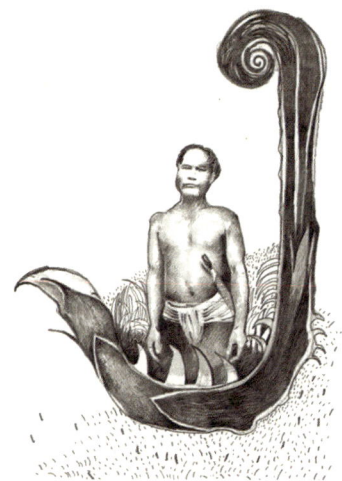

Jawbone. Used as handle for the gangsa or gongs. Scott noted, when he studied the Madukayan Kalinga: "One house, for instance, has gongs with handles made from the jawbones of a headman of Lias, two Japanese soldiers, and a Huk." (Scott 1966, 105).
See also: Gong.

Jegjeg *(IBA)* also **Yogyog** *(IFU).*
Earthquake.
See also: Gingined; Yumogyog ad Dalom.

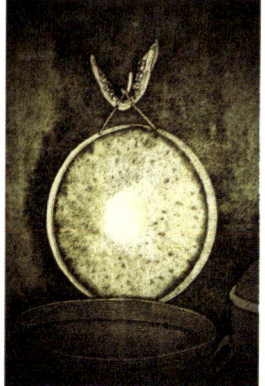

Artwork by Sultan Mangosan, 2014.

Joe Rice. A former private first class in the US Army who came to the Philippines. He then married a Japanese woman, retired in Baguio City, and opened a wholesale food shop in Abanao. He invented the tiklis and the bamboo box to hold strawberries. (Halsema 1991) FYC
See also: Tiklis.

John Hay, Camp. The military reservation in Baguio City set up by the civilian colonial administrators to protect the summer government operations. It was a disguised agenda to protect the gold mining prospectors that would eventually grow into one of the world's largest mining operations. Camp John Hay (CJH) became the most popular R&R center for American troops in the Far East to re-energize

Jabbar, the Wonder Dog. A German Shepherd owned and raised by Sonny San Pedro of Baguio. Jabbar was a regular on *Seeing Stars with Joe Quirino,* where he would perform new tricks almost every other week. He played 'Sandy' in the musical *Annie,* with Lea Salonga as the little orphan. Jabbar also played roles in the movies of Fernando Poe Jr. and Niño Muhlach. He also loved to perform in many parades in Baguio. He died at the age of 16. There followed two more Jabbars. FYC
See also: Dog-eating.

Jabjab *(IBA).* To fan. Manjabjab means 'it is breezy.'

Jail. The Coldest Jail in Luzon happens to be the Baguio City Jail. As an ominous billboard in the 1950s along Kennon Road used to tell visitors, Mountain Province is the 'Vacation Center of the Philippines.' Yet awaiting you, according to the billboard, were landslides, narrow roads, blind curves, 100 traffic policemen and yes, the coldest jail in Luzon. What a way to welcome visitors. But that's truth in advertising. FYC
See also: Kennon Road; Landslide.

Jakjak *(IBA).* A sieve or to sift or shake.

Jamjam *(IBA).* To advise or reprimand.

Japanese generic business. The shops owned by the Japanese in Baguio before World War II were remarkably only prefixed with 'Japanese' (or maybe the English names were). So there is a Japanese Bazaar, Japanese Candy Store, Japanese Watch Repair Shop, Japanese Store, and Japanese Bakery. (Cheng 1997).
See also: Cabbage King.

Jasjas *(IBA)* also **Yasyas** *(KAN).* Breath. Manjasjas means to breathe. DLD.

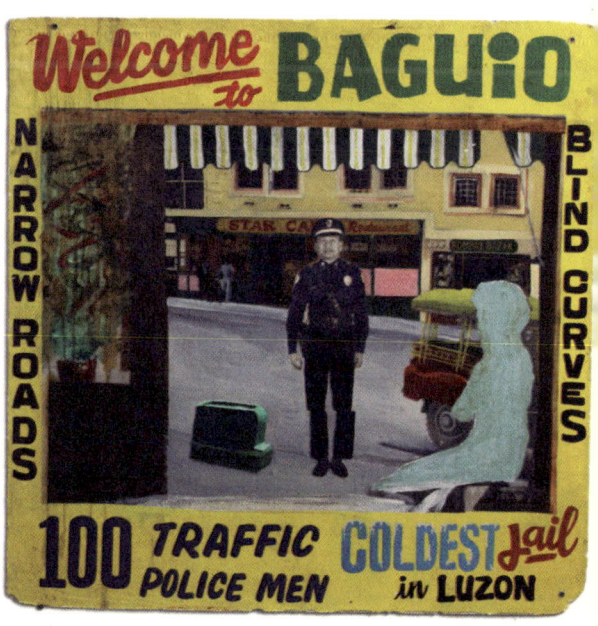

Artwork by Santiago Bose, C. 1990s.

GIs on furloughs during the Vietnam War. It was turned over to the Philippine Government in 1992 when the Pinatubo eruption effectively evicted the US bases, and eventually punctuated by the Philippine Senate's decision not to renew the US Bases treaty. It then became a private resort run by mega real estate developers from Manila – which renewed its 50-year lease with the developer, BCDA. One is advised to read the 19 conditionalities imposed by the Baguio City council. With its quaint cottages-cum-fireplaces and its 18-hole golf course, CJH was a Little America for locals who could not afford a trans-Pacific air ticket to the 'Land of Promise.' KT
See also: AFRTN; "Blue Seal" Yosi Quotas; Hay, John Milton.

Jones, Isabela. Place in Isabela named after William Jones, an American anthropologist who stayed and studied the Ilongots in 1909. He was apparently well-loved and on his last day with them, while crossing the river that would bring him back home, his head was taken by the same people who loved him. Ilongots were said to take heads not as a trophy but to gain the amed (spirit) of the victims and in so doing gain the respect and admiration of the community.

They also take heads sometimes, as in the case of Jones, because of rage born out of grief. FYC.
See also: Haight's Place; Headhunting (the tale); Hunt, Truman; Pre-white; Tribes.

Jueteng. The first jueteng (illegal numbers game) in Baguio was the 'Pak kap pio.' Leung Chiw was said to have introduced this numbers game in the

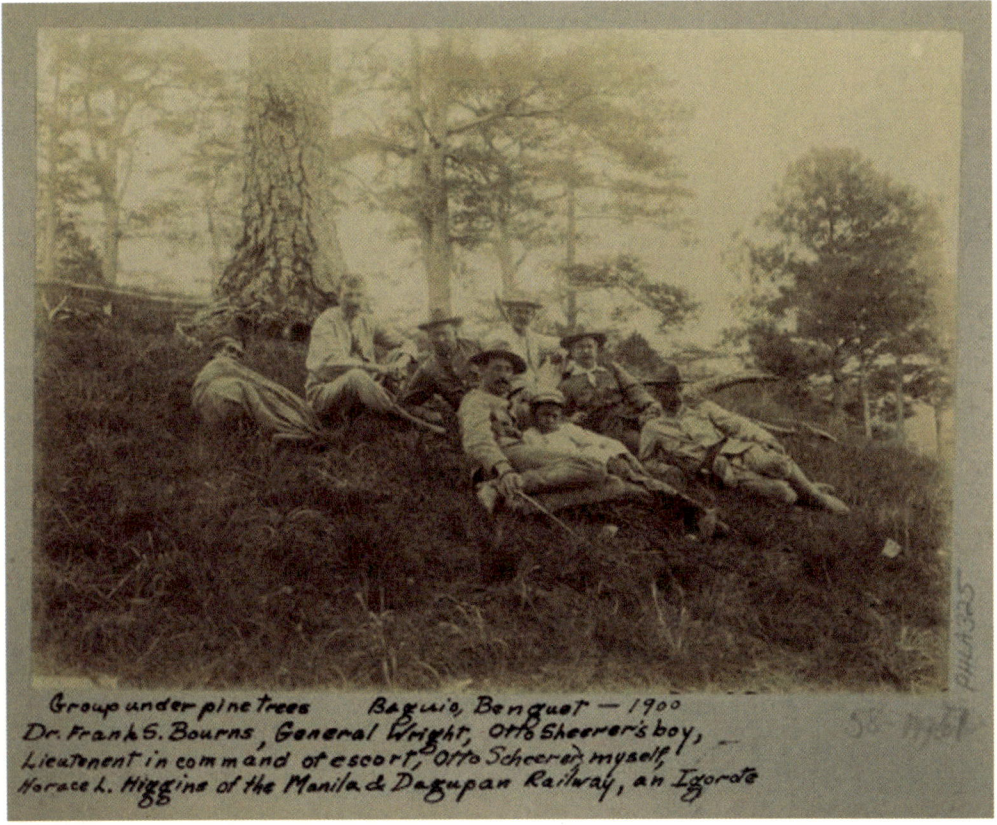

Photograph of "group under pine trees, Baguio, Benguet, 1900. Dr. Frank S. Bourns, General Wright, Otto Sheerer's boy, Lieutenant command of escort, Otto Sheerer, myself, Horace L. Higgins of the Manila & Dagupan Railway, an Igorote." Courtesy AV Cating Family Collection.

1960s where you choose ten numbers from a row of eight characters. There were two draws a day. When Leung died, the Filipinos took over jueteng. In the 1970s and 1980s, the biggest jueteng draws came from Baguio and Itogon because of the mines. When the mines dwindled, jueteng shifted to Benguet especially in Buguias where vegetable farming was very lucrative, and in the capital of La Trinidad where vegetables were traded. Jueteng also became popular in Tabuk, Kalinga and Bangued, Abra. The daily take of jueteng operators in Baguio (where the financiers came from Pampanga and Laguna provinces) is PHP2 million. In Ifugao, jueteng was not as successful because the houses are in small clusters that are far from each other, and the Ifugaos bet only two to five pesos. FYC.

Opposite page: Advertisement of Ivory Soap depicting Igorots carrying cases of soap, c. 1910s. Courtesy AV Cating Family Collection.

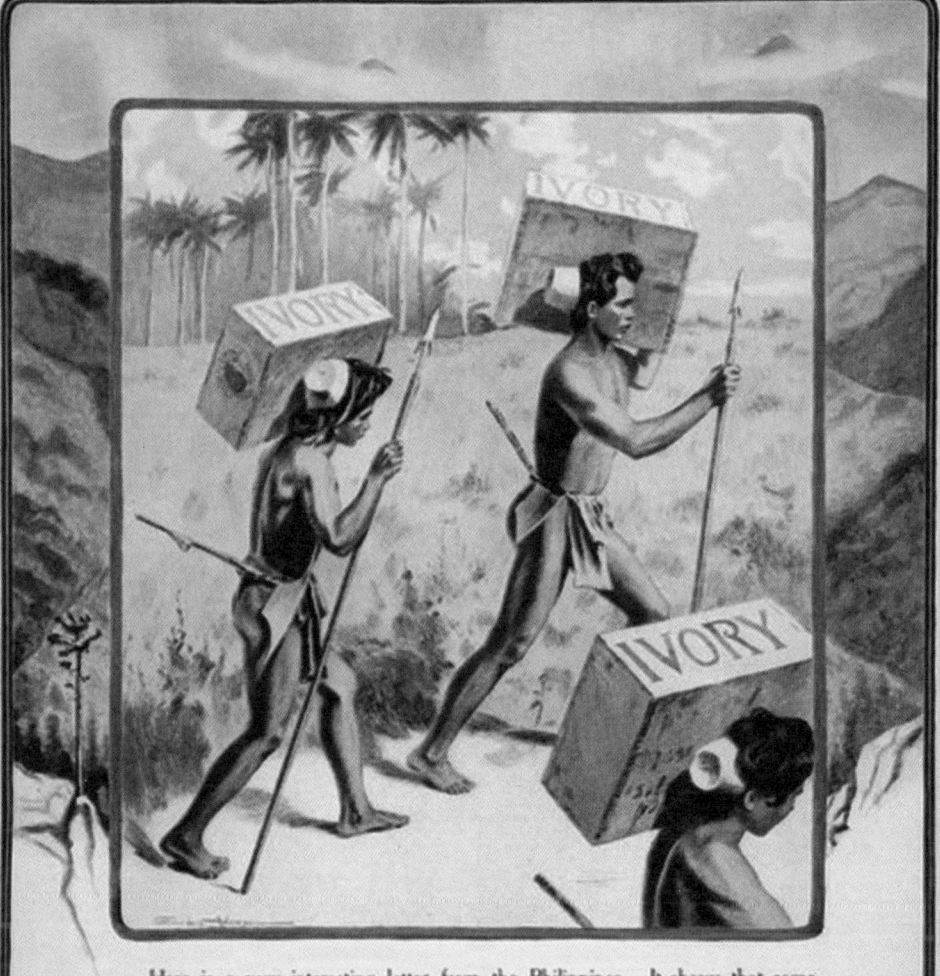

Here is a very interesting letter from the Philippines. It shows that some people like Ivory Soap so much that they have it brought *nearly half way 'round the globe for them.*

"Enclosed is a photograph which I have recently taken in the town of Bontoc, in north central Luzon, with the idea that you may be able to use it as an advertisement of Ivory Soap.

Ivory Soap is furnished by the Philippine Government for each of the seven Igorrote Industrial Schools under my supervision. At first the pupils did not like it, but now, if the teachers do not keep it under lock and key, the boys carry it home.

The soap, after being landed at Manila, is put on board a little coasting vessel and in a couple of days reaches the town of Vigan, 300 miles north. At Vigan, begins a one hundred mile journey into the extremely wild and mountainous country, which is the home of the Igorrotes. As it is impossible for wagons to make this trip over the mountains, the cases are carried on the backs of pack animals for the first three days, at the end of which time they reach the town of Cervantes, the capital of the province of Lepanto-Bontoc. From Cervantes to Bontoc, Igorrote carriers are used, as the mountain trails are very steep.

The photograph represents an actual, bona fide occurrence. The men are taken in their every-day costume. The little basket hats on their heads serve as pockets. The axes in their belts are used as implements of peace, or as weapons of war. The spears are their constant companions, and the hats, axes, spears, and the "Gee-strings" 'round their waists are all of home manufacture."

It is not necessary for *you* to send eleven thousand miles for a cake of Ivory Soap. It is on sale in nearly every one of the three hundred thousand grocery stores in the United States.

Ivory Soap . . . . 99 44/100 Per Cent. Pure.

How can you face your problem when your problem is your face?, Mark Tandoyog, mixed media, 30x20 cm, 2006.

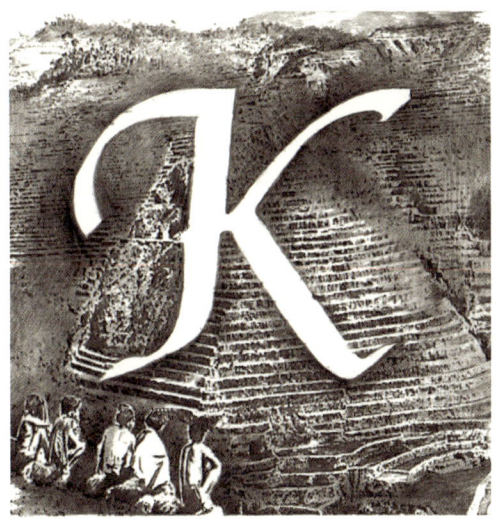

Kabaggaang *(ITN)* also **Pinaing** or **Pinating.** *"In many Tinguian villages, one finds a stone or some stones strategically located at the sungaban (entrance). Sometimes, these are kept under the trees. These are not just stones; they are the community guardians which have a power of their own... As guardians of the community, the kabaggaang/ pina-ing/ pinat-ing are installed in the entrance of the purok (village) to defend the people from man-made or natural calamities like sickness, famine and drought. Those who live near the entrance say that they sometimes hear sounds of an enraged bull especially during night. They believe that kabaggaang fights with the enemies who want to attack the community. They also say that these stones intercede for them. When there are gatherings in a purok... an Apo Baket always rubs coconut oil on each kabaggaang before the tadek (dancing) takes place. This is to make them part of their community celebrations and so that the latter will continue to shield them from harm."* (Sumangil, 2003, 2).
See also: Tadek.

Kabalo *(KAN).* For the Kankanaey it is lawa (bad or prohibited) to say anybody's name when burying a dead person. If it is necessary to call one's attention, the speaker replaces the name of the person he is calling with Kabalo. One would say, *"Iyawat mokod san pala ay Kabalo [Hand me the shovel, Kabalo]."* DOS.
See also: Inayan.

Kabasilya. How Igorots in the 1900s pronounced 'cabecilla,' their peers who were selected to enforce American edicts in the village level. The kabasilya was given an 18-inch whip to enforce authority. FYC.
See also: Pre-white; Tribes.

Kabayan Mummies. Kabayan is *"one of the Municipalities of Benguet Province in the Cordillera Mountain Ranges of northern Luzon. The municipality is recognized as a center of Ibaloi Culture. The Ibaloi, the dominant ethno-linguistic group, of Kabayan have a long traditional practice of mummifying their dead. Mummification began prior to the Spanish colonization. Individuals from the higher societal stratum of the Ibaloi of Kabayan used to be mummified through a long ritual process over a long period of time. The process of mummification using salt and herbs and set under fire may take up to two years. When the body is finally rid of body fluids, the mummy is placed inside a pinewood coffin and laid to rest in a man-made cave or in a niche dug-out from solid rock. During the Spanish period, Christianity spread and took a foothold in the mountains of Benguet and the practice of mummification and cave burial was abandoned. The remains are then placed in wooden coffins and interred in man-made burial niches in rocks or rock shelters and/or natural caves. Strategically located in the mountain slopes of the municipality of Kabayan, more than 200 man-made burial caves have been identified and 15 of which contain preserved human mummies."* (UNESCO World Heritage Center 1992-2014).
See also: Apo Annu; Enmity between the Igorots and Christians, The Beginning of; Lumiang Burial Cave.

Kabunian also **Cabunian, Kabunyan, Kabonyan.** In earlier records of prayers, songs and conversations, Kabunian in pre-Christian texts meant any of the following: a group of deities, a man/woman of superhuman abilities, a place of deities, the sun and/or moon. Moss in Kibungan translated 'buni' to mean prayers, and in Mayoyao 'mumbuni' to mean a common word for praying or sacrifice. Barton in Kalinga translated Cabunian as *"those to whom sacrifices are offered."* Lambrecht in Ifugao translated this same word as *"the place of the deities."* Jenks in Bontoc mentioned Lumawig, otherwise known as Funi or Kambunyan, as the supreme being. Eugenio Bayang who wrote the prayers of Sagada in 1955 referred to kabonyan in the plural. Simon Aquino of Besao wrote *"Kabunian"*

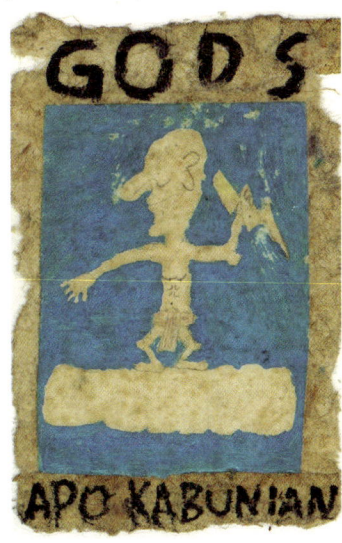

Artwork by Kabunyan de Guia, 1991.

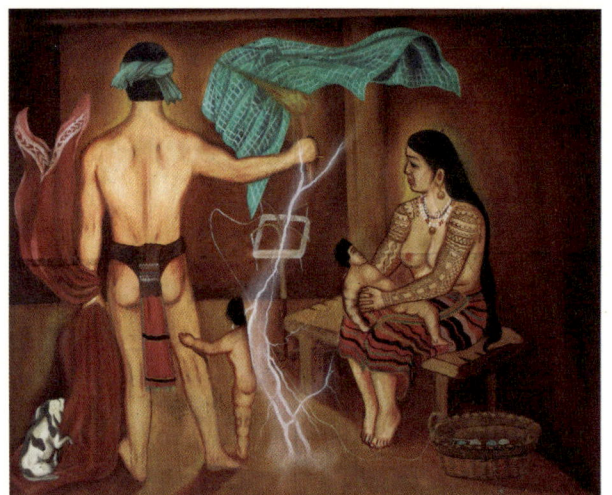
Artwork by Chris Mero, 1990.

in some prayers and "a Kabunian" in others (Scott, 1966, pp. 134-143) Ask any young person now and they'd say Kabunyan refers to God, the 'Igorot God' in a monotheistic sense. GAD.

Kabunyan had six wives.

(1) The first marriage was in Gawa-na.
No mention of his first wife's name.

(2) His second marriage was to Kabunyan-bugan.
His children from the second marriage were:
Liddum
Indan-no
Mon-gadang
Mon-tayyom
Gin-nomom

(3) The third marriage happened at Hubuwan.
No mention of his third wife's name.
The children from his third marriage were:
Amgaling-nan
Gin-nomon
Natudoh

(4) The fourth marriage was at Dagah-na.
No mention of his fourth wife's name.
The children from the fourth marriage were:
Dinok-ligan
Bugan
Naam-ma
Kin-nodan

(5) The fifth marriage transpired at Kay-ang.
No mention of his fifth wife's name.
The children from the fifth marriage were:
Amduy-yan
Halibubu
Ginipaan
Kabigat
Wigan

(6) The sixth and final union was at Kiangan.
No mention of his last wife's name.
The last fruits were:
Tad-ona
Wigan
See also: Doligen ed Kabunian; Si; I-langit; Kadaklan; Kain.

Kadaklan *(TIN)*. Lit. The greatest.
(1) *"A powerful male spirit, who lives in the sky, created the earth, sun, moon, and stars. The stars are only stones, but the sun and moon are lights. At times Kadaklan enters the body of a favored medium, and talks directly with the people; but more frequently he takes other means of communication.*

Oftentimes he sends his dog Kīmat, the lightning, to bite a tree or strike a field or house, and in this way makes known his wish that the owner celebrate the Padīam ceremony.... All other beings are in a measure subservient to him, and his wishes are frequently made known through them.

Thunder is his drum with which he amuses himself during stormy weather, but sometimes he plays on it even on clear days. Makaboteng, also called Sanadan, is the guardian of the deer and wild hogs. His good will is necessary if the dogs are to be successful in the chase; consequently he is summoned to many ceremonies, where he receives the most courteous treatment. In one ceremony he declared, 'I can become the sunset sky.'" (Cole (1922) 2004).
(2) A barangay in Barlig, Mountain Province. Its forests are home to many kalaw (hornbill).
See also: Kabunian; Tinguian Spirits.

Kadso *(KAN/BON)*. Washing of hair, not necessarily with soap or shampoo. It is also the term for a natural shampoo found in the mountains: a bluish, grayish sticky soil that produce very little suds but leaves a clean moisturized feeling on the hair and scalp after washing. PAD.
See also: Igod.

Kaduduwa *(ISN)*. The spirit that leaves the body of the dead. It is similar to the Tagalog's kaluluwa which is also spirit but in Isneg, the duality (duwa) of body and spirit is emphasized. FYC.
See also: Ab-abiik; Pattaliat.

Kain *(ILN)*. Ilongot cosmology is influenced by Christianity as their supreme deities are brothers Kain and Abal, who lived in the skyworld among the sun and stars. They traveled by lightning and thunder. Inevitably, they fought and Abal, who was stronger, came to earth and created the lowlanders. Kain settled on the mountains and created the Ilongots and other mountain tribes.

Because Kain was a head-taker, the Ilongots also became head-takers. Unlike other Cordillerans, the Ilongots did not bring home the heads but either left them where they cut them or threw them in the river. FYC.

See also: Bureau of Non Christian Tribes; Enmity between the Igorots and Christians, The Beginning of; Kabunian; Remontados.

Kakala *(KAL)*. Ritual payment, more often the head of an enemy, which was the main motif of most ceremonies.

See also: Headhunting (the tale).

Kalasan *(KAN)*. The high-elevation cloud forest dominated by oak in Buguias and nearby towns.

Kalabog-kalabog-Buguias-patatas! *(KAN)*.
This is the cheer of Buguias participants in any division or regional sports meets.
It has been popularized by Buguiasians in jamborees, sport events, or any local gathering of different municipalities. 'Kalabog-kalabog' is the onomatopoeic sound of falling potatoes. As potatoes are considered the trademark of Buguias' agricultural livelihood, the crop has been always associated with the place and the people. CCA.

See also: Buguias Cocktail; Buguias Patatas; Buguias Soil; Loo.

Kalajo *(IBA)*. Lit. Welcome! The Ibaloi word for invitation; from the root verb, 'kala,' which means 'come.' The attached pronoun, 'jo,' is the plural 'you.' In rituals, it is used to invite various spirits to take part in the feast or offering. (Ballard 2011, 222) SKW.

See also: Pitik.

Kalang *(ITN)*. A carabao-shaped wooden box. Food and alcohol (usually rice or sugarcane wine) placed inside are for the spirits. Spirits do not dwell here but the headbands of the mediums are often placed there for added potency. The kalang is attached to the roof. Offerings are usually done before the men go on a hunt. FYC.

See also: Iwaxan.

Kalanguya. *"Their identity and ethnic label [Kalanguya] had not been fixed in any of the historical or ethnological literature of Spanish and American colonial times. The people who carry [the name] and who share a language are now spread out across the contiguous areas of the provinces of Benguet, Ifugao, Nueva Vizcaya, Nueva Ecija and Pangasinan. This... is the result of their movements as swidden cultivators, as well as of the arbitrary political boundaries drawn and re-drawn by Philippine governments since American times... The word Kalanguya is said to originate from the Kalanguya sentence, 'Kallay ngo ya?,' which means, 'Why is that?' and is sometimes used as an expression of surprise or puzzlement. According to Patricia Afable (1989), residents of Kayapa, Nueva Vizcaya prefer to be called Kallahan because their Kankana-ey neighbors use the phrase 'Kallay ngo ya' to make fun of their speech. Founders of the Kalanguya Tribal Organization insist that the label Kalanguya connotes peace, because the phrase is also used to rebuke someone who has done wrong. On the other hand, Ikalahan literally means 'from the forest' or 'people of the forest'. The term has its roots among their Ibaloy neighbors who settled the lower slopes of Mt. Pulag, and referred to the mossy oak forests as kadasan. Thus, the i-kadasan, or i-kallahan are the people from the mossy oak forest; just as the i-baloy, are said to originate from an area which was covered by a plant known locally as baloy... The Kalanguya... trace their descent to "Tinek,' this being the name not only of a settlement but also of a larger region that includes the Ahin and Kadaklan headwaters, the Mt. Pulog heights and the Matunu headwaters region known as Danggu.' (Afable 1989, 157.)"* (Perez 2010, 38-39).

See also: Dang-ah; Inum'an.

Kaling *(KAN)* also **Panispis** *(KAN/BON)*, **Fanisfis** *(BON)*. Indigenized from 'Japanese fish,' it refers to dojo loach usually found in the rice terraces. It is said to have been introduced by the Japanese farmers such as Iwama, a grocer in Baguio, and Okui of Sagada in the 1920s. PAD/FYC.

Kalsa *(IBA)*. A small cymbal held in the left hand and struck with a wooden stick. The kalsa works as a counterpoint to the solibao (long wooden drum). The palas (two iron sticks) are also played simultaneously in Ibaloi rhythm. FYC.

See also: Music.

Kalu-os *(ILO)*. A local version of the luge. The board varies in size and depends on spare cut-out wood available from house construction. Kalu-os is played on a steep road where children climb up the road and slide down repeatedly. Oil, candle wax or floor wax, and crushed gumamela flowers are the most popular lubricants for the bottom of the board to make it slide faster. While sliding, children often wear their slippers on their elbows or palms to use as brakes or to push themselves off the top of the slope. As with the luge, players may slide down in various positions: standing, sitting, and even lying down on their tummies head first. HZK.

See also: Bongtot; Butubutu-Ukiuki; Play.

Kamal *(IBA)*. Cooperative work. This refers to the gathering of neighbors to help someone who has a project involving heavy labor, which can last for days. The host butchers an animal for those who come to work. Rice wine is also served. If there is leftover meat, it is given to the workers to take home. (Ballard 2011, 228) SKW.

See also: Baddang; Ob-obbo.

Kamaling *(KAN)*. Used to describe the center of towns in the Western Mt. Province. In Sagada, it would refer to Poblacion. TDH.

Kaman gangi *(KAN)*. Lit. Like a gangi. Traditionally, gold dust placed on a gangi (terra cotta concave plate) is refined by melting it over burning charcoal. After the process, the gangi naturally turns black. Hence, Kankanaeys use kaman gangi to describe dark things or people with a dark complexion. NEP.
See also: Dayasan; Pansejew.

Kamma i Kungnga *(IFU)*. Kamma and Kungnga are characters in Ifugao a'apo (stories for children) usually told to send children to sleep. Kamma literally means old and Kungnga, young. There are many versions of this story. In one story, they are co-tillers of a habal (swidden farm) where they plant gube (watermelons) that are stolen by Lablabuut. They use a tagtagu (mannequin) made of paste to catch Lablabuut but he tricks them and convinces them to throw him into a pond which is revealed to be the thief's kingdom.

Another story has it that they are brothers sent to clear out the habal. Their parents took turns in bringing them food but the mother always brought stale food for Kamma and good food for Kungnga. Kamma then decided to become a bird after calling upon the magical birds to give him a beak and wings. As a bird, Kamma got even with the mother by bringing her rotten fruits while the best ones he gave to Kungnga and their father. The father and brother were able to catch Kamma and brought him back and turned him into a man again. RHK.
See also: Three Orphans of Sagada, The; Ullalim.

Kammid *(KAL)*. Ritual where the grandparents officially recognize their grandchild at six months of age. A bead bracelet or necklace is given to the child who must wear it for life. A pig or chicken is slaughtered during the kammid. FYC.
See also: Gobgobbao; Linayaan.

Kangkang *(ISN)*. A kind of cramp that affects the whole body, but more especially the fingers and toes, and ends in death.

Kaon ya Teteg *(KAN)*. Kaon is the formal wedding engagement between a man and a woman. This is followed by the teteg (wedding celebration) that is presided over by a mambunong. The couple wear only casual clothes during the occasion. At the wedding party, a native pig or two is butchered and the pork is cooked in a large wok over an open fire. On the night of the teteg, it is forbidden for the new couple to sleep together until the ritual is finally over the next morning. NEP.
See also: Bayas; Bet-bet; Mambunong; Nantoltolo; Ngilin; Peshit.

Karayan Libeg *(ILO)*. Lit. Murky river. The Abra River in Cervantes (whose headwater comes from Mount Data, Bauko) is called Karayan Libeg. Mine tailings are also said to contribute to its murkiness. DOS.
See also: Cervantes; Chico.

Kassap *(ISN)*. A common herb used in black magic, causing a whole ricefield to lie in ruins.

Katekateg ad U.S. *(KAN)*. Lit. Just like in the U.S. It is a common description used in Besao town where conversations are often peppered with English – e.g. *"Adiyak nakaali ad yesterday ta nen-cry si baby [I wasn't able to come yesterday because baby cried]"* or *"Ad Besao e, katekateg ad U.S. Nan breakfast mi ah, kumbasa. Nan tukduan mi ah, electric chair [In Besao, it's just like in the U.S. Our breakfast is squash and we sit on electric chairs]."* JBC.

Kato *(IBA)*. Small and button-like mushrooms.
See also: Ibbaw; Tabayong.

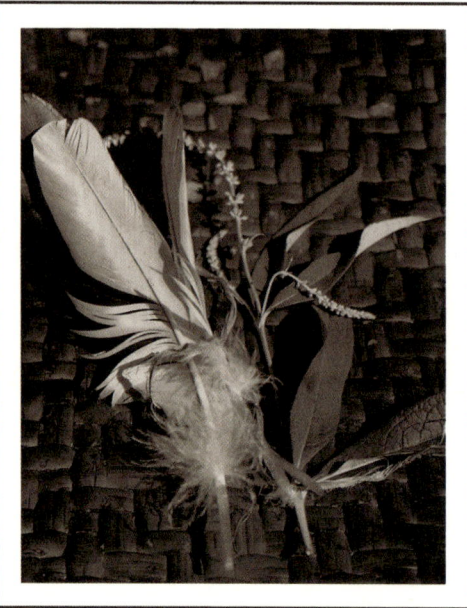
Photograph of a bundle of *Kawkaw*. Photograph by Tommy Hafalla.

Kawkaw *(KAN)*. A bundle of feathers taken from a sacrificial chicken at a ritual and then tied with local sage. The kawkaw is used during blessing ceremonies. TDH.

Kayan. According to church records, the first mission school in the Cordillera was set up in Kayan, Tadian in 1660.
See also: Bureau of Non-Christian Tribes; Episcopalianism.

Kayangga *(KAL)*. Red hibiscus. Worn by Kalinga headhunters and ritual specialists during headtaking feasts as a sign of martial power,

sexual attractiveness, tribal prominence, and eloquence. FYC.
See also: Kulatod.

Kayngot *(IFU)*. To bite one's lower lip as a sign of anger or displeasure.

Kennon Lion. The huge lion monument located at Camp 6, Kennon Road, was the mascot of the Baguio Lion's Club. It was commissioned by then club president Luis L. Lardizabal, who was also Baguio City Mayor at the time. After being 'shaped' from a lime outcrop, Anselmo Day-ag rendered it into a lion. It was finally finished in 1972. It has since been repainted multiple times after an agreement between the city, the Lions Club, and Davies Paints Philippines. FYC.
See also: Day-ag, Anselmo; Indi-genius; Kennon Road.

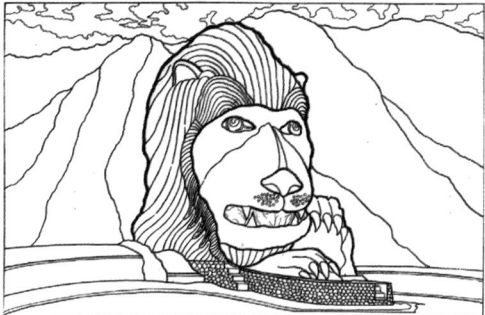
Illustration of **Kennon Road**. Illustration by Sirk Deuda.

Kennon Road. First known as Benguet Road, it was first estimated that it would cost only US$65,000 to build (with extra USD10,000 as a margin of safety). Its construction eventually cost more than US$2 million with US$100,000 annual funds for repair. Construction was started in January 1901. The first major American roadwork of the 20th Century, it opened for regular service in March 1905. Its first officer-in-charge was Capt. Charles Mead but after a *"disastrous start,"* he was replaced by Major Lyman Kennon in 1903, who added features such as permission for wives in the camp, a band to serenade the workers, and weekend dances to complement the existing casinos and saloons. When Benguet Road (later renamed as Kennon Road) was finally opened, there were hardly any Baguio residents to welcome the workers and travelers. In 1909, Baguio became a chartered city and Summer Capital of the Philippines, and by 1913, there were already several hundred buildings in Baguio. FYC.
See also: Baguio Oil; Halsema Highway; Jail; Kennon Lion; Leonard Wood Real; White Elephant.

Kerol *(IBA)*. Thunder.
See also: Kimat; Thunder.

Ket-an *(KAN/BON)*. A hard-shelled snail with a slim, long and pointy shell. It is dark brown or black in color and found in rice paddies. PAD.
See also: Agudong id Manitong; Atubang; Bisukol; Falokag; Golden Kuhol; Lisdeg.

Kidlos *(KAN)*. A thanksgiving ritual done in Besao just after childbirth. The grandparent or any old person in the household, gets a small piece of cooked etag on a stick and says a prayer of thanksgiving for the safe delivery of the baby, and intercedes for the mother to produce enough breast milk for the baby. When the woman is in labor, somebody in the household already boils the etag. If all the immediate family members are present, this meat can be mixed with chicken to make pinikpikan for the whole family to eat together. Otherwise, the etag is just cooked with beans for the family meal. PAD.
See also: Etag; Kidlos di bakas; Kiya; Pinikpikan; Putting; Teknag.

Kidlos di bakas *(KAN)*. Ritual for abortion with prayers for the health of the mother. PAD.
See also: Kidlos.

Kimat *(ILO)*. According to a Benguet legend, Kimat (Lightning) was the son of Kido or Amkidol (Thunder) and a Benguet woman named Bugan. The son was literally divided but whenever his two halves were joined, lightning occurred. When an Igorot (or a tree or any property) is struck by lightning, a liyaw is performed so it won't strike again. The person struck should not be touched but left for two to three hours to allow Kido to heal what he did. To disturb the body could cause death. FYC.
See also: Apang; Bangan; Kadaklan; Kimat; Liyaw; Longayban; Thunder.

Kimata *(BON/KAN)* also **Gimata** *(KAN)*. A pair of two huge bamboo baskets joined to a pat-ang (wooden crossbar). A Bontoc man can easily carry a hundred pounds with the kimata. FYC.

Kineykhey *(BON)* also **Inab-abosang** *(KAN)*. A traditional dish of glutinous rice boiled with camote as its sweetener, prepared for occasions like rest days, New Year's, or family celebrations. PAD.
See also: Boko; Camote; Intum; Sinalupsop.

Kiya *(KAL)*. Children barking like dogs in front of a newborn baby boy as a ritual.
See also: Kidlos; Putting; Teknag.

KKK. Other than the white supremacist Klu Kux Klan and the 1890s Kataas-taasang, Kagalang-galang Katipunan ng mga Anak ng Bayan (KKK) or the Philippine revolutionary group against the Spaniards, KKK is also known as Kilusang Kabataan ng Kabundukan, a group of Cordilleran student activists in Manila before Martial Law (and

Hi-Act or Highland Activists before that). Later, it became known as the more radical Kilusang Kabataan ng Kordilyera. FYC.

Km. 26 Guerrilla Saddle 66th Infantry Battalion Rice. Red rice with porkchops and vegetables. Not only is it the longest name for a roadside dish but it is also a historical one, as Saddle is the name of the place where many Japanese troops died in battle against the 66th Infantry Battalion, composed of American and Igorot guerrillas. FYC.

Km. 53. The former Highest Point in the Philippines' Highway System at 7,400 ft. above sea level. It is located along the Halsema Highway at Cattubo, Atok, Benguet. In the past, the highest point was at 7,800 ft. The Cattubo spot is a story of bad tourism management. Before the 1990s, the highest point was marked by a huge concrete mortar with a dying pine tree beside it. The Department of Tourism thought of building a view deck and a restroom, blocking the sign. Then someone decided to put up a store beside it. Then the Department of Public Works and Highways decided to put up their own sign a few meters away. Right now, the highest point marker is in Tinoc, ifugao. FYC.
See also: Halsema Highway.

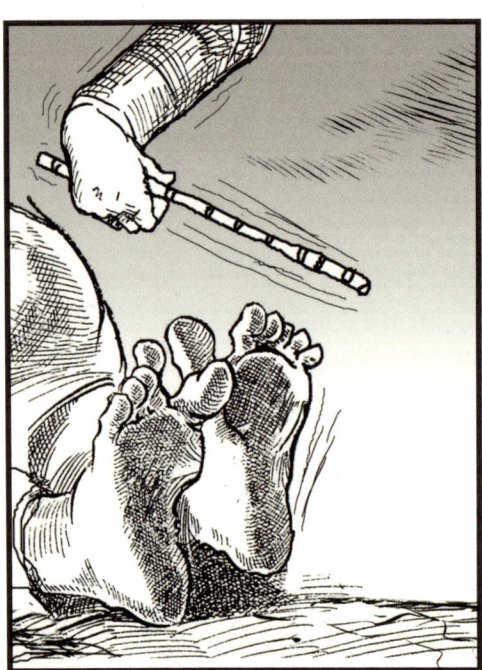

Illustration of Kolkol-is. Illustration by Benjie Mallari.

Kolkol-is *(KAN)* also **Dagdagay.** Foot *"reflexology"* using sticks, done by young boys for adult men in the dap-ay. At home, young girls can also do it to their fathers. The soles of people were thick in the past as they didn't wear any shoes or slippers; thus scratching with the sticks was not painful to them. PAD.
See also: Dap-ay.

Komboy. Generic Baguio word for porter. Although the "Komboy" YouTube video by Wilson Lingpawen depicts all porters as 'komboys,' the term is more specific to the porters at the Baguio City Market who deliver vegetables from the Hangar section. They have their own wooden handcart or kariton. These karitons are designed with the wooden 'stay' (the post in front) and the back end with 'flip-flop rubber sole' brakes so it can manage to descend the steep Hilltop road without much problems. Steer clear of the path of a komboy and his fully-loaded kariton. FYC.

Korta *(KAN).* The act of digging root crops such as carrots and potatoes. The latter is the largest crop of Benguet. DOS.
See also: Buguias Patatas.

Koto ni Shontog *(IBA).* Lit. Lice of the mountains. A poetic description for cattle roaming on the mountains.
See also: Divang.

Kub-kuba *(KAN)* also **Akhifay** *(BON)*, **Chanipan** *(BON).* (1) The bark of the puspos tree that is flattened and softened by beating, and then used as a napkin during menstruation and after giving birth. It is reusable (can be washed), absorbent, deodorant and it facilitates healing of the perineal wound from childbirth. PAD.
(2) This bark may still be used today when a person is given the traditional funeral rite in which the deceased is seated in a death-chair for the duration of the wake. The kub-kuba bark is used to tie parts of the deceased's body, to secure it to the chair. TDH.
See also: Sangadil.

Kudo *(KAN).* Lit. Poor. It is a custom in the Cordilleras that if a man is courting a lady, he should always say he is kudo even if it is false humility. DOS.
See also: Buaya Economic Classes.

Kulatod *(KAL).* A warrior's helmet with feathers, hibiscus, and bougainvillea. It is made and given by women.
See also: Akipur; Apang; Bayoyok; Duwao; Kayangga; Panglao.

Kuliteng *(ITN).* An all-bamboo guitar. First, strips are made around the tube between the bamboo nodes and then these narrow strips are raised as strings and tuned accordingly. These are beaten with sticks or plucked with the fingers. FYC.
See also: Abistong; Dew-dew-as; Gong; Music.

Kung Mangarap Ka't Magising. Lit. When you dream and then wake up. The start of the movie *Kung Mangarap Ka't Magising* (1977) (known in English as *Moments in a Stolen Dream*), would put a smile on most Baguio residents who lived here in the pre-EDSA Revolution years. The scene shows a young man waking up to the sound of AFRTN (Armed Forces Radio and TV Network), which brought American tunes to American servicemen all over the world. Residents of Baguio, the site of Camp John Hay, listened to AFRTN not only because it gave us the Top 40 hits two weeks before Manila, but also because it gave us news that was sometimes critical of the Marcos government. Watching *Kung Mangarap Ka't Magising (KMKM)*, the 1977 movie of Mike De Leon, brings back a Baguio someone might wish to return to. *KMKM* tells the story of De Leon as a biology student who wants to be a musician and then meets a young woman on the verge of a breakdown in her marriage. They briefly fall in love and then break up to live out the rest of their lives separately. The essence of Baguio romance is captured in the scenes showing actor Christopher de Leon playing the piano with the Apo Hiking Society band in UP Baguio, having a picnic with actress Hilda Koronel among the limestone outcrops of Dominican Hill, and walking in the rain along Outlook Drive.

Poster of the movie *Kung Mangarap Ka't Magising* by Mike De Leon, 1977. Theatrical release poster.

We asked movie reviewers what movie was the most evocative of Baguio, *Kung Mangarap Ka't Magising* came out on top.

Rolando Tolentino, the dean of the UP College of Mass Communications and author of various critiques on the movie industry, chose *KMKM* because, for him, it depicts a *"picturesque Baguio that makes you fall in love, fall out of love, and gives you melancholia to make the loss linger."* Tolentino also chose *Dear Heart* (1981) starring Sharon Cuneta and Rowell Santiago as students in Brent International School, as well as another Mike De Leon movie, *Kakabakaba Ka Ba?* (1980), a satire about lovers played by Christopher De Leon and Charo Santos, caught in a search for cocaine by Chinese agents and Japanese drug lords using fake nuns as drug mules. Tolentino also chose Kidlat Tahimik's *Bakit Yellow ang Gitna ng Bahaghari?* (1994), a documentary about the Baguio filmmaker's sons amidst the country's political awakening that led to the first EDSA Revolution.

Simon Santos, son of the artist Malang and the owner of Video 48 in Quezon City, which houses the most extensive collection of old Filipino movies and memorabilia, also chose *KMKM* for the distinctive Baguio scenery. Santos also chose *Baguio Fever*, a 1959 comedy starring Nida Blanca and Nestor de Villa; *Daigdig Ko'y Ikaw*, a 1965 film starring Fernando Poe Jr. and Susan Roces; and *Bato sa Buhangin*, a 1976 movie again starring FPJ and Sharon Cuneta. Santos said that the changes in Baguio across the decades can be discerned in these movies.

Mauro Tumbocon, San Francisco-based writer on movies and popular culture, chose *KMKM* because it wasn't touristy and didn't use the popular Baguio tourist spots to convey the Baguio mystique. Tumbocon also chose *Magandang Gabi sa Inyong Lahat* by Lupita Aquino-Concio as his other Baguio film favorite. This 1976 movie was about a balikbayan played by Nora Aunor who met her former boyfriend played by Tirso Cruz III.

Mario Hernando, another respected movie critic, also chose *KMKM* as his best Baguio movie favorite, as well as Cirio H. Santiago's 1961 movie, *Mga Yakap na Walang Bakas* starring Nestor de Villa and Aura Aurea, and Chito Roño's 1996 *Istokwa* starring Mark Anthony Fernandez and G Toengi.

Only New Jersey-based film archivist and film blogger Jojo de Vera did not choose *KMKM*. He instead chose Peque Gallaga's 1995 *Baby Love* starring Edu Manzano and Anna Larrucea; Baguio-born Tata Esteban's 1995 thriller, *Alapaap* starring Tanya Gomez and William Martinez; Celso Ad Castillo's 1987 movie, *Mga Lihim ng Kalapati* starring Isadora, Tanya Gomez, and Marissa Delgado; *Nakaw na Pag-ibig*, a Lino Brocka 1980 adaptation of Theodore Dreiser's *An American Tragedy* set in Baguio and starring Nora Aunor and Hilda Koronel; and Romy Suzara's 1980 *Sa Init ng Apoy* starring Rudy Fernandez and Lorna Tolentino. FYC.

See also: Abong; AFRTN; Baguio (the movie); Banaue: Stairway to the Sky; Big Bird Cage; Igorota: The Legend of the Tree of Life; Irisan (the movie); John Hay, Camp; Mumbaki; Vacacionista.

Kunsisal. How Igorots in the 1900s pronounced 'consejal' or the subregional deputies to the American lieutenant-governors. The kunsisal was given a baston or a swagger stick as symbol of his administration. FYC.

Kunyas *(KAN)*. Cold chisel, used for mining or splitting wood.

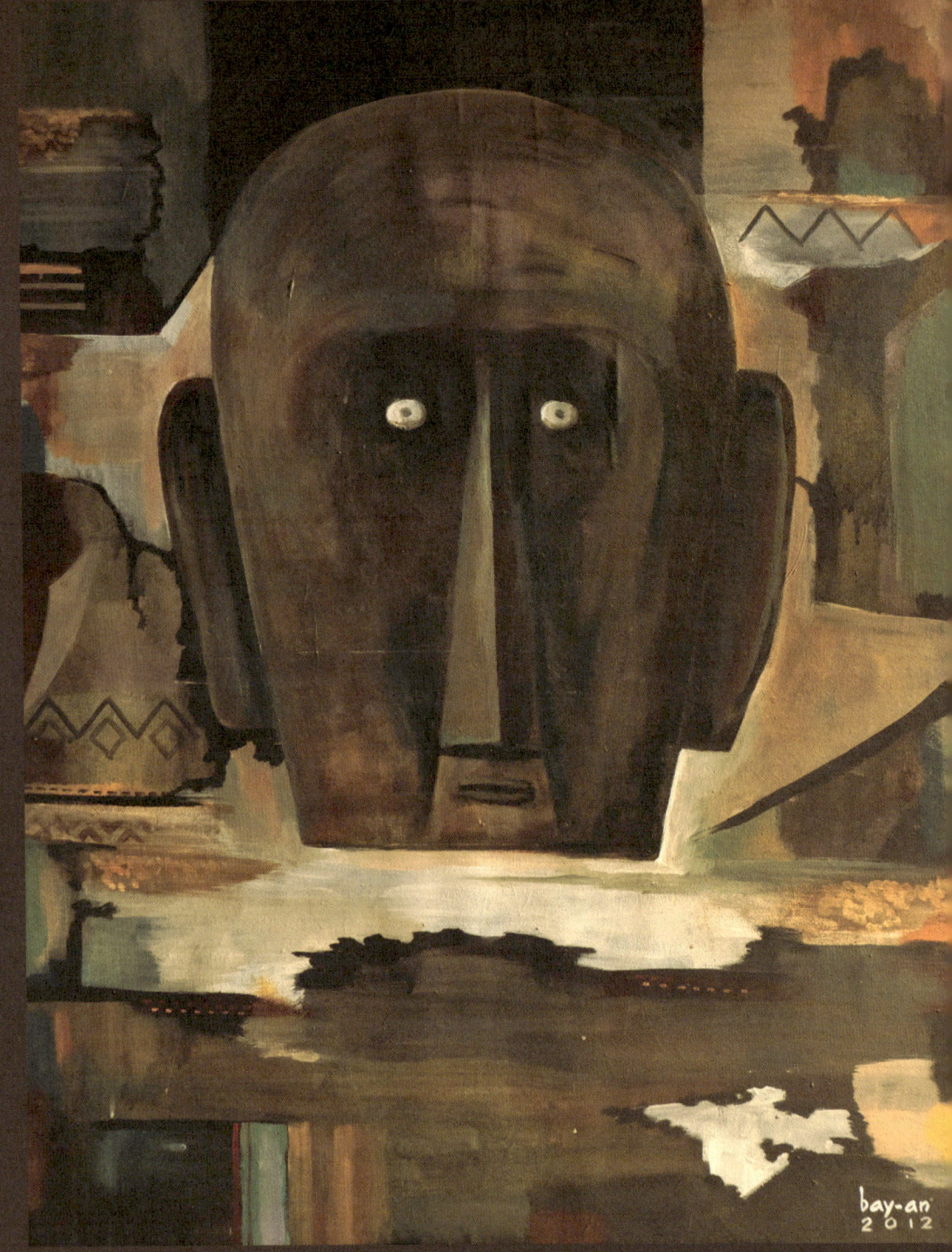

Untitled, Roland Bay-an, oil on canvas, 96x141 cm, 2012.

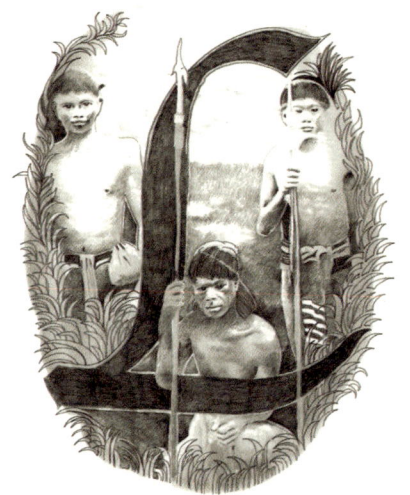

Labeg *(KAN)*. Omen often brought by the sight of animals like birds or snakes. These omens are taken into consideration when intending to travel – e.g. if one leaves one's house to travel and a bird flies by over one's left, it is a bad omen but if it flies by over one's right, it is deemed auspicious. The same applies to passing snakes. DOS.
See also: Bangon; Ichaw; Sangbo.

Labun *(IFU)*. To bury a dead infant or small child as they are too young to be placed on a death chair.
See also: Sangadil.

La Casita. A dim-lit nightclub on Harrison Road during the 1950s. Clients could buy a 'stateside' cocktail with hostesses to 'table' with for cozy conversation or dancing. KT.
See also: Chaparral; O-O.

Lady Valerie. The mysterious organist of the lobby of Pines Hotel in the 1970s who won over the love and lust of many Baguio machos. She was actually Valentino Rios Torillo, born in Rosario, Cavite. Before that, her claim to fame was her brother Eagle Scout Antonio Torillo, one of the Boy Scouts of the 11th World Jamboree who perished when their KLM plane exploded over the Indian Ocean on July 1959. In the 80s, Lady Valerie reinvented her image to become the Ballroom Queen of the Philippines. She died in 2020. FYC.

Lakko *(ISN)*. The way a dog sleeps.

Laktaw *(ITN)*. *"Laktaw is a word which means 'to pass over'. This practice which exists among Tinguians demands a younger brother or sister to pay his/her older sibling with beads or an amount of money for getting married ahead of them. The payment is called panglaktawan. The council of elders asks for it and hands it over to the older brother or sister. The fine varies depending on the economic status of the payer."* (Sumangil 2003, 70).
See also: Iuya.

Lalong *(ISN)*. Red rooster tied to a beam before it is sacrificed for the tungtung (dialogue ceremony).
See also: Say-am; Tongtongan.

Landslide. Benguet has been tagged the most landslide-prone province in the whole country, with Ifugao and Mountain Province close behind in the ranks. No surprise there. But nothing more surprising than what happened on July 14 to 15, 1911 when 880 milimeters of rain fell within 24 hours. All in all, 2.234 meters of rain fell in four days causing a landslide of 1.5 million cubic meters of earth and rocks along Kennon Road which created a dam 30 meters deep. When the dam broke, it flooded La Union and Pangasinan, spoiling their rice harvest. Many of the mines closed because of the landslide, and Kennon Road, already a headache to build, had to be rebuilt again. (Corpuz 1999, 152) FYC.
See also: Gingined; Jail; Jegjeg; Kennon Road; Manginadu; Poy-do.

Landusan *(ISN)*. An Isneg spirit that brings about extreme poverty. The impoverished said to be under its spell are called malandusan.
See also: Iwaxan; Kalang.

Lang-ay *(KAN/BON)*. [1] In Bauko, this refers to meat.
[2] In Sagada, Besao, and Bontoc, this may also refer to wet-nursing.
[3] 'Maki-lang-ay' means eating in the house of a relative or friend when visiting in another place.
[4] Since 2004, Lang-ay became the name of the annual festival celebrating the foundation of the new Mountain Province. All the ten municipalities of the province gather for a week, with one of its days falling on the seventh of April (Foundation Day of the province), for cultural activities and food and wine festivities. PAD.
[5] In Ifugao, lang-ay means joyful conversations though this term is used mostly in Hudhud recitations. FYC.
See also: Hudhud.

Lapat *(ILO/ISN)*. Lit. Taking over. Among the Apayao Isnegs, when one dies, the spirit dwells first in the lake, river, hunting ground, or forest. A lapat is therefore performed by a clan or family member. No one is allowed to enter, hunt, fish or gather wood or fruits from the lapat area. Anyone caught in the lapat area would have to pay cash or with properties like antique beads, valuable tapestry, or jewelry. Those who were not caught but violated the lapat will be harmed by the anitos or spirits. The spirit would stay in the lapat area for a year or two, after which, the area can again be entered. The lapat is seen as one of the reasons why Apayao remains partly pristine. FYC.
See also: Ampasit; Ayyew; Madmad; Pikut.

Last No-Pant-On-Day. During the 1904 St. Louis Fair, then-Secretary of War William Howard Taft, who spent years as Governor General of the Philippines, was against the spectacle of the popular Igorotte Village. He wrote the organizers: *"The President has heard severe criticism of the Igorottes and wild tribe exhibit on the grounds that it verges towards the indecent. He believes either the Igorottes and wild tribes should be sent home or that they should be more fully clad."*

Taft actually wanted to stop the freak show because he said that the Philippines should be more than that. The U.S. press thought otherwise and said that the savagery and spectacle were what made the Philippine Village a hit. The St. Louis Post-Dispatch headlined: *"Whoop! How the People Rush to See the Igorottes Before They Put the Pants On."* The subheadings included: *"Dear Governor, Please write and Say What is the Last No-Pant-On Day."*

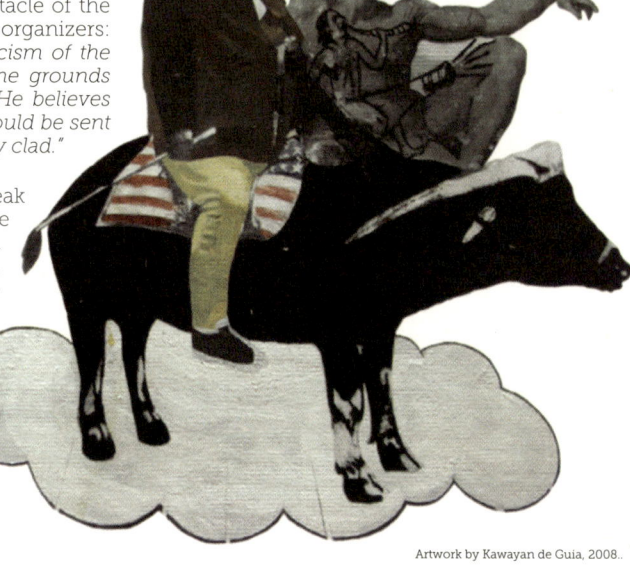

Artwork by Kawayan de Guia, 2008..

Poet Clark McAdams wrote:

Blessings on thee, little man,
Living on the Eden plan,
In thy unaffected way,
Drawing thousands every day.
Wild as winds, and free as air,
You're a winner at the Fair.
Ah, is that the monthly draft?
No, it is a note from Taft.
Of what pressing circumstance Does he write?
The Igorottes! They must wear pants!
The Igorottes must wear clothes! Impossible! Ten thousand No's!
Four billion nits! Twelve billion Can'ts! Great Cesar, anything but pants!

The Last No-Pant-On-Day did not materialize. (Vaughan 1996, 219) FYC.
See also: Dog-eating

Lennek *(KAN).* New moon. Not a good time for planting, traveling, and weaning animals. DOS.
See also: Balikawkaw; Beska; Moon Craters; Seddag; Teke.

Leonard Wood Road. One of the most popular roads of Baguio, it was named by then-Mayor Eusebius Halsema after his hero. In his last term as Governor of the Moro Province in March 1906, Wood was responsible for the Battle of Bud Dajo, an extinct volcano six miles from Jolo, Sulu. Because of Wood's imposition of the cedula, many of the Moros rebelled and holed up at Bud Dajo. A battle ensued with the Moros armed with kris, spears, and boulders against the Americans with guns and fixed bayonets. Only six of the 800 to 1,000 Moros survived, many of the dead were women and children. There were 21 Americans killed. Wood was questioned about this but he was still promoted to Chief of Staff of the US Army and Governor General of the Philippines. He also started the ROTC (Reserved Officers Training Course) which survived for a century in the Philippines. Wood planned to die in Baguio but he died of a brain tumor in the US. (Halsema 1991, 186) FYC.
See also: Halsema Highway; Kennon Road.

Lepanto Igorots. This ethnographic group name and place name was lost when the Lepanto sub-province of the old Mountain Province got dissolved. The Lepanto subprovince used to consist of the towns of Ampusungan, Angaki (now Quirino, Ilocos Sur), Bagnen, Bangao, Bauko, Besao, Cervantes (now belonging to Ilocos Sur), Cayan (now Tadian), Concepcion, Mankayan, Sabangan, and San Emilio (now also belonging to Ilocos Sur). Lepanto now only refers to the mining area run by the Lepanto Consolidated Mining Company (LCMCo). DOS.
See also: Mountain Province.

Libek *(KAN).* The milling of sugar cane, which used to be a common crop in Sagada. The begnas di libek is still performed today, but without the sugar cane milling. This demonstrates a ritual practice that persists even though the social and economic basis for the ritual has changed. TDH.
See also: Bayas; Begnas.

Liblibayu *(IFU).* Deities that cause stomach aches and intestinal pain because they may have been offered rice wine but the meat and other food offerings were forgotten. They then proceed to

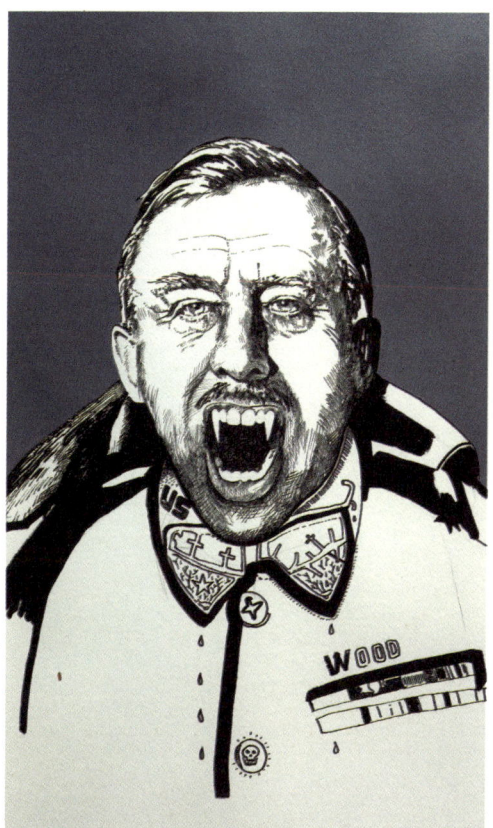

Leonard Wood. Artwork by Kawayan de Guia.

stick their invisible spears into the stomachs and intestines of their victims. The complete offering is often called atang. FYC.

Libuo *(KAN).* Clouds.
See also: Cloud Atlas; Finabdas.

Liga *(ISN).* "The women wear a little head axe in their hair, which, blade and handle together is from 12 to 16 cm in length. It is in the Bontoc form and serves for household work, for the skinning of fruit, cutting-up of cane, basket-weaving, etc." (Schadenberg 1975, 156-157).

Liget *(ILN).* Energy, force, passion that stirs the heart and animates the natural world. It is fused with beya (knowledge) in the Ilongot's concept of purposed-ness. Or, fused with upug (focus, concentration), you have the concept of beauty. "Concentrated liget is what makes babies, stirs one to work, determines killers, gives people strength and courage, narrows vision," said anthropologist Michelle Rosaldo (1980, p. 49) in "Knowledge and Passion." The Rosaldo couple studied the Ilongots for decades, particularly their headhunting practice. Michelle Rosaldo said that the culmination of liget and upug is headtaking.
See also: Headhunting, the Tale.

Likon *(IFU).* Long grass formed into a ring and placed on the head to soften the impact of carrying heavy loads on the head. FYC.
See also: Taraki.

Linayaan *(KAN).* This ritual has a lot of versions. In Agawa, Besao, this is kasal di kodo (poorman's wedding ceremony). It can be done anytime within one month from the birth of a child and after the umbilical cord has fallen off. But it is only for a firstborn child. It is a celebration of the marriage of the parents and thanksgiving for the birth of the child. A pig is butchered and relatives and umili (people in the village) are invited to eat lunch. The guests also give gifts to the couple and the baby (these are not separate gifts). PAD.
See also: Buaya Economic Classes; Gobgobbao; Kammid.

Lingling-o also **Wising** *(KAN).* An ear pendant. Its shape is a thick ring with a slit such that it can be hooked into a pierced ear. While jade (nephrite) is one of the most common materials used for lingling'o across the Philippines with ancient examples found in the caves of Palawan and Cagayan, the most characteristic materials used for lingling-o in the Cordillera are gold, silver, or brass. They are seen as signs of fertility and nobility.

Lisdeg *(KAN/BON).* A hard-shelled snail found in rice paddies. PAD.
See also: Agudong id Manitong; Atubang; Bisukol; Falokag; Golden Kuhol; Ket-an.

Literature:
Searching for Contemporary Cordillera Literature

My search for Contemporary Cordillera Literature began with piling books that I associate with the term on my desk. Sinai Hamada's *Collected Short Stories* (1975); Luisa Igloria's collections of poetry; the Baguio Writers Group's two book projects *The Baguio We Know* (2009), a collection of creative non-fiction, and *Baguio Calligraphy* (2010), a collection of poetry and short fiction; the Ubbog journals (2011, 2012, and 2016), independently-published by the Ubbog Cordillera Writers; some of the Cultural Center of the Philippines' *Ani Literary Yearbooks* dedicated to the Cordillera or with entries that have a decidedly Cordilleran flavor; and the textbook *Filipino's Writing* (2001), edited by Bienvenido Lumbera and which includes a section on Cordillera Literature. I stare at the diverse pile, and ask myself, why do I associate these books with Contemporary Cordillera Literature? Is it because they all relate, in one way or another, with the word Cordillera?

Is that all?

I feel that I only confused myself. So in the tradition taught to me by the university, I start anew and look into the individual words.

'Contemporary' in literature may vary in meaning. Simply, it means current. But current can mean 10 years ago to the present, or the 21st century, or 100 years up to now. Contemporary may also mean a point in time which had influenced the direction of present affairs, such as World War II. On the other hand, contemporary literature may also mean the use of themes that are still relevant to the readers of today. I unearth Sinai Hamada, the first published writer that hails from Cordillera. National Artist Francisco Arcellana once called Hamada's most well-known work "Tanabata's Wife" the "finest Filipino short story ever written." Another National Artist, F. Sionil Jose, was said to have asked, *"Is there Baguio writing after Sinai Hamada?"* These statements are interesting because much of Hamada's fiction was first published in the 1930s, which is almost a century ago, and therefore very old. My haphazard book-piling system tells me that I consider Sinai Hamada a contemporary Cordillera writer though, for his works resonate with themes that many Cordillerans continue to grapple with today – love, identity, change – and with relatable Cordilleran characters – pragmatic, stoic, straightforward. But Hamada is only one writer, and my pile asserts that he may be the first, but he is not the last.

The next word that needs meditation is 'Cordillera.' In my mind, Cordillera literature can mean two things: either literature written by the people of the region that is known as the Cordillera Autonomous Region or literature that is set in any part of it. The first is problematic in terms of what is meant by 'people of Cordillera.' Does it mean that the writer must be a member of one of the indigenous ethnolinguistic groups of the region? What about writers whose ancestors were migrants to the Cordillera like many Ilocanos and Pangasinense and who now consider a specific part of Cordillera home? Many have asked the same questions, and the distinction between 'Igorot' and 'Cordilleran' is often tossed around. 'Igorot' is used to refer to members of the indigenous ethnolinguistic groups of Cordillera, while 'Cordilleran' refers to individuals who do not necessarily belong to any of these groups but nevertheless have come to consider themselves as natives of the place. In both cases, Cordillera is considered as home.

But there are also works that are written by non-Cordillerans which are associated with Cordillera Literature. Amador Daguio's

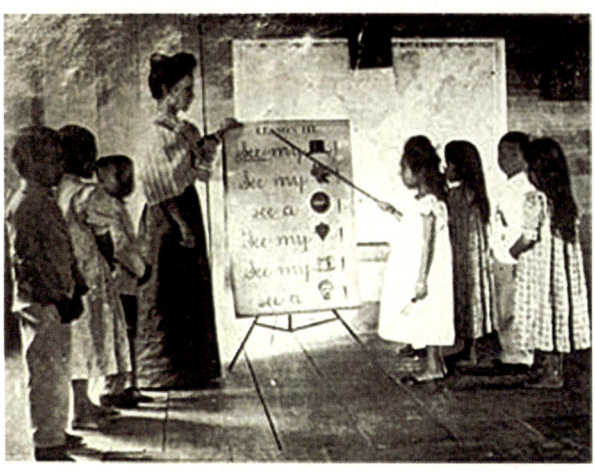

Photograph of schoolchildren and a Thomasite teacher in the Cordillera.

"Wedding Dance" is a prime example. Part of Amador Daguio's formative years were spent in Cordillera, specifically Mountain Province, but it is not home for him and he claims Ilocano as his ethnicity. And yet, "Wedding Dance," his most-anthologized short story, talks about a specific Igorot practice, divorce, and it is set in a specific part of the Cordillera, Mountain Province. However, identifying Cordillera literature by setting can also be problematic in the face of works which utilize the place but people it with characters who are basically tourists – visitors to the place who eventually leave after having taken in some aspect of the culture and atmosphere in their most simplistic, one-dimensional permutations. Cordillera, in these works, therefore becomes limited to strawberries and pine trees, or men and women wearing traditional attire as everyday wear or simply as a range of mountains. There may also be literary works that narrativize lives which have left the Cordillera homeland to migrate somewhere else but nevertheless still carry with them a memory of the place and all that it entails. Luisa Igloria, now living in the United States, comes to mind.

Language is also a matter of concern when one talks about Contemporary Cordillera Literature. Should Cordillera Literature be attributed to works written in the indigenous languages alone? After all, Cordillera is home to seven major ethnic groups, the Ibaloi, Bontoc, Kankana-ey, Kalinga, Itneg, Ifugao, and Isneg. Each group has a distinctive language of its own with a rich resource of folklore. However, the Cordillera has also had an extensive relationship with the English language, originally because of its American colonial experience, but which has now become the first language of choice in many middle-class households. And then there is the lingua franca Ilocano. It is therefore not exceptional to encounter Cordillerans, both Igorot or otherwise – who could comfortably switch between three, four or more languages – Ilocano, Filipino,

English and their indigenous languages – within one conversation. Consequently, it should be unsurprising to encounter Contemporary Cordillera literature in well-written English or Filipino.

So, what is Contemporary Cordillera Literature? I turn to look back at the pile on my desk, which is no longer overwhelming and now seems very little. Some of the books are excavated from the library or borrowed from friends, and some are bought over the years. But they are only a limited assortment of what comprises Contemporary Cordillera Literature, for there are many more scattered between the pages of other dusty anthologies and collections waiting to be unearthed and claimed. There are more carefully printed in school journals and local newspapers waiting to be acknowledged. There are others written in personal notebooks that are recited and performed during Spoken Poetry Nights or Days, reminiscent of the oral traditions of the Cordillera. And there are the blogs and Facebook posts, which continue to engage with a community, as the storytellers of old used to do before the written form became privileged. Regardless of what is meant by the individual words or the language used, Contemporary Cordillera Literature is an inexhaustible series of texts that primarily aims to tell the never-ending stories of Cordillera and its people. RLP

Little Alaska. Places in Benguet especially along the Mountain Trail such as Sinipsip and Natubleng in Buguias, or Sayangan, Atok where temperatures drop to as low as five degrees celsius. In these places, andap (frost) often forms in January or February causing leafy vegetables to wilt, burdening farmers. CCA.
See also: Baggat Udan; Buguias Patatas; Duyayu, Halsema Highway; Sinipsip.

Little America. Baguio City.

Little Baguio. (1) There are many places all over the Philippines that call themselves *"Little Baguio"* for their mountainous topography and cool climate. Among the Little Baguios are Don Salvador Benedicto, Negros Occidental; Kalsangi in Polomolok, South Cotabato; Cambigang, Sibuyan Island, Romblon; San Fernando, Bukidnon; Malico in the border of San Nicolas and Sta. Fe towns in Pangasinan; Lingap Kalikasan in the Science City of Muñoz; Malita, Davao del Sur; San Vicente, Palawan; Valencia, Negros Oriental; Anilgalan, San Remigio, Antique; Caibiran, Biliran; and Luisana, Laguna. The most famous of them all is the Little Baguio shopping district in San Juan City.
(2) The fighting name of Constancio Baguio, a boxer from Oroquieta City, Misamis Occidental who was active from 1980 to 1990 and whose highest rank and prominence was when he lost in the World Boxing Council International Light Flyweight title fight in 1987. FYC.

Lituku *(IFU/KAN/BON).* Referring to rattan, but mostly to the super sour rattan fruit which has a shell that seems to have been woven in the rattan strands used for basket weaving. FYC.
See also: Raut

Liwliwa *(KAN).*
(1) A term that loosely translates as 'let the mind wander.' It is a type of chant that expresses prayer, but can also become a form of entertainment. It is a way of telling stories – e.g., during a wedding, the elders may advise the couple on married life or people may tell stories about the couple's courtship. TDH.
(2) A drinking spot along Magsaysay Avenue, Baguio City that is as wild as it is dingy and real. It is where the Igorot drunk will always be happy.

Liwliwot *(IFU).* Drunken walk if just liwot. If liwliwot, it means your mind is whirling, that's why you are walking either from side to side or going around in an aimless spiral after too much basi or baya. FYC.
See also: Basi; Baya; Butong; Nafutengak; Siniktiman.

Liyaw *(KAN).* A ritual performed wherein a small pig is offered at the uma (swidden farm) to counter the disease called gyodongor (stagnant growth). FYC.
See also: Kimat.

Loakan Road White Lady. An urban legend. A woman in white standing at night at the side of the road usually in front of the cemetery across from the Voice of America compound, or near the junction to Greenwater where a huge pine tree used to grow in the middle of the road. She would suddenly appear in the back seat of a cab, private car or even inside the Philippine Military Academy bus, only to disappear. This Baguio City icon has been featured in numerous magazines, books, news programs, and documentaries cementing her place at the top of the ghost pop charts! CPM.
See also: Baguio Ghost Stories; Chainus; Guirey.

Longayban *(KAN).* A figure revered as the most beautiful woman. Her name is often sung in modern Kankanaey love songs. According to mythology, Longayban is a demi-god, the daughter of Gatan (god of lightning) and the mortal Bangan. Longayban is the sister of Kabigat. In Kalinga, a beautiful lady is known as Mandiga, a name taken from the Ullalim. DOS.
See also: Aginaya, Panginomnoman ki; Bangan; Headhunting (the tale); Iddaya; Inhabian; Kimat; Ullalim.

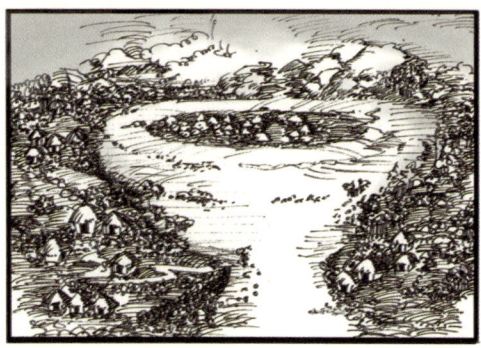

Loo. A village in Buguias regarded as the Potato Capital of the Philippines. It is an old Igorot settlement and was first spelled as Lo-o (though its amphitheater shape actually does resemble half of a toilet bowl). FYC.
See also: Buguias Patatas; Kalabog-kalabog-Buguias-patatas!

Lourdes Grotto. Anyone who has been to Baguio must have counted the 212 steps leading to the Lourdes Grotto atop Mirador Hill (some devotees even climb these concrete steps on their knees holding candles that drip on their sides). After offering candles at the statue of the Virgin Mary and posing for photographs, it's off to other tourist spots. Some might notice the gates above the grotto and wonder where they lead to. But the gates seem to be always locked. The Mirador Jesuit Villa can be found there and is one of the last secrets of the city. After being opened to the public in 2002, it has become a retreat house for tired souls. In 1876, Don Manuel Scheidnagel, the gobernador politico-militar of Benguet, stood on the hill and called it 'El Mirador' for its form and the view which still allows you to see La Union, Pangasinan, and Benguet. Then in the 1890s, Fr. Miguel Roses, then the rector of Ateneo de Manila, turned the place into a sanatorium for sick Jesuits (1,500 meters above sea level). Ateneo de Manila would soon build a meteorological and seismic observatory atop Mirador Hill in 1900. In 1906, the Jesuits purchased 327,881 square meters of Mirador property for a mere PHP1, 093 in a public auction where, a year later, they built a simple three-room house. Seven years after the purchase, the Lady of Lourdes was created by noted sculptor Isabel Tampingco who earlier also made the statue of San Ignacio in Intramuros. In 1918, the construction of the 212 steps ensued.

During World War II, the Japanese soldiers occupied the hill and at the end of the war, the Americans carpet-bombed the city and the villa was destroyed. Fr. Leo Cullum in 1952 rebuilt the villa with architect Gines Rivera, the designer of Ateneo. At the same time, the Jesuit theologate in Shanghai had to transfer to Baguio because of the Communist takeover. For years, the villa had been the refuge of the Chinese Jesuits.

The grotto would be made-over by Fr. Jose Algue in the early 1960s to become a must-see for Baguio tourists and pilgrims. Even the Catholic Bishop Conference of the Philippines held their meetings there twice a year.

In 2002, the Jesuits handed the management of the villa to Christian Life Community Inc. The grounds were modified for soul-searching, and the former volleyball court turned into a huge sand labyrinth patterned after that of the 13th century Chartres Church. Stone lamps and tree stumps and flat rocks were randomly situated in the wide garden for solitary reflections. They have 89 rooms available for guests. There are conference rooms, a chapel, and a mess hall. Most of the features, needless to say, are spartan. Gates are closed at 7PM but you can negotiate with the guards to let you in before 9PM. So if you see a Zen monk tracing the labyrinth, it is not a ghost. FYC.

Lover's Moon. The saudade (melancholic longing) brought about by a cheap song in a foreign place. Expounded by writer Pico Iyer using Glenn Frey's Lover's Moon: *"But in the midst of all this, it was Lover's Moon that took me to a little café in Baguio in the Philippines, where pretty kids were getting up on stage and adjusting their guitar straps while the streets around them collapsed... It was Frey's aching voice of transport ('I'm dancing with a memory') that reminded me of the many (too many) lovely new friends and hopes I'd met along the way, so many of them ready to hitch themselves to a star if only it could carry them away from what they knew."* (Iyer 2010) FYC.
See also: Amazing Grace; Batawa; Cowboy; Nan Layad Nan Likhatan; Pure Country; Waynasdi.

Lubug *(IFU)*. To disrupt festivities by causing trouble or starting fights. Like the Filipino word lubog (sink), your status in the village will sink for every lubug you get yourself into. FYC.

Luktap *(IFU)*. "Unaggravated adultery; adultery unaccompanied by great scandal and by insults to offended spouse." (Barton 2012)
See also: Dagdagas; Daladag; Mandeki.

Lumiang Burial Cave. One of the various burial caves in Sagada located on the way to the famous Sumaguing Cave. It is unique among the other caves because it is the only burial cave that was blessed by Rev. John A. Staunton, the first American Anglican missionary priest to have arrived in Sagada in 1904. According to old folks, Rev. Staunton blessed this burial cave because he too believed that Jesus Christ was once put and buried in a tomb inside a cave, and thus a cave is accepted as a burial place. (Piluden 2004, 98) DOS.
See also: Apo Annu; Episcopalianism; Kabayan Mummies.

Luna, Joaquin. In October 1913, Luna became the first person from the lowlands to be appointed as Mountain Province Governor.
See also: Pitapit.

Lungos *(KAL).* Sharing game after hunting. Usually, Kalinga people hunt in groups accompanied by a hunting dog. If the hunt is successful, the game, like a deer or wild boar is shared among the hunters. The head, neck, and a leg part of the hunted animal will be given to the hunter who owns the dog; other parts will be divided equally amongst the other hunters. If hunters (in groups or not) meet along the way, there is no question that they should share whatever they hunted. (Weygan 2011) HZK.
See also: Saga-ok; Tambo.

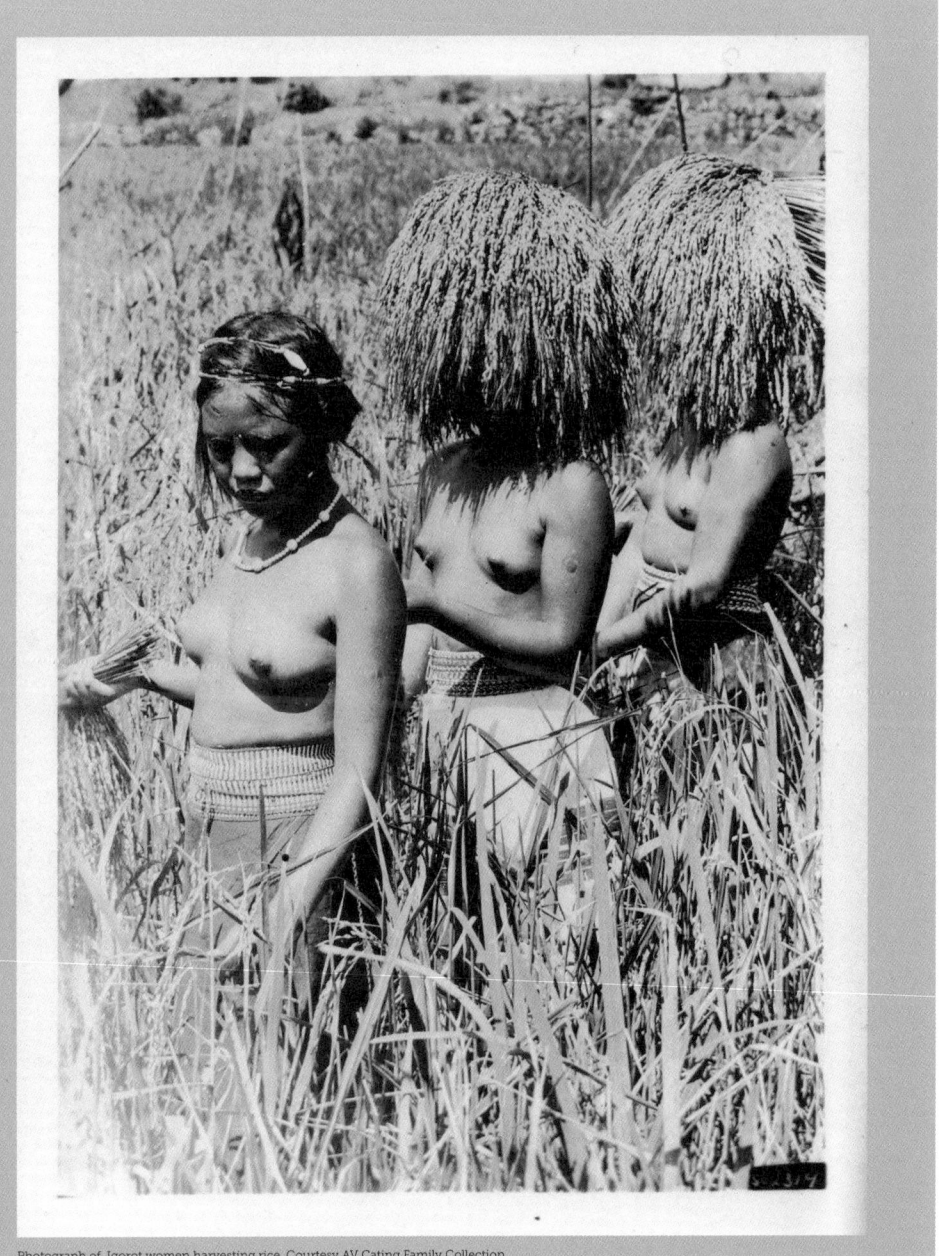

Photograph of Igorot women harvesting rice. Courtesy AV Cating Family Collection.

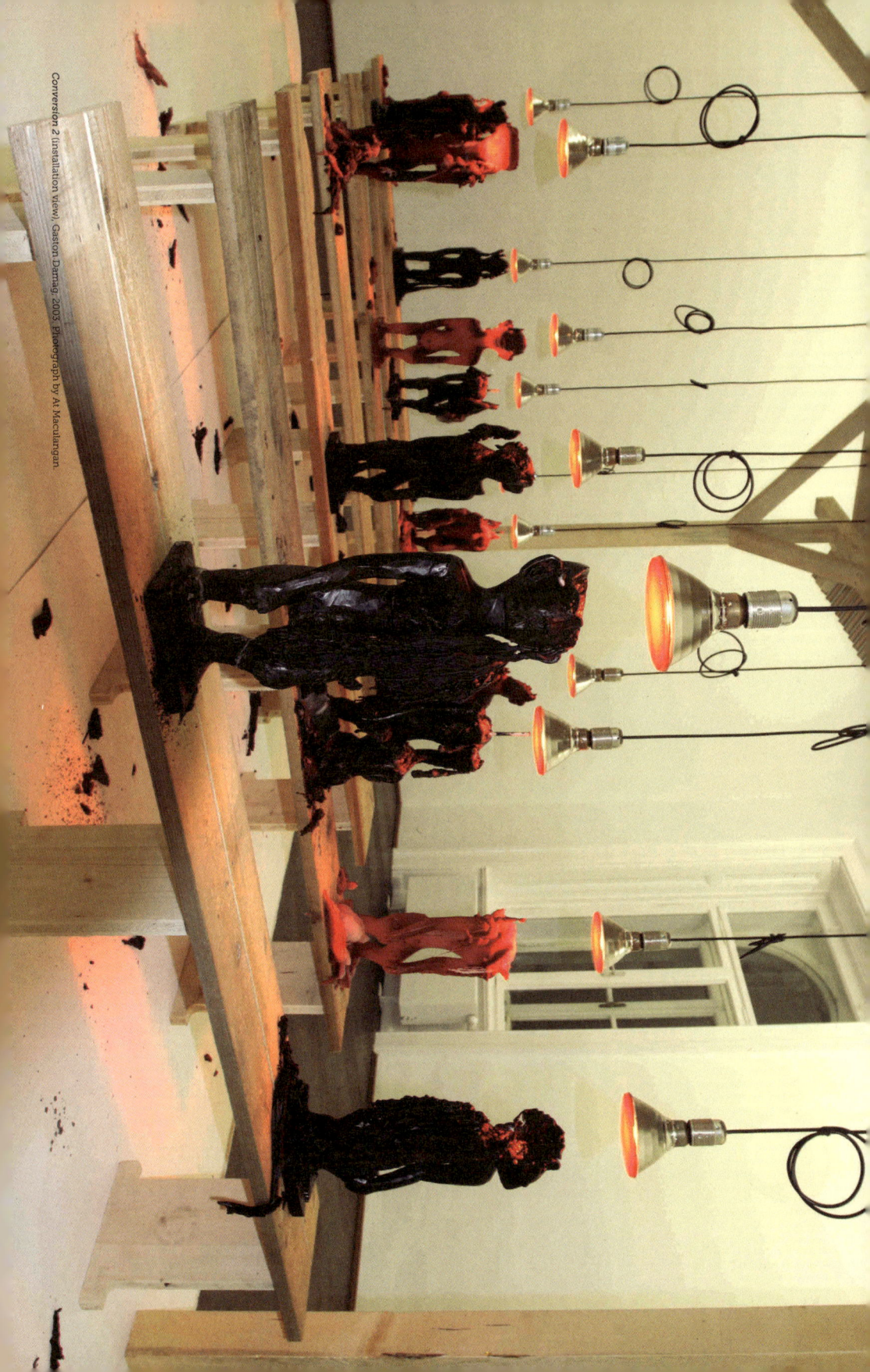

Conversion 2 (Installation View), Gaston Damag, 2003. Photograph by Al Macullangan.

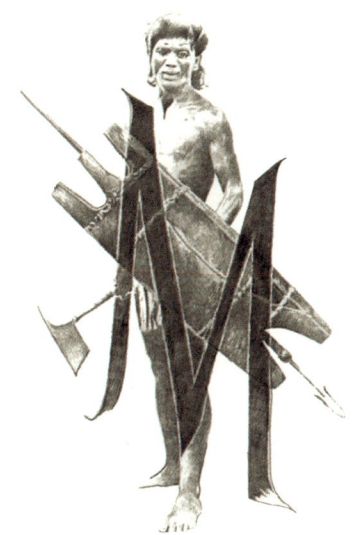

Mabukag (KAN). It describes the taste of the perfect swelling of the starch granules, especially upon biting into a boiled or steamed potato, sweet potato, yam, corn or squash. CCA.
See also: Camote.

MacArthur and the Igorot Soldiers. "Many desperate acts of courage and heroism have fallen under my observation on many fields of battle in many parts of the world. I have seen forlorn hopes become realities. I have seen last-ditch stands, and innumerable acts of personal heroism that defy description. But for sheer breathtaking and heart-stopping desperation, I have never known the equal of those Igorots riding the tanks. Gentlemen, when you tell the story, stand in tribute to those gallant Igorots. As members of the Philippine commonwealth, they have proved to be excellent fighting men." (Gen. Douglas MacArthur as quoted in New York Times Feb. 23, 1942 edition).
See also: Balweg brothers; Hunt, Truman; Tribes.

Madmad (IBA). A lay person's prayer made directly to a deity – sun and moon, spirit owners, ancestral spirits, Kabunian, and, in recent times, to God. This is prayed before violating domains owned by spirits, such as beginning mine operations, cutting a tree, crossing a stream, walking a trail, asking permission or praying for protection from a falling tree, etc. The madmad is also prayed before tongtong or a peace conference to settle disputes between contending parties. In gracing a meal (taja), the mambunong prays (bonong) while elders can be heard praying madmad. This can also refer to informal conversations with spirits. (Ballard et al. 2011, 286, 542) SKW.
See also: Aginaya; Ampasit; Lapat; Mambunong; Panginomnoman ki; Tree Cutting.

Ma-donkey-an (KAN). Lit. To cause to have a donkey. This word is used when stocking vegetables on an elf or a similar vehicle, such that it grows a hump on its back. GAD.

Maenang boom. "Just what it sounds like: mining boom, a term familiar to all Igorots and perhaps most lowlanders." (Chamber of Mines of the Philippines 1939, 204).
See also: Alonso Martin; Quirante.

Mahimunu (GAD). A spiritual conciliator shaman who examines signs.
See also: Dorarakit; Maingal; Mambunong; Manpapayad; Mansib-ok; Mumbaki.

Ma-id (KAN/BON). Nothing or none.
See also: Wada.

Ma-imdong (KAL). Shy.
See also: Shy Mango.

Maingal (GAD) also **Maingel.** Lit. Brave. A brave man and a shaman who exorcises by fighting with ghost-deities or carangat to make them surrender. In Bontoc, maingor or mengol is a brave warrior.
See also: Carangat; Dorarakit; Mahimunu; Mambunong; Manpapayad; Mansib-ok; Mumbaki.

Mallawallawa (KAN). Someone zealous enough to follow all religious taboos.
See also: Inayan; Ukas.

Mamapteng (IBA). Beautiful, pretty or lovely.

Mambabaga (KAL). Spokesman.

Mambudang (IBA). Animals locking horns such as bulls.

Typescript of 'Igorots Cited By MacArthur,' Associated Press, February 23, 1942. Courtesy Associated Press and AV Cating Family Collection.

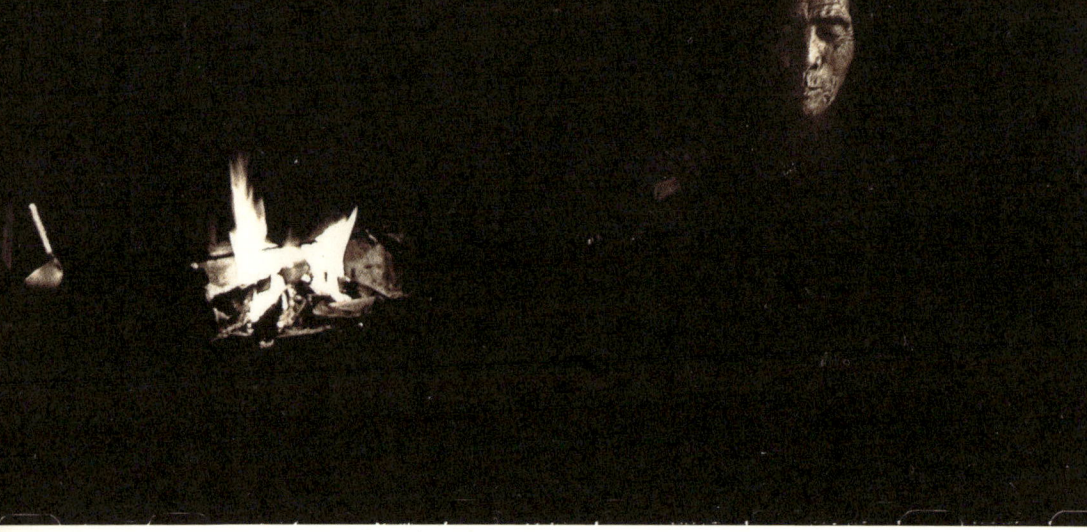

Portrait of Kabigat, a *Mambunog*, 1984. Photograph by Tommy Hafalla.

Mambunong *(KAN)*. Native priest. These spiritual practitioners, either male or female, come from the nabiteg or poor class in the community as a rule. Their role in the community is important for they are sought by anyone, rich or poor, when their services are needed. They officiate the rituals as messengers between man and the spirits or Kabunian. It has been observed that the mambunong, consented to by Kabunian as the people's spiritual leader, is naturally charged with the duty of playing messenger every time a community member seeks a communication with Kabunian or other minor gods. While it is in the hands of the Kadangyan (rich families) that Kabunian is said to have entrusted the responsibility of worldly leadership, the spiritual needs of the community rest in the hands of the mambunong. A person has to accept becoming a mambunong if the opportunities warrant that he has to become one. There are several ways in which a person may become a mambunong. Among these are by heredity, succession, or popular choice. NEP.
See also: Buaya Economic Classes; Dorarakit; Kabunian; Mahimunu; Maingal; Manpapayad; Mansib-ok; Mumbaki.

Mampay *(KAN/BON)*. In songs and chants *"Sia mampay, wen mampay,"* which translates as *"Yes, that is true. I agree,"* or *"Yes, I already told you,"* is often used as a refrain when an affirmation is awaited. For example, in a marriage gathering when an elder sings his/her pieces of advice to the newlyweds. Usually, when an individual is singing ad lib, everyone joins in the part of the singing of the *"Sia mampay, wen mampay."* It is also an expression of affirmation in everyday conversations. GAD.
See also: Ngilin; Salidummay; Ullalim.

Mandeki *(IBA)*. To have an illicit relationship.
See also: Dagdagas; Daladag; Luktap.

Mandesangat *(IBA)*. Super-hot and spicy.
See also: Amkis; Sichot.

Manerwap *(BON)*. Rain-calling ritual in Bontoc usually performed in April or May when a drought is imminent. Young men of the village converge at the ato with their sokod (shield and spear) and hike very silently in a single line towards Mt. Sagmayao or Mt. Kaman-olo. When they reach the summit, they start a bonfire and play the gangsa and the leader prays to Lumawig for rain. The next day, they descend, and after a compulsory bath in the river, they end in the ato and again play the gangsa. FYC.
See also: Dap-ay; Fakil; Gangsa; Tengngay.

Mang-gabi *(ISN)*. To abstain from gabi (taro) or even rice while in mourning.

Manginadu *(KAN)*. To pour or rain heavily.
See also: Landslide.

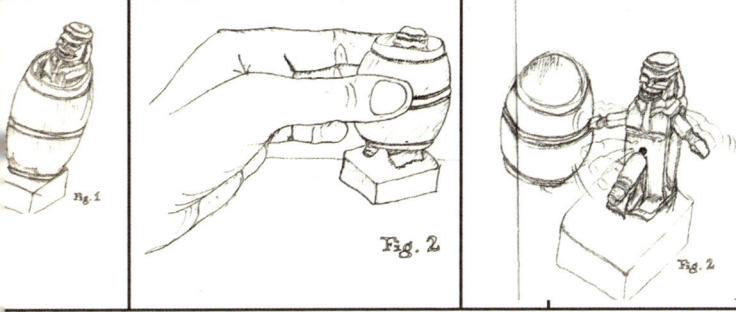

Illustration of a popular souvenir called **Man in the barrel**. Illustration by Abbie SJ Lara.

Man in the barrel. A popular souvenir in the Baguio Market especially in the 1970s. A more prurient version of Jack-in-the-box, it is a male wooden figure whose penis would spring erect when the barrel is taken out. Exact origin is unknown although there is a dick-in-a-box from the late 1800s where the original man-in-a-barrel is said to have been Diogenes the Cynic. Baguio theater artist EV Espiritu and his Tropang Paltok staged a Man-in-the-Barrel event (with actual whitened men in paper mache barrels), to dramatize reproductive health awareness in 2006. FYC.

See also: Duggong ti Intsik; Penis ashtray.

Manpapayad *(KAL)*. A fortune-teller.

See also: Dorarakit; Mahimunu; Maingal; Mambunong; Mansib-ok; Mumbaki.

Manshowa-showa *(IBA)* also **Manduadua** *(KAN)*. To be doubtful or unsure. Manshowa, however, means to divide into two.

Mansib-ok *(KAN)* also **Mansip-ok** *(IBA/KAN)*, **Manop-ok** *(BON)*. The mansib-ok (diviners) diagnose the cause of illness or afflictions of a person. They are named or labeled differently according to the medium that they use. A manbuyon uses metal in his or her divination. A mansib-ok determines the cause of something through prayers or vision. The manbaknew uses water, gin or rice wine. The man-ila or man-anap communicates with souls or other spirits. The diviners are as important as the mambunong in the community. They are generally consulted in times of illness or difficulties because they can see what others cannot. They can predict a future occurrence, determine the causes of people's maladies or misfortunes, or recommend measures to cure or remedy human problems and afflictions. The findings or diagnoses of a mansib-ok are not always final unless proven by the following precautions or activities: (a) Consult several mansib-ok and see that their findings tally with each other; (b) The findings must be isib-ok or idengaw to the sick patient. This entails chewing the root of a dengaw (sweet flag grass [*Arocus Calamus L.*]) to release its sweet aroma and then praying over the head of the sick while rubbing chewed dengaw over the head. Signs of recovery after a few days mean the diagnosis is probably correct and a ritual may be performed; (c) Tapuy (prepared from kintoman [red aromatic rice]) is stored in a jar while a prayer is recited invoking the spirits who may have caused the person's sickness. These spirits are informed that there is an on-going preparation for the prescribed ritual based on the diagnosis. They are also asked to show signs of recovery if the diagnosis holds true. If there are signs of recovery, the ritual may be pursued. NEP.

See also: Dorarakit; Iwa; Mahimunu; Maingal; Mambunong; Manpapayad; Mumbaki.

Mansion House. When Architect Daniel Burnham left the Philippines, he chose Architect William Parsons, who studied at Yale, Columbia and L'Ecole des Beaux-Arts, to realize his visions for Baguio and Manila. Among the structures Parsons built for Baguio were Brent School (completed 1909) which was made mostly of wood (Brent's principal office, the Ogilby Hall, is the oldest existing wooden structure in the city) and Mansion House, which Parsons designed for the Governor General in 1908. Mansion House was first used by Governor General Forbes and became the summer residence of the Philippine Legislature until it was turned over to the Philippines during the Commonwealth. It was destroyed in World War II and was rebuilt in 1947. Its gate was modeled after that of Buckingham Palace. FYC.

Marapait. Marapait, the wild sunflower, is the emblem of Baguio's Panagbenga Festival. The marapait is the harbinger of cold in Baguio. They bloom (and they do by hundreds of thousands on the mountainsides of the city) only when the weather reaches a certain low temperature. The local bee industry depends on them, and their interlocking roots literally hold up the mountains. Marapait, a term derived from pait (bitter) is in reference to its bitter medicinal leaves, is used by Igorots to treat wounds. FYC.

See also: Igorot; Panagbenga.

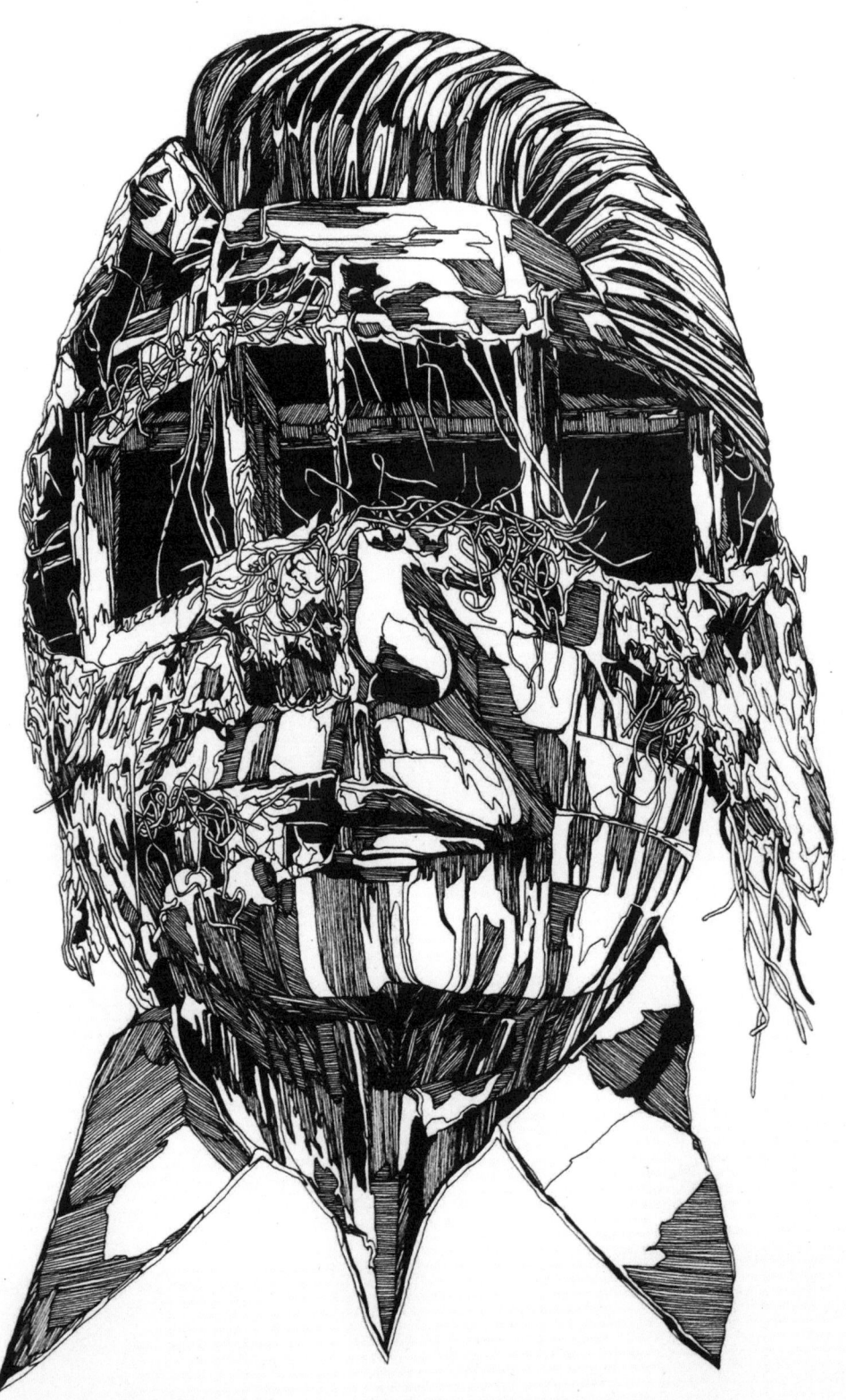

Untitled (Malakas) by Pio Abad, screenprint, 45x35 cm, 2017.

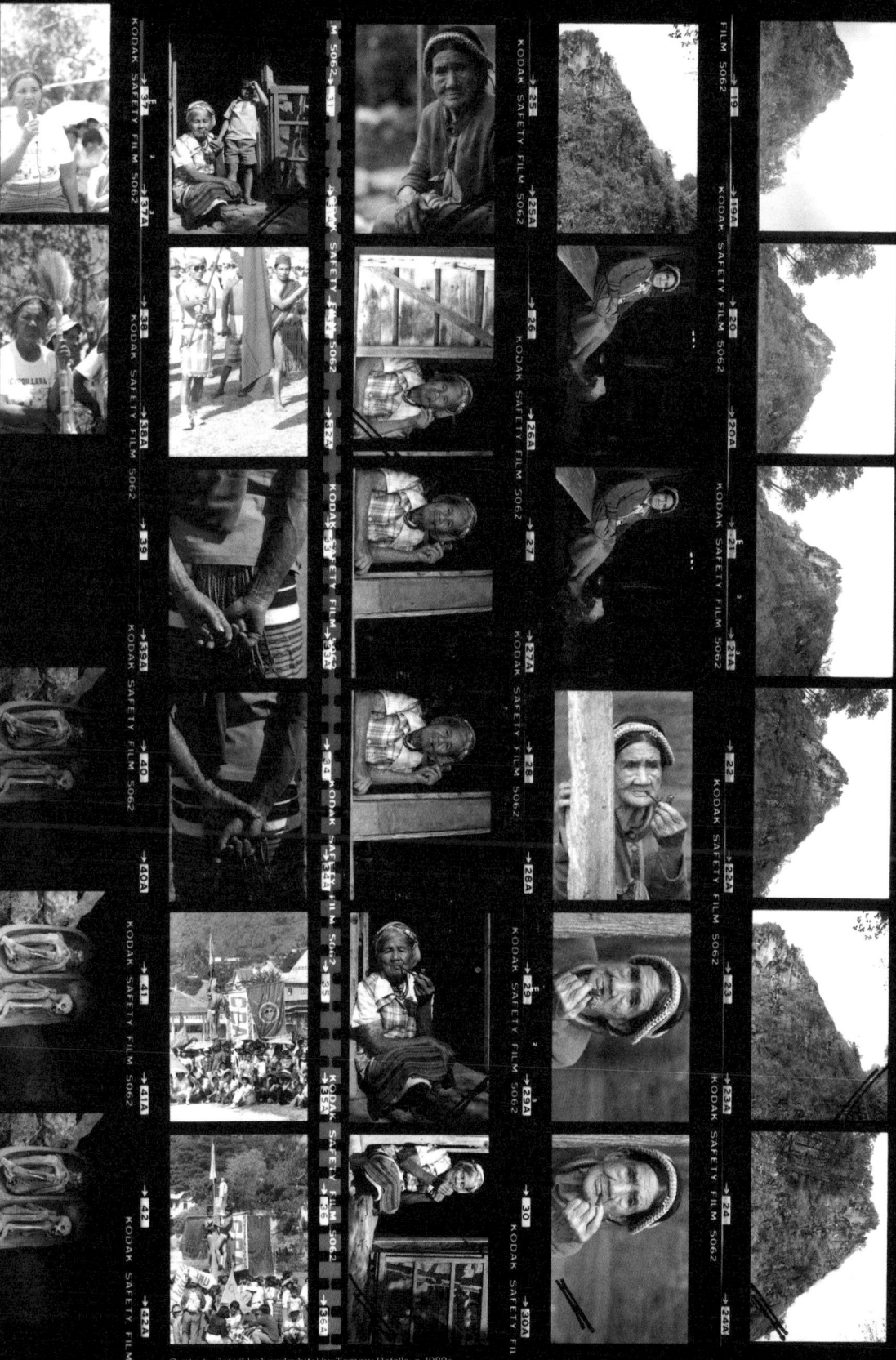

Contact prints (black and white) by Tommy Hafalla, c. 1980s.

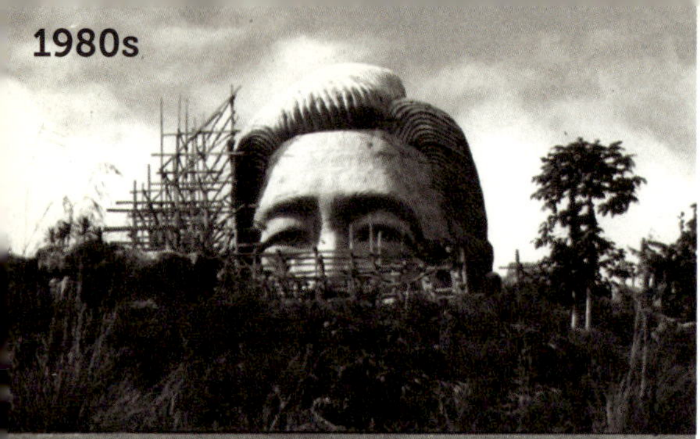

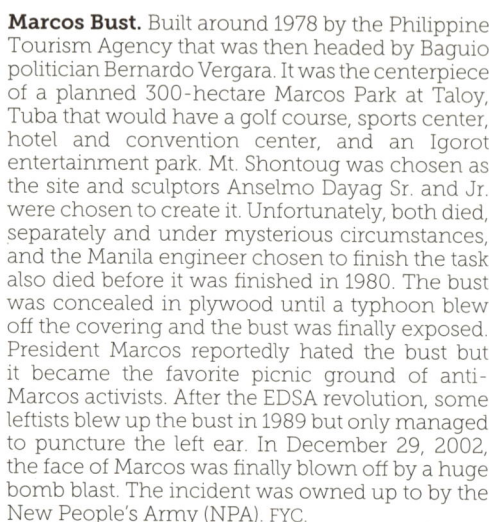

1980s

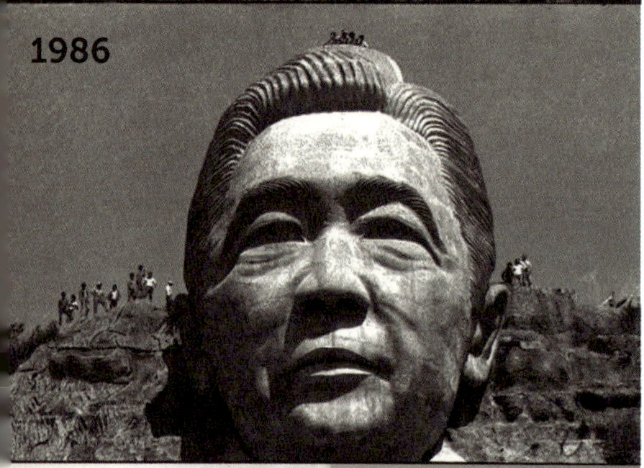

1986

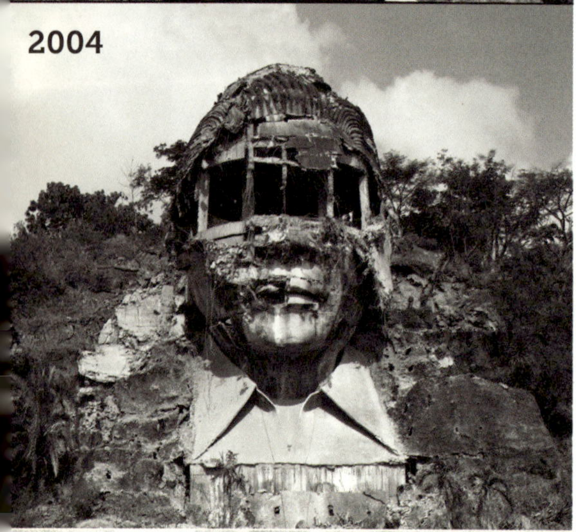

2004

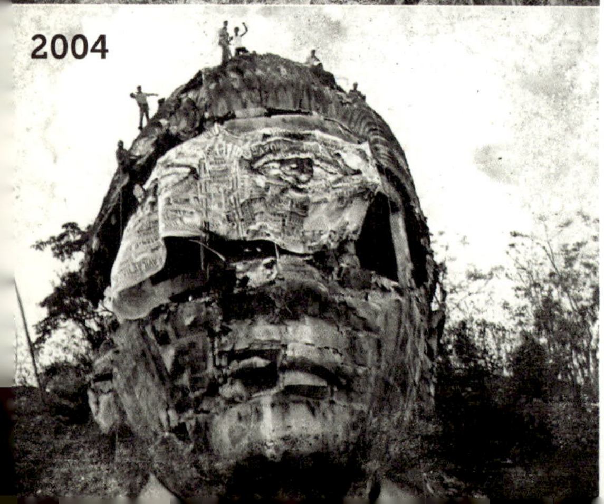

2004

Marcos Bust. Built around 1978 by the Philippine Tourism Agency that was then headed by Baguio politician Bernardo Vergara. It was the centerpiece of a planned 300-hectare Marcos Park at Taloy, Tuba that would have a golf course, sports center, hotel and convention center, and an Igorot entertainment park. Mt. Shontoug was chosen as the site and sculptors Anselmo Dayag Sr. and Jr. were chosen to create it. Unfortunately, both died, separately and under mysterious circumstances, and the Manila engineer chosen to finish the task also died before it was finished in 1980. The bust was concealed in plywood until a typhoon blew off the covering and the bust was finally exposed. President Marcos reportedly hated the bust but it became the favorite picnic ground of anti-Marcos activists. After the EDSA revolution, some leftists blew up the bust in 1989 but only managed to puncture the left ear. In December 29, 2002, the face of Marcos was finally blown off by a huge bomb blast. The incident was owned up to by the New People's Army (NPA). FYC.
See also: Day-ag, Anselmo; Igorot; Marcos Gerrymandering; Marcos Mask.

Marcos Gerrymandering. For decades, the Congress had been ignoring the creation of a Cordillera region, but in 1966, then-President Ferdinand Marcos approved the division of the old Mountain Province into Ifugao, Benguet, Mountain Province and Kalinga-Apayao. Why Kalinga and Apayao were not separated can be explained by looking at a map of the region where the two provinces together resembled the profile of Marcos complete with his signature hairdo. On Valentine's Day, February 14, 1995, Republic Act 7878 separated Kalinga and Apayao, resulting in the beheading of the 'Marcos head.' FYC.
See also: Marcos Bust; Marcos Mask; Mountain Province.

Marcos Mask. In May 2004, a week before the elections, young Baguio artists led by Kawayan de Guia and Ferdie Balanag decided to collect election banners, streamers and posters confiscated by the Commission on Elections for being oversized and create a huge collage of a pair of eyes to replace the bombed-out eyes of the Marcos Bust in Taloy, Tuba. Before the 'masking,' a concert led by Jose 'Pepe' Smith was held inside the skull. FYC.
See also: Marcos Bust; Marcos Gerrymandering.

Martial Law Plant. A fast-growing vine which can overrun fish ponds, farms, and banana plantations. It can choke banana, according to a Philippine Information Agency (PIA) report in 1993. The vine was called 'Martial Law plant' because farmers in Mountain Province first spotted it right after President Ferdinand Marcos proclaimed Martial Law in September 1972. It is described as having leaves similar to the sayote but smaller and bristled. However, it is said to be medicinal and can treat wounds. After the PIA report was published, then-President

Photographs of the Marcos Bust in different stages of its evolution.
Courtesy J. Liverod (first from top), Roberto Yñiguez (second and third from top), and Kawayan de Guia (bottom).

Fidel V. Ramos, who was one of Marcos' men in 1972, decided to conduct an investigation on the Martial Law plant. The Department of Science and Technology found that the vine isn't toxic and, as the farmers had attested, is even medicinal. FYC.
See also: NPA Plant; Sayote.

Masaflora. Cordilleran name for passion fruit (Passiflora). The egg-shaped fruits (one variety is orange and the other deep purple) come from vines that often climb pine trees. The orange variety is sold in Atok and Sayangan (along the Halsema Highway) and in Baguio where they are strung on a string, while the deep purple variety, deemed unattractive to sell and with a very sour to tangy taste, is confined to the city's secret gardens and in small communities across the mountains where they are considered 'native' as opposed to the sweet orange variety. FYC.

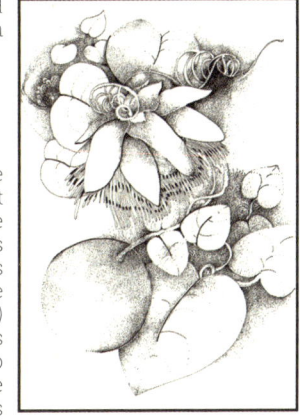
Artwork by William Magtibay.

Maxabbat *(ISN)*. To boil salt water to acquire the salt.

Mendayaw *(KAN)*. "'To praise' does not appear in Montane oral literature and is presumably a modern borrowing from another dialect, but is used in this sense in ordinary conversation." (Scott 2011, 202).

Mendoza, Benjamin. Bolivian artist who almost killed Pope Paul VI when the latter landed at the Manila International Airport on November 27, 1970. Mendoza stabbed the Pope twice and he said that he could have dealt the deadly blow had his hand not been parried by then President Ferdinand Marcos's deadly karate chop. Mendoza was kept at the Bilibid Prison, left in seclusion almost all the time. Before this assassination attempt, Mendoza was an art teacher in Baguio. His prized pupil was famous Baguio artist Willy Magtibay who was in Grade VI when he was taught by Mendoza at Cecile Afable's Ato Bookshop in 1969. Magtibay said that Mendoza spent most of the time talking about surrealism and Che Guevara. He referred to his teacher's assassination attempt as performance art. Magtibay visited Mendoza in prison and said that Mendoza was teaching art classes to children of prisoners before he was deported to Bolivia. FYC.
See also: Afable, Cecile; Ato Bookshop.

Menlemlem *(KAN)* also **Inlemlem** *(BON)*.
(1) *(KAN)* Whole day drizzling.
(2) *(BON)* Typhoon weather.
See also: Inhabian; Is-is.

Menoken *(IBA)*. To know what to do next after the reading of the gall bladder of a chicken slaughtered for ritual.
See also: Cañao.

Michongpit *(BON)*. Broken or crooked nose.

Million Dollar Hill. Tomoyuki Yamashita or the Tiger of Malaya was captured in Kiangan, Ifugao in September 2, 1945. An obelisk was erected on the Million Dollar Hill near the Kiangan Museum. The Million Dollar Hill is now only soil overgrown with grass. But in 1945, it was a hill bombarded with so many bombs that it was collectively worth a million bucks. FYC.

Moma *(IFU/IBA/KAN/BON)* also **Nganga** *(KAN/ILO)*. In the Cordillera, moma chewing is attributed to the Ifugaos. The folks usually have their taluwan with them which contains all or one of the following: a piece or two of moma (areca nut), some sheets of hapid (betel leaf), a tabayag that holds the lime powder made of burned aggudung (a kind of shell), and sometimes tuhlab (stem of the betel leaf), puduh (fruit of betel plant), and tobacco. In the yard of a typical Ifugao abode, an areca palm is present and the vine of the hapid can be found climbing on a tree nearby. People would usually share ingredients while casually socializing. However, the practice is not of the Ifugaos alone. Historians write that one of the very first things that Magellan saw when he first landed on an island of what would later become the Philippines, were inhabitants chewing areca nuts. Areca chewing is also common among ethnic groups found in Asia and the Pacific. It is not surprising then, that it was easily adopted by other communities such as those in Benguet and Mountain Province. Some say that the proliferation of chewing started with the Ifugaos who were involved in the stone walling of farms and roads along the Halsema Highway. Others say that it was when people converged to work in the mines or the flower gardens in Bahong, Benguet. In Baguio City, it is no longer just the Ifugaos who buy the moma packets from the city

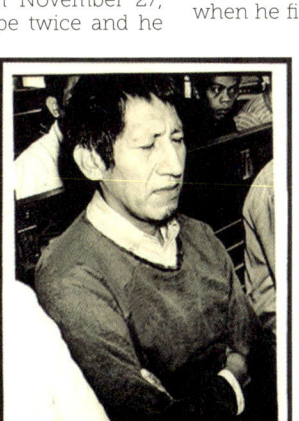
Photograph of Benjamin Mendoza from the Baltimore Sun.

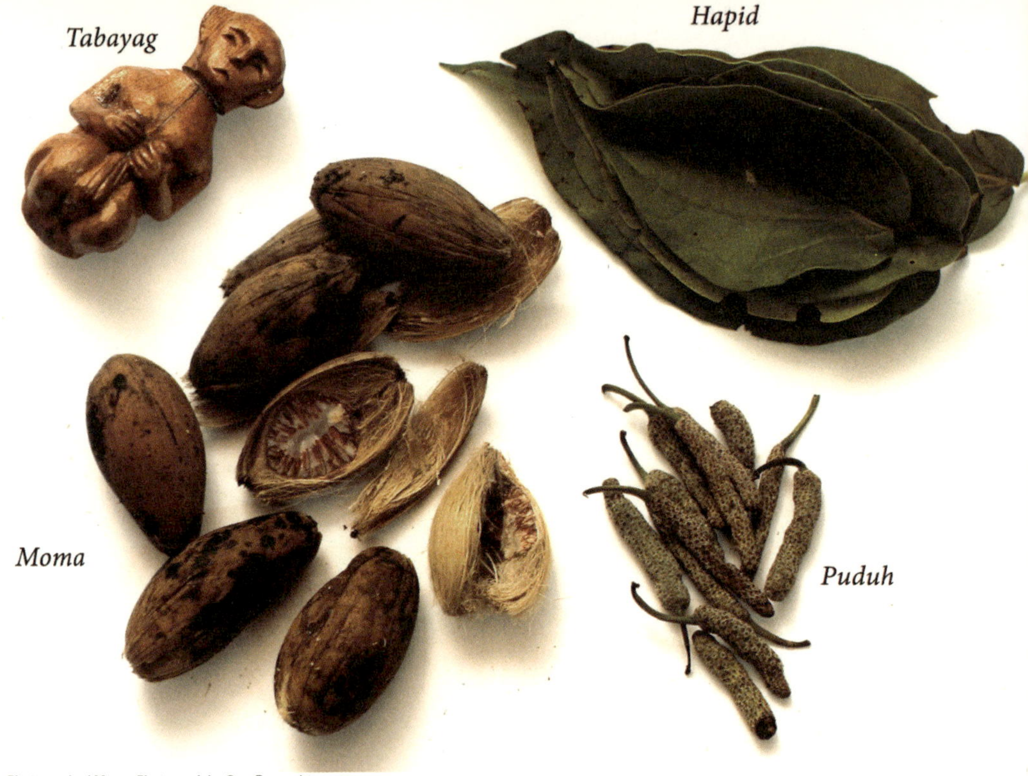

Photograph of Moma. Photograph by Gary Buenavista.

market. In fact, it has become a common sight to see moma packets sold on almost every street corner in the town center. Even the city's most pristine public spaces are splattered with the red moma spit. RFK.

See also: Halsema Highway; Hidit; Moma by myself; Moma for peace; Ngalngal; Tabayag

Moma by myself. The Ifugaos love to ask themselves, *"Tubi or not tubi?"* Tubi means chewing moma with someone or with a group. Also tubi is used when a boy offers moma to the parents of the girl he wishes to marry. If the parents accept the moma, then *"tubi"* becomes *"I do."* FYC.

See also: Hidit; Moma; Moma for peace; Sukarno.

leaf. Both are then supplied by the priest with lime. They proceed to chew betels and the priest prays with *'Ye are chewed, Betel Leaf, Areca Nut, and Lime. Let not them who were enemies be afflicted with coughings, shortness of breath, quick-coming fatigue, bleeding from the nose, nor labored breathing. Let them, instead, be like gold, which tarnishes not; like the tail feathers of the full-grown cock, which never touch the earth; like the waters of the river, which never cease coming; like Talal of Ambuaya, who ate his own children, yet was not afflicted by the hidit. Let them be as active as the waters of Inude (a cataract) or the feathery plumes of the cogon and runo grass. Let them be like the rising sun, like the Cobra of the White Mountain, like the Full-grown Cock of Dotal, like the Hard Stone of Huduan. May their*

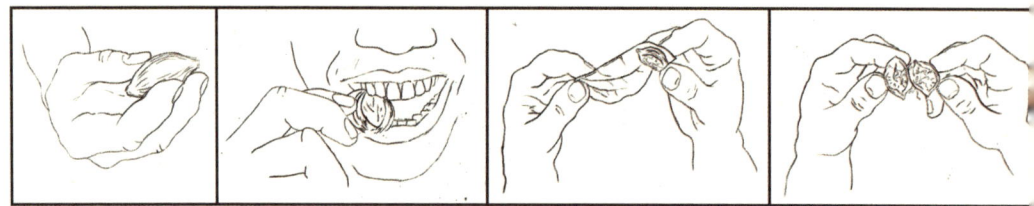

Moma for peace. *"The chewing of betel quids together by reconciled enemies is the essential part of the peace-making ceremonies especially in Ifugao... The priest takes position between the two (as yet) enemies. One of the enemies then gives the other an areca nut, and the courtesy is returned by the enemy giving the other a betel* *enemies stand aside from them in fear. May their valor be heard of in all the hills.'"* (Barton 2012).

See also: Hidit; Moma; Moma by myself; Sukarno; Tabbi.

Monastery. In 1978, Mike Parsons and Nida Dumsang set up a small print shop along Brent

Road, Baguio City. They experimented on various pulps from local plants. When they became more or less successful, they set up the Dontoug Foundation to teach papermaking and book art. Mike Parson's house and print workshop up on TipTop was called Monastery.
See also: Paper; Parsons, Mike.

Moon Craters. *"Once the sun and moon fought. The sun said, 'You are moon, not so good; if I give you no light, you are no good.' The moon answered, 'You are sun and very hot. I am moon and am better. The women like me very much, and when I shine they go out doors to spin.' Then the sun was very angry and took some sand and threw it on the moon, and that is why there are dark places on the moon now."* (Cole (1915) 2004).
See also: Headhunting (the tale).

Moore, Lina Espina. Born and raised in Cebu, she became a reporter for the Manila Times. She married Kip Moore, a logging executive for a business that provided timber to mines in Benguet. They settled in Mt. Data in Bauko. While there, Lina shifted to writing fiction and wrote short stories about her new mileu and the novel *Heart of a Lotus*. Kip Moore, who also happened to be a great photographer, died in 1976. Lina later wrote other works, including two novels and two collections of short stories. She returned to Cebu where she died in 2000. FYC.
See also: Daguio, Amador; Haight's Place; Hamada, Sinai; Mt. Data.

Mosaic:
The Baguio City Mosaic

In the introductory essay to the collection, *Cartography: A Collection of Poems on Baguio* (1992) Baguio poet Maria Luisa Aguilar-Cariño (now publishing as Luisa Igloria) gives a short account of the various displacements that have transpired throughout the course of the city's history. Accounts by Spanish expeditions which were able to penetrate the Cordilleras contain records of Igorot settlements which were headed by either a chieftain or an elder. The history of what is now known as Baguio City began with the migration of one such Igorot settlement composed of four families – the Carantes, Cariño, Molintas and Pinaw-an – to an area which eventually came to be known as Kafagway. (Cariño 1992, 67).

In later years, with the colonization of the Philippine islands by the Americans and urbanization and development after the war, waves of migration from the lowland provinces to Baguio City occurred, and the original settlers were displaced and marginalized. Baguio as place has been forged in the furnace of the confluence of cultures and its story finds echoes in the present-day geographical terrain.

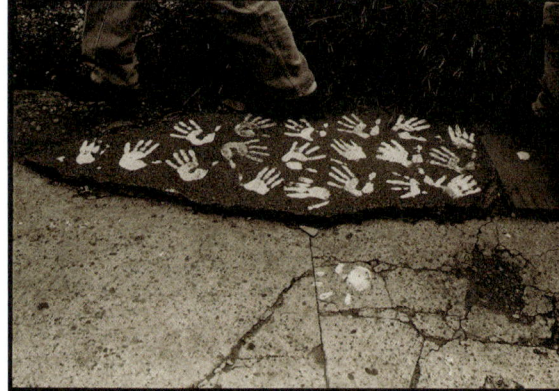
Photograph of a Baguio City sidewalk. Photograph by Tommy Hafalla.

"Baguio city is a construct.

"Beyond the images of leisure and romance is a place whose history is replete with displacement and reconfiguration. History will relate how the old pasturelands of the local Ibaloi elite or baknang were taken over by the colonizers, leaving the former disenfranchised and relegated to the fringes. ...

"Road names reflect the intriguing amalgamation of native and outsider: Kennon road (after Lyman Kennon, road builder) feeds into Kisad (referring to spirit possession of the mambunung or priestess) road, which lies along one side of tourist landmark Burnham Park (named after Daniel Burnham, Architect of Chicago); Wright park (named after Luke E. Wright, member of the Taft commission to explore Benguet), is contained in an old Igorot village Pacdal (local word for "log for crossing" although others claim the name derives from Pacshal, meaning, wood arranged in lattice pattern to form a corral)." (Subido 2009, xiii).

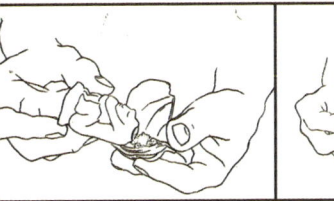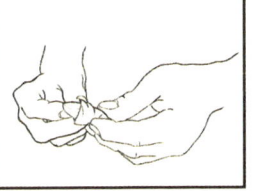
Illustration on how to prepare **Moma**. Illustration by Kawayan de Guia.

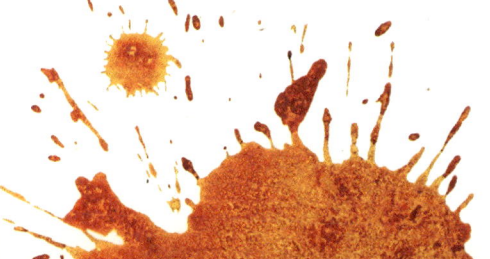

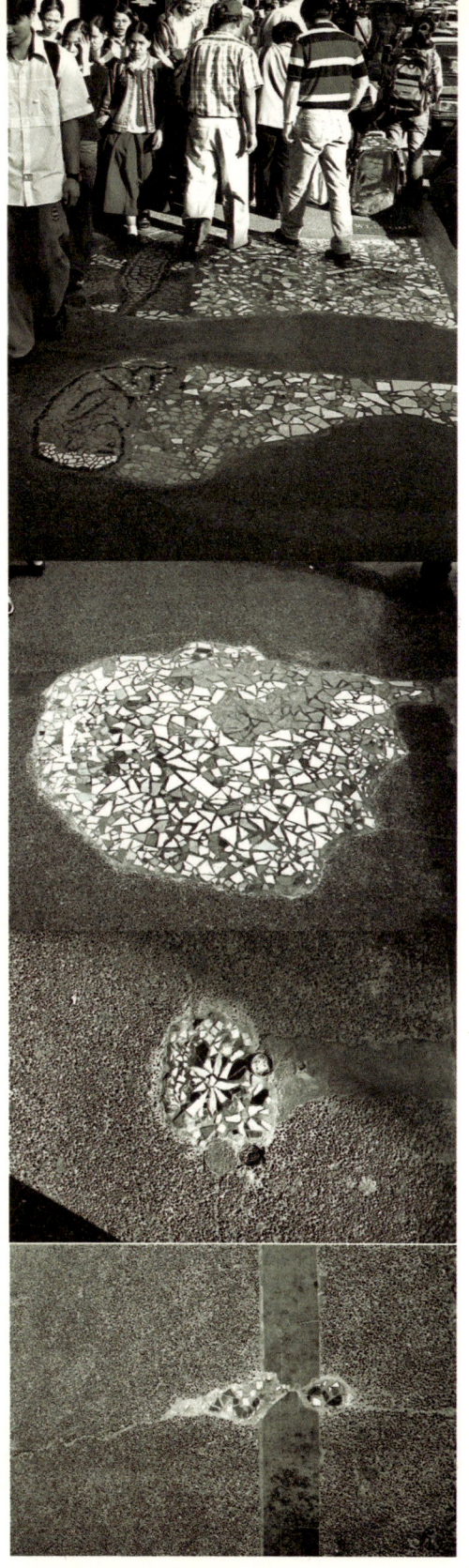

Historical experience and geographical location as 'gateway to the Cordilleras' have imbued the place with a hybrid character, with numerous and diverse ethnic groups and cultures existing alongside each other in 'cultural simultaneity.' For postcolonial theorist and critic Kumkum Sangari, cultural simultaneity is a condition which results from the blending, intermingling and melding of various, at times discordant and conflicting aspects of the diverse cultures flung into the vortex of encounter. It is the result of both convergence and contradiction, assimilation and resistance (Sangari 1990, 217).

Simultaneity is indicative of the resilience, adaptability and persistence of culture and its people, even in instances of unequal power relations such as that of colonizer and colonized, where the one culture seeks to efface that of the other. In Philippines, western colonialism has resulted in cultural simultaneity that is manifest in the coexistence of empirical science and folk belief; the concurrence of logic and "superstition"; a syncretic religion, which combines western and indigenous beliefs and practices; and the contemporaneousness of traditional customs and modern ways of life.

Baguio as place is a cobbling together of these various, at times dissonant, shards into a vibrant and colorful bricolage.

Sometime in the mid-2000s, the community of Baguio artists, along with a motley group of the city's denizens came together in a grand collaboration to repair the cracked sidewalk pavement of Session Road, the city's main thoroughfare. The result of the grand collaboration was a Session road mosaic, where an assortment of bits and pieces of broken multi-colored tiles and other found materials were cobbled together into a colorful whole by a similarly motley group of people from a variety of backgrounds and persuasions.

The collaborative event took on the mien of a town fiesta. A call was made for contributions – not for pecuniary support – but for shards of broken tiles or other materials that could be incorporated into the mosaic that would encompass the sidewalk that lined both sides of the entire length of the road, along with the invitation to participate in the mosaic project. Community members responded in droves, all eager – perhaps literally and figuratively – to embed themselves into the landscape of this place they called 'home.'

For some time, the Session Road mosaic provided an additional tourist attraction at the city's central business district. Walking along the sidewalk, you felt a heightened consciousness of the ground beneath your feet. Pedestrians were compelled to slow down – at times come to a complete stop – to be able to fully take in various features of the larger work intermittently spread along the path. The mosaic provided Baguio residents already familiar with the details of the mosaic an

Photographs of the Session Road sidewalk mosaic.
Photographs by Kawayan de Guia and Wig Tysmans.

opportunity to turn the 'touristic gaze' on visitors to the city whose eyes were enrapt by the ground on which they walked – it allowed the 'natives' the opportunity to gawk at those who would, under 'normal' circumstances, be gawking at them. However, its existence was short-lived. When the rainy season came, incidents of pedestrians slipping on the mosaic tiles began to emerge, so a non-slip coating was applied to the tiled areas of the sidewalk. However, reports of accidents continued and, to forestall any future untoward events, government decided to take action. The administration decided that the Session Road mosaic was a 'public hazard,' and had to be removed. It was an ironic chicken-and-egg situation – what government had forgotten to make a clean breast of in laying full blame on the community mosaic for the accidents that had befallen pedestrians, was that it was precisely the administration's negligence that initially spurred on the idea of the mosaic project. Pedestrians had suffered accidents from the severely damaged sidewalk, which the city government had not taken any action to repair for the longest time.

The Session Road mosaic has since been replaced by a 'more refined,' 'neater,' and 'pedestrian-safe' commercial tile finish. And, with the removal of the mosaic, the landscape was once again altered, and the people that had been 'embedded in the land,' were, yet again, 'displaced.' Nonetheless, the original project had provided a glimpse into the narrative that pervades Baguio City, and intimation into the continuing challenges that face the residents of this place of encounter, where individuals continually contend with various forces, and face a gamut of experiences and influences which are at once variegated and diverse.

Today, the remaining vestige of the Session Road mosaic will be found along the sidewalk on Session Road, marking the entrance to La Azotea building owned by the De Guia family of artists Kidlat, Kawayan and Kabunyan, and their parents Katrin and Kidlat Tahimik, a.k.a. Eric de Guia. This building is home to the Victor Oteyza Community Art Space (VOCAS), located on the top floor. GTS.

This essay also cobbles together portions of the writer's dissertation papers in progress, "Cultural Simultaneity, Memory and the 'Myth of Authenticity';" "Baguio the Poetry of Place," "Tessellated Lives: VOCAS and the Politics of Place," as well as and portions of the exhibit notes written for a UPB Fine Arts student Exhibit for the National Commission on Culture and the Arts (NCCA) titled "Tessellated Lives."
See also: Waiting Sheds.

Motit *(KAN)* also **Alima-ong, Amonin, Ingaw, Kolang, Musang, Silay.** Palm civet cat. Now valued in Sagada where their droppings (they love to eat ripe Arabica coffee berries) are collected and sold in Manila as kape alamid (similar to kopi luwak) at a very steep price. FYC.

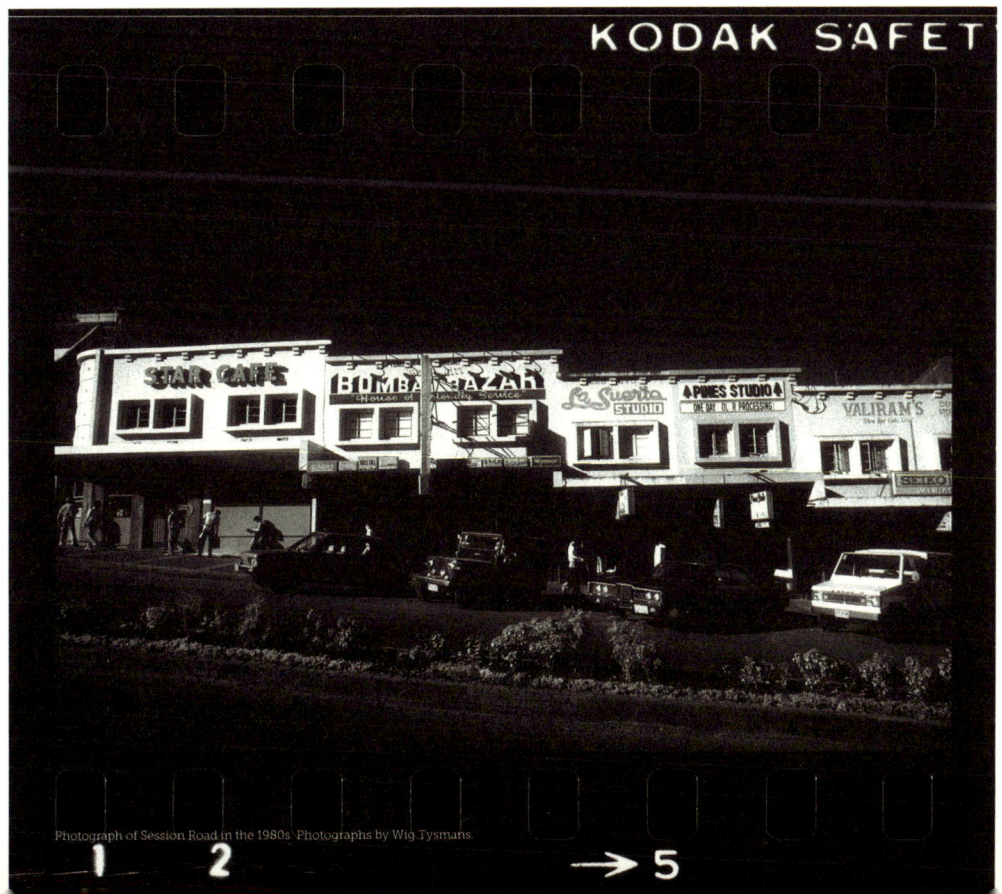
Photograph of Session Road in the 1980s. Photographs by Wig Tysmans.

Mountain Province. During Spanish times, Northern Kalinga, Kiangan, Ifugao, Benguet, Cabuagan and Amburayan belonged to one commandancia while Bontoc, Western Ifugao and Southern Kalinga were in another. In 1907, Mountain Province became the super province with Bontoc-Lepanto-Amburayan, Ifugao, Kalinga, Benguet and Apayao as sub-provinces. A year later, Mountain Province was subdivided into the sub-provinces of Benguet, Bontoc, Ifugao, Lepanto, Amburayan, Kalinga and Apayao. Later Amburayan was joined with Bontoc and Lepanto with Benguet. Since 1925, Mountain Province felt that being lumped into one Mountain Province and getting the same allotments as the other much smaller provinces was unfair and so bill after bill was submitted to chop the Mountain Province into smaller provinces but these were ignored. In 1965, Mountain Province was divided into three legislative districts: First District comprising the present Mountain Province except for Besao, Tadian and Bauko towns, Kalinga and Apayao; the Second District comprising Baguio and Benguet; and the Third District comprising Ifugao and the towns of Tadian and Bauko. In 1966, however, then President Ferdinand Marcos approved Republic Act 4695 where the old Mountain Province was divided into Benguet, Ifugao, the new Mountain Province, and Kalinga-Apayao. If you looked at the old Kalinga-Apayao, you could see the silhouette of Marcos. To confound the situation, during the Martial Law years, the city of Baguio, Benguet, Mountain Province and Abra belonged to the Ilocos region while Kalinga-Apayao and Ifugao belonged to Cagayan Valley. FYC.

See also: Marcos Gerrymandering.

Mt. Clitoris also **Mt. Mogaw.** An unusually-shaped hill located within Tadian, Mountain Province that looks like a woman's clitoris in the middle of a valley. A better view of its peculiarity can be seen from high areas in Tadian and Bauko, Mountain Province and in Cervantes, Ilocos Sur. DOS.

See also: Doligen ed Kabunyan, Si; Mt. Data; Mt. Polis; Mt. Pulag; Mt. Santo Tomas.

Mt. Data. The highly forested area in the Mountain Province from which emerges the headwaters of the Abra River, the oldest river in the Philippines, and the Gran Chico River. Both of these rivers were among the major reasons for the Cordilleran revolution during the Marcos Administration due to major infrastructure projects that would have affected the region's life and resources.

See also: Cellophil; Chico; Mt. Clitoris; Mt. Polis; Mt. Pulag.

Mt. Polis. Located at the boundary of Mountain Province and Ifugao. Mt. Polis is 2,255 meters high. The landscape is mossy forest, pine forest, and mixed montane forest. Over the years the area earned the reputation of being a place where hold-uppers lurk. But in recent times, the robberies have dwindled. It is also a favorite of birders. Here you can find the Mountain White-eye, Chestnut-faced Babbler, Metallic-winged Sunbird, Mountain Leaf-Warbler, Little Pied Flycatcher, Mountain Verditer-Flycatcher, Island Thrush, Philippine Swiftlet, Luzon Bush-Warbler, Luzon Water-Redstart, Blue-headed Fantail, Elegant Tit, Philippine Bulbul, Sulphur-billed Nuthatch, Citrine Canary-Flycatcher, Mountain Shrike, Mountain Tailorbird, White-browed Shortwing, Greenbacked Whistler, Flame-crowned Flowerpecker, Olive Tree-Pipit, Flame-breasted Fruit-Dove, White-cheeked Bullfinch, Montane Racquet-tail, Tawny-breasted Parrotfinch, Grand Rhabdornis, Whiskered Pitta, Red Crossbill, Snowy-browed Flycatcher, Luzon Scops-Owl, Bukidnon Woodcock, Long-tailed Bush-Warbler, Benguet Bush-Warbler, and flocks more of other such pretty names. (Perez 2012).

See also: Doligen ed Kabunyan, Si; Ikik; Mt. Clitoris; Mt. Data; Mt. Pulag; Mt. Santo Tomas.

Mt. Pulag. Pulag means 'bald.' It is the name of the highest mountain in the Cordillera, located in Benguet. At 2,930 meters above sea level, it is the third highest mountain in the Philippines. It is a popular hiking and camping destination for mountaineering groups and tourists who often make their ascent to the peak before the crack of dawn hoping to catch the spectacular sunrise. To the Ibaloi, Mt. Pulag is spiritual homeland. The souls of their ancestors reside on the mountain. The mossy oak forests of Mt. Pulag were once the traditional hunting grounds of both the Ibaloi and the Kalanguya peoples. Mt. Pulag is the habitat of several endemic species and it is a recognized Important Bird Area. Although Mt. Pulag is a national park and a protected area, its ecosystem is under siege from the expansion of commercial vegetable gardens by migrants, Ibaloy and Kalanguya alike, and the heavy unchecked traffic of hundreds of tourists and mountaineers and their careless behavior. PLP.

See also: Doligen ed Kabunyan, Si; Mt. Clitoris; Mt. Data; Mt. Polis; Mt. Santo Tomas.

Mt. Santo Tomas. True to its saintly name, this mountain in Tuba, Benguet, turns one into a religious pilgrim when one climbs its peak. Bikers and amateur climbers before arriving at its highest point at 2256 meters above sea level would chance upon Stations of the Cross before great views of vegetable gardens, strawberry farms, a water reservoir, and the whole of Baguio City. Often, the mountain is mistaken as *"that mountain with Mickey Mouse ears"* because of two circular radars that are propped on top of Mt. Cabuyao. The Ibalois of the past called the mountain 'Adagut [lichen].' At the peak of this mountain are towering satellites for television, radio, and cellphones. But amidst these bundled structures at the narrow peak, is another cross. From a 360-degree view, one can see La Union (southwest), and the Lingayen Gulf and Philippine Sea (south). This mountain is a huge welcoming sight when entering the mountainous Cordilleras

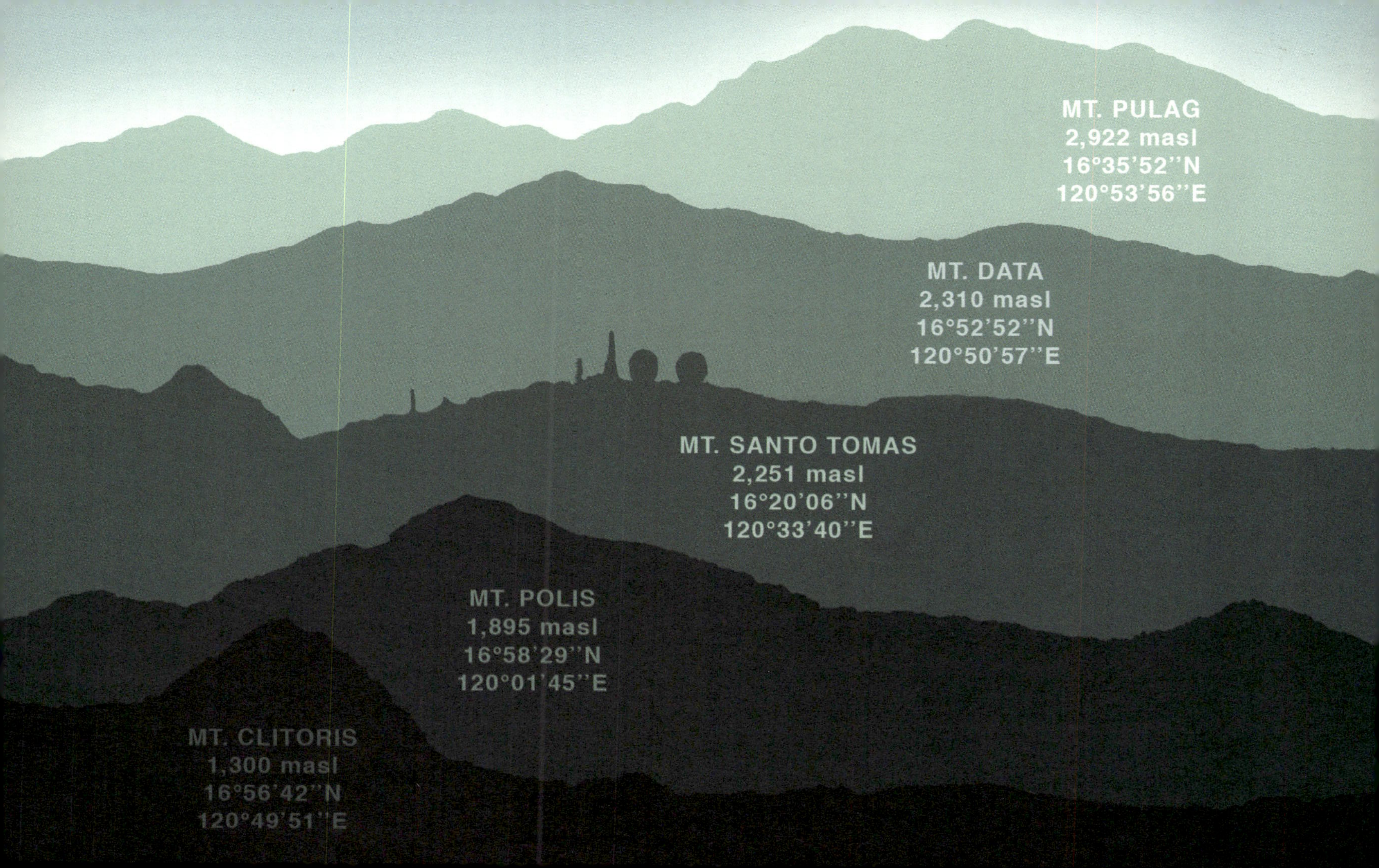

MT. PULAG
2,922 masl
16°35'52"N
120°53'56"E

MT. DATA
2,310 masl
16°52'52"N
120°50'57"E

MT. SANTO TOMAS
2,251 masl
16°20'06"N
120°33'40"E

MT. POLIS
1,895 masl
16°58'29"N
120°01'45"E

MT. CLITORIS
1,300 masl
16°56'42"N
120°49'51"E

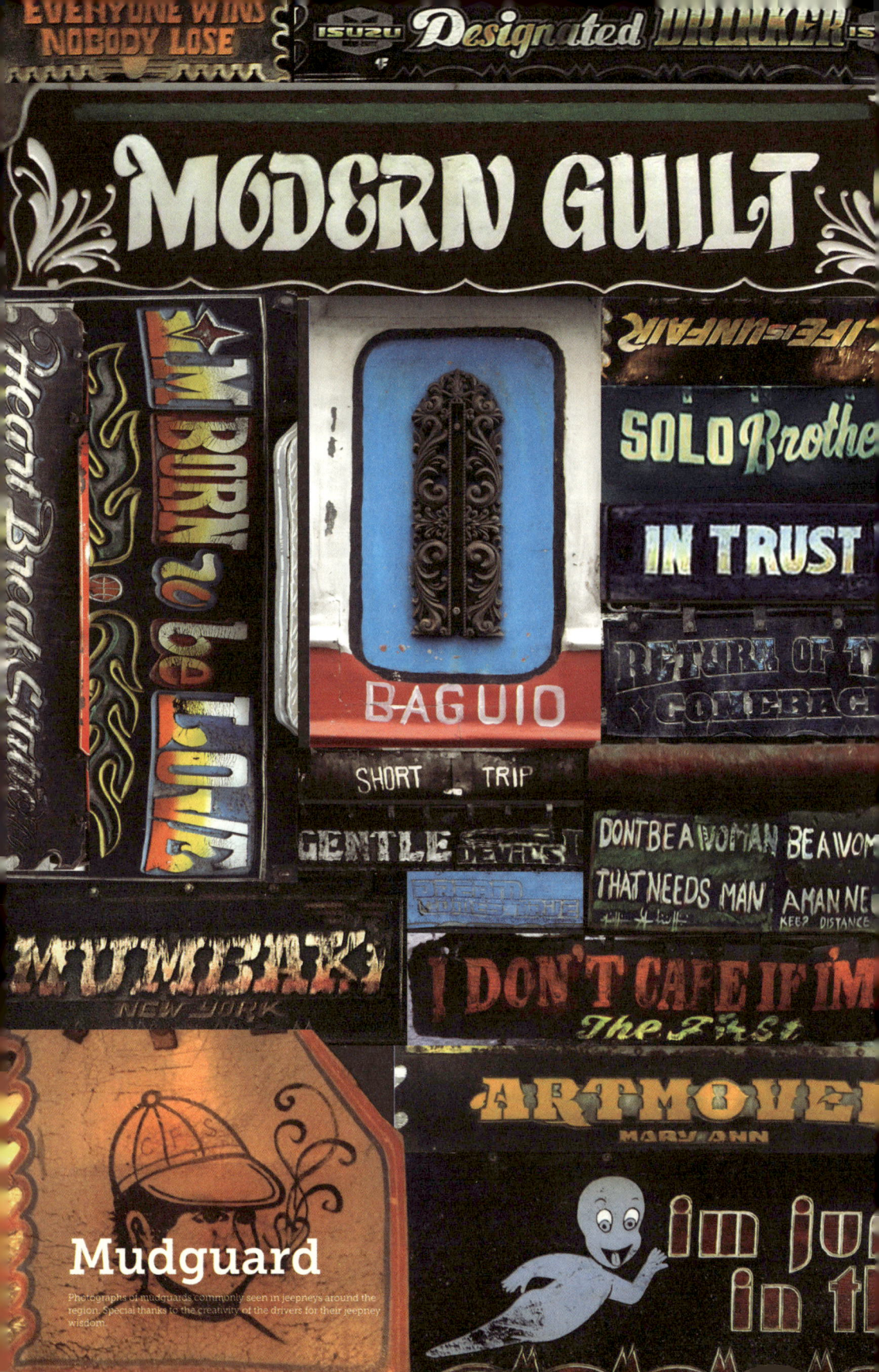

Mudguard

Photographs of mudguards commonly seen in jeepneys around the region. Special thanks to the creativity of the drivers for their jeepney wisdom.

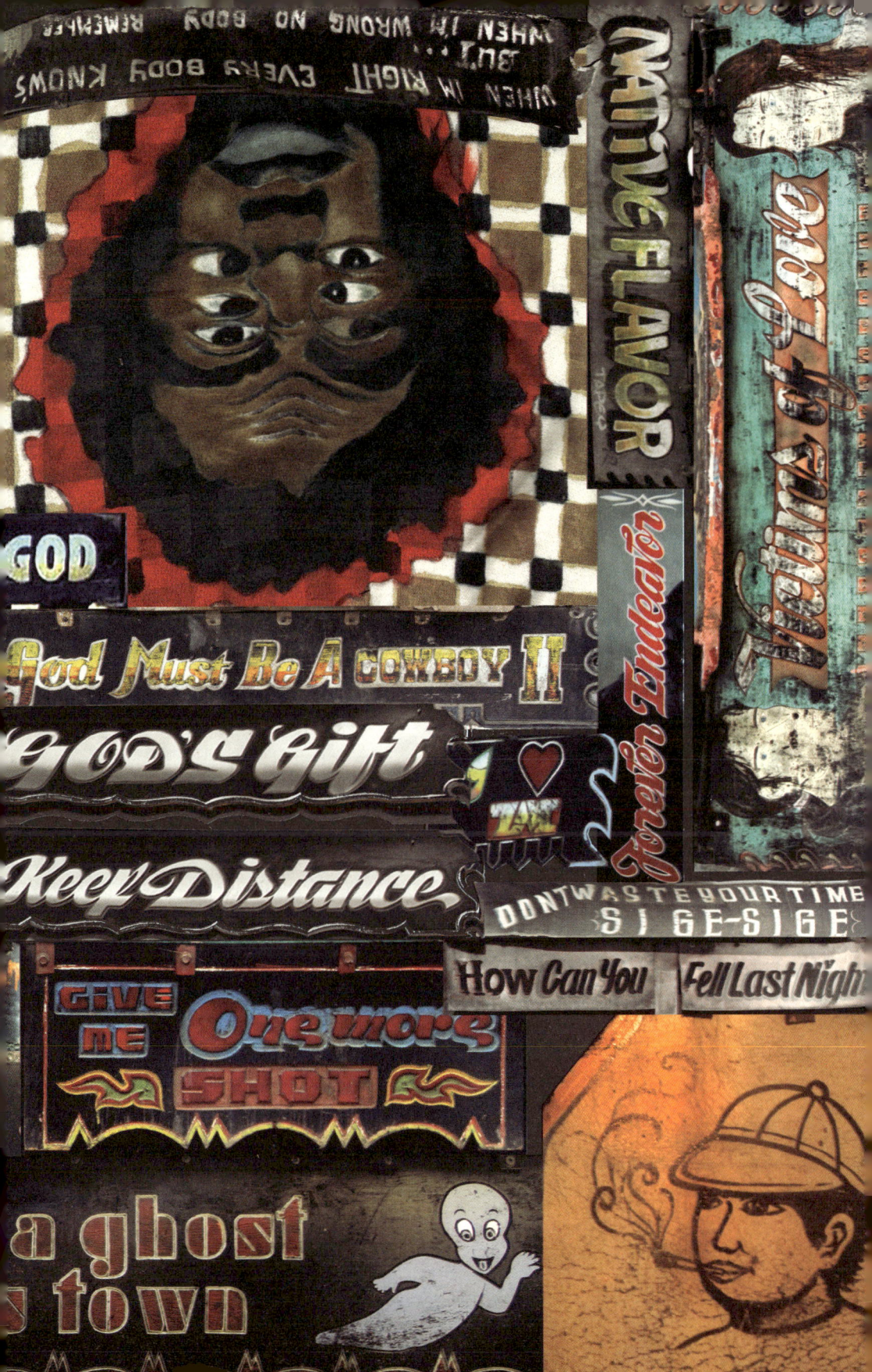

from the lowlands via Kennon Road, Quirino, or Marcos Highway. HZK.

See also: Doligen ed Kabunyan, Si; Mt. Clitoris; Mt. Data; Mt. Pulag.

Mumbaki. [1] The mumbaki is an Ifugao spiritual authority whose task is to perform or recite baki prayers to deities and act as representative for the spiritual needs of the people. A mumbaki may perform the following: (a) ask for protection or blessings for warriors before and after going to war/headhunting; (b) heal unexplainable illnesses and diseases caused by harmful spirits; (c) appease dead ancestors who are disturbing the living family members and instead ask them to give blessings; (d) call back the spirit of a person that was taken by the unseen; (e) call for blessings for planting seasons.

[2] A 1996 Antonio Perez film about a doctor who planned to go to the US but had to go back to Ifugao due to the death of his father who was a victim in a tribal dispute. His community expected him to lead the battle. HZK.

See also: Dorarakit; Igorota: The Legend of the Tree of Life; Kung Mangarap Ka't Magising; Mahimunu; Maingal; Mambunong; Manpapayad; Mansib-ok;

Music.
Cordillera Soundscapes

Reverberating through the soundscapes of continents, countries, cities and villages, music has been connecting communities in geographically separate but similar worlds. Cordilleran music transcends the physical and moves to a higher dimension. Present from birth to death and the afterlife, music here heals, nourishes and bridges the physical to the spiritual world. It bonds strangers, unites enemies, constructs identities and strengthens a community's solidarity.

In the Cordillera, each province and ethno-linguistic group has *"its own political and social structures, divisions of lands, agricultural rites, feasts and music"* (Maceda 1998). Traversing mountains, valleys, rivers, and villages are the brilliant reverberations of the flat gongs called the gangsa, the wide range of sounds from bamboo instruments, community singing, and the various chants that not only mark the life cycles of each community but also their everyday lives. Music is characterized by spontaneity, improvisations, pulsating rhythms, and resultant melodies. Melody is usually pentatonic and while rhythm is of utmost importance, the sounds produced by metal and bamboo instruments result in different layers of sonic colors that give life to a vibrant musical tradition.

The entire community participates in music making. There is no distinct demarcation between performer and audience. The gong ensembles, which play for hours, involve most of the men in the community, and now sometimes, the women too. Music is an oral tradition and the community acknowledges the importance of leadership and tradition in the process of transmission and innovation. Musical practices and knowledge are learned through participation. Innovations accepted by the community today, and practiced by the community over time, become traditions in the future. The youth actively watch rituals and performances and learn along the way. Each young boy still learns the gangsa through observation and the use of mnemonic devices to learn the rhythms.

Another important component of music-making is dance. Music and dance are integral in festivities such as weddings and harvest rituals. Exciting and vigorous, dance among the Cordillerans plays a big role in binding the community. Dancers move around in a circle, the males imitating the movements of a rooster chasing a hen.

Dancing in a circle is symbolic. The circle, a universal symbol for eternity, is omnipresent in celebrations. Rituals begin when participants huddle in a circle. Going beyond this, the physical circle in which music is played also has a symbolic relationship with time, very much different from the Western concepts of music which are concerned with temporal logic and tonal resolutions. Southeast Asian music, renowned ethnomusicologist Jose Maceda has theorized, is *"absorbed in another concept of the world, another measure of time, not a linear,*

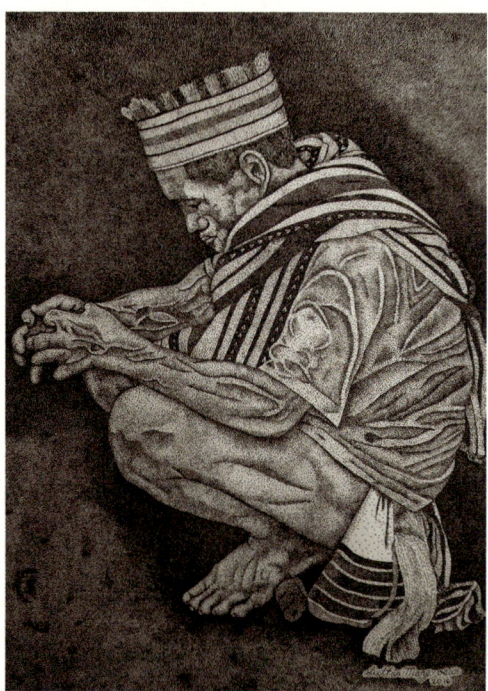

Artwork by Sultan Mang-osan, 2014.

cause and effect entity of logic and matter, but a metaphysical world" (Maceda 1986). It is this concept of time which impels the inner life of Cordillera music. Ostinato, a repeating melodic pattern, and drone, a note or sound continuously played in a performance, produced by gongs and drums give a sense of a longer and a more fluid musical time.

It was said that *"Ifugao elders, when asked about the beginning of the hudhud, would simply answer: Handih wandi! which means, "Long time ago!" or "Since time immemorial"* (Dulawan 1985). This very concept of time, exemplifying indefiniteness and eternity, permeates a musical culture whose songs range from something like the hudhud, an epic song which can last for days, to the lewlewa or liwliwa, a leader-chorus chant which may last for hours or a short chant or prayer barely lasting a minute which is recited by a male elder after the puta, the ritual of hacking an axe on a carabao's back before a wedding.

Songs and chants are also common in the Cordilleras. Responsorial singing is prevalent. Songs are mono-linear, characterized by vocal ornaments – slides, mordents, pulsating rhythm, syllabic singing style (Maceda 1958) and distinct bodily gestures. With the contrast between long, drawn-out songs and short chants, music can both coalesce and dissolve the passage of time in the many days that characterize a typical Igorot celebration. Example of songs are the ba'diw of the Ibaloi. It is sung poetry in leader-chorus style. The hudhud of the Ifugao is a sung epic about the story of Bugan and Aliguyon from courtship to marriage. The ullalim of the Bontoc and Kalinga are stories of adventure to entertain and ease the tired. The Bontok ayyeng is an extemporaneous song sung by male elders. The salidommay is sung in solo or chorus by women and it is most often about love. The baya-o is a song about the good achievements of the dead. The dawak of the Kalinga is sung by the mandadawak, a female ritual specialist who can cure sickness inflicted by the anitos, or ancestral spirits. The daing is a debate song between sexes while the Sagada lewlewa or Ifugao liwliwa are responsorial songs sung during harvest, in between calling of spirits and marriage celebrations.

The exuberant gangsas are instruments of prominent stature. They are played in weddings, harvest ceremonies and peace pacts. In an Ibaloy ensemble, the gangsas are usually joined by the solibao, a conical drum, and metal sticks. In Sagada weddings, young boys skillfully play and swivel the gangsa in an elaborate display of gong twisting. In most parts of the Cordillera region, it is commonly practiced that when the set of gongs are brought out for the first time for a wedding celebration, a group of men perform a ritual involving the playing of gongs with 'open' sounds, ebullient and ringing. Some musical styles of gangsa playing are the traditional takik, balangbang, binnaniwan and the modern boogie-boogie, a style based on the boogie dance.

Other musical instruments are the Sagada panpipes called the diw-as, the nose flute called kalleleng. The Kalingas have the balingbing, also known as bungkaka, a bamboo buzzer equivalent to the pakkung of the Ibaloi. The patang-ug are quill-shaped bamboo tubes while bamboo stamping tubes of various lengths are called the tongatong. The ulibao is a bamboo Jews harp and the patatag are xylophone staves. The kolitong/kulibit or kolesing are polychordal zithers. The whistle flute is called the olimong while the tongali is a nose flute. The pattung of the Ifugao are percussion yoke bars. The Bontoc dew-dew-as, diwdiw-as or diwas are bamboo panpipes which are equivalent to the saggeypo of the Kalinga.

Music as an experience should not be taken out of its social context. It is more than just an acoustic phenomenon. More importantly, it belongs inside its community, as a living and breathing tradition. It is enmeshed in the mountains, the rice fields, and the expanse of sky – in constant communication with the revered anitos. Music helps in the construction and preservation of the history of the Igorot. Though not written, the Igorot story rings loud and clear in the songs, chants, dances and beats of the gangsa, not only in the ili but also in the cities where they now reside, or even in other parts of the world. RA.

See also: Country Music; Cowboy.

Music:
What is Cordillera Music?

Dumay Solinggay (DOS) interviews Matti Camfili (MC) of Salidummay Band, and singer Ingrid Payaket (IP).

Interview with Matti Camfili

DOS: What is Cordillera music for you and do you consider yourself a Cordillera musician?

MC: Of course, I consider myself a Cordillera musician. Any musician may claim that they are a Cordillera musician with whatever music they are creating. But for me, my own standard in calling someone a Cordillera musician is whether the music embeds something that promotes our identity as a people. Kasi, even with the fast changes in the music styles right now, you can still distinguish something Cordilleran. A Cordillera music obviously integrates an element from the traditional music like the chants, the musical instruments, and also the content having to do with the Cordillera ethno-scape and the past, present, and future situations of the region.

DOS: How do you classify your music genre and when did you start getting involved with it?

MC: I grew up in the ili listening to songs and chants during community occasions in the ab-abfungan. And while growing up, I came across recorded music. I was in grade six when I first heard the recorded album of Salidummay and I remarked, "wow, naisabsabali (unique)!"

I met the group in Saint Mary's School in Sagada sometime in 1993-1994. I was so happy to listen to them live, which heightened my interest to learn their music. When I came to study in Baguio in the late 1990s, I had the opportunity to join them and learn about creating music.

DOS: How did the music of Salidummay evolve?

MC: The first generation of Salidummay involved Judy Cariño and Ani Bonggaoen. According to them, the inception of this kind of music started way back in the 1970s. They were students then and they wanted to go to the communities to understand the issue regarding the Chico River Dam project funded by the World Bank which was being implemented by the late President Marcos. The chorus singing of the old women protesting against the project caught the interest of the students including Manang Judy and Manang Ani.

One of the specific songs was the Pasil, Chico, *Tanudan/ lumubwat tako losan/ Ay, ay, salidummay* [sings]. The Pasil, Chico, Tanudan are the communities where the tributary of the Chico river passes along. *Sayang nu adik ilaban/ti taon nataguan ay ay* [sings]. We should fight for our ancestral land. This song caught Manang Julie's interest to understand traditional music used for protest. But, siempre, Manang Julie actually articulated that they could not sing the song the way the elders sung. So the least thing that they could do was to capture whatever they could catch and they developed from that. They accompanied the songs with instruments and they recorded them because their sole objective of learning the songs is so other people would hear about the struggle.

There was initially a good reaction to their music. One comment that hit them was, *"Wow! They sound like Indians."* They were inspired with that comment and tried composing more, accompanying their music with the guitar, then the flute and later on, they also used gongs.

After that, the demand increased. People were

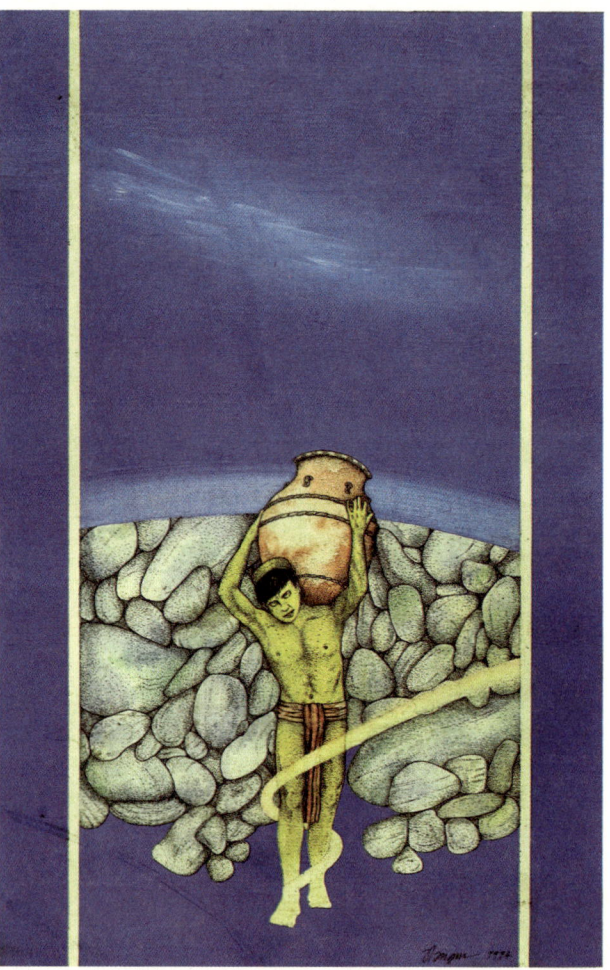

Man-aawit si Kinarcho (The Jar Bearer) by Ged Alangui, acrylic and ink on canvas board, 43x28 cm, 1994.

saying, *"More songs! More songs!"* and until now a lot are still asking, *"Apay awan pay ti barbaro [Don't you have new pieces]?"*

DOS: Were there ever apprehensions questioning the use of instruments especially the gongs?

MC: There was one time when we were invited to perform in Itogon. The elders were a bit strict – they said that we could not play the gongs unless there was a ritual. We had to be selective with our choice of songs. But it's different when we perform in schools. There, we are well and easily accepted.

DOS: Why do you think they were open to accepting your music?

MC: I think because the music talks about them. They can easily relate with the songs because the content is something of their experience. For instance, when we went to Dalican, Bontoc, we sung the "Balay," it is a song depicting the situation of the urban poor community here in Baguio that had problems with demolition issues. Someone cried when we sung that and we learned from that person that their house in Baguio was demolished.

DOS: How do you label your music?

MC: For our group, we call it salidummay music, and from there we try to define salidummay, which for us simply means 'traditional music' with innovation. Of course, some people take issue with the word 'traditional,' which they equate with 'pure.' For us though, what matters is the acceptability of the community.

There is a fulfillment in contributing in the preservation of the musicality of the Cordilleras while innovating so the younger generations could relate as well. It's also fulfilling that we are raising awareness with this kind of music. But the most fulfilling experience for me is when we go to the community without other agenda than to learn with them. The very humbling experience we can derive from this is when we can communicate different concerns and talk about different issues. And from there we ask, "What do we do after this?"

It is a mission for us to enliven the spirit of Cordillera music as an avenue of discourse about social issues. For us as a people, we cannot separate ourselves from music and we cannot separate our music from our reality, thus we cannot separate ourselves from what's happening around us. That is when we say that music is an integral part of the lives of the people of the Cordillera.

DOS: What makes your music distinctly Cordilleran?

MC: I think one of its distinctions in terms of its musicality is that it's based from the traditional songs of the Cordilleras that are most commonly pentatonic in scale, and the integration of different indigenous musical instruments. I think that's what makes it distinct aside from that it talks about the Cordilleras. Although recently we composed songs that are not limited to Cordillera concerns alone. We included wider issues, for example, songs in solidarity with international friends because we have the same concerns as indigenous peoples.

DOS: How do you think you can get along with the choices of the younger generation who are into 'introduced' music?

MC: I think Salidummay is the pioneer when it comes to innovating from traditional music in as far as recording is concerned. When the songs became popular, others also tried to innovate from their own traditional music.

DOS: Who are your audience?

MC: That's an interesting study to look into because I find it inappropriate to generalize that the older people have a bigger acceptability or appreciation with this music. I saw children in the community who are listening to it although many of them are engaged in pop music.

DOS: Do you feel like you hold some responsibility in letting the younger generation listen to this kind of music?

MC: Of course! We want the young people to become aware of the different community issues. And there is also this responsibility to reach out to the younger people, as fast as we can sana. This issue is also a recurring concern for us. Sometimes we assume that our audience grew tired of our music and are just opting for introduced music like pop. Hence we ask ourselves, do we adjust for them?

DOS: What is your sentiment about the appreciation of young people for pop music? Is it something bothersome?

MC: We cannot remove the fact that one genre of music influences the other. But if pop music is dominating the scene, it tends to suppress the other forms and genres of music. Diversity should be the very ideal situation. It would be good that even if there are introduced pop music we can still listen to traditional and salidummay music. I actually also like pop music that talks about relevant matters.

DOS: Can you say that at this point, urban Baguio is predominated by pop music?

MC: I think not yet as of now. They're probably at par with each other.

Carla Rosito: I don't think so because I don't see any venue for traditional or salidummay music. Although it's good that they teach it in schools. Unless you consciously expose your children to this kind of music – there is no venue.

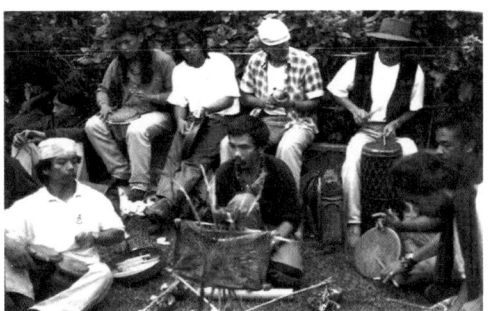

Members of the *Baguio Arts Guild* playing drums., c. 1990s.

DOS: Do you have a vision of what kind of Cordillera music would be here 10 or 20 years from now? Were you able to reflect on the trend?

MC: It would be interesting to plot what would happen. As of now, there is still a demand to popularize salidummay songs. Many are still interested to learn and many are still demanding new songs from us. So how would things be? Would we still be here 20 years from now? – maybe Ingrid's album would be what's on top by then [giggles].

Interview with Ingrid Payaket

DOS: What is Cordillera music for you and do you consider yourself a Cordillera musician?

IP: I guess I am because I am a product of the Cordillera. We may not be specifically singing Cordillera songs all the time but since I'm a Cordilleran by blood, I guess yes, I am a Cordilleran singer.

With my observation, Cordillera music is strongly influenced by country songs because we were occupied by the Americans. Most Cordillerans are fond of patterning after country music or replacing the lyrics of the country music with lyrics in the native language. But there are also authentic Cordillera songs like Babagto. There are also Ibaloi songs but I forgot. There is also the salidummay choral composition of Ma'am Rio Pablico. I guess, the contribution of Cordillera music to choral arrangement is the use of native language and the use of the pentatonic scale, which most traditional, especially Asian music, are scaled on.

DOS: How do you classify your music genre and when did you start getting involved with it?

IP: I guess I belong to a cross-over of classical and pop. I was initially introduced to the choir and the placement of my voice is actually soprano. In college, our choral arrangement was very classical. My a capella group now mostly sings pop songs and I am the soprano.

DOS: Who are your audience?

IP: Since currently we're doing contemporary a capella arrangements, it can be appreciated by the oldies and the younger generation. Kasi with a capella, we can arrange old songs which the older audience can appreciate, and the contemporary pop is what appeals to the younger audience.

When I say contemporary, I mean *"yung uso ngayon [what's in right now]"* like Bruno Mars, Ariana Grande.

DOS: When you joined *Pilipinas Got Talent*, you said you were a proud Igorota. Did it ever

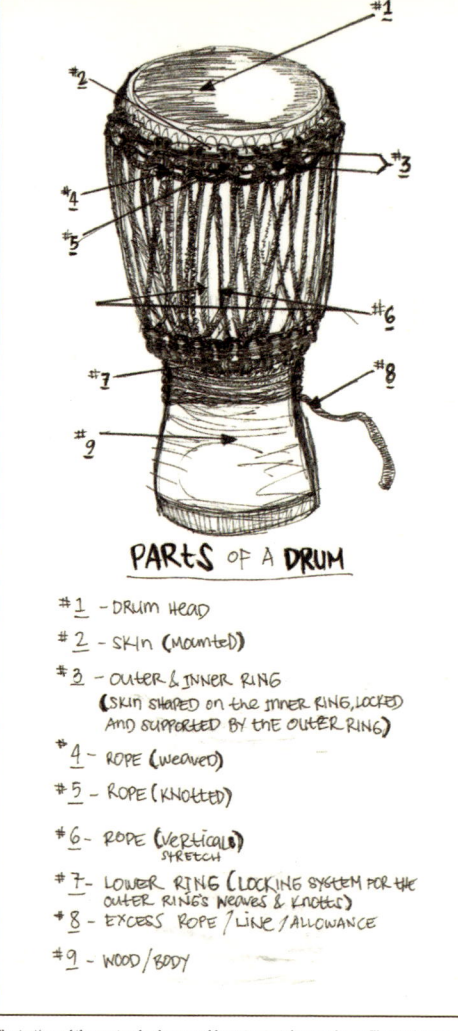

Illustration of the parts of a drum and how to stretch your drum. Illustration by JV Romawac.

cross your mind to you to make music which represents the Cordilleran 'identity?'

IP: Actually it's one of the ideas I've been pondering about that's why I wanted to travel around the Cordillera to see what really makes Cordillera music. Although, based on my observation, Cordillera music leans more towards country music but I wish we could discover song writers who could freshen the existing Cordilleran songs to make it appealing to the younger generation.

When you say Cordillera music, one person that comes to mind is Lourdes Fangki, dubbed as the queen of Cordillera songs. She's one of the artists I know who made original songs and the popular one is the *Nan Layad Nanlikhatan*. There was one time when I had a set and they were requesting for that particular song.

I think we like country songs because of the

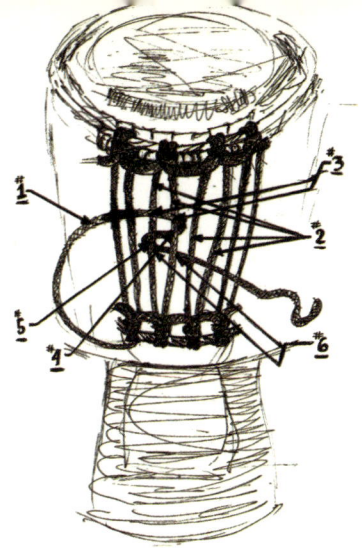
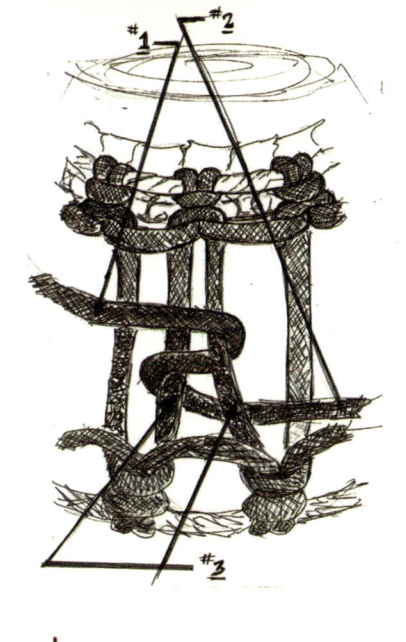

storytelling within the lyrics. We like songs that have stories.

DOS: What other steps would you like to take to broaden your musical world?

IP: I have always wanted to travel around the Cordilleras just so I could get an idea and of course to know myself better so I could create something that we could call 'our own.' Because anywhere you go, you would like to represent something that's 'sariling atin.'

When I was in college, I was exposed to broadway musicals. We performed *Beauty and the Beast*, and *The King and I*. I was hoping for an agency or a certain department that would push for musical plays showcasing our own stories – we have so many stories to tell. We did one with the Department of Tourism, the play entitled *Lumawig* which ran for several shows. It was hard to put it together and we had difficulties in terms of musical instruments. But I think, the only way to develop it is to do it step by step. So that if there are tourists who come and they ask what Cordillera is about then we have something to show to them.

When my a capella group performed in Manila, one of the songs we performed was "Salidummay," which became the crowd favorite. Imagine a song from the Cordillera that they could not understand became the most appreciated.

DOS: How do you see your career in five years or ten years? Which development would you like to move forward to?

IP: I really could not say. But for music, I really hope that in one way or another we could help push forward the identity of Cordillera music. I wish we could produce more materials, produce more songs heard on the radio. I wish we could have more song writers that could merge traditional and pop music together – and of course, I wish there would be more musical plays.

DOS: Your inspiration?

IP: Love for your hometown, talaga. Because once you dedicate yourself, whatever talent you have, to your people, what you give will always come back to you. DOS.

Unearth by Nona Garcia, oil on canvas, 242x335 cm, 2015. Courtesy Nona Garcia and Singapore Art Museum Collection.

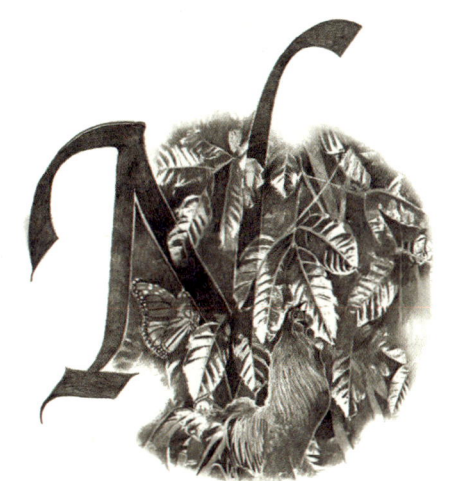

Naanannongan *(KAN)*. Haunted. Made ill by ghosts. Related to Anong, the Kanakanaey word for religious rites and sacrifices.
See also: Baguio Ghost Stories; Nabat-ing.

Nabat-ing *(KAN)*. *"A victim of spirit possession."* (Scott 2011, 149).
See also: Naanannongan

Nafutengak *(BON)*. Lit. I'm drunk.
See also: Butong; Liwliwot.

Namati *(ILO)*. Lit. Has believed. A believer in Christ – to differentiate from Adi Namati: non-believer or pagan. DOS.
See also: Paganu.

Namwaw *(KAN)*. The extinct Benguet-Kankanaey term for 'Thank you.' CCA.
See also: Bontoc Kiss; Iya-iyaman.

Nan Layad Nan Likhatan. Lit. A Love Beset with Difficulties. A love song every Bontok knows in sleep, when drunk, or while walking a narrow foot path between two waterlogged rice fields and balancing on their head a load of camote. Composed in fun by a group of Bontoks, one of whom was Christopher Oakes, the song revolves around the tragic love of an Ilocano man for a Bontok maiden. The man was rejected by the maiden but the song was accepted by many listeners. The melody was adopted from *When "There's Love at Home"* by John Hugh McNaughton. "Nan Layad," as it is also referred to, was first sung in public by Bontok high school students in 1947, and has grown in popularity exponentially in the years that followed. The first to cover the song was Pedro Chinalpan, a Dangwa Bus conductor of the Baguio-Tabuk route, who sang on the bus to keep him from sleeping and to entertain his passengers or put them to sleep. Lourdes Gomeyac (a.k.a. Lourdes Fangki) made this song a sensation in music bars and public performances in Baguio where other Cordillerans learned the song by heart and loved it as much as the Bontoks. GAD.
See also: Amazing Grace; Lover's Moon; Waynasdi.

Nantoltolo *(KAN)*. Refers to a Kankanaey couple or family who performs a traditional Kankanaey thanksgiving ritual involving the butchering of three pigs for Kabunyan. For the Kankanaey, performing this traditional practice is a serious observance and in conformity with Kankanaey spirituality. This is also a way of gaining public eminence in Kankanaey communities, for it is a sign that the nantoltolo have become well-off. However, in performing the ritual, a Kankanaey couple should have first undergone the teteg (traditional Kankanaey baptism), which is the prerequisite of the toltolo. NEP.
See also: Bayas; Kaon ya Teteg; Peshit.

Narda's. Before 1975, Narda Capuyan's hobby was weaving on her mother's loom. In 1975, Narda was introduced to ikat, a Southeast Asian tie-dyeing technique unfamiliar to Cordilleran weavers. She began to incorporate ikat into Cordillera loom weaving, recruiting more weavers, and turning the fabric to clothes. She then opened Narda's, and by 1982, was already being featured in Bloomingdale's in New York City. After ikat, Narda's is now into tapestries made from rags and haute couture using natural fabrics such as loofah, piña, and abaca. FYC.

Natalaw *(ISN)* also **Fangawur** *(KAL)*. Coward.

Nemnem *(KAN)*. Clifford Nobes, an Episcopal missionary in the Cordillera before World War II described nemnem as *"thought, idea, will, intention, mind, plan, purpose, and brain."*
See also: Ugali.

New Baguio Theater. One of the three theaters owned by Antonio 'Tonying' Hipolito Geneta of La Union and Bulacan. The other two were Embassy Theater in Pureza and Empire Theater in Mandaluyong. Tonying was acknowledged as the King of Ukay-ukay (second-hand clothes which used to originate mostly from the US via Manila after World War II). In its first decades, New Baguio Theater at the end of T. Alonzo Street, Baguio City, was a respectable movie house at the outskirts of the central business district. In the 1970s, it began showing double reruns of mostly the action star FPJ and other Filipino stars, and in the 1980s, soft-porn movies. People would endure the bedbugs on the seats to wait for the end of the movies to catch the often hard porn footage taken out by the government censors. It was defunct even before the 1990 earthquake. FYC.
See also: Baguio Cine; Gingined; Pines Theater; Plaza Theater; Ukay-ukay.

Ngabis *(KAN)*. Leaving one's house or place, usually before dawn for work or for any other very important matters to attend to. Nangabis is the past tense of ngabis while mangabis means to ngabis – e.g. *"Mangabis kami si bigat ay sumaa ed ili. [We'll pack our things very early tomorrow to get to our hometown]."* NEP.

Ngadngad *(IBA)*. Reddened eyes.

Ngaful *(IBA)*. Puppy.

Ngafus *(IBA)* also **Ngepos.** Last flicker of light or the burning end of a stick or coal.

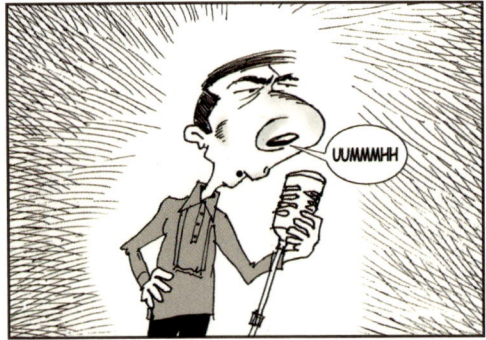

Ngak and other Kankanaey noise sounds *(KAN)*. Ngak means to screech or shriek. Ngakngak means to howl like a dog. Ngalutungut means to murmur or grumble. Ngang means to snarl or growl. Ngangak means to cry or weep. Ngangang means to pronounce incomprehensibly. Nganget means to scold or rebuke. Ngasngas means to crunch. Ngek means to grunt like a hungry pig. Ngekngek means to rattle or clatter. Ngeng means to hum noisily. Ngengeng means to talk through your nose or talk when you have colds. Ngiak means to ngangak noisily. Ngik means to ngek like piglets. Ngikngik means to chirp or squeak. Ngokngok is for a pack of dogs ngakngaking together. Ngongok means to ngek generically. Nongnong is to quietly observe all these. FYC.
See also: Ngaful; Nganga; Ngangak.

Ngalngal *(ILO)*. Lit. Masticate. A recent popular term for moma mostly among Ibalois. The Ibaloi have already taken on betel nut chewing as much as the Ifugaos, Kalingas and those from Mountain Province. JST.
See also: Moma.

Nga-nga *(IBA)*. Primarily refers to a baby. When the old speak of the younger people, they refer to the young as nga-nga. When old people behave like a child, as in senility, they are referred to as nga-nga. (Ballard, 2011, p. 317) The word is onomatopoeic with a baby's cry. SKW.

Ngangak *(BON)*. Dumb.
See also: Ngak and other Kankanaey noise sounds.

Ngantoy? *(IBA)* also **Ngentoy?.** A one word sentence that is used to ask what someone's problem is. What's the matter? If used at the beginning of a question, it asks the reason for something or some action or situation. Why...? (Ballard 2011, 317) SKW.

Ngilin *(IBA)*. ⁽¹⁾ These are non-working days following a burial, observed by the whole community out of respect for the deceased. Or, non-working days observed by a couple following their marriage. Special ngilin are declared by the elders of the community. Ngilin are also celebrated by work gangs in the mines. During ngilin, people are especially alert for omens.
⁽²⁾ **Ngilin** or **Lawa** *(KAN)*. Taboo. Most rituals have taboos attached, and failure to observe them is traditionally believed to bring misfortune, such as unhappiness to a couple that doesn't observe wedding taboos. Ngidinen also forbids the use of a ritual object for ordinary use, such as a blanket restricted for use at a tayaw (traditional Igorot dance).
⁽³⁾ *(IBA)*. The traditional wedding ritual is also called ngilin. Details of the ritual vary from locality to locality. One version holds the wedding feast in the evening. A pig is butchered and rice wine is drunk. Ba'diw (chants) are recited as advice for the couple, then there is the sekep (the entry of the groom into the bride's family house) for more advising. Historically, the new couple would not leave the house until the fifth day, when an elder calls them to wash their faces. They can then go to the fields to work. They are then a married couple. It is at the ngilin, if not before, that the tonton (tracing of lineages) takes place to be certain that the bride and groom are not related. (Ballard, 2011, p. 321) SKW.
See also: Amolo; Asbayat; Bayas; Kaon ya Teteg; Sichot.

Nginin *(KAN)*. *"Evil spirits inhabiting caves, harmful to pregnant women or setting hens."* (Scott 2011, 152).
See also: Alan; Ampasit; Banig; Bengao; Carangat; Darupaypay; Ibwa; Paniaw; Pasang; Tinguian Spirits.

Nikimalika *(BON)*. *"Bontoc expression among older people for describing those who went on early journeys to [Malika]."* (Afable, 2004, p. 446). The biggest of the fairs in America, the 1904 St. Louis World Fair, brought 1,000 Filipinos to Missouri of which over a hundred were Igorots. The Igorot Village with its dog feast was the fair's blockbuster. According to Afable, over 200 more Bontoc Igorots went nikimalika from 1905 to 1913. That these Igorots demanded to be paid and were paid (except for Hunt's wards) made them the first OFW (Overseas Filipino Workers). FYC.
See also: Dog-eating; Hunt, Truman; Nikimalika; Timicheg.

Niyek *(IBA)* also **Liyek** *(KAN)*, **Miyek** *(BON)*. A brown, winged termite-like insect that swarm at night from February to May (Ballard 2011, 311). These insects (ephemera) die the next day, leaving behind their wings. When fried, they make good pulutan. SKW.
See also: Abu-os; Asocena; Babate.

No wada asok, wada watwat *(KAN)*. Lit. If there's smoke, there's meat. In Igorot communities, a never-ending column of smoke means a traditional festivity or an important occasion. It is also a form of invitation for the community members to go to the party. These days, some Igorots have become wiser: they use a blowtorch to char a butchered pig to lessen the smoke signal. NEP.

See also: Igorot; Watwat.

NPA Plant. A month after the Martial Law Plant came out in the news in 1992, this plant also surfaced in the news and was said to have come from Pinukpuk, Kalinga. Similar to the Martial Law plant, the NPA (New People's Army) plant also looks like a greener and smaller sayote and can also strangle other plants. It was called the NPA plant because the military had a hard time eradicating the NPA guerrillas in the area where this plant thrived. FYC.

See also: Martial Law Plant; Sayote.

Num-a *(KAN)*. Vegetable farm among Benguet-Kankanaeys where potatoes, cabbage, carrots and the like are grown for market. It is the basic production facility in vegetable growing. Farms may be owned and operated by a single individual, or a financier whose workers are called 'supplies.' A num-a can be a holding of any size from a fraction of a hectare to several hundred hectares. During the early times, the process of acquiring a num-a was through voluntary labor among the early settlers in the community. The wider an individual has toiled, the bigger his share of the land. Nowadays, a farmer is entitled a num-a through inheritance or procurement. CCA.

See also: Buguias Patatas; Sayote.

Nya ngay, pards?. The 'Watsup?' greeting. A warm, friendly opening gambit into a casual conversation. It is the Cordilleran equivalent of the Filipino 'Kamusta?' FYC.

See also: Yes Ngarrud!

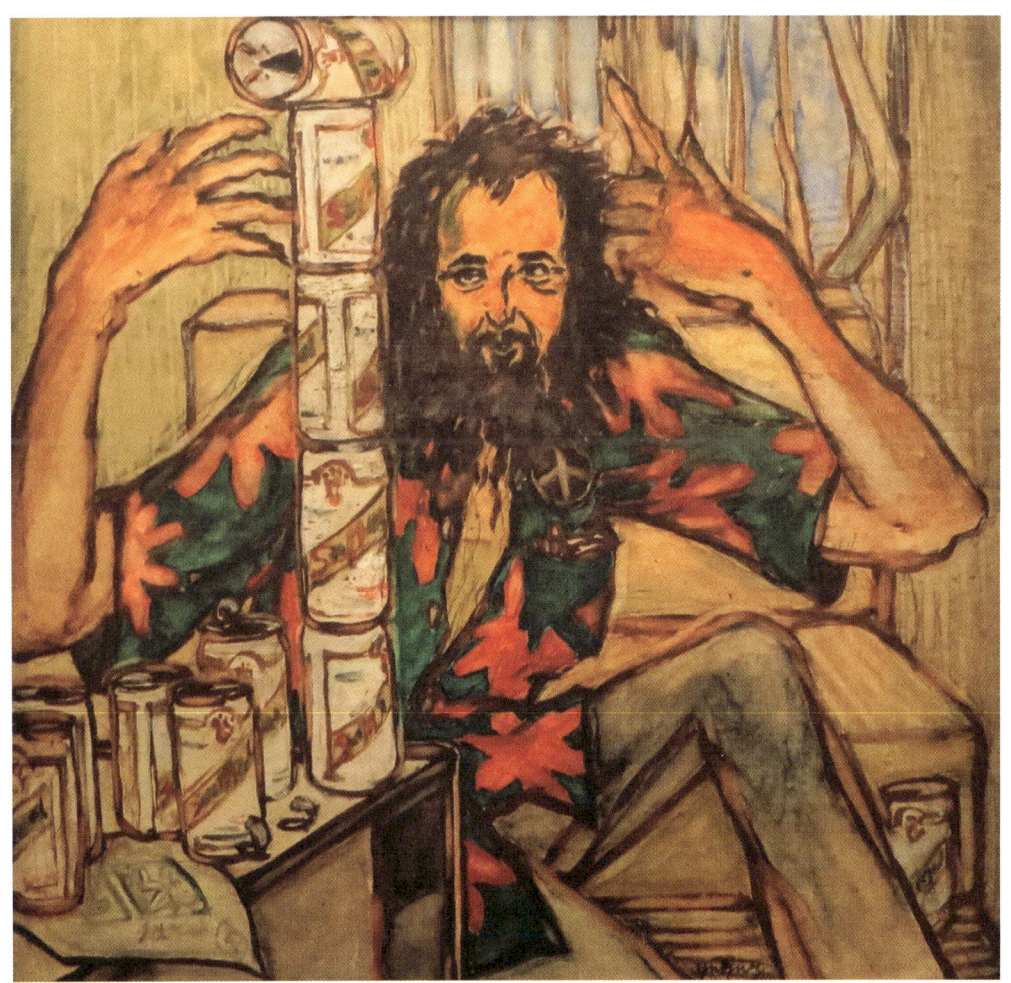

Portrait of Pepito Bosch by Sonny Yñiguez.

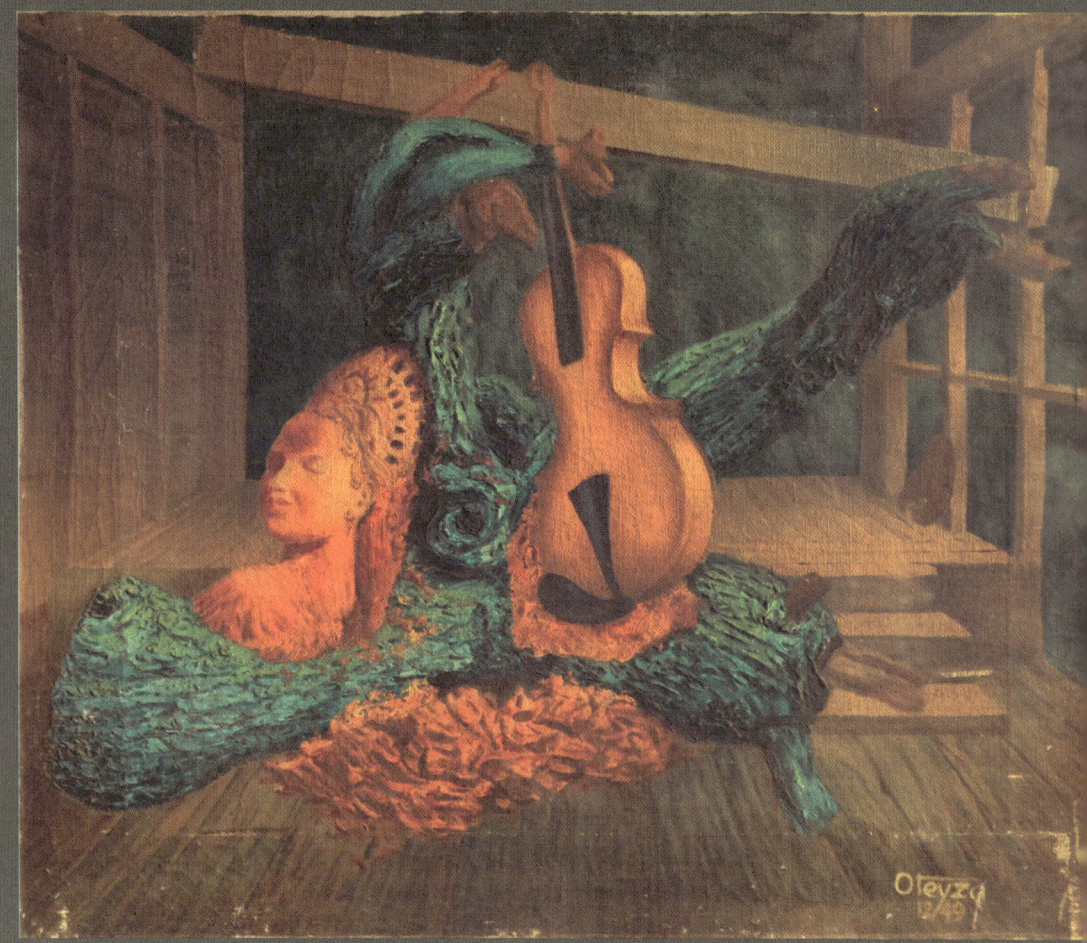
Untitled, Victor Oteyza, oil on canvas, 1949.

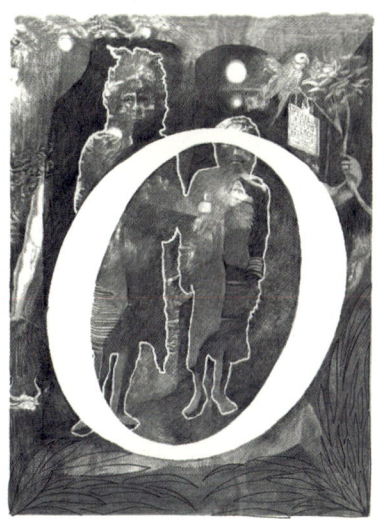

Ob-ob *(KAN)*. Lit. Spring or spring pool. Ceremony to increase the water in the spring.

Ob-obbo *(KAN)* also **Og-ogfo** *(BON)*. Lit. Cooperation. (1) Similar to the Filipino 'bayanihan' or cooperation, it is a practice in farming communities where help is extended in planting or harvesting mountain or terrain rice. Those who performed the ob-obbo are either given two to three bundles of rice each as badang (help) after the planting or called an alagey (standing), after the harvesting. FYC.
(2) The Igorot value of helping and sharing work.
See also: Adoyon; Baddang; Kamal; Tambo; To-ned.

Ochichi *(BON)*. Hind legs of animals.

Og-okhod *(BON)*. Story, storytelling, or narrative.

Ohayami. Bus line plying the Baguio-Ifugao route. It is the Ifugao Imayaho (the owner's family name) reversed to sound Japanese.

Okab *(BON)*. Small basket for collecting grasshoppers. The bigger basket is called owas.

Okat! *(BON)*. Gesundheit! Bless you!
See also: Banan.

Old Pagoda. A curio shop on Session Road run by Mrs Chan (we only knew her by that name), a Chinese fortune-teller with a strong Mandarin accent. She would sell you anything from antique Ming dynasty porcelain jars to teak abacus calculators to Japanese bayonets. But the greatest treasure you could walk away with would be knowing how your life would move henceforth or her metaphors of your character (eg. *"you are the happy-go-lucky crane flying over the fat content chickens – with the butcher sharpening his knife."*) KT.

Ongakanak *(BON)*. Lit. I am a serial liar.

Ong-ong *(KAL)*. Necklace of agate beads and later, of any multi-colored beads. In Kalinga, the new plastic multi-colored beads worn during traditional festivities are made of melted plastic spoons and forks from popular fast food chains like McDonald's and Jollibee's.
See also: Apang; Bungol; Dalanasip; Fukas.

O-o *(KAN)*. Ritual in which sacrificial meat is shared among the rich.
See also: Buaya Economic Classes; Watwat.

O-O. Double O. Short for 'Old Orchestra' as it was part of the orchestra of a theater that went out of business in the 1980s. It was revived as a nightclub in the 1990s and in the middle part of 2000 became the Baguio Country Sounds (BCS), the biggest country western club in Baguio. O-O the nightclub has since been relegated to a smaller space on the left of BCS. FYC.
See also: Chaparral; La Casita.

O-od. The name for the outlet of Sagada's underground river.

Oo(h) *(IFU)*. To suck on something like sugarcane stalk.

Oppak *(BON)*. Outer husk of sugarcane.

Oppas *(KAL)*. Healing ritual.

Otak *(IFU)*. A large knife, almost always carried by the Ifugaos. It is used in war or in work; commonly called throughout the Philippines as 'bolo' in both English and Spanish. (Barton, Ifugao Law).

Otek *(IBA)*. (1) Small.
(2) *(IBA/KAN)*. A small pig.
(3) Name of a street in central Baguio.
(4) *(ILO)*. Brain.

Oteyza, Victor. (1913-1979). A Baguio-born, self-taught artist who is among the pioneers of Philippine Modern Art. Migrating to Manila after World War II, Vic joined the Philippine Art Gallery (PAG) Artists who dabbled in modern abstract paintings. He was the only Baguio boy amongst the 13 modernists barkada like H. Ocampo, V. Edades, R. Tabuena and Cesar Legaspi (who acknowledged Vic convinced him to become a painter). As a breadwinner, he was not prolific like his peers – who respected him as a "painters' painter." He joined an advertising firm and created radio soap operas like *Ilaw ng Tahanan* and *Gulong ng Palad*. (He had written plays while studying engineering in UP). His most successful series was *Tawag ng Tanghalan* the equivalent of *American Idol* in the 50s. He emigrated to Washington D.C., then tried to go back to painting until he was too weak and died of emphysema in 1979. His last solo show in Manila was at Galerie Bleu in 1978. His paintings were included in the Homage to the 13 Moderns at the Metropolitan Museum of Manila. His siblings honored him by building the Victor Oteyza Community Art Space (VOCAS) in Baguio to promote art of the Cordilleras. KT.

Ovodan *(IBA)*. A sharpening stone.

Owik *(IBA)*. The ceremonial way of killing a pig: thrusting a slightly pointed stick into the side of the pig and thence into the heart (but ideally not through it). Also, the instrument used, esp. made of guava wood. When they owik a pig, it should face the house where the ritual takes place and its head should point towards the rising sun or upstream or wherever the mambunong says. (Ballard 2011, 342) SKW.

See also: Abang ni keshel; Mambunong; Peshit.

Oyok *(IBA)*. To stoop, to be meek or submissive, or to yield.

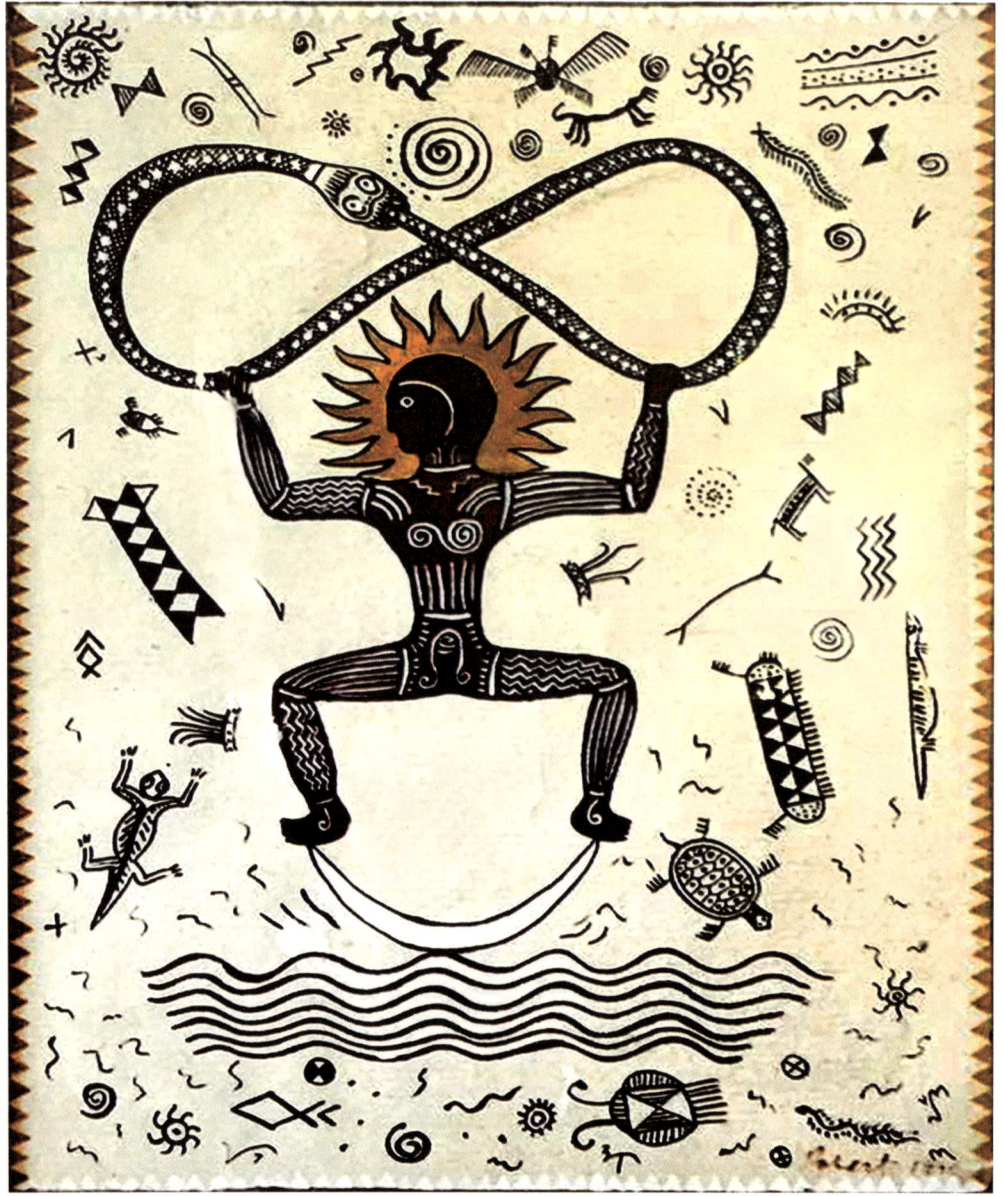

Artwork by Roberto Villanueva, 1991.

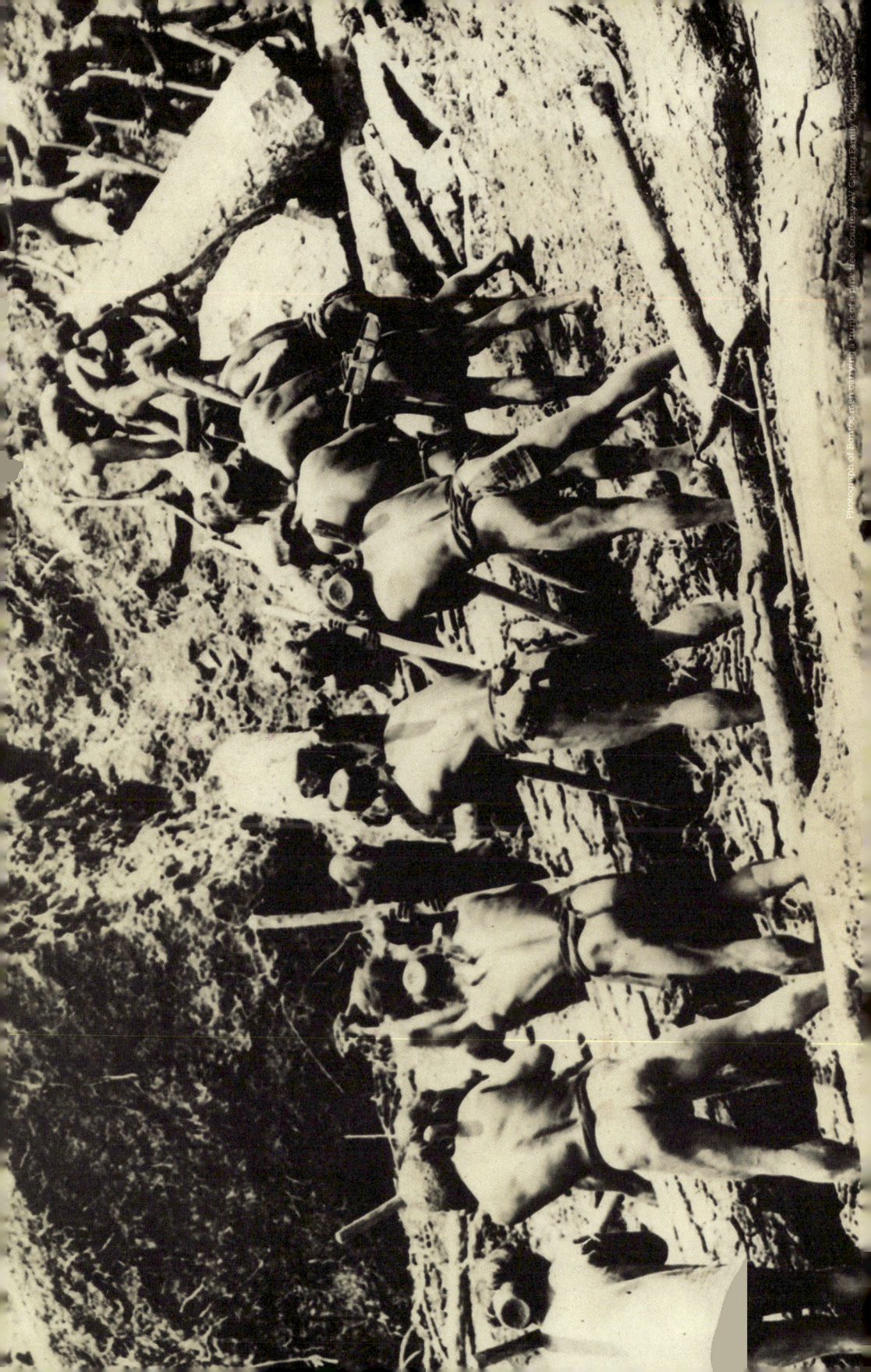

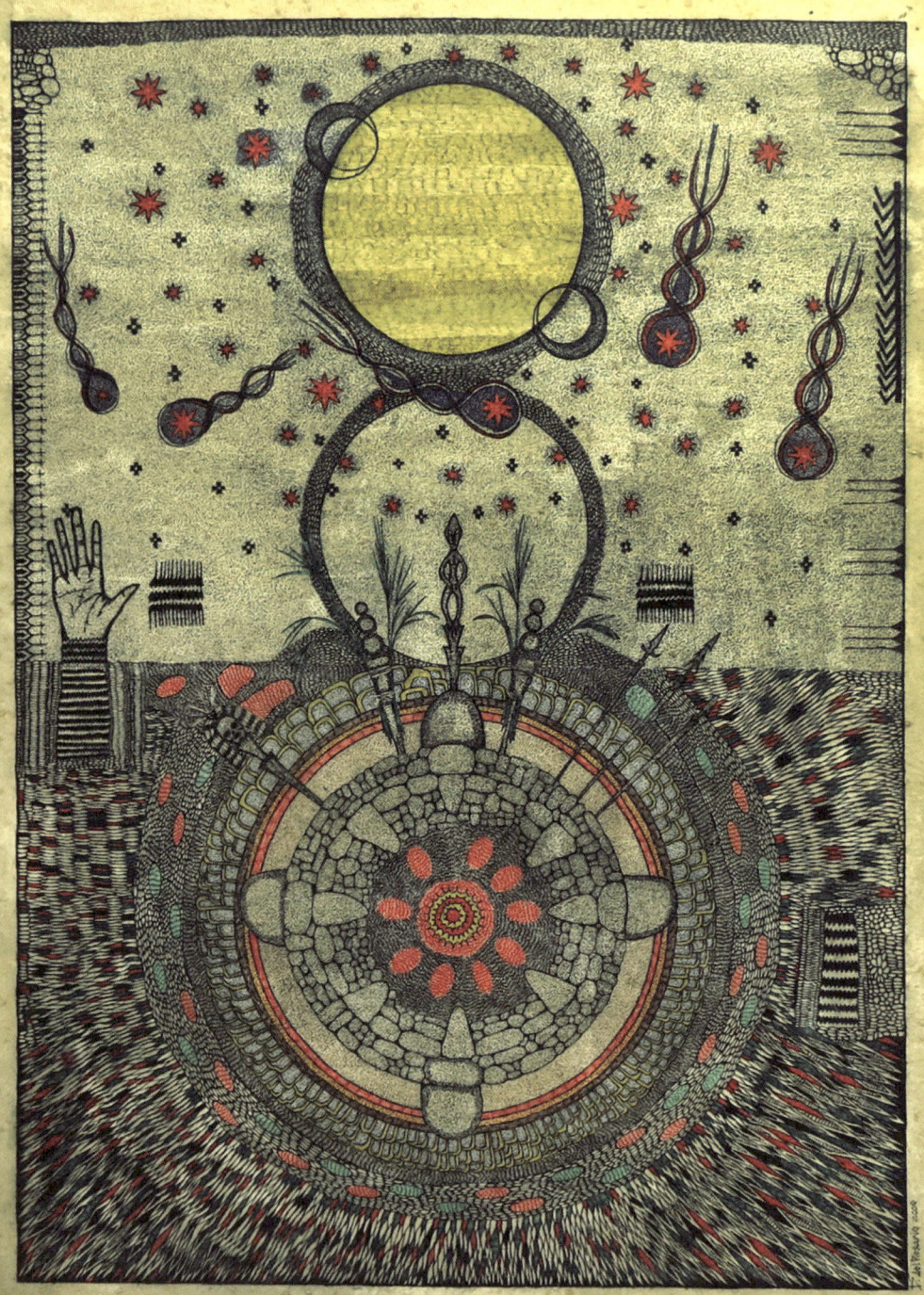

Artwork by Demi del Rosario., 2000.

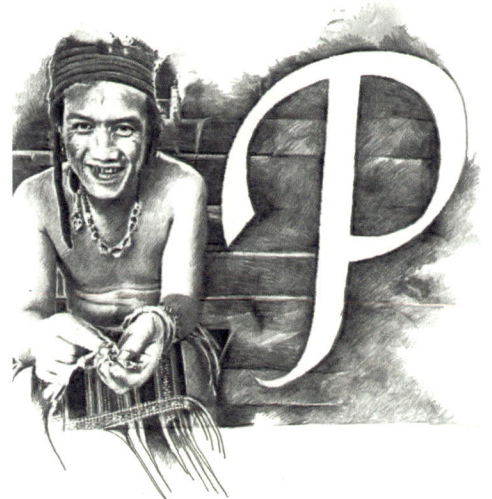
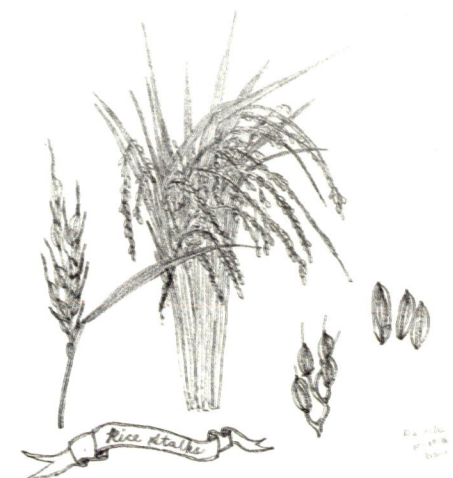

Pa'chas *(KAL)*. Symmetrical.

Padang *(IFU)*. Silver anklets.
See also: Bitog.

Padpadaya *(KAN)*. *"A kind of bewitching in which a lover in one village calls to the ab-abiik of a desired lover in another, causing his sickness."* (Scott 2011, 153).
See also: Ab-abiik; Ayag; Ayak; Hidit; Pasang; Pattaliat.

Paganu *(KAN)*. A person who practices the traditional rituals of appeasing ancestral and natural spirits. Borrowed from the English word, 'pagan.' DOS.
See also: Ethnographic Mapping; Namati.

Page *(IFU)*. Indigenized from the Ilocano pagay (rice), it refers to rice from rice terraces to differentiate it from bakan (rice from swidden fields). FYC.
See also: Tinawon.

Pahang di Munhab-i *(IFU)*. An Ifugao ritual performed either twice or thrice during pregnancy. Still being practiced now, this one-evening family affair is done inside the home, facilitated by a mumbaki. A chicken or pig is sacrificed, depending on what is available. Prayers are offered for the well-being of both mother and baby, especially during birthing. RBB.
See also: Mumbaki.

Pakkaw *(ISN)*. (1) Raiding boast similar to Kalinga's palpaliwat. It means 'to shout' or to extol exploits in headhunting while riding the spirit of Anglabbang.
(2) To curse in shouting so that the object of the curse may eventually hear it. FYC.
See also: Palpaliwat; Sagawsaw; Salopey; Say-am.

Palpaliwat *(KAL)*. Lit. Shouting tune. Raiding boast.
See also: Pakkaw; Say-am; Ullalim.

Palutput *(IFU)*. Spattering defecation.

Panagbenga *(KAN)*. The non-traditional annual flower festival of Baguio City. Created to spike tourist arrivals in the dead period between the two peak seasons of December and Holy Week, Panagbenga later became bigger than the two peak seasons. It was one of the first secular festivals in the country and became a model for other local festivals in almost every town and city in the country. One of the top five festivals in the country in terms of visitors, Panagbenga has come to mean the season for the budding of flowers although it really refers to the stage of conception of rice in the agricultural cycle. Alternatively, it also refers to a dance in the headhunting rituals of Kabayan, Benguet. FYC.
See also: Tinawon; To-ned.

Panamdamman *(ISN)*. A remembrance, souvenir, or keepsake.

Pangat *(KAL)*. (1) Traditionally refers to prominent citizens like famous head-takers whose leadership comes from their recognized authority in the village. Recently, this form of recognition has also been bestowed upon prominent elders as long as public respect is earned. It can also be inherited by the eldest son or daughter depending on communal acceptance. FYC.
(2) Also refers to a peace pact holder.
See also: Buaya Economic Classes.

Panglao *(ISN)*. A headdress made from the skull of the scarlet hornbill attached to a wicker

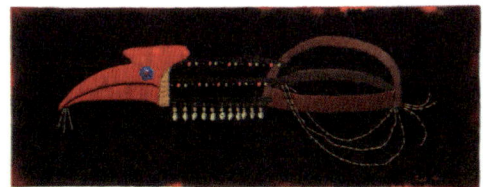

Artwork by Tioan Medrano, 2014.

headband. Wearing it indicates that one has taken the head of an enemy. FYC.

See also: Akipur; Apang; Bayoyok; Duwao; Kulatod.

Paniaw *(KAL)*. Spirits that dwell in stagnant green ponds. They like to bring pregnant women and small children to their underwater abode.

See also: Alan; Ampasit; Bengao; Darupaypay; Ibwa; Nginin; Pasang; Tinguian Spirits.

Pansejew *(IBA/KAN)*. Gold panning. The most common mining method among Igorots. It was said to have been practiced vigorously in the 16th Century. Sand from the rivers was placed in a sadjewan (rectangular pan) and then shaken, allowing the gold dust to settle at the bottom. Gold was cleaned, wrapped in cloth and placed over flames to be molded into a coin and bartered. Sejo means to pan gold. Nansayo is panned gold. FYC.

See also: Dangtey; Dayasan; Kaman gangi; Saga-ok; Tonglo; Usok.

Papa *(KAN)*. Lit. *"Whipping a chicken to death. Also, the fifth day of the wedding season, when local relatives are invited to eat."* (Scott 2011, 153).

See also: Pinikpikan.

Papanam? *(ILO)*. Lit. Where are you going? A universal greeting in the Cordillera especially to those waiting by the road or passing each other by while in a hurry, like ants.

See also: Umayam?

Papatayan *(ISN)*. The exact spot on the pig through which the heart is pierced. Not to be confused with Patpatayan. FYC.

See also: Papattay.

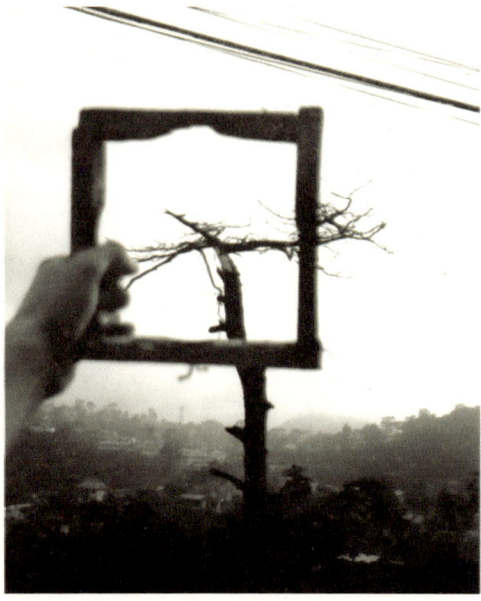

Photograph of *Patpatayan*. Photograph by Kawayan de Guia.

Papattay *(BON)* also **Patpatayan** *(KAN)*. It is the most sacred place in Igorot spirituality as it is where direct communication with Kabunian or Lumawig is achieved. It encompasses a whole hill or mountain with a dead tree (likely struck by lightning) in its midst. The tree itself may be called the Papattay. It is customary not to build houses near it or to bring fish. These bear an odor unnatural to the mountain. In the Papattay, only prayers for protection or blessings are sought, matters that are not man-made, and matters that greatly involve the whole community, i.e. more rain or bountiful harvests and protection against natural disasters. It is not allowed to perform rituals or ask for prayers regarding sickness in the Papattay as these are caused by anitos, meaning, these are earthly matters. There are also specific sacred sites for dealing with spirits that cause sickness (mostly near creeks and springs), ancestral spirits that cause grave illnesses (a tiny house or structure is built on the ground, usually where the clan settlement is located), or to pray for safe childbirth (in certain areas on mountain slopes). RAC.

Paper:
Cogon grass paper

Cogon grass paper's very beginnings go back to Sagada, 1977 in the person of one Julia White of Albuquerque, New Mexico. She appeared one day in Tiaong, Quezon, having just come from Sagada. She was in transit, killing a month, returning home for her brother's wedding. Then learning shiatsu in Japan and teaching English in Taiwan. In her backpack was a five-page purple repro of a handwritten instructional "How to Make Paper from Weeds". It was meant as a preschool activity and it was very basic. All that month, Julia and I made paper, using the book as our guide. By the time she left, we had the rudiments in action, with very poor samples from the farm's backyard weeds.

Basically, one somehow breaks down the weeds into pulp, disperses the pulp in a tub of water, and draws a screen stretched on a frame through the slurry, drawing out a layer of pulp which when dried turns into a sheet of paper that may be peeled free from the screen. The pulp was the key: different plant materials produced unlike pulps and papers. On my own, I would go on to try other weeds, corn and coconut husks, cannabis stalks, orange peel, etc., boiling them in a little caustic soda (lye from the hardware), washing and beating them with a piece of wood on a chopping board. For the hardy banana stalks (saba), I shifted to an antique stone grinder that was lying around on the farm. The resulting banana papers were the most striking; they had the makings of onion skin. I carried my samples to Manila. Pepito Bosch was always the first to see them.

Visiting Baguio the following year, Santi Bose was the first to call me a 'papermaker,' and my fate was locked. Later, I would set up shop in Sagada, first in Maryhurst in Bangaan, then at Ben and Sol Longid's in town. I worked with garami (stalks of mountain rice), pine bark, and maguey. All made beautiful papers. Two Kankaney boys helped me turn the plant material into pulp.

A local elder dropped by once and asked, *"Can I make a living from that?"* Not yet, I admitted. *"Can I make rolling paper?"* he followed, and I noticed he was smoking tobacco with a torn-off piece of newspaper.

Above all, while in Bangaan, I would discover how to transfer wet paper from a mosquito screen to the bare pinewood walls of Maryhurst, by way of an intermediate, finer screen (a silkscreen). I held workshops at St Joe's for the orphans and at St. Mary's. The school's submissions of handmade paper at the science fair in Bontoc that year would win prizes, I heard. Nida Dumsang came up from Baguio to represent Mike Parsons and Duntog Foundation. Mrs. Killip also dropped by.

She asked whether I could make toilet paper. *"Two rolls a day when all the family is home!"* I demurred. It was too much work, I said, for her intentions.

Back in Baguio, I next set up at km. 6 Asin Road, at Briccio Santos' place near the old Jesuit retreat house. There I would make my first papers from cogon grass (Imperata cylindrica) that covered the mountain side, and I learned to ply papers together into thicker sheets. My helper was a mute Kalinga teenager. One day, Peachy Prieto brought a group of deaf-mute children for a workshop. Their joy at it was heat-warming.

In 1980, Adelaida Lim had a paper tub waiting for me at their home, and I would make paper there for a spell, mostly in collaboration with Santi Bose who was testing his hand at etchings, woodcuts, and rubber cuts, which I would then print on my papers on Laida's etching press.

After a stint in Bacolod for an outreach with Roberto Villanueva and Jaime de Guzman organized by Maring Llamado, and then at Kido Kalaw's in Puerto Galera, I returned to Tiaong in 1983 to set up the Tiaong Paper Workshop. That was after Ninoy Aquino's assassination. In Tiaong, we now boil cogon grass, 25 kilos at a time, with a kilo of lye. We beat our pulp with mortar and pestle (the kind for pounding rice). Our tubs are open-top wooden boxes on legs lined with tarp stapled on and we dry our papers on marine plywood boards that hang from hooks in a wood fire heated room when the sun is absent. The largest cogon paper we have ever made measured 30 by 75 inches.

I lost touch with Julia White soon after she left in 1977, and realized that she knows nothing of these paper things that she has wrought.LS.

Paracelis. (1) The border town of Mountain Province that is also where the Gaddang – who prefer to be identified as Baliwon and Balangao – communities are settled. It is the farthest municipality from Bontoc, the provincial capital.
(2) (See Easter Weaving Room).

Parsons, Mike. Son of the famous guerrilla leader 'Chick' Parsons, Mike Parsons decided to stay and live in Baguio City. He started his artistic career as a filmmaker in the 1960s with such black-and-white experimental films as *The Wall* and *Las Munecas*. He also acted in noir films like Eddie Romero's 1966 film, *Passionate Strangers*. He eventually ventured into papermaking and was making paper in Baguio and in Kabayan. FYC.
See also: Paper; Monastery.

Parti *(ILO)*. Lit. Butcher. This means (and is also pronounced the same as) 'party.' In the highlands, when one says they are going to a parti, it could mean butchering pigs and inviting the whole community (especially when in the rural areas). JST.

Pasang *(KAN)*. (1) A fertility ritual. It is believed that the temporary infertility of a partner occurs when he or she attracts and is married by a tumungaw (malevolent spirit).
(2) A sickness caused by spirits that possess the power to inflict sterility and drowsiness. There are two types of pasang: pasang di tumungaw (underworld spirit) and pasang di Kabunian (skyworld spirit). Pasang di tumungaw occurs when symptoms show that the person is always sleepy even during daytime. If this happens, it is believed that the spirit of the person may have been taken by the tumungaw as a spouse. This is usually manifested in the dreams of the person, which may be about being in a wonderful relationship with a person he does not know. Chicken serves as the sacrificial animal for this ritual, but pigs may also be used if the case warrants it. For the pasang di Kabunian, the symptoms do not mean physical sickness but that the ability of a couple to bear children is affected. For example, a newlywed couple may not be blessed with a child even after quite some time trying it out. As a practice, a couple would often consult medical doctors but if a doctor cannot find anything wrong with either of them, the couple might then consult a mansib-ok. When a mansib-ok finds out the cause of the problem, he or she recommends that the couple carry out a bigger ritual in which the pasang (healing ritual) will be incorporated. NEP.
See also: Ab-abiik; Alan; Ayak; Bengao; Darupaypay; Hidit; Ibwa; Nginin; Padpadaya; Paniaw, Pattaliat; Pudung; Tiw-tiwong.

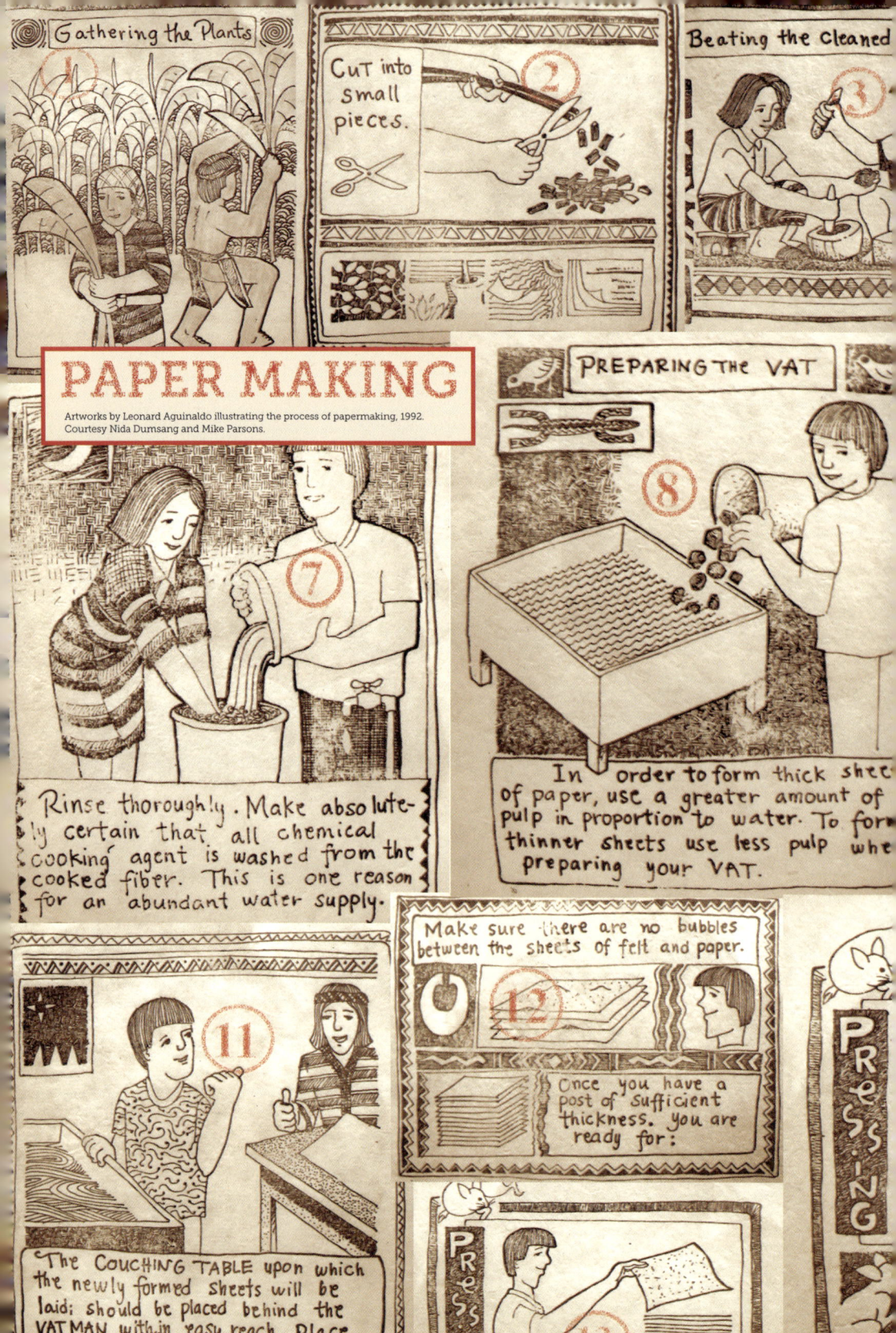

PAPER MAKING

Artworks by Leonard Aguinaldo illustrating the process of papermaking, 1992. Courtesy Nida Dumsang and Mike Parsons.

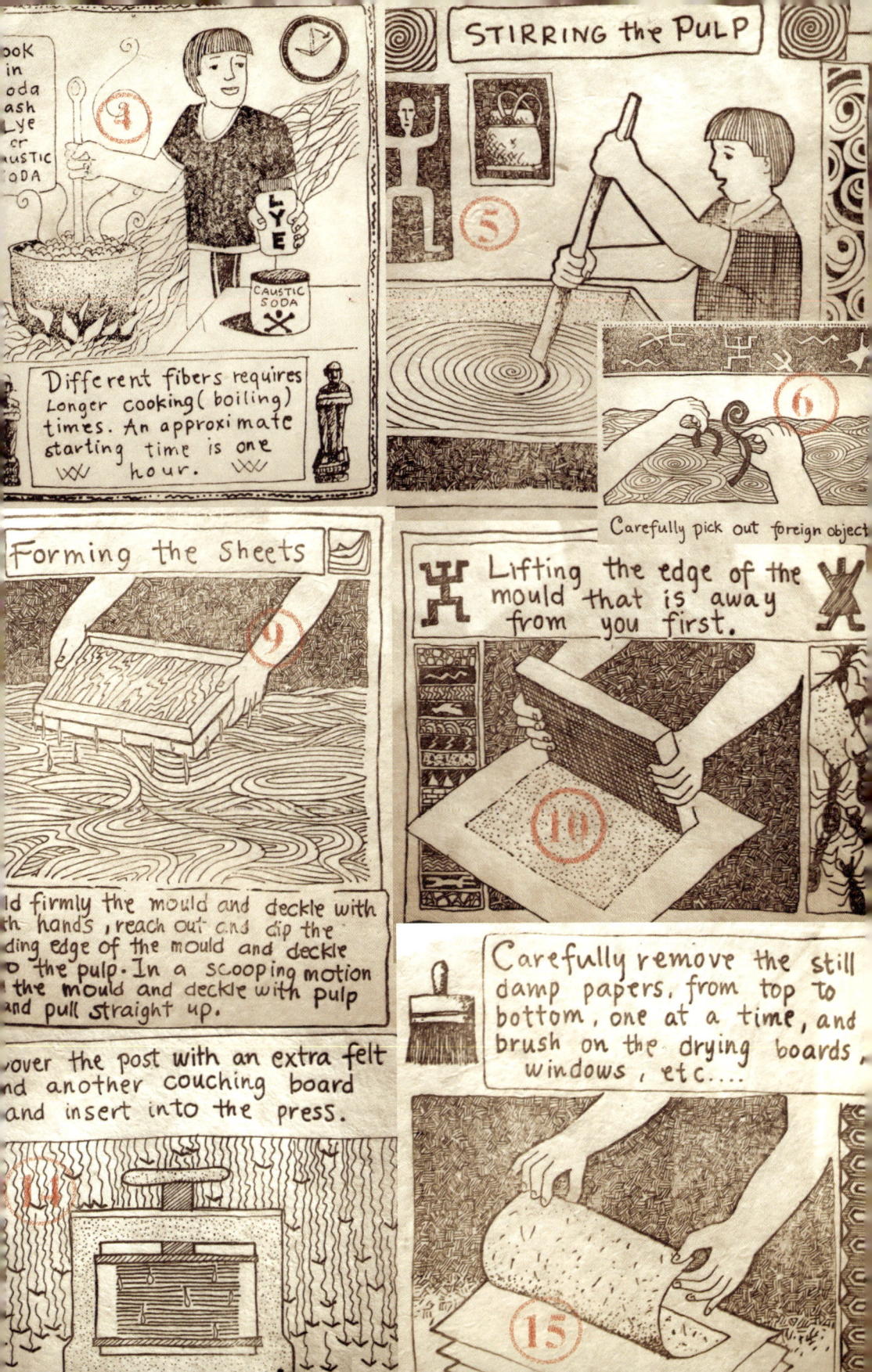

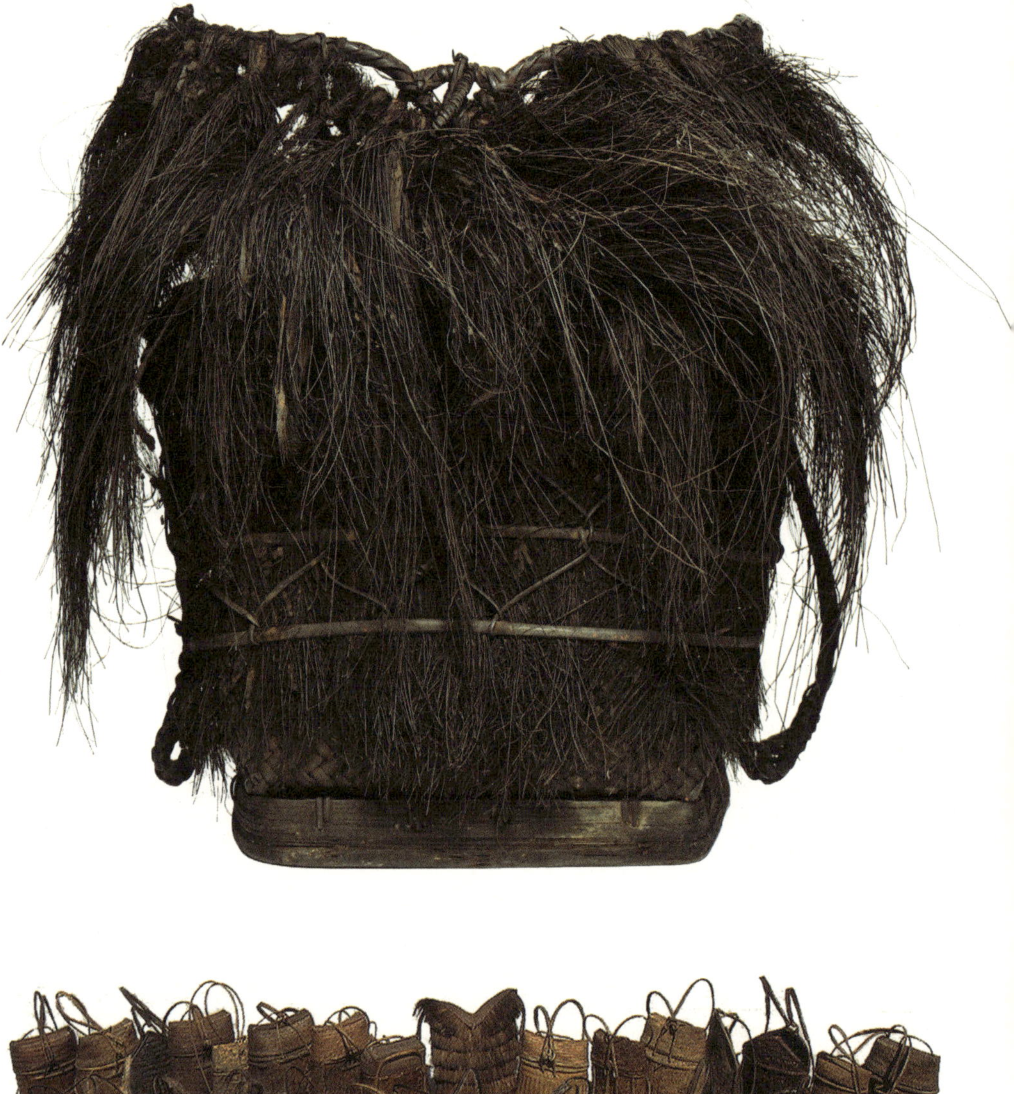

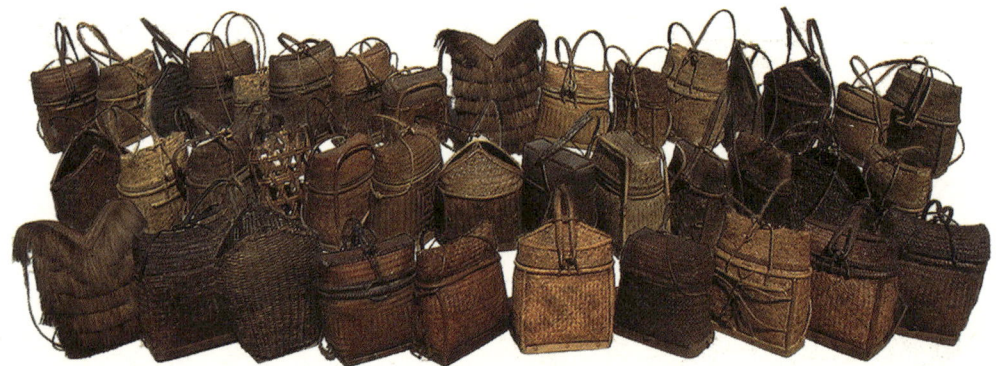

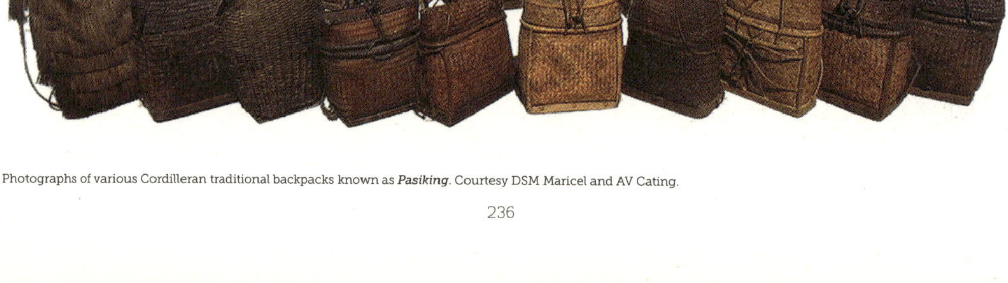

Photographs of various Cordilleran traditional backpacks known as *Pasiking*. Courtesy DSM Maricel and AV Cating.

Pasiking *(BON/KAN)* also **Sangi** *(BON)* **Lagpi** *(ITN)*, **Hagupit** *(IFU)*, **Bango** *(IFU)*. The traditional backpack of the Cordillerans. It is woven of rattan and can last for a very long time although the straps have to be occasionally repaired (which was not a problem when most people knew basic rattan weaving). It has many designs and each has its name. New versions of the pasiking are woven out of plastic strips and even wiring plastic salvaged from the mines. FYC/RAC.

Pasok *(KAN)*. "The ceremony in which scarecrows are fixed in the fields." (Scott 2011, 153).
See also: Bading; Faked.

Paterno Cave. In Ambongdolan, Tublay are two caves. One is the Bengaongao (echoing) Cave, a cave so spacious that the community there would sometimes hold their masses inside. The Japanese troops were said to have stayed there during the war. The other cave was named after Emilio Aguinaldo's Chief of Staff, Gen. Pedro Paterno, who stayed there while the revolutionary government chiefs were escaping from the Americans. Paterno Cave is similar to Alice's rabbit hole: a small hole serves as an entrance to chambers that get bigger every time you enter. FYC.

Patpatok *(KAN)*. Meat.
See also: Bingit; Watwat.

Pattaliat *(GAD)*. Rites in which something is offered to the spirits in exchange for the soul of a sick person without ritual segregation on the part of the victim (in the Cordilleras, sickness is believed to happen when the ab-abiik of a person strays or is taken from him or her), as compared to the Pangacau or rites in which the soul of the sick is ritually stolen from the spirits. FYC.
See also: Ab-abiik; Ayag; Ayak; Hidit; Kaduduwa; Padpadaya; Pasang; Pudung.

Patupat *(ILO/BON/KAN)*. Adopted from the lowlands, this is a delicacy in many Cordillera villages and is made of glutinous rice with coconut milk that is wrapped in banana leaves in the shape of a pyramid or tube before it is steamed. PAD.
See also: Sinabalu; Tufu.

Pawa *(IFU)*. Forbidden words among Ifugaos. Uttering these at night may induce the speaker to dream of them, and such dreams may bring bad omens or cause more harm. For example, apuy (fire) should be substituted with its nemesis, danum (water), or laah instead of puul (torching area), as a dream of a burning mountain means the rice will not mature. Use the less common word for carabao, 'dappug' instead of 'nuwang,' as dreaming of carabaos could give you arthritis when you grow old. Carabaos in dreams could also mean that rats will eat your rice when you grow lazy. Other omens of rats eating rice include a dream of weeding your rice, so replace paguey (growing rice) with gulun (spear rice) at night. Lastly use "lonah" instead of 'goday' for landslide, as a dream of landslides may mean not only crop failure but also that a family member may die soon.

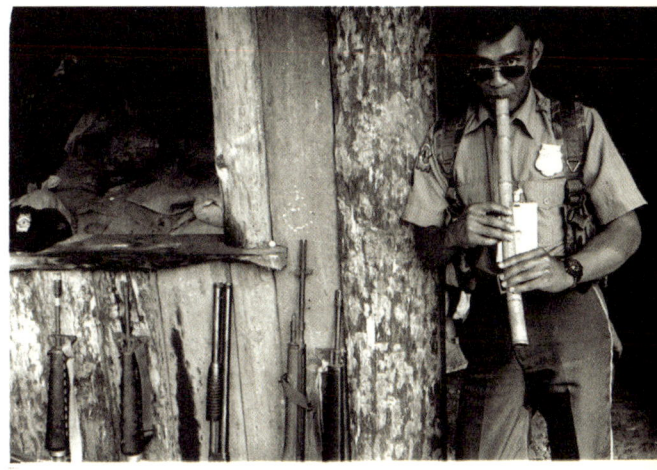

Photograph of one of the Peace Zones. Photograph by Ashley Jude.

Peace zone. Sagada, Mt. Province and Tomiangan, Tabuk, Kalinga were among the 11 Peace Zones established around the nation during the subsequent Aquino and Ramos administrations. The concept of the "peace zone" was proposed by the Social Democrats (SocDem) during the Cory Aquino Administration through the Coalition for Peace. A peace zone indicated the absence of both the New People's Army (NPA) and the Armed Forces of the Philippines (AFP) for they are not allowed to establish their headquarters or their presence in the zone. Only police officers, the Citizen Armed Forces Geographical Unit (CAFGU) – the local armed forces, and the Cordillera People's Liberation Army (CPLA) are allowed to be positioned in the peace zone. Sagada is the only successful Peace Zone in the country, especially as it has radically turned into one of the foremost tourist destinations in the country. The peace zone of Tabuk was called the "Zone of Life" as it became a haven for members of warring tribes within the province. DOS.

See also: Asin, Republic of; Balweg brothers; Cellophil; Chico; Dulag; Macli-ing; Mt. Data; Vochong.

Penis ashtray. It is a popular souvenir item from Baguio since the 1960s. The wooden penis perched on an ashtray comes in many sizes. The origin may have been from Japanese farmers and carpenters before World War II, as there are similar souvenir items from the Shinto Kanamara Matsuri (Festival of the Steel Phallus) held at the Kanayama Shrine in Kawasaki, Japan every spring. FYC.

See also: Duggong ti Intsik; Man in the barrel.

Persimmon. There is a cause of contention as to who brought it to the Cordilleras. Afable in *Japanese Pioneers In The Northern Philippine Highlands*, says that it was brought by the Japanese farmers who worked on Kennon Road (Afable 2004), while Cheng & Bersamira in *The Ethnic Chinese in Baguio and in the Cordillera*, insists it was through Chinese farmers (Cheng and Bersamira 1997). Persimmon in the Cordilleras are now found mostly in Sagada and Bauko. The persimmon sold in Baguio as 'Sagada persimmon' actually comes from China. FYC.

See also: Gayunan.

Pes-ay *(KAN)*. The first harvest, which is usually done by the kadangyan. People will not harvest their rice until the kadangyans perform the pes-ay. Symbolically, it is the first cutting of the rice. A pig is butchered in the rice fields and then brought home to be cooked. On the way home, they pass by an elder's house and everyone brings etag there.

See also: Apoy; Buaya Economic Classes; Etag; Hagabi; Immuya-uy; Tinawon; To-ned.

Peshit *(IBA)*. A prestige feast celebrated by the wealthy. A great number of pigs are butchered in multiples of three, including other larger animals. People from far away villages are invited and the feast lasts many days. The peshit is sometimes celebrated multiple times, each one greater than the one before. Traditional culture endorses entrepreneurism and hard work as long as successful people also honor their ancestors and celebrate feasts for the benefit of their neighbors. Ritual feasting at one's level of capability is said to be rewarded by the ancestors with more success. (Ballard 2011, 374) SKW.

See also: Cañao; Kaon ya Teteg; Nantoltolo.

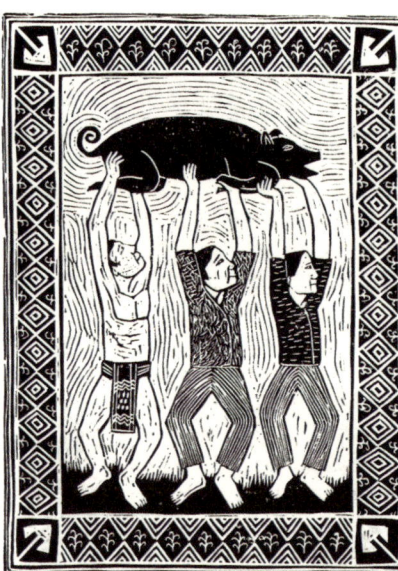
Artwork by Leonard Aguinaldo, 2013.

Pig. (1) A very important ritual animal all over the Cordillera Region. In Benguet and Ifugao, the black native pig called derrem (also tilem) is important for divination in any undertaking, from the opening of new mining tunnels to embarking on a political campaign. A good augury (boton) of the gall bladder and liver of the butchered pig would be auspicious. In Benguet, the town of Tublay is the traditional source of these black pigs. During election campaigns, some unscrupulous hog dealers would dye their pigs black to make them more expensive. Among the Bontocs, there are different terms for pig. The generic is fotog but there are also fatui (castrated male), laman (wild), and chakau (red haired). Pig swill is called tud-tud while its pen is called kongoan. Among the Tinguians, the pig is known by its Ilocano term, babuy. In Ifugao, it is also babuy but at night it is forbidden to use the word or else you will have a terrible dream. Instead of "babuy," use "allama" (crab) because dreaming of killing a pig means a child will be killed depending on the size of the pig. Same thing with killing a laman, which is also wild pig in Ifugao. Use its other term, bangul, instead. While hunting in the forest, when you spot a laman or bahil, don't call these terms but instead call them "manu" (chicken) because the bagawah (worker spirits) will inflict sickness on you.

(2) Name of one of the 25 Suyoc Igorots who went to the St. Louis World's Fair in 1904. Pig was 30 and married to Sendican, who also went to the fair. But he already had a mining claim back home so after the fair, Pig went back home to Suyoc and died in 1928. FYC.

See also: Cañao; Tilem.

Pikat *(ISN)*. The sap of the jackfruit that is used to catch birds.

Pikut *(ISN)*. An enchanted area in Conner, Apayao that covers a river and its surroundings. It is believed to be guarded by three spirits: an old man, an old woman, and a child. Sightings of huge animals that disappear in front of everyone are common experiences there. Fishing and the cutting of trees and bamboo are prohibited. Shouting and laughing are not allowed. Children never swim in its river. People can only pass by the place quietly to go to their fields. Those who have gone against these prohibitions get mysterious illnesses and can die. GAD.

See also: Ampasit; Lapat; Madmad.

Pilpilak-Taltalak *(KAN)*. Lit. Money-toy car.
(1) One characteristic of most Cordilleran languages is the repetition of word segments to intensify or emphasize that word. Hence, taltalaga is an intensified form of the Tagalog 'talaga' which means 'really' or 'very.' For example, when one wants to emphasize the size of something,

one would say, *"Nagdakkedakkel"* or *"Nagdakkel taltalaga!"* The repetition could be further repeated for further emphasis, as in *"Nagdakkedakkedakkel!"* Aside from repetition, one could also lengthen the enunciation of the first vowel of the root word: *"Nagdaaaaakkedakkel!"* When a Kankanaey appreciates your work, saying, *"Gawigawis taltalga [It's really very good],"* you can reply, *"Salasalamat"*; or, if you are overwhelmed with gratitude, *"Salasalasalamat."* JBC.

(2) Such words come to illustrate the Buguias way of talking, e.g. *"Bumulodak kod si pilpilak mo ta way ilakok si taltalak. [Could I borrow some money so I could buy a simple car]."* Among Buguiasians, the manner of repeating a particular syllable is a habit to emphasize the intensity of one's action – e.g. One says, *"man-ame-ames"* [Lit. take-a-bat-bath] after a tiring, sweaty day. The emphasis though in *"Bumulodak kod si pilpilak mo ta way ilakok si taltalak"* is made in a lighter tone so as to cover the fact that a big amount of money is involved. The lender then may say, *"Wat pig-piga di nabay-bay-an sin pil-pilak ko et ya"* [Lit. How little-little is left-left of the money-money I have]." CCA.

See also: Iya-iyaman.

Pinakpak *(KAN)*. Rice boiled with sliced camote that was once popular in western Mountain Province where rice was scarce. The camote acts as an extender. Once cooked, the camote is mashed with a bakkong (wooden ladle) to spread its sweetness and to make sure it is eaten and not pushed away from the plate. PAD.
See also: Camote.

Pinit *(KAN)* also **Oyokan** *(IBA)*. Wild berries.

Pingel *(IBA)*. A barangay in Baguio which got its name from where wild animals or livestock were made to engage in tupada (betting fights). Its early settlers were natives who owned vast tracts of pasturelands for cattle. Occasionally, for recreation, the animals were brought to fight in this area called pinget.

Pink Ponies

The Pink Ponies of Wright Park are a new and yet entirely unique attraction to the city of Baguio. But the ponies themselves have been present for a very long time. The first instances of the common use of horses in the Cordilleras can be traced back to the early 1700s. The Ibaloy originally used ponies for cattle herding, as status symbols, and in their rituals. The arrival of the American colonizers changed the Ibaloy relationship to land and cattle therefore changing their relationship with the ponies. Though horse paths were integrated in the development of Baguio City and surrounding areas, horses were mainly used by those that could afford them or by military and government officials.

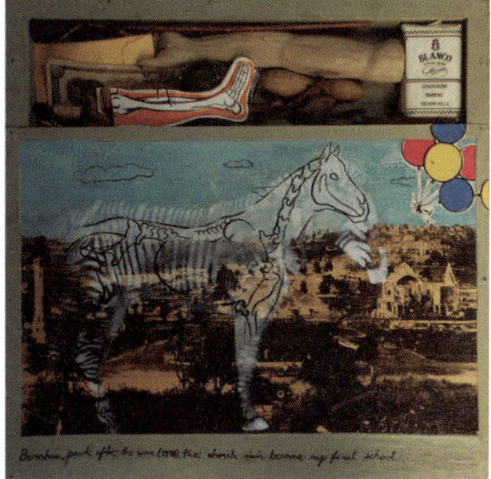

Artwork by Kawayan de Guia as part of the *Baguio Day Series*, 2008.

The recreational use of horses in Benguet began during the time of the American occupation. The status and use of horses by the people of the Cordillera gained popularity again after World War II with the introduction of cowboy culture. The people of Baguio took quickly to the style of cowboy hats and country and western music. It was at this point that Baguio residents began to rent their horses out to tourists while dressed as cowboys in Burnham Park. Today, most if not all the ponies within the city limits are used for purely recreational purposes. They can be found for rent in the areas of the Baguio Country Club, John Hay, Green Valley, Wright Park, and outside of Baguio, in La Trinidad. Eventually, the 'cowboys' that took care of the horses became known as the pony boys.

Riding horses (or at least having a photograph taken with one) has become a tradition for tourists visiting Baguio. There are many riders that come back year after year to visit the same pony boys and their horses. Some pony boys and their customers have even developed a bond that has lasted through generations.

The Pink Ponies have become a symbol of Wright Park and the Baguio tourist. The pony boys say that the pink color makes a horse more attractive to children and also makes it appear to be of a more gentle nature. The pink dye that is normally used is a cheap one that the pony boys call *"Number 13."* This dye requires constant reapplication and has a tendency to wash off easily. Due to this fact, pink horses in shower caps can be observed during rainy days in Wright Park.

The Pink Ponies are the most distinct example of the attention-catching devices that the pony boys use in order to get riders to choose their horse out of the multitude that are available, but they are not

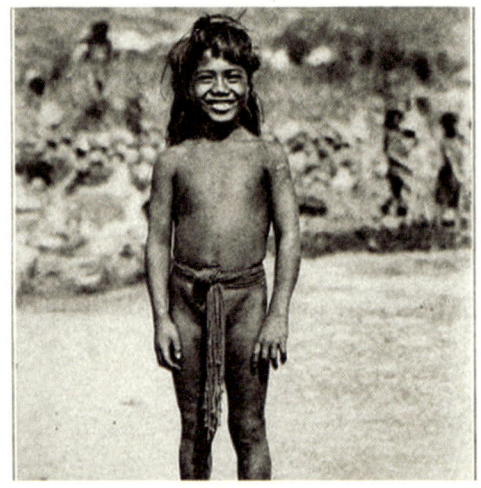 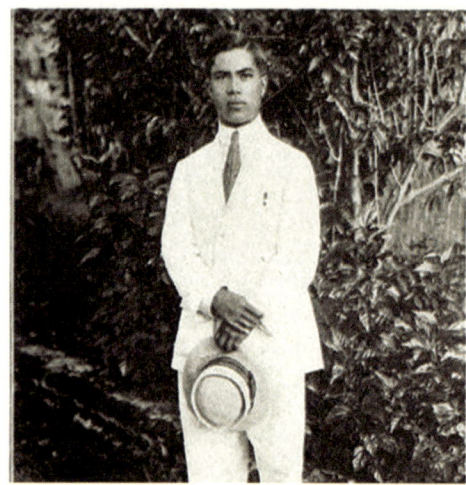

Photograph of *Pitapit* also known as Hilary Clapp. Photograph by Dean Worcester.

the only devices used. Aside from other bright colors like purple and orange, the pony boys also use more subtle colors like black or brown to add distinct markings to the horses, and in some cases change the color of the entire horse. Plastic markers in the shapes of stars, diamonds and hearts with neon names or images of cartoon characters and other elements of pop culture are also utilized to catch the eye of potential riders.

Pink Ponies have become quite a common sight and have gained popularity even in other riding parks. It is still quite bizarre though to come across a pink horse grazing in the fog by the side of the road. When one chances upon such a sight, one cannot help but wonder if the Pink Pony is actually a unicorn in disguise. That being said, I'm sure it's only a matter of time before the pony boys start producing horns for the white horses in Wright Park. FLP.
See also: AFRTN; Burnham Park; Cowboy; Horse-watering trough; John Hay, Camp.

Pinten *(KAN)*. Spirits of the dead ancestors who died in accidents or were killed during a war. DOS.
See also: Dentan.

Pinuneg. Blood sausage. Versions of blood sausages are considered a delicacy all over the world. Pinuneg is an anticipated portion of the food that is shared when a pig is slaughtered for a special occasion in the Cordillera. Making blood sausage is simple but requires many pairs of helping hands, which adds to the fun of getting it done. When the pig is slaughtered, collect the blood in a basin. Empty and wash the intestines thoroughly. Before the blood coagulates, mix in chopped ginger and onions, perhaps a chopped chili or two and a few scoops of diket (raw, glutinous rice). (Every cook will have his or her own variation of what to add to the blood.) Knot one end of the intestines and slowly pour in the blood mixture. Keep massaging the intestines so that the blood gets down to the other end. (No need to suppress giggles as you do this). When the intestines are full, knot the end carefully and gently add the coil of blood sausage into an already boiling cauldron of meat and broth. About thirty minutes later, fish out the coil of pinuneg, slice into bite-sized or three-inch portions and pass it around with a bowl of soy sauce and chili. PLP.
See also: Burnham Park; Cowboy; Etag; Food; Horse-watering trough; Inasin; Intum; John Hay, Camp; Safeng.

Pitapit. The native name of Hilary Clapp. He was made a poster boy by Dean Worcester for his book, using a before picture of a young Pit-a-pit with long hair and wanes (G-string) in Bontoc, and an after picture of him as a young doctor in Manila where he matriculated with the sponsorship of American missionary Rev. Walter Clapp, from whom he got his name. He became the District Health Officer of the old Mountain Province in the 1920s and became one of the first Igorot intelligentsia. He was appointed by the Japanese as the first highlander governor of Mountain Province, although some said he aided the Japanese resistance fighters. He died at the end of World War II.

Artwork by Matilda Glass.

His daughter Florence Clapp became a student activist, a leader of the group BIBAK, editor of the Gold Ore, and exponent of Igorotism. FYC.
See also: Cariño, Dr. Jose; Igorot; Luna, Joaquin; Mountain Province; Wanes.

Pitik *(KAN)*. The act of praying when drinking rice wine or any alcoholic beverage. Before drinking, a small amount of liquor is poured to the ground as offering to the unseen spirits who are among the people drinking. DOS.
See also: Apag; Basi; Bayas; Fuas; Iwa; Liblibayu.

Plastic fantastic. *"Repurposed plastic has been extracted from the waste stream"* and used by Igorots to make everyday objects such as tabayag (lime containers), baskets, pasiking, bolo handles, fish traps and beads for many decades now (McKay, forthcoming). The practice of making beads began with melting down old toothbrushes, but now makes use of a variety of other forms of waste, including discarded CD cases and plastic spoons and forks from Jollibee. Strands of plastic replica beads are on sale in Baguio City. Strung according to Kalinga traditional patterns, but used by other ethnic groups to denote Igorot identity. These beads replicate strands of glass and stone heirloom trade beads. The plastic beads recreate the distinctive bright colours of a set of beads made from stone, ceramic and glass used as a currency to exchange for goods and services during the colonial era (16th to 20th centuries). However, these new 'plastic' crafts are often dismissed as 'fakes' or examples of cultural decline. In 2012 Ruel Bimuyag, Kawayan de Guia, Padmapani Perez, and Deirdre McKay mounted the exhibition *Everyday Objects* in the Bencab Museum, which used the materiality of plastic to reveal the network of shifting relationships in which these contemporary, everyday objects are embedded. *"By juxtaposing utilitarian objects with multiple purposes, craft objects, and the tools used to make them, with recognized tribal art pieces, [they] asked audiences to confront their expectations for indigenous authenticity, temporality and value."* (ibid.) DM/PLP.

Plaza Theater. One of the 'big three' 'first class' theaters in Baguio City that was located at the market plaza (where all jeepney lines converged). Eventually it turned into a 'second-run cinema' (cinemas showing Tagalog movies or old gangster flicks on a double program). It became the most popular cinema for the miners coming to Baguio for their Sunday break. They would watch from first screening at 9AM until late afternoon (sulit ang ticket). Then at 5PM, there would be a big exodus to catch the last jeeps back to Balatok and Antamok mines. If you sat beside miners in an afternoon show, you would get a preview of the dialogue, a few seconds before John Wayne uttered them on the screen (or, the hero's line *"Get outta my way!"* – complete with lip synch!). KT.
See also: Baguio Cine; New Baguio Theater; Pines Theater.

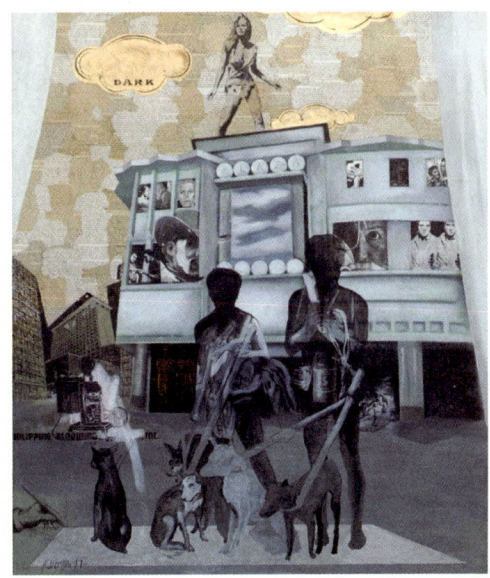
Plaza Theater, Kawayan De Guia, mixed media, 135x113 cm, 2011.

Pokingang *(KAN)* also **Lanot** *(ILO)*. (1) Morning glory (Ipomoea violacea). The vine is found in the Cordilleras along cliff walls or down walls. Some users would pulverize the vines and add water and then drink at least three glasses of the mixture to get high. But the more efficient way is to ingest the seeds as that's where the hallucinatory potency really is. The seeds contain a naturally occurring tryptamine (Lysergic Acid Amide [LSA]) which gives a high like LSD.
(2) Children use the vine and chop them into two-inch lengths to make slingshots. FYC.

Polo *(SPA)*. (1) Labor services during the Spanish times.
(2) A game apparently played by the Americans at Polo Field, located near Wright Park, Baguio City.

Pow-wow: Dance of the Philippine Igorots. Piano piece composed by Paul Rubens in 1904 with the companion liner notes: *"When the Igorottes first arrived at St. Louis the cold weather made it necessary to keep them indoors. With the advance of spring these children of the Philippines were taken out into the sunshine. Forming into bands, or clans, these Indians of the Archipelago continued the performance until compelled by those in charge to stop for rest."* Other Tin Pan Alley piano pieces are the *Igorrote Dance* and *My Igorrote Sue*, both composed by Frances Dekressien Brady in 1905. FYC.
See also: Dog-eating; Igorot; Igorotism.

Poy-do *(KAN)*. Landslide or something big falling in your direction.
See also: Landslide.

Presidente *(SPA)*. (1) As used in the reports of the

Philippine Commission, it refers to the municipal president or the head of the municipal council – e.g. in Tinglayan, Kalinga, the god Kabunian is seen as the presidente of the anitos.

(2) Presidential table, referring to the main table in any occasion. FYC.

Pre-white. Keesing's term of Cordillera before the coming of Europeans and Americans.
See also: AFRTN; Annual Headhunter's Fund; Jones, Isabela; Nikimalika; Squaw men; Thomasites; Tribes.

Pucay, Eugene. Decades ago, there was a Thomasite named Arthur McCann who taught at the Mountain Province High School (now Baguio City National High School) and coached a baseball team which later became one of the best in their league. His best player was Eugene Pucay Sr., who soon became a city councilor and helped organize the YMCA, Masons, Boy Scouts and other organizations in the city. The Eugene Pucay Cup for baseball was organized in his honor. FYC.
See also: AFRTN; Pre-white.

Pudung *(IFU)*. [1] It is the spirit possessed by a person that can cause illness to another, similar to the concept of the amling or annong of the Ilocanos. One who is afflicted by an illness due to a pudung will be referred to as "kinalat di pudung (bitten by a pudung)." Illnesses usually come in the form of stomach disturbance, general feeling of weakness, and rashes or inflammations in any part of the body including the scrotum. The infliction can be due to an unwanted or unwelcome (intentional or unintentional) contact with the possessor of the spirit. It includes using something owned or previously used by the possessor of the spirit, trespassing into the confines of the possessor, and even eye contact. To heal the illness, it is advised that the inflicted should ask for healing from the possessor of the pudung. The healing process called the bugi means blowing a mouthful of air on the affected part after chewing moma. Other possessors heal those inflicted by applying their saliva onto the affected part of the body. The illness usually subsides right after the bugi. Some possessors of the spirit use this power to guard their valuables such as their ricefield, their pond, their things at home, and even their firewood left in the forest. Kind ones usually make manifest their pudung with a runo with its leaves knotted and then placed conspicuously on the valuable they are trying to protect. This should warn people that a pudung is on guard. RHK.

(2) (See Purchos).
See also: Ab-abiik; Ayak; Moma; Padpadaya; Pasang.

Pumapa-ot *(IFU)*. Woodcarver. Munpa-ot is to carve.
See also: Aginaya; Panginomnoman ki.

Puraw *(ILO)*. Lit. White. [1] Caucasian.
(2) Ginebra San Miguel (GSM). The Cordillera region has the highest per capita consumption of GSM gin in the country. The puraw is an alternative to tapuey during rituals and celebrations. DOS.

Purchos *(KAL)* also **Purhos** *(KAL)*, **Porong** *(IBA)*, **Pudong** *(KAN)*, **Pujong** *(KAL)*, **Alpud** *(IFU)*. [1] It is a knotted runo grass used as a warning not to trespass. Children in every Kalinga village are very familiar with this sign. HZK.

(2) *(IBA)*. A knotted piece of sapsap used as a 'no trespassing' marker. It may be placed over the path to a house when the people are away or observing ngilin and nobody is allowed to visit. It is also usually placed along the trail to rice fields at harvest to keep spirit owners (and some say, rats) from harming the grain. It is also seen on community assets such as water sources and forests, or on one's cargo to say that it has not been abandoned. A porong is placed on the house where a baby has been born to drive away spirits, or is carried by mothers who bring their children to the fields as an amulet to protect them from the ampasit spirit owners. (Ballard 2011, 394-424) SKW.

(3) *(IFU)*. *"Runo stalks with the blades tied in a loop. It is an 'ethics lock,' and denotes private property. Used by placing near or on whatever it is desired shall remain unmolested; as, for example, a sugar-cane thicket, cord of wood, house in the absence of owners, rice field in dispute, and so forth."* (Barton 2012).
See also: Ampasit; Bengao; Dila anito; Inhabian; Pudung; Runo; Sapsap.

Pure Country. A 1992 film about a country singer portrayed by country singer George Strait, who grew tired of his celebrity status and made his way back to where he came from and found his true love. The movie made Benguet's biggest video stores, like Horizon and Pink and Gray, purchase multiple copies as they always ran out of it because the copies were either stolen or never returned. The movie was so big back in the 90s that most vegetable farm truck owners painted and labeled their automobiles, *"Pure Country." I Cross my Heart*, one of the songs featured in the movie, is one of the favorite wedding songs in Benguet. HZK.
See also: Cowboy; Lover's Moon.

Puting *(BON)*. A thanksgiving ritual in Bontoc done after the umbilical cord falls off from the baby. A native chicken is butchered and cooked with etag and with or without etab. Family and relatives share the meal. PAD.
See also: Etab; Etag; Kidlos; Kiya; Teknag.

Puto *(KAN)*. Used as a verbal clue to ask someone suspected of lying – e.g. *"Mang put-puto kan sa met? [Are you trying to fool me?]"* JST.
See also: Pilpilak-Taltalak.

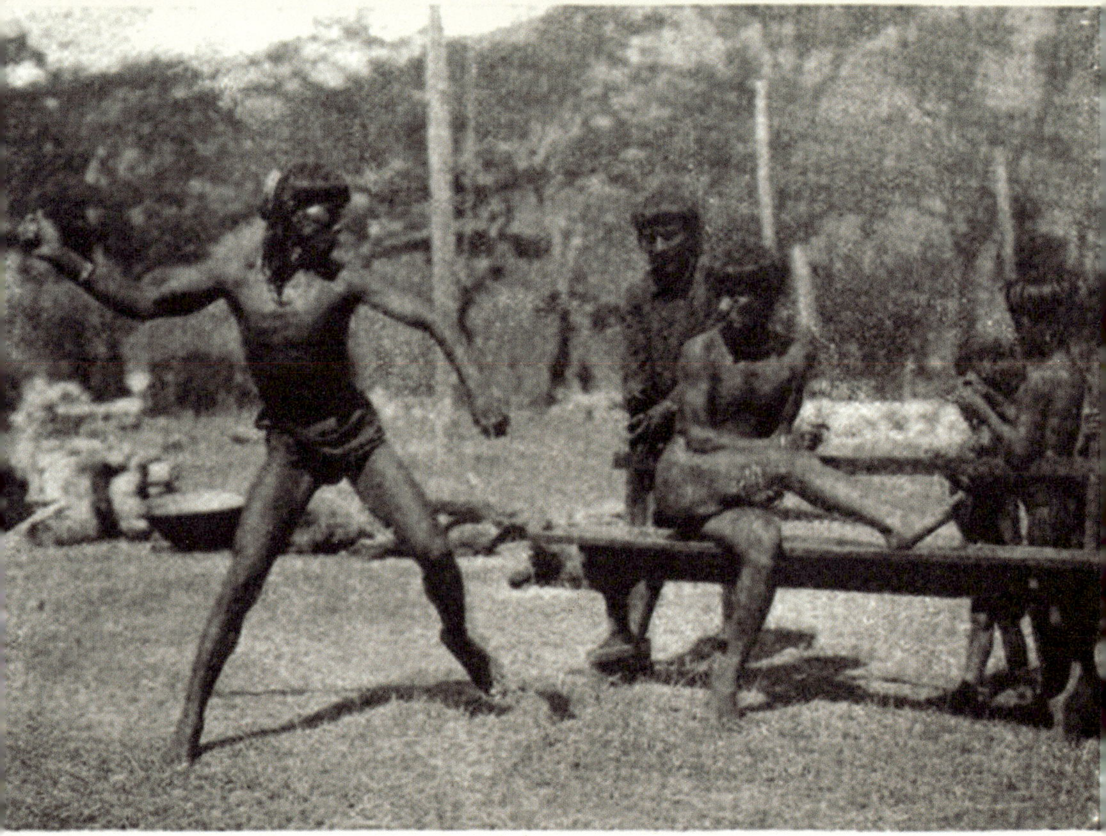

BONTOC IGOROT SLAPPING GAME
Third position: the striker ready to deliver his blow

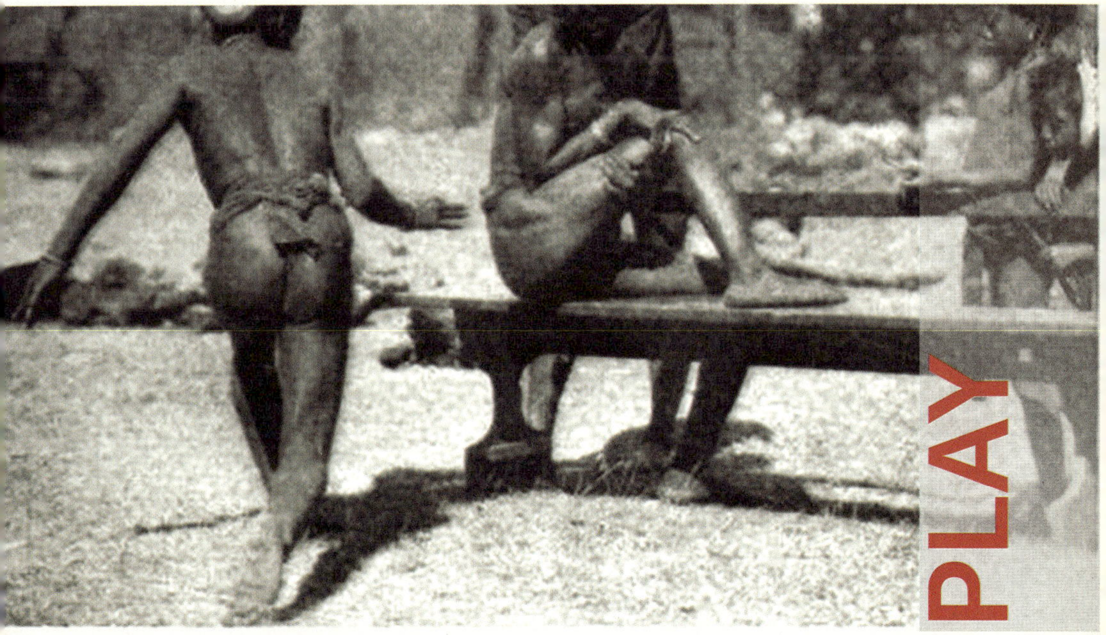

aphs of the *Bontoc Igorot Slapping Game*, 1911. Courtesy National Geographic Magazine.

BONTOC IGOROT SLAPPING GAME
Fifth position: just after the blow. The man struck does not look happy

PLAY

Rene Aquitania at Play

A man prances back and forth on the hand railings of an overpass. He larks around with the polluted air of the city below. Balancing high above the roaring traffic, he pretends to catch the diesel-fumes with plastic bags, whose ends he knots together to make balloons. These, he tosses to a group of youth, who excitedly start a fray.

The man is Rene Aquitania, a Baguio artist and father of four. His balloons do not just protest the dirty urban air, but also encourage children to make toys from things they find and to play with the wind. *"There was never any money [in what we did]. But your heart was really full. [Bilog na bilog ang puso mo!] You could sleep with a smile on your face!"* he says.

In our age of consumerism and media overload, such types of games are supplanted by 'gaming' – withdrawal into the cyber world. Cheap plastic toys replace the handmade rag-dolls, the improvised bottle cap 'dama' boards, the vehicles assembled from wood scraps, tin cans and rubber. Parents, who once used to play with their kids, are now harassed for time. They need to make money to buy all the things they feel their family must have living in that 'iron cage.'

The expression *"iron cage"* was coined by Max Weber. Almost a hundred years ago, this German sociologist expressed misgivings about the course the industrial revolution and its ideology of rationalization mapped out for society. He criticized said modern philosophy for dehumanizing people, degrading them to 'cogs in the machine' and trapping them in an 'iron cage'

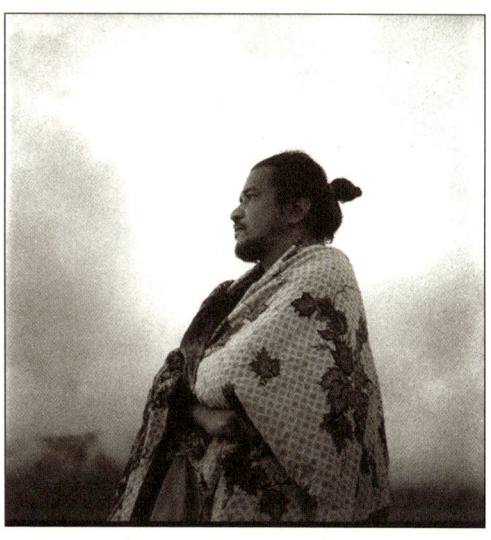

Portrait of the artist *Rene Aquitania*. Photograph by Kidlat de Guia.

of bureaucracy and materialism (Allan 2005, 177).

At the time Weber wrote this, Cordilleran kids still played with seeds and braided ropes into shapes (tinubtubong). They whistled on leaves (menkigug) and whirred wooden discs on cords producing shrill sounds (balinggeg). They walked on stilts (akkad), flew kites (ulaw) and spun a great variety of spinning tops, such as the bawet and the salugat, the small pandokay, the big-bellied pusase, and the two-headed patlongay, to name but a few (Vanoverbergh 1982). Their playthings were fabricated from nature, or were their bodies. They flicked pebbles from reed tops with their eyes closed and hopped long distances in a squatting position (Simms 1908). They also practiced challenging ritual games during harvests.

Some of those indigenous games are revived in Cordilleran schools nowadays (Bontoc Festival 2009). For example, the one where several girls twine together one of their legs (always on the same side) and hop around in circles, singing. The one who loses her balance first would leave the game and the last standing would win. Other games have fallen out of memory, like the one observed by the American anthropologist S.C. Simms in Bontoc, in the year 1903. He described how three girls would stand on their heads, put their feet together in the center and chant, while rhythmically changing their leg position until one after the other would lose balance, to their great merriment. Simms also described a *"slapping game,"* where one man wedged himself on a narrow platform and offered his upper leg and thigh to an opponent, who smacked it full force with the hand. Designated judges examined the

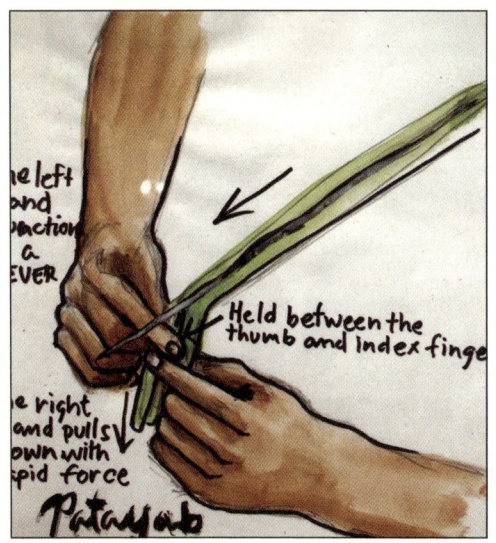

Artwork of Rene Aquitania on games and toys in the Cordillera.

signs of apparent injury in order to determine the winner.

A generation later, another US anthropologist, Morice Vanoverbergh (1982) ploughed the mountain trail in search of the passtimes of the Cordilleran child. He encountered word games (itakem and kalapa), riddles, talking with the hands (mekullup) and guessing what was hidden in another's palm (menkitkit-ug). There were also games that refined physical balance, speed and coordination. For example, mengaldo – catching a piece of wood alternately with the back and the palm of the hand; menpakgaok – whirling on one foot around one's own axis while cradling the other leg to the body; menpikpiko – a finger catching game; and menninnin – balancing a cane on one finger. He also witnessed war games, such as wrestling while holding the opponent with one finger, mud battles among whole villages, foot boxing, and tug of war.

Rene Aquitania, whose son Kudip is 12 years old (at the time of writing), decided to put on his own hiking boots and journey along the Halsema Highway in quest for Cordilleran games and toys. Asking around among the youngsters, he found them shrugging their shoulders: What should they care about their grandparents' toys? Deep in Kankanaey country, however, he found that boys still played with the slingshot, called a pal-siit. Kids there also raced on stilts (kadang-kadang, akkad in Vanoverbergh); fought blowgun (sur-surtok) wars; and skillfully spun the baw-et' or top – as in Vanoverbergh's time. The older boys showed the artist how to select a branch from a tree to carve the top, which was shaped like a cone and had a rounded bottom for spinning. Like its commercial version, but without a nail at the tip, the baw-et' was spun by means of a string.

Aquitania soon met another type of the Cordillera top – the tiyo'ngan from Ifugao. Fashioned from the fruits of a special heirloom tree called the Palayon, this spinning device operates without a string. Instead, it uses a thin bamboo stick for setting it off. It takes great effort to pierce the hard Palayon fruit and insert the stick, upon which one places the bamboo between one's palms and rubs them very fast to spin the tiyo'ngan. The spinning process recalls the old way of starting fire by friction, twirling a wooden stick in a hole filled with tinder.

Further on along the Halsema Highway, off the road in Bugias, Aquitania met an old man at a sari-sari store. *"Manong, do you remember any toys that you had when you were young?"* he asked. *"We had no toys, we had to work in the fields,"* said the man, echoing Vanoverbergh (1982). But the artist kept on prodding and the old man, eventually, began to share. The boys used to play *"Cañao-cañaoan,"* he said. In this play-enactment of community rituals, the boys cut a

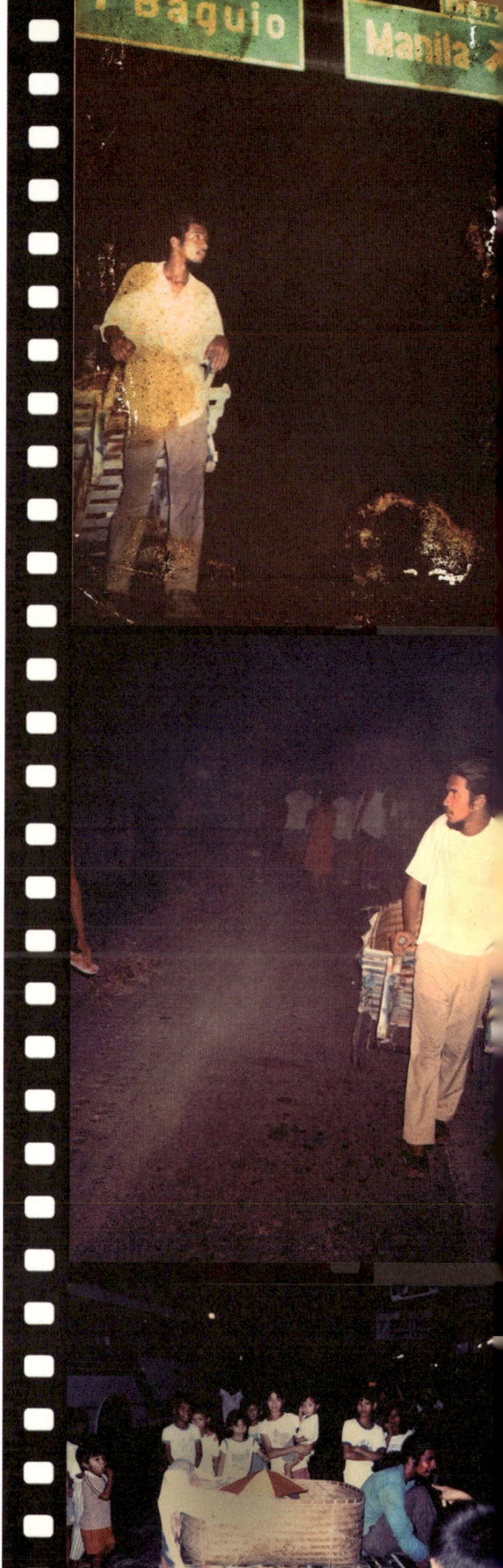

Contact prints of the artist *Rene Aquitania* at play, 1987. Courtesy Katrin de Guia.

banana trunk and pretended it was a sacrificial animal. One child was designated to play the shaman. He prayed over the 'pig' and slaughtered it with his helpers. Then, they cut the banana stalk into pieces, cooked it, and distributed it among the *"villagers,"* according to the customs of their place. The boys also fashioned toy guns from twigs and wood and shot small seeds from hollow reeds, the old man said.

In Sagada, Aquitania found some women who were willing to share their childhood memories about toys: the girls would make ornaments from flowers, the women said. The blooms of the seasons were their toys and they fashioned themselves pretty earrings and necklaces or garlands. They would also dig for clay and shape little people and animals and cooking ware. They would even carry around their family tinagtago (similar in appearance to the bulul, given as gifts to newlyweds, for their house) like babies in a sling. They also used jump ropes made from camote (sweet potato) vines.

Elsewhere in Bontoc, the artist was told of some 'dangerous games' (which may have their origin in ancient ritual practices). During harvest, young men threw stones at each other. Trying to dodge each other's projectiles, the youths did not stop until one of them drew blood. That was the end of the game for that day.

In yet another village, Aquitania was shown a toy made from flattened bottle caps, which the people called tay-tayek. A string, adjusted to fit the arm span of a child, was looped through two holes in the metal disc, which was positioned in the center of the loop. Holding each end of the loop in one hand, the child pulled the string to its outward most limits. In the process, the string would coil and the bottle cap would spin. When the rotation stopped, the string was released, then immediately pulled again. The inward/outward motion made the bottle cap gyrate faster and faster until it began to 'sing.' It was the toy Vanoverbergh called balinggeg – a prehistoric device once used to induce trance.

In search for more indigenous toys, Aquitania left the trodden paths. Off Halsema, in the hills, he encountered Ibaloy people. Asked for their toys, the children showed him little balls (bula-bula) that were skillfully woven from coconut leaves and used for catching, target practice and tagging each other. He was also shown a curious sound-producing device: A banana stem the length of an arm was stripped down to a fist thick core. Within finger-length gaps, small four-sided pieces (around one centimeter deep) were carved from the stem and carefully twisted into an upright position. Stuck to the trunk by some remaining ligaments, these flaps made a loud noise when struck by a quick hand that moved along the banana stem: *"Prarak!" "Prarak!"*

Returning from the Halsema, Aquitania's notebook brimmed with sketches and notes. On the one side, there were games and toys that could be well found along some street sides of Baguio City: Pat-patos – the throwing game and its variations, where stones are aimed at a tin can in the hope to hit and trip it over unless a 'catcher' manages to avert the attack; lastico – the ubiquitous rubber band that functions as all-around plaything throughout the Philippines; the two-wheeled scooter made of scrap wood and bits of rubber tires; and the mobile 'ground helicopter' made from two interlocked tin cans. There is also the four-wheel makeshift car, where the driver's feet are the stirring device. However, where in the city such vehicles are for racing and fun, they are used for transporting firewood and drinking water over stony trails along the Halsema.

Aside from local toys modeled after playthings from industrial countries, Aquitania was also able to sketch some fragile Cordilleran toys – things that would hardly survive the bus ride from the Halsema into Baguio City. Like the twisted sayote leaves that are used to play pal-lot – a kind of a 'cockfight'; or the weeds for a cloverleaf fight, where the long, thin stems of the red clover are stripped down to tiny fibers that are swung to catch the opponent's leaf and skillfully tear it off its fragile filament. Slightly more sturdy but equally ephemeral would be the batayab – the tiger grass spear. To make this indigenous toy, one cuts a section of grass from a stalk and peels most of its blade from the middle rib. A small part of blade remains at the end. Holding the stalk loosely, the player removes the last bit of grass fiber with a

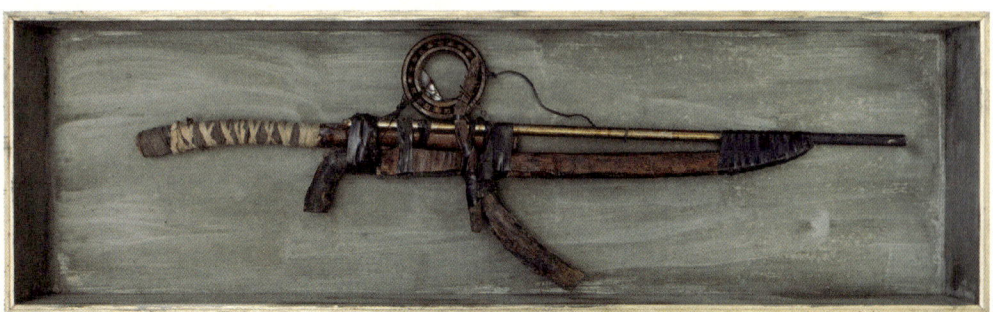

Patibong (part of a series), Rene Aquitania, box construction, 46X152 cm, 2018.

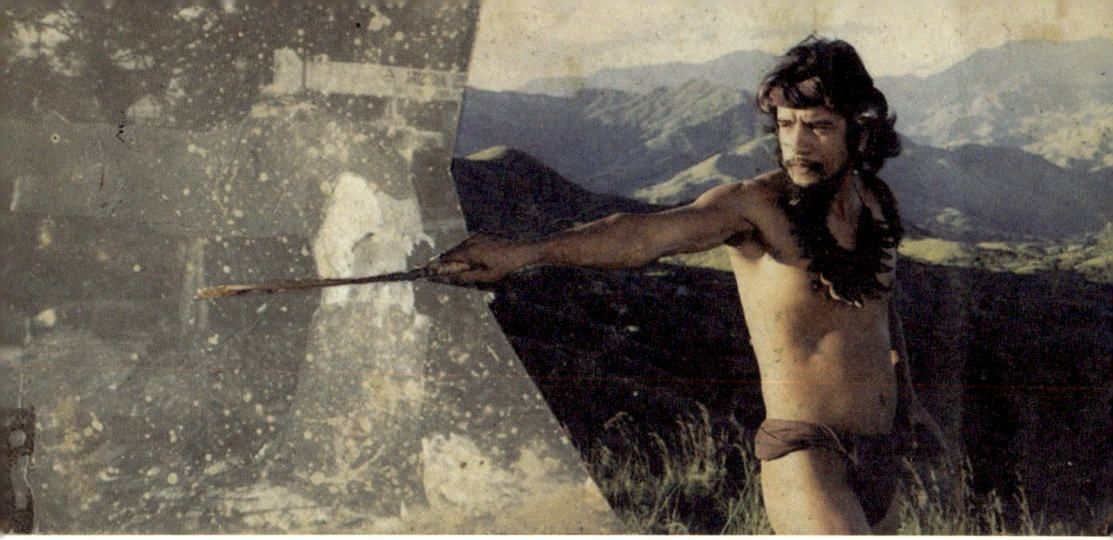

Portrait of the artist *Rene Aquitania* taken behind-the-scenes during the filming of a French movie in Tanay, Rizal, Philippines.

quick flip of his fingers in a way that the now bare middle rib will fly – *"Zzzzingggh!,"* like a spear.

Ephemeral playthings like these would escape most Philippine urbanites wheeling along the paved paths of provincial landscapes, electronic gadgets in hands. But Rene Aquitania is a Filipino culture bearer. He has time to look and wait and see and find. Even the fragile things that taste like centuries bygone.

Aquitania grew up as the youngest of eight, the son of a folk healer and a policeman. When he was small, he remembers that he played with elves and unseen beings instead of trucks and guns. By the time he entered school, he knew more tales about Filipino folk heroes than about Superman. Due to his mother's healing lineage, the invisibles played with him and he played with them. He is still played by them today. He says, what he knows, he did not learn in school.

As a youth, he began to follow his artistic calling. He performed in the streets unannounced, and exhibited art in public corners. He hung cute little things to dangle in the wind – made of leaves or paper or cut-up coke cans – He gathered street urchins and blew soap bubbles with them, cleaned up dirty city grounds and painted paper murals on walls. Doing so, he acted on his belief that artists must try and find solutions for the problems in their communities. That, even if an artist cannot change much in one time, at least he could say that he tried.

Aquitania found like-minded friends in the Baguio Arts Guild (BAG). Here, cultural workers from all artistic fields shared the vision of art as public event: art that reached out to people beyond institutions and galleries; art defined by process, not by product; and art that ultimately affirmed communities. By choice or by default, the initiators of such art took on the function of conscience in the groups with which they mingled.

Aquitania, ever the animator, the jouster and the jester, had long adopted such art as his personal style. With his informal, indio-genius ways, he had organized a number of 'no-budget' community festivals in Baguio: People sang, danced, built altars, played music, cooked, ate, and slept in the park. Citizens donated food, water, firewood and tents. Artists offered free workshops to children, created mandalas and transformed dumping grounds into gardens. The magic of art as a movement and an agent of change prevailed. At the vortex of these activities was Aquitania. Like the charismatic leader of a Kapatiran, a Filipino spiritual brotherhood, his secret as a game master was the ancestral skill of fusing energy. As he wandered about commenting on installations, tending the fire, organizing food, initiating workshops, performing skits, painting and playing instruments, he was living art, breathing art, being art. And he showed others how to do that!

When Aquitania mobilized his friends, it was always the 'we' that won – a 'we' that included all age groups and social strata. In his systemic waste-none approach, no one was pitted against another. It was all about learning things through engaging with each other, one's community, and the environment.

In our solipsistic techno-world, Rene Aquitania wants his 12-year-old son to play games that build physical, mental and social skills – talents that enliven the community. He believes in the value of reviving the traditional Cordillera games of old. That's why he traipses through the Cordillera mountains – to learn from those who still remember how and what their parents and grandparents used to play. KatDG

See also: Bongtot; Butubutu-ukiuki; Kalu-os; Tocucan Bridge.

Shoeless Gentleman

Rene Aquitania has no audience. He never chose his audience. His gallery was on the streets and alleys, and his material ranges from every little thing that could turn big: what you have forgotten, discarded, or left behind? Even the very floss you use in between your teeth. He has the magic to turn nothing into something and that something into nothing. You would be left perplexed if you don't pick up quick, but you would come home a few thoughts richer – boggled if you may, but it will haunt you until the point strikes right through you.

This is what he's been doing over the past 30 years. Now he is a devoted father to his 12-year-old son, Kudip. You would find the Rene-and-Kudip tandem turning up at the same places, performing art one minute, and in the next, carving out Kudip's imagination to take a stick as seriouly as a sword. But these are fast-changing times that have been taken over by technology. Rene's antics wouldn't work anymore, the way they once did with other children – as if there was no magic in Kudip's eyes whenever Rene tried to make something to entertain his son.

Rene was bothered by this: that back in the old days, all it took was one's imagination to come up with the most ingenious games that educated children outside the four walls of a school. This is what led him to come up with this project. He realized the importance of those hand-made toys, where there was a process of creation which made one love the final toy even more. Those games that posed as playful interactions amongst children and in some characteristic ways defined the community. If there was a crack in that sense of community, what would be left for the future?

As he went around the Cordilleras, he collected stories and toys from old folks. He also created a stage where parents were asked to teach their children the kind of games they grew up with when they were still young. It was in this artist's charisma (which he always had) where you felt safe to try something new and fun! I was only six years old when I met him for the first time. He was playing with street kids, giving workshops, and leading everyone's imagination to its optimum elasticity.

Rene's practice is mostly informal. We would create public art; murals in forgotten spaces or installations, and there was practically no limit to what we could do when he was around. His performances were just as inviting and had the complexity of instilling fear and a thrill and disturbance. Initially, you would think that you could do all the things that he did. It looked so easy – but you didn't really know how hard it would be to follow him, how much practice and body control it took to be like Rene. There was always fear and excitement in learning from Rene, but it was ever so highly diverting. His tricks expanded one's horizon beyond age and class and gender – if one believed in any of those categories at all – it did not matter to this artist. He was one of the best teachers one could ever have and he had this independent drive and spirit that nobody or nothing could hold down.

Rene has a way of delivering the most basic of things as appearing larger than life. But he could also show the most intricate ones in their most archaic form. Raised by a mother who is a healer, Rene tried to transform her practice into art: an art that became his own. He is a healer in his own right, cures where he senses conflict, and creates one if there is a need for something to be cured – is that what it takes to defragment this so-called modern society? KDG.

Photograph of the artist **Rene Aquitania** in a performance. Photograph by Ed de Guia.

Rene Aquitania: Walking Still

Spanning around three decades of work from performances to paintings and installations, Rene Aquitania's largely undocumented body of work transforms the mundane into inventive critiques of pressing political and social realities. Within the tradition of "artist as the art," his work, notably in performance, captures the power of a minor gesture or movement, repeated or even elaborately designed, to easily reconstruct a 'whole' reality, or present cultural meanings hidden in the noise of daily modern life. This performance process is a thorough or even taxing procedure that Aquitania seems to cloak behind the spontaneity of his performances. But it is also a procedure, or even a spiritual undertaking, that can be glimpsed from mountain healers in the Cordillera, a place Aquitania calls home. The procedure can also be described as the creation of a myth.

Katrin de Guia in her book *Kapwa: the Self in the Other* (2005), describes Aquitania:

> "Culture-bearing Filipino artists like Rene often remain at the fringe of the commercial art market circuit – by choice.
>
> In the Eastern sky looms the Morning Star. The Western horizon swallows the sickle of the waxing moon. The neighborhood is empty and quiet.
>
> Somewhere, in a dark deserted street, a tall dark figure lays out a large circle of charcoal about the width of the asphalted lane. With slow sweeping movements, he creates a crescent out of broken glass within the circle. A few street people watch in sleepy daze, while the artist pours denatured alcohol over his work and sets it ablaze. He waits until the flames have recoiled into ember, and then dances barefoot in the glass and the glowing remains.
>
> The Baguio artist Rene Aquitania called this installation performance: "Welcome to the Fire Ox." When later asked why he presented it in the dead of the night in a deserted street, the artist answered, "I just wanted to let them know that I'm still around!"

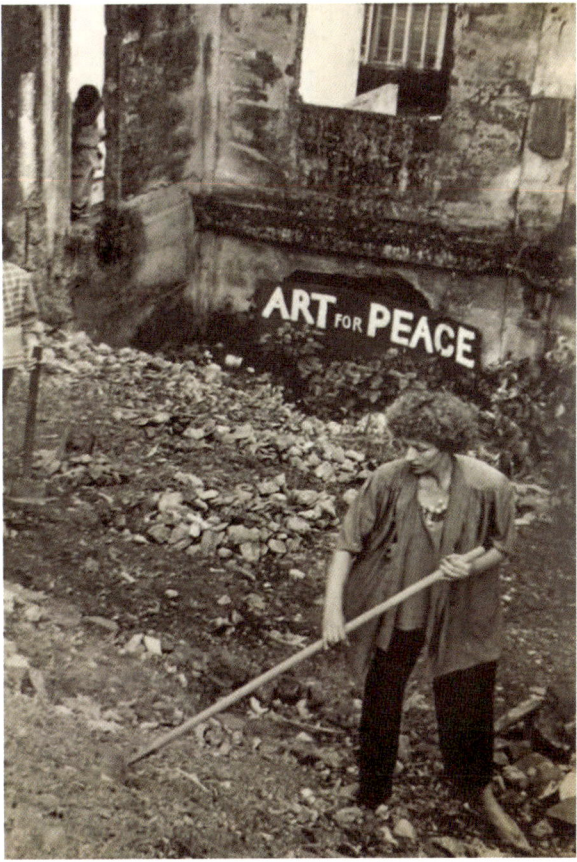
Photograph by Ernie Enriquez. Courtesy Ernie Enriquez.

From his 1986 performance project *Lakaran*, where he walked from Baguio to Makati with a kariton, to co-founding the Baguio Arts Guild a year later, performance rituals and meditations in galleries in Baguio and Manila including the Cultural Center of the Philippines' Little Theater, acting in films by Kidlat Tahimik and Raymond Red, building a bamboo bridge patterned after the Tocucan Bridge in Bontoc for AX(iS) Art Project 2011, exhibiting playful sketches on traditional games as part of AX(iS) Art Project at the Singapore Biennale 2013, and his recent tarot card paintings and influence on established and emerging Baguio artists like Kawayan de Guia, Aquitania has built a vibrant presence in the arts.

For the length of time that Aquitania has meandered between gallery floors, streets, forgotten places, even spirit worlds, negotiating the realms of performance art and ritual practice, his work has solidified him in the canons of Baguio Art and perhaps a collective Philippine Art that still struggles to find its footing at the doors of the country's many forgotten islands and mountains. RAC.

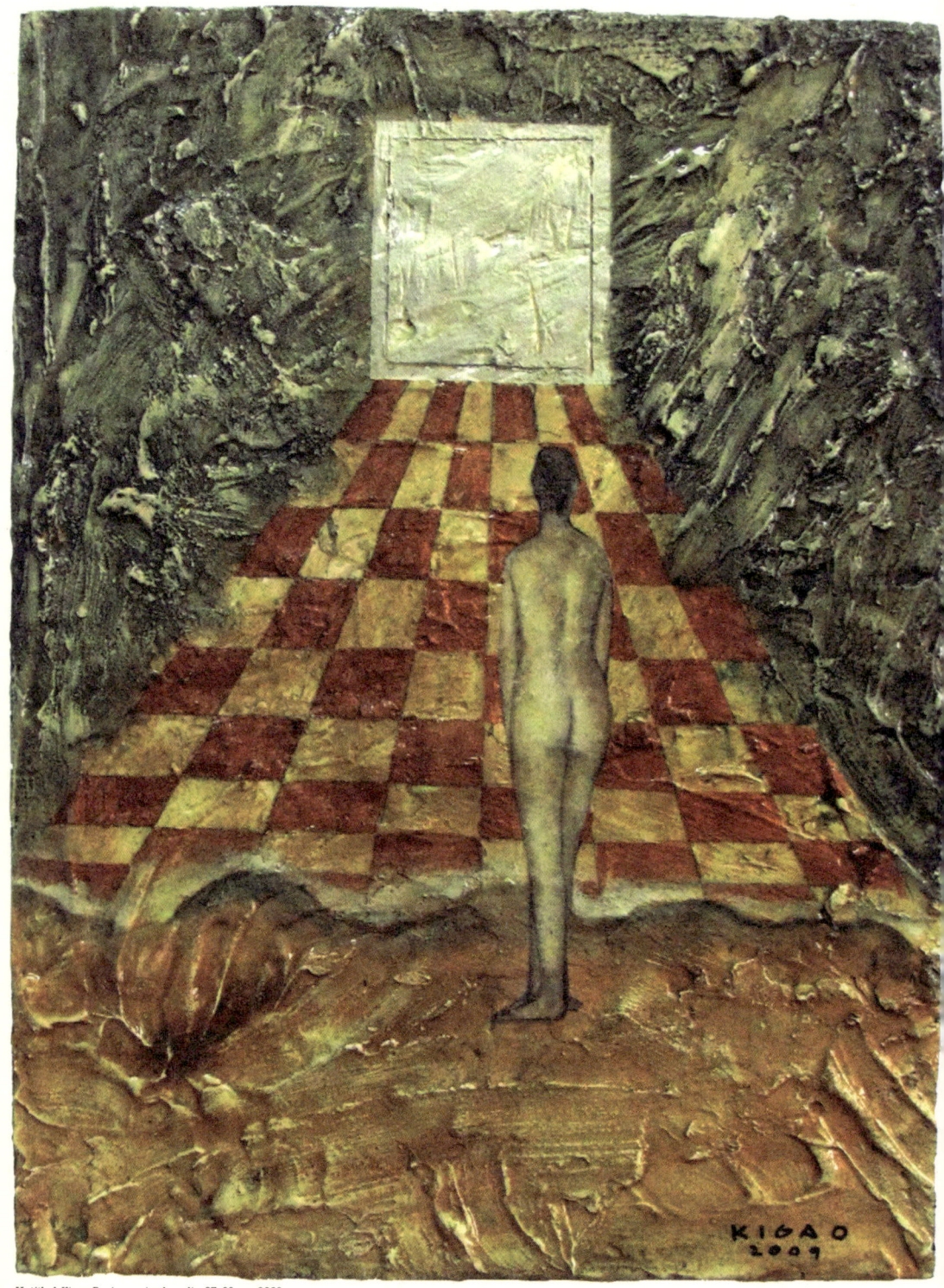
Untitled, Kigao Rosimo, mixed media, 27x22 cm, 2009.

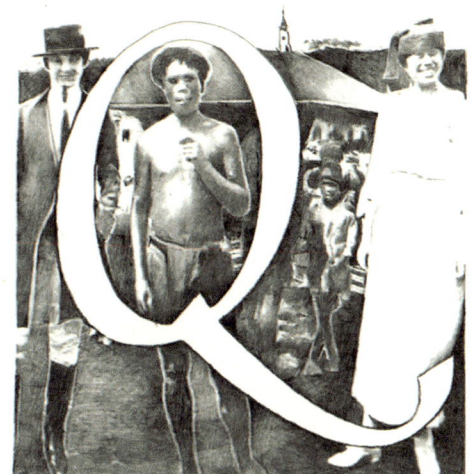

Qua *(ISN/KAN/ILO)* also **Kuwa**. Lit. Property or belonging. (1) In Baguio Ilocano, it is a verbal mannerism verging on a tic, and can mean anything, i.e. *"Quangai? [you know what I mean?],"* *"Niqua [Him/Her who, specifically, is tacit and unspecified],"* *"Tiqua [What we should do and you know what I mean],"* and *"Qualattan [You know and that's it or let's just go with that]."*

(2) Used when referring to the sexual organ. FYC

See also: Butubutu-Ukiuki.

Quan Nga Yen. A man who had a plucky story similar to many Chinese in Cordillera. His father was a foreman during the construction of Kennon Road and later became a cook at Camp John Hay. Quan Nga Yen married a Tublay woman and became a miner for King Solomon Mines there. He became the first Chinese to start a vegetable plantation in Paoay, Sayangan. FYC.

See also: Cabbage King; John Hay, Camp; Kennon Road; Sayangan.

Quartz also **Fulilising** *(BON)*. That the old Bontoc people had a word for it shows that gold deposits must indeed be plentiful in that area.

Quezon Gamble. In 1938, President Manuel Quezon, a frequent Baguio visitor, found out that a new pit for cock-fighting was planned for La Trinidad, Benguet. To let *"Igorots retain their child-like simplicity and innocence,"* Quezon decided to stop the construction until he was dissuaded and made the cockpit *"for lowlanders only."* But because of this prohibition, many Ibalois and Kankanaeys later turned out to be inveterate gamblers, frequenting not only the cockpits in Benguet but also the casinos in Manila and other places. FYC.

Quiangan. Spanish name for Kiangan, Ifugao. Quianganes referred to the inhabitants.

Quiangan Bread. Bread pudding on boxes traded for old newspapers by old Igorot women who went around Baguio City since the 1960s until the 1990s. They would measure a fair trade ratio by one dangkal (the length of breadth of their fingers) of newspapers to eight Quiangan breads. FYC.

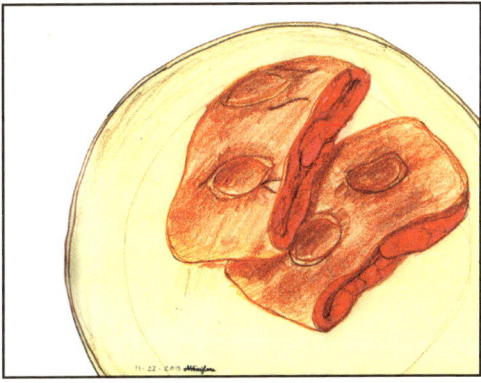

Illustration by Abbie SJ Lara.

Quiangan Line. The tendency to follow someone in front of you as if you are walking along the edge of a rice terrace. It is close to the Ifugao term 'oltog' which means a group walking in line or even aligned objects. FYC.

Quirante, Alonso Martin. In 1624, Don Alonso Martin Quirante led 1,800 men from Aringay to Antamok to investigate the gold mines there. After five months, Quirante decided that the gold there was of inferior quality and dismantled his garrison, not knowing that the Igorots hid the real mines from him. FYC.

See also: Baguio Gold; Maenang Boom.

Quirino Bridge. The four-span bridge (formerly the Banaoang Bridge) in Bantay, Ilocos Sur, which traversed the Abra River was built by Muneo Teraoka (A.K.A. Charles Teraoka) of Baguio. It was built before World War II and was so durable that it was only destroyed by Typhoon Feria in 2001, when one of the spans was rammed by cut timber brought down by the swollen river. Other major projects by Teraoka, who married a Filipina, are the Saint Louis Girl's High and Notre Dame Hospital in Baguio, both still standing. He died in 1941. His son Carlos Bautista Teraoka and daughter Marie Dolores were the only survivors of atrocities committed both by Japanese soldiers and American forces as they were deported to Japan as "illegal aliens." Both were repatriated in 1954 and Carlos became an Honorary Consul to Japan until 2011.

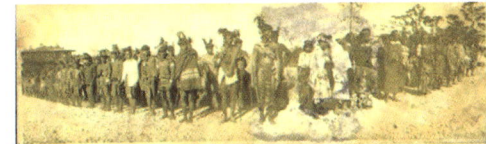

Courtesy AV Cating Family Collection.

Untitled, RJ Fernandez, C-type print, 62x78 cm, 2012. Courtesy RJ Fernandez

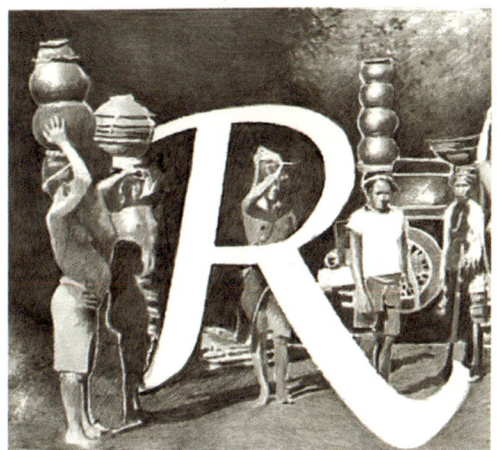

R. Rolling the Rs. There are no entries for R in the dictionaries for traditional Kankanaey, Ifugao, Bontoc or Ibaloi. When one is given the American name 'Rocky,' it becomes 'Lucky' to the elders who when asked to say 'Rabbit' will say 'Love-it.' FYC.
See also: Swan.

Rabit *(ISN)*. Caught with a fishhook.

Radam *(ISN)*. Vision problem, either near-sightedness or far-sightedness.

Radio spittoon. The Yankee colonial administrator's acknowledgment (resignation?) that Baguio's moma-chewing Igorots were a fact of life: concrete spittoons along downtown Session Road. These structures (the size of half a balikbayan box) were cast in cement to look like a 1950s radio (complete with 'speakers' and 'knobs' embossed on the sides). Spittoons were spaced apart every 20 meters to give nganga chewers a chance to obey the No Spitting Ordinance. A colonial surrender to the 'kultur' taste buds that were impossible to quell. KT.
See also: Moma.

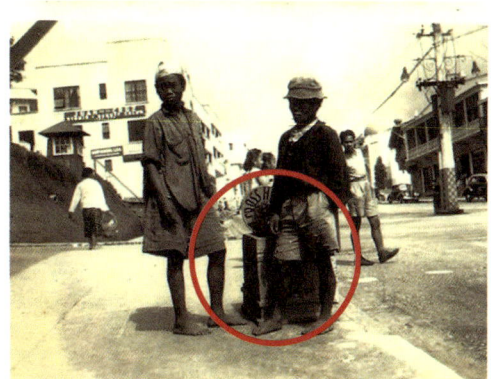

Photograph of two Igorot men beside a *radio spittoon* along Session Road. Courtesy Virginia de Guia.

Rainforest. Code name for a special area in Baguio's Burnham Park where the queer community hooked-up during the night especially pre-smartphones and social networking sites. Due to extensive police watch of the area in 2010, the area is no longer as it was used. It became an arid desert. Very dry. No longer wet.
See also: Burnham Park.

Rancherria de los Igorottes. In 1887, Parque del Buen Retiro, Jose Rizal's favorite park in Madrid, was the site of the Exposición de Filipinas of 1887. Included in the exhibition were *"samples of Philippine peoples"* such as the Igorots, Manobos and Negritos. In a letter dated June 6, 1887, Rizal wrote to his best friend, Ferdinand Blumentritt: *"I have worked hard against this degradation of my fellow Filipinos that they should not be exhibited among the animals and plants! But I was helpless. One woman has just died of pneumonia... and the newspaper El Resumen has made a smutty wisecrack about it! I would rather that they all got sick and died so they would suffer no more. Let the Philippines forget that her sons have been treated like this – to be exhibited and ridiculed."* Rizal said to Blumentritt that *"from what I understand, it is not an exposition of the Philippines at all but only of the Igorots."* But Denis Richard Byrne in his 2007 book, *Surface Collection: Archaeological Travels in Southeast Asia* said that of the 44 representatives of ethnic minorities in the Madrid Exposition, only eight were Igorots. And the Igorots created the Rancherria de los Igorottes. The woman whom Rizal mentioned to have died was a Muslim. FYC
See also: Dog-eating; Igorot; Igorotism.

Raut *(ISN)*. Rattan strips.
See also: Lituku.

Reavis, Tex. A photo of Reavis panning gold is displayed at the Benguet Corporation function hall in Balatoc, Itogon, Benguet. He was said to go to Pines Hotel whenever he filled up his bag with gold dust and would treat anyone in the bar. He would stay at the bar and leave only when the equivalent of his gold dust had been consumed. But it was also said that he never set foot in the mines and he was just a locator of a claim in Itogon. In his Supreme Court battle against Jose Fianza, who claimed the site because his ancestors had been mining on it, the Court sided with Reavis. It was Fianza who had been supplying him with the gold that he splurged in Pines Hotel. FYC

Remontados *(SPA)*. Lit. Renegades. Igorots who went down to the Christian settlements and then returned to the mountains to go back to their pagan ways. FYC.
See also: Bureau of Non-Christian Tribes; Cayat; Enmity between the Igorots and Christians, The Beginning of; Kain.

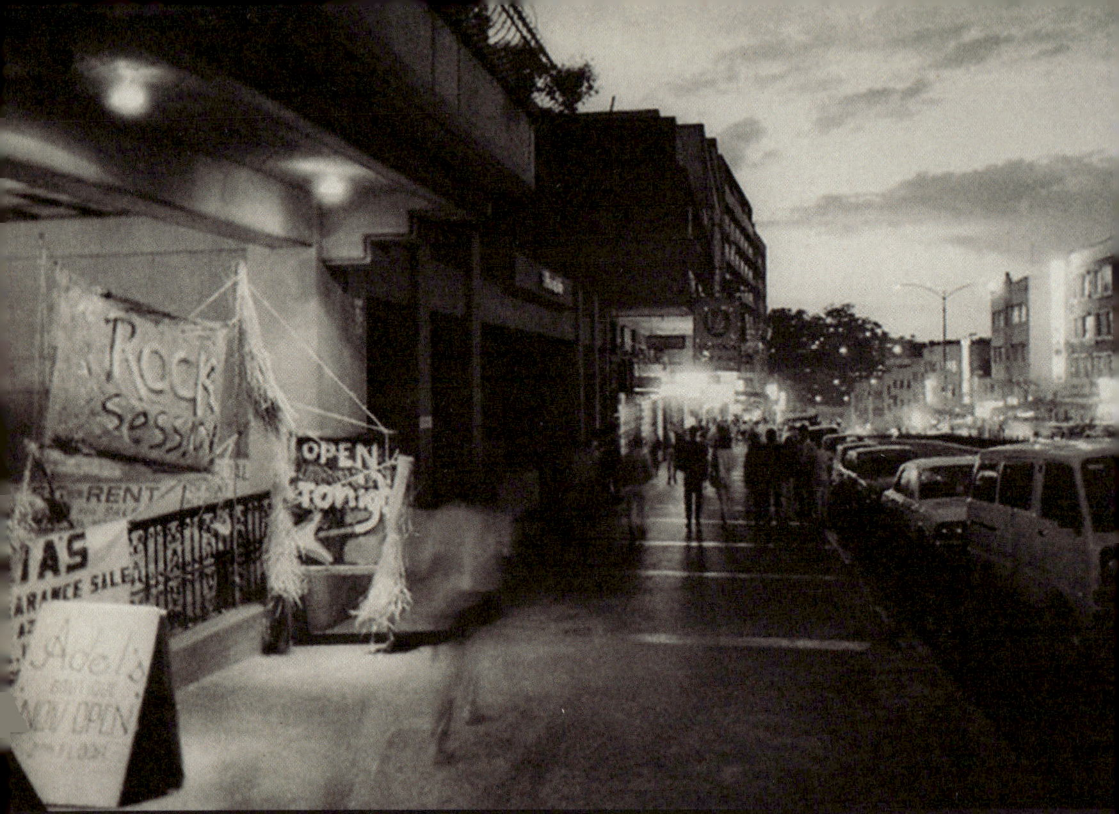

Rock Session.

THE BLANK

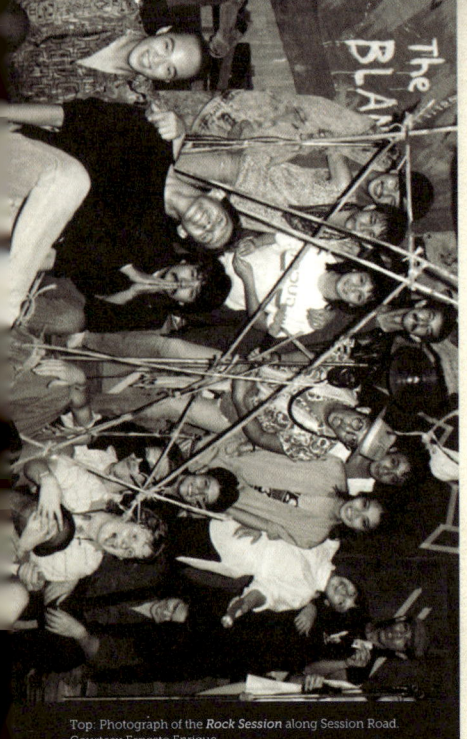

Top: Photograph of the *Rock Session* along Session Road.
Courtesy Ernesto Enrique.
Bottom: Photograph of one of the *Rock Session* nights.
Courtesy Ernesto Enrique.

There i was.. just been drinking my second to the last pale... i knew then that i am again walking the way home along strech of four kilometers cement underneath my shoes... i did'nt give a damn. that was ROCK Session. Between a pale and a taxi fare. i chose a pale. So there i was dancing as Grace Nono, belching out lore-ree to the nite. In the corner of my eye I caught a glimpse...... what a sight. this girl.... So being with carnal manifestation, and i would walk up to her and said... i said would you dance with me? she did! There we where Oblivious to the world around us. at that moment it was indeed a Shiva Shakti. a Dance, dance and Dance !!! We were just having a lot of fun !!!!
Till an NBI agent her bodyguard just pulled me out grabbing me by my back... shoved me out!.. and i said whats wrong with you we were just dancing !!! He pulled out his pistol and said I am attorney Malik from the NBI ! i said So? (i knew i irritated him i am a tiny bit artist. and he was tall dark and ugly). Having said it they threw me inside a 1967 Beatle. i was just there for twenty minutes.... they did'nt know what to do with me.... I said what am i here for with an agonizing projection they were talking mumbling arguing... till someone I am sorry He opened the door and let me out... then they got in and drove away!!! What? a few years later I met him again in Hyatts swimming pool..... and I said Hello! would you like to dance?........ remember me. He just smiled and hid behind her girlfriend..... My friend from the gang i just let that slipped ma oras ka rin joking ako no!
years later i read that he got shot at in a drug deal and died.. .. ...

Kawayan 2018

Wall around Mayoyao station

Photograph of a wall around the Mayoyao Station in Ifugao. Courtesy John Tewell

Romulo, Carlos P. Pulitzer Prize-winning reporter, war hero, one-time President of the United Nations General Assesmbly and long-time Foreign Minister of President Marcos. Carlos P. Romulo (CPR) once applied at Baguio Brent School and was rejected. We don't know if this had an effect on CPR when he wrote in his 1943 book *Mother America* that *"The fact remains that the Igorot is not Filipino... and it hurts our feeling to see him pictured in American newspapers under such captions as 'Typical Filipino Tribesman.' We passed laws in Philippine legislature forbidding pictures under such captions to be taken out of the Philippines."* It was only in 1953 that someone pointed this out to Alfredo Lam-en, who then wrote a letter to the editor of the Philippine Free Press criticizing the passage. (Finin, 2005, p. 180-181). The incident had wide repercussions even until the present, despite CPR's apology, and it was said that it caused him to withdraw from running for the presidency of the Philippines. FYC.

Rosy cheeks. The pain when you were a child and lowlanders would pinch your cheeks for looking like a strawberry. 'Red cheeks' do not mean that upland Cordillerans have more oxygen in their blood than lowlanders; it just means that they can have as much as ten times more nitric oxide which causes the dilation of blood vessels. This in turn allows blood to flow more freely to the extremities and aids in the release of oxygen to tissues. This is the reason for rosy cheeks in the uplands, and is not to be confused with Asian Flush. FYC.

Runo *(ILO)*. Tiger grass reeds that when dried and cleaned become pa-o (runo sticks) that are then strung, joined, or woven together to make mats or screens for floors and walls.

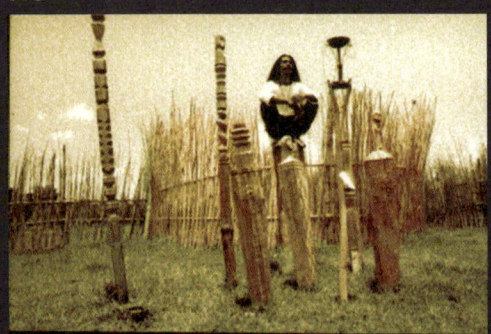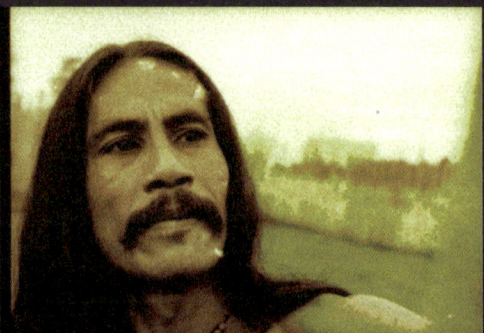

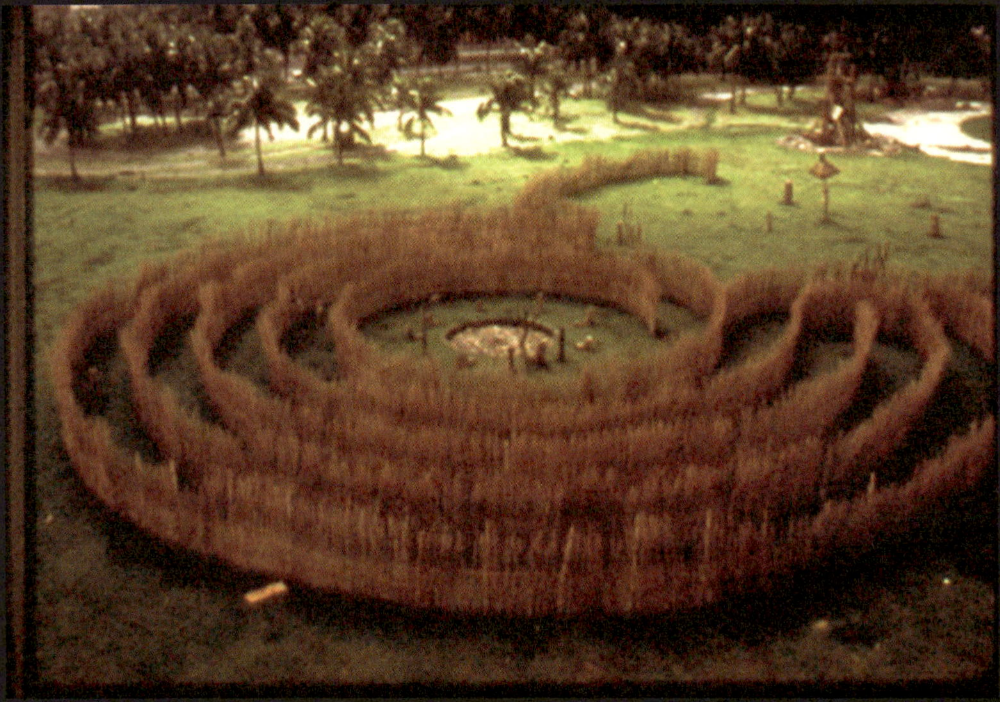

Top: Photographs of Roberto Villanueva.
Bottom: Video Capture of Roberto Villanueva's runo installation at the Cultural Center of the Philippines. Courtesy Rica Concepcion.

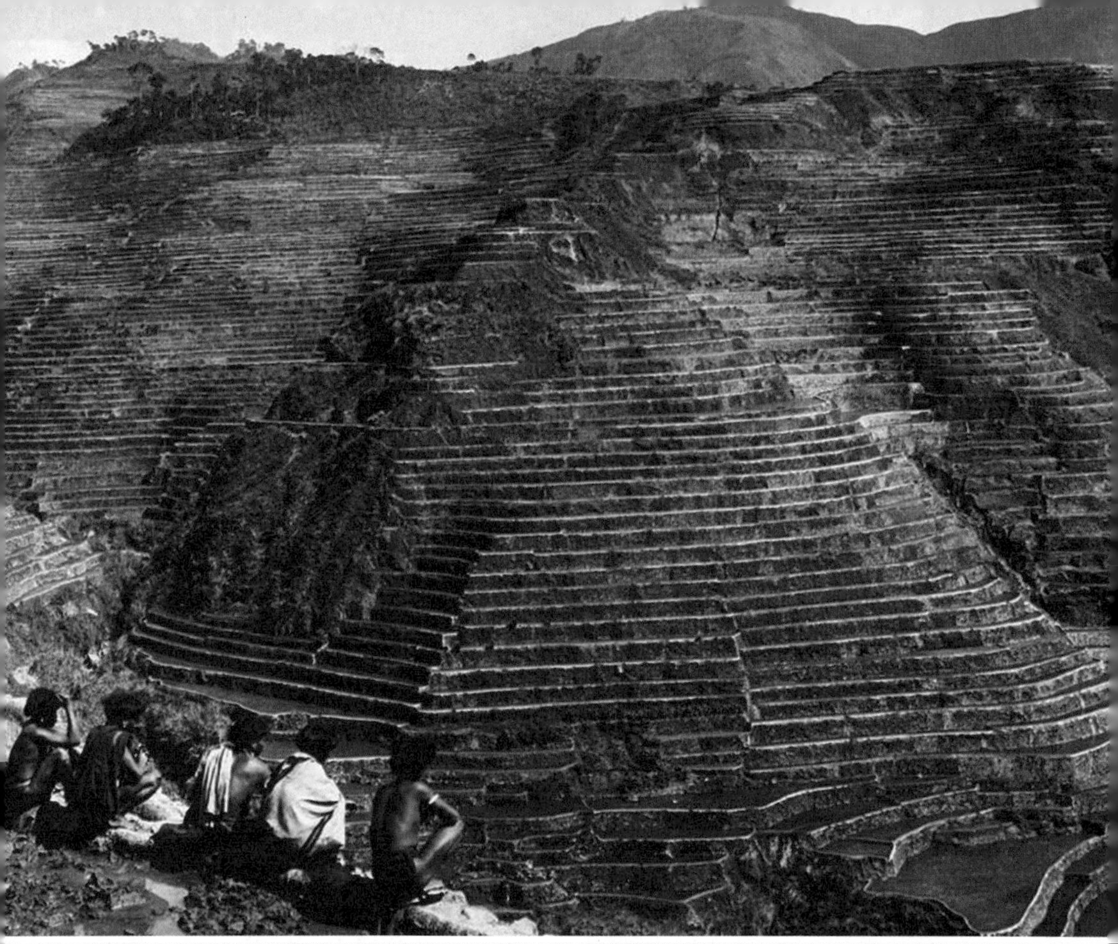

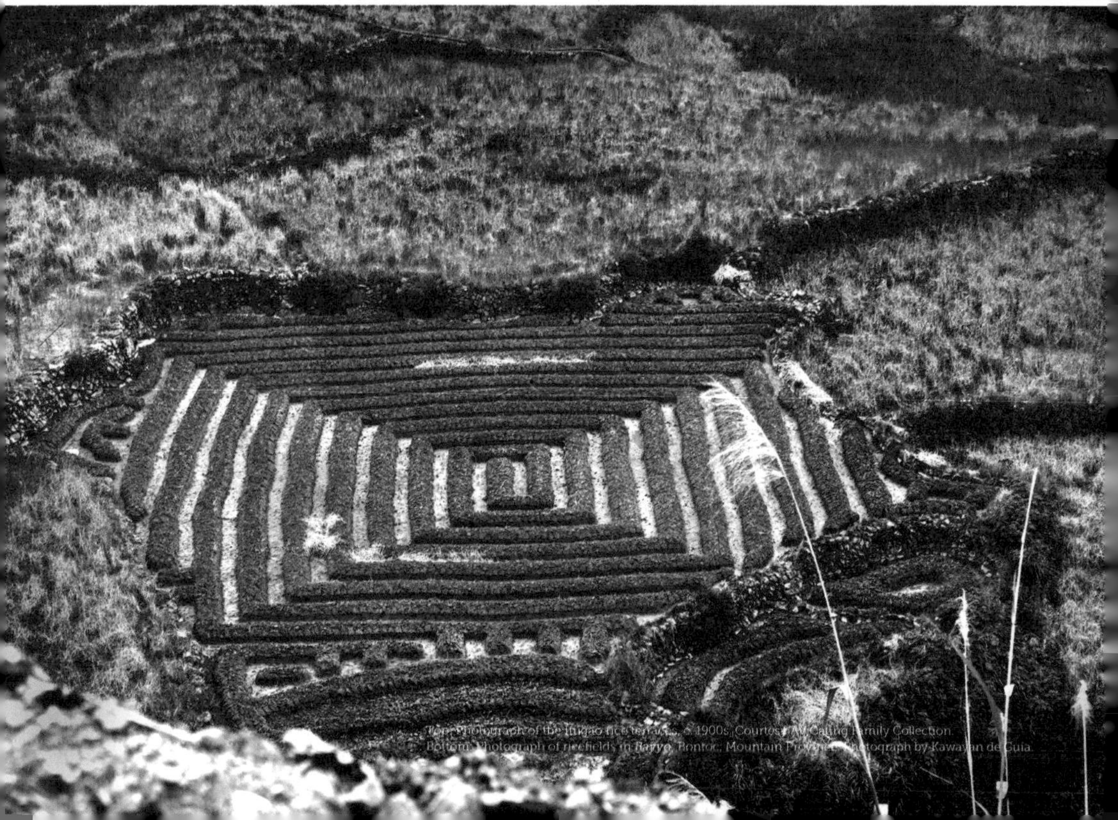

Top: Photograph of the Ifugao rice terraces, c.1900s. Courtesy of the Calling Family Collection.
Bottom: Photograph of ricefields in Bayyo, Bontoc, Mountain Province. Photograph by Kawayan de Guia.

Man Sinup, Willy Magtibay, watercolor, pen and ink on paper, 2013.

Sabusab *(KAN)*. On the third day of the begnas, the elders carry the heads of the sacrificial animals – the pig, the dog, and the chicken – and they bring water, a bolo, and put all their buwaya in a winnowing basket, and they take these to the dap-ay for the palis. TDH.
See also: Bangon; Bedbed; Begnas; Buwaya; Dap-ay; Iyag.

Sadkik *(BON/KAN)* also **Satkik** *(KAN)*. Indigenized from 'hotcake,' it is any homemade pancake or hotcake, popular in Bauko and Bontoc, where it is sold in bus terminals. Also popular is "sinamon napudot [hot cinnamon rolls]," which are sold at the fringes of the Baguio market. NEP.
See also: Barako.

Sadshak *(IBA)*. Happiness. Although in Baguio Ilokano, this means 'I am sad.'

Safeng *(BON)* also **Tengba** *(KAN)*, **Sabeng** *(KAN)*. Juice from fermented raw camote or cassava. This sour drink used to be very popular in Bontoc as it is an excellent thirst-quencher and good for colds, flu, stomach problems, and a hangover. It also increases breast milk. When corn is in season, the cob is added. Sometimes leftover animal bones are boiled and added to make the aroma stronger. One used to freely ask for safeng in Bontoc, and in some villages, a jar of safeng is left outside the house for anyone to drink. PAD.
See also: Abungol; Aw-aw; Bakkay; Camote; Sinaplak.

Sagada Ceramic Center. In 2001, Archie Stapleton Jr., son of an Episcopalian missionary who was based for a long time in Sagada, went back to Sagada with Jaime de Guzman. With land and a building donated by Thomas Killip and funding by Ella Lyman Cabot's trust, they set up a gas-fired kiln and trained a new batch of Sagada residents as ceramicists. The new potters like Lope Bosaing, Siegrid Bangyay, and Tessa Baldo, among others, are characterized by their inventive forms using the simplest of high-fired natural glazes and incorporating twigs and bamboo for handles. The SCC works have been exhibited in Baguio and Manila. FYC.
See also: De Guzman, Jaime.

Sagada Lunch. A famous, or rather controversial, food eatery found in the backrstreets of Baguio, on Dagohoy Street and its annex at Rajah Soliman. It allegedly used to serve dog prior to the Animal Welfare Act. It also serves pinikpikan. In the late 1990s, Koreans were said to have also eaten dogmeat on the second floor of Sagada Lunch. Other so-called dog eateries are those found on Katipunan Street and a popular spot on Marcos Highway. Some animal rights activists and law enforcement agents would pose as dog eaters so it was a game of cat-and-mouse or rather cat-and-dog for them and the waiters. FYC.
See also: Dog-eating.

Sagada Weaving. Located at Nangonogan, Poblacion in Sagada, the weaving shop started only in 1968 and is now the biggest local employer of weavers, churning out hundreds of woven bags, wallets, runners, caps and many others. Its distinctive local weaving designs, a stripe, a diamond and two half-diamonds forming an X of any two colors was granted a patent certificate in 2011, the first such patent to be awarded in the province. The shop has also shifted to dobby-weaving to make it easier to replicate traditional Cordilleran weaving designs like the pinilian and bird's eye. The dobby is a mechanical attachment on a loom that controls the harnesses, or the frames holding the heddles in position, to allow the weaving of the geometric designs. FYC.
See also: Cloth Dyes; Easter Weaving Room; Tapis; Wanes; Weaving.

Saga-ok *(KAN)*. The sharing of blessings with folks, especially the women and elders, by pocket miners who have been lucky in finding gold veins in their tunnels. Sharing is done by letting people work with the miner in exchange for gold ore. People say that a miner who doesn't follow this unwritten law of the community will suffer from bad mining luck or that the unrefined gold will suddenly disappear because the source deposit is enchanted. Makisaga-ok means to join the saga-ok. NEP.
See also: Dangtey; Kaman gangi; Lungos; Pansejew; Usok.

Sagawsaw *(KAN)*. A curse that can make someone crazy. DOS.
See also: Chapilang; Pakkaw; Salopey.

Saklot girls. Women paid to sit on the laps of videoke habitués especially in Mankayan and Buguias, Benguet. FYC.

Salabao *(ISN)*. A traditional name still used up to the present to refer to someone witty and small, the characteristics of the ancestor from whom this name originated. A small boy given this name who proves his wit can be complemented with, "*Salabao ka nga talaga! [You really are Salabao!]*" GAD.
See also: Ambit, Ambot, Amboy; Apugay.

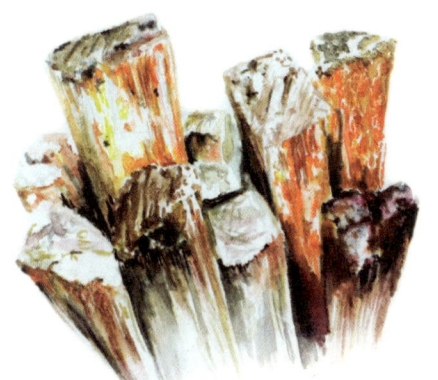

Saleng *(BON/KAN)* also **Halong** *(IFU)*. The resinous or fat part of pinewood used as kindling.

Saleng Productions. This is the 'drama' maker of the radio station DZWX Bombo Radyo Baguio, which in 2007 provided the Ilocano radio drama productions for the rest of Northern Luzon. Its productions include *Pagsarmingan* (Mirror), *Laughingly Yours, Bianong, Doming Mabalin Amin, Kapitana Orang* and *Once There Was A Love*. These radio drama serials are the favorite of ukay-ukay (secondhand clothes) sellers. FYC.

Salip *(ISN)*. Dance usually performed during weddings, on the 40th day after a death, and at fiestas and community gatherings. The dance is accompanied with music created by slapping the gongs with the palms. The fast movement of the feet goes with the fast beat of the gongs. The arms are extended sideways throughout the dance. GAD.
See also: Bontoc Boogie; Challichog; Tadek.

Salopey *(KAN)* also **Halope** *(IFU)*. A curse. If you have been having bad dreams lately, if you are always unlucky with your ventures, or if you are sickly for no apparent reason, somebody must have put a curse on you. Talk to an elder healer, i.e., a Mansib-ok, about your experience and he or she will suggest ways to send the curse back to where it came from. Sinalopey means to experience a salopey curse. DOS.
See also: Mansib-ok; Pakkaw; Pattaliat; Sagawsaw.

Salupin. Indigenized from cellophane, referring to a plastic bag.

Sambag. Indigenized from 'handbag,' referring to any bag.

Samfu *(KAL)*. Whenever people observe the disappearance or the decrease of the water from springs, they believe that, in order to bring the water back, a ritual offering must be made to appease the spirits of the water source. The ritual, called samfu, is usually performed by an old man. Samfu involves the butchering of a chicken or a pig or even a humble offering such as an egg. The main feature of the ritual is the invocation of the old man, appeasing the spirits of the water, asking forgiveness for the disrespect done unto them, and a plea to bring back the water. The signs of samfu are left at the spring. Depending on what was offered, the sign could be the chicken's head, pig's jaws, and eggshells hung on sticks. This serves as a warning to everyone to refrain from polluting the water again. (Weygan 2011, 51-52). DOS.
See also: Ampasit.

Samiklay. An Igorot pirate and bandit who was known to have pillaged villages in the towns of Bontoc, Sabangan, Bauko, and Buguias in the 1800s. He stole rice and animals and he and his gang were reputed to have cut off peoples' heads if his wishes were not granted. He also kidnapped children and asked for gold, woven blankets and animals as ransom. Villagers from Buguias and Bauko escaped him and moved to the neighboring mountains of the Malaya Ranges, along Cervantes, Ilocos Sur. Samiklay settled and built a house in Loo in Abatan, Buguias, Benguet. Stories of his crimes and the exact area of his abode are still remembered by old folk to this day. DOS.

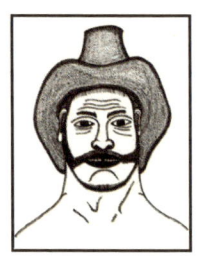

See also: Great Ifugao War; Hunt, Truman; Loo; Timicheg.

Samoki. Formerly Kidlaa, a barangay in the current municipality of Bontoc. The name change is attributed to American colonizers who referred to this village as *"smoky"* from the constant firing in ovens used for baking earthen pots, which this village was long ago famous for. Separated from Poblacion by a bridge over the Chico River, Samoki people have had a characteristic way of speech that is slightly different from the other side of the bridge. For example, people from Bontoc Ili (formerly Churyaa) would refer to a snake, a river and a sandal as uweg, wanga, and sandal, respectively, while those same words would be uwar, wangar and sandar for Samoki villagers, thus a joke arose that Samoki should actually be *"Samoker."* GAD.

Sangadil *(BON/KAN)*. The death chair. In Bontoc, Ifugao, and

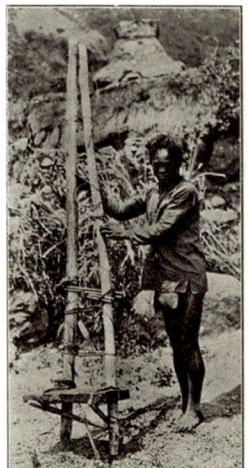

Photograph of *sangadil* or death chair, c. 1920s. Courtesy AV Cating Family Collection.

other mountain communities, the kadangyan who have attained a significant stature in the community's welfare are put on the sangadil upon death.

Sangbo *(KAN)*. This ritual is offered to Kabunian in appreciation of good fortune. Some omens are regarded as signifying good fortune, and it is believed that bad luck will fall upon those who do not perform the sangbo after receiving these omens. Sangbo is considered to be a Kankanaey formula for success. The Kankanaeys believe that ancestral spirits or the spirits of recently departed relatives can make their living relatives wealthy by sending them omens subject to wise interpretation of the man-ila and the performance of the sangbo ritual. Such omens can be unexplained phenomena or observed in dreams. In one incident, a Kankanaey family once observed that during a ritual, a family member dreamt that he was given a bundle of iwik (pointed wood pegs used for killing pigs during rituals) by one of his ancestors. Later, the mambunong and the man-ila interpreted the dream as a good omen. The sangbu was then performed to accept whatever blessings the iwik omen would bring them. Sometime after, the family observed that whenever they planted carrots, the prices went up. The luck was attributed to the iwik dream. Other signs for which the sangbo can be performed include bee hives inside and outside the house, entry of snakes, odd insects that enter the house, or birds entering the house during or after a ritual and staying for a while. NEP.
See also: Ichaw; Kabunian; Labeg.

Sapon. Japanese. Indigenized from the Filipino word Hapon.

Sapsap *(IBA)*. Reed or runo whose sharp-edged leaves have many uses in the Ibaloi culture: (a) its green leaves are used as agpay required in shilos ceremonies where the living relatives hold feasts to appease the spirits of their ancestors; (b) its leaves, when knotted at the end, are placed in certain areas as porong; (c) its leaves are used in the last part of the siling (Ibaloi funeral rite), when the mambunong dips sapsap in water and wasiwas (waves) it over the deceased's family; (d) it is used to heal wounds; (e) its shoots are eaten raw as a salad; (f) its mature leaves as roofing material, particularly as the peded, or the first layer. (Ballard 2011, 424) SKW.
See also: Agpay; Mambunong; Purchos; Runo; Tangay.

Sarsarita ni Uncle Pete *(ILO)*. Lit. Stories of Uncle Pete. In the 1970s to 1980s, children would hurry back to their homes at 6PM (right after the motion-freezing Angelus) and listen to Uncle Pete on DZWT as he rehashed Aesop's fables, stories of Lola Basyang and other tales in Ilocano. After 15 minutes, it was back to fun and games but with a little bromide from Uncle Pete in mind. FYC.
See also: Angelus; DZWT; Saleng Productions.

Saxo *(ISN)*. Any matter that flows through the nose and mouth of a corpse.
See also: Sangadil.

Say-am *(ISN)*. Ritual dedicated to Anglabbang, the tutelary spirit of headhunters. Once held to celebrate a successful headhunt, it is now the main festival during Apayao's founding day on February 14. The say-am's headhunting origin is supplanted by the sacrifice of a dog head, the splitting of coconuts and the tungtung, where the dorarakit dance in a trance on a large boulder encircled by warriors. The entire village participates in the say-am with the men shouting the maxaroroy (war cry) while pounding the boulder with their bamboo poles, and the women holding head axes and rice bundles while showering the men with rice. FYC.
See also: Dorarakit; Headhunting (the tale); Lalong; Pakkaw; Palpaliwat; Tongtongan.

Sayangan. A popular stop-over for buses and vans along the Halsema Highway, located at the northern end of Sayangan. Its name was derived from the number of so-called cabarets and gambling areas in the area in the 1960s: wives would tell their husband-farmers not to go to this place because their money would be 'sayang [wasted].' Because of the constant nagging and the truth it bore, the place gradually became known as Sayangan. DOS.
See also: Halsema Highway.

Sayay *(KAN)*. Paracelis betel bag worn by men around their necks. It is a red cloth bag filled with their betel nut, lime and tobacco. FYC.
See also: Moma; Paracelis.

Sayote. This Mexican plant was introduced to Baguio by Mariano Oteyza, grandfather of Kidlat Tahimik and the country's forestry chief. Now, sayote haciendas are a common thing not only in Baguio but in Tuba, Tublay, and Kapangan where they cover certain highly-valued plants. Like the Taiwanese and Thai, Cordillerans love to turn the sayote tops into salad or phat yot sayongte (stir fried sayote tops) and, like the Brazilians and Indonesians, Cordillerans love to add the fruit in a stew or tinola. Sayote is also known as the Baguio lifesaver because adding it to sardinas makes an instant meal. Not only in the pre-import liberalization Philippines but also in Australia, there is a rumor that fastfood apple pie is actually sayote with apple sauce. This rumor still persists down under because sayote does not get soggy like apple when cooked. Sayote plantations use the fruit as hog feed. Ketchup and spice sauce manufacturers also order it to use as extenders for their products. FYC.
See also: Baguio Bean; Binaod; Buguias Patatas; Camote; Num-a; Zucchini.

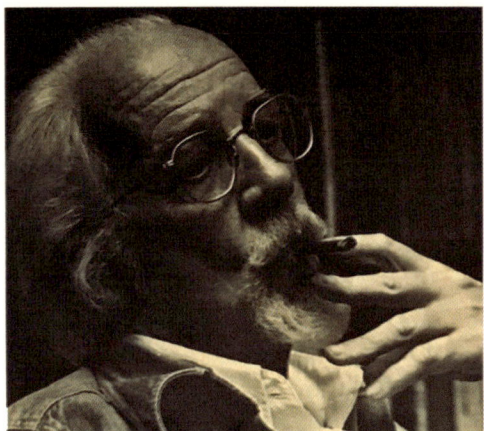

Photograph of **William Henry Scott**. Photograph by Eric de Castro.

Scotty. William Henry Scott wrote 15 books on anthropology, history and ethnography, mostly on the Cordilleras. He arrived in Sagada in 1954 to become an Episcopal missionary and stayed there for the next 40 years. He taught Igorots to be proud of themselves and even fought the Marcos regime, which caused him to be detained. He fought for Cordillera autonomy even before it became popular. He loved the Cordillera more than most Cordillerans. He died in October 1993 and we dedicate this 'Uncyclopaedia' to him. FYC.

Seddag *(IBA)*. Moonlight or moonshine.
See also: Balikawkaw; Beska; Lennek; Moon Craters; Teke.

Self-Determination. The right of a group to determine its own future including form of government, i.e. the Cordillera's assertion for autonomy or at least the original proposal embodied in the 1987 Constitution. The organic acts for Cordillera autonomy were watered down and both acts were rejected in two plebiscites. FYC.

Session Road. The main thoroughfare of Baguio City's Central Business District.

Sheket *(IBA)*. [1] To cause something to adhere or to stick like rice to a pot.
[2] A very sharp knife that when thrown, sticks into the wood without bouncing off.

Shy Mango *(IBA)*. *"how to spot an ibaloi: they are the guys who stays near the walls of a room in a social gathering, and jaz smiles(ngishit) if ask to go in front. They point to one another when called, (sikam ga!).;they say "eh eh" instead of i'm sorry.;they always use the word "timing".;they have "wat wat" on the inside pocket of their jacket carried on one shoulder, and a toothpick protruding from their mouth,(this is when they come from a party.).;"* – comment left on the blog *From the Boondocks* by user sahiy ya ibadoi ngo', 2006.
See also: Ingat; Ma-imdong; Taraki; Watwat.

Sichot *(KAL)*. Chili. It is said that Kalingas always eat with sichot. The only time that a Kalinga cannot eat with sichot is during ngilin. During childbirth, spicy food is not allowed to be served and be eaten because it will make the birthing wound more painful. HZK.
See also: Amkis; Food; Inasin; Mandesangat; Ngilin.

Sidey *(KAN)*. A community healing ritual usually done every five years, or when many children have been falling ill in the community. Widespread illness among children is taken to mean that the ancestors are feeling neglected, and so a ritual must be performed. TDH.
See also: Begnas.

Sigsig *(IBA)*. To splinter or to chop wood into splinters.

Sikki *(ITN)*. *"A newborn baby is usually put on top of an inverted winnowing basket for the rite of sikki. The mammaltot (traditional midwife) carries the infant and starts the ceremony by saying: 'Sikki, sikki, your name is Ommi. May you grow up handsome/beautiful, healthy, generous and kind to everybody! Sikki, sikki.'"* (Sumangil 2003, 12).

Silag *(KAN)*. Woven rattan field hat.
See also: Suklong.

Silang, Gabriela. First known Filipina to lead a revolution against the Spaniards. She is often regarded as the Joan of Arc of the Ilocandia. She was born a mestiza, of Ilocano and Spanish descent in Santa, Ilocos Sur in 1731. She was adopted by a businessman who married her when she turned 20. Their marriage ended after three years when her husband left. After five years, she got married again to the Ilocano rebel Diego Silang. She was his adviser in the collaboration of Ilocano rebels with the short-lived British occupation to expel Spaniards from Vigan, Ilocos Sur. Diego Silang was later assassinated by the order of the royal church and authorities in Manila. Gabriela, in her rage, fled to the mountains of Abra to re-establish their troop and convince the Itneg communities to join their revolution. They went down to Vigan on the eve of September 10, 1763 but were awaited by a battalion of Tagalogs, Kapampangans, and Ilocano warriors assembled by the Spaniards to fight against them. Many lives were lost from her forces but she and her uncle, Nicolas, were able to escape. They would be caught weeks after on September 29 and were summarily hanged in Vigan. The present feminist political party Gabriela was named in her honor. A rumor about Gabriela Silang's descent interests many Itnegs today. It was known to many that her mother was Ilocana, but some claims are surfacing now that she was actually the daughter of a Itneg woman who was raped by a Spanish priest based in Pidigan, Abra. This was kept secret by the community to protect the Church especially since she was declared a National Heroine. Today, some Itneg researchers are proving that she is of Itneg bloodline. DOS.

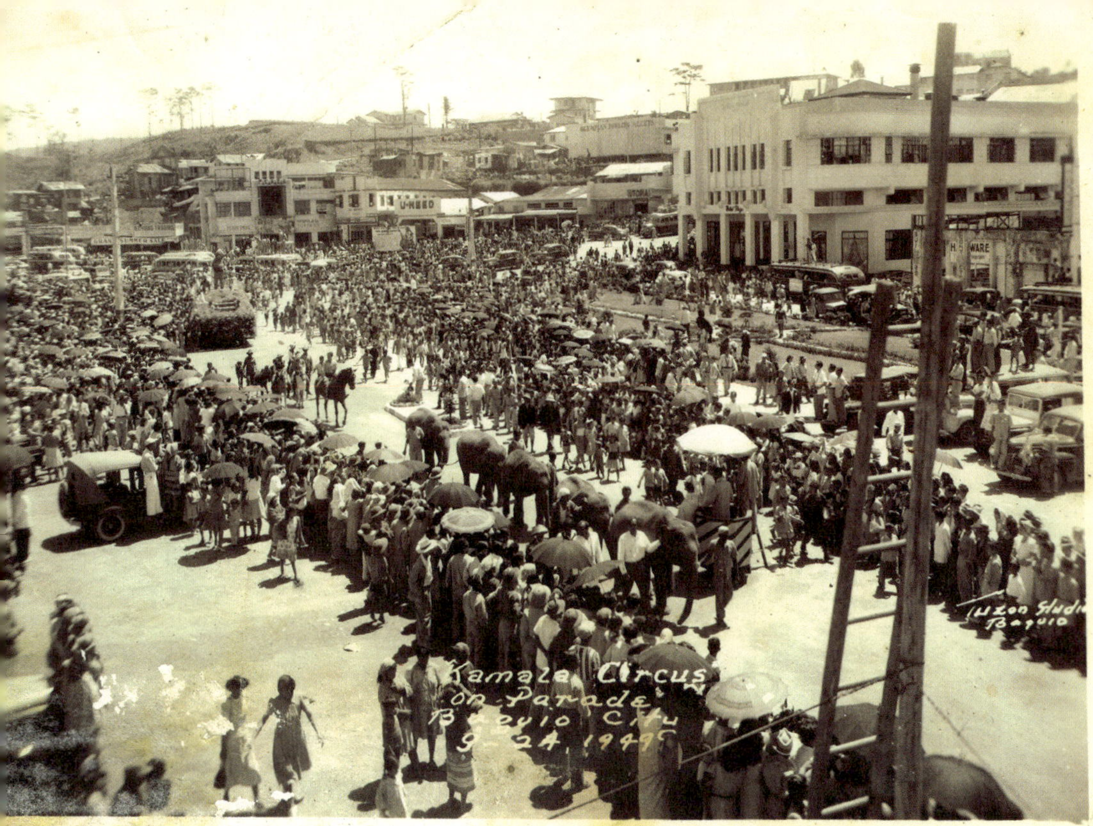

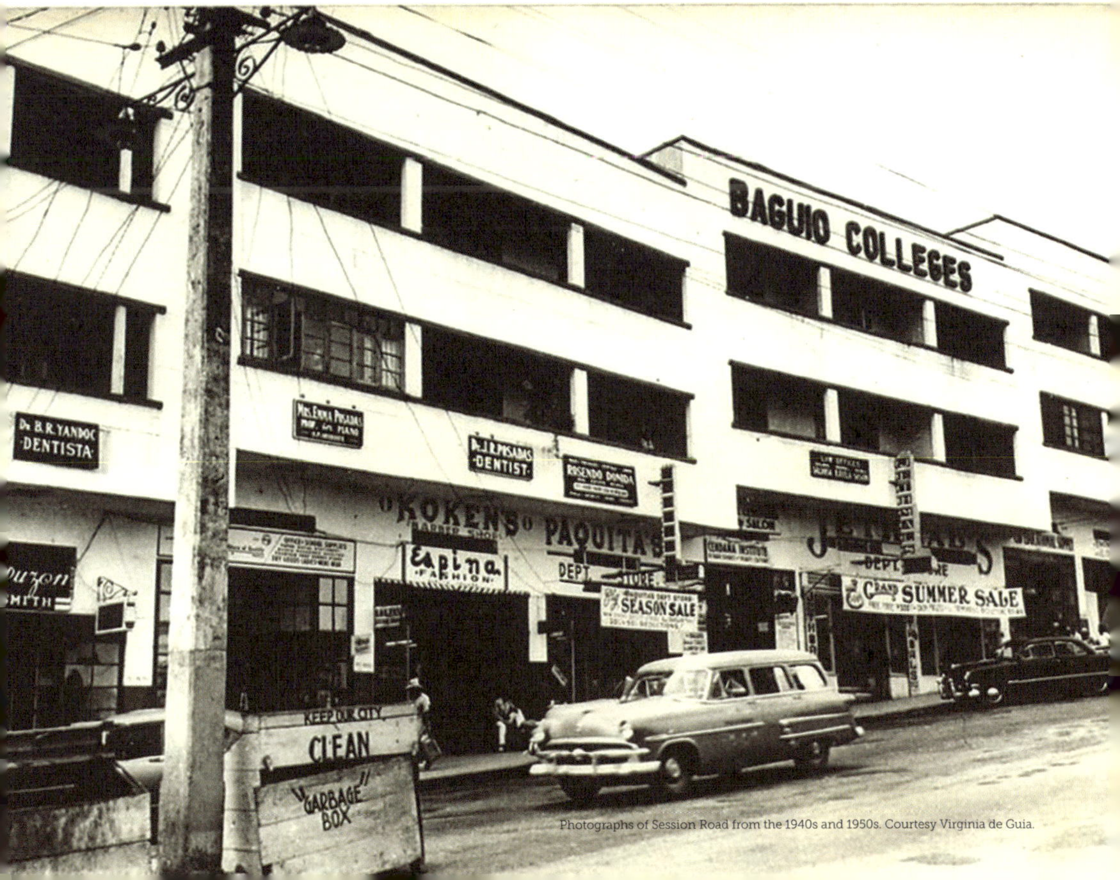

Photographs of Session Road from the 1940s and 1950s. Courtesy Virginia de Guia.

Silap *(KAN).* Coconut shell bowls.

Silay. [1] *(KAL).* House lizard. Be careful not to kill it for it may carry the soul of pigs. [2] (See Motit).

Silipanes. A lost tribe said to be those now from Halipan in Ifugao. *"The Silipanes are a stout and sturdy people who differ greatly from their neighbors, the Kiangans... Among these natives untouched by any civilization, you find excellent physiques; the women have very good figures, especially well-developed bosoms."* (Schadenberg 1975, 167).

Simtik *(KAN).* Smack lightly or smacking of tongue and lips.

Sinabalu *(ISN).* An Isneg delicacy prepared with sticky rice, coconut milk, and salt. Sticky rice is first soaked in water then drained. Coconut milk and salt is added. The salt serves to balance the umami of the coconut milk. A young bulo (bamboo) is then lined with leaves of an arukek (a wild tree). The sticky rice is cooked in this container over a bonfire. GAD.
See also: Patupat; Tufu.

Sinag-et *(ISN).* Among older Isnegs, sinag-et refers to a condiment of mostly native chilies cooked with a little bagoong (fermented salted shrimps) and green onion leaves. Among the younger generations, this word has evolved to also mean dishes cooked with lots of chilies and tomatoes. Fish or beans like patani or fresh cardis are mixed with chopped tomatoes. Prepared without oil or water, chili and salt are added to the beans or fish. This is then placed in a young bulo (a type of bamboo), lined on the inside with banana leaves. The filled bamboo is heated at the edge of a bonfire. When cooked, a wooden stick is used to lightly pound the bean/fish mixture. This is then poured out from the bamboo and served. Beans and fish and other similar dishes cooked this way are also called binasal. GAD.
See also: Food; Intum; Sichot; Sinaplak.

Sinalupsop *(KAN).* Ground boko made into a pudding.
See also: Boko; Camote; Kineykhey.

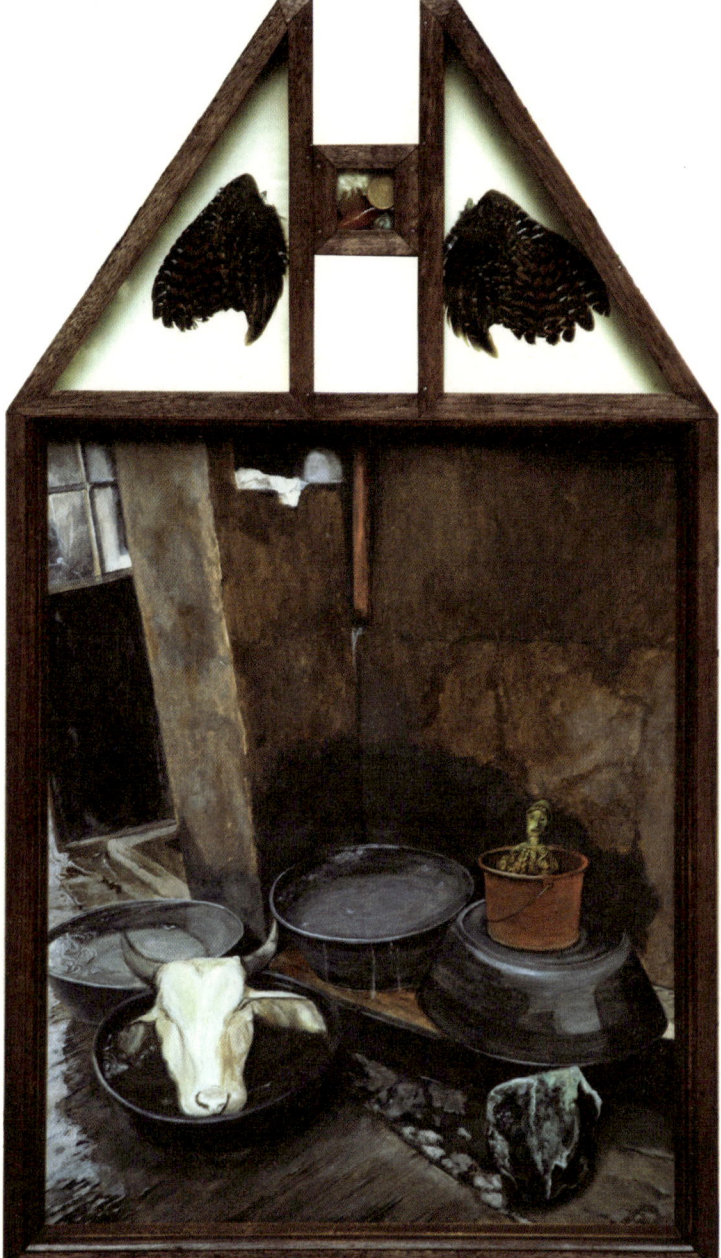

Artwork by Rocky Cajigan depicting a scene of the *Slaughter* area in Baguio City.

Sinan-adom *(KAN)* also **Sinangad-um** *(BON)*. (1) When people say sinan-adom, it usually refers to a conversation with words so deep that only the elders would understand, in the same way that today's English speakers do not readily understand Old English. (2) It refers to the ancient or very old ways, i.e. wearing an indigo wanes. TDH.
See also: Agay-o.

Sinaplak *(BON)*. A dish among the Bontoc villages near the river banks consisting of rice and gadew (small river fish) boiled in plenty of safeng. When the rice is cooked, the watery mixture is strained and the soup is served separately. This is prepared on occasions like the celebration of the start of the planting season or after a funeral when men would go to the river and catch gadew. Only a handful is served per person so it doesn't need to be served on a dish. It is served directly on the hand or on wide leaves. PAD.
See also: Food; Intum; Safeng; Sinag-et.

Siniktiman *(KAN)*. A tangy Cordilleran dish in which pinikpikan (especially its soup) is mixed with etag and tapuey. The dish is also a perfect appetizer and when served as a soup for a Cordilleran drinking spree (mostly with gin), it guarantees that drunkenness will be achieved twice as quickly. HZK.
See also: Butong; Liwliwot; Nafutengak; Pinikpikan.

Sinipsip. A sitio that is part of both Bakun and Buguias, Benguet. Back when Dangwa was the only busline plying Halsema Highway, Sinipsip was the only stopover. It got its name because the chill would seep through your bones (Sinipsip is on a major windpath). Colder than Sinipsip, however, is Madaymen at the foot of Mt. Osdung in Kibungan, which is the highest inhabited village in the country. FYC.
See also: Little Alaska.

Sipsipnget *(ILO)*. Lit. Darkness. A common Baguio expression is *"Apay taga-Barrio Sipsipnget ka? [Are you from some dark village],"* which really means *"Are you so out of touch that electricity has not reached your place?"* Sipsipnget was the original name of Baguio City's Barangay Hillside but it had to be changed because of its proximity to Camp John Hay and a dark jungle cannot be a neighbor to an American rest-and-recreation area. FYC.
See also: John Hay, Camp; Slaughter.

Slaughter. One of the biggest barangays (villages) in Baguio. So named because it was and still is, despite the new zoning law, the site of the city's abattoir. It is the best place to eat meat stew and innards in Baguio, considering the ambiance. Various attempts have been made to deodorize its name: from *"Hidden Valley"* in the early 1980s, to Santo Niño in the late 1980s, only because a women's group there erected a shrine of the Santo Niño (Baby Jesus) near their basketball court. The shrine was later demolished to give way to the village hall. It is now more formally (and macabre-ly) known as Santo Niño Slaughter. FYC.
See also: Sipsipnget.

Spear Blades. *"The one most common is called 'fal-fěg.' It is a simple, single-barbed blade, and ranges from 2 inches to 6 inches in length. This style of blade is the most used in warfare, and the smaller, lighter blades are considered better for this purpose than the heavier ones. The fang-kao, or barbless lance blade, is next common in use. It is not a war blade, but is used almost entirely in killing carabaos and hogs. There is one notable exception to this statement – Ambawan has almost no other class of spear. These blades range from 4 to 12 or 14 inches in length. The other two blades, si-na-la-wi-tan and kay-yan, are relatively rare. The former is quite similar to the fal-fěg, except that instead of the single pair of barbs there are other barbs – say, from one to ten pairs. This spear is not considered at all serviceable as a hunting spear, and is not used in war as much as is the fal-fěg. It is prized highly as an anito scarer. When a man passes alone in the mountains anito are very prone to walk with him; however, if the traveler carries a si-na-la-wi-tan, anito will not molest him, since they are afraid when they see the formidable array of barbs."* (Jenks 2005).
See also: Anito.

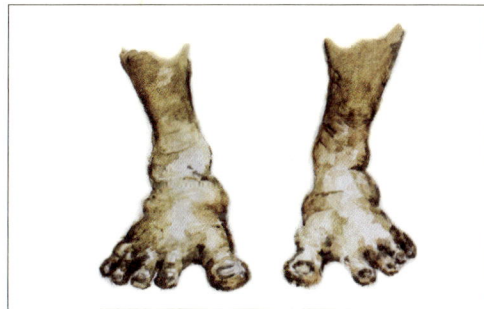

Illustration by Matilda Glass.

Splayed feet. Also known as casco feet or in Bontoc, fa-wing. It is the inturning of the toes, said to have been a result of mountain (and tree) climbing since the toes have become the claws for secure footing. Also common among the Igorots of yore is the enlargement by the basal joint of the toe caused by bunions and bruises. Recently, the popularity of ukay-ukay Birkenstock and Crocs have made splayed feet fashionable. FYC.

Squaw men. Americans who married Igorot women in the 1900s were called Squaw men. They were discriminated against by fellow Americans.
See also: AFRTN; Annual Headhunter's Fund; Haight's Place; Hunt, Truman; Nikimalika; Pre-white; Thomasites;

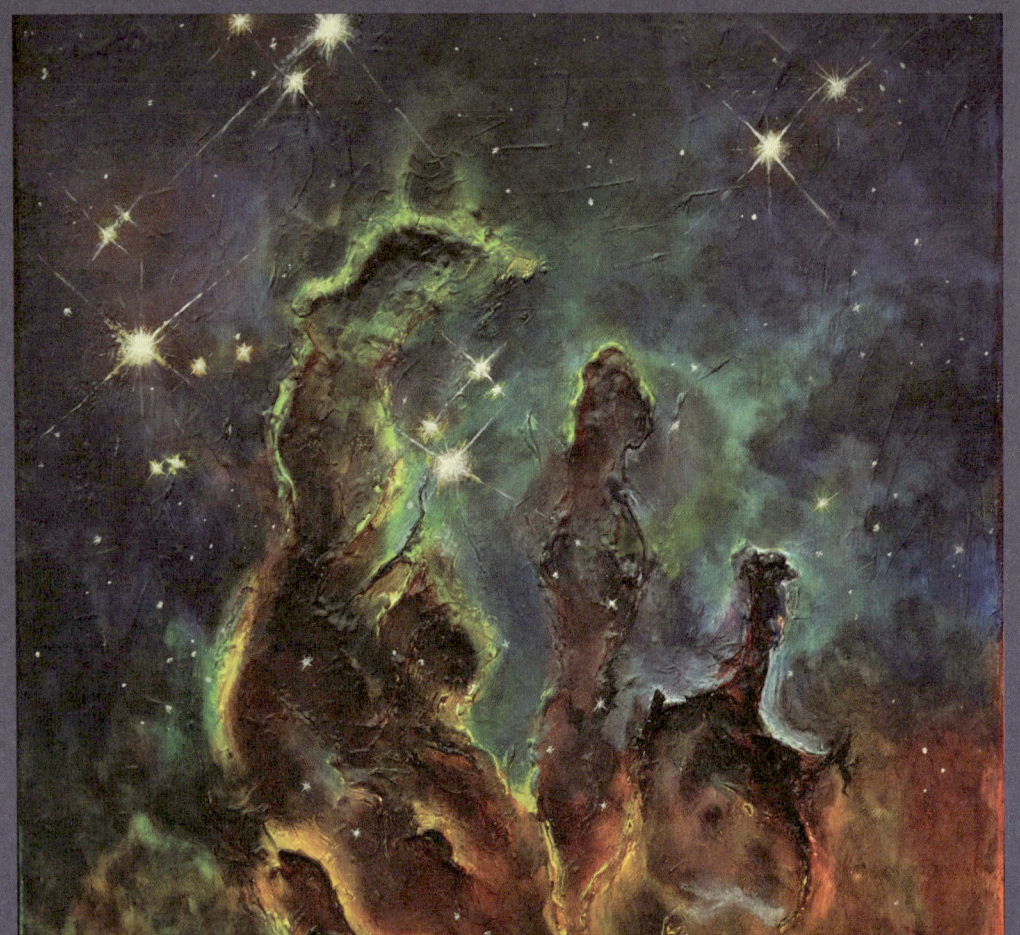

Artwork by Solana Perez, 2019.

Stargazing:
The Best Way to Observe Stars

I was asked to write an article on the *"best way to observe stars"* in part because I have been observing them for over half a century, and in part because I have been an avid amateur astronomer with all sorts of telescopes. Yet with the credentials of having all my telescopes, personal observatory, and countless images of deep space, I still think the best way to observe stars is with nice grass under a clear dark sky.

I like to go high on a hill-top away from bright city lights, during a clear dark night with little more than a warm jacket and a like-minded friend to lie flat on my back, on a patch of grass, facing only the sky. All lights have to be turned off to let your eyes get fully dark-adapted and sensitive to the delicate glow of starlight streaming in from very far far away. On your back, one experiences the sky in a manner that cannot possibly be felt while standing up and looking at the sky with neck awkwardly tilted back. On your back you will see the vastness of the sky to your left, to your right, directly above, on top of your head, and down to your toes. You will feel yourself silently hurtling among the stars while attached to a big lump of spaceship-earth behind you. And to think there is actually another hemisphere of stars behind you and that lump of dirt you are stuck to! The utter all-encompassing vastness of the star-filled sky becomes quickly and intimately apparent in the supine position. I have found myself holding my breath at the stark beauty of countless points of light dusting the dark backdrop of infinity. And being in the high Cordilleras above the dense and obscuring atmosphere of the lowlands makes the experience feel even closer. Behold the heavens!

A point eventually comes when staring at the light of the night sky makes you feel one with what is being stared at. A point comes when you realize you are staring God in the face and He is looking back at you with your own reflection. You realize that in the vastness of it all, stars are mere specks of dust, recycled matter and energy in an endless dance of transformative permutations that somehow, in this particular space and time, took the shape of one staring up at itself on a dark grassy hilltop, enjoying the best way to observe stars. JN.

Strawberries. *"Benguet is the finest place on Earth: I cannot say too much of the beautiful climate and fine views. I had a large plate of strawberries from Mr. Petrelli's farm at Trinidad which had an exquisite flavor. And I saw at the farm what I never expected to see in this country – genuine peach tree in bloom."* (Executive Secretary Arthur Fergusson, January 4, 1908).
See also: Galvey, Gullermo; Xandaro, Eduardo.

Strike & Spare Bowling Lanes. Mabini Street in Baguio was the 'bowling lane' of the city with three bowling alleys (Aurora, Colorado, and Strike & Spare [S&S]). These bowling alleys were always full during the weekends. When the country was going tenpin (Baguio produced a national tenpin bowling champion in Bec Watanabe), Baguio was still duckpin country because most of the customers, mostly mine workers, loved the small granite and shale duckpin balls. Not to mention that the suki (regular) pinboys would sometimes group your pins so that a strike was easily achieved, or, they would kick the pins not hit by the ball. The July 1990 earthquake destroyed the Aurora theater/bowling/billiard building while the lanes of Colorado and S&S became warped and are now defunct. Today, one of the duckpin bowling alleys in Mabini is still in operation (with the last duckpin holdouts in the Philippine Military Academy and in the mining communities). FYC.
See also: Gingined.

Sudsud *(KAN)*. To tell a tale or story or piece of gossip in a sing-song way.
See also: Tayubtub.

Sukarno. The title of a video production made about the traditional engagement practices of the Isneg. Materials for moma, or betel nut chewing, are used in the ceremony. In the video, a woman gives a seed (bua) to the man, while the man gives the lime (apog) to the woman. When a man and woman have exchanged such items in an engagement ceremony, the community recognizes their union and no other man/woman attempts to woo or court the engaged person. GAD.
See also: Moma; Moma by myself.

Suklong *(KAL)*. A warrior's woven hat. When it falls, all fighting will stop and no one will take advantage of the cessation until the suklong is picked up, then the fighting resumes. FYC.
See also: Akipur; Apang; Bayoyok; Duwao; Kulatod; Panglao; Silag.

Suma *(ISN)*. A common woody vine which is used to cure snake bites by chewing the bitter stem and spitting it on the wound.
See also: Pokingang.

Sumursurot si ug-ugali *(KAN)*. Lit. Following the traditions and practices or worldviews. It refers to Kankanaeys who believe and follow the Kankanaey ways of life. NEP.
See also: Ugali.

Survivance. Anishinaabe critic and writer Gerald Vizenor's (2008) term for survival, endurance, and the repudiation of dominance often seen in contemporary Cordillera texts.
See also: Historical Trauma Response; Igorotism; Imperialist Nostalgia.

Suwit *(KAN)*. A special weighing scale for etag. THD.
See also: Etag; Food; Inasin.

Swan. Juan, indigenized by the Bontok, according to William Clapp's dictionary.
See also: Kaling; R. Rolling the Rs.

Stonecutting. *"Man sees a woman walking at night near the guardian stones. She refuses to talk and he cuts her in the thigh. She vanishes into the stones. Next day it is seen that one of the stones is cut. Man dies."* (Cole (1922) 2004)

Swardspeak

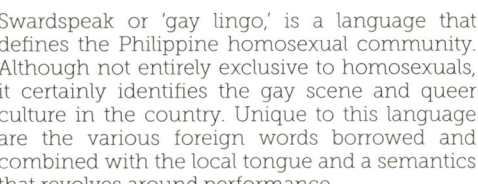

Swardspeak or 'gay lingo,' is a language that defines the Philippine homosexual community. Although not entirely exclusive to homosexuals, it certainly identifies the gay scene and queer culture in the country. Unique to this language are the various foreign words borrowed and combined with the local tongue and a semantics that revolves around performance.

Words in this language rely heavily on how they are performed by the speaker. It is not what one says that matters but how one says it. Swardspeak is characteristic of pop and Philippine gay culture and has thus been developed along with being gay in the Philippines: humor and wit, snark and sarcasm, flair and finesse, and gossip and secrets fill sentences punctuated with a swish of the hips and a 'broken' wrist.

Eventually, swardspeak reached the indigenous North where various communities have their own, depending on the local languages they speak. For the indigenous homosexual speaker, swardspeak necessitates a double performance: the Igorot as both an indigenous and colonial identity is coupled with the swardspeaking performance. Interestingly, the words borrowed by the sward from the foreign are also words of the colonizers. The Igorot is spoken into the language making the indigenous colonial experience not only an identity remembered but also borrowed and performed. What matters then is not how it is spoken but on who is speaking. KC
See also: Vakla.

Weaving Cultures, Dissolving Boundaries

"Banit!" My grandfather clearly repeated the word so I could write it down. Banit is an arm-length size of a cone made of woven coconut leaves used to wrap salt. With this packaging, the salt could withstand the melting heat of the sun along the riverside of the Rio Abra and the damp coldness of the highlands when the Ilocano traders carry it and find their way to the Igorot communities in the mountains. There were two trade routes that were taken by Ilocano and Igorot barter traders. The earlier pre-Hispanic routes were the Candon-San Emilio-Angaki (now Quirino, Ilocos Sur)-Besao-Bontoc and the Candon-San Emilio-Angaki-Cervantes-Tadian-Bauko. In the late 19th century, the interest of the Spaniards in Suyoc gold led to the development of the Tagudin-Suyo-Cervantes-Mankayan trail into a road, which became known as the Spanish Trail. The Igorot traders exchanged their gold, copper, honey, wax, rattan, cured deer meat, and other forest products (Wilson, 1953, p. 88) with lowland salt, handwoven textiles, and earthen jars. *"Nakakariton da."* Grandfather remembers that the Ilocanos used wagons dragged by carabaos to transport their trade.

Beginning with the creation of the Mountain Province under American rule in 1908, highland-Igorots have been the favored focus of ethnology and anthropology for their previously un-colonized culture. This drawing of arbitrary geo-political and artificial cultural boundaries is attributable to Dean C. Worcester, member of the Philippine Commission and Secretary of the Interior. It has led to a dichotomy between the highland-Igorots and the lowland Christianized Ilocanos. An enmity developed from the misrepresentation of Igorots as uncivilized, while on the other hand, Ilocanos were described as weak for falling under the rule of the conquistadores. Often, the enmity is so strong that a generative discourse on the shared history of lowlanders and highlanders ought to be reclaimed. The salt trade provides major evidence of a mutual relationship between the two cultures.

"Nabalor san asin ed-idi." Salt was valuable then. Before the Igorots learned to make counterfeit Spanish coins out of copper, which was abundant in their mines, gold, rice, and salt were used as currency. In the olden times, one could exchange gold or a hectare of a rice-field for several banit of salt.

In those days, the mountain dwellers wore loincloths made from the beaten bark of a tree. When the trade relations between the two communities strengthened, the Ilocanos provided the Igorots with woven loincloths and skirts. The craft of weaving was adopted by the

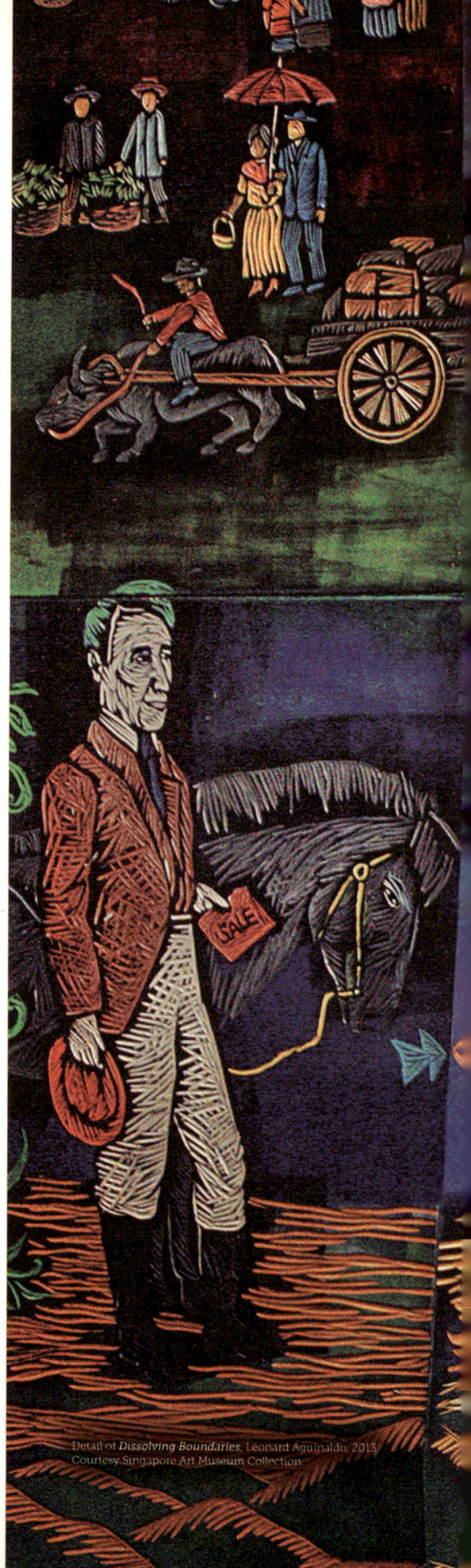

Detail of *Dissolving Boundaries*, Leonard Aguinaldo, 2013. Courtesy Singapore Art Museum Collection.

SALT TRADE

mountain dwellers and up to now, is considered one of the important industries of highland material culture.

Trade between the highlanders and the lowlanders was healthy except during events of misunderstanding. Flaymegh and Scott (1978) recovered an Igorot-Ilocano Peace Pact that dates back to the year 1820. The document is in fact a peace pact entered into for the purpose of *"restoring the highland-lowland trade,"* which had been broken off three years before after the death of an Igorot in Tagudin and the retaliatory killing of an Ilocano in Bangar. Agustin Decdec of Cay-ang (now Kayan, Tadian, Mountain Province) together with 18 others with Igorot names are signatories to the agreement with 60 Spanish-named Ilocano signatories of Tagudin, Ilocos Sur. It was further noted that the 1820 peace pact was based on earlier peace pact agreements between the two aggrieved parties.

Intermarriage between the ethnic communities of the lowlands and the highlands was part and parcel of the trade. For example, it has been claimed that the Abayas of Candon are descendants of the Igorota Abay, from Lamaoan, whose sister is Ganggang-a, who is married to Casindo. The story goes that since it was not possible to prosper agriculturally in Lamaoan, Ganggang-a and Casindo went in search for a good place and found Besao in the highlands. Ganggang-a's siser, Abay, chose to go down to lowland Candon and got married there. After three generations, the population of Besao grew to 300. The elders decided that they were strong enough in numbers to go down to barter in the lowlands. This journey was led by Maksil, the grandson of Ganggang-a. When they reached the coast, a lowland father and a son were shocked by their appearance. The father ran away but the Igorots captured the young boy whom they brought home. Years later, the young boy, Quiño, grew up and felt homesick so he decided to visit his family. When he went down to Candon to his parents, he asked about the whereabouts of the Igorot woman Abay. He learned that he was actually a descendant of hers (Robertson 1914).

The spiritual relationship between the lowlanders and highlanders is also tied to salt. Its importance was not only in flavoring and preserving food, but in rituals. Etag, a salted and smoked pork, is ever present during rituals. It is part of the offerings to the spirits. In Sagada, Mt. Province, rituals cannot go on if there is no etag. Sangadil, the mortuary practice done by noble-blooded Igorots involves washing the dying person in brine. Once dead, the person is tied to a chair and smoked. It stays seated for days as relatives come to pay their final respects. Sangadil was only performed for the noble and rich class, those who could afford the lowland white gold: salt. The famous mummies of Kabayan, Benguet may have also used salt in the mummification process.

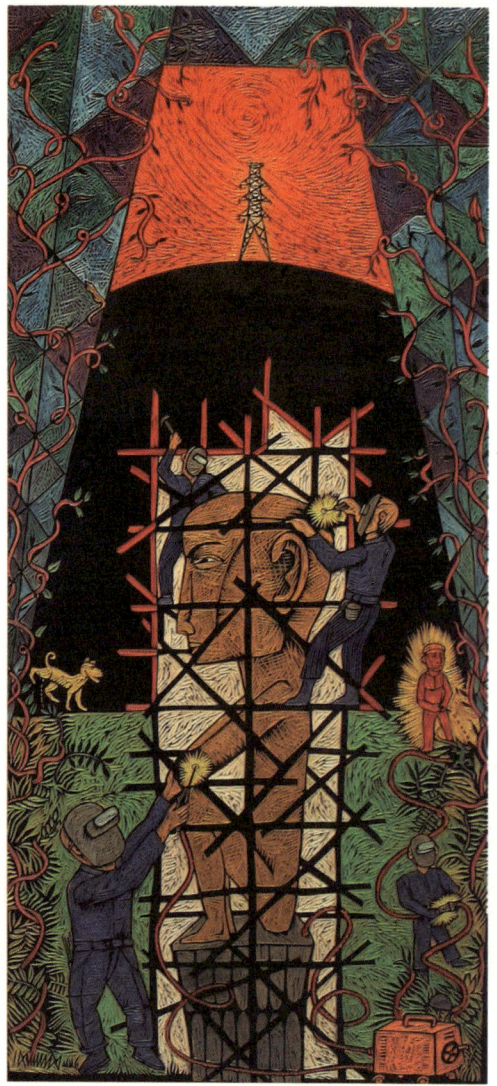

Power Lines, Leonard Aguinaldo, handcard carved rubber (ukir), 91x46 cm, 2006.

These past connections have become memories that have depreciated in value as did the value of salt. We inherited an ethnic dichotomy from our colonial past that for some artists like Leonard Aguinaldo, is important to tackle in his work by redirecting the audience's gaze towards a shared grassroots history.

Leonard Aguinald was was born and raised in the upland city of Baguio but traces his ancestry to Candon in the lowland Ilocos region. . His parents moved to the mountains for trade. Aguinaldo's early works often shows the highland and lowland cultural in panoramic canvasses of

Opposite page: *Specimens ca. 1900s*, Leonard Aguinaldo, mixed media, 51x132 cm, 2014.

rubber cuts colored with strong hues of acrylic.

One of his major works was a bicycle journey through the communities of Benguet to research and listen to the stories of Igorot elders. He created pieces of art from these stories and instead of displaying them in galleries in the cities, he spoke to the local governments of these communities if he could have his works shown in their municipal halls, barangay halls, or public schools. *"I borrowed those materials from them so I had to bring them back. Bagi da met [the stories are theirs, not mine],"* he said when asked why he felt the need to do the traveling art exhibit.

A man of few words, he speaks his thoughts by carving images on rubber to create narratives of Igorot rituals, stories he heard from elders, and everyday experiences along the streets of Baguio. His themes are often grounded in cultural symbols and ancestral imagery. He is an avid researcher of the past. He often draws the themes in his work from stories of the past told to him by his grandmother during his visits to the lowlands as a young boy.

Leonard Aguinaldo is among the Baguio-based award-winning visual artists who have contributed to forms of art that are distinctly Cordilleran. He was an artist-in-residence at the Vermont Studio Center in the US in 2009. He was recognized as the Best Emerging ASEAN Artist in 2004 and garnered the Grand Prize in the ASEAN Arts Award sponsored by Philip Morris in Bangkok, Thailand. He was also a Cultural Center of the Philippines' Thirteen Artists Awardee in 2003, and received the Special Selection Award for the SEA Art Festival Installation Contest at the Busan Biennale 2002 in South Korea.

Although he is an Ilocano by blood, his yearning for belonging to the mountains of his birth led him to create art where he would find his own roots linked to the historical culture of the highland-lowland trade relationship. He may have trodden paths across the world farther than he ever expected to reach but he still longs to trace the trails his ancestors traversed. He remembers his grandmother's stories of trade when they used to travel via La Union to go to Baguio to exchange their products with the native Igorots. She also told him stories of the old salt trade, which she had heard from her own elders. He retells these stories in his rubber-cut art installation entitled *Dissolving Boundaries,* a replica of a specific Kandong Tree.

This was a tree in a village on the coast of the West Philippine Sea, under which, centuries ago, Igorot traders would rest and display their wares for Ilocano traders. This village is now known as Candon. The Kandong tree had branches extending far from its trunk, and its wide shade served as an umbrella for traders. At present, a church now stands where the Kandong tree used to shade commerciantes. The pre-Hispanic historical link of the Ilocanos and the Igorots in Candon was buried underground by Catholicism. This too, Aguinaldo succinctly illustrates.

The tree is used by Aguinaldo as his central metaphor in his installation. On the trunk of the artist's installation are traces of the present map of the long trails that his Ilocano ancestors had trodden to get to the Igorot mountain villages. He wove the threads of stories he heard from his grandmother into pictures. The pictures are elaborately carved and are as intricate as the handwoven textiles that were once exchanged for cured deer meat. In one, men are sitting the Igorot way, their buttocks resting on their calves with both feet planted on the ground to support their weight and keep them balanced; their expressions indicate anticipation of a good exchange. Anup, or the highland hound dogs are portrayed as traveling mates of the Igorots. A panorama of the highland landscape converges with the lowland scene of seas, boats, and Spanish buildings.

Aguinaldo's ancestral memory brings us to a space where the old is caught in nostalgia with the presence of the new church scene. The work itself is a display of both forgetting and longing. The pain of remembering a lost past is tempered with some humorous details of barking dogs, instructions on how to cook pinikpikan (a chicken dish best served when flavored with etag) and how to process etag with salt. In this detail, salt, the lowland white gold traded under the Kandong tree, emerges as the major element that fused and preserved the mutual relationship of Ilocano and Igorot societies.

Aguinaldo's Kandong Tree, his biggest work in terms of size and historical importance, is his own way of weaving the two cultures together and dissolving their superficial boundaries – his means of paying homage to the two societies that reared him not only as a human being but also as an artist. DOS.

See also: Enmity between the Igorots and Christians, The Beginning of.

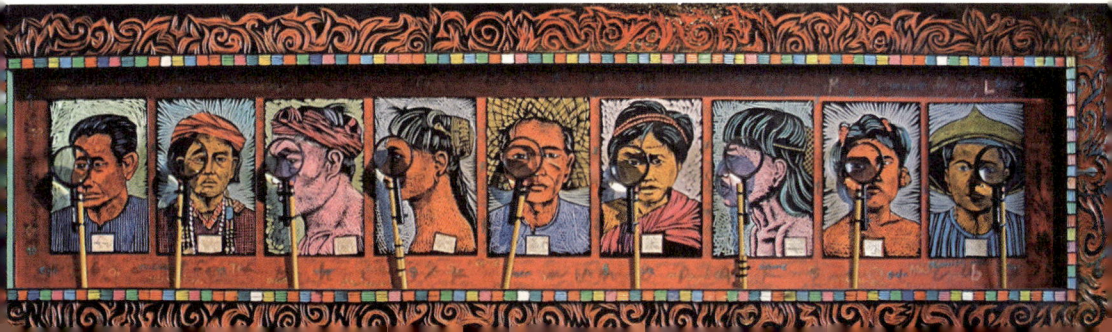

The Vibrant Colors of Silence

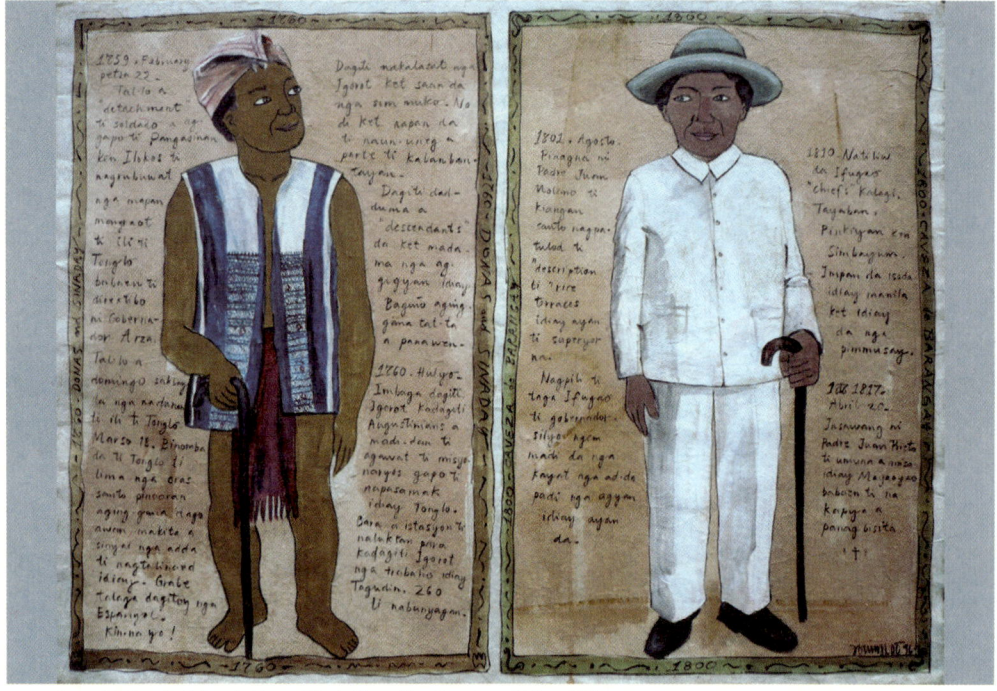

Benguet Costume (part of a series), Leonard Aguinaldo, acrylic and brush pen, 46x61 cm, 1996.

In 1993, traveling village to village on a bike for over a year, Baguio artist Leonard Aguinaldo collected the myths of Benguet folks and depicted these with tempera on large panels of handmade paper. Neatly rolled up in his pasiking (the Cordilleran equivalent of the modern-day backpack), he exhibited his works in those communities, in spaces like public schools and barangay halls.

This early work of Aguinaldo (transporting myths on his bike) parallels the old salt trading routes, in the sense that the way in which information and vital resources were disseminated to the outside world did not compromise local traditions. Rather, such trading preserved a way of life that was built on exchange or barter. The paramount value of salt is like the art that represents the roots of the Cordilleras. In this project, both are presented as an intertwined, organized whole.

I know Leonard to be a man of few words, but there is a sort of deliverance in his works that bursts in the most vivid of colors that I can only liken to dreams. It would be safe to assume that the process he chooses to create such mastercrafts, using wood/rubber cuttings, is almost like turning these dreams into reality. It is like letting a beautiful secret out in the open for others to turn into their own.

Others would use stamps as templates for their pieces but, to Leonard, they are the actual representations of his ideas. This reverse approach to rubbercuts somehow leaves me perplexed in a good way, as it reminds me of the kind persona in Leonard, one that is playful, humorous, and young, but is enclosed in a man so composed and silent.

Leonard's works paint a thousand words with stories passed on by Cordilleran elders – stories that have long been in transit through ancestral oral traditions. Through Leonard's hands, they are left tangible for the imagination. However, many of these stories, if not told correctly (if at all told), can transmit an erroneous version of the truth.

If you allow Leonard to give you the only version of the truth there is, all you have to do is use your eyes and let your heart do the walking. Walk to the "Tree of Life" that bears the fruits of these elders and their laborious trade that shows the importance of roots over fruits.

What Leonard does is to clear a path to that very tree forgotten by others – nowadays, along less-traveled roads. It would be a shame to pass by it. As long as all the nuclei of heritage remain ripe on the branches of Leonard's tree – for us to pick and pass on – then, others could taste it too – while it is still capable of bearing fruit. KDG.

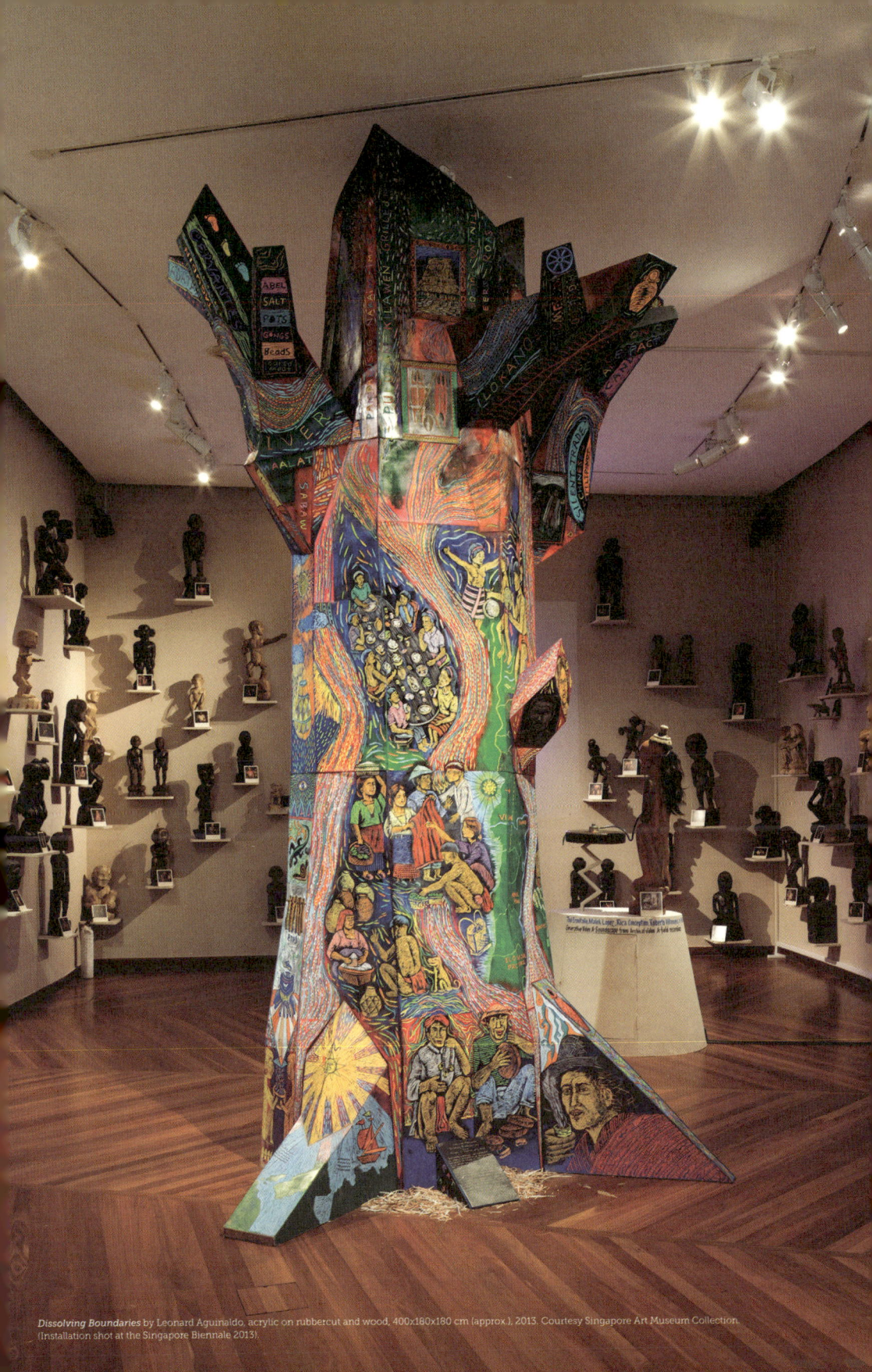

Dissolving Boundaries by Leonard Aguinaldo, acrylic on rubbercut and wood, 400x180x180 cm (approx.), 2013. Courtesy Singapore Art Museum Collection. (Installation shot at the Singapore Biennale 2013).

The Speed of Shant

Discussions about speed in terms of sound traveling through air can be easily defined through a gesture of scientific equations. But to define speed through the reinterpretation of life in collected hours of sound, what would it entail, most especially if it is a particular way of living that is being described?

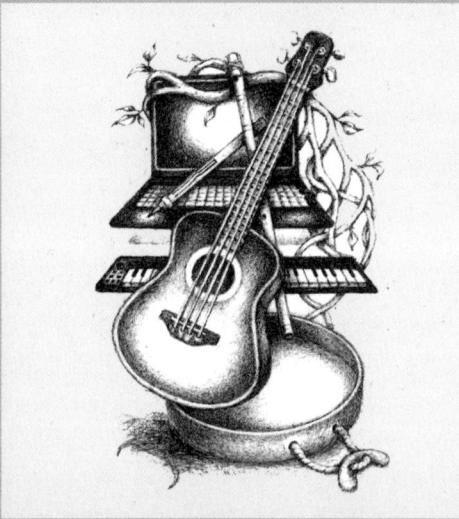

Illustrations by Shant Verdun. Courtesy Shant Verdun.

From *Inner Nature* (1990), Shant Verdun's maiden voyage into creating sonic expressions, we can surmise that there would be two major things to consider:

1. The manner in briefly discussing something that has come out justifiably experimental, from a four-track cassette tape recorder and indigenous instruments; and,

2. To come up with something equally important, almost religious, and a realistic gestation of actual events, one has to live purely for the potential of the sound he wishes to reproduce for mass consumption (if there is ever any intention to make it for that). Fortunately, there's a lot of supporting evidence that Shant has made such artistic donations to the world based on the life he has led through the years.

We fast forward to 23 years later, Shant Verdun begins a reiteration of a life he has lived. A 24-hour collection of sounds and inflictions, just about enough to state (without explicitly having to do so) a perfect marriage between stories, lives, and a world of frequencies put together. Before one delves into a category so expansive and yet simple in the ears of many, aside from the umbilicus that is entertainment to art, there is a question that begs to be answered and that is: what does sound really do to us?

Sound and the Mind

Depending on the four kinds of wave patterns our brains respond to, there are certain bonus effects we can get from sound. The sound responsible for changing brain activity measured in electroencephalography (EEG) can be helped by various forms of brainwave entertainment, one of which, is listening to Binaural beats and exposing yourself through a certain pattern of frequencies for your brain to fall into a specific wave pattern, that has corresponding effects whether it be as simple as relaxation or advanced resonance to certain stimuli.

In filmmaking, the use of Infrasound below 20 Hz (inaudible to the human ear), is induced to create emotions of fear, anxiety or awe; with a very thin line ranging from inaudible to loud, a sudden shift in higher frequencies of infrasound can cause vibrations in certain parts of the body.

Just how are these frequencies and the action-responsive brain able to work in full effect together? The age-old question on whether our emotions precede cognition or vice versa can be helped through a simple, logical framework: sounds are heard, emotions are felt, and therefore we act.

Sound and Memory

Every facet of our senses is a tool to revisit an essence of the past. Anything can trigger a vision of yesterday. But what is the relationship of sound and memory?

Involuntary autobiographical memory or Proustian Memory is where everyday activities easily transport us to a portion of the previous, without any conscious effort. According to Marcel Proust, an odor, texture or sound becomes a vehicle to recover memories of the past. Music that we hear from a certain period in our lives can trigger reactions and behavioral changes depending on the memory linked to the song.

As of hearing something familiar, our emotions are triggered and there would be a predictable set of responses and feelings due to those sounds, e.g. the sound of the bustling city provides a feeling that is preoccupied and busy because of

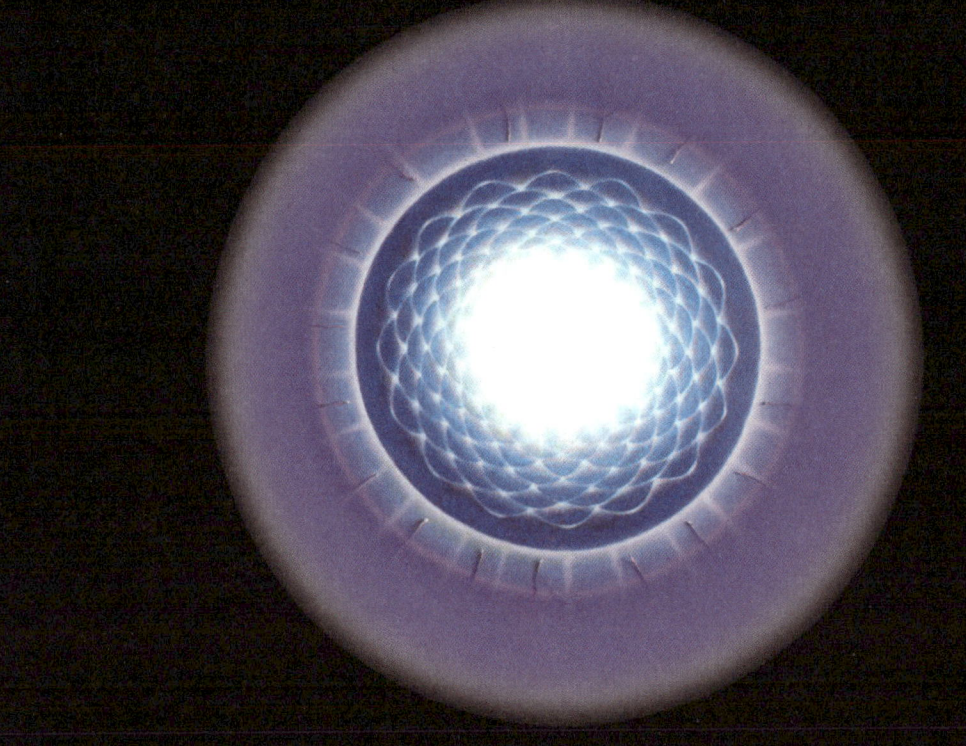

SOUND

its cosmopolitan surroundings with fast cars that run on an explicitly studied framework; while the sound of nature gives a more relaxed vibe, uplifting, connected to a way of life that is loose, natural and mystical. Whichever way you may want to put it, the cycle of reactions depending on the stimuli will produce pretty much the same results: memory, emotions, actions.

Sound, Mind and Memory

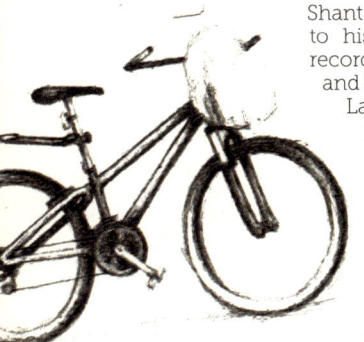

Shant grew up listening to his father's gifts of records from traveling and building airplanes. Latin music and percussive pieces were the main themes of these records from his childhood, and this is heavily evident in Verdun's more recent works. Perhaps this is partly an attempt to recreate an essence of his youth; as any artist would, who is influenced deeply by a certain kind of music. Now the percussive twists of the Northern Cordillera sounds are incorporated in his works, indigenous and not exactly veering away from that music he was accustomed to growing up. This Northern music retains a sense of the present as he chooses to live in the Cordilleras, with a way of life that is a preservation of sustainability and a maintenance of a sense of Higher Self.

Shant says, of the place, culture and mountains in which he now lives: *"It's quite remarkable to observe in the Cordillera how its ancient culture is interwoven in the daily life of the present communities. The rituals, dances, and music are still being practiced in the local communities in spite of the presence of the church and the school. I see two paths converging; the ancient way and the modern way. The ancient way calls for connection with the Higher Spirit or Self, the Controller of Nature and the whole creation. The modern way is going the opposite way, towards materialism. It's a path of cutting off our connection with our Higher Self...."*

His punctuated imagination coupled with today's technology become facets of a prism. *Sangharaw* is a 24-hour project in which the artist attempts to express through a *"soundscape-collage[...] the contrast between the ancient way and the modern way in the context of the Cordillera culture."*

All 24-hour recordings of nature and music were archived during the same hour it is played in the piece. Reminiscent of the influence of Raga music where only a particular set of modes can be played during specific hours of the day, this is a way of recounting the cycle of man's life on a grander scale with the limited number of hours he is given in a day. The manner in which sound was captured through the element of chance is very much similar to the nature of field recording; a perfect match to the indigenous culture that rests on a conduct that is associated with results inspired by fate. Some of the sound tracks are from wedding rituals, harvest rituals, and simple everyday events involving routine activities.

"The idea is to create the mood of the hours of the day by constructing sound collage intertwining with sounds of Cordillera rituals and music based on the life cycle of the culture," Shant explains.

We can only speculate this way of life, of intertwining rituals and sounds, to be Shant's axis. As a Buddhist well-versed in the Dharma, his work is a tale of going back to the basics; a way of life that is reminiscent of the past and reaches a certain minimalism, not unlike having his foot in the door of modernity, but always knowing where his roots remain. A way of existing that comes back again for another day, tomorrow in the name of survival. Or is it his subtle tug of fighting for a way of life that he is adamant to never forego? Perhaps the possibility that all of his artistic offerings would only survive when someone takes the time out to listen?

Perhaps there is a bit of obsession with the thematic reappearance of cycles in the piece when you listen to it, but this is almost like when fate responds to the precision of choices we all would make, given an opportunity to make another, so with the chances we take and choose to capture and keep with us forever, and others that we let go. That is the basic strength that is part of the indigenous beliefs that the Cordilleran Culture clasps tightly to its center.

It may be overwhelming to listen to, but with pure concentration and faith that it is the closest to being – or even beyond living under the guidance of the Northern Spirits, it is because there is an attachment between the artist and the practice to a reverence and strength that solely relies on destiny; a piece woven by time and circumstance. There goes our conductor, Mr. Verdun on his bike, needing no introduction nor an encore, just going where the wind takes him as he turns experience into sounds that go round and round, ready to repeat itself by design. AOM

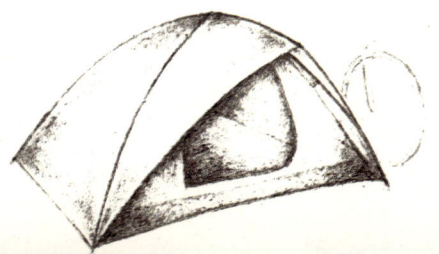

Shant Wants to be Alone

A year before Shant stepped into his cave to create *Sangharaw*, I was working on my *Bomba* project, which had a sound component and the original score was done by Mark Zero. Unfortunately, it had gotten lost, so I casually asked Shant for some help. I tried to explain to him the concept of my work. He listened intently and then disappeared. Two weeks later, as I was still rushing with my work, he said, *"Here it is, you want to listen to it?"* A week or so went by and one night exhausted and alone in the studio, I remembered Shant's work and pressed play. My jaw dropped and I remember swearing – not only did he understand my concept in its entirety, he also had done it in only two weeks time. He had turned my vision into sound.

It has been almost 20 years (as of this writing) since Shant released a serious work: *Inner Nature* (c. 1990) and produced by Lampas Isip Production. This first album was followed by *Invisible Link* (c. 1993), which was composed for the Lab Project, a dance collaboration between Myra Beltran and Rico Labayen. Elsewhere, Shant also scored films for my father's Sunflower Cooperative and worked with my mother in Lampas Isip projects. In some ways, he's like an uncle to me. I grew up seeing him around the house and lived with him for a time. There was always music when he was around and he gave me some of the best gifts I could remember: cassette tapes and the love for music.

As far as I can remember, Shant always had his headphones around his neck, carrying a microphone or a recording device. This was the time when not everyone had access to this kind of equipment: a Nagra, DAT, tinkering with the Moog, pairing it up with bamboo instruments, or whatever he found lying around that made a sound: a glass or a spoon, sounds made by man, the very breath and hiss – all of which are only being used in today's version of experimental music (at least locally). He has always subsisted on sound, like it was the food of his very soul, and experimented with it before most of us had an awareness of the genre called sound art. Shant has been independent this whole time and that's probably why his work never made its way into your frequency.

Shant has an air to him that would bring him near people but never close enough. He would be in our company and yet there was a relevant distance he so preserved without trying. This is not to say he is impenetrable. In fact, he is one of the more sensitive people out there (maybe because he is a vegetarian?). But it is just in his nature to find the balance between standing out and blending in without changing – just being.

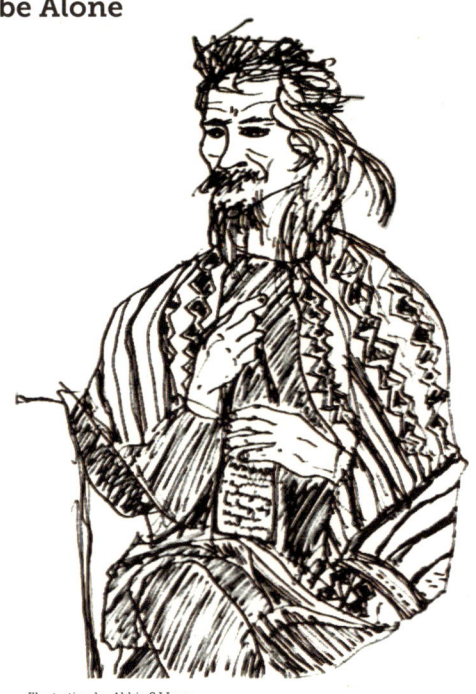

Illustration by Abbie SJ Lara.

I wouldn't say that his mode of transport is really the bicycle. It is more as if he sort of travels through sound. I say this since his recordings of the things he stumbles upon are put on record while he rolls on his bike. If you've heard any of his works, you'd know what I'm saying. But truly, only god knows what passes through his ears.

Fortunately, the overly-ambitious 24-hour Singapore Biennale piece *Sangharaw* that he created as an homage to *"one day in a life,"* or the cycle of Samsara, is his insight into the existence of man from the cradle to the grave. Now it can be experienced. This piece was completed in real time, likened to the hours that he depicted in the same way a clock would do. Of course I was nervous to know that three weeks before the show, this piece was still being worked on. Half the time he was unreachable, just somewhere in his cave, concealing his best kept secrets from us who were sweating bullets in anticipation.

Shant wants to be alone. Because he has to be alone. But in these moments, he is not idle. He is listening and recording the sounds we sometimes don't realize we make – the things we take for granted only to turn into gold. And this is what *Sangharaw* is: the daily voices that speak to us that we do not hear, and the musings of what we have and yet don't know we do. Sometimes it has to take another ear for one to hear, or to talk about someone else to get a true reflection of how we see ourselves. KDG.

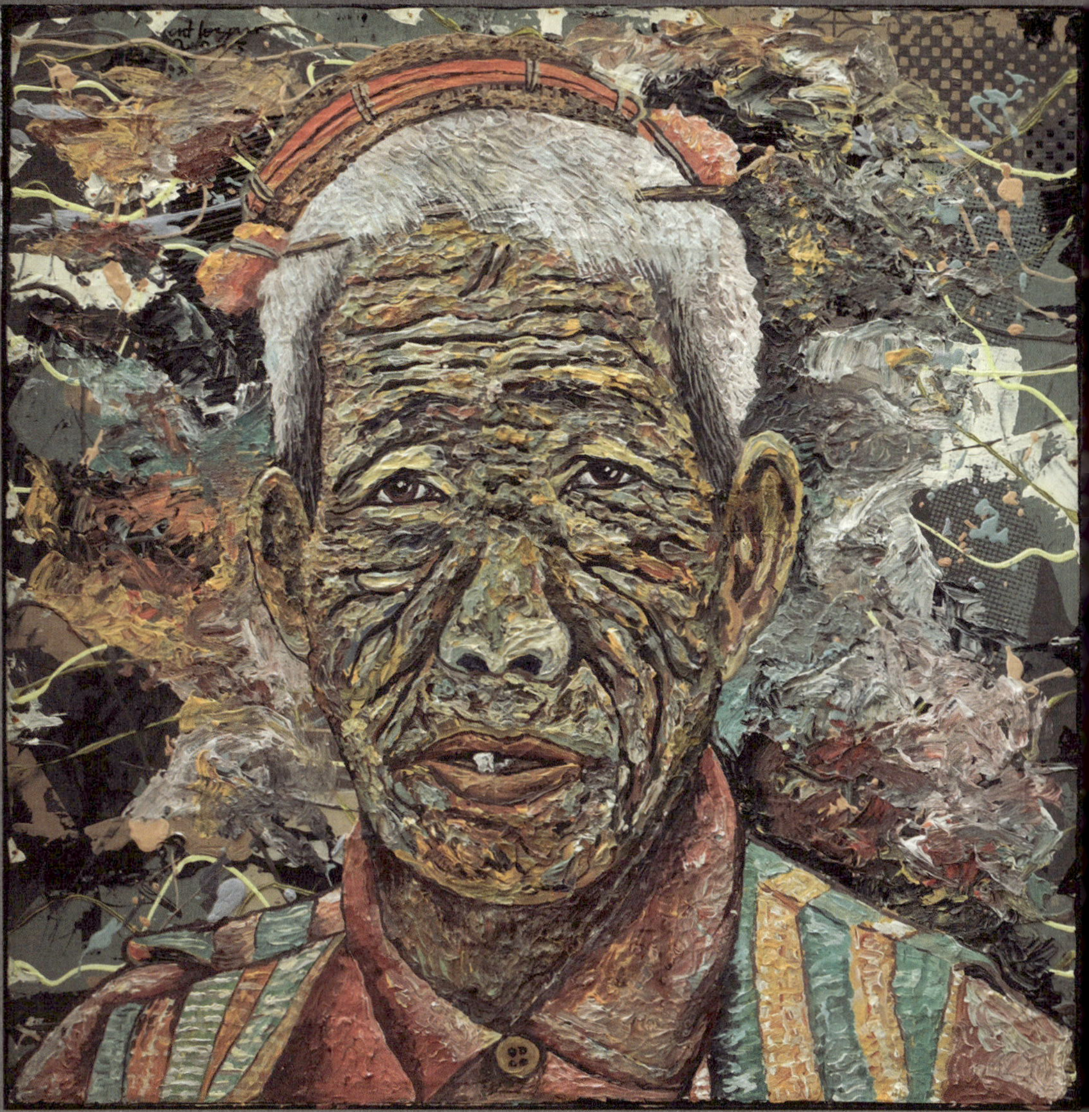

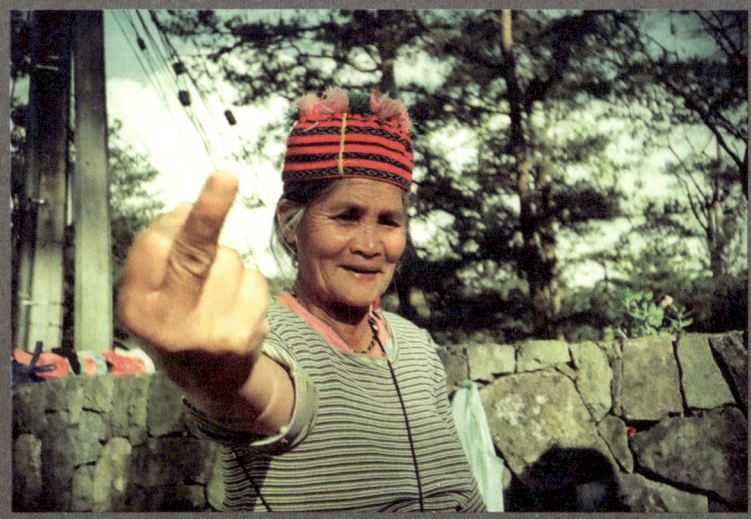

Top: *Untitled*, Ari Lozano, mixed media, 61x61 cm, 2013.
Bottom (right): *Mean Lolas*, Jed Escueta, 2002.

Tabayag *(IFU)* also **Agapuxan** *(ISN)*. Receptacle for lime used for moma. It may be made of bone, wood, carabao horn, or desiccated gourd. In the case of agapuxan, it is made of the fruit of the limbokbokaw tree. The artist BenCab's tabayag collection was compiled into a book and can be seen at the BenCab Museum in Asin, Tuba. FYC.
See also: Ethnographic Mapping; Moma

Tabayong *(IFU)*. The hallucinogenic effect of eating magic mushrooms.
See also: Ibbaw; Kato.

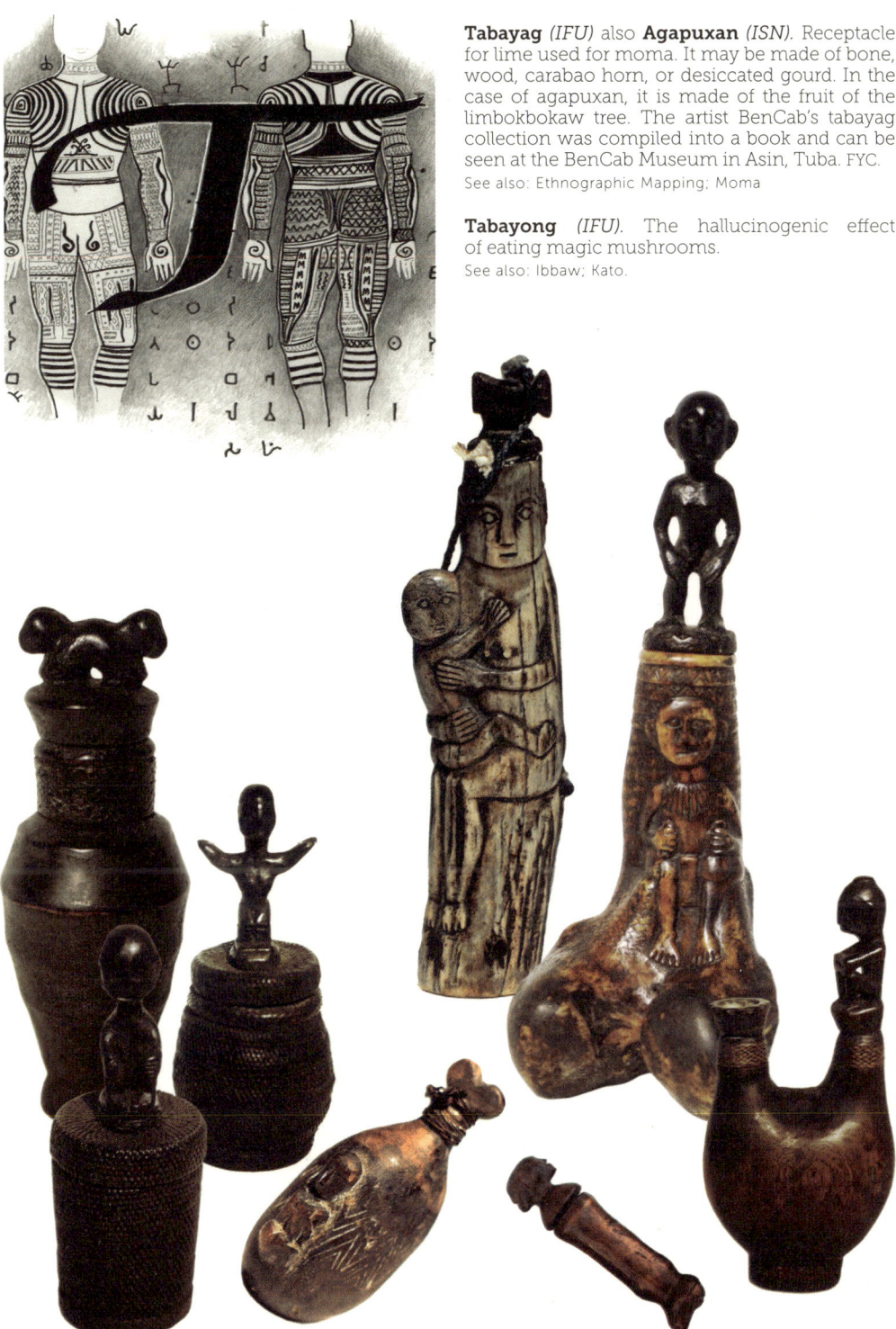

Photographs of different kinds of *Tabayag*. Photograph by Gari Buenavista. Courtesy BenCab and Kawayan de Guia.

Tabbi *(ISN)*. A piece of a betel nut. See also: Moma.

Tablangan *(ISN)*. The mountainous part of Conner, Apayao inhabited purely by Isnegs. Tablangan can be reached after an hour's walk from the lowland highway in Malama, the capital of Conner. The remoteness and relative isolation allows the Isnegs there to subsist mostly on their own resources. Their land is known to be abundant with rice, bananas, and coffee. Most of their wares are hand-made, including a range of woven rattan items. GAD.

Tadek *(ITN)*. "The music for this dance usually is made with three gangsas and a drum. The gansas are pressed against the thighs of the players who kneel on the ground. Two of the coppers are beaten with a stick and the palm of the hand, while the third is played by the hands alone. The stick or left hand gives the initial beat which is followed by three rapid strokes with the right palm. A man and a woman enter the circle, each holding a cloth about the size of a skirt. The man extends his cloth toward the woman, and bringing it suddenly down, causes it to snap, which is the signal to begin. With almost imperceptible movement of the feet and toes and a bending at the knees, he approaches the woman, who in a like manner goes toward him. They pass and continue until at a distance about equal to the start, when they again turn and pass. Occasionally the man will take a few rapid steps toward the woman, with exaggerated high knee action and much stamping of feet, or he will dance backward a few steps. At times the cloth is held at arm's length in front or at the side; again it is wrapped about the waist, the woman always following the actions of the man. At last they meet; the man extends his hand, the woman does likewise, but instead of taking his, she moves her own in a circle about his, avoiding contact. Again they dance away, only returning to repeat the performance. Finally she accepts the proffered hand, the headman brings basi for the couple to drink, and the dance is over. The man sometimes ends the dance by the sharp snapping of his cloth, or by putting it on his extended arms and dancing toward the woman, who places her cloth upon his." (Cole (1922) 2004). Variations of tadok are also danced in many parts of the Cordillera.
See also: Bontoc Boogie; Challichog; Salip.

Tagalog palaka? Tagalog kabayo? *(FIL)*. Asked by urban Cordillerans to make fun of peers who always speak in Tagalog. *"Tagalog palaka?"* means *"Tagalog frog?"* and *"Tagalog kabayo?"* means *"Tagalog horse"* but they are actually wordplay puns for *"Tagalog ka pala [Are you really Tagalog]?"* and *"Tagalog ba kayo [Are you Tagalog]?"* JBC.

Ta-in di gayang *(KAN)*. Lit. Crow feces. A variety of taro with dark-colored shoots.

Takba *(KAN)*. In every ritual, each person has a personal takba in which to put rice. If you go on a hike, it's what you bring. A person has to have their own takba to participate in a ritual. The takba is used in different ritual situations. There's a takban di pinteng (spirit basket), which is brought out during begnas. It's a takba that has its own personality. At every begnas, the takba must be fed. In the takba there are several containers which are brought out during the begnas to feed the spirit basket. Everything inside each container is replaced with fresh etag and tapuy. If a feeding is missed, or if someone sells it, someone in the family will fall ill. The repercussions are almost

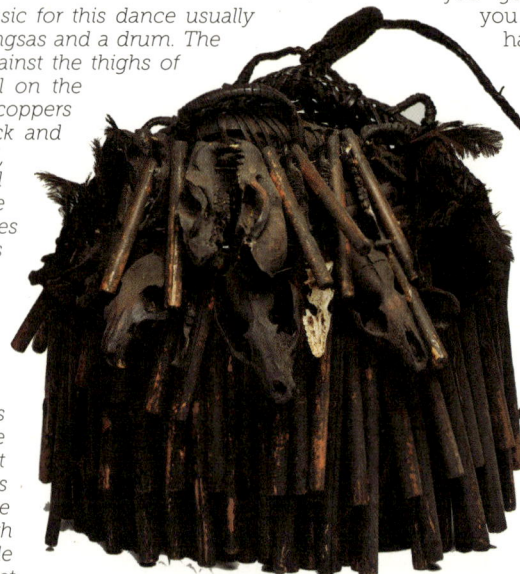
Photograph of a vintage *Takba* Photograph by Ompong Tan.

instant. Those who have a spirit basket have the honor of being seated in a sangadil when they die. A takba is usually inherited from ancestors. TDH.
See also: Begnas; Etag; Pinten; Three orphans of Sagada, The.v

Take side. A Kankanaey reader of the signage would understand it in his own language to mean *"defecate there"* if read aloud in Kankanaey phonation (takki sidi). DOS.

Talampunay.
[1] It is a common name for a ubiquitous shrub in the Cordillera also known as 'angel's trumpet' or 'brugmansia.' Making it into a tea can give you terrifying rather than pleasurable hallucinogenic effects: paralysis, confusion, tachycardia, diarrhea, migraine, insanity, and even death. One anecdote, related by Sagada journalist Alfred Dizon was that of three Israeli vacationers who

stayed in St. Joseph Inn in Sagada and drank talampunay tea. They almost drove the nuns nuts there when they jumped from a two-storey window again and again. Finally, they became comatose and were taken to St. Theodore's Hospital for three days. They were unaware of what had happened to them when they woke up. FYC.

(2) There once was a bookstore called Angel's Trumpet housed in the art deco building of Café Amapola. The shop was run by the late intellectual and writer Jorge Arago, who personally curated the books. The selection ranged from classics such as the Mahabharata to comic books such as Barefoot Gen, long before manga became all the rage. PLP.
See also: Ato Bookshop and Art Gallery; Zilch Café.

Talang *(ISN)*. Pine tree, especially its soot that is used as tattoo pigment.
See also: Batang; Fatang.

Taliwan *(KAN)*. A bamboo container with a lid used to carry tapuy or sabeng during rituals that involve walking to the sacred places. TDH.
See also: Safeng.

Talungango *(IFU)*. Pretending to be listening even if your mind or eyes are elsewhere or everywhere. FYC.

Tambo *(KAN)*. Social obligations. During begnas, community members give anything that they can give: rice, tupig, bread, food, drinks, chicken. They bring their contributions to the dap-ay. After everything is done, during the tuling, when people are going home, everyone is given a share of the contributions. This is an example of the culture of sharing and redistribution in the Mountain Province. TDH.
See also: Begnas; Dap-ay; Lungos; Ob-obbo; Tupig.

Tangay *(KAN)*. Refers to the flower or leaf of a tangayen (hibiscus). It is a very important part of rituals, especially the begnas. Among the gumamela plant is where snakes like to live. The spirit of the snake is included in the ritual by bringing the tangay. TDH.

Tangeb *(KAN)* also **Tangfan** *(BON)*. To cover with a lid.
See also: Tuk-kab.

Tangkil *(KAN)*. An armband that is usually worn with the buwaya and the takba. No ordinary man can wear a tangkil unless he's been through the rigors of life and survived. TDH.
See also: Abkil; Buwaya; Takba; Three orphans of Sagada, The.

Tapis. A wrap-around woven skirt used by Igorot women. It is held by a bakget. Every ethnolinguistic Igorot community has different designs, patterns, and colors. For Kankanaeys, the dominant color is red; the Bontocs, green; the Ibalois, an alternating red and black checkered with yellow, green and red; the Ifugaos, red and black; the Kalingas, orange to red; the Apayaos, blue; and the Itnegs, white.

The wearing of tapis has various meanings. In some ethnolinguistic communities like the Kankanaey, when the tapis is worn with the wrap ending on the left, it signifies mourning. In contrast, end-flap on the left is how the Kalingas normally wear their tapis every day. Inspite of the differences, the universal rule of wearing it is to wear it below the knee. A lot of women cultural performers, and especially those who join beauty pageants wear their tapis above the knee – a curious display of 'exoticism.' DOS.
See also: Bakget; Cloth Dyes; Weaving.

Taraki *(ILO/KAN)*. Bold and brave, gutsy and spunky. An employment ad in one of the wagwag/ukay-ukay shops said: *"Wanted wagwag seller. Uray haan a napintas basta taraki. [Wanted wagwag seller. Never mind being pretty so long as taraki]."* Among others, to be taraki means to cross seven mountains without complaint, to eat dog meat with gusto, to always lend a hand, to butcher a chicken for pinikpikan or even dog and pig for ritual, to carry heavy loads on your back or on top of your head, and to be smart and not shy. However, being a Shy Mango doesn't necessarily mean one is not Taraki. DOS.
See also: Shy Mango; Ukay-ukay.

Tayangtang *(IFU)*. Sun at its zenith. This is a good sign for headhunters because the sun god on top means they will not fail in their aim. FYC.
See also: Headhunting (the tale).

Tayubtub *(IFU)* also **Tayuktuk**. A talkative person, especially when conversing with another tayubtub.
See also: Sudsud.

Team Lakay. The leading mixed martial arts (MMA) stable in the country composed mostly of Igorots who once excelled in wushu under popular martial arts movie actor Tsing Tsong Tsai. FYC.

Teke *(KAN)*. Full moon. It is a good time to celebrate and hold a cañao. Everybody gets festive, perhaps because of the 'lunatic' energy. DOS.
See also: Balikawkaw ; Beska; Cañao; Lennek; Moon Craters; Seddag.

Teknag *(BON)* also **Tatag** *(KAN)*. A ritual done just after childbirth to make the baby brave and not easily frightened or startled. A wooden stool is dropped or slammed on the floor to make a loud noise. One can see the baby reacting. This could be a good hearing test for the newborn. PAD.

See also: Kidlos; Kiya; Puting.

Tengngay *(BON).* One time, the spring at Tengngay suddenly dried up. When the villagers consulted the manop-ok, he said that the spring dried up because it felt slighted that the people were always fighting over water. The spring decided to go to Tinglayan in Kalinga (about 40 km from Bontoc). To court the spring back, the men of the village went to Tinglayan and scooped water from their escaped spring and put it in a pouch. They went back without stopping so that the water would not escape. When they reached Bontoc, they performed the necessary rite and prayed to the water spirit not to leave them again. Days later, water came back to the spring at Tengngay. FYC.

See also: Fakil; Manerwap; Mansib-ok.

Tengshal *(IBA).* To cut branches off a tree.

Thomasites. As employees of the Philippine Bureau of Public Education, the first American teachers arrived in the Philippines in August of 1901; dubbed the 'Thomasites' after the USS Thomas (just one of the many ships bringing teachers and troops to the Philippines) that delivered a batch of 530 teachers to Manila. One teacher, Mary H. Fee, arrived on the UST Buford one week before the USS Thomas docked in Manila Bay and took charge of welcoming and preparing housing for the large group of arriving Thomasites. After a short orientation period and just twenty days since their arrival, the group were sent out to the provinces.

A year later, they numbered around 2000. By then, there were 225,000 students enrolled, with 3,400 Filipino teachers installed. The conditions with which the teachers worked varied: from the metropolitan areas to remote rural areas with little contact with 'civilization.'

The duties of the teachers were to teach a minimum of five hours a day, to instruct the Filipino teachers-in-training, to organize and implement adult education evening classes, to supervise the barrio teachers, and to act as liaison with the town's priest and mayor or administrator. Pay was good, ranging from USD75 to USD125 a month, but was often late and not in US currency. It was a daunting mission; Cholera, Typhoid, Malaria, and Small Pox were just some of the diseases the teachers died from. A few years later, a group of teachers were ambushed and killed on an outing outside Cebu. But they continued to come out to the Philippines to teach, their mission: one of planned obsolescence by teaching and training Filipinos to take their jobs. Within a few decades, they achieved their goal. In 1937 Time Magazine reported *"Their crowning accomplishment was the training of the nucleus*

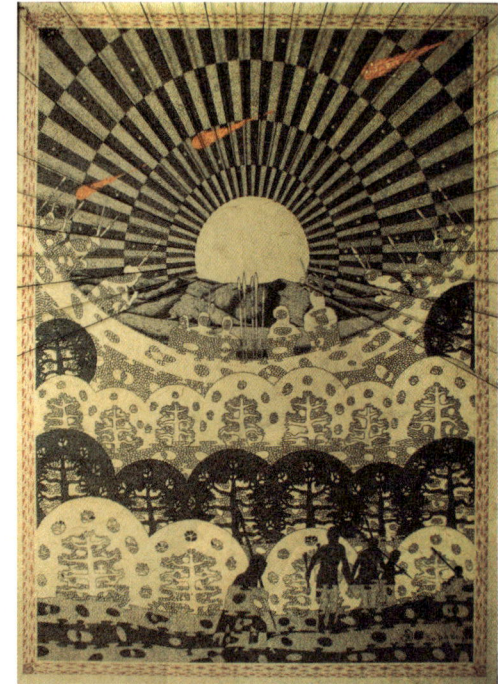

Artwork by Juan Franco Sabado, 1997.

of 25,000 English-speaking Filipino teachers who now staff the island schools." MW.

See also: Teachers Camp.

Three Orphans of Sagada, The *(KAN).* The three orphans of Sagada were two boys, Palakawan and Boaken, and one girl, Bugan. Their parents died when they were very young and they were left with an uncle. They were becoming a burden to the uncle's family. The uncle locked them up in the agamang and left them there to die.

One day the family noticed that all the cockroaches and rats were coming out of the agamang. When they opened it, the three children were alive and well and they had grown. They were feeding on the cockroaches and rats that entered the agamang. They were brought out of the agamang but the uncle continued to treat them as burdens. He left them to live outside of the house. He did not feed them. The three orphans would go eat with the chickens and the pigs when the animals were fed.

One day, the two boys ventured out into the mountains. They were good hunters. They would bring home the birds that they had caught and give them to the family. They began to be useful to the family, so the family would often send them hunting. But they would soon be part of the start of the conflict between Sagada and Besao – because of the hunting.

One time they hunted in Ampacao and a group

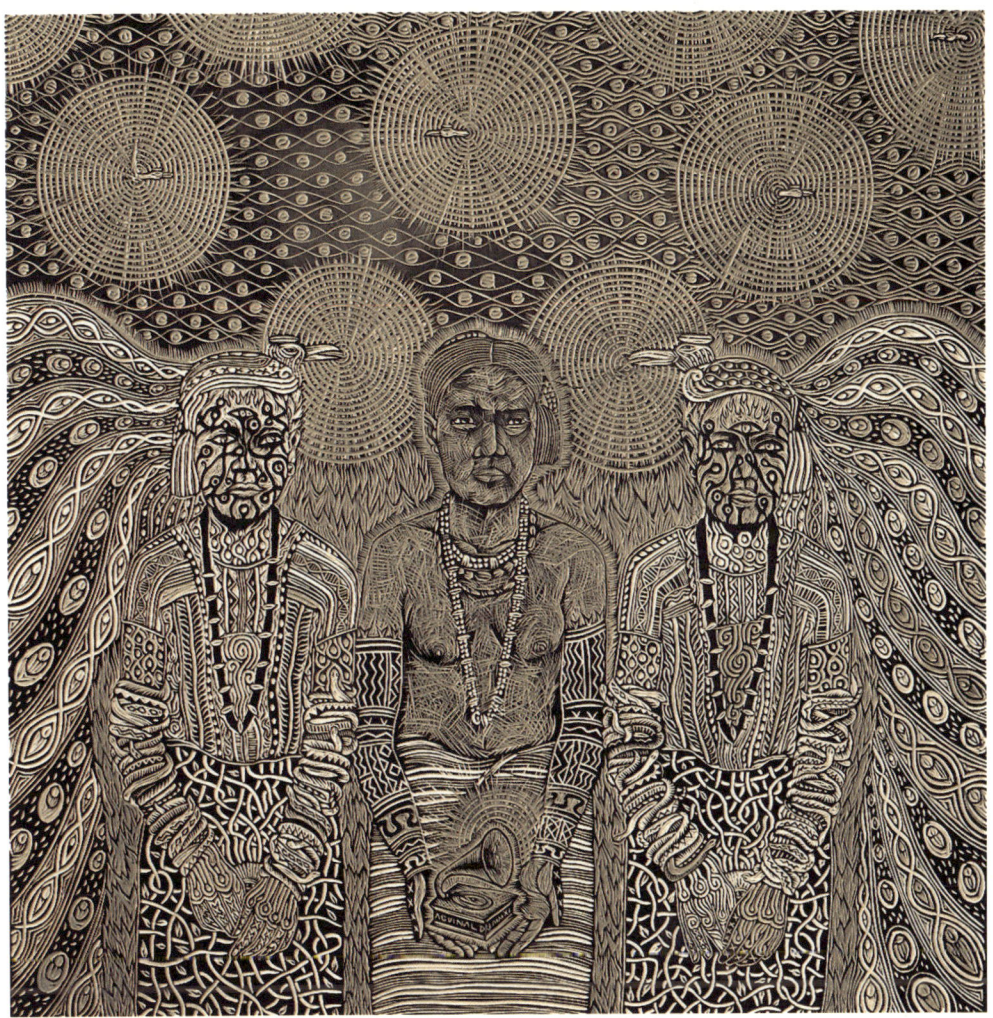

Artwork by Leonard Aguinaldo, 2011.

of Besao men stopped them and took all the birds that they had caught. Every time they would go up, the men of Besao would do that. The orphans cursed them and the birds turned into stone. That's why the takba for the dangtey has stones marked like birds.

Bugan, on the other hand, was very good at fishing. The two boys wondered how their sister could come home with baskets full of fish every time she went to the river. When the boys went fishing, they would only get two or three fishes each. They spied on her one time. She removed her clothes and went into the water. When the water touched her nipples, fish came and swam around her. She then used her tapis to collect the fish. She caught her brothers watching her and she was angered. Bugan told them, *"I will turn myself into a crow."* They begged her not to turn into a crow. They said, *"If ever you turn into a bird, turn into an idaw and warn us if bad omens are coming."* That's why in rituals, they look for the idaw.

As the story goes, life was hard for the two remaining orphans. They made a pact with each other to go up to the mountains, and that if they reached a river crossing, they would go separate ways. The first one to find a monster that would eat them to end their misery, would call the other one. They reached a crossing where on one way, it was murky and the other one, clear. They separated ways. The one who followed the murky water found a big crocodile entangled in a vine. The boy went into the water, removed all the vines and freed the monster, and talked to it and said, *"I will call my brother. Eat us to end our misery."* The crocodile spoke and said, *"No, call your brother and I'll show you how to go through life. Go up the mountain. When you see a rock, call your brother and I will teach you."* Then the brothers met and the crocodile said to them, *"You* go up that bamboo, up to its tip." One brother went up, and when he reached the tip, he fell into the water, into the abyss and did not return. Same with the other brother. But they had entered a different realm. When they came back out of the water, they came back with the buwaya necklace, the tangkil and the basket. The crocodile said, *"Now you've seen life. You go back and teach them what you've learned."*

In other, similar versions of this story, the brothers met a python and the python created a vortex and that's how they went into the abyss. The story of the Three Orphans is the basis of many of Sagada's rituals. TDH.
See also: Aginaya, Panginomnoman ki; Allang; Buwaya; Dangtey; Doligen ed Kabunian, Si; Kamma i Kungnga; Takba; Tangkil.

Three Witches. These three women were already legendary before they formed their 'coven.' Virginia de Guia was the first woman vice-mayor and acting-mayor of Baguio right after the war. She was a movie star and an exemplary debater who once beat President Ferdinand Marcos in a national contest. Cecile Afable was a scion of the famous Cariño clan in Baguio, a university instructor, a bookstore owner, and a fictionist and journalist whose column was one of the longest continuing weekly columns in the world until her death in June 2012. Her high school classmate, Leonora San Agustin, was the first woman chemical engineer in the country and a long-time curator of the Baguio-Benguet Museum until her death in November 2011. They were in their 80s when they were at the forefront against Baguio's mis-development projects. They would continue tio do so well into their 90s. They were eloquent in leading rallies against wrongful projects like overpasses and the Taiwanese take-over of Camp John Hay. They represented the Baguio residents' desire to make Baguio the better city they wanted it to be. FYC.
See also: Ato Bookshop and Gallery; Daguio, Amador; Hamada, Sinai; John Hay, Camp.

Thunder. Barton (1949) thought that thunder came only as 'loud' and 'over loud' until he went to Ifugao and learned that kidul or kodyam (thunder) can be classified as:

*"Binabaan: Toothed thunder
Bumayugbug: Shaking ground and house thunder
Dumunguwol: Like the cry of a startled pig thunder
Nginalakngakan: Intermittent rattling thunder
Ngumalakngak: Rattling thunder
Umalolot: Throbbing or vibrating after a thunderclap
Umalakaak: Rolling thunder
Umalogo-og: Deep rolling thunder
Umungngul: Diminishing end of a peal thunder
Umunuwol: Thud-like falling tree thunder"* FYC.
See also: Kimat.

Tiklis *(KAN).* Large bamboo contraption for carrying vegetables.

Tilem *(KAN).* Black pig. Sought-after ritual animal.

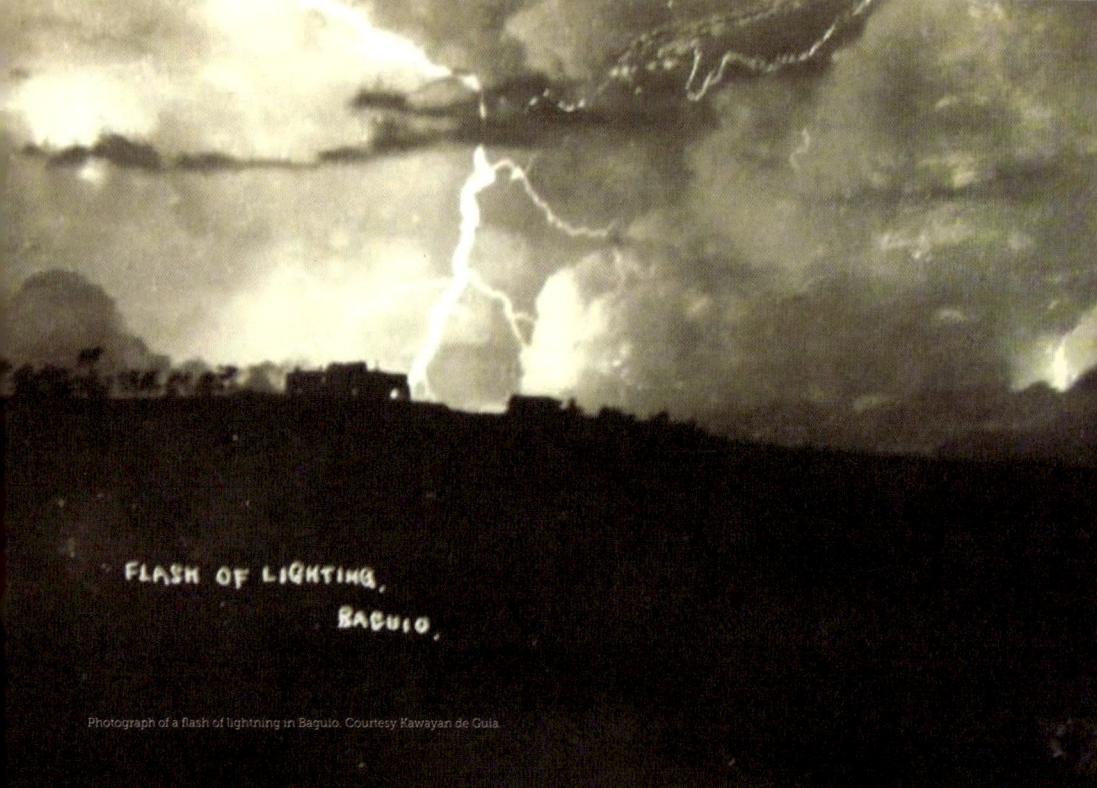

FLASH OF LIGHTING, BAGUIO.

Photograph of a flash of lightning in Baguio. Courtesy Kawayan de Guia.

Time. [1] How Baguio people pronounce *"taim"* which means *"your shit"* in a good way.
[2] Used by Cordillera people in the phrase *"time first"* which means *"time out."*

Timicheg. One of 50 Igorots brought to Ghent in Brussels for the city's 1913 World's Fair. After a few months of being displayed in the Igorot village, Timicheg died of tuberculosis and was buried in a Ghent cemetery. A century later, Ghent's Street Names Committee decided to name a tunnel after *"a little man who lost his life there (1913 Ghent World's Fair) in miserable circumstances."* Timicheg Tunnel allows pedestrians and cyclists to pass under the railway tracks near Gent-Sint-Pieters station. FYC.
See also: Dog-eating; Hunt, Truman; Igorotism; Nikimalika; Samiklay.

Tiw-tiwong *(IFU)* also **Tim-timo** *(IFU)*. [1] A spirit that has gone astray but is destined to come home.
[2] To not be able to find one's way in a known trail on a hill or mountain, or in a forest. It may happen to one person or a group. It is caused by unseen being or beings who intend to send a message or are merely playing around. A person spellbound is called natiw-tiwong. To escape the spell, one asks for help from ancestors who have passed. A natiw-tiwong sometimes cannot recall getting lost even upon retuning home. Sometimes, a person never makes it back. The term is used in Banaue, Ifugao and thereabouts. In other places where Tuwali is spoken, it is called Tim-timo. RHK
See also: Ab-abiik; Ayag; Ayak; Evin; Pasang; Ulliyan.

Tinguian Code of Conduct. *"It is bad manners for a man to sit with his legs far apart or to expose all of his clout, or for a woman to sit on the floor with one leg drawn up. A person should not walk about while others are singing or dancing. Basi should never be drunk, until it has been offered to everyone present, especially the elders. Always call before entering a house. Never enter a dwelling, when the owner is away, and has removed the ladder from the door. Never enter a village dirty; stop and bathe at the spring before going up. Only dogs enter the houses without bathing."* (Cole (1922) 2004).

Tivangdal *(IBA)* also **Tibanglan** *(IFU)*, **Atifangan** *(KAL)*, **Tunnapo** *(KAN)*. Tree fern (*Cyathea contaminans*) which grows up to four meters tall with a trunk of about 15 cm. Because its top resembles a human head when fully matured, it is sometimes cut and used as a substitute human head in festive cañaos. The presence of tivangdals means water is plentiful in an area. Among the Kalinga, stripping the trunk would show whorls similar to scars from wounds inflicted by the enemies. The Ibaloi call the fern tendrils johjohkow.
See also: Alam-am; Cañao; Balangbang.

To Be A Man. An American movie filmed in the Philippines in 1961. Cordillerans rallied against the film because of some characters wearing G-strings that were referred to as *"lousy monkeys"* and released under the name *Cry of Battle*.

Tocucan Bridge. Many years ago, half of the village of Tocucan in Bontoc would become

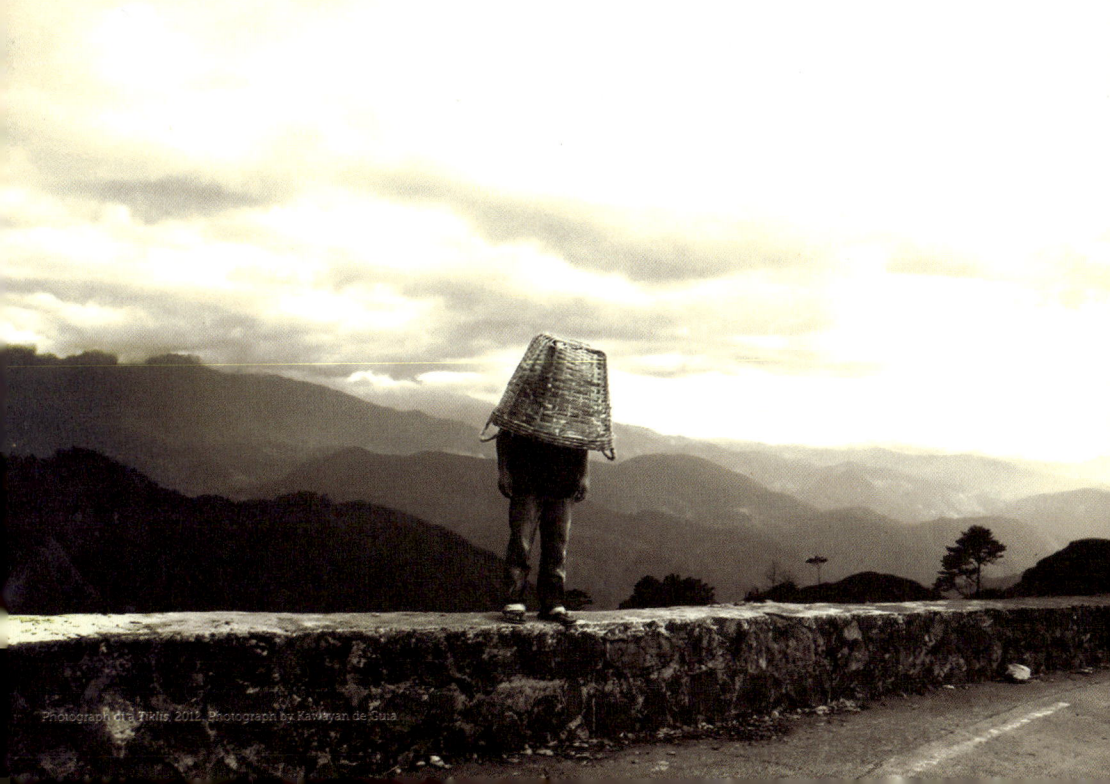
Photograph of a Tiklis, 2012. Photograph by Kawayan de Guia.

isolated once the rains came in and the river waters rose. They would build a 'monkey bridge' made of huge pine logs strapped together into the shape of an 'A.' Some of the villagers would fall while making this bridge and die. Coordination and faith were the keys to making the bridge. Later, a metal hanging bridge was constructed and the unified sacrifice went to naught. Performance artist Rene Aquitania, however, did not forget the lesson of the Tocucan Bridge and *Tocucan* became his landmark performance. FYC.

See also: Architecture; Play.

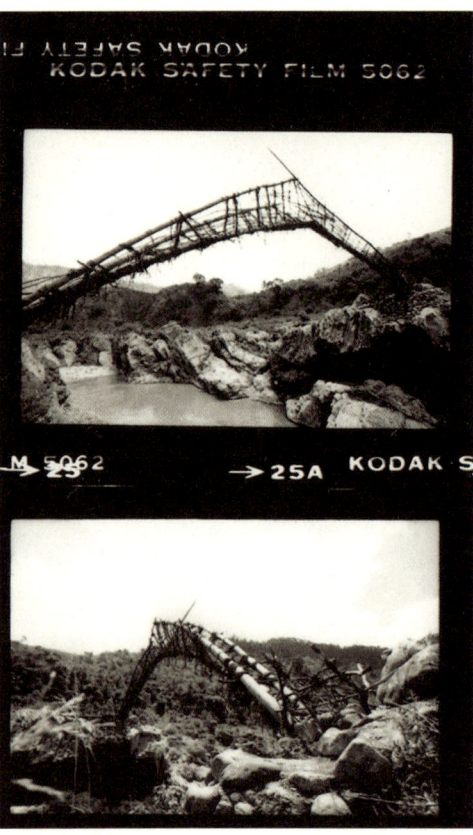

Contact prints of the Tocucan Bridge, 1981. Photograph by Tommy Hafalla.

Tokwifi *(BON)*. Star. Because of 'wifi,' it has become a favorite name for internet cafes and videokes in the Cordillera. FYC.

See also: Batakagan.

Tomo *(KAN)*. Prayer against itching, boils, and other skin diseases.

See also: Dog-eating.

To-ned *(KAN/BON)*. Lit. Transplant. *"The time and ceremony of beginning the community transplanting of rice."* (Scott 2011, 155).

See also: Adoyon; Baddang; Chinamwi; Ob-obbo; Panagbenga; Pes-ay; Tinawon.

Tonglo. Once the richest village in Benguet because of gold trading. The Spaniards attacked Tonglo for five straight days in 1759, killing 200 villagers and razing the whole village to the ground. The scorching was so complete that up to now, no one can pinpoint the exact location of Tonglo. FYC.

See also: Baguio Gold; Dangtey; Galvey, Guillermo.

Tongtongan *(KAN)*. The indigenous court system of the Kankanaeys. It is traditionally composed of male elders who arbitrate suits like murder, divorce, and settlement, and then prescribe penalties. Membership in the tongtongan is achieved by prestige, but recently, the term has been generalized – i.e. Tongtongan ti Umili, a left-leaning civil society group in Baguio active in Baguio issues like autonomy, environment, and development aggression. FYC.

See also: Lalong; Say-am.

Topload. To ride on top of a jeepney to enjoy the view and escape road dust. But beware of low-lying branches that might make you fall off. FYC.

Topside. The mansion of Governor-General Cameron Forbes in 1906 where he used to entertain Manila millionaires in order to get them to invest in Baguio City. It was located at what is presently the Good Shepherd Convent. FYC.

Tree Cutting. When the Ikalahans intend to cut a huge tree, they start a bonfire beside it. If the fire dies, the Ikalahans see it as a sign that there is a spirit protecting the tree and they abandon their intention. FYC.

See also: Aginaya, Panginomnoman ki; Ambaboy; Ampasit; Batang; Fatang; Madmad.

Tribes. The Americans employed what Tania Li (2000) called *"the tribal slot,"* in which the colonial bureaucracy used classifications produced by missionaries, academics, travelers and the likes of Worcester, to place people in the Cordillera within an *"administrative grid"* (Finin 2005). The Igorot tribal slot therefore means that American colonial policy lumped them with the American Indians and so the Igorots were grouped as tribes. FYC.

See also: AFRTN; Annual Headhunter's Fund; Hunt, Truman; Jones, Isabela; Kabasilya; MacArthur and the Igorot Soldiers; Nikimalika; Pre-White; Squaw men; Thomasites; Worcester, Dean.

Tsuli *(BON)* also **Duli** *(KAL)*. *"The wearing of the vertebrae of the snake is widespread in mountain areas in Northern Luzon, predominantly among the Bontoc, where it is called tsuli and in Kalinga, where it is called duli. These are worn by most women for a variety of reasons: to enhance fertility, to cure ailments, to facilitate ease of childbirth, to relieve backaches, to act as a powerful charm against evil spells, and to give protection from lightning. In Bontoc, most elderly women wear their tsuli, which are strung together and worn, as*

a headdress or necklace." (Salvador-Amores 2013, 68).
See also: Apang; Fukas; Xaranait.

Tubbob *(IFU)* also **Tuppaya** *(KAN)*. A way of beating the gong. The men are seated or kneeling and they beat the gong with the palms of their hands, open or the fisted. TDH.
See also: Gangsa; Music; Tadek.

Tudtud *(ILN)*. (1) A story, especially a known story. (2) A myth or fable.
Aginaya, Panginomnoman ki; Doligen ed Kabunian, Si; Kamma i Kungnga; Three Orphans of Sagada, The.

Tufu *(BON)*. Popular in Bontoc and Sadanga, this rice cake is made by wrapping some glutinous rice in woven sugarcane leaves. In Sadanga and Mainit, it is mixed with black beans. This is boiled until dry and can keep for some days without spoiling. It has no added salt or sugar and is now available commercially at the Bontoc Sunday market. PAD.
See also: Patupat, Sinabalu.

Tuk-kab *(KAN)*. To open, especially during a ritual — i.e. a jar of tapuy wherein the spirits are addressed during the process of opening. When the elders are done, they have to close it. TDH.
See also: Tangeb.

Tuling *(KAN)*. The main day of the begnas. All the men involved in the march go to the water source. In Sagada, Mountain Province, there are two major water sources: Tudey and Getdangat. All the men bathe for ritual cleansing. They then go to the tutulingan, the sacred spot beside the waters. They invoke the spirits and then they go back to the patpatayan and make offerings to the pinading again. TDH.
See also: Ambaboy; Begnas; Emes; Papattay.

Tulud *(IFU)*. "*A ceremony of witchcraft, in which, following the recitation of a myth for magic purposes, the characters of the myth recited are made to perform, or declare their will to perform, the desire of the priest.*" (Barton 2012).

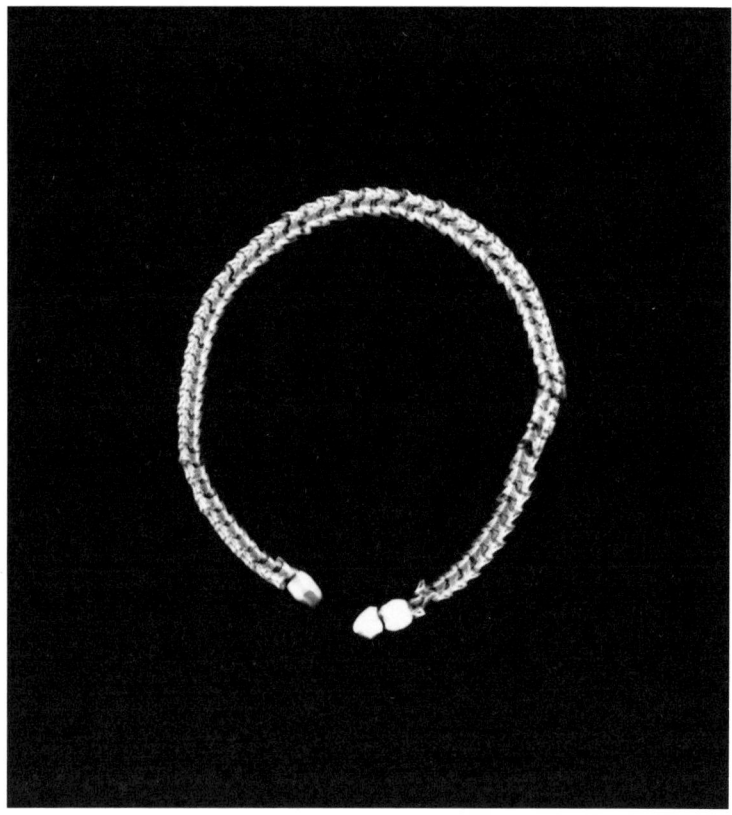

Detail of **Recovery** by Nona Garcia, X-ray and lightbox, 2014. The work shows the X-ray of a *Tsuli*. Courtesy Nona Garcia.

Tumba Tumba Liquor Store. No one can beat this pre-WWII store along Session Road. Owned by Ma Siw Mo. It was named after the Ilocano effect of too much liquor. *"Tumba tumba"* means *"falling down repeatedly."* FYC.

Tupig *(KAN)*. Rice cooked in a basket made out of sugar cane leaves. Usually made during begnas. They bring the tupig to the dap-ay where it is redistributed.
See also: Begnas; Tambo.

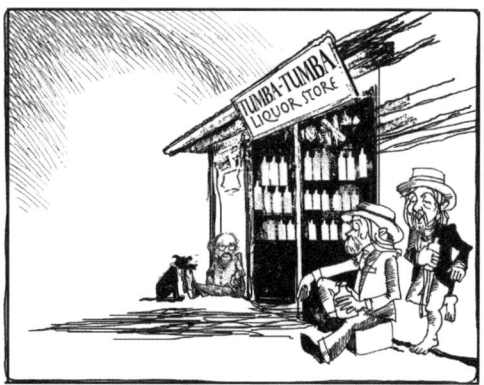

Fathoming Fang-od, Tattoo Artist

What you seek and what you sipat.

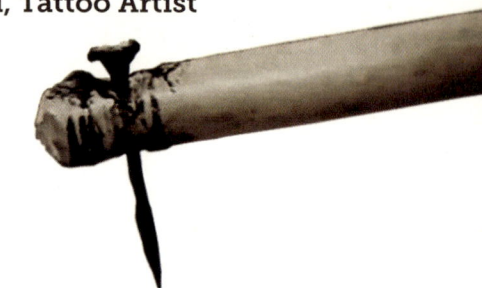

A man and a woman arrive in Buscalan, Tinglayan, Kalinga with the same intentions as many visitors before them. One is to get a batok, a hand-tapped Kalinga tattoo, the other is to meet warriors.

It is not difficult to meet the first objective. Buscalan, an upland village of barangay Butbut, in the jurisdiction of the municipality of Tinglayan, province of Kalinga, has suddenly drawn local as well as international pilgrims because of one woman who has arguably captured the traveller's imagination.

Fang-od, a mambabatok (tattoo artist) living near the mouth of the village, is the reason many people troop to Buscalan. Her reputation has grown to legendary stature, shared in countless stories and photographs on social media and the blogosphere. In online accounts, her age ranges from 90 to 100, and she is sometimes referred to as a 'living treasure' of the Philippines. Though by Fang-od's own admission, she could not be 90 years old. Her art is described as 'traditional,' 'ancient,' and 'indigenous.'

Despite the effort of scholars, researchers, and well-meaning sectors to redirect misconceptions, the second goal for visiting Buscalan – to meet *"warriors"* – embodies a popular image about the 'essential' Igorot. If one thinks that the people of the Cordillera wear loincloths every day, it is not difficult to stretch the imagination further to think that these G-stringed tattooed warriors are also out to hunt heads. The expectation of a weekend thrill in some exotic landscape with equally exotic people drives adventurers to endure rough travel over great distances.

Ruel Bimuyag, a photographer and cultural guide, has had the privilege and good fortune to make 96 trips to Buscalan over the past six years. His many returns have been fueled in part by his realization that, to be with Fang-od is to put oneself in the presence of a master.

Visitors' expectations, when driven by popular images of a 'savage' Cordillera, often result in the grave misunderstanding of a place and its people. As a guide, Bimuyag sees to it that visitors are briefed on what to expect and how to behave when they reach the community. Imagine the couple's disappointment when they asked to see the 'warriors' and Bimuyag pointed to a man pinning clothes to a line. Bimuyag then fuels the irony by impishly saying, in jest of course, that the tattoos of these warriors are found in their privates.

Bimuyag is a culture-bearer in his own right – Ifugao by birth, Kalinga by marriage, and a tireless student of the various cultures of the Cordillera that he has become intimate with through his travels and photography. For Bimuyag, *"local knowledge"* should serve the interests of the community more than those of the tourists. *"It's a delicate balance,"* Bimuyag says. Indeed, the act of bridging the cultures of his guests and their hosts is an art in itself. He thinks that the demand to visit Fang-od in Buscalan is owed much to the fact that she has become recognized by many as a *"national treasure"* on the one hand, and on the other hand, the speculation that she may not have many years of tattooing left in her life.

The opportunity to avail of the art of Fang-od is a privilege sought by a whole range of individuals: from tattoo enthusiasts to those who want to be able to say that they made the trip to Buscalan and withstood the pain of a traditional tattoo under Fang-od's hands. Buscalan has become part of the itinerary of tattoo connoisseurs who go on world pilgrimages, getting hand-tapped tattoos in Hawaii, Thailand, and Malaysia, to mention a few of these special destinations. Bimuyag says his role as a guide is to see to it that the privilege of getting a tattoo from Fang-od is properly obtained.

For instance, there is the matter of sipat. In Kalinga, sipat generally refers to compensation for any service provided. It is an object that is exchanged; often it is something symbolically valuable. For a warrior the sipat would be a bolo; the most formal sipat for a healer would be an orange agate bead. It is important that the appropriate sipat be given to a healer, so that her abilities will not be reduced. Bimuyag's wife, Irene Bawer, gave Fang-od a death blanket as sipat for the full-sleeve tattoo she received on her arm. Since Irene hails from Mabilong, a weaving village of Lubuagan, Kalinga, the death blanket was deemed an appropriate exchange. Furthermore, it is believed that giving a person a death blanket preempts death itself and lengthens the recipient's life. For Irene, the decision to be tattooed by Fang-od was a decision to acquire cultural property as a Kalinga woman.

Bimuyag points out that most visitors to Buscalan have only cash to offer Fang-od as compensation or sipat. As a bridge between cultures and across naivete or ignorance, Bimuyag teaches Fang-od's

Photographs of of *Fang-od*, a mambabatok or tattoo artist from Kalinga, 2011. Photographs by Tommy Hafalla.

TATTOO

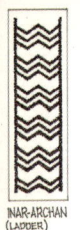
INAR-ARCHAN
(LADDER)

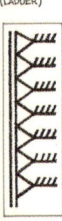
TIBUL
INALAPAT
(PERM. PLANT IN FOURS)

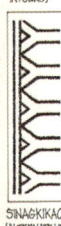
SINAGKIKAO
(ALTERNATE LINES)

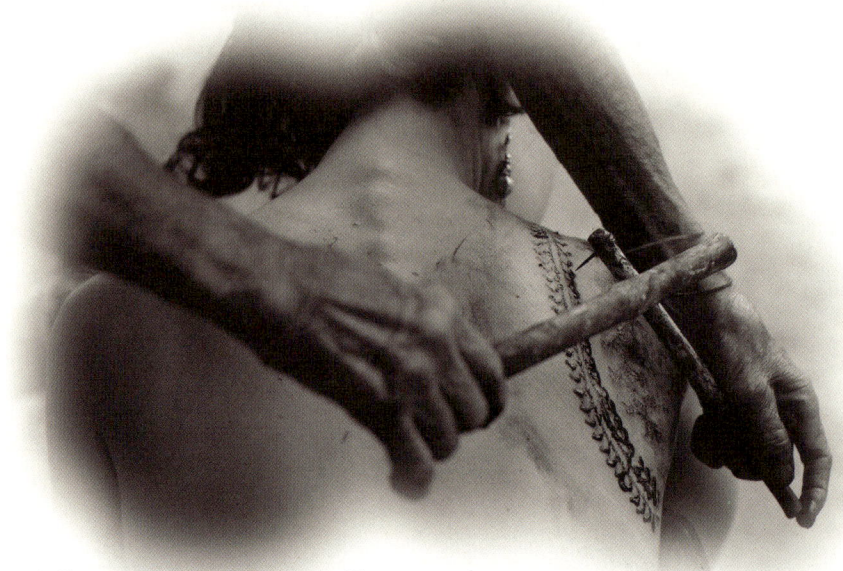
Photograph of *Fang-od* tattooing a woman. Photograph by Ruel Bimuyag.

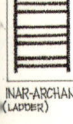
INAR-ARCHAN
(LADDER)

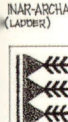
BINUNGA
(FERN W/ FRUIT)

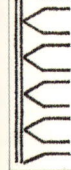
TIBUL
(HINDLEG)

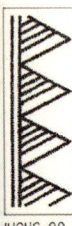
INONG-OO
(COILED SNAKE)

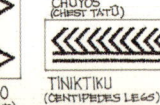
CHUYOS (CHEST TATU)
TINIKTIKU (CENTIPEDE'S LEGS)

visitors how to give properly. Discussions over the price of a tattoo are a delicate matter. He explains that it must be done discreetly and respectfully. It's not as simple as mindlessly handing over payment to a cashier.

Furthermore, it is customary in Kalinga that an animal be sacrificed for an event such as the completion of a house, a purchase, an exchange, or an agreement. This is called payalos; it refers to the ritual animal itself. A tattoo is a person's permanent property. Bimuyag says that it is not necessary that all of Fang-od's clientele offer a payalos, but if they are able to do so, it is much appreciated by Fang-od and the community that partakes of the feast. When Ruel and Irene asked Fang-od what payalos she would prefer for Irene's tattoo, she requested a dog. A pig is the more common payalos. People in Buscalan were surprised, as a dog was a break with tradition. No one could recall that this had ever been done before. Bimuyag attributes this to Fang-od's being not only a tattoo artist, but a *"total artist,"* one who thinks out of the box – sometimes inexplicably.

Aside from her skill and creativity as a tattoo artist, Fang-od also chants and can play the nose flute and mouth flute beautifully. Sometimes she chants while tapping ink into a visitor's skin, her own ullalim of a tattooist. Little known to others, Fang-od is a healer in some respects. The marks of a tattoo are believed to have healing properties in certain contexts. The rashes of a skin disease are contained in a simple tattoo circle, to keep them from spreading. Tattoos were also believed to prevent goiter, back when it was common across the mountains. Finally, infertility can be reversed with a tattoo. It is said that a woman from Manila, childless after eight years of marriage, was tattooed by Fang-od and she bore a child the following year.

As a photographer, Bimuyag observes that Fang-od is *"accustomed to being photographed."* He believes it is part of her instincts as an artist. *"She fixes her hair and her appearance before she begins work. When you start to shoot, you become like a ghost to her,"* he elaborates. What people may not realize, as they submit themselves to the steady, rhythmic hammering of the thorn and soot into their epidermis, is that Fang-od has experienced the full spectrum of the cultural tourism they so avidly pursue, from shallow to skin-deep to penetrating. Once upon a time, as a young woman, Fang-od was one of the Igorots posing for photos at the entrance to the Baguio Botanical Garden. From accepting a mere pittance for becoming some tourist's exotic Other in a photograph, recognition of Fang-od's artistry has made her and the Kalinga tradition of tattooing among the most sought after cultural icons of the Cordillera.

Tattoos in the eyes of the beholder

Traditionally, tattoos are an indicator of a warrior's status in their society. Episodes of inter-village warfare and head-taking in Cordillera history result in the blurring of the lines between the real and the imagined. To this day, Kalinga are perceived to be fierce warriors and headhunters. Because of this simplistic stereotype, it becomes particularly jarring for visitors to see Kalinga men taking care of children or engaged in domestic chores (as with a 'warrior' seen hanging clothes on a line).

For women, the tattoo is an adornment, a means to enhance the female body. It is said that in a courtship gathering, men will likely gravitate towards women adorned with tattoos than to those who are not. Fang-od tells the women who come to her for tattoos that even in death they will stand out among their ancestors because their tattoos will shine.

While Fang-od is not by any means the last of the Kalinga tattoo artisans, she is most likely the best, and yet, interest among locals in having their bodies marked is waning. This is because of the stigma brought to bear on individuals wearing these marks on their bodies, no doubt perpetuated by the Western 'civilizing' process.

Local men watching Fang-od at work on a tourist's skin say that while she can still find use for her skill, they are no longer inclined to have tattoos on themselves because they do not want to be called 'headhunters.' Local women a generation younger than Fang-od have some scathing comments on tattooing hinged on the biblical argument that the body is a temple of God, and therefore should not be subject to violations and alterations such as the sporting of tattoos. The process of conversion of the Cordillera people to Christianity is of course a significant factor in the decline of the practice of tattooing in the Cordillera. The 'pagan' label is one of the most potent weapons introduced by the missionaries.

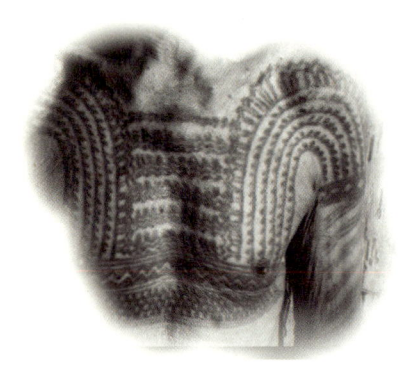

Photograph of a Kalinga warrior with his tattoos. Photograph by Ruel Bimuyag.

Locals would soon make the distinction among themselves between the Christians and those who are 'still pagan.'

Such remarks about tattoos belie the role of Fang-od in the community. She is possibly Buscalan's largest income-earner, and although she wields no political influence, Fang-od readily and quietly provides cash in loans or donations whenever needed in their close-knit community.

Though some Buscalan men and women may not be enthusiastic about the batok for themselves, they recognize that the community derives value from Fang-od's artistry. And it is not simply economic value that Fang-od contributes to Buscalan. More significantly, her very life sets a singular example for the people around her. From her early forays into posing for tourists and inking tattoos, to the tragic endings of her love affairs (her ex-lovers' names are tattooed on her arms), through to her current status as an artist and living treasure, Fang-od demonstrates how one person can venture forth in life, endure and become something or someone beyond one's imaginings. The manner in which she has lived her extraordinary life – this is what makes her so quietly luminous. This sets her apart.

There is another significant distinction in Kalinga society that Fang-od's artistry brings back to light; that between dinuras – people without tattoos – and people with tattoos. The tattooed ones always danced first when the gongs were played in local festivities. Women with tattoos walked ahead on main trails; dinuras women followed behind or took side trails. To have a tattoo, to elevate oneself from the dinuras, meant at least two things that commanded respect within the community: one, you were able to endure the pain, and two, you were capable of giving the proper sipat for a batok. RR/PLP.

See also: Tattoo Designs and Descriptions; X-mark tattoos on faces.

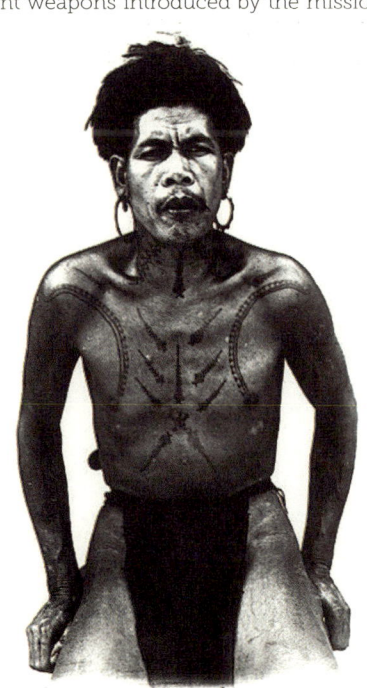

Photograph of a Kalinga warrior with his tattoos. Phototgraph by Dean Worcester.

TINULIPAO (SNAKE SKIN)

TINATALAAW (DAY AND NIGHT)

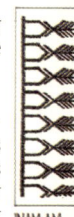
INAM-AM (FERN PLANT)

CHILLAG (SNAKE'S BELLY)

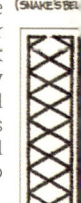
SINASAO (CRISS-CROSS)

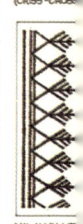
NILAWHAT (FERN PLANT)

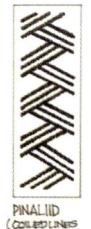
PINALIID (COILED LINES AROUND THE ARMS)

GAYAMAN (CENTIPEDE)

TABWHAD (SNAKE)

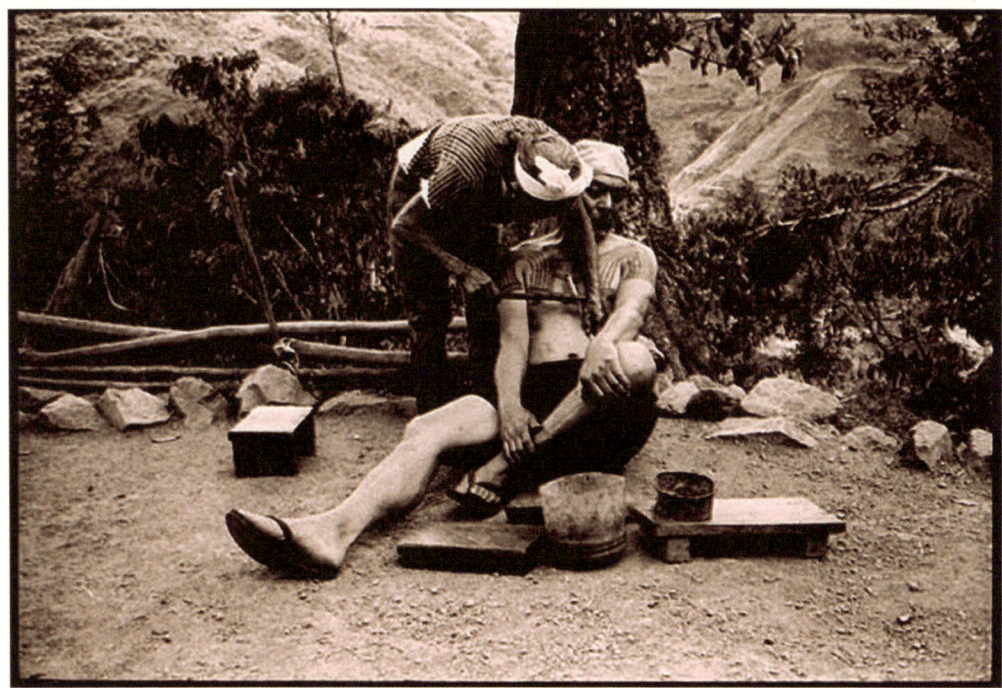

Photograph of *Fang-od* tattooing photographer Tommy Hafalla. Photograph by Roland Rabang.

Hand-tapped Taboo

I recall 15 years ago, when the woodcarving villages were still thriving. It felt like 'a little Ifugao' had been carved out of Asin, a few miles outside Baguio. This place, called Boblé, became an independent 'cultural center.' It was not your usual exoticized gongs/bahag performance space. It had a big part of the gut of the motherland; and I, along with the people who circulated at Boblé, witnessed the birth of a new generation of culturally aware Cordilleran artists and artisans.

Unlike generations past, there was a sense of pride in being 'Igorot,' literally being 'mountain people' – which had become derogatory through the Spanish and misuse by lowlanders. But this time around the Boblé, I saw a new brand of identity. The Boblé was an independent collective, where Jason Domling (Antadao, Sagada, Mountain Province), Marjorie Amla (Naneng, Kalinga), Ruel Bimuyag and Gilbert Gano (Hapao, Ifugao), among others, would be found (and were part of the same 'cultural dance troupe'). Little did they know that they would find each other in a quest for defining Cordilleran identity.

Around the same time, my father, Kidlat Tahimik, with Lopez Nauyac (Ruel's grandfather), had just re-ignited the ritual 'Punnok' in Hapao. Punnok is a harvest ritual and a manner of thanksgiving – playfully in a tug-of-war across a river among three village teams. Alongside this celebration, we, the Baguio artists, would give workshops, exhibits, installations, and film screenings. This is where Ruel Bimuyag and Tommy Hafalla would cross paths and develop a strong bond.

Cordilleran photographer Tommy was one of my mentors in this medium. I had spent several years following in his footsteps. One characteristic of Tommy is his sensitivity to his subjects. Unlike other photographers we see around today, you wouldn't find Tommy whipping out his 'weapon of choice' to take a shot. He would immerse himself completely – until he felt it was right to capture that moment. This has been his practice for over 30 years.

Ruel, carries the consciousness of the ancient culture within him. Give him a camera and he is able to produce an archive of the Cordilleras and the changes in it, as well as, of what remains of it. He becomes a keeper of the intersecting path where stories of the old pass through, aurally (which is the original way) and visually (with the gift of technology). If you pair these two in the heart of the times, you can see and hear the right (total) picture.

These days, Ruel is everywhere. Top-loading on jeepneys along the mountains of the Cordilleras, or biking the trails on wheels of all sizes. There is hardly one moment that you find him still. He is your ultimate guide – to knowing the ins and outs of the highlands and the people . Being married (with three boys) to Irene of Lubuagan's famous Bawer clan, this gives him access to the Kalinga hinterlands, where Maria Fang-od of Buscalan can be found.

Known to many as just 'Fang-od,' she is one of the last artisans who performs the ancient practice of hand-tapped tattooing. Today, with tattooing a normal accessory, she has become quite popular. Just around a couple decades ago, her craft was considered a taboo. Selectively, tatooing by Fang-od was only done to mark a ceremonious event in one's life as a Cordilleran.

Ruel, being the guide for travellers of all origins, has noticed an upsurge, a faddish need to have Fang-od on their skin. So he begins to question where and when the tattoo seeking began. But, as he finds more material about how ingrained tattooing is in Cordillera culture, he begins to voice his own understanding of what it means to belong to these mountains: *"The hand-tapped tattoo is the ultimate art that you will bring to your deathbed. And it will glow – as your physical being fades away... these indelible patterns will carry your spirit forward into the next realm."*

As we witness the growing fondness for traditional hand-tapped tattoo, we also ask the question: are we losing our identity or are we regaining it?

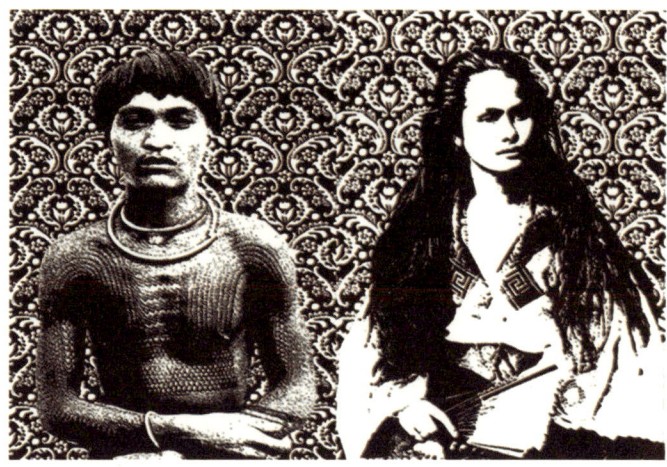

Artwork by Vincent Navarro, 2014.

Tommy Hafalla describes the immense pain he experienced when his tattoo was done: *"It brings you back to the source of your existence... that your only salvation remains in the entrancing sound of the tapping... coupled with Maria Fang-od's humming – like a mother – the comfort she brings, like your first memory."*

Lest we forget, Fang-od is not the only one who can produce these markers of northern heritage. Yet she remains the only one that tattoo seekers line up and travel from far-off shores to see. Perhaps what sets her apart from her peers is a particular experience to be had only between her gentle tapping hands and their skin.

This is in the now. But by the time Maria Fang-od passes on her craft – to her niece and her generation, will we ask the same questions again? Or will the tattoos of this generation be enough to tell the entire story – of where it all began? KDG.

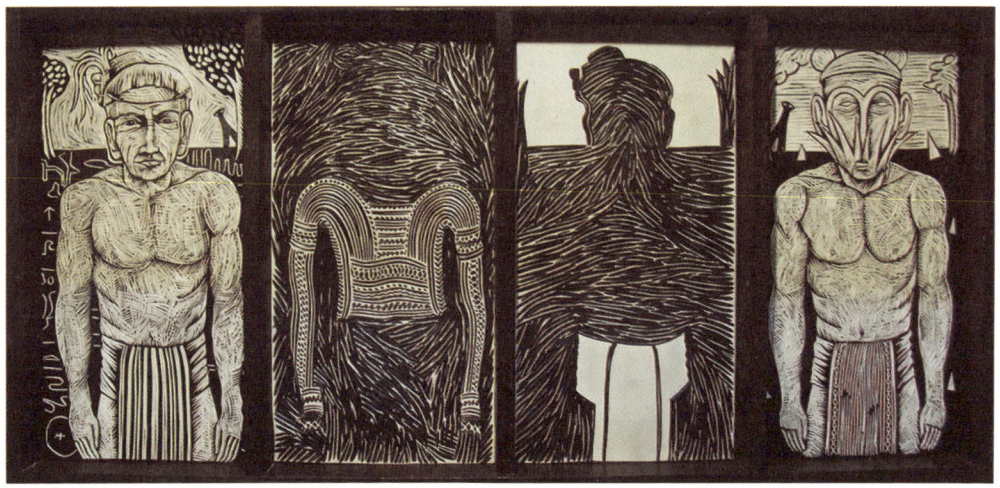

Untitled, Leonard Aguinaldo, mixed media, 46x101.5 cm, 2010.

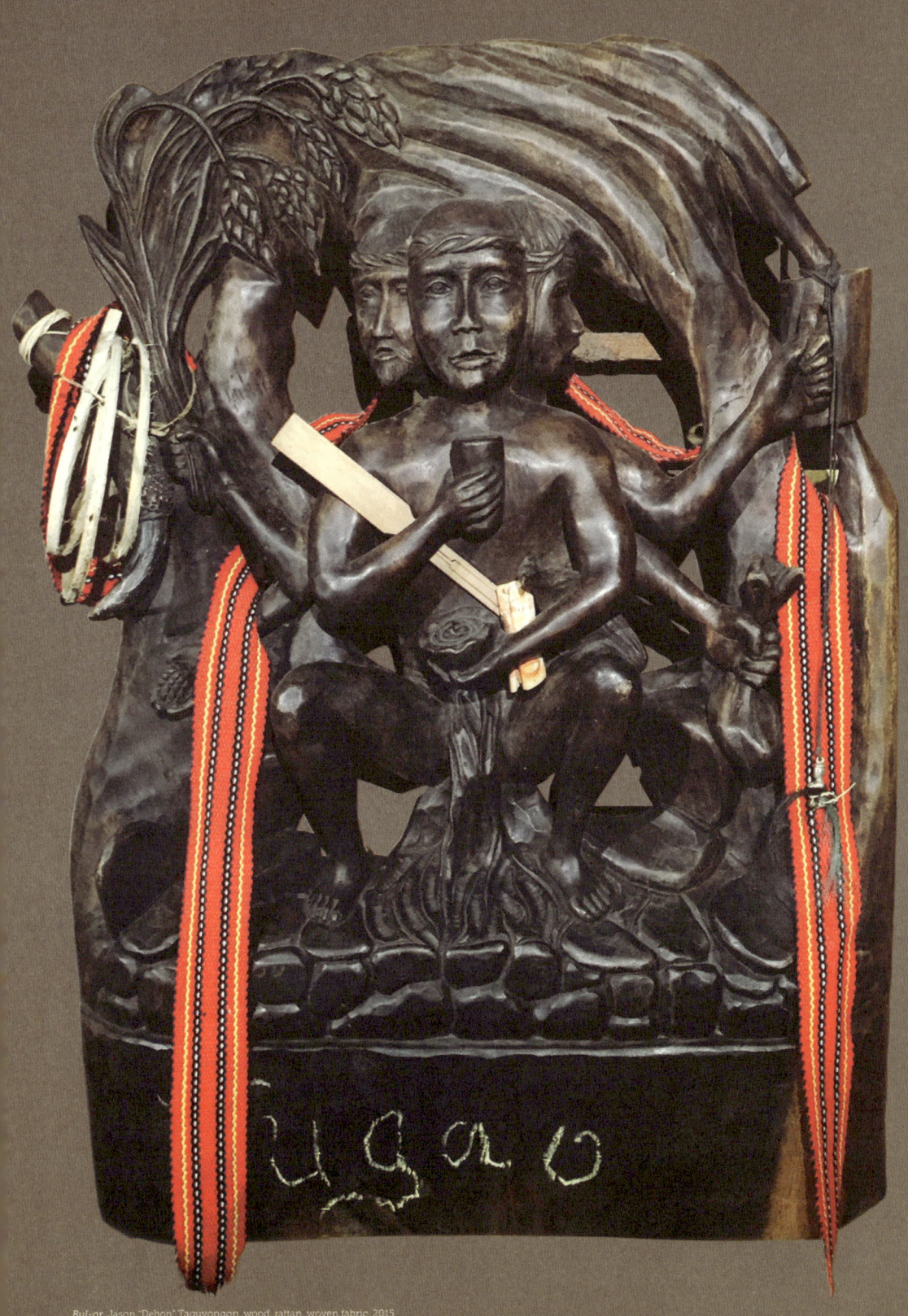

Bul-or, Jason "Dehon" Taguyongon, wood, rattan, woven fabric, 2015

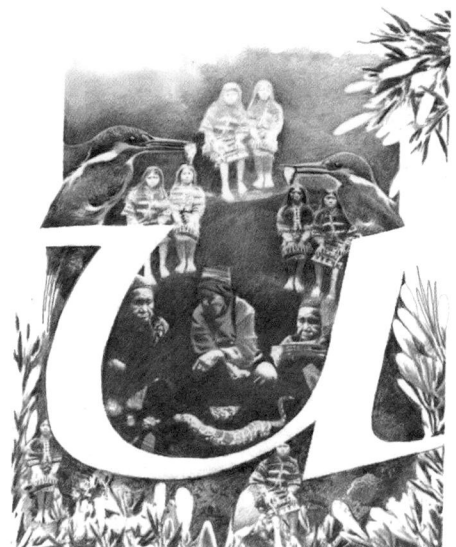

Ukas *(ISN)*. Freed from taboo, loosened.
See also: Inayan; Mallawallawa.

Ugali *(ILO)*. Basic nature, habit, way of life, or custom.
See also: Nemnem; Sumursurot si ug-ugali.

Ullalim *(KAL)*. Epic or the chanting of it during the palpaliwat. The ullalim has episodes on courtship and marriage, moral duty, warfare, leadership, superheroes, and magical objects, and could go on for four days. Parts of it are sung by mothers to put their children to sleep or by grandparents to make their grandchildren sleepless in suspense. The provincial festival of Kalinga has been named the *Ullalim Festival* since 1996. FYC.
See also: Gotad; Hudhud; Kamma i Kungnga; Mampay; Palpaliwat; Salidummay.

Ulliyan *(ISN)*. To be wandering about after having lost one's way.
See also: Ab-abiik; Ayag; Tiw-tiwong.

Umali ka. Lit. You come. Kankanaeys, Kalingas, and Ifugaos use this to say, *"Do enter."* The phrase has since been adopted by the local tourism offices to mean, *"Welcome."* DOS.

Umayam? *(BON/KAN)* also **Umeyam?** *(IFU)*. Lit. Where are you going? Instead of a greeting, Igorots say *"Umayam?"* to each other when meeting along the way. Since there is no equivalent of 'Hi' or 'Hello' or 'Good day' in the local language, *"Umayam?"* almost serves the same purpose of showing you care about a person you meet and wishing him/her well. In earlier times, during tribal wars, this was the most important question to ask people you met along the way. This was one mechanism to ensure that people in the community knew where you were at any given time. In the event that you didn't come home that night, or when you were expected to return, community members had a way of knowing where you intended to go or where you could possibly be, and could start searching from that lead. GAD.
See also: Papanam?; Tiw-tiwong; Ulliyan.

Uncle/Auntie. While lowland Filipinos would use mama/ale to address strangers who are older, highlanders use uncle/auntie as a sign of respect. JST.

Unsek *(KAN)*. Camote tops and other shoots gathered to be steamed or sautéed. DLD.
See also: Camote.

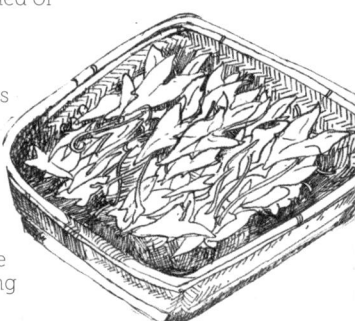

Unting *(GAD)*. Items of supernatural importance made to hang in various spaces of the house. A house is not a Gaddang house unless there are unting hanging around. FYC.

Usok *(KAN)*. Mining tunnel.
See also: Dangtey; Kaman gangi; Pansejew; Saga-ok.

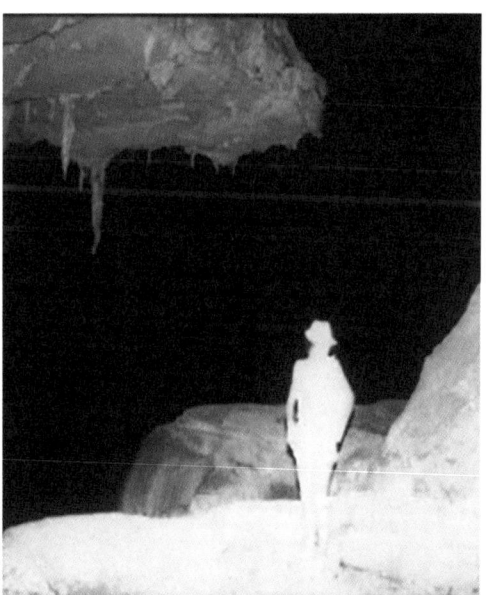

Photograph by Roberto Villanueva, c. 1980s.

Utum *(KAN/BON)* [1] *(BON)*. Your stake on something such as when you say *"Ngag man nan utum?"* or *"Mangutum? [What's it to you?]"*
[2] (See Intum).

Ukay-ukay

The used clothing business in Baguio City started after World War II when undistributed relief goods where subsequently sold by enterprising individuals at the old Hangar Market. The peak of the trade, however, occurred in the mid-1990s when a number of women from the Cordillera Region, who found themselves working in the former Crown Colony that was Hong Kong, sorted and packed used clothing and shipped them to Baguio City to be sold at the Hilltop section of the city market. Most of these women were working in Hong Kong as nannies or domestic helpers.

It was a timely endeavor since Baguio was just reeling from the devastation that the killer quake wreaked on the community in 1990. A number of women left the region to work overseas since jobs were scarce, and these same enterprising women saw a business opportunity in selling used clothing back in Baguio. The similarity of Hong Kong's climate with Baguio's ensured that the merchandise would be appreciated and bought by the community who were looking for affordable items given the economic hardships of that period. Prior to the earthquake, there were a number of viajeros or businessmen posing as tourists who would shop in Hong Kong and sell their goods back in Baguio. But after the earthquake, these businesses, many of them located at the Maharlika Shopping Center, were affected.

The term 'ukay-ukay' (Lit. dig, dig) came about during the peak of the trade when the used items were sprawled in piles or boxes on the streets and sidewalks and customers had to literally 'dig' into the piles to choose which items they would purchase. It was in these makeshift 'stalls' that items could be purchased for as low as PHP10. These stalls were open only during weekends but soon gave way to all-week establishments in rented stores due to local clamor for the secondhand merchandise.

Another moniker for the trade is 'wagwagan,' derived from the area where the Wag-wag variety of rice was sold, next to which, used clothing vendors set up their wares. 'Miss Saigon' was also briefly used; a shortened version of the pun Miss Saigon-da Mano derived playfully from the Spanish phrase segunda mano, meaning secondhand. This was after all during the time when Philippine sensation Lea Salonga (and a bevy of Filipino talents) wowed the West End in the Cameron Mackintosh musical of the same name.

Not surprisingly, tourists caught on to ukay-ukay and developed a penchant for it as well. It came to the point when lowlanders would trek to Baguio purposely to shop at the ukay-ukay. The rise in ukay tourists was reported in several national dailies during this period. The locals who had basked in the affordability of designer goods attribute the rise in prices of ukay-ukay to these tourists who would not haggle and unabashedly exclaim how 'cheap' the designer goods were, considering their actual value when bought brand new. The vendors, having observed this behavior (and who probably concluded that they were on the losing end of the business), did their research. Hence, it was not uncommon to see the vendors, some of them men, reading back issues of fashion magazines like Vogue, Elle and Mademoiselle, if only to acquaint themselves with these designer goods in the hopes of pricing their ukay based on their former values as brand new items.

The term 'selection' was introduced at this time. The importers of these goods would invite their 'distributors' on scheduled days when new shipments would arrive so as for them to have 'first digs' when these boxes were opened. These distributors would 'select' items that they deemed most saleable in their respective stores. These 'selected' items were priced higher because of their condition and 'pedigree' as designer items.

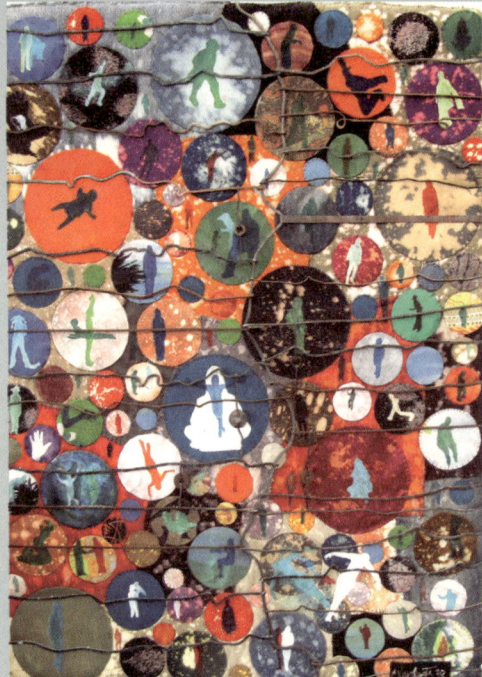

Phoenix Cage, Carlo Villafuerte, mixed media, 106x76 cm, 2010.

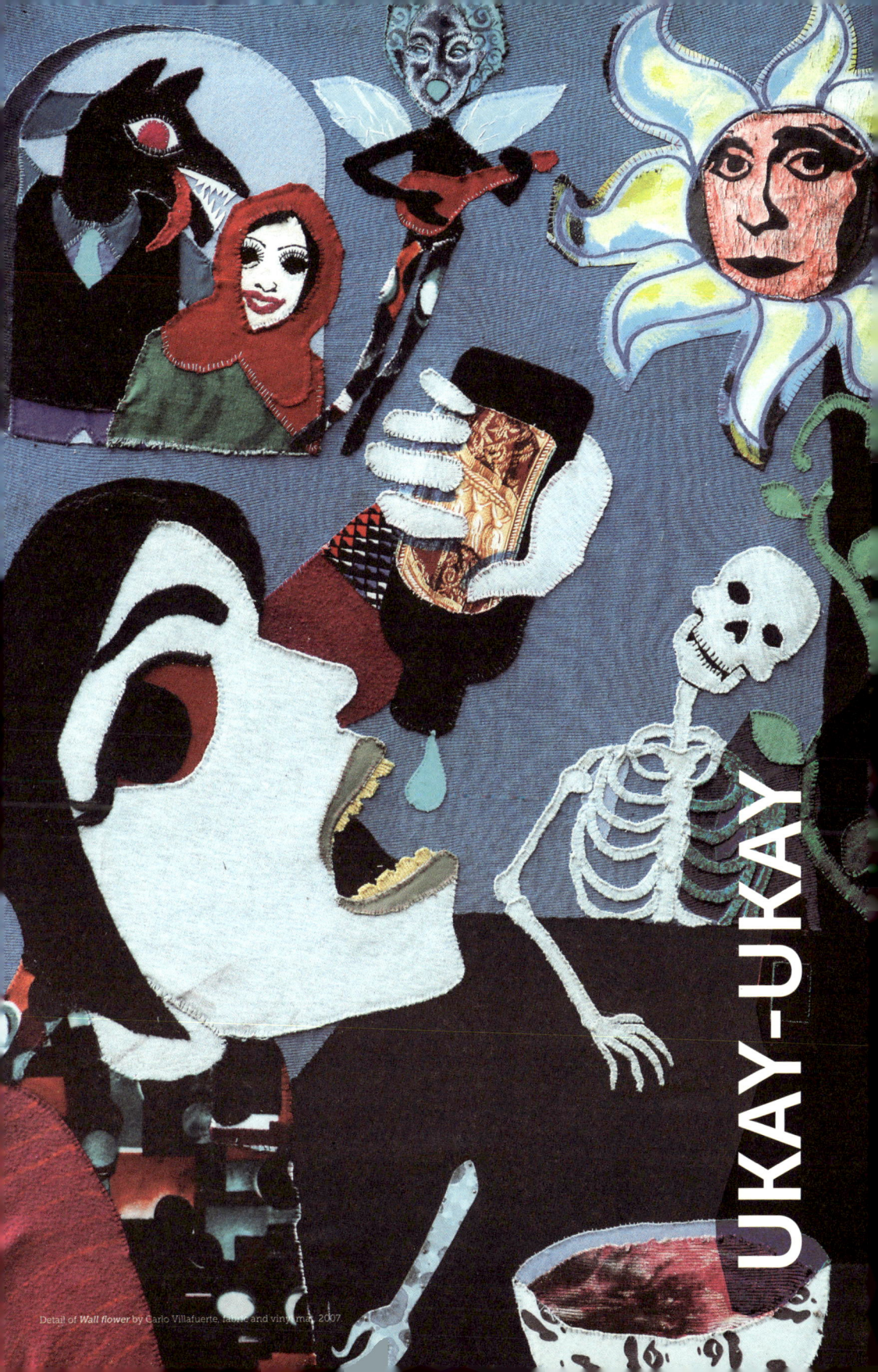

Detail of *Wall flower* by Carlo Villafuerte, fabric and vinyl mat, 2007

UKAY-UKAY

What was once a motley of used clothing displayed in a carefree manner soon became a variety of 'specialized' shops. Because of this 'selection' process, some ukay-ukay shops opened, exclusively selling designer handbags, shoes, children's clothes, women's and men's wear, shoes, toys, Christmas décor, houseware, and blankets.

Ukay-ukay shops expanded and were no longer confined to the area of the Baguio public market known as Hilltop. Soon, other shops opened in Bayanihan, U-Need, Harrison Road, and Skyworld. Old movie houses or any available space in Baguio's Central Business District soon gave way to stalls leased out for the used clothing business. Even some residential neighborhoods were not spared. Not long after, the used clothing trade spread out of Baguio into neighboring La Trinidad and other towns further up North in the Cordillera; and inevitably, the provinces in the lowlands and Metro Manila. Most of these businesses were set up by families originating from Benguet and the Mountain Province.

Ukay-ukay in Baguio is still a robust business today. To give way to the vendors, the local government has even granted them the use of half of Harrison Road during the evenings. It seems the trade in secondhand clothing is unfazed by the presence of giant malls. Neither is it threatened by the occasional 'spin' in the national dailies that ukay-ukay goods are a source of disease or a conduit for illegal trade.

Enter Carlo Villafuerte, a 35 year-old artist, born and raised in Baguio City. Villafuerte is known for his artworks that mainly make use of fabric from used clothing. Exhibiting his works since 2010 (to date he has made a total of 30+ pieces), he was actually 'discovered' by Kawayan de Guia sometime in 2004. During this period, Villafuerte sold his one-of-a-kind functional goods on the street with other artists. He made handmade bags, painted t-shirts and other souvenir items, which he fashioned from old leather goods and other clothes, including clothes left behind by his ex-wife. Out of frustration from the failings of his marriage, he had cut up his wife's clothes and then was hit with the inspiration to 'create' something from the mess. A sort of epiphany, since he likely contributed to the failed marriage, it was also up to him to 'salvage' what was left.

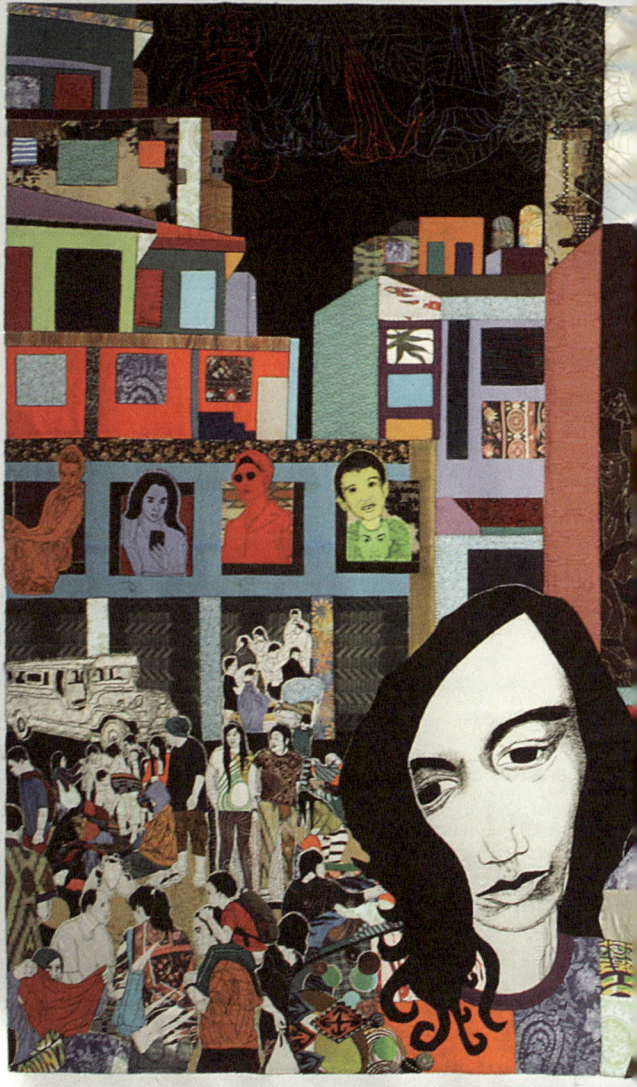

Villafuerte's pieces are large and constructed solely by his hands. No machinery is used but a needle and a pair of scissors. This is evident in the detail and the almost obsessive-compulsive feel of the artworks – the equidistant blanket stitching, the mix-match of textures, and the profusion of bright colors.

Villafuerte says that when he buys used clothing, his main criteria in his 'selection' process is color (having a preference for purple), print, texture, and lastly, the price of the clothing. He usually does not have any concept at first when he decides to do an artwork, rather he lays out the pieces of used clothing on the floor and he lets them 'speak' to him. He does not do any studies beforehand, but plunges straight into making the

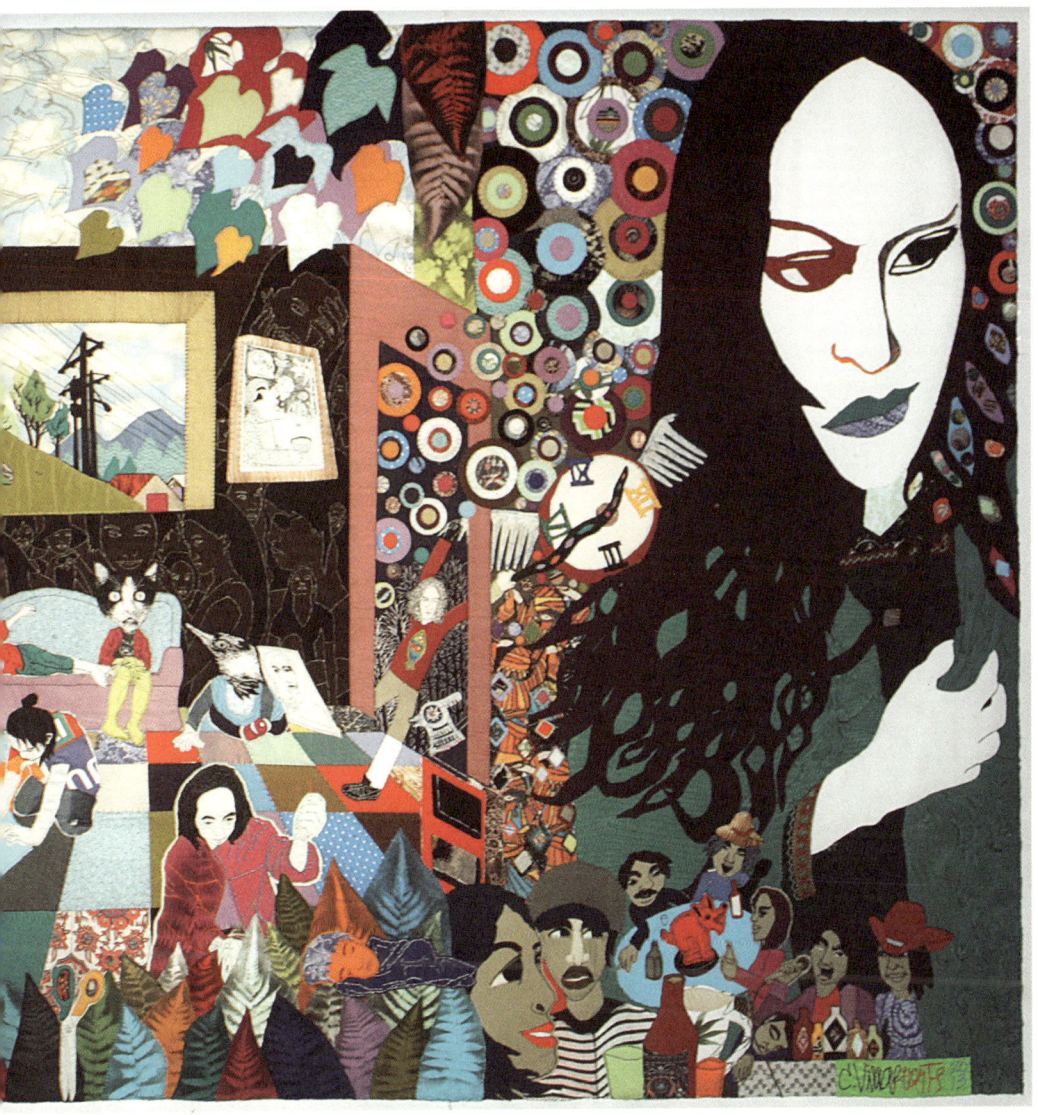

Wag-wag Wonderland by Carlo Villafuerte, fabric and vinyl mat, 244x355 cm, 2013. Courtesy Singapore Art Museum Collection.

artwork. Sometimes, in the middle of a work-in-progress, if he does not like what he has done so far, he goes to the extreme of unstitching everything and starting all over again.

It was only for the AX(iS) Art Project contribution to the Singapore Biennale 2013 that Villafuerte created an artwork with a pre-determined theme: ukay-ukay. It is a stunning 12 by 8 feet triptych mounted on linoleum (easier to roll for shipping). Working on linoleum inevitably made it more difficult and time-consuming for Villafuerte who, true to his artisanship, had hand-sewn the entire artwork. No glue or other adhesive was used.

Entitled *Wag-wag Wonderland*, Villafuerte proudly states that this piece is his homage to the ukay-ukay trade. He also considers the piece to be a milestone in his career as an artist. It was his first time to exhibit outside of the Philippines and is his largest work to-date. The piece includes a self-portrait and unlike his early artworks where he would incorporate found objects, in this case, the triptych was entirely made from secondhand fabric. It evokes the mélange of colors, textures and even the cacophony of the ukay-ukay experience.

Villafuerte says his medium and philosophy is patience. *"I used to see wagwagan with my business eye, now I see it differently through the eye of my heart,"* he adds. An apt statement reflecting the synergy of the ukay-ukay trade and this Baguio Artist's experience. MM.

Colossal Imprints

The popular 'ukay-ukay' trade (sale of relief items, used clothing) in Luzon is mostly in the hands of a few families from Sagada, who turned millionaires through the trade. The word 'ukay' derives from the term 'hukay' which means to dig, or sort through massive wholes. In ukay-ukay, heaps of varied, colorful clothing are offered to people in stalls or on the streets for rummaging.

Items bought in the ukay-ukay are also the base-material for Carlo Villafuerte's creations. Through the tedious task of sewing, the artist assembles quilt-like, wall-bound works, embellished with embroidery. His pieces are depictions of fantasy on fabric. They display a distinctive sense of perception in terms of color and imagery. His mesmerizing and playful works of art narrate a childhood come full-circle: fruition after years of exposure to textile scraps while the artist's mother supported her family as a seamstress in a sweatshop in Baguio's Export Processing Zone.

There might be more than just one way to describe Carlo Villafuerte. I first met him selling little crafts and items along Session Road – the typical, if not the only, means of living for many young, aspiring artists. During the day, and sometimes also at night, such commerce would magically convert into music jam sessions of sorts and I would hang out there and interact with newcomers and mainstays. Then one day, I got to spend a bit of time with this quiet man.

A friend pointed out the content of Carlo's work – which to me had strength and potential. It was a different technique altogether and somehow, he had a way of telling stories through a medium not used much by artists nowadays. Little did we know that he himself had a story to tell, and it just might have been one of the more interesting ones I'd heard in a long while.

Sometimes being able to make a living as an artist comes close to a once-in-a-lifetime contract with luck. It's hard. Carlo, having two children and one more on the way, began to involve himself more with the Baguio artist community. After long days of selling crafts, he would somehow end up in our circle.

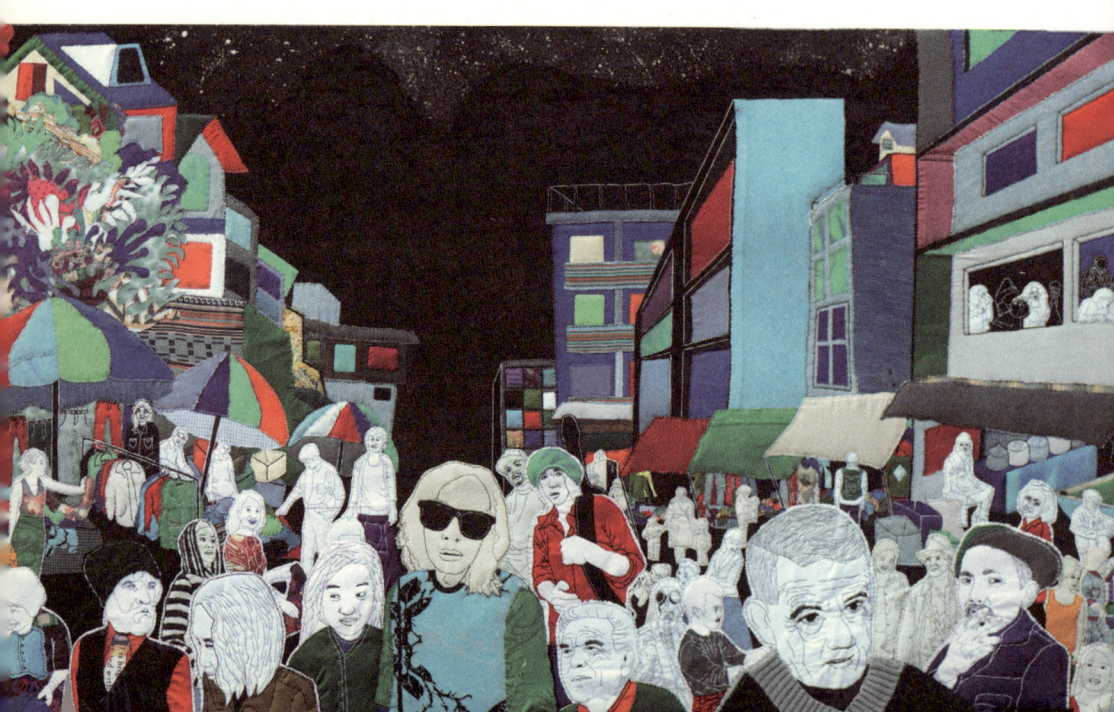

Upon realizing how brilliant his work could be, given some encouragement – in the form of a regular offer to produce works that were not the fruits of formal art training – we put him in a show at the Victor Oteyza Community Art Space (VOCAS). In this, his first solo show, we were just blown away with what he had done. His work was about how an artist had arrived at his own brand of originality. We felt a greater audience would need to see and feel it.

Carlo works in a humble and humbling space, cramped and small, which doubles as home for his family. Here, he puts together small sections of 'fabric-canvas' and often, due to space constraints, doesn't quite see the entire picture. It is not far from how many of us truly look at life, except that the bigger picture from where he stands is a tangible masterpiece that needs no introduction for one to make out whole.

Getting too engrossed with your work, especially when it doesn't make money, is sometimes not a real problem. But when you have a wife and kids, the whole economy of a promising artist is somehow predestined to doom. This is what happened to our friend here, who came home one day to his kids and a missing wife.

Soft-spoken and pensive, he got a pair of scissors, then started shredding and cutting his wife's clothes in rage and frustration – stitching the remnants of his broken self into narratives, becoming a storyteller. In this way, he filled the void inside of him by creating worlds that tells his exact story, but in colors that invites the outsider to feel at ease with a total stranger, just by a single look. KDG.

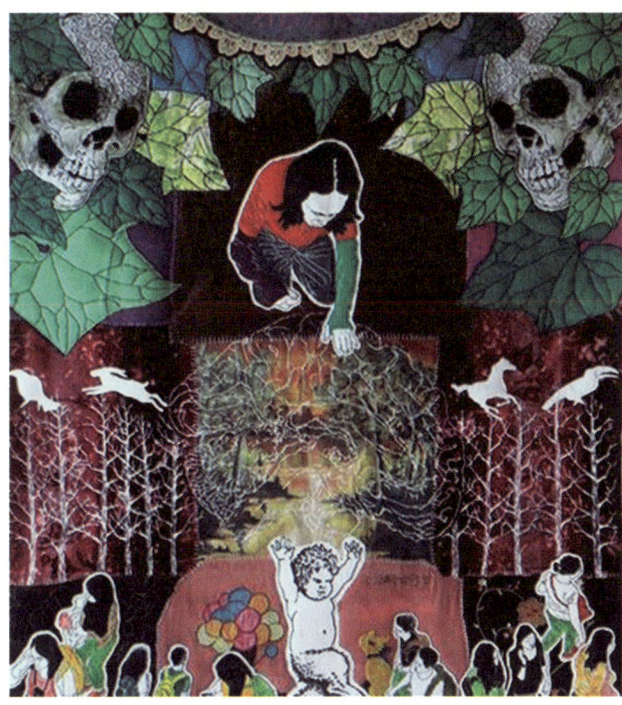

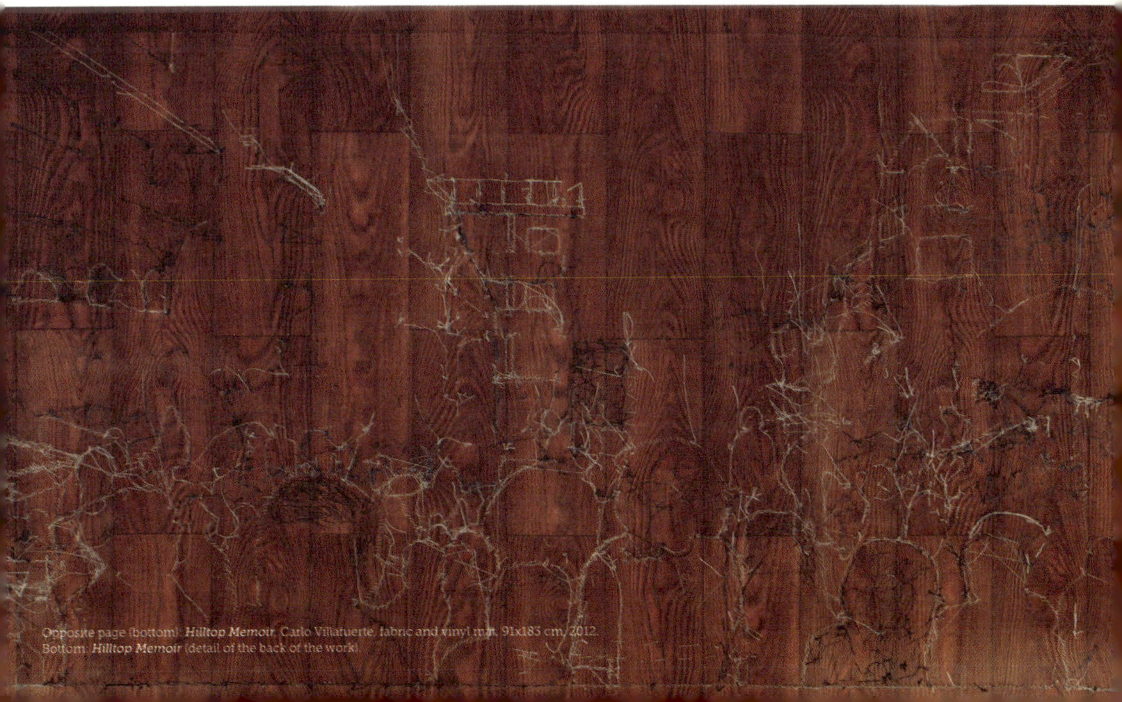

View from the Bayabas Tree, Carlo Villafuerte, fabric and vinyl mat, 125x100cm, 2016.

Opposite page (bottom): *Hilltop Memoir,* Carlo Villafuerte, fabric and vinyl mat, 91x183 cm, 2012.
Bottom: *Hilltop Memoir* (detail of the back of the work).

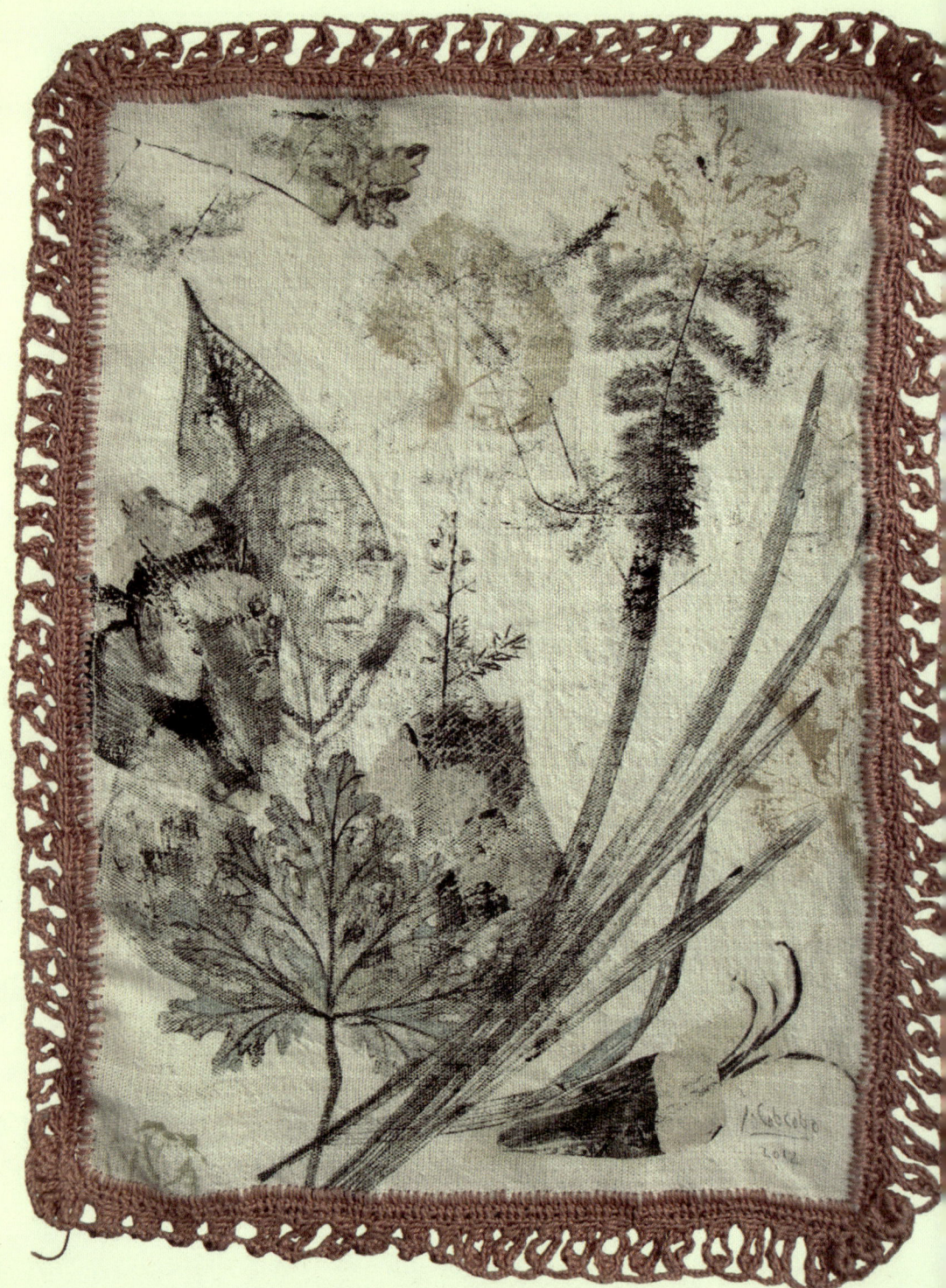

Lydia Romawac, Glamorous Lola, Joey Cobcobo, monoprint, 32x24 cm, 2012. Courtesy Joey Cobcobo.

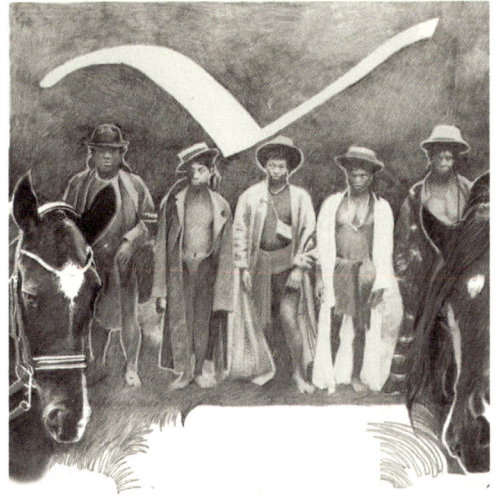

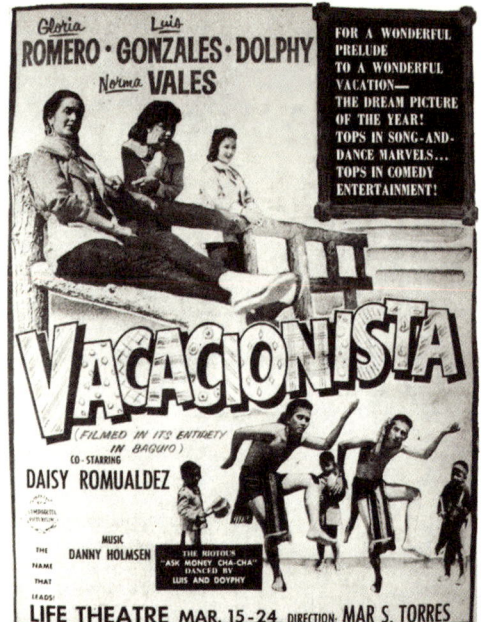

Poster of the movie *Vacacionista*, 1955. Theatrical release poster.

Vacacionista. By the 1950s, Baguio had become a movie back lot. Where else could actor Rogelio dela Rosa wear his woolen coats anyway? *Vacacionista*, released in 1955, was the first movie entirely shot in Baguio starring Gloria Romero, Luis Gonzales, Dolphy, Norma Vales, Daisy Romualdez, and Etang Discher (before she became the Vincent Price of the Philippines). The racist dance, "Ask Money Cha Cha," should be taken in context, though.

From *Vacacionista*, we got the term *"bakasyonista"* to refer to local tourists mostly from Southern Tagalog who would come up for Christmas aboard mini buses for a very hectic two-day tour of Baguio; staying in apartment houses instead of hotels, and bringing everything with them, including their food and coconut charcoal. FYC.

See also: Abong; Baguio (the movie); Banaue: Stairway to the Sky; Big Bird Cage; Igorota: The Legend of the Tree of Life; Irisan (the movie); Kung Mangarap Ka't Magising.

Vakla *(FIL)* also **Bading.** A term for members of the queer community. In queer communities, use of the label denotes a loose affirmation of affinity. But it is also used as a homophobic derogatory label in communities with very pronounced cultural roles for men and women.

See also: Swardspeak.

Vicente Chan. There was a councilor in Itogon who called for an adjournment of their meeting because of one man. *"Who is it?,"* the presiding officer asked. *"Vicente Chan,"* the councilor said, provoking laughter because *"Vicente Chan"* sounds like *"bisin ti tiyan"* which means *"hungry stomach"* in Ilocano. Vicente C.S. Chan was the principal of the Baguio Chinese Patriotic school in 1948 and organized the Mt. Farmers Association of Chinese and Igorot Farmers. FYC.

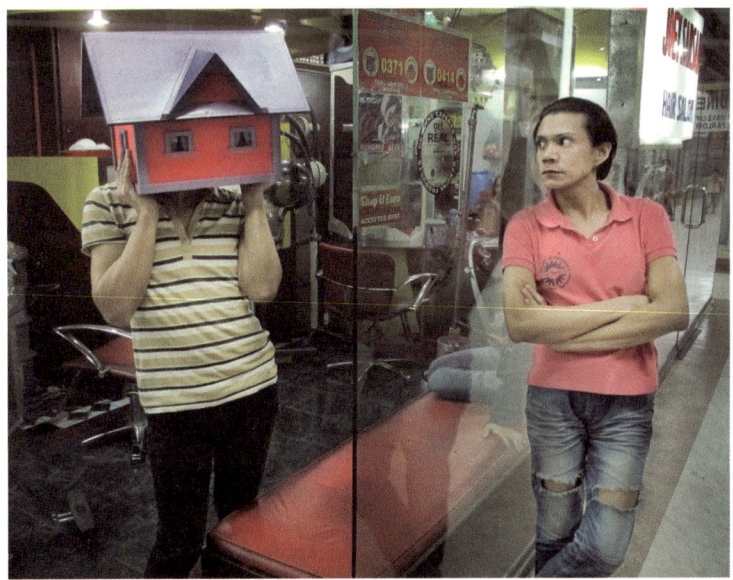

Photograph of a Salon at the Maharlika Livelihood Center in Baguio City. Photograph by Kawayan de Guia from the *Candy House Series*, 2011.

VOCAS (Victor Oteyza Community Art Space). An art exhibition center in the heart of Baguio in memory of the pioneer modern art painter from Baguio in the 1950s. VOCAS seeks to encourage new artists from the North (especially Baguio and the Cordilleras) by affording them a venue to show paintings/sculptures, original music, poetry readings, plays etc. With a flamboyant atmosphere of organic architecture (no blueprints) VOCAS is a hub of new talents in Baguio who love to jam with indigenous gongs and drums. It is located at the 5th Floor, L'Azotea Bldg., 108 Session Road.KT.

Vochong *(KAL),* also **Bodong** *(KAL),* **Pochon** *(BON),* **Peden** *(KAN),* **Pechen** *(BON).*
[1] *"A socio-political institution that dates back to the Pre-Spanish colonial years. It is a bilateral fraternal relationship between two specific ethnic communities living in the Gran Cordillera mountain range. Since an ethnic community may have as many as a couple of dozen kabodong [co-peace pact] communities, the total number of peace treaties may reach 3,000, thus constituting an interesting complex web of bilateral and multilateral relations and crisscross of interconnectedness that is unique. The vochong requires a very cautious process that envelops the entire community. It follows a generally prescribed traditional process that is guided by the customary laws and the histories of the involved communities. The rites and symbols are as important as the provisions of the pagta, the code of vochong. There are two reasons why two communities venture into a vochong relationship: to expand friendly relations into a bilateral fraternal alliance, and to solve a serious conflict or erase tensions between their people. After the initial peace-forging celebration, there are again two reasons for reliving the entire peace-seeking process: to restore a pact severed by a violation of any provision of the pagta and the chernat. The latter, which is usually conducted every three or four years, aims to strengthen the brotherhood and review the provisions of the pagta to delete useless articles and incorporate new ones that are relevant to the changing times."* (Weygan, 2001, p. 36).
[2] Vochong was the term used by the oppositionists against the Chico and Cellophil industrial projects in forging a wider network of bilateral peace pacts among the binodngan (peace pact holding) communities in Kalinga, Mountain Province, and Abra. Known as the 1st Vochong Conference in St. Bridget's in Quezon City in May 1975, it was a major step in using indigenous systems in fighting modern woes. FYC.
See also: Butu; Cellophil; Chico; Mt. Data; Peace Zone.

Volontarios *(SPA).* Volunteer police or guards, especially those in Benguet in the early 1900s.

Voyeurism. In Bauko, it is said that a child who witnessed the sexual intercourse of their parents would soon get sick and die. In Sagada, if such a union was witnessed by a child, the intercourse would be fruitless. FYC.

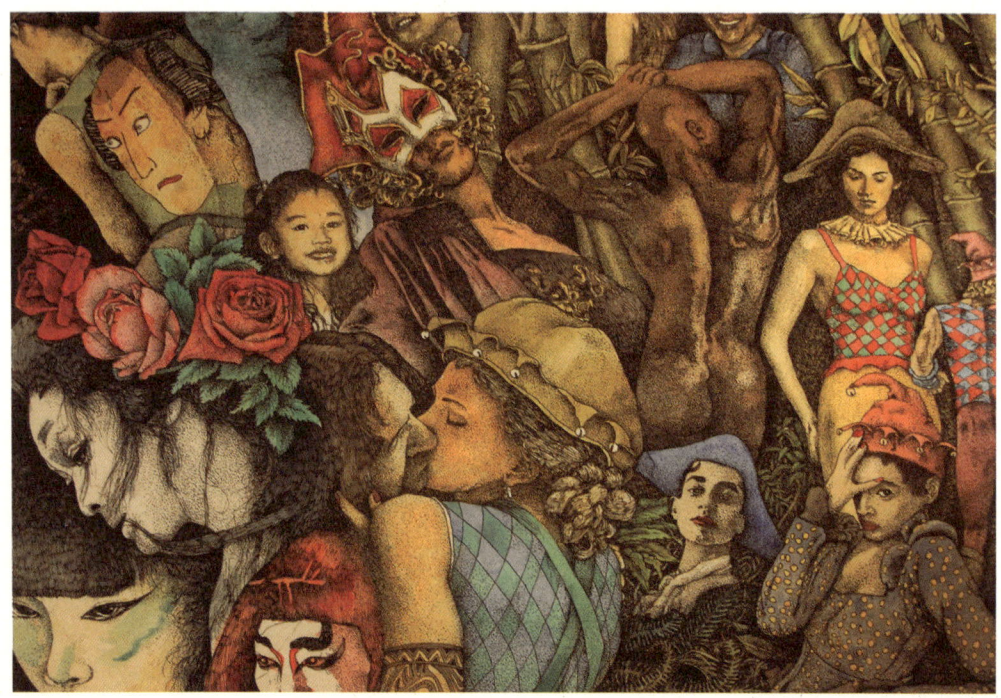

Artwork by Iñong Geslani, 2009.

Opposite page: ***Untitled***, Cenon Rivera, oil on wood, 108 x 78 cm, c. 1952.

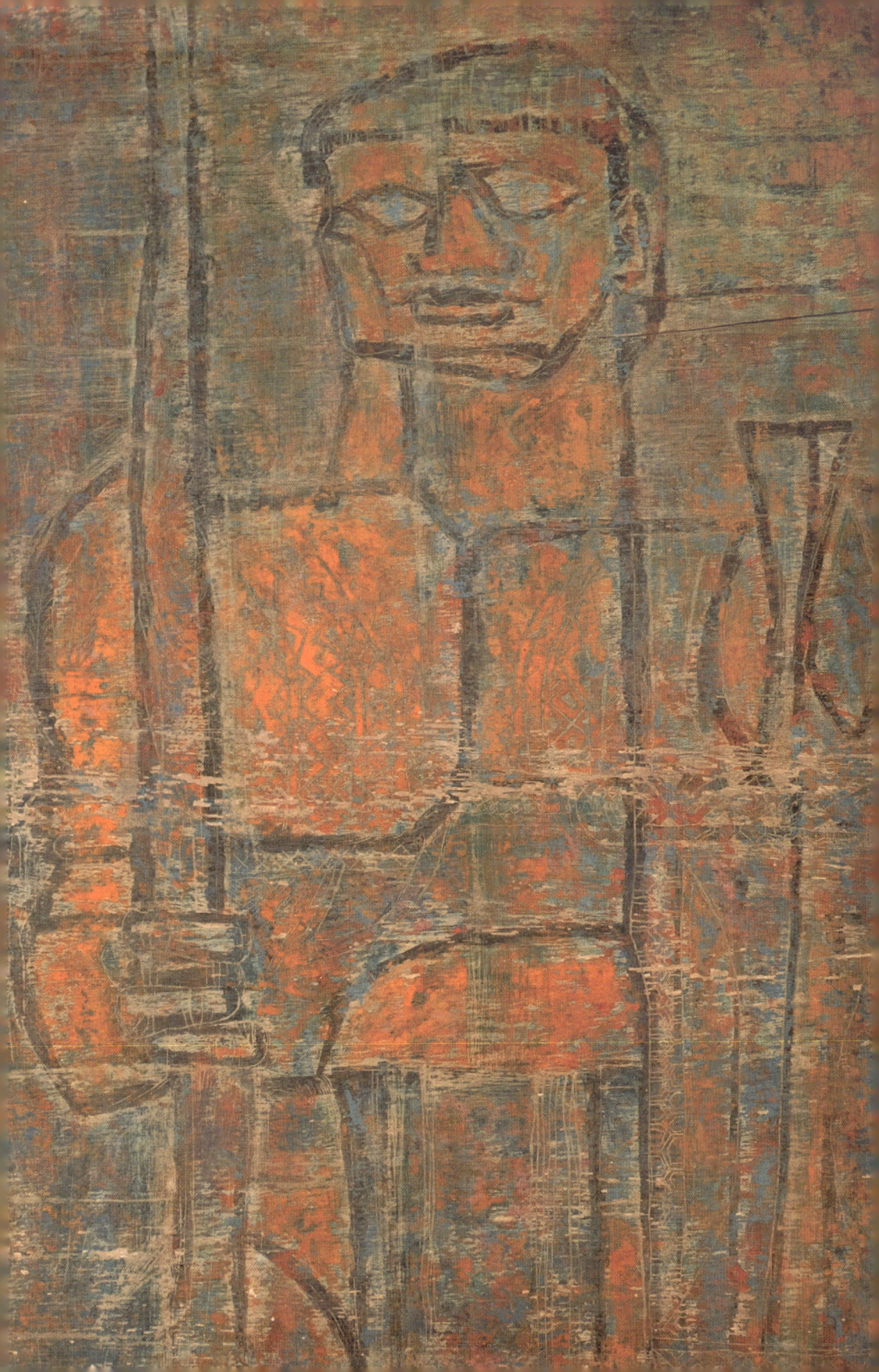

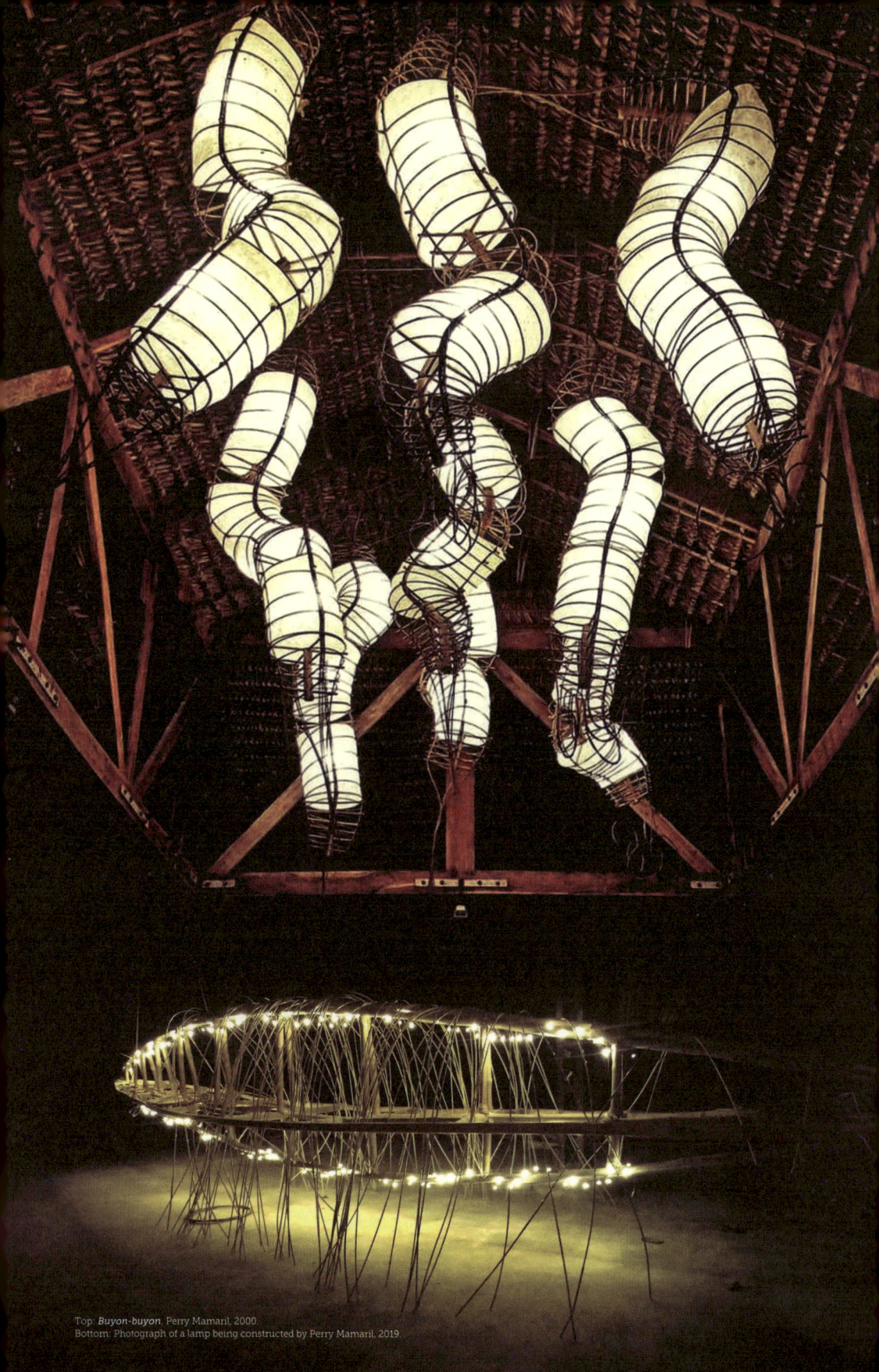

Top: *Buyon-buyon*, Perry Mamaril, 2000.
Bottom: Photograph of a lamp being constructed by Perry Mamaril, 2019.

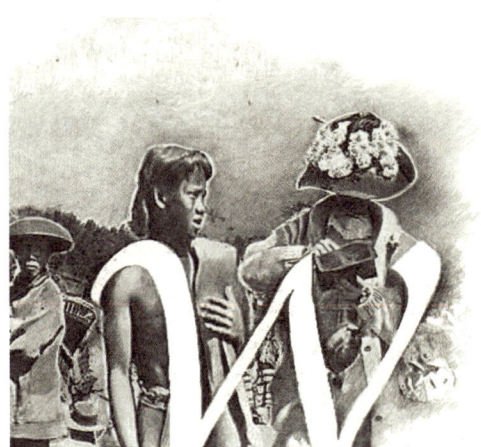

Wada *(KAN/IFU)* also **Waday** *(BON)*. Lit. There is. As in the expression *"Ay waday elf mo? [Do you have an elf?]"*
See also: Elf; Ma-id.

Wading *(KAN)* also **Gadew** *(KAN)*, **Gadiw** *(BON)*, **Kachiw** *(BON)*. A small river fish that sucks on stones to feed, and navigates by resisting the river's current. It was probably the most common river food before the introduction of other freshwater fish and seafood to the markets in the mountains. Locals used to catch wading by hand or by woven nets and contraptions. Today, a local would wear a car battery like a backpack and armed with a net and a stick with a metal end wired to the battery, would wade in the river and electrocute them under the river stones to let the fish float towards the net.
See also: Intum; Sinaplak.

Wanes *(BON/KAN)* also **Ba-ag** *(KAN)*, **Wanoh** *(IFU)*. A woven loincloth worn by Igorot men. It comes in various colors, patterns, and designs that distinguish one ethnolinguistic community from another. The most dominant color is red except for the Itneg's wanes which is mostly white.

When wearing a wanes, Igorot men display their buttocks and muscular bodies because only their loins are covered.

To wear the wanes is said to be very easy. One is told to follow this Kankanaey riddle: *"Yakang en Yapot, inputipot, insiglot [Yakang and Yapot, looped, then tied]."* OK. Perhaps learning how to wear it is actually as complicated as trying to answer the riddle. DOS.
See also: Agbaxan; Igorot Tail; Iniwitan; Weaving; Tapis.

Washing. (1) The act of drinking a light alcoholic drink (usually beer) after consuming copious amounts of hard liquor or spirits.
(2) Having a beer during a bad hangover. JST.

Washington Hotel. Stood where the Laperal Building on Session Road, Baguio City stands today. The Washington Hotel became the first concentration camp run by Japanese forces during the start of World War II, after Baguio became an Open City on December 27, 1941. Foreigners (mostly Chinese, Americans, and Indians) were rounded up and brought there. Later, they were transferred to Camp John Hay and Camp Holmes (now Camp Dangwa). The Americans were later brought outside the city to the University of Santo Tomas Interment Camp. FYC.
See also: John Hay, Camp.

Watwat *(KAN)*. (1) What's watwat? It used to mean raw or blanched pork given to those who attend a cañao but now has also come to mean any food (surprisingly, in one instance, canned sardines) distributed to guests during a feast. A paper plate is now usually wrapped in cellophane (replacing woven rattan containers or leaves) so the watwat can be brought home easily.
(2) In Abra, watwat means stretching the body to prepare for a siesta. JBC/NEP/RBB.
See also: Bingit; No wada asok, wada watwat; Patpatok.

Way ka's kugkugay mo *(KAN)*. Lit. Live your own life. A popular expression.

Waynasdi *(KAN)*. An idiomatic expression likened to the Filipino expression, *"Bahala na [leave it up to celestial fate]."* Waynasdi became more popular not only among the Kankanaey but also among non-Kankanaey speakers through Margaret Locano's hit song "Waynasdi" from the *Bigis* album. Although the song's melody is patterned after the country song "Why not me?," it has become so popular that Kumyoung karaoke added the song to its *Original Pilipino Music (OPM) list Vol. 5*. NEP.
See also: Amazing Grace; Cowboy; Lover's Moon; Nan Layad Nan Likhatan; Waiting Sheds.

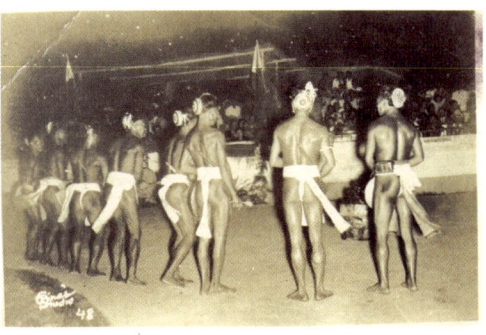

Photograph of Igorot men in their *Wanes*, c. 1940s.
Courtesy AV Cating Family Collection.

307

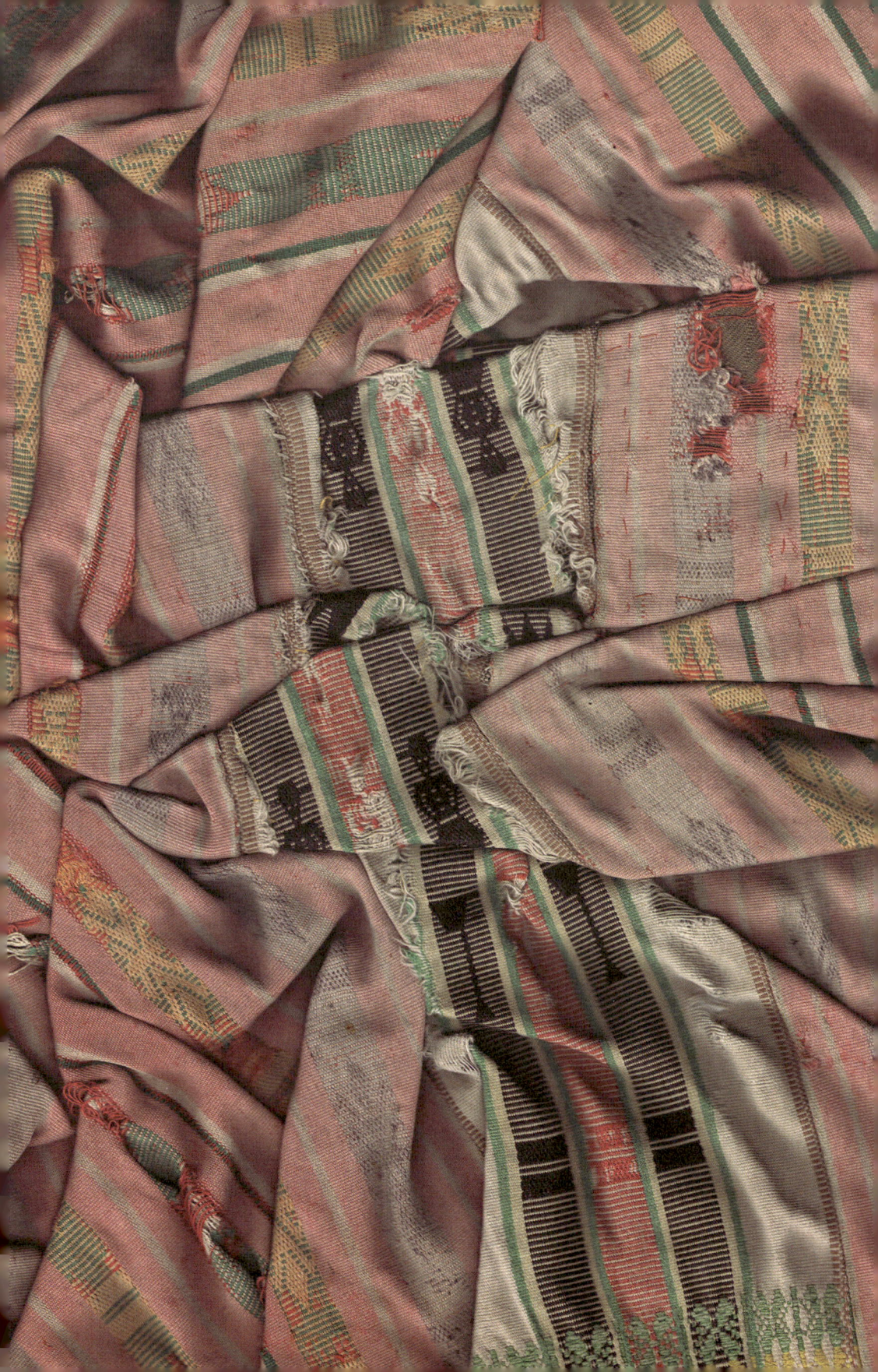

Weaving:
The Way of Weavers

Some anthropologists contend that weaving is an undervalued realm of artistic expression. This is true of the Cordillera, where the craft is the domain of women and its practice is seasonal, taking place when the planting and harvesting do not take up their time. In the work of women, weaving is merely an adjunct to the tasks of farming, and yet textiles are an integral part of Igorot culture. Women express their creativity and distinctiveness in the art of weaving.

Cloth is involved in life from birth to death, in sickness and health. A baby is cocooned in cloth. The sick are wrapped and healed in it. Couples are clasped in it, and at death one is buried in it. Identity can be expressed when the members of a group make and wear clothing that distinguishes them from others. Styles of dress indicate different ethnic origins. As an art form, textiles are embedded in all aspects of life from quotidian situations to ritual events.

The production of cloth is an occupation of women, a creative power that they possess. Women cultivate cotton, spin, dye, and weave it. Further, they trade their products as they please. Beginning at the age of ten or earlier, daughters learn the craft from their mothers. When mothers pass on their skills, they transfer technology that involves expertise about materials and ways of learning. The legacy of weaving is not just cloth or a physical product. Weaving, as it passes from mother to daughter, is a social practice that carries a continuity of culture. Acknowledged as having specialized skills, expert weavers obtain prestige and economic benefits from weaving.

The earliest types of cloth in the Philippines are very likely beaten bark cloth. Cotton was brought in by Chinese traders during the late Sung dynasty. When the Spanish colonizers first encountered the coastal Ilocanos, white cotton textiles were in common use. In the Cordillera, it appears that the Itneg and Gaddang were among the first to take up weaving, although the exact date has not been established. The Ifugao, Bontoc, Kalinga, and Kankanaey, according to some research, may have appropriated weaving only in the 18th century.

Presently, textiles may be classified into two categories: ritual cloths, and textiles produced for the tourist market. Innovations in contemporary production are implemented not only for economic gain and increased social standing but also to define cultural identity. Crafts formerly made for local use and trade are now increasingly earmarked for commercial sale due to the impact of tourism. Textiles tell stories of identity, economics, and social change.

Among the Ifugao, Kankanaey, Bontoc, Kalinga, Gaddang, and Itneg (the Cordillerans who

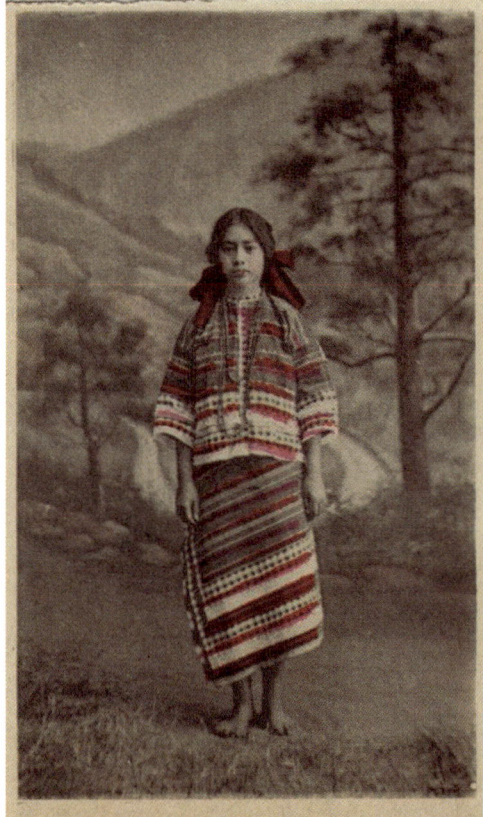

Photograph of Ibaloi woman wearing traditional clothing.
Courtesy AV Cating Family Collection.

weave their own cloth), the common weaving technology is the back strap loom, a primitive yet intricate operation. (The Ibaloi and the Ilongot did not weave). Unlike the upright loom, the back strap loom is portable so its place of operation can be relocated easily from inside the house to outside, under the bright warm sun of the mountains. The Kankanaey words for body tension back strap weaving are 'impaod,' 'impagod,' or 'pinnagod,' meaning strapped.

In back strap weaving, the woman's body forms part of the loom. Her spine, curved in a soft S, maintains the web in tension and dictates the cadence of creation. Her hands insert the weft in the shed and pick up the threads that define a motif. The weaver's mind is a creative one, the mind of one who makes things.

The weaving patterns worked into the weft design and the stripes set in the warp, articulate an innate awareness of mathematical operations involving principles of symmetry and order. Cordillera textile methods might be called primitive but the construction of their cloth is far from simple.

By means of bamboo poles, reeds, and pinewood sticks, the warp threads are fastened to a cross timber of a house, or a tree trunk. A belt attached

Opposite page: Photograph of traditional Cordillera *tapis* from Mountain Province.

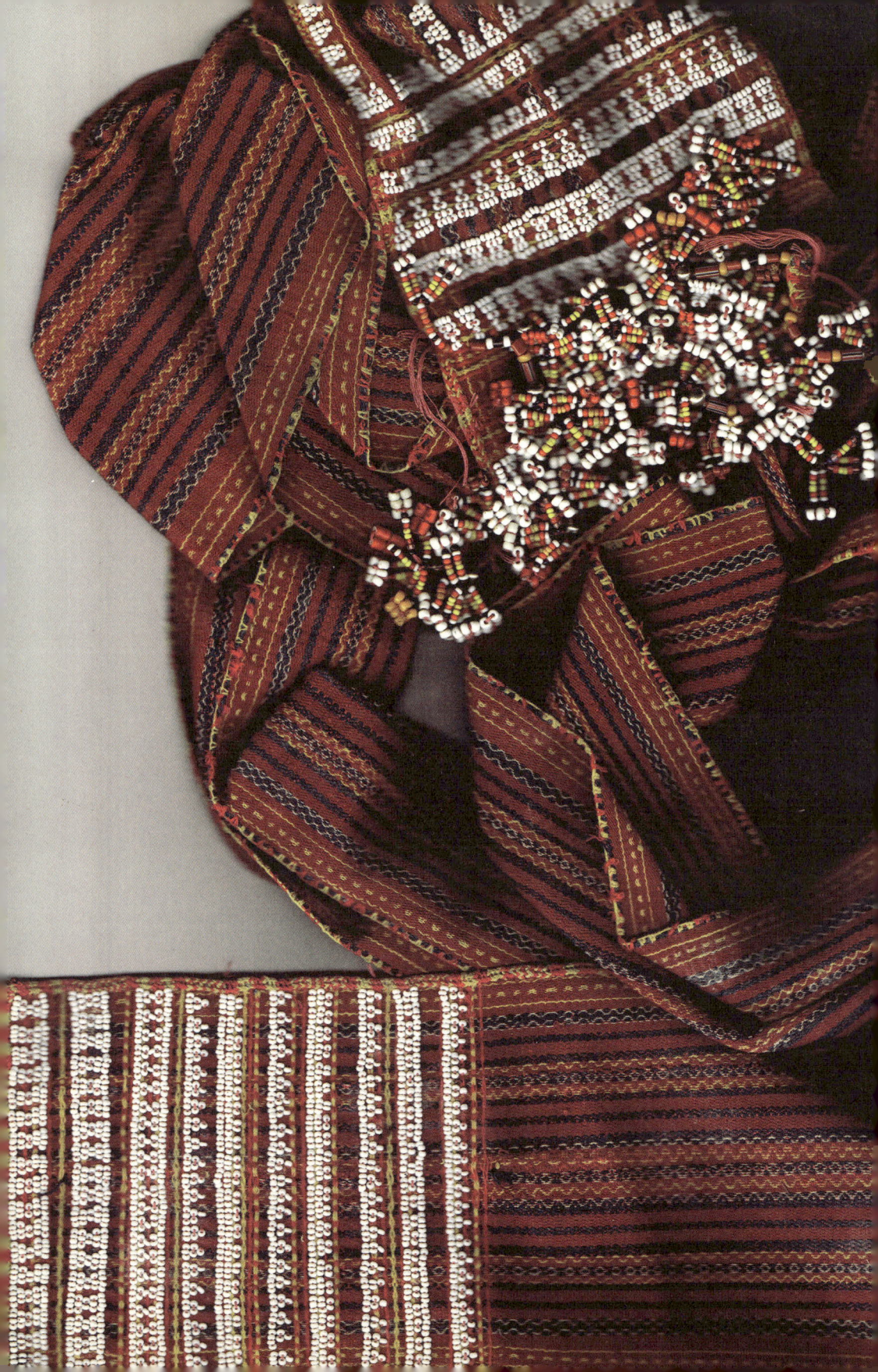

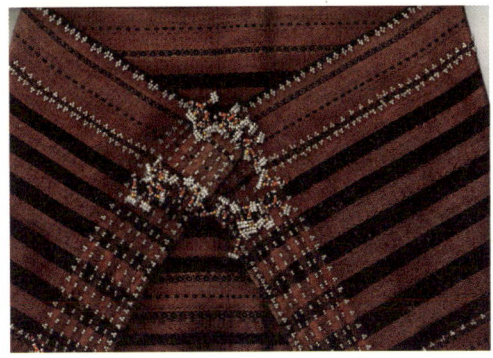

to the near roller and passed around the waist of the weaver keeps the web stretched. By raising one of the heddle sticks, the shed is opened then a knife-shaped wood batten is inserted into the opening. The batten, when turned sideways, enlarges the shed to allow a shuttle with weft thread to be shot through. The warp is changed by raising heddle sticks alternately or in a designed sequence. When performed by experts, back strap weaving looks deceivingly easy. The required discipline is invisible to the observer as is the centered and concentrated mind. A weaver, as she works and makes her creative decisions, has to be well-tempered, like a musician playing on strings – not too tense nor too lax.

According to Fr. Francis Lambrecht (1955), a CICM missionary, the weaving process in the Cordillera *"is intricately related to the domain of ritual."* In Ifugao, ceremonial textiles – simple striped cloths – are essential for the effective conduct of the rites of passage of birth, marriage, death, and healing. Religions practiced in the Cordillera require appeasement of the ancestors. It is believed that continuous sacrifices of animals and material goods such as blankets and other pieces of clothing brings prosperity and well-being to the community.

In the Cordillera, it is possible to tell apart ethnic groups by styles of dressing and weaving. The Ifugao practice a plain weave with simple and elegant warp stripes for their ceremonial cloths. Early ritual textiles were produced from bast fibers extracted from the local mulberry tree. These pieces are exchanged in ceremonial events.

In the 1930s, Roy Franklin Barton (1938) recorded the autobiography of a weaver named Bugan who cultivated cotton, gathered wild indigo, and traded her works in neighboring communities. Bugan's cotton was spun by rolling the fibers on her bare thigh with the palm of her hand. This ancestor of today's Ifugao weavers can be imagined seated in the lower part of her dwelling, under the family room, industriously making clothes and blankets. Her descendants continue to work in the same manner.

Opposite page: Photograph of a traditional Gaddang *wanes* from Mountain Province.
Top: Photograph of a traditional Gaddang cape.
Right: Photograph of a Gaddang cape and *tapis* from Mountain Province.

With increased tourism to the Banaue rice terraces, a World Heritage site, the Ifugao also produce textiles intended for sale to their visitors. These include table runners resembling loincloths, place mats, wall hangings, and various small items that can be easily packed for the tourists to take away with them.

In the 1970s the ikat method was introduced in Ifugao, ostensibly for the tourist trade. They produced yardage and blankets employing traditional motifs like the six-pointed star, lizards, bugs, and flowers. Using natural and synthetic dyes, they managed to depict houses, granaries, shields, and other symbols of Ifugao life. Ikat, an item produced for the market, co-existed with textiles woven for ritual use.

The town of Sagada, which hosts a viable tourist industry, is currently experiencing a resurgence of upright loom weaving aimed at visitors. New

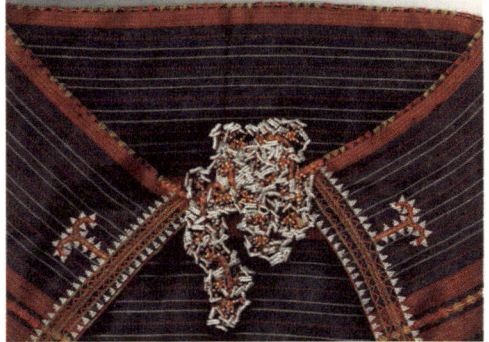

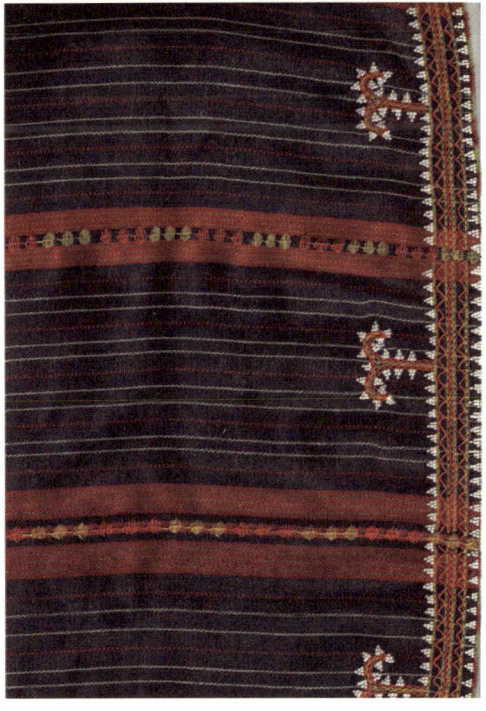

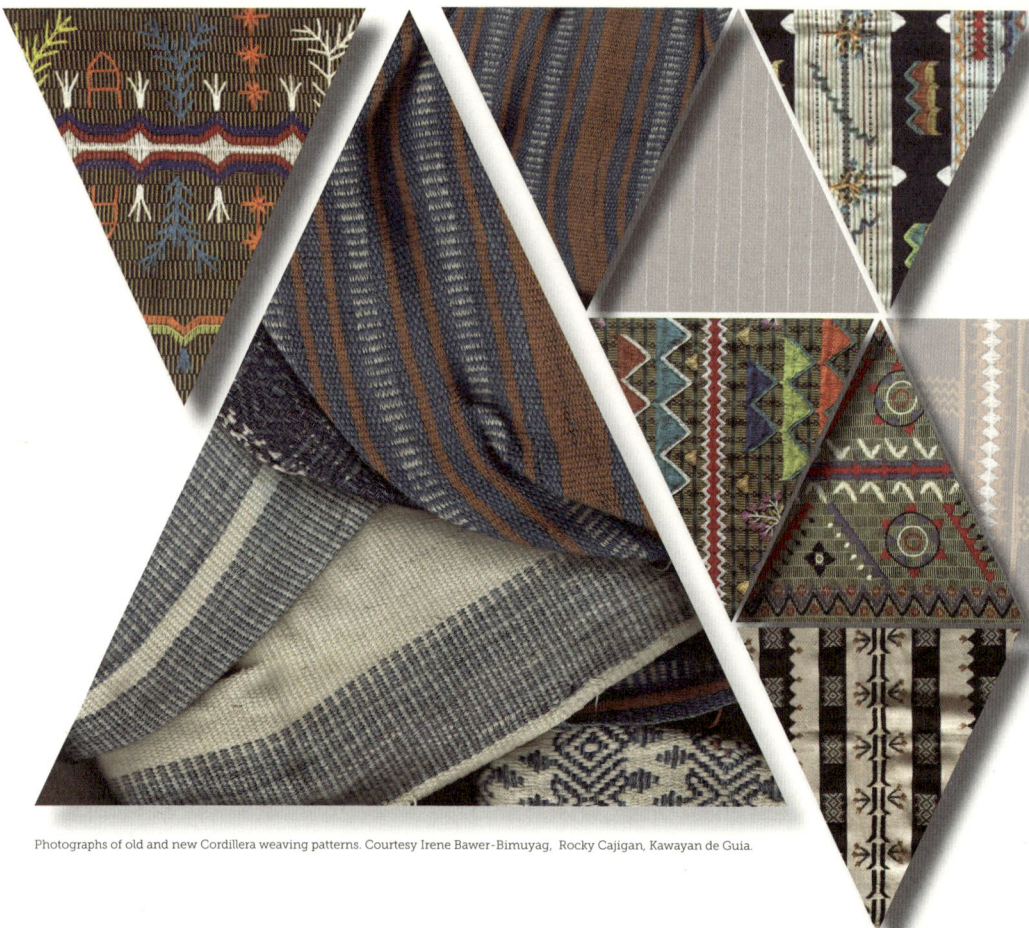

Photographs of old and new Cordillera weaving patterns. Courtesy Irene Bawer-Bimuyag, Rocky Cajigan, Kawayan de Guia.

weavers are encouraged to take up the enterprise because of brisk sales. Indeed, Sagada woven wares like backpacks, bags, vests, and belts are spotted all over the world – in the Paris metro, the bike lanes of Amsterdam, and the immigration lines of the Narita Airport. These commercially produced items are imbued with traditional Bontoc motifs in contemporary colors.

The active weaving centers in the Mountain Province are Samoki and Can-eo in Bontok, Sagada, Sabangan, Besao, and Paracelis.

The blankets produced by Kalinga weavers have specific uses and functions. For instance, there is the lilabey or widow's blanket which, aside from keeping widows warm, swaddles babies for the ritual to celebrate the first born child. The silambituwon with its six-pointed star theme, is their funeral blanket because it is believed that the dead become stars. Other items worn and produced by the Kalinga are beaded betel nut bags and bags for carrying fertility amulets.

The weaving communities in Kalinga are in Lubuagan and Dacalan.

Writing in 1921, the linguist Otto Scheerer described the Itneg of Abra as wearing *"turbans made of the bark of the balete tree."* They wove their own clothes made of cotton that they grew. Formerly, they produced threads from flayed bark which they *"twisted on the naked thigh under the palm of the hand"* (Cole 2004). They dyed their yardage using herbs and berries.

Itneg women presided over the manufacture of cloth from growing the cotton, the sourcing of barks, to spinning and actual weaving. The men made the tools – loom sticks, the spindle, batten and the various apparatus for fluffing the cotton and winding skeins.

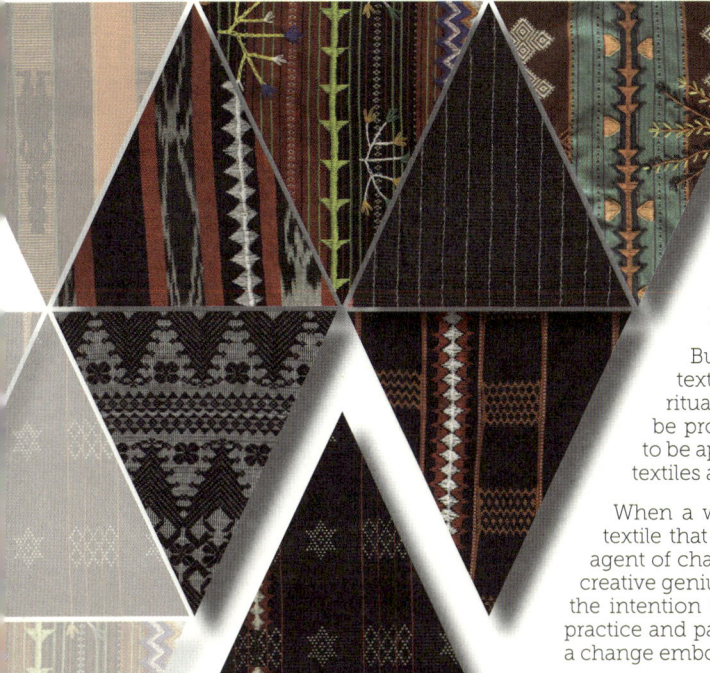

spinners, dyers and weavers – have been exploited of their labor and products, to the advantage of the colonizers and buyers. This trend, together with a lack of appreciation for the creativity that goes into the making of handwoven textiles, continues into the present with the tourist demand for ever cheaper items, no matter how shabby.

But traditional and ceremonial textiles will endure for as long as rituals are held. They will continue to be produced as long as ancestors need to be appeased because, in the Cordillera, textiles are linked to customs and identity.

When a weaver in the Cordillera creates a textile that is a work of art, she becomes an agent of change. Her work is an expression of creative genius and her art is fully invested with the intention to change the world even as the practice and patterns may remain the same. It is a change embodied in the continuity of her art.

Ifugao Weaving

An important Ifugao ceremonial textile is the funeral blanket. This piece, which is woven and used exclusively for burial, is said to have three parts: the center and two identical sides. Lambrecht (1955) identifies the two central panels as the *"body."* The right side panel is the blanket's *"back"* while the left, the *"stomach."* The supplementary weft patterns of the top and bottom of the middle section, or *"body"* is referred to as *"that which has been repeatedly beaten with a stick."* These raised motifs are compressed into the cloth by firmly beating the batten in the shed after inserting the weft thread. Since the products of back strap weaving tend to be narrow (not wider than the weaver's hips), several panels are stitched together to make wider pieces of clothing such as skirts and blankets.

Baguio City in Benguet is the center of market-driven weaving. Although the Ibaloi by tradition did not weave, many women engage in it, producing items for contemporary use such as table napkins, placemats, throw pillows and yardage for clothing. There are now weavers in the municipalities of Kabayan and Kapangan as well.

The Easter Weaving School, in the 1920s, began to operate a vocational department for girls, teaching back strap weaving. Its purpose was to 'reawaken' the traditional art.

Most weaving produced currently is done with synthetic fiber – either acrylic or polyester blended with cotton. Cotton, which is now rare, is imported from either China or India. The cultivation of cotton declined during the Spanish tobacco monopoly.

For centuries, Filipino artist-producers – the cotton farmers, yarn

Photograph of women wearing traditional Cordillera weaving. Courtesy AV Cating Family Collection.

Mountain Province Weaving

In the Mountain Province, the wrap around skirt with its three panels makes the Bontoc woman. Composed of red, white and black bands, this piece of apparel requires three loom set ups as each panel has its own set of defined patterns. The ladies also wear distinctive belts that distinguish single women from married ones. There is also a belt for newly delivered mothers, to hold their stomachs in so they can stand and walk erect.

Kalinga Weaving

The Kalinga hand woven niluslusong cloth has a floating weft design that is characterized by chevrons (called matmata, meaning eye), zigzags, and lozenges. The niluslusong style is achieved by a method similar to twill weaving. Supplementary continuous weft patterns, embroidery and beading with mother of pearl shells and old coins are the distinguishing marks of Kalinga textiles.

Gaddang Weaving

The most elegant clothing is that of the Gaddang, a people closely related to the Kalinga. These handsome men wear loincloths, short upper garments, and capes that are embroidered and embellished with small white beads. The edges of their cloth lengths have special finishes appearing to be corded. Indigo and narra red are the vegetable dyes they employ. They also make bark cloths called tayak.

Abra Weaving

These days, the Itneg of Abra work on the upright loom, unlike other Cordillera weavers. Their pinilian, similar to the Kalinga niluslusong, is a continuous supplementary weave or floating warp cloth which is produced in Peñarubia, Manabo, and Langiden. Pinilian is also produced in Santiago, Ilocos Sur. The transfer of the technology in recent times was spearheaded by Corazon Agosto, the Ilocana doyenne of weaving. AML.

See also: Bakget; Igorot Tail; Tapis; Wanes.

White Elephant. What Baguio City is according to the Philippine Free Press. *"It has all the earmarks of that distinguished mammoth, even to its being 'white.' For, so far as the great mass of the Filipino people are concerned, Baguio might as well be a resort to the moon... Furthermore, like the aforesaid distinguished mammoth, Baguio has a prodigious appetite. Its 'chow' thus far, expressed in dollars and cents, must run somewhere in the neighborhood of three or four or five million pesos."* The latter amount referred to the cost of building Kennon Road. FYC.

See also: Annual Headhunter's Fund; Baguio, The Naming of; Gateway to Wonderland; Kennon Road.

Worcester, Dean. Known as Bokeg to the locals. A six-foot-four-inch Zoology professor from the University of Michigan who first came to the Philippines in 1887 and returned in 1890 for a two-year study. He is why the University of Michigan has one of the most extensive collections of Igorot artifacts and photos. He later published *The Philippine Islands and Their People*. He became a member of the Philippine Commission and later the Secretary of Interior in 1906. He was said to have created the most tremendous impact on how Americans perceived Igorots with his mapping, classification and publications on the Igorot *"tribes."* (Finin 2005)

See also: Annual Headhunter's Fund; Bureau of Non-Christian Tribes; Ethnographic Mapping; Tribes.

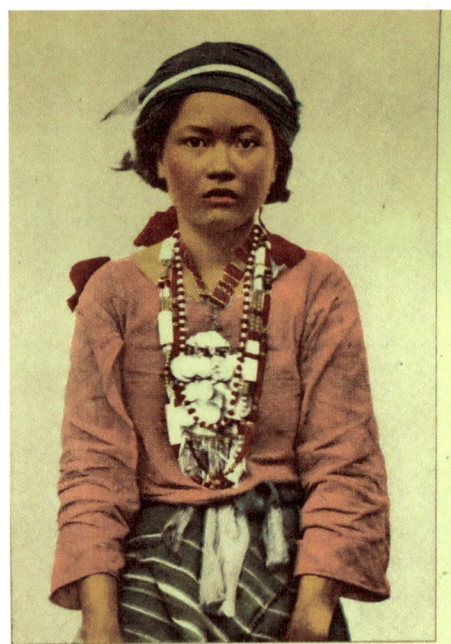

A WILD TINGIAN GIRL OF APAYAO

Note the peculiar mother-of-pearl ornaments and the blade of the miniature headaxe thrust into the hair. Among this tribe a blue thread tied around a girl's ankle is a sign that she is unmarried.

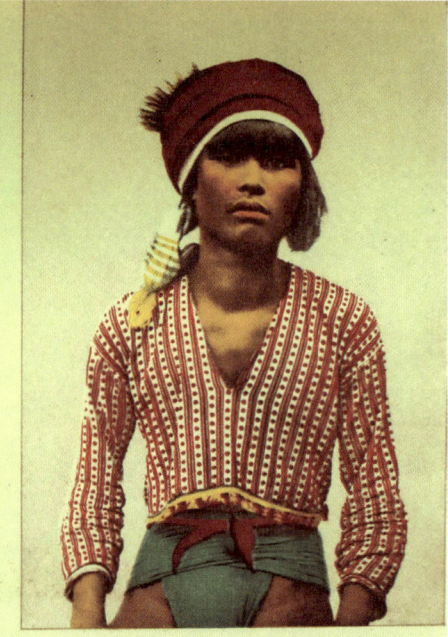

A WILD TINGIAN OF APAYAO

The Tingian man's loin cloth is almost invariably blue and in his upper garments he exhibits a decided partiality for gay colors, especially for red and yellow, two colors usually combined in his turban. As a rule he does not cut his hair and is not above supplementing the natural growth by such a feminine addition as a switch.

Portraits of Itnegs in traditional dress. National Geogrpahic Magazine.

Woodcarving:
Carving and Other Tools *(IFU)*

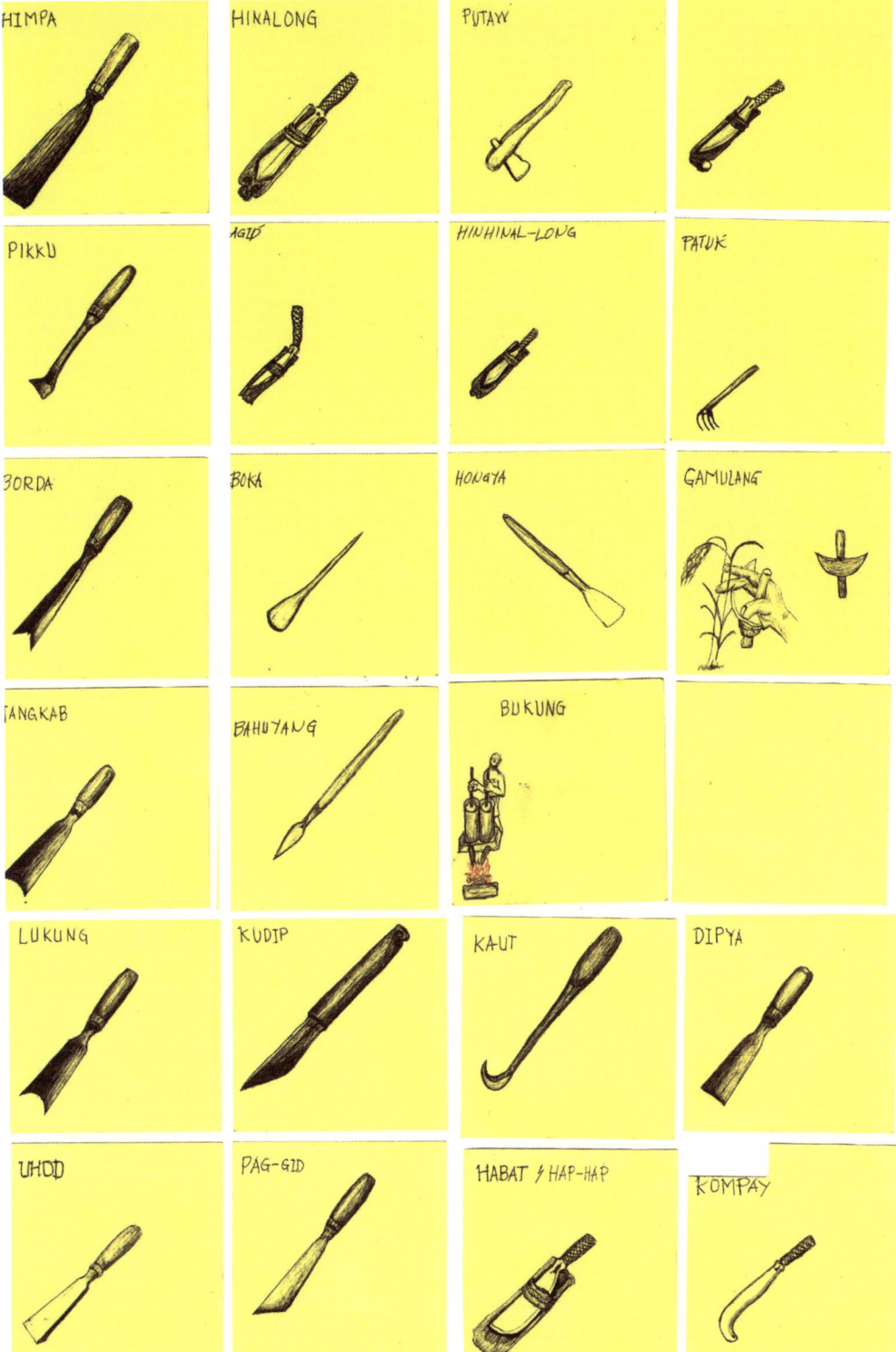

Illustrations of different carving tools. Illustrations by woodcarver Jason "Dehon" Taguyongon.

WAITING FOR WAITING SHEDS

Among the Kankanay of the Philippine Cordillera, Waynasdi might as well be a magic word. Contracted from *"Oway Na Isdi,"* it translates to *"Bahala Na"* in the Tagalog of the lowlands. *"Bahala Na"* loosely translates as, *"Leave it up to God."* Waynasdi is uttered when waiting, such as for the result of an exam you studied well for, when switching to a new job without knowing if the new job will be better, or, when separating from a partner you struggled with for a dozen years.

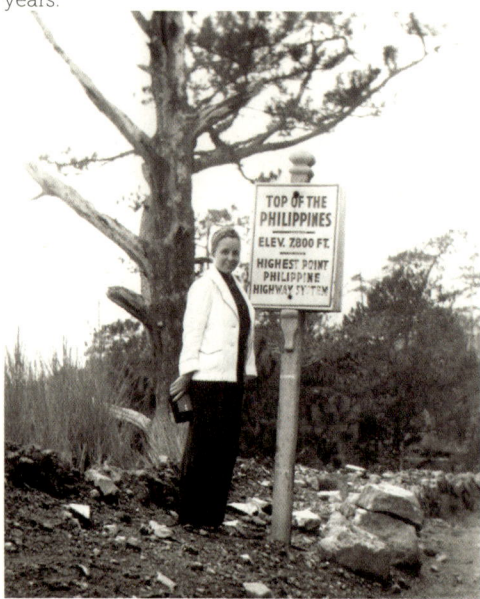

Photograph of a woman along the Halsema Highway, c. 1930s.

Waynasdi also expresses the uncertainty in the life of farmers who, after back-breaking soil preparation and planting, wait for the grains to grow well until ready for harvest, hoping that the drought, the storms, and the pests, will ravage distant Pluto but never their own fields and gardens. On a lighter note, Waynasdi captures your feelings when you're not sure if the kite you made will fly, or if the dish you're experimenting with will turn out palatable or even edible. Popular in videoke bars frequented by Cordillerans, "Waynasdi" is also a Kankanay song first performed by Margaret Paleng Locano, to the exact tune of the country song "Why Not Me?" by The Judds. Far from The Judds' pining song about wanting to be loved, Locano sings about a hard-working and devoted woman doubting her future with a worthless husband she's thinking of leaving. When asked what tomorrow will be like, Waynasdi – much like que sera, sera – is a perfect answer. Waynasdi has the power to calm fraying nerves over unforeseeable, uncontrollable outcomes, to assure that things are best in whatever state and order we experience them, even if we might not think so at the moment those things are happening.

Waynasdi, as it is known in the Cordilleras, encapsulates the spirit of waiting sheds along the Halsema Highway, and possibly, too, that of all the waiting sheds in the world.

A waiting shed's basic structure involves a roof and four posts. Variations occur with the material, the size, the walls, the seats, the design of the roof, and the finishing. Although most sheds are steel and concrete structures, there are some sheds that make use of old, discarded bus roofs supported by four wooden posts. The latter are usually made by community people using locally-available resources that they don't have to buy or pay for – the steel and concrete waiting sheds are usually built with funding allocated by local governments. Some sheds have roofs of cement and some of galvanized iron that provide a deafening audio experience when the rain pours hard. An average shed can fit at least eight people standing or a dozen squeezed tightly together. Bigger ones accommodate motorcycles parked beside sacks and sacks of commercial fertilizers. Some sheds have three completely closed walls, while some have windows. Others are open from the waist up. Most sheds have seating areas so people don't stand the whole time they are waiting. Roofs can either be slightly slanted (to have a wider opening) or can be flat, parallel to the floor. Sheds with more generous funding show off a painted finish while lesser endowed ones make do with the bare cement they're left with. Each shed is as different from the others as one thumbprint is different from the next. The century-old Halsema Highway, leading to the interiors of the Cordillera, hosts more than fifty waiting sheds on its almost 150-kilometer stretch.

There are a hundred and one purposes for waiting sheds in the Cordillera. Primarily, these are intended as road-side shelters from bad weather, temporary storage space for farm supplies and/or produce, and waiting areas for rides to the city or deeper into to the interior of the region. Distinct two-storey waiting sheds, also called loading platforms, make it more convenient to unload luggage and other cargo from the tops of jeepneys or buses onto the second-floor and down to the ground through a staircase. Sheds located far from residential areas turn into drinking places, and dating and party venues for young people avoiding adult supervision and restrictions. Waiting sheds are also structures for corruption. Clever politicians use the walls of these sheds to promote and popularize their names and to increase name recall come the next election. Wily proponents and contractors use the construction of waiting sheds as opportunities to siphon taxpayers' money into their own wallets, as is

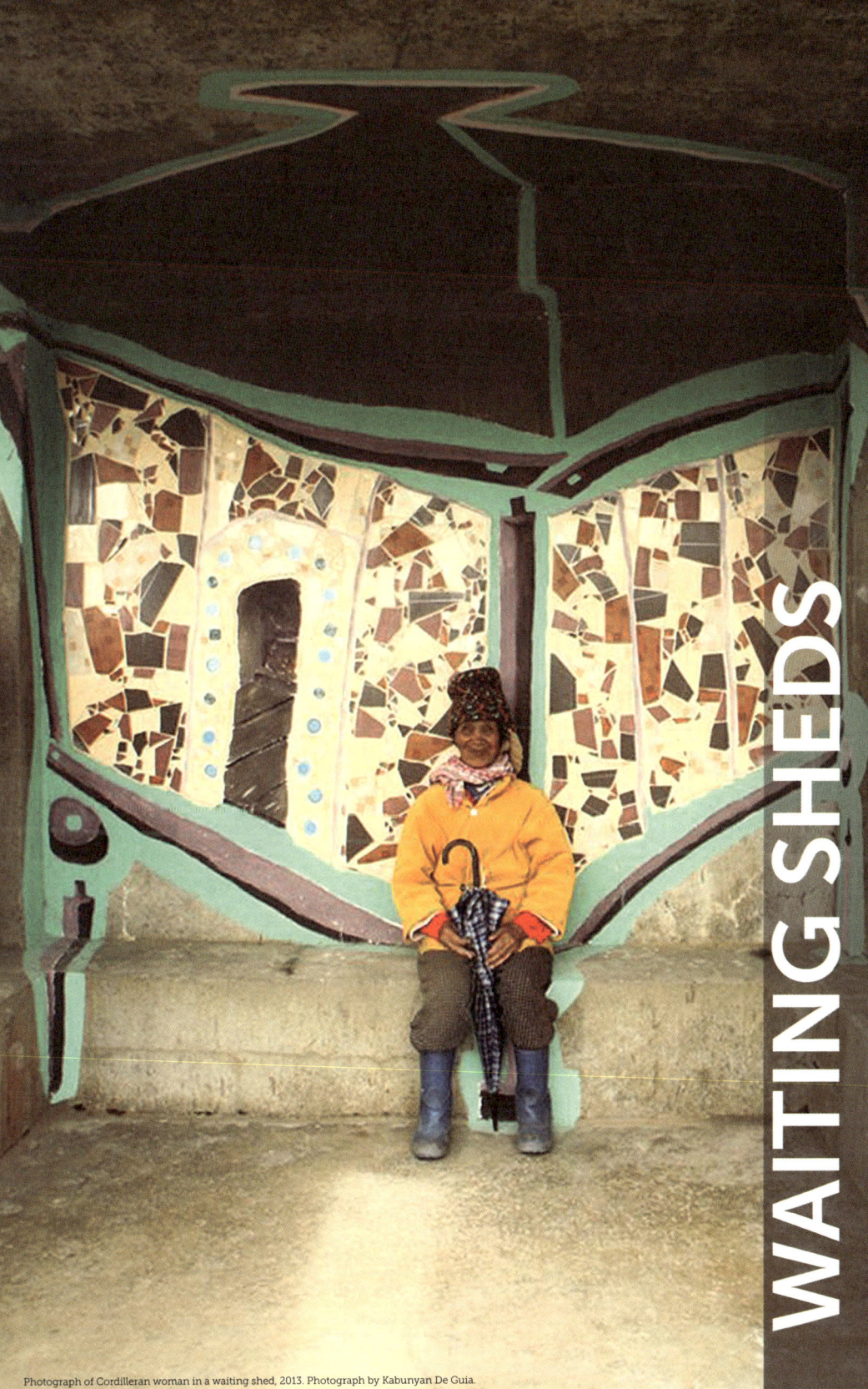

Photograph of Cordilleran woman in a waiting shed, 2013. Photograph by Kabunyan De Guia.

WAITING SHEDS

done with most government infrastructure projects in the country.

But it is the ordinary community people that use these sheds daily. A sudden rain may change plans for people passing through and impose an indefinite waiting time inside the sheds. The last bus to the city might already be full of sacks of vegetables picked up from farmers in earlier stops, and a farmer's haul of sacks in one shed may have to wait until the next day. A particular public ride expected at a certain time may come early, on time, late, or, in rare but possible instances, may not come at all. In a region where time is dictated by the seasons (and not by the bundy clock), the state of mind that is Waynasdi allows for effective coping in waiting shed situations.

These sheds proved to be the perfect match for the work of the Mighty Bhutens, a trio of tile mosaic artists: Kabunyan De Guia, Oliver Olivete, and Guiller Lagac. Their main working philosophy is Bathala Na, another version of Bahala Na that highlights God (Bathala in Tagalog). Filipino psychologist Alfredo Lagmay interprets Bahala Na as indicative of the improvisational personality of the Filipino people, which allows them to cope and thrive even in unstructured, indefinite, unpredictable, and stressful situations (De Guia, 2005, 85). Using already discarded, broken tiles from tile shops, the resulting work of The Mighty Bhutens is largely affected by the tile colors available and the accidental shapes of broken shards. They *"jam with the cosmos"* as one of them succinctly puts it.

The Mighty Bhutens created murals of different themes in five municipalities along the Halsema Highway, one waiting shed in one municipality per day. The mosaics they pre-designed for the waiting sheds changed during the actual installation. Depending on the weather, the unexpected adjustments in size, the other people they randomly worked with, the available time, and other unforeseen factors, their murals evolved from plans to different actualities. Joining them in this project, several artists and artist-collectives from the Cordillera and Manila transformed over thirty sheds into their unique expressions of art.

Kabunyan de Guia and Oliver Olivete were first classmates and then both drop outs in Fine Arts at the Baguio campus of the University of the Philippines. They met Guiler Lagac in the so-called wider University of Life, while learning to mosaic on-the-job for the Victor Oteyza Community Art Space, also in Baguio City. After participating with Baguio artists on the mosaic project along Session Road in 2005, the three of them decided to continue to work together, with tile mosaic as their medium. They use improvised tools like old rubber slippers for grouting and rags for cleaning their finished worked. They named their group The Mighty Bhutens and started making tile mosaic murals in public places, business spaces, and inside the homes of clients.

When asked about why they chose the name Mighty Bhutens, they gave at least three versions, or more, depending on the degree of permanent goofiness they're in. The shared version says buttons were involved when they first met and they wanted a strong name so from Mighty Buttons, they decided The Mighty Bhutens would give it a serious-but-not-so-serious twist. In another version, they wanted to make a band, and in one of their friend's films, where the leading man sings country songs in a bar, they entered The Mighty Bhutens in the bar's line-up of performers. Of course they neither performed in the film nor in real life, but the name stuck. The other version is a green joke. Yet another version, also obviously another joke, involves the lovely Bhutan.

With three creative minds and three separate personalities, humor keeps them working together, and helps them to disregard previous disagreements for the next big laugh; for the Mighty Bhutens know what to take seriously and what can be laughed out of their way. The origin of their name is something they can forever joke about. Before starting work in a shed, one of them performs stunts, or parodies a pathetic local actor, while the others draw a funny figure in chalk – not to be included in the mural. They play with whatever they can play with; but they know work. During the last hour to finish, each of them concentrates on one corner, quietly applying grout or fixing a misplaced tile or cleaning the completed parts. In the end, the permanent mosaic mural in someone's living room, in an outdoor space of a restaurant, on the fountain of a public park, or in this case the waiting sheds along the Halsema Highway, are works of art.

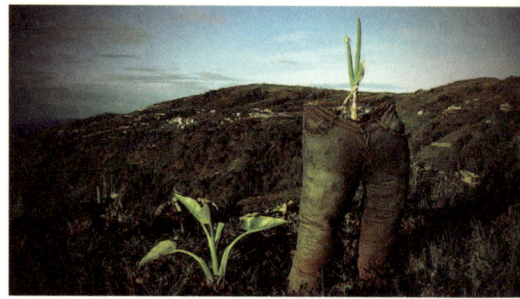

Photographs along the Halsema Highway during the Waiting Sheds project, 2013. Photographs by Kabunyan de Guia.

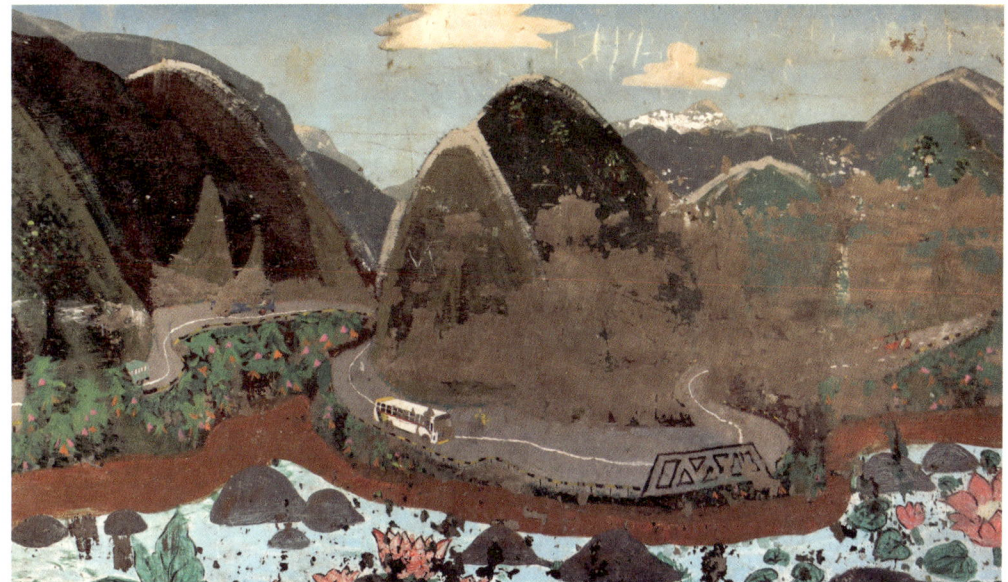

Photograph of a school mural in Calasipan along the Halsema Highway, 2013. Photograph by Kawayan de Guia.

In waiting sheds, humor is also necessary, as The Mighty Bhutens demonstrate. Waynasdi and its Tagalog counterpart Bathala Na combine effectively with humor. Otherwise people could pass out, add to premature white hairs and increase chances of heart failure while dealing angrily, impatiently or too seriously with the unpredictable unknown. Such is not the case in the waiting sheds along the Halsema Highway, with The Mighty Bhutens, or at least whenever and wherever Waynasdi magic is at play. GAD.

See also: Halsema Hijinks; Mosaic, Waynasdi.

THE MIGHTY BHUTENS

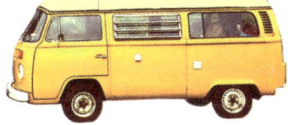

The rainy season was closing in, and no funds were sprouting out. By then, we had already determined what the 13 projects would be and everybody anticipated to act on it, for a deadline due October, and we were three months near dead.

Since *Tiw-tiwong: The Odds to Unends* (the culminating exhibition in Singapore Biennale 2013) was based on the *AX(iS) Art Project: To the End of the World* road-trip along the Halsema Highway in 2012, we decided to head back to the very highway where it all began. We went pledge-in-hand with the words "*art access for all.*" The Mighty Bhutens joined us in their Volkswagen and did the first waiting shed – the embryo for all of the would-be 36 sheds, finished in just six months.

The main point was to expound on these dilapidated waiting sheds that were scattered across the 150 km highway, stretching from Baguio to Bontoc. With the initiative coming from the playful Mighty Bhutens bunch (now very responsible fathers who could not take more than a week off), it was a way for other artists and other individuals with limited time to boot, to participate in the project.

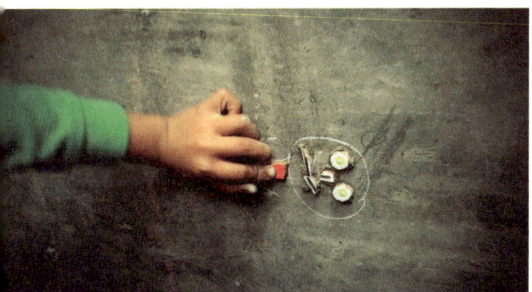

What is a waiting-shed along the Halsema? Basically a cube with a roof. A three-dimensional physical space where the fourth dimension is Chance or Luck: When is this bus going to pass by? Or is it ever going to? Questions in mind, the weather conditions also come into play. The worst time being the rainy season. There's the risk of landslides accompanied by the cold that settles down one's spine and does not intend to leave. But such a shed is also a place where people find each other by accident. One might end up sharing stories and necessities, cigarettes, betel nut, and sometimes silence.

To produce the sheds project was a logistical nightmare: Where to stay? Who to talk to? How to talk them into letting us into their community? Perhaps even sleep over for the night? Nobody took a shower (because there were no showers). It was collective bathing by the river or wisik-wisik (or a splash of water here and there) if we chanced upon a stream. But we had good food. Fresh vegetables and smoked pork readily available from the richness of the vast Halsema. The produce continued to roll as we met farmers along the way.

Painting the sheds was organized like a military command, with only four vehicles at our disposal and passenger loads from a low of 15, and at times peaking to 40 artists as they came and went.

A typical day would begin with a breakfast of sweet potatoes, fried rice and a piece of dried fish, then dismantling the tents and breaking up the camp. An advance party would proceed, ensuring that the permits in the next town were given on time, as well as establishing the necessary links between the artists and the locals. With their tools and materials, the remaining group would then be dropped off – okay, scattered if you will – at times between 50-kilometer distances for the farthest sheds. On good days, we would complete over six sheds, and on slow days, only three.

Often, the artists would spend around eight to ten hours finishing just one shed. Sometimes, you would see 50 school children participating in the project, interacting and helping the artists. In other times, you might sense the irate old folk or find a local drunk interrogating the artists, asking about the work, almost ready to kick the artists out for stepping into their territory. Some of us were made to confront the stereotype of a leftist, or a 'crazy' creative, or doing some sort of self-rehabilitation through art. But when the sheds started to take shape, these same people would wear the same smiles we did.

We would end the nights in bare minimum artist-campsites (sometimes in schools) with hot stew, swigging bottles from one end to the other, and guitars and drums loud enough to invite other passers-by. There were long exchanges of stories about the day's events. Some nights, these would stretch on, until it was time to break camp again without much sleep. This went on for over a week, until finally, all sheds were ready and done.

We could approximate around what time or decade each shed was built, or under whose political mandate, just by the condition of the concrete, or how it was built. During the time of former President Marcos, the shed walls were at least a foot thick in diameter, solid enough to withstand artillery fire; others, perhaps during Fidel Ramos or Gloria Macapagal-Arroyo's reign, had walls that were a whole lot thinner, like they had osteoporosis and can't be salvaged – that they'd have to be wholly knocked down. Some areas had not one but two of these sheds, sitting right next to each other as if they were the only eureka moments of that place. That revealed to us that the waiting sheds were a tangible display of corruption that was being passed down from one political dynasty to the next. The lowest example of infrastructure-projects corruption.

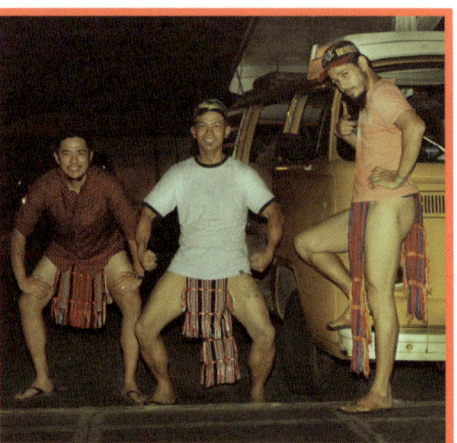
Photograph of the Mighty Bhutens members (L-R) Oliver Olivete, Guiller Guilac and Kabunyan de Guia.

The pictures tell very little of what exactly happened. The project could look like a huge jinxed-artists club looking for something to doodle on, but it was the backbone of this whole undertaking – including this book – and it is a direct representation of the idea that no one is limited by anything, and everyone is invited to participate. It was a roving school where we refueled our cultural deficiencies from the locals and amongst ourselves, as we shared with the locals what we knew. But what did we know? It would be prudent to say that the art was only an excuse to mingle and educate ourselves with things we would never have learned had we taken another highway system as our 'canvas.'

And what did we learn? It was learning about the language of resilience the Cordillerans have carried along with them since forever, being survivors of culture, and innovators, bearers of culture, and spiritual guides. A very strong Cordilleran trait is the art of perfect timing that is embedded in waiting; the value of circumstance, one that leaves things to chance. All this time, until the moment I am writing this down, I have stopped asking when this bus is going to pass by, or if it ever will. The answer is this very book; as your guide, our guide, and our vehicle to exploring the world we have come to know. KDG.

Opposite page: Photographs of the different waiting sheds along Halsema Highway, 2013.

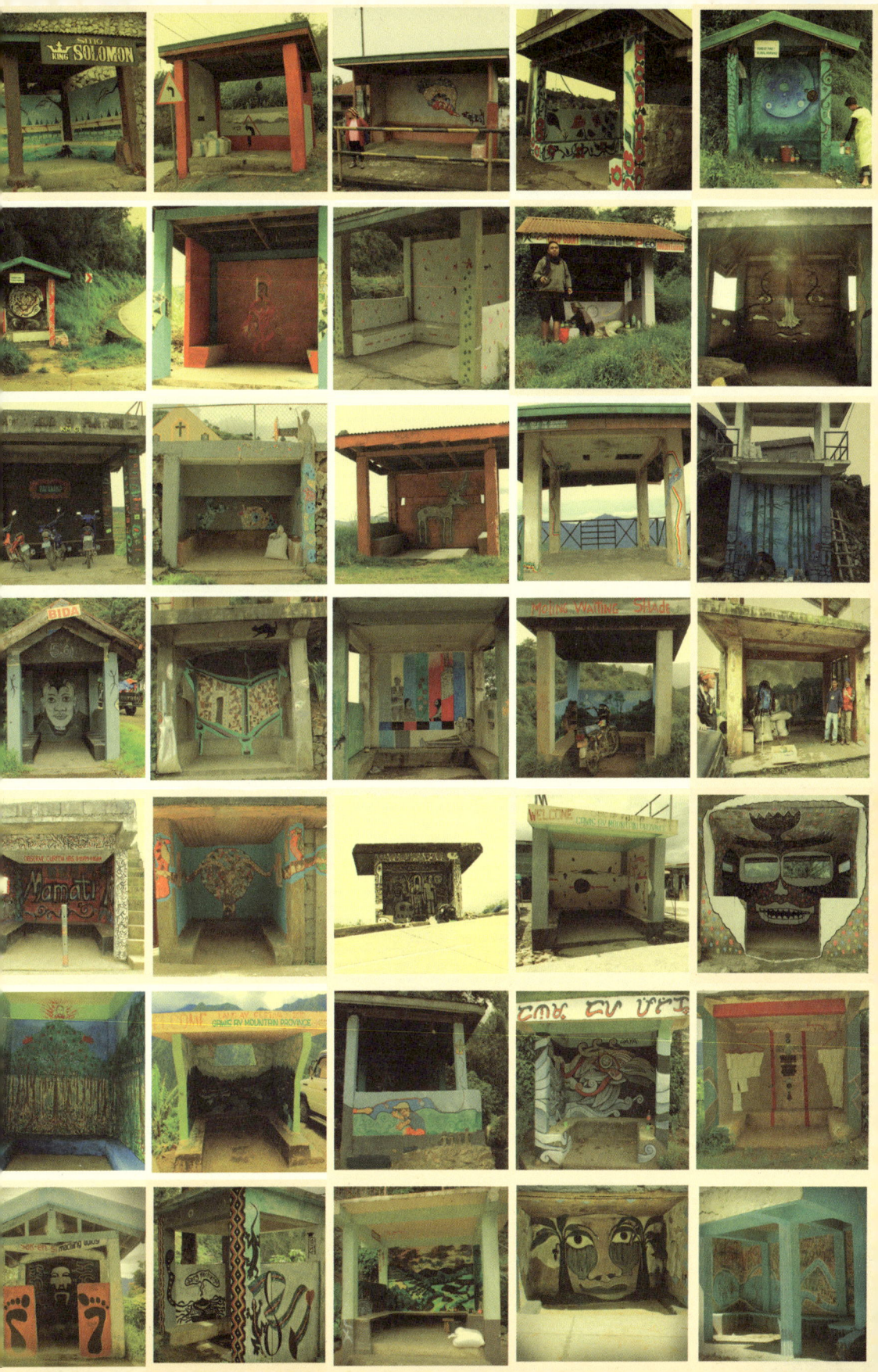

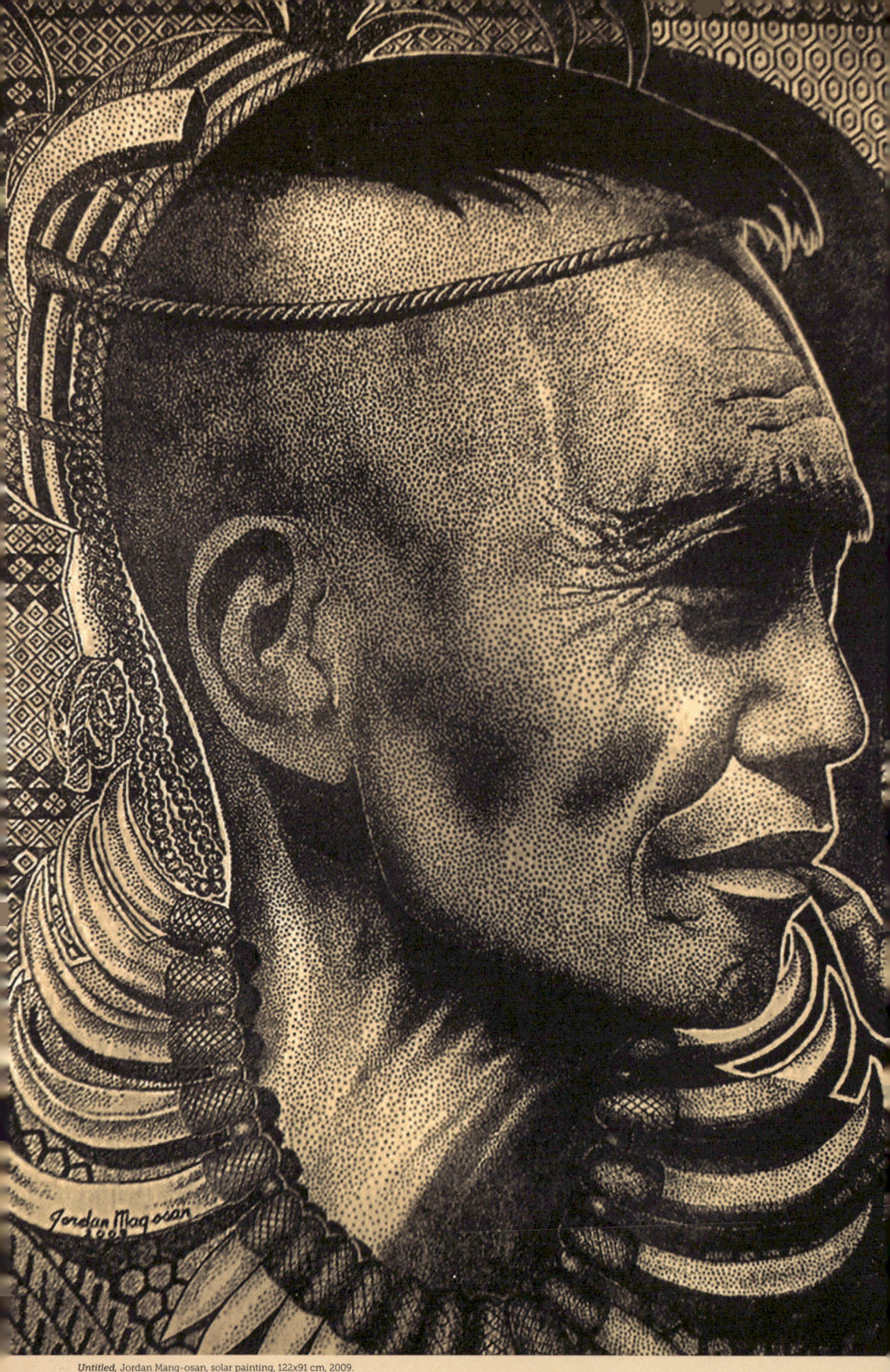

Untitled, Jordan Mang-osan, solar painting, 122x91 cm, 2009.

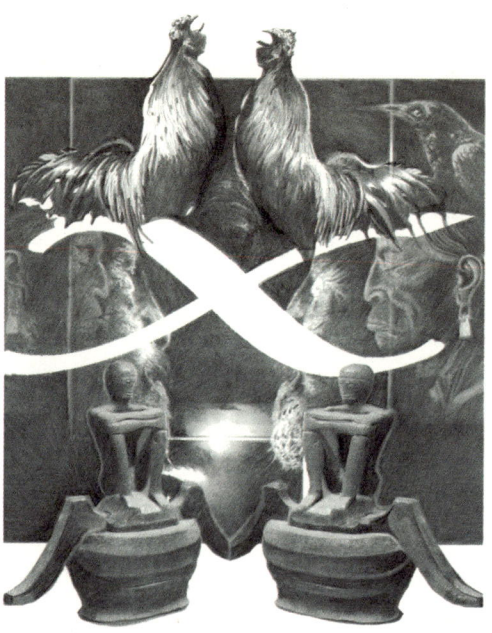

Xaberno *(ISN)*. Government. Indigenized from 'gobierno.'

Xabi *(ISN)*. Night.
See also: Xidam.

Xamata *(ISN)*. Black dye obtained by wetting the crushed thick bark of the kadig tree or the fresh stem of the xamat herb. The dye is used for blackening teeth.
See also: Cloth Dyes; Fallai.

Xandaro, Eduardo. Xandaro was the Comandante Politico Militar de Bontoc when the 1898 Philippine Revolution broke out on the 12th of June. In July, the Filipino revolutionaries invaded La Trinidad, Benguet, and the few Spaniards that were there found refuge in Bontoc. Xandaro made Sagada his last homestand, and when the Filipino revolutionaries arrived on September 3, 1898, the Sagada residents offered them the head of Xandaro for PHP1,000 but Comandante Xandaro had already escaped and the Spanish occupation of the Cordillera had thus ended. FYC.
See also: Galvey, Guillermo.

Xaranait *(ISN)*. Beads which an older Isneg shaman would press on the forehead of her potential successor. Before this, the shaman would pour sweet-scented oil on the young girl's forehead. The shaman would then blow over the xaranait with her cupped hands so that the spirit of healing would be transmitted to the girl who would tremble and shake all over. This is the first consecration of the young girl in the Isneg rite of consecration called ipuwan. The girl would then become the assistant of the shaman in her seances. (Demetrio 1973, 133) FYC.
See also: Apang; Dorarakit; Tsuli.

Xerox, ading, xerox?. Along Bonifacio Road, Baguio City, in the section between two universities, are hawkers for the many photocopy shops that line the sidewalk. They approach you by extending their hands especially if you are holding a book and ask rather imposingly, *"Xerox, ading, Xerox?"* Be ready to shake your head a dozen times. Every stall has a hawker asking the same question. DOS.

Xidam *(ISN)* also **Napat-a** *(KAN)*. Dusk.
See also: Xabi.

X-mark tattoos on faces. On the face of a woman, the ling-ling-ao (X-marks) are meant to confuse the alan-alan especially if the woman is pregnant or when headhunting just took place. Among Bontoc men, the X-mark is tattooed on the nose and both cheeks to indicate that he was a participant in head-taking.
See also: Alan; Tattoo; Tattoo Designs and Descriptions.

Xoho *(ITW)*. Tears.

Xomot *(ITW)* or **Fakiu** *(BON)*. (1)*(ITW)*. Moss. Xomotxomotan means to be covered with moss. (2) *(BON)*. Moss or algae.

Xonut *(ISN)*. Thorn-like bristles protecting the shoots of fan palms.

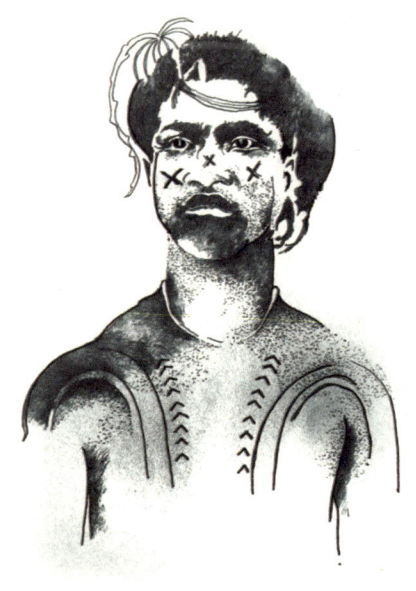

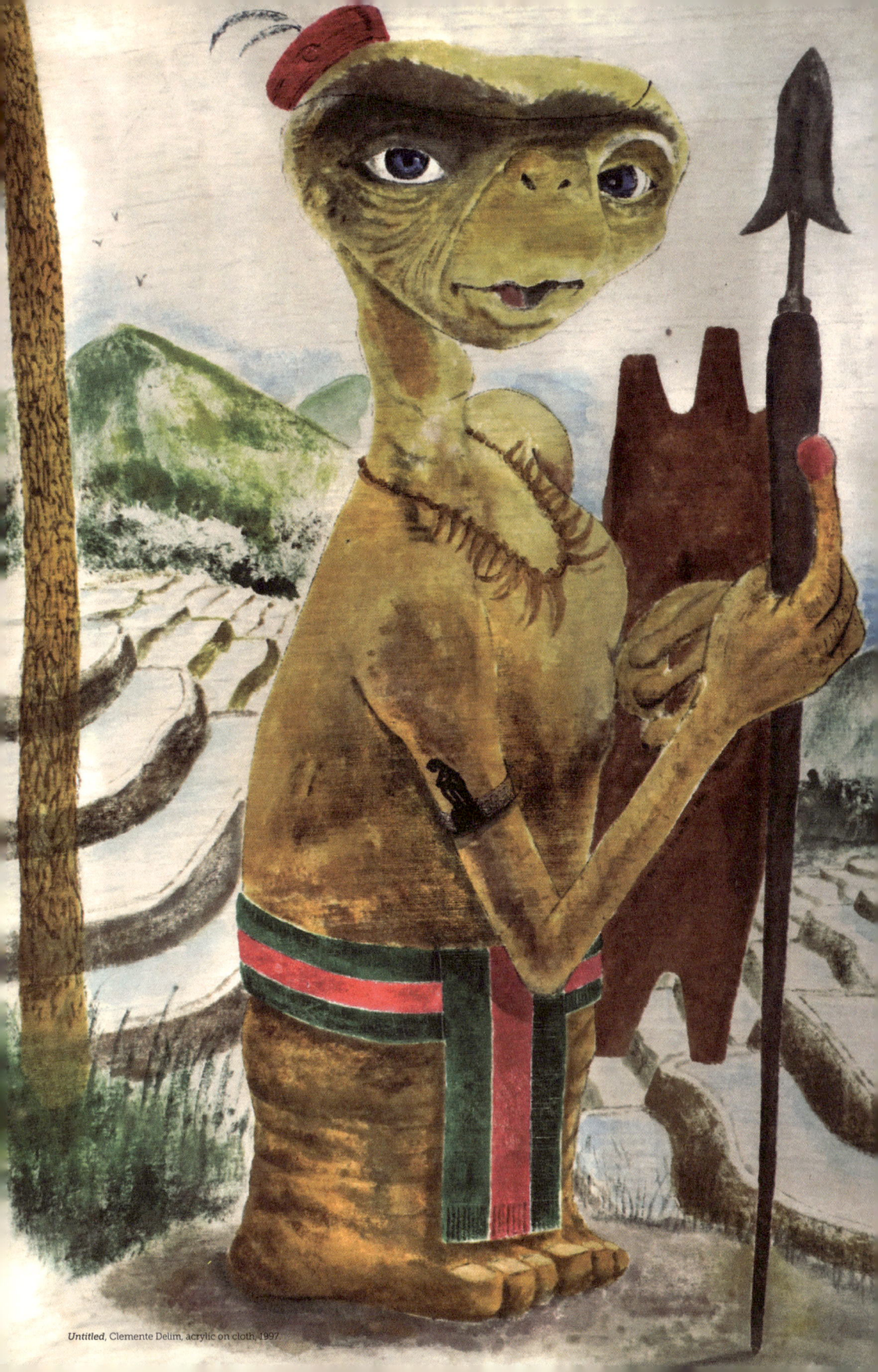

Untitled, Clemente Delim, acrylic on cloth, 1997

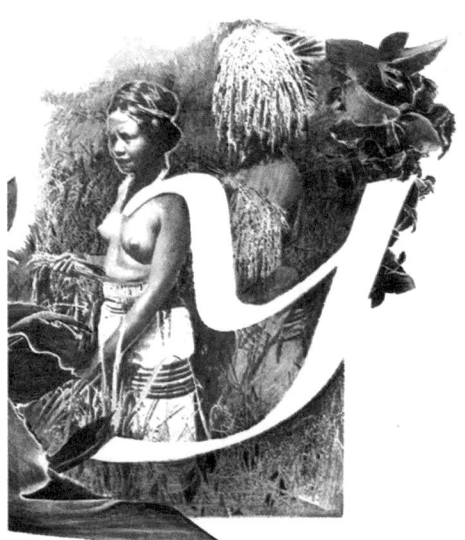

Yadok *(IFU)*. Penile erection.

Yakingking *(IFU)* also **Yaking**. Hopping on one leg.
See also: Haking.

Yamashita Treasure. When Gen. Tomoyuki Yamashita was retreating to his last stand in the Cordillera region at the end of World War II, rumors had it that he buried his war booty of gold and jewelry somewhere along the way. It was said to be so big that President Marcos used it as an alibi to explain how he was able to live in luxury. People insist that the bulk of the treasure has not yet been found, and so the digging continues. If there is the Kankanaey truism that *"Where there's smoke, there's a cañao"* then there is also its treasure-hunting corollary, which is *"If there's digging, there's Yamashita's treasure."* So far, the areas where diggings have taken place include:

1) Bayanihan Hotel, Baguio
2) Yamashita Cottage near Brent
3) Camp John Hay's Bell House and other areas in the base
4) Burnham Park including the lake
5) The digging for the sewer along Session Road
6) Baguio General Hospital
7) The foundations for the flyovers and overpasses in Baguio
8) Baguio Cemetery including the grave of Chainus Guirey and some old Japanese
9) Beckel in La Trinidad and other areas in LT
10) Buguias
11) Ifugao particularly Kiangan
12) Nueva Vizcaya
13) Aurora.
FYC.

Yanay ay! *(KAN)*. An expression that connotes disbelief, shock, boredom, disgust, irritation or annoyance as in *"Yanay ay! Makapaseyep mo? [Yanay ay! This makes me fall asleep?]"* NEP.
See also: Yoy!

Yaw. A distinctly Besao tic word to precede a statement that is a feeling of apology, remorse, disappointment or sadness depending on how you say it or whether it ends with a rising or falling intonation. There's a common joke that goes (with a sing-song intonation), *"Yaw, yaw, yaw ay kanan di iBesao. [Yaw, yaw, yaw, says the person from Besao]."* PAD.

Yayas *(ILO/KAN/BON)* also **Ayas** *(IBA)*. Cicada. The larger breeds (Annual Cicada) usually appear during summer towards the beginning of rainy season, making the Cordillera mountains sing. During this time, people fry them for food. The smaller breeds are found in remote parts of the mountains and can be caught by making a repeated *"tic-toc"* sound using your tongue and the roof of your mouth. The sound attracts the insects. Difficult to find but easy to catch, children consider them a treasured toy. HZK.
See also: Baka baka.

Yes ngarrud!. The ultimate Bag-lish (Baguio English) 'accommodative' expression which denotes agreeing to the other's opinion. It is the opposite of a negating parry like *"Awww, come on... that will never work!"* KT.
See also: Nya ngay, pards?

Yoy! *(ISN)*. A popular expression among the Isnegs that precedes or follows a statement of disbelief, mercy/pity, surprise, awe, anger/irritation, or joy at accomplishing something. The intonation varies to suit the emotion expressed by the statement it follows or precedes. This can also be used to call someone's attention such as in *"Yoy! Here it is!,"* and to precede an affirmation *"Yoy! I told you so!"* GAD.
See also: Yanay ay!

Yumma Gam-o. The old name of Hapao that is still mentioned during old ritual prayers. RBB.

Yumogyog ad Dalom *(IFU)*. Lit. Earthshaker from the underworld. The bringer of yogyog.
See also: Gingined; Jegjeg.

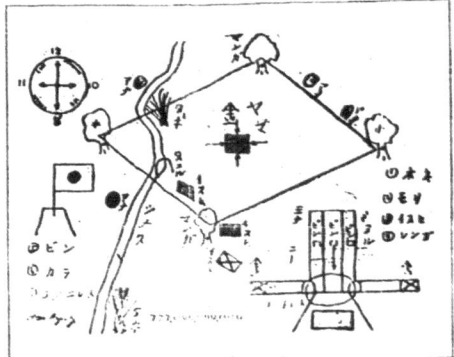

Map of the Yamashita Treasure.

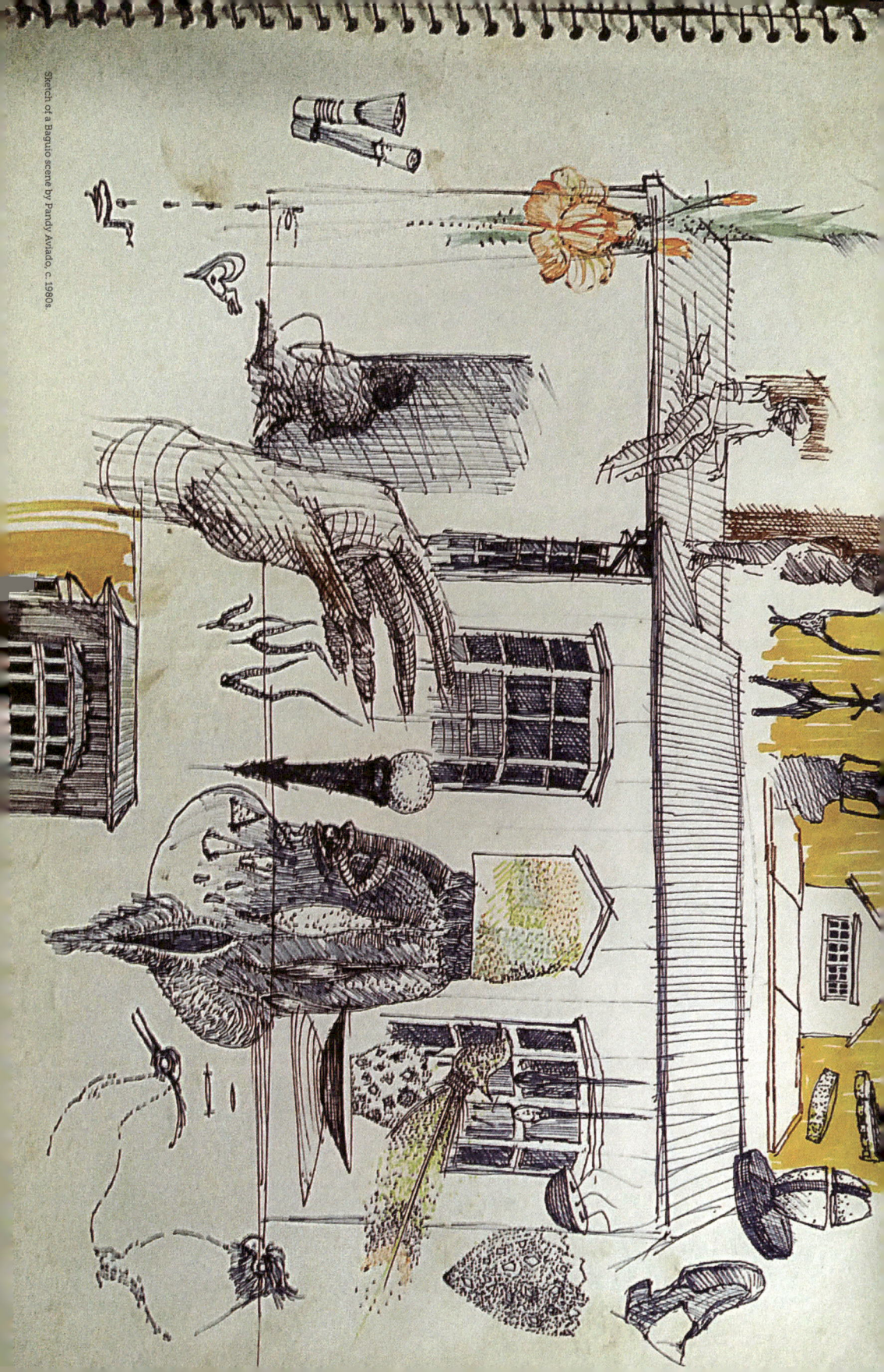

Sketch of a Baguio scene by Pandy Aviado, c. 1980s.

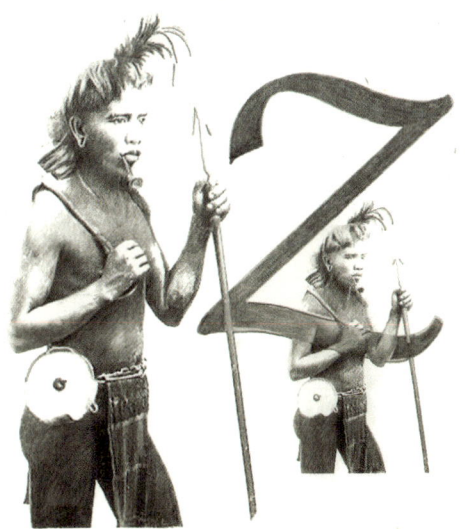

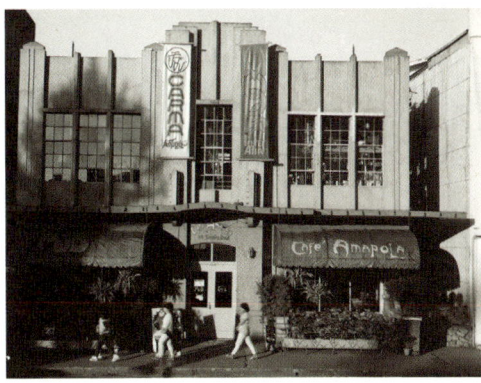

Photograph of the Amapola Building, said to be the same building where the café at Kilometer Zilch was located. Photograph by Ernesto Enrique.

Zacatera *(SPA)*. Grassland.

Zambals. In the 1600s, 'Zambals' was used by Ilocanos to refer to anyone from Pangasinan, whether he/she was a lowlander or a highlander. The Zambals were the first tour guides, escorting travelers headed into uncharted territories, which often happened to be in the Cordillera. They were not exactly friendly though. The Zambals were also famous then for head-taking. FYC.
See also: Headhunting (the tale); I'waks.

Zeroth Law of Thermodynamics (Sagada style). If there is a house or major forest fire, expect the weather to become very cold the night after. Also, it is believed that if your house were to burn down, you must sleep overnight under the stars. If you slept in someone else's house, that house would burn next. FYC.

Zigzag Road. *"Few countries give the observer a deeper feeling of historical vertigo than the Philippines,"* Benedict Anderson (1997) wrote in his review of *Noli me Tangere* for the London Review of Books. This is certainly true, historically and literally, of Zigzag Road (A.K.A. Kennon Road), which has the most dizzying road curves in the country, perhaps second only to the Halsema Highway. FYC.
See also: Halsema Highway; Kennon Road.

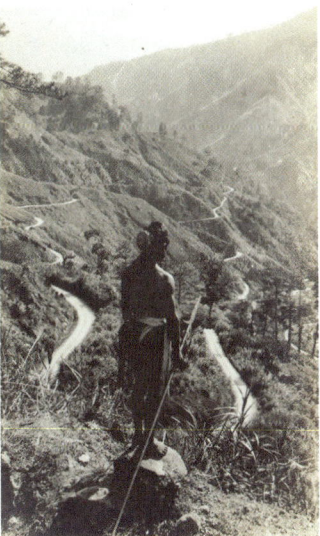

Photograph of Kennon Road. Courtesy AV Cating Family Collection.

Zilch Café. When the poet James Fenton (1986) wrote about the Snap Revolution for Granta, he talked about the *"Café at Kilometer Zilch,"* run by an artist named Johnny. The café is said to be the now defunct Café Amapola and Johnny is Briccio Santos. But that information couldn't be said during the essay's publication. *"Johnny had put his premises at the disposal of the (Cory) Aquino campaign and now that the election is over he was exposed and is in danger. The local KBL men had been making threats. There were scores to settle, as there were all over the country."* The basement of the Amapola Building was the headquarters of the Cory Aquino for President Movement. The volunteers worked hard for free, but the food and drinks were the best. Many artists gave support, some clandestinely. After the 'life in hiding,' the Snap Revolution was realized (Baguio Cathedral was the city's EDSA) and the café at Kilometer Zilch emerged victorious. FYC.
See also: Bontoc Café; Fireplace.

Zubieta, Ramon. Dominican Fray Ramon Zubieta was one of only four missionaries in the Cordillera when the new commandancias were created in 1889. The others were Augustinian Fray Mariano Garcia in La Trinidad, Father Perez in Cervantes, and Father Malumbres in Kiangan. Zubieta was sent to Kalinga and he recommended that Lubuagan become the capital there. FYC.
See also: Bureau of Non-Christian Tribes; Enmity between the Igorots and Christians, The Beginning of; Remontados.

Zucchini. A deep-green summer squash introduced in Benguet in the 1990s. Alternative spelling at the Baguio market and among Baguio's sidewalk vegetable vendors include: sukini, zukini, suckinee, sookini, zookini, sutchini, sokini, zuchini, zukinee, suchini. FYC.
See also: Baguio Bean; Buguias Patatas; Camote; Sayote.

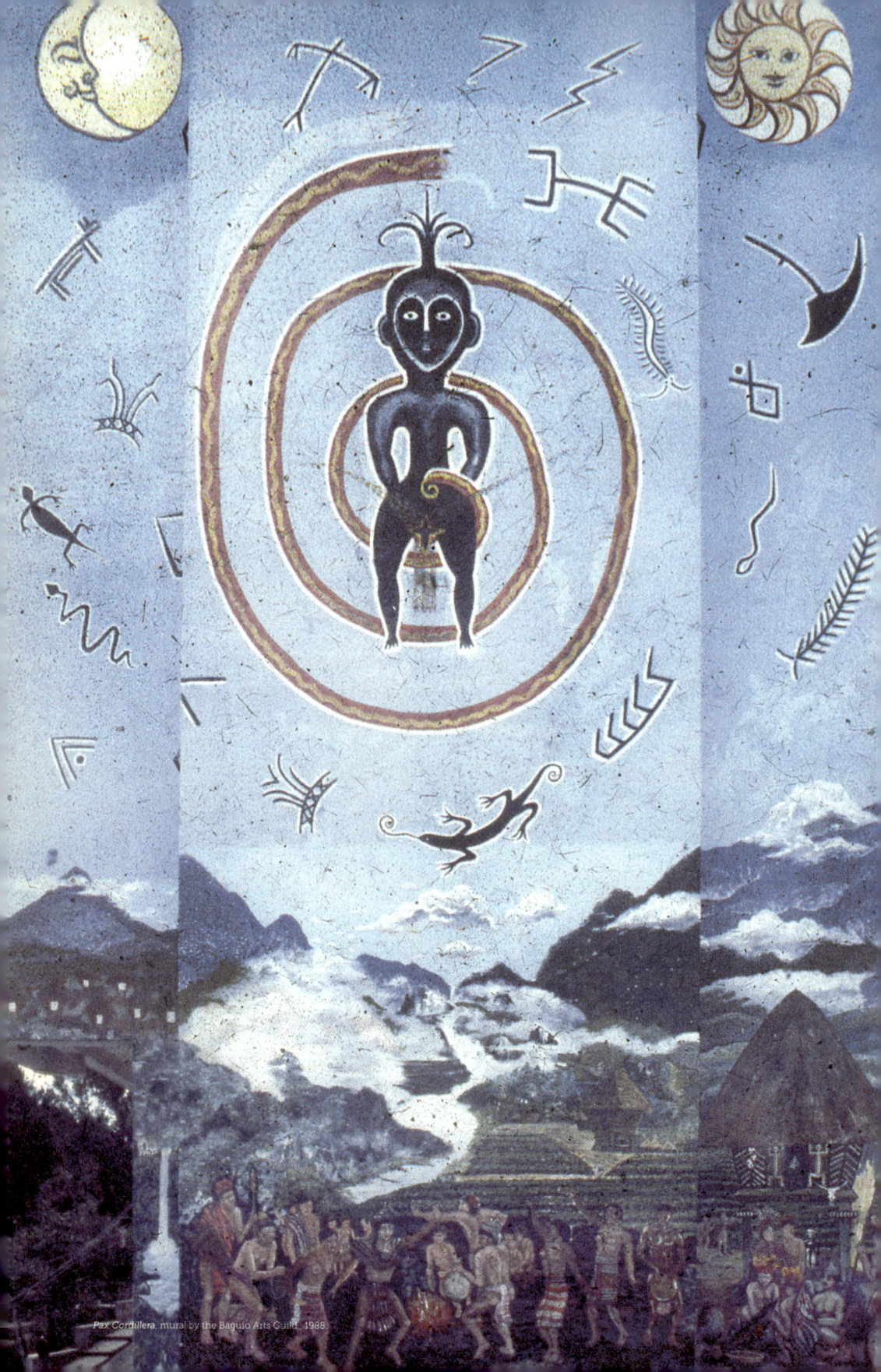

Pax Cordillera, mural by the Baguio Arts Guild, 1988.

Topic Lists and Category Notes

Agriculture

Soil, Earth, Work, Life, Cycles.

Allang	Camote	Faliling	Page
Apoy	Challichog	Gaganayan	Panagbenga
Bading	Chicken Dung	Gengen	Pasok
Balkah	Chinamwi	Gipi	Pes-Ay
Begnas	Darupaypay	Hudhud	Rice Terraces
Buguias Cocktail	Dentan	Kassap	Tinawon
Buguias Soil	Divang	Korta	To-Ned
Buwaw	Elf	Libek	
Cabbage King	Elle't	Ma-Donkey-An	
Calendar	Faked	Num-A	

Ancestors/People

Artists, trailblazers, proud leaders, colonialists, rebels, heroes, crooks, odd characters, givers of life, takers of life. The beloved, but also the reviled.

Afable, Cecile	De Guzman, Jaime	Little Baguio	Silang, Gabriela
Aginaya, Panginomnoman ki	Dog-Eating	Luna, Joaquin	Silipanes
	Dulag, Macli-ing	Mendoza, Benjamin	Sound
Apo Annu	Ethnographic Mapping	Moore, Lina Espina	Tattoo
Apugay	Fischer, Bobby	Narda's	Team Lakay
Baguio Arts Guild, The Future of	Gagaban	Oteyza, Victor	Three Witches
	Galvey, Guillermo	Parsons, Mike	Timicheg
Baguio Arts Guild, The History of	Gong	Pig	Ukay-Ukay
	Guirey, Chainus	Pitapit	Vacacionista
Balweg Brothers	Haight's Place	Play	Waiting Sheds
Bangan	Halsema, Eusebius	Pucay, Eugene	Worcester, Dean
Bose, Santiago	Hamada, Sinai	Pumapa-Ot	Xandaro, Eduardo
Cabbage King	Hay, John Milton	Quan Nga Yen	Zambals
Cariño, Dr. Jose	Hunt, Truman	Quirante, Alonso Martin	Zubieta, Ramon
Carlos Bulosan's Failed Kodak Moment	I'wak	Quirino Bridge	
	Igorot	Reavis, Tex	
Cayat	Indi-Genius	Romulo, Carlos P.	
Cielo, Marky	Joe Rice	Salabao	
Cowboy	Kalanguya	Salt Trade	
Daguio, Amador	Lady Valerie	Samiklay	
Dangwa	Leonard Wood Road	Scotty	
Day-ag, Anselmo	Lepanto Igorots	Shaman Wars	

Animals

From endangered to engendered.

Ab-Abo	Bees of Tinoc	Ikik	Motit
Abeb	Belbelting	Jabbar, The Wonder Dog	Ngaful
Ahu	Bisukol		Niyek
Alipatpat	Buaya	Kaling	Ochichi
Ambiyongan	Co-Op	Kennon Lion	Otek
Antatadul	Cowboy	Ket-An	Papatayan
Ating-Nganganu	Dog-Eating	Koto Ni Shontog	Pink Ponies
Babate	Feclat	Lakko	Silay
Bading	Goat	Lalong	Tilem
Baka-Baka	Golden Kuhol	Lisdeg	Yayas
Bakkat	Ichaw	Mambudang	

Baguio

- "Blue Seal" Yosi Quotas
- AFRTN
- Agrix
- Angelus
- Ato Bookshop and Gallery
- Ayuyang
- Baguio (The Movie)
- Baguio Amusement Committee
- Baguio Arts Guild, The History Of
- Baguio Boy
- Baguio Cathedral
- Baguio Cine
- Baguio Convention Center
- Baguio Distillery
- Baguio Express
- Baguio Ghost Stories
- Baguio Gold
- Baguio Newspapers Before WW II
- Baguio Oil
- Baguio, The Naming Of
- Banaue: Stairway To The Sky
- Benguet Auto Lines
- Bontoc Bar
- Bontoc Café
- Boom Boom Chack Chack Man
- Burnham Lake
- Burnham Park
- Cariño, Dr. Jose
- Casa Vallejo
- Cayat
- Chaparral
- Concrete Pine Tree
- D&S Fine Food Store
- Dog-Eating
- DZWT
- Easter Weaving Room
- Entako Menlabak
- Ethnographic Mapping
- Faithhealing
- Fireplace
- Fischer, Bobby
- Gateway To Wonderland
- Gingined
- Guirey, Chainus
- Half-Way House
- Hamada, Sinai
- Hole In The Wall
- Horse-Watering Trough
- Iddaya
- Jabbar, The Wonder Dog
- Jail
- Japanese Generic Business
- Joe Rice
- John Hay, Camp
- Jueteng
- Kennon Lion
- Kennon Road
- Kung Mangarap Ka't Magising
- La Casita
- Leonard Wood Road
- Loakan Road White Lady
- Man In The Barrel
- Mansion House
- Marcos Mask
- Mosaic
- New Baguio Theater
- O-O
- Otek
- Panagbenga
- Paper
- Penis Ashtray
- Pines Hotel
- Pines Theater
- Pinget
- Pink Ponies
- Plaza Theater
- Polo
- Radio Spittoon
- Rainforest
- Rock Session
- Sagada Lunch
- Saleng Productions
- Santiago Bose
- Shaman Wars
- Sipsipnget
- Slaughter
- Stargazing
- Strike & Spare Bowling Lanes
- Teachers Camp
- Team Lakay
- Thomasites
- Three Witches
- Topside
- Tumba Tumba Liquor Store
- Ukay-Ukay
- Vacacionista
- Vicente Chan
- VOCAS
- Washington Hotel
- White Elephant
- Zilch Café

Body & Self

Shapes, sizes, colors, mannerisms, personalities, body parts, sensations.

- Ab-Abiik
- Agbaxan
- Ala
- Aliwan
- Anglit
- Ayut
- Baak
- Betnek
- Bikutkut
- Busil
- Butu
- Chayag
- Chinuyas
- Denas
- Digdiga
- Divag
- Engnga
- Enoto
- Ensiluak
- Fallai
- Fikek
- Fungais
- Ganga
- Gisgisto
- Gutti
- Haking
- Hangkuku
- Hegyat
- Hukhuk
- Igorot
- Igorot Tail
- Ilablab-Ak
- Inaw
- Jasjas
- Jawbone
- Kadso
- Kaduduwa
- Kangkang
- Kayngot
- Kolkol-Is
- Liget
- Liwliwot
- Mamapteng
- Mang-Gabi
- Michongpit
- Nafutengak
- Natalaw
- Nemnem
- Ngadngad
- Ngalngal
- Ngangak
- Ongakanak
- Oo(h)
- Otek
- Oyok
- Paganu
- Palutput
- Pudung
- Qua
- Radam
- Rosy Cheeks
- Sadshak
- Salabao
- Salopey
- Saxo
- Simtik
- Splayed Feet
- Talungango
- Tattoo
- Tomo
- Vakla
- Watwat
- X-Mark Tattoos On Faces
- Xoho
- Yadok

Cosmology/Otherworld

- Ab-Abiik
- Abig
- Aggabau
- Alan
- Ampasit
- Animbanan
- Anito
- Bagong
- Banan
- Bangan
- Banig
- Bata-Ey
- Binokbok
- Bulayaw
- Bungkaka
- Carangat
- Darupaypay
- Daya
- Dila Anito
- Dinet-Aean
- Engnga
- Flat Earth
- Hidit
- I-Langit
- Ibwa
- Iddaya
- Inhabian
- Ininop
- Iwaxan
- Kabaggaang
- Kabunian
- Kadaklan
- Kain
- Kimat
- Landusan
- Liblibayu
- Loakan Road White Lady
- Longayban
- Mahimunu
- Maingal
- Mambunong
- Manpapayad
- Naanannongan
- Nabat-Ing
- Namati
- Nginin
- Paniaw
- Papattay
- Pasang
- Pattaliat
- Pawa
- Pig
- Pikut
- Pinten
- Pudung
- Salopey
- Three Orphans Of Sagada
- Tinguian Spirits
- Tiw-tiwong
- Yumogyog Ad Dalom

Environment

The world around us.
The world within.

- Alingasiu
- Ambuklao Dam
- Attifungalin
- Ayyew
- Baggat Udan
- Balikawkaw
- Batakagan
- Batang
- Beska
- Buguias Soil
- Bulayaw
- Butigi
- Calendar
- Cellophil
- Chico
- Cloud Atlas
- Concrete Pine Tree
- Dakitan
- Dalagadag
- Duyayu
- Finabdas
- Gaganayan
- Gu-Wab
- Hinag
- Ikik
- Is-Is
- Karayan Libeg
- Kerol
- Landslide
- Lapat
- Lennek
- Libuo
- Manginadu
- Menlemlem
- Ngafus
- O-Od
- Ob-Ob
- Pa'chas
- Pikut
- Poy-Do
- Seddag
- Stargazing
- Tengshal
- Thunder
- Tokwifi
- Tree Cutting

Film

- Abong
- Baguio (The Movie)
- Baguio Cine
- Banaue: Stairway To The Sky
- Big Bird Cage
- Bontoc Eulogy
- Igorota: The Legend Of The Tree Of Life
- Indi-Genius
- Irisan
- Kung Mangarap Ka't Magising
- Mumbaki
- Pure Country
- To Be A Man
- Vacacionista

Folklore

- Abu-Os
- Aginaya, Panginomnoman Ki
- Agudong Id Manitong Ala
- Dayapan
- Doligen Ed Kabunyan, Si
- Emla
- Flood, The Story Of
- Hunger
- Iyu Myth
- Kamma I Kungnga
- Longayban
- Moon Craters
- Og-Okhod
- Pig
- Rock Session
- Sarsarita Ni Uncle Pete
- Stonecutting
- Sudsud
- Ta-In Di Gayang
- Tengngay
- Three Orphans Of Sagada, The
- Tree Cutting
- Tudtud
- Yamashita Treasure
- Zeroth Law Of Thermodynamics

Food & Drink

Abungol
Agkufangfangfang
Allang
Amkis
Asocena
Aw-Aw
Babate
Baguio Bean
Bakkay
Barako
Basi
Bayas
Binaod
Bingit
Boko
Camote
Daneb
Demshang
Dog-Eating
Duggong Ti Intsik
Etab
Etag
Feclat
Food
Gammal
Gayunan
Golden Kuhol
Ibbaw
Ice
Ice Cream
Ikik
Inasin
Inaw
Ingat
Intum
Itikmanokpato!
Iwa
Kidlos
Kineykhey
Km. 26 Guerrilla Saddle
   66th Infantry
   Battalion Rice
Lang-Ay
Mabukag
Mandesangat
Mang-Gabi
Maxabbat
Moma
Niyek
No Wada Asok,
   Wada Watwat
Oo(h)
Page
Papa
Parti
Patpatok
Patupat
Pinakpak
Pinikpikan
Pinit
Pinuneg
Pitik
Puraw
Quiangan Bread
Sadkik
Safeng
Salt Trade
Sayote
Seddag
Sichot
Sinabalu
Sinag-Et
Sinalupsop
Sinaplak
Siniktiman
Strawberries
Ta-In Di Gayang
Tabayong
Tabbi
Tufu
Tupig
Uka
Washing
Watwat
Zucchini

Forms of Speech & Utterances

Abang Ni Keshel
Affrom
Agay-O
Anina
Anuka
Arn
Au-Auni
Awanen
Aye
Baddarong!
Digdiga
Divag
E
Gawis
Ilablab-Ak
Inayan
Iuya
Iya-Iyaman
Kaman Gangi
Katekateg Ad U.S.
Ma-Id
Mendayaw
Namwaw
Ngak and other
   Kankanaey noise
   sounds
Nya Ngay, Pards?
Og-Okhod
Okat!
Pa'chas
Pakkaw
Palpaliwat
Pilpilak-Taltalak
Puto
Qua
R
Sadshak
Sinan-Adom
Sudsud
Swardspeak
Tagalog Palaka?
   Tagalog Kabayo?
Taraki
Wada
Way Ka's Kugkugay Mo
Waynasdi
Xaberno
Yanay Ay!
Yaw
Yes Ngarrud!
Yoy!

History

Ambuklao Dam
Annual Headhunter's
   Fund
Asin, Republic Of
Baguio Amusement
   Committee
Baguio Cathedral
Benguet Auto Lines
Besang Pass,
   The Battle Of
Bontoc Elections
Bureau Of Non-
   Christian Tribes
Burnham Lake
Burnham Park
Cabbage King
Cariño, Dr. Jose
Casa Vallejo
Cayat
Cellophil
Chico
Company 1, 48th
   Infantry
Concrete Pine Tree
Dark-Hued New
   England Town
   Meeting
Dulag, Macli-Ing
Enmity Between
   the Igorots
and Christians,
   The Beginning Of
Episcopalianism
Ethnographic Mapping
Fakwit
Galvey, Guillermo
Gateway To
   Wonderland
Great Ifugao War
Guirey, Chainus
Halsema Highway
Hamada, Sinai
Hay, John Milton
Historical Trauma
   Response
Hunt, Truman
Ice
Ice Cream
Igorot
Igorot Workers Welfare
   Association
Igorotism
Imperialist Nostalgia
Japanese Generic
   Business
John Hay, Camp
Kabasilya
Kennon Road
KKK
Kunsisal

Landslide
Last No-Pant-On-Day
Leonard Wood Road
Luna, Joaquin
Macarthur and
    The Igorot Soldiers
Marcos Bust
Marcos Gerrymandering
Million Dollar Hill
Mountain Province
Nikimalika
Paterno Cave

Peace Zone
Pitapit
Polo
Pre-White
Presidente
Quezon Gamble
Quirante, Alonso Martin
Rancherria De Los
    Igorottes
Salidummay
Salt Trade
Self-Determination

Silang, Gabriela
Squaw Men
Survivance
Teachers Camp
Thomasites
Timicheg
Tonglo
Tribes
Vochong
Volontarios
Washington Hotel
White Elephant

Worcester, Dean
Xandaro, Eduardo
Yamashita Treasure
Zubieta, Ramon

Material Culture:

Clothing and Adornments

Abkil
Akipur
Aneb
Apang
Bakget
Bang-Gor
Barangal
Bayoyo
Bedbed
Bitog

Bungol
Cloth Dyes
Dalanasip
Duwao
Ear Stretcher
Fukas
Gold Earrings
Hopot Hi Hoho
Igorotak T-Shirt
Iniwitan

Kub-Kuba
Kulatod
Lingling-O
Narda's
Ong-Ong
Padang
Panglao
Sagada Weaving
Silag
Suklong

Tangkil
Ukay-Ukay
Wanes
Weaving

Material Culture:

Everyday Objects

"Blue Seal" Yosi Quotas
Aban
Atubang
Ayum
Baliw-A
Banaue Vespa
Bimtak
Bitoto
Bukatot
Bungbung
Bungkaka
Chayag
Concrete Pine Tree
Dayasan
Duvilvil
Elf
Falokag
Fuas

Gongot
Hihim
Hikot
Ice
Idus
Igadan
Igod
Ingat
Jakjak
Jawbone
Kadso
Kimata
Kunyas
Liga
Likon
Man In The Barrel
Okab
Otak

Ovodan
Panamdamman
Paper
Paper Making
Pasiking
Penis Ashtray
Plastic Fantastic
Quartz
Raut
Sagada Ceramic
    Center
Saleng
Salupin
Sambag
Sayay
Sheket
Silap
Spear Blades

Tabayag
Tiklis
Tsuli
Xamata

Material Culture:

Ritual Objects

Agba
Agpay
Anginaman
Apag
Bangibang
Bangkilay

Bangonan
Bulul
Buwaya
Chapilang
Dinakyat
Gagaom

Hagabi
Kabaggaang
Kabayan Mummies
Kalang
Kawkaw
Kub-Kuba

Suwit
Takba
Taliwan
Xaranait

Movement

Where are you going? Where did you come from? Omens for setting out on a journey.

Ejew	Halsema Highway	Liwliwot	Salt Trade
Evin	Igorotism	Ngabis	Topload
Fakwit	Iyu Myth	Ohayami	Yakingking
Fungais	Labeg	Quiangan Line	Papanam

Music

AFRTN	Hib-At	Pow-Wow: Dance of	Sound
Cowboy	Music	the Philippine Igorots	
DZWT			

Music:
Dance

Bontoc Boogie	Country Music	Headhunting Dance	Salip
Challichog	Folk Music	Panagbenga	Tadek

Music:
Instruments

Abistong	Chokang	Gong	Kuliteng
Bungkaka	Dew-Dew-As	Kalsa	Tubbob

Music:
Songs/Chants

Amazing Grace	Baya-O	Humlun	Ullalim
Asbayat	Cherwasay	Mampay	Waynasdi
Badio	Dujung	Nan Layad Nan	
Bah'diw	Gehhehhe	Likhatan	
Batawa	Hudhud	Salidummay	

Places

Ato Bookshop and Gallery	Chaparral	Karayan Libeg	Mt. Santo Tomas
Baguio Cine	Chico	Kayan	Narda's
Balbalasang	D&S Fine Food Store	Kennon Road	New Baguio Theater
Bangbangbang	Dinet-Aean	Km. 53	O-O
Bangued!	Doligen ed Kabunyan, Si	La Casita	O-Od
Batawa	Fireplace	Lepanto Igorots	Papattay
Besang Pass, The Battle of	Gu-Wab	Little Alaska	Paracelis
Bontoc Bar	Haight's Place	Little America	Paterno Cave
Bontoc Café	Half-Way House	Little Baguio	Peace Zone
Bontoc Studio	Halsema Highway	Liwliwa	Pikut
Buaya	Hole in the Wall	Loo	Pines Hotel
Buguias Cocktail	Ifugao	Lumiang Burial Cave	Pines Theater
Buguias Soil	Irisan	Mansion House	Pinget
Burnham Lake	John Hay, Camp	Marcos Bust	Plaza Theater
Burnham Park	Jones, Isabela	Million Dollar Hill	Polo
Busol	Kabayan Mummies	Mountain Province	Quiangan
Casa Vallejo	Kadaklan	Mt. Clitoris	Quirino Bridge
Cervantes	Kalasan	Mt. Data	Rainforest
	Kamaling	Mt. Polis	Sagada Ceramic Center
		Mt. Pulag	

Sagada Lunch
Samoki
Sayangan
Sinipsip
Sipsipnget
Slaughter
Strike & Spare Bowling Lanes
Tablangan
Teachers Camp
Tengngay
Timicheg
Tocucan Bridge
Tonglo
Topside
Tumba Tumba Liquor Store
VOCAS
Yumma Gam-O
Zacatera
Zigzag Road
Zilch Café

Plants

Agakong
Amkis
Baguio Bean
Bangonan
Batang
Bengao
Buguias Patatas
Busad di Kaiw
Butubutu-Ukiuki
Camote
Concrete Pine Tree
Dila Anito
Etab
Fakingol
Fatang
Fire Tree
Fo-o
Folu
Fulifug
Gayunan
Ibbaw
Kalabog-Kalabog
Buguias Patatas
Kalasan
Kassap
Kato
Kayangga
Kub-Kuba
Lituku
Marapait
Martial Law Plant
Masaflora
Npa Plant
Oppak
Page
Persimmon
Pikat
Pinit
Pokingang
Raut
Runo
Sapsap
Sayote
Strawberries
Suma
Ta-In Di Gayang
Tabbi
Talampunay
Talang
Tangay
Tinawon
Tivangdal
Xomot
Xonut
Zucchini

Play

Bongtot
Butubutu-Ukiuki
Fagfagto
Kalabog-Kalabog
Buguias Patatas
Kalu-Os
Play
Pokingang
Saleng Productions
Sarsarita ni Uncle Pete
Strike & Spare Bowling Lanes
Yakingking

Ritual

Ames
Amolo
Apag
Apoy
Ayag
Ayak
Baliw
Bangibang
Bangkilay
Bangon
Banuwat
Baya-O
Bayas
Bayoyo
Bedbed
Begnas
Bet-Bet
Binaod
Bingit
Binokbok
Cañao
Casna
Chanchanag
Dakodak
Dangtey
Daw-Es
Dentan
Dog-Eating
Dorarakit
Dujung
Es-Eset
Etag
Ethnographic Mapping
Fakil
Gobgobbao
Gotad
Hidit
Hogop
Hulin
Ininop
Inorngang
Iyag
Kabayan Mummies
Kakala
Kalajo
Kammid
Kaon Ya Teteg
Kidlos
Kidlos Di Bakas
Kiya
Labun
Lalong
Lapat
Libek
Linayaan
Liwliwa
Liyaw
Madmad
Manerwap
Menoken
Mumbaki
Nantoltolo
Ngilin
O-O
Ob-Ob
Oppas
Owik
Padpadaya
Pahang Di Munhab-i
Papa
Papatayan
Papattay
Pasang
Pasok
Pattaliat
Peshit
Pig
Pinikpikan
Pitik
Pudung
Puting
Sabusab
Samfu
Sangbo
Sapsap
Say-Am
Sidey
Sikki
Sukarno
Takba
Tambo
Tangay
Teknag
Three Orphans Of Sagada, The
Tilem

Tomo
Tukkab

Tuling
Tulud

Ufo
Ukas

Social Life

Who are you? Who am I?
Who am I in relation to you?
Who are you, in relation to who?
Perceptions of Others
How "Others" see "Us"
I see you, you see me
Give and take
How we relate
Where you belong
How to, how we, how do, how you?

Abeggan
Adivay
Adoyon
Ambit, Ambot, Amboy
Anthropology, Questioned
Ayot
Ayyew
Baak
Baddang
Baggha-An
Balballo
Begnas
Bontoc Kiss
Bosesero
Buaya Economic Classes
Buguias Cocktail
Bulbulagaw
Bungot
Busol
Butong
Butu
Cañao
Carlos Bulosan's Failed Kodak Moment
Cayat
Chinuyas
Cowboy
Dagdagas
Dakodak
Daladag
Dang-Ah
Dangas
De Vega, Juan Manuel
Digdiga
Dog-Eating
Edakdakian
Edang
Engnga

Enmity between the Igorots and Christians, The Beginning of
Es-Eset
Fagfagto
Fire Tree
Fireplace
Fogwah
Gannawa
Gawis
Gisgisto
Gobgobbao
Gumassilang
Gutti
Hagabi
Headhunting Requirement
Hegyat
Hidit
Ifugao Marriage and Courtship Taboos
Igorot
Igorotism
Iho
Ikik
Ilablab-Ak
Ili
Immuya-Uy
Imok
Imperialist Nostalgia
Inayan
Indi-Genius
Ishemshem
Iuya
Iya-Iyaman
Jamjam
Jones, Isabela
Kabaggaang
Kabalo
Kalajo
Kamal

Kammid
Kaon Ya Teteg
Kayangga
Kolkol-Is
Kudo
Laktaw
Lang-Ay
Liget
Linayaan
Liwliwa
Lubug
Luktap
Lungos
Ma-Imdong
Madmad
Mahimunu
Mallawallawa
Mamapteng
Mambabaga
Mambunong
Mampay
Mandeki
Mang-Gabi
Manshowa-Showa
Moma
Moma by Myself
Moma for Peace
Mumbaki
Nafutengak
Namati
Namwaw
Nantoltolo
Natalaw
Nga-Nga
Ngantoy?
No Wada Asok, Wada Watwat
Nya Ngay, Pards?
Ob-Obbo
Ongakanak
Oyok
Padpadaya

Paganu
Pakkaw
Palpaliwat
Panamdamman
Pangat
Pansejew
Papanam
Parti
Peace Zone
Peshit
Pig
Pilpilak-Taltalak
Pinikpikan
Pitik
Puraw
Purchos
Puto
Qua
Radio Spittoon
Rancherria de los Igorottes
Remontados
Sadshak
Saga-Ok
Sagawsaw
Saklot Girls
Salabao
Saleng Productions
Salopey
Salt Trade
Sapon
Self-Determination
Shy Mango
Sinan-Adom
Squaw Men
Sukarno
Sumursurot si Ug-Ugali
Survivance
Swan
Tagalog palaka? Tagalog kabayo?
Talungango

Tambo	Tinguian Code	Vakla	Waynasdi
Taraki	Of Conduct	Vochong	Zambals
Tattoo	Tongtongan	Voyeurism	
Tayubtub	Ugali	Way Ka's Kugkugay Mo	

Social Spaces & Physical Structures

Eating, meeting, courting, waiting, sleeping, dreaming.

Abong	Bale	Dangdangan	Papattay
Allang	Baruti	Dap-Ay	Purchos
Ambuklao Dam	Bontoc Bar	Datil	Rainforest
Anido	Bontoc Café	Ebgan	Waiting Sheds
Ato Bookshop And Gallery	Burnham Park	Hihim	
	Chapai	Ili	
Ayuyang	Chaparral	Kamaling	

Time

Au-Auni	Faliling	Tayangtang	Waiting Sheds
Cah'sheman	Fire Tree	Teke	Xabi
Calendar	Gaganayan	Time	Xidam
Dalagadag	Lennek	To-Ned	

Nuanced accounts of Cordillera Culture, with a Touch of Humor

(Advisory: Entries quoting foreign descriptions of Igorots in the olden days are great fun to read aloud with an affected foreign accent and a grain of salt.)

Bontoc Disco	Ear Stretcher	Ngak and Other	Time
Bontoc Kiss	Goat	Kankanaey Noise	Tokwifi
Bosesero	Headhunter's Drink	Sounds	White Elephant
Buaya Economic Classes	Hopot Hi Hoho	Pilpilak-Taltalak	Xerox, Ading, Xerox?
	Humlun	Pokingang	Zeroth Law of
Buguias Cocktail	Igorot Tail	Qua	Thermodynamics
Bulbulagaw	Iho	Quezon Gamble	
Bungot	Jail	Quiangan Line	
Caddies	Katekateg ad U.S.	R. Rolling the Rs	
Carlos Bulosan's Failed Kodak Moment	Last No-Pant-On-Day	Radio Spittoon	
	Loo	Sipsipnget	
Dark-Hued New England Town Meeting	Ma-Donkey-An	Spear Blades	
	Mudguard	Tagalog Palaka?	
	Marcos	Tagalog Kabayo?	
Domoguing	Gerrymandering	Take Side	

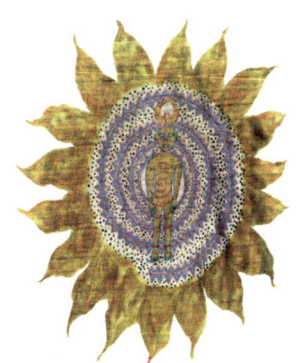

References

"Expedition of Comandante Guillermo Galvey to Baguio in 1829." 1962. *Unitas* 35 (1): 129.

Abad, Gemino. 2003. "Amador T. Daguio: A Turning-point in Filipino Poetry from English." *National Commission for Culture and the Arts*. Accessed August 21, 2013. http://www.ncca.gov.ph/about-culture-and-arts/articles-on-c-n-a/article.php?i=29

Afable, Patricia O. 2004. "Journeys from Bontoc to the Western Fairs, 1904-1915: The 'Nikimalika' and Their Interpreters." *Philippine Studies* 52 (4): 445-473.

---. 2004. *Japanese Pioneers in the Northern Philippine Highlands: A Centennial Tribute, 1903-2003*. Baguio City: Filipino-Japanese Foundation of Northern Luzon, Inc.

Afable, Patricia O. and Cherubim A. Quizon. 2004. "Rethinking Displays of Filipinos at St Louis: Embracing Heartbreak and Irony." *Philippine Studies* 52 (4): 439-444

Allan, Kenneth. 2005. *Explorations in Classical Sociological Theory: Seeing the Social World*. Thousand Oaks, CA: Pine Forge Press.

Anderson, Benedict. 1997. "First Filipino." *London Review of Books* 19 (20): 22-23. Accessed June 9, 2019. http://www.lrb.co.uk/v19/n20/benedict-anderson/first-filipino

Arboleda, Pia. 2007. "Rekindling the Fires of the Ator: Significance and Revival of the Ifiallig Ub-ufok." Abstract *in Inter: A European Cultural Studies Conference in Sweden, 11-13 June 2007*. Accessed June 9, 2019. http://citeseerx.ist.psu.edu/viewdoc/download?rep=rep1&type=pdf&doi=10.1.1.137.7587.

Bagamaspad, Anavic and Zenaida Hamada-Pawid. 1985. *A People's History of Benguet Province*. Baguio City: Baguio Printing and Publishing Co., Inc.

Baggo, Jude. 2013. "Diaries from the Field: Tinoc, a Paradise in Peril." *Nordis*, August 25. Accessed June 9, 2019. http://www.nordis.net/?p=16337

Baguio Police Department. 1959. *Baguio Guide*. 3rd ed. Baguio City: Standard-Vacuum Oil Company and the Baguio City Police Department.

Ballard, Lee, with Chimcas Ameda, Gonzalo Tigo, Vicente Mesa, and Patricia Afable. 2011. *Ibaloy Dictionary, Phonology, Grammar, Morphophonemics*. Compiled by Lee Ballard. Baguio City: Dinteg, Inc and Cordillera Studies Center.

Barton, Roy. (1919) 2012. *Ifugao Law*. Urbana, Illinois: Project Gutenberg. http://www.gutenberg.org/ebooks/40807.

---. 1946. "The Religion of the Ifugaos." *American Anthropologist* 48 (4, Part 2): 1-219.

Beyer, William G. 1981. "Ifugao Art." *Event Catalogue, Manila Oriental Antiques Exhibition and Auction* 1: 50-58.

Bose, Santiago. n.d. "Baguio Grafitti." *In the BAG* 1. Accessed June 9, 2019. http://members.tripod.com/in_the_bag/graffiti.htm

---. 2002. "Baguio Grafitti." In *Vestiges of War*, edited by Angel Shaw and Luis Francia, 260-267. New York: New York University Press.

Bulosan, Carlos. 2006. *America is in the Heart*. Pasig City: Anvil Publishing Inc.

Brody, David. 2010. *Visualizing American Empire: Orientalism and Imperialism in the Philippines*. Chicago: University of Chicago Press

Byrne, Denis. 2007. *Surface Collection: Archeological Travels in Southeast Asia*. Plymouth, U.K.: AltaMira Press.

Cabrera, Benedicto. 1991. *In the Land of the Headhunters: Being an Account of a Summer Holiday in Baguio, 1924*. Manila: Fullmoon.

Carino, Ma. Luisa. 1992. "Cartography; A Collection of Poems on Baguio." *Verge: Journal of the University of the Philippines Baguio* 5, no. 1-2 (December): 67-86.

Castro, Bel S. 2008. "Food, Morality, and Politics: The Spectacle of Dog-eating Igorots at the 1904 St. Louis World Fair." In *Food and Morality – Proceedings of the Oxford Symposium on Food and Cookery 2007*, edited by Susan R. Friedland. Devon: Prospect Books.

Chamber of Mines of the Philippines. 1939. "A Glossary of Philippine Mining Terms." *Philippine Mining Yearbook* 1 (1): 199-205.

Cheng, Charles and Katherine Bersamira. 1997. *The Ethnic Chinese in Baguio and in the Cordillera Philippines*. Baguio City: Cheng and Bersamira.

Coben, Herminia Meñez. *Verbal Arts in Philippine Indigenous Communities: Poetics, Society and History*. Manila: Ateneo de Manila University Press.

Cole, Faye-Cooper. (1915) 2004. *Traditions of the Tinguian: A Study in Philippine Folklore*. Urbana, Illinois: Project Gutenberg. http://www.gutenberg.org/ebooks/12545.

---. (1922) 2004. *The Tinguian*. Urbana, Illinois: Project Gutenberg. http://www.gutenberg.org/ebooks/12849.

Corpuz, Arturo G. 1999. *The Colonial Iron horse: Railroads and the Regional Development of the Philippines, 1875-1935*. Manila: University of the Philippines Press

De Raedt, Jules. 1996. "Buaya Headhunting and its Rituals: Notes from a Headhunting Feast in Northern Luzon." *In Headhunting and the Social Imagination in Southeast Asia*, edited by Janet Hoskins. Stanford: Stanford University Press.

---. De Raedt, Jules. 1993. *Buaya Society*. Baguio: University of the Philippines: Cordillera Studies Center.

De Vega, Juan Manuel. (1903) 2005. "Expeditions to the Province of Tuy." *In The Philippine Islands 1493-1898*, vol. 14, edited by Emma Blair and James Robertson. Urbana, Illinois: Project Gutenberg. http://www.gutenberg.org/ebooks/15445.

Demetrio, Francisco, S.J. 1973. "Philippine Shamanism and Southeast Asian parallels." *Asian Studies* 11 (2): 128-154.

Dulawan, L. S. 1985. *Ifugao Baki: Rituals for Man and Rice Culture*. Nueva Viscaya: Saint Mary's College of Bayombong.

Dyer, Thomas. 1980. *Theodore Roosevelt and the Idea of Race*. Baton Rouge: Louisiana State University Press.

Ellis, George. 1982. "Arts and Peoples of the Northern Philippines."In *The People and Arts of the Philippines*, edited by Fr. Gabriel Casal and Regalado T. Jose, Jr., 183-263. Los Angeles: Museum of Cultural History, University of California Los Angeles.

Fenton, James, and Bill Buford. 1986. "The Snap Revolution." *Granta* 18 (Spring): 33-155.

Finin, Gerald. 2005. *The Making of the Igorot: Contours of Cordillera Consciousness*. Quezon City: Ateneo University Press.

Flaymegh, John, and Scott, William Henry. 1978. "An Ilocano-Igorot Peace Pact of 1820." *Philippine Studies* 26: 285-295.

Florendo, Maria Nelia B. 1999. "Tracing Historical Confluences in Lowland-Cordillera Relations". Paper presented at the 20th Annual Conference on Local and National History of the Philippines National Historical Society, U.P. Baguio, 21-22.

Fong, Jimmy B. 2007. "Batawa: Constructing Identity Through Country Music in the Philippine Cordillera." Paper presented at INTER: A European Cultural Studies Conference in Sweden, 11-13 June 2007. Linkoping: Linkoping University Electronic Press. Accessed June 9, 2019. http://www.ep.liu.se/ecp/025/013/ecp072513.pdf.

Fry, Howard. 1983. *A History of the Mountain Province*. Quezon City: New Day Publishers.

Geertz, Clifford. 1973. *The Interpretation of Cultures: Selected Essays*. New York: Basic Books.

Halsema, James J. 1991. *E.J. Halsema, Colonial Engineer: A Biography*. Quezon City: New Day.

Hoffie, Pat. 2003. "Santiago Bose: Magic, Humor and Cultural Resistance." *Planting Rice.Com*. Accessed September 18, 2013. http://www.plantingrice.com/content/santiago-bose-magic-humor-and-cultural-resistance. Archived at Internet Archive, accessed June 9, 2019. https://web.archive.org/web/20170608043245/http://www.plantingrice.com/content/santiago-bose-magic-humor-and-cultural-resistance.

Ingersoll, Joshena. 1971. *Golden Years in the Philippines*. Palo Alto: Pacific Books.

Iyer, Pico. 1989. *Video Night in Kathmandu: And Other Reports from the Not-So-Far East*. New York: Random House

Jenks, Albert Ernest. (1905) 2005. *The Bontoc Igorot*. Urbana, Illinois: Project Gutenberg. http://www.gutenberg.org/ebooks/3308.

---. 1970. *The Bontoc Igorot*. New York: Johnson Reprint Corporation.

José, F. Sionil. 1968. *The God Stealer and Other Stories*. Quezon City: R.P.Garcia

Keen, W. W. 1926. "Human Tails -- A Statement and a Correction." *Science* 63 (1631): 359-360.

Leith, Andrew. 1938. *The Geology of the Baguio Gold District*. Manila: Bureau of Printing

Lewis, Martin W. 1992. *Wagering the Land: Ritual, Capital, and Environmental Degradation in the Cordillera of Northern Luzon, 1900-1986*. Berkeley and Los Angeles: University of California Press.

Maceda, Jose. 1958. "Chants from Sagada Mountain Province, Philippines." *Ethnomusicology* 2 (2): 45-55.

---. 1975. "A Preliminary List of Vocal Music in the Philippines as Recorded in a Collection of Tapes at the Department of Asian Music, University of the Philippines." In *Dialogue for Development: Papers from the First national Congress of Philippine Folklore and Other Scholars*. Cagayan de Oro: Xavier University Press.

---. 1986. "A Concept of Time in a Music of Southeast Asia." *Ethnomusicology* 30 (1): 11-53.

---. 1998. "Upland Peoples of the Philippines." In *The Garland Handbook of Southeast Asian Music*, edited by Terry E. Miller. New York and London: Garland Publishing.

---. 1998. *Gongs and Bamboo: A Panorama of Philippine Musical Instruments*. Quezon City: University of the Philippines Press.

Magannon, Esteban. 1984. "Cognition of Time, Change and Social Identity: Kalinga History and Historical Consciousness." In *History and Peasant Consciousness in Southeast Asia*, edited by Andrew Turton and Shigeharu Tanabe, 235-265. Osaka: National Museum of Ethnology.

Malanes, Maurice. 2013. "In Cordillera, Resilience vs. Piracy." *Philippine Daily Inquirer*, March 12. Accessed June 9, 2019. http://newsinfo.inquirer.net/372451/in-cordillera-resilience-vs-piracy.

Maso, Miguel S.J. (1910) 2006. *Catalogue of Violent and Destructive Earthquakes in the Philippines 1599 to 1909*. Urbana, Illinois: Project http://www.gutenberg.org/ebooks/18556

Newell, Leonard E., comp. 1993. *Batad Ifugao Dictionary*. Manila: Linguistic Society of the Philippines.

Nike Programme. 2007-2010. *Ifugao-English Dictionary*. Ifugao: Nike Programme.

Ocampo, Ambeth. 2008. "Details that Breathe Life into History." *Inquirer.net*, September 24. Accessed October 13, 2013. http://opinion.inquirer.net/inquireropinion/columns/view/20080924-162481/Details-that-breathe-life-into-history

Palencia, Joaquin G. 1998. "Art as Life: The Ifugao Bul-ul". *Tribal Art* (Spring): 52-63.

Parker, Luther. 1919. *My Philippine Pictures and Other Poems*. Manila: Methodist Publishing House.

Perez, Padmapani L. 2010. "Deep-Rooted Hopes and Green Entanglements: Implementing Indigenous Peoples Rights and Nature-Conservation in the Philippines and Indonesia." Leiden: Faculty of Social and Behavioural Sciences, Leiden University.

Pilapil, Virgilio R. 1994. "Dogtown U.S.A.: An Igorot Legacy in the Midwest." *Heritage* 8(2): 15-18. Accessed June 9, 2019. http://www2.webster.edu/~corbetre/dogtown/fair/igorot.html

Piluden, Dina. 2004. *Death and Beyond*. Quezon City: Giraffe Books.

Prentice, Claire. 2014. *The Lost Tribe of Coney Island: Headhunters, Luna Park, and the Man Who Pulled Off the Spectacle of the Century*. New York: New Harvest.

Reed, Robert. 1989. *City of Pines: The Origins of Baguio as a Colonial Hill Station and Regional Capital*. Baguio: A-Seven Publishing

Reid, Lawrence. 1961. "Dancing and Music: Notes from Guinaang, Bontoc, Mountain Province, Philippines." *Philippine Sociological Review* (1961) 9:55-82. Accessed June 9, 2019. http://www2.hawaii.edu/~reid/Combined%20Files/A02.%201961.%20Dancing%20 and%20Music.pdf

Robertson, James. 1914. "The Igorots of Lepanto." *Philippine Journal of Science* 9 (6): 465-529.

Roll, Christian. 1974. "Rice gods of the Ifugao." *Arts of Asia*, January-February: 20-29.

Rosaldo, Michelle. 1980. *Knowledge and Passion: Ilongot Notions of Self and Social Life*. Cambridge: Cambridge University Press.

Rosaldo, Renato. 1996. *Culture and Truth: The Remaking of Social Analysis*. Boston: Beacon Press.

Roxas-Lim, Aurora. 1973. "Art in Ifugao Society." *Asian Studies* 11: 47-75.

Salvador-Amores, Analyn. 2013. *Tapping Ink, Tattooing Identities: Tradition and Modernity in Contemporary Kalinga Society, North Luzon, Philippines*. Quezon City: University of the Philippines Press.

Salvador, Analyn Ikin V. 2005. "Bark from the Pan: Decoding the Spectacle of Dog-Meat Eating in the 1904 St. Louis Fair and in the Cordillera." Paper presented at the Doreen Gamboa Fernandez Food Symposium 2005: Vanishing Food in the Philippines, Filipinas Heritage Library, Makati City, August 27.

Sangari, Kumkum. 1990. "The Politics of the Possible." In *The Nature and Context of Minority Discourse*, edited by Abdul JanMohamed and David Lloyd. 216-245. New York and Oxford: Oxford University Press.

Santos, Ramon. 2005. *Tunugan: Four Essays on Filipino Music*. Quezon City: University of the Philippines Press.

Schadenberg, Alexander. 1975. "Tribes Living in the Interior." In *German Travelers on the Cordillera (1860-1890)*, edited by William Henry Scott, 140-160. Manila: The Filipiniana Book Guild.

Scheerer, Otto. 1975. "On Baguio's Past." In *German Travelers on the Cordillera (1860-1890)*, edited by William Henry Scott, 173-218. Manila: The Filipiniana Book Guild.

---. 1975. "On Baguio's Past." *In German Travelers on the Cordillera (1860-1890)*, edited by William Henry Scott, 173-218. Manila: The Filipiniana Book Guild.

Scott, William H. 1958. "Some Calendars of Northern Luzon." *American Anthropologist* 60 (3): 563-570.

---. 1962. "Cordillera Architecture of Northern Luzon." *Folklore Studies* 21. 186-220.

---. 1966. *On the Cordillera: A Look at the Peoples and Cultures of the Mountain Province*. Manila: MCS Enterprises

---. 1974. *The Discovery of the Igorots: Spanish Contacts with the Pagans of Northern Luzon*. Quezon City: New Day Publishers.

---. 1982. "The Creation of a Cultural Minority." In *Cracks in the Parchment Curtain and Other Essays in Philippine History*, 28-41. Quezon City: New Day.

---. 1988. "Introduction." In *Notices of the Pagan Igorots in the Interior of the Island of Manila*, by Father Francisco Antolin, translated by William H. Scott. xii-xix. Manila: Corporacion de PP. Dominicos de Filipinas, Inc.

---. 1993. "The Origin of the Word Igorot." In *Of Igorots and Independence*, 41-70. Baguio City: ERA.

---. 2011. *A Sagada Reader*. Republished ed. Quezon City: New Day Publishers.

Simms, S.C. 1903. "Bontoc igorot Games." *American Anthropologist* 10: 563-567. Accessed June 9, 2019. http://archive.org/stream/jstor-659686/659686#page/n1/mode/2up

Subido, Grace Celeste T. Ed. 2009. "Intoduction: A Baguio State of Mind." In *The Baguio We Know*. xiii-xvi. Pasig City: Anvil Publishing.

Sumangil, Pura, ed. 2003. *Practices and Tradition of the Tingguians of Abra*. Bangued, Abra: DWCB Abraeniana Institute and Research Center.

Tapang, Bienvenido Jr. 1985. *Innovation and Social Change: The Ibaloy Cattle Enterprise in*

Benguet. Social Science Monograph Series vol. 5. Baguio: Cordillera Studies Center, University of the Philippines Baguio.

UNESCO World Heritage Center. n.d. "Kabayan Mummy Burial Caves." UNESCO World Heritage Center. Accessed June 9, 2019. http://whc.unesco.org/en/tentativelists/2070/

Vanoverbergh, Morice. 1972. *Isneg-English Vocabulary*. Honolulu: Hawaii University Press.

---. 1982. "Kankanay Games: A Lexicon." *Asian Ethnology* 41: 97-107. Accessed June 9, 2019. http://nirc.nanzan-u.ac.jp/nfile/1162

Vaughan, Christopher. 1996. "Ogling Igorots: The Politics and Commerce of Exhibiting Cultural Otherness, 1898-1913." In *Freakery: Cultural Spectacles of the Extraordinary Body*, edited by Rosemarie Garland Thomson. New York: New York University Press.

Vega, Juan Manuel de. (1903) 2005. "Expeditions to the Province of Tuy." In *The Philippine Islands 1493-1898*, vol. 14, edited by Emma Blair and James Robertson. Urbana, Illinois: Project Gutenberg. http://www.gutenberg.org/ebooks/15445.

Vizenor, Gerard, ed. 2008. *Survivance: Narratives of Native Presence*. Nebraska: University of Nebraska.

Voss, Joachim and Erlyn Ruth Alcantara. 2005. *Ritual/Life: Sagada Photographs 1976-1982*. Baguio: A-7 Publishing.

Wesley-Esquimaux, Cynthia and Magdalena Smolewski. 2004. *Historic Trauma and Aboriginal Healing*. Ottawa: Aboriginal Healing Foundation. Accessed June 9, 2019. http://www.ahf.ca/downloads/historic-trauma.pdf

Weygan, Andrew. 2011. *Ukali*. Baguio City: CVM.

Wilson, Lawrence L. 1953. "Occupational Acculturation in the Mountain Province." *The University of Manila Journal of East Asiatic Studies* 3 (1): 87-96.

Yoneno-Reyes, Michiyo. 2011. "Unsettling 'Salidummay:' A Historico-Ethnography of a Music Category." PhD. Diss., University of the Philippines.

Filmography

Abong: Small Home. 2003. Directed by Koji Imaizumi. Japan and the Philippines: NPO Salubong.

Alapaap. 1984. Directed by Tata Esteban. Philippines: Aces Films International, Oro Vista Motion Pictures, & Rare Breed.

Ang Daigdig Ko'y Ikaw. 1965. Directed by Efren Reyes. Philippines: FPJ Productions.

Azucena. 2000. Directed by Carlos Siguion-Reyna. Philippines: Reyna Films.

Baby Love. 1995. Directed by Peque Gallaga and Lore Reyes. Philippines: Regal Films.

Baguio Fever. 1959. Directed by F.H. Constantino. Philippines: LVN Pictures.

Bakit Dilaw ang Gitna ng Bahag-hari? 1994. Directed by Kidlat Tahimik. Philippines.

Balikbayan#1: Memories of Overdevelopment. 2016. Directed by Kidlat Tahimik. Philippines.

Banaue: Stairway to the Sky. 1975. Directed by Gerardo de Leon. Philippines: N.V. Productions.

Bato sa Buhangin. 1976. Directed by Pablo Santiago. Philippines: FPJ Productions.

Bontoc Eulogy. 1995. Directed by Marlon Fuentes. Philippines: Corporation for Public Broadcasting.

Dear Heart. 1981. Directed by Danny L. Zialcita. Philippines: Sining Silangan Production.

Gojuman-nin no Isan [The Legacy of the 500,000]. 1964. Directed by Toshiro Mifune. Japan: Mifune Productions Co. Ltd., Takarazuka Motion Picture Company Ltd., & Toho Company.

Igorota: The Legend of the Tree of Life. 1968. Directed by Luis Nepomuceno. Philippines: Nepomuceno productions.

Irisan. 1952. Directed by Manuel Silos. Philippines: RDR Productions.

Istokwa. 1996. Directed by Chito S. Roño. Philippines: MAQ Productions.

Kakabakaba Ka Ba? 1980. Directed by Mike De Leon. Philippines: LVN Pictures.

Kung Mangarap Ka't Magising. 1977. Directed by Mike De Leon. Philippines: LVN Pictures.

Magandang Gabi sa Inyong Lahat. 1976. Directed by Lupita Aquino-Kashiwahara. Philippines: Premiere Productions.

Mga Lihim ng Kalapati. 1987. Directed by Celso A. Castillo. Philippines: FLT Films International.

Mga Yapak na Walang Bakas. 1961. Directed by Cirio H. Santiago. Philippines: Cirio H. Santiago Film Organization.

Mumbaki. 1996. Directed by Butch Perez, produced by E.M. Cautico. Philippines: Neo Films.

Nagkaisang Landas. 1939. Directed by Carmen Concha. Philippines: Parlatone

Nakaw na Pag-ibig. 1980. Directed by Lino Brocka, produced by Juan Antonio Marcos. Philippines: Associated Entertainment Corporation.

Perfumed Nightmare [Mababangong Bangungot]. 1977. Directed by Kidlat Tahimik. Philippines.

Pure Country. 1992. Directed by Christopher Cain. USA: Warner Bros.

Sa Init ng Apoy. 1980. Directed by Romy Suzara. Philippines: Trigon Cinema Arts.

The Big Bird Cage. 1972. Directed by Jack Hill, produced by Roger Corman, Cirio H. Santiago and Jane Schaffer. USA: New World Pictures, Roda Film Productions.

The Passionate Strangers. 1966. Directed by Eddie Romero. Philippines: MJP.

Till I Met You. 2006. Directed by Mark A. Reyes. Philippines: GMA Films and VIVA Films.

To Be A Man. 1963. Release title: Cry of Battle. Directed by Irving Lerner. USA: Allied Artists.

Vacacionista. 1956. Directed by Mar S. Torres. Philippines: Sampaguita Pictures.

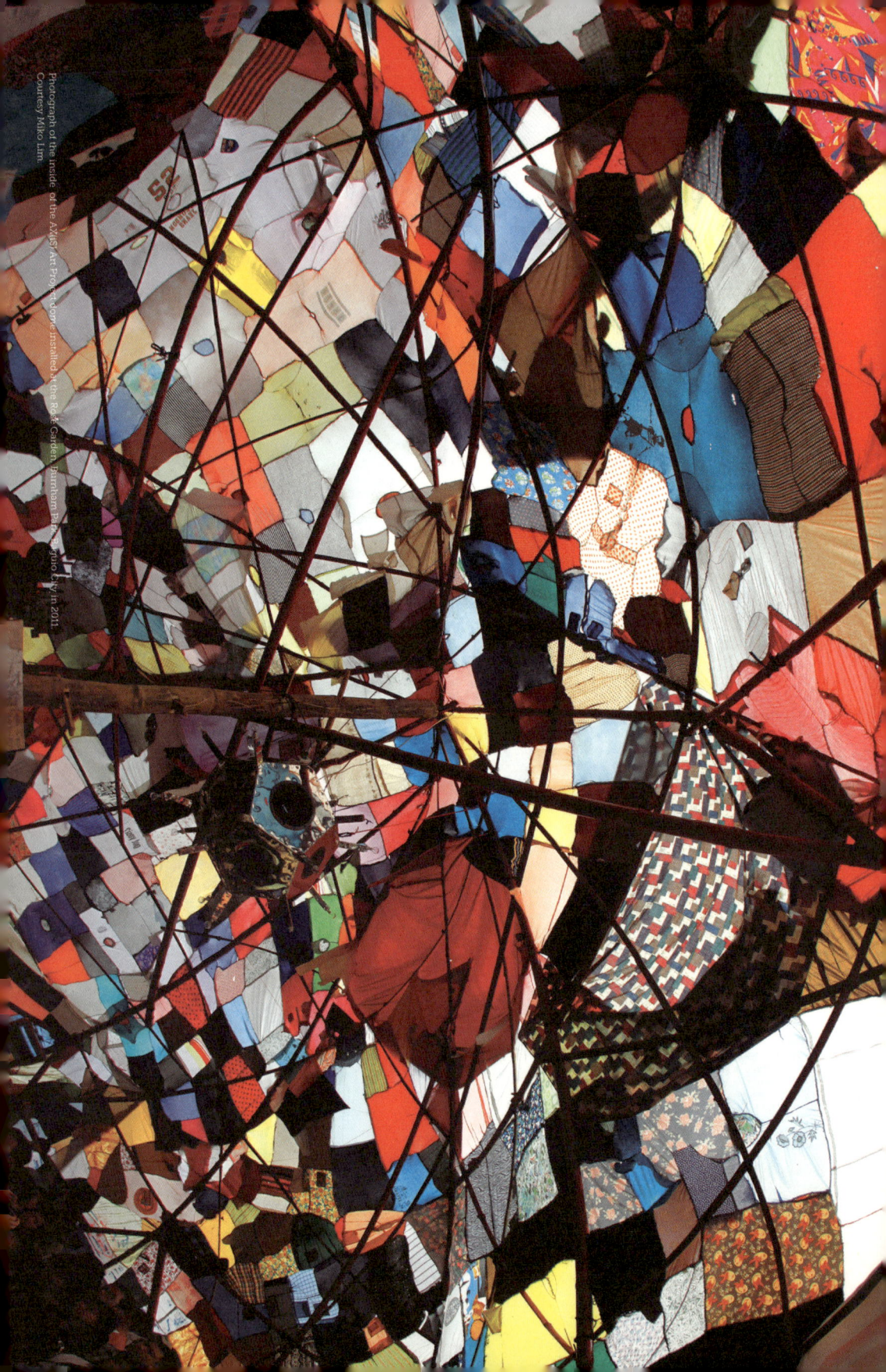

Photograph of the inside of the AMAST Art Project dome installed at the Rock Garden, Burnham Park, Baguio City in 2011. Courtesy Miko Lim

Afterword

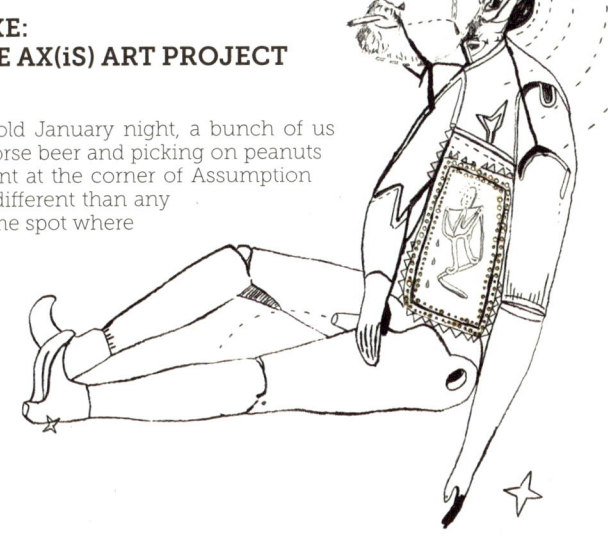

REFLECTING ON THE AXE:
A BRIEF HISTORY OF THE AX(iS) ART PROJECT

What were we thinking? One cold January night, a bunch of us found ourselves drinking Red Horse beer and picking on peanuts in Mandarin, a Chinese restaurant at the corner of Assumption and Session Road. This was no different than any other day. Mandarin was the prime spot where artists, writers, drunken lawyers, Baguio old-timers and college students found themselves after a long day. No one really ate unless they were nursing a hangover – the hot chicken noodle soup was always on stand-by for that purpose. Mandarin is gone now, a true loss for the city, closing its doors on the 1st of January, 2015.

You would often start there, sitting alone, and as the hours and bottles ticked away, the tables and chairs would slowly interconnect into a giant mass as more and more people came in and joined. Ideas, politics and gossip were exchanged, eaten up and chewed over by a strongly opinionated assortment of Baguio characters. If you weren't familiar with them, you might wonder, *"How do these guys get along?"* They were all very different from each other, from different backgrounds and walks of life, everyone from 16 year-olds to 65 year-olds in a constant discourse – arguing, laughing and sometimes crying.

All our ideas were cooked there (at least mine were) in the chop suey atmosphere on the second floor of this aging Chinese restaurant.

On one of those late nights in 2011 AX(iS) was born and this was our mandate: We believe access to art should go beyond those already active in the art community. We intended to produce an art festival that would inspire community involvement and that was total and non-exclusive in its presentation. The use of public spaces and the opening of artists' studios to the general public would be ways of fostering that kind of involvement. The artists would come from different backgrounds from different parts of the country, and would collaborate using all of their different forms of art. The heart of the festival would lie in a tent made from used clothing and found textiles. The tent would be erected in Burnham Park, serving as the main venue for the festival activities.

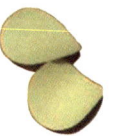

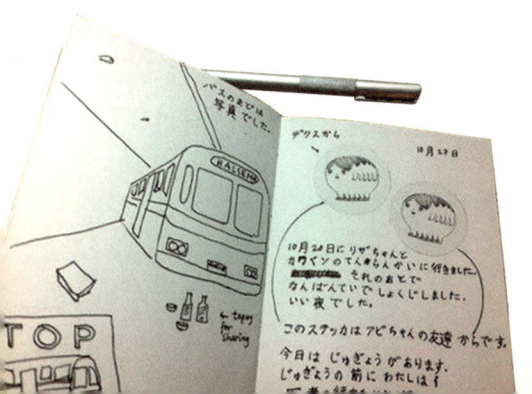

Artwork by Kidlat Tahimik

The AX(iS) tent was a two-week long sewing project. Those sewing sessions traveled around many universities, art spaces, and public parks in Baguio and encouraged citizens and students to participate in creating it. I asked volunteers to bring personal textiles to be incorporated. While sewing, people talked and shared stories, all threaded in the act of creation. An informal discourse emerged into various subjects: art, the environment, and political issues.

Yes! An art project can be an axe! A tool that can cut barriers and break down walls – the barriers that divide, separate, and segregate society. This creative tool called Art would be the weapon of choice to show what lay behind the cliché perceptions of a manicured world. This was a desperate attempt to connect the different perspectives of various creative art practices. Whether it was a blind weaver from Viscaya, the work of woodcarvers from across the city, or the underground electronic music of Lirio Salvador and Elemento, a wide variety of creative individuals and groups participated during the 13-day DIY art festival.

The festival's title was *An Accident Waiting to Happen*. It took off with *Ipitik*, another festival. Celebrating the richness of the highland Cordilleran culture, the sound of 108 gongs cried out over Baguio's traffic. It carried an overpowering energy of young G-string-fueled power! Over the next two weeks, the celebration was reinforced by informal workshops ranging from hand-tap tattooing to rattan weaving. Teddy Co's Cinema Rehiyon took place, which for seven days showed films on Baguio, one film designated for each of the last seven decades. Artist talks and concerts were constantly happening. The music ranged from WSK's infused noise and sound art to more traditional beats and instruments. The culmination of different energies came together just like the coalescing chairs in Mandarin restaurant.

The colorful hand-sewn tent was the hub of the festival. But the energy would spill out over the whole city. The festival T-shirt featured a print of a map of Baguio City and said in bold letters read "YOU ARE AX(iS) ART PROJECT." With over 300 artists participating in an attempt to juxtapose the ancient with the contemporary, the whole city became a playground where site-specific installations sprung. Vacant lots, greenhouses, dirty alleys, and abandoned buildings were venues to exhibit and perform. One such place was Transient Studio, the deserted old wooden library at Scout Hill in Camp John Hay, which housed the artist Chris Yniguez and Ubbog, a small group of young Cordilleran writers and artists that wrote and published in their mother tongues.

After a week, the festival grounds looked like a tent city and, in spite of third world sound system conditions, the concerts, readings and dancing continued each night until the wee hours of the morning. The spontaneous energy of our community had been tapped and it knew no limits. Every day, it would intensify a little bit more. The foot traffic of the festival grounds averaged 5,000 people a day. It was overwhelming and we were outnumbered and understaffed. Everyone involved became a multitasking volunteer who performed a juggling act of activities to keep the festival afloat.

As the 13th and final day of our powwow came to a close, a sense of relief could be seen on everyone's faces. We had finally reached the finish line on a marathon of art and organization. As soon as it ended, the first summer rains started to pour down onto the hot festival grounds – a much needed cleansing for the exhausted force called AX(iS). Soon after we found ourselves in our beds reflecting on the colorful storm that had engulfed us.

The project had naïvely been conceived to be a biennale. AX(iS) 2011 was a demonstration that we could deliver and host a one of a kind art festival, one that was based on the legacy of the notorious Baguio Arts Festivals held by the Baguio Arts Guild in the

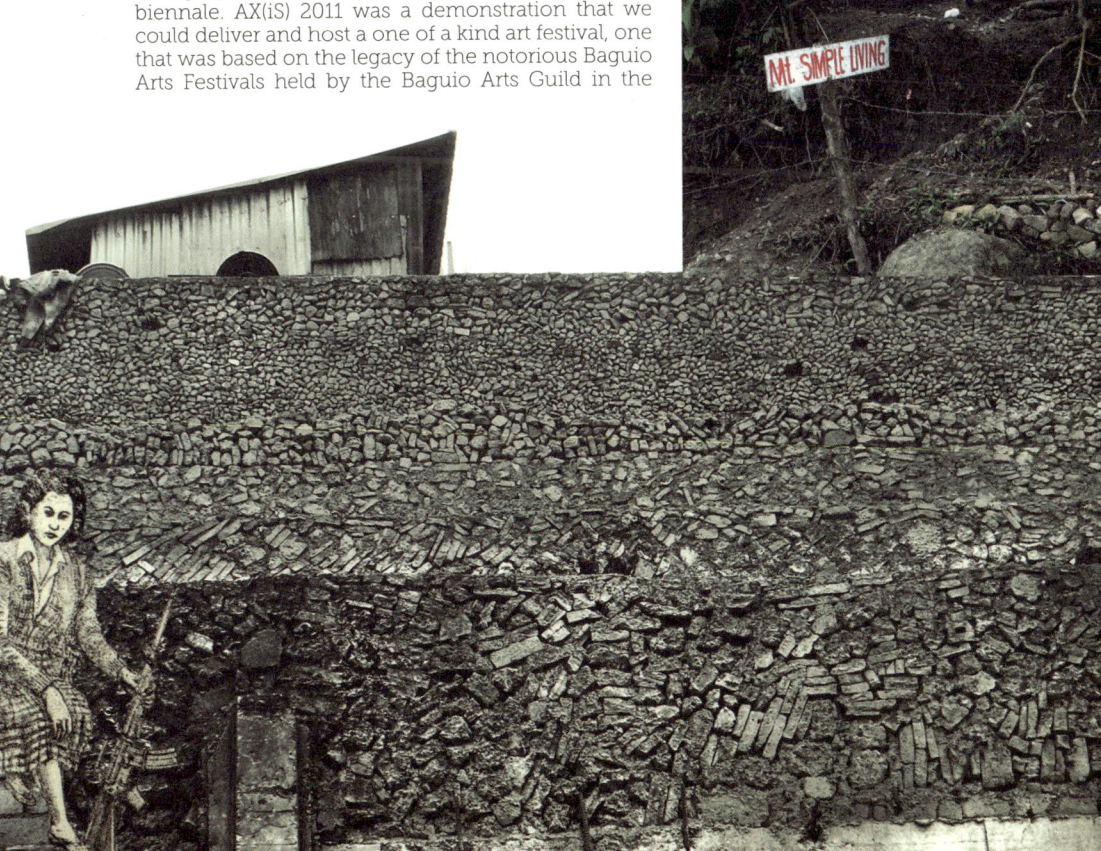

early 1990s. Then, they had the brave and playful initiative to deliver such a platform, which happened to be the first of its kind in Asia. We would hold on to that torch.

With the AX(iS) festival, a beam of white light passed through a crystal prism and projected all the colors of the rainbow, a glimpse of the possibilities for us and the city; and although succeeding AX(iS) initiatives did not, in the end, take that form again, that festival still stands as a starting point and inspiration.

THE OLDEST PINE TREE VS. THE SUPER MALL

Later that year the oldest pine tree in Baguio was dying. An Australian biologist had wanted to measure its exact age, drilled holes into its core, and in the process killed it. Bravo! The tree had been a special place that we would visit occasionally to continue our after-hours conversations. Simultaneously, SM, the consumer, plastic giant had bigger plans to expand its shopping territory and planned to cut down 182 trees.

Everyone once again found themselves at Mandarin to discuss plans on how to deal with the de-greening of Baguio City. The plan was to transform the 500-year old pine tree that had died, into a memorial totem pole.

Out of the woods, five Ifugao carvers brought forth the image of Iddaya, an Ifugao goddess that represents maternal generosity. Every night, alongside the carving, Baguio's artists once more found themselves together – playing music, showing films and occasionally even handing out hot soup. Kidlat Tahimik's *Banal Kahoy* or *Holy Wood* was shown. AX(iS) regathered.

During one of those days, along with other cultural and environmental groups, we spontaneously held a lightning rally in front of the expanding SM super-mall in the hopes of saving the 182 full-grown pine trees in the center of town. When we managed to block the main road to the mall, their security intensified and we were suddenly facing a barricade of guns and shields. Never has a giant corporation seen so much resistance from the people of this city. The protests continued for many

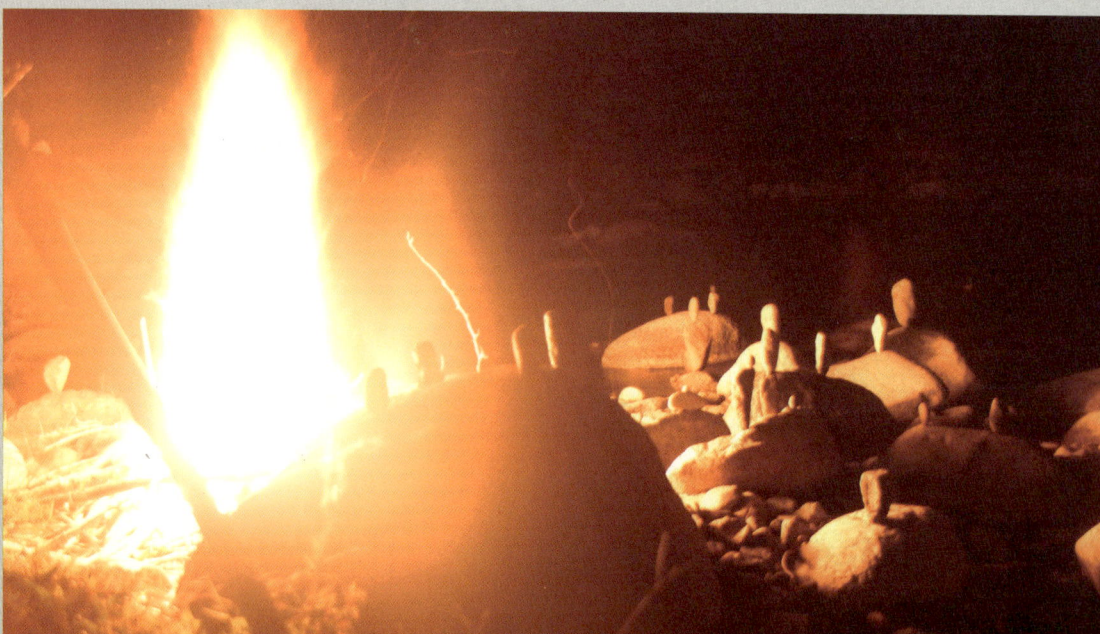

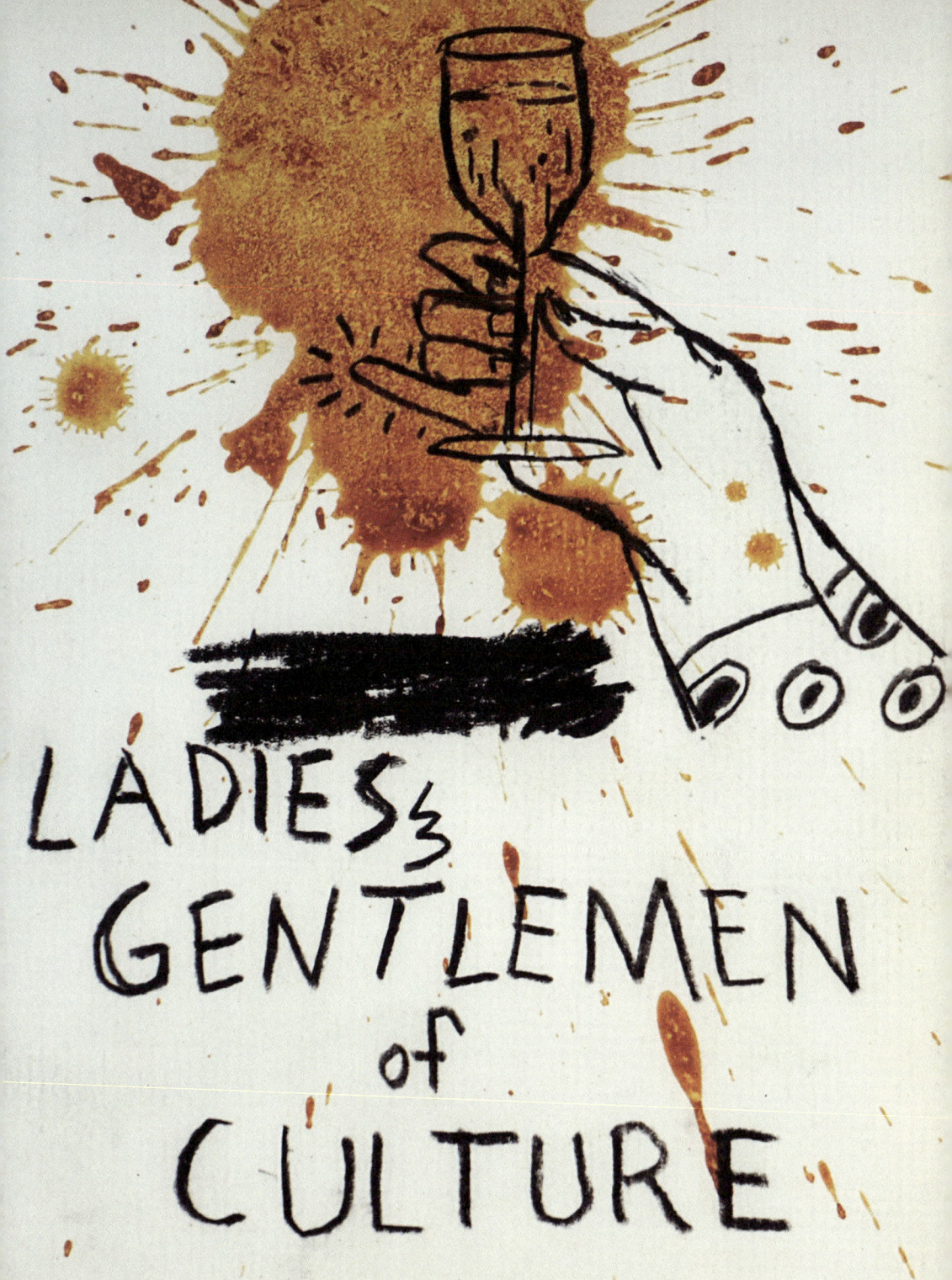

months but, in the end, big money won and their plans pushed through. The trees were cut on the night Pope Francis came to town. What an irony!

The transformation of the former oldest tree into a public artwork was also an attempt to show the city that art and culture were integral parts of the city's landscape and played an important role in society.

THE BUS IS BORN

Then, the following year, we developed a proposal in which we decided to step away from the city and try to engage with the smaller communities located on the length of the Halsema Highway. A week-long art caravan was suggested.

We chose a bus as a central image for the project. Our caravan would be a repurposed Dangwa bus. Since our activities were going to be held along the mountainous highway, what better image to portray the spirit of perseverance than one of those iconic, rickety, old vehicles from the company which was the first operator to plow the Halsema route?

After various sources of funding fell through, we were in a tight spot. We had no money, no gas ,and no bus. But we had a plan, and just in case the world was really going to end on 12-12-2012 according to our 'pop osmosis' of the Mayan calendar, it wasn't such a bad idea to end it up in the mountains. Our slogan became *AX(iS): To the End of the World.*

In the end we were saved by a fifty print run of a four-plate silkscreen image of our bus. It was circulated out to close friends and family members who were sometimes forced to buy the artwork. It was an impetus to support our art caravan. It was a hard sell but those were the times and it made our project possible.

We recycled the recycled cloth that had formed the dome of our tent in the 2011 festival, this time transforming it into the shape of a bus.

Two weeks before our journey kicked off, Rocky Cajigan and I drove up and down the highway countless times talking to barangay officials, village elders, and local authorities to prepare them and secure locations. By the time of the scheduled departure, we were ready and we even had a real bus. Thanks must be given to Ernest Dangwa for making that possible.

The bus-tent and the planned weeklong caravan were launched at MO_Space in Manila. The exhibition opened with rice wine and gongs played by a motley crew of Baguio artists. Installations of scattered objects in the gallery simulated what to expect during the weeklong trip. The details of our eventual journey can be found in Joyce Toh's essay in this book titled "Halsema Hijinks."

In turn, *AX(iS): To the End of the World* became the template for the work we presented at the Singapore Biennale in 2013, and the artists and iconic subjects that were part of that show became the backbone of this book.

The title of this book is *Tiw-Tiwong* – a spirit that has gone astray but returns again, sometimes after years of distant travel and delay. And as in our title we, AX(iS) Baguio Artists, have finally arrived to share our stories. With this book, we have made it. We have come back home. Our story can be shared to future generations and live on.

When a story is told, a myth is born. KDG.

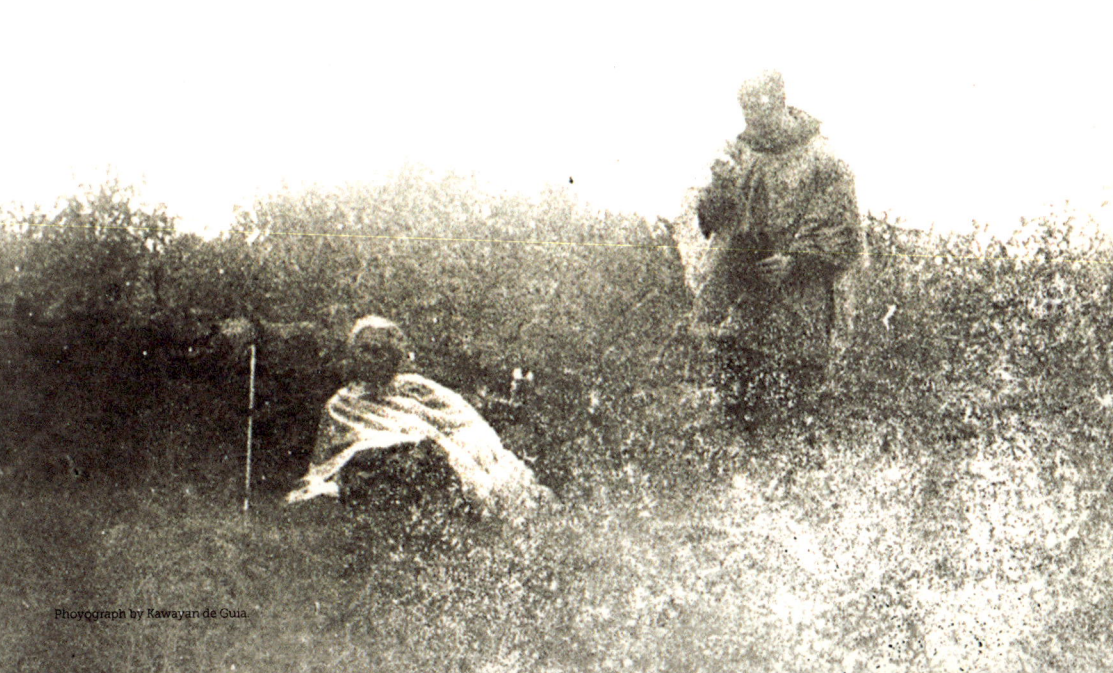

Phoyograph by Kawayan de Guia

Appendices

Appendix A:

TEXT / CAPTION FOR THE AX(iS) EXHIBITION AT THE SINGAPORE BIENNALE 2013

AX(iS) Art Project
Established 2011, Baguio City, The Philippines

Tiw-tiwong: The Odds to Unends, 2013

Mixed media installation (13 art activities & artworks) and *Uncyclopedia* (book)
Dimensions variable
Collection of the Artists
Singapore Biennale 2013 commission

In a journey of unpredictable means to uncertain ends, finding 'the' way was never going to be straightforward. This was especially so for the AX(iS) Art Project – a 'vehicle' carrying travellers of disparate ilk and like – as it navigated its way through mountain terrain and twists of time. The name of this project, *Tiw-tiwong*, comes an Ifugao term that broadly translates as "getting lost" but it also carries nuances of a passage into other worlds, of wondering and wanderings, and of a return to complete unfinished business after being long astray.

Arriving at its eventual destination, *Tiw-tiwong: The Odds to Unends* can be considered a multi-pronged collaborative art project that summons the potency of history, as well as indigenous knowledge and practices, to open up the story of Baguio and the Cordilleras during a time of flux. Fuelled by the concept of "Art Access for All" — the belief that art is not exclusive and, therefore, posited outside the confines of institutional norms — the project involves over 150 participants and is driven through 13 art activities, several of which were in collaboration with local communities along the 90 mile-long Halsema highway in the Cordilleras mountains.

Commissioned by the Singapore Biennale 2013, *Tiw-tiwong* straddles a parallel existence across two locales, occurring as projects in-situ within Baguio and the Cordilleras, and also as an exhibition of artworks and documentation at the Singapore Art Museum. They include Leonardo Aguinaldo's investigation of the history of the salt trade; the late Santiago Bose's painting assessing the colonial damage wrought upon native land use and practices; Ruel Bimuyag's documentation of Maria Fang-Ud, an 80-plus indigenous tattoo practitioner, and Carlo Villafuerte's tapestry that weaves a personal narrative from the story of Wag-wag (surplus clothing) trade in the Philippines. Here, BenCab's drawing capturing the many faces of the different ethno-linguistic groups also sits alongside 86 *binulols*, self-portraits by traditional woodcarvers more accustomed to deploying their craft, not for 'art', but rather to produce objects for ritual or tourist consumption. Meanwhile, Rene Aquitania's handmade toys and games transmit old ways-of-knowing from parent-to-child through the act of play, while media artists Tad Ermitaño and Malek Lopez, together with Rica Concepcion, communed with ones dearly departed in the Last Gong Maker.

The Mighty Bhutens worked with several artists and schools to rehabilitate 32 waiting sheds along the Halsema, even as another site was being transformed in the back alley of Baguio – the Katipunan dog eatery found new existence as a 'restro' museum dedicated to the culture of canine cuisine. Mark Zero investigated the perplexing popularity of country and western music in the mountains by re-imagining record covers of the Abatan Records press, and Shant Verdun composed a 24-hour soundscape to voyage through the infinite loop of night and day. Bringing a cycle to an almost-end, filmmaker and artist Kidlat Tahimik also premiered "Memories of Overdevelopment", a film 33-years in the ever-making about the 'first' circumnavigation of the world.

The project culminates in the "Uncyclopedia", an A-Z survival guide that tackles key topics addressed by the artworks, as well as several others. Categorized alphabetically like an encyclopaedia, the publication consciously critiques the surfeit of half-truths, falsehoods and misinformation that came about under the guise of national education.

With artists, writers and cultural activists as the chroniclers of change, the project is an urgent and collective remembering of histories and inscribing of indigenous ways of living and communal knowing, and a call to action to protect the resources that are still with us today. Through the act of sharing, it also seeks to activate the transference of fragile knowledges to a generation that is yet-to-come. As such, it is a tribute to ancestors who have passed on, a lament for things lost, but it is also a celebration and a carnival – a gathering of spirits, where the past, present and future come to party, parlay and play.

JTH / AX(iS)

AX(iS) Art Project
Tiw-tiwong: The Odds to Unends, 2013
Mixed media installation (13 art activities & artworks) and Uncyclopedia (book)
Dimensions variable
Collection of the Artists
Singapore Biennale 2013 commission

ARTWORKS & CAPTIONS

Leonardo Aguinaldo
Dissolving Boundaries, 2013
Acrylic on rubbercut and wood
390 x 180 x 180 cm (approx.)
Collection of Singapore Art Museum (Formerly Collection of the Artist)

Salt has traditionally been a precious commodity for the inland communities of the Cordilleras as procuring it required arduous journeys overland prior to the opening of the Halsema Mountain Trail. Yet the salt trade was also more than an exchange of commerce and commodity: it engendered interactions amongst people of disparate backgrounds and locales. A famous tree named Candong once served as the meeting point where lowland and highland traders met, but was cut down by the Spanish during their colonial rule. In the place of the felled tree, they built a church and named the town Candon. The towering sculpture by Aguinaldo pays tribute to the lost tree and the images cut into the rubber vinyl retrace the route of the salt trade as well as depict the myriad uses of salt in the Cordilleras. Many of the stories depicted here were collected by the artist through conversations with community elders, in an effort to remember, revive and transfer these rich tales that root Cordilleran heritage.

Rene Aquitania
Ay-Ayam (To Play), 2013
Drawings and mixed media objects
Various dimensions
Collection of the Artist

Games, toys and playing are integral in enabling each child to learn and navigate the terrain of growing up. For performance artist Rene Aquitania, a father himself, traditional games and toys are also indispensible in rooting the individual in his or her heritage and cultural past. In the Cordilleras, toys were often fashioned from the simplest, most available materials: leaves, wood, bottle caps, tin cans, and crafting these childhood playthings was also a process of passing ways of knowing from parent-to-child. Today, these hand-made toys are becoming increasingly 'rare' as they are bypassed in favour for their commercially produced counterparts and tech games.

Ruel Bimuyag
Dinuras: Fathoming Fang-Od, 2013
Sound, photo-documentation
Dimensions and duration variable
Collection of the Artist

Hailing from the indigenous people of Butbut in Kalinga, Maria Fang-od is one of the last traditional tattooists in the Cordilleras. Over 90 years old, she continues the tradition of batok (tattooing) and inks the body by hand-tapping the patterns into the skin, producing the rhythmic beat from which the term 'tattoo' originates. Ruel Bimuyag has documented Maria Fang-Od for the last decade, and observed a spike in the clientele of this once-dying art. Once the preserve of warriors and protectors of the community, the painful body marking is now actively sought by young urbanites and foreign travellers, who perhaps quest to belong to a tradition much older than what modern life offers.

Santiago Bose
Bury My Soul in the Chico River, 1981
Mixed media: cement, wood, metal
124 x 122 cm
Collection of National Gallery Singapore (Formerly Collection of Imelda A. Bose)

Rivers and waterways are precious resources amongst rural communities and the Chico River has long been regarded as a lifeline of the Cordilleras, especially by the Kalinga people who live on its banks. During the Marcos regime, a series of hydro-electric dams was proposed, whose construction would have drowned many traditional villages, and with it, the burial of entire indigenous cultures and displacement of thousands. Against military threats, protests by local people delayed and eventually prevented the construction. Producing this work at a time when the protests were on-going, Santiago Bose – whose practice revolved around issues of self-determination, indigenous rights and anti-colonial struggle – depicts a people who fought to protect their natural heritage and ancestral domain.

Ben Cabrera
I, Baguio, 2013
Acrylic and pencil on handmade paper
152 x 305 cm
Collection of the Artist

A portrait of a complex and ever-changing city, this drawing is an ethnographic portrayal of the people involved in the growth of Baguio City. Built during the American colonial period, Baguio is just over 100 years old and this gateway to the Cordilleras has become a melting pot of cross-faded bloodlines from the indigenous people of the highlands and the lowlands, as well as of Japanese and Chinese migrants who came to trade. National Artist Ben Cabrera, who is Pampangueno by blood, retraces the origins of the people of Baguio, where everybody is by assessment, an adopted son or daughter of the city. I-Baguio literally means, "I am from Baguio".

Tad Ermitaño, Malek Lopez, Egay & Rica Navarro, Roberto Villanueva & Shalla Montero
Gangsa (The Last Gong Maker), 2013
Archival video footage and OSC programming, sound, bulol, gong
Dimensions and duration variable
Collection of Singapore Art Museum (Formerly Collection of the Artists)

The gangsa (gong) is the ultimate instrument of convergence in the Cordilleras, and this work brings together artists from across the divide of time and the mortal plane. Working with a master gong maker, Ernesto Carino, the late artist Roberto Villanueva started the project 'The Last Gong Maker' some 20 years ago. Villanueva's art, which centred on community and communal collaborations, indigenous cultural traditions, as well as ephemeral and ritualistic practices, were integral in defining Baguio art in the 1980s. This work begins with found film footage of Carino, which was shot by Rica Conception and the late Egay Navarro. Using Open Sound Control programming, Tad Ermitaño and Malek Lopez – two pioneers of new media art – have introduced an interactive component into the raw footage, spawning a sonic and visual representation that reveals the late master gong maker at work.

Katipunan Aso-ciation
Katipunan: A-Resto-Art, 2013
Site-specific installation in Katipunan eatery (Baguio); mixed media objects (Singapore)
Dimensions variable
Collection of the Artists

In modern urban life, the dog is oft-regarded as faithful pet; within other contexts and cultures, it has signified a host of other meanings. In the Cordilleras, the dog is the highest form of animal sacrifice and its meat has long been a part of the northern diet, sustenance in harsh and barren mountains. The Katipunan dog eatery, located behind the Baguio market, has been a hub for miners, vegetable dealers and land workers for years, and more recently, as a space for artists and writers. For SB2013, part of the eatery was converted into a 'museum', to retrace and examine the history, myths and sensitivities surrounding the subject of dog-meat consumption. The term Katipunan – which comes from the root word tipon or pagtitipon, means 'to gather' – was the name used by the revolutionaries fighting the Spanish and Americans during colonial rule.

The Mighty Bhutens and Halsema Hijinks artists
The Halsema Mosaic, 2013
Site-specific installation in 36 waiting sheds (Halsema Highway, Cordilleras); mosaic and photo-documentation (Singapore)
Dimensions variable
Collection of the Artists

The exhibition 'Tiw-tiwong' takes off from last year's 'AX(iS): To the End of the World', a journey by artists on board the rickety, if iconic, Dangwa bus along the Halsema Highway. For many locals, such buses are the only means of transport along the mountain road. Because of unreliable schedules and accidents occurring, waiting in such sheds was an exercise of 'never-knowing' that could stretch from hours into days. Moreover, the proliferation of hastily built sheds in some areas also point to the misuse of funds by officials, and thus, these ubiquitous cement boxes have come to signify a peculiar vortex of time and money. In this project spearheaded by The Mighty Bhutens, who worked with several other participating artists, 36 desolate waiting sheds have been converted into colourful spaces.

Kidlat Tahimik
Memories of Overdevelopment Redux: A Castaway's 33-year Celluloid Journal, 1980–2013 version
Film and mixed media (stone, wood, found objects)
Dimensions variable
Collection of the Artist

Memories of Overdevelopment reveals Kidlat Tahimik's penchant for the 'might-have-been' stories involving Enrique de Malacca's circumnavigation of the world with Portuguese navigator, Ferdinand

Magellan. Playing upon the inter changeability between master and slave, and the notion that destiny and destination are not necessarily pre-determined, Tahimik – who often films sans script – leaves to accident, synchronicity and chance, how individual events may unfold and eventually turn out. In an instance of life and art echoing each other, the narrative of Memories has also become confusingly and intimately intertwined with the twists-and-turns of Tahimik's life. Thus the installation in the gallery comprises of found and adapted objects, as well as old and obsolete film media – much like the artist's own abode. Growing to become Tahimik's life-long obsession to complete the work-in-ever-progress, Memories comes almost full-circle in 2013, some 33 years after it began.

Shanto Verdun
Sangharaw (One Day), 2013
Sound, duration: 24 hours
Collection of the Artist

A confluence of found and created sounds, ambient music, Sangharaw is a 24-hour soundscape to voyage through the infinite loop of night and day. An aural echo of the Dap-ay (the stone circle), the work courses through the individual points of the day, even as it locates the listener in the rhythms of life in north Philippines, allowing the chance encounter of rituals and traditional performances. Like the rippling of micro-cosmos within the macro-cosmos, silence, sound and music circle to create a temporal journey in which the single moment resonates and reverbs in the second, minute, day, month, year and millennium.

Carlo Villafuerte
Wag-wag Wonderland, 2013
Fabric and vinyl mat
199 x 355cm
Collection of Singapore Art Museum (Formerly Collection of the Artist)

Baguio is known for its abundance in wag-wag stores (surplus or second-hand clothing, sometimes also known as ukay-ukay). Carlo Villafuerte, having been raised by a mother who worked in a textile export processing zone and with no formal training in art, possesses an intimate understanding of fabrics and textiles. Villafuerte has created an intricate hand-sewn tapestry from wag-wag that stitches a personal narrative together with the story of Baguio. Scenes of the night market are interwoven alongside the artist's imaging of the self: as a single father, as an artist in the present moment and in older years to come.

Woodcarvers from Ifugao and the Cordilleras
Binulol: Carved Selves, 2013
Wood, 86 figures
Various dimensions
Collection of the Artists

The iconic bulol is the most used figurative image of pre-colonial Philippines. Often misconstrued as a rice god, it is actually a carved portrait of a person for ritualistic purposes. Probing what the bulol is today, the project garners 86 figures by wood-carvers from more than 40 villages in Ifugao and other parts of the Cordilleras. While the self-portrait is an established genre in fine art, it is rarely the subject for traditional artisans who are more accustomed to deploying their craft to produce objects for religious, ritualistic purposes or tourist consumption. Continuing the old tradition, the 60 wood-carvers created the figures as portraits, but they have also departed from the past, for here they have carved and chipped away to capture likeness and expression of the self. The figures – self-portraits – are known as binulol created in the likeness of a bulol but not used for ritual purposes.

Mark Zero
Re+Covered, 2013
Collage on 29 vinyl disc covers
19 x 19 cm (each)
Collection of the Artist

Abatan – a small town in the middle of the mountains whose name literally means 'crossroads' – has been the point of contact for miners, vegetable dealers, traders and villagers. After American colonialists established Baguio as their summer headquarters, came the gradual popularisation of cowboy culture in the Cordilleras. In the 1970s, Abatan Records press was set up, where musicians recorded countryand-western songs in native tongue, and produced 45 rpm and 35rpm records until the late-1980s. As these records were played in jukeboxes, they had no record covers. Here, archivist, DJ and music enthusiast Mark Zero imagines and creates fictitious covers for these records, honouring unsung heroes forgotten by time.

Appendix B:

MARKETS OF RESISTANCE 2014

Markets of Resistance was a collaboration between AX(iS) Art Project and the Institute for Heritage, Culture and the Arts at the Philippines Women's University (PWU), under the direction of Angel Velasco Shaw. The activities connected with the project took place over the best part of a year in 2014-15. They included the immersion of a group of PWU Fine Arts and Design and Communication Arts students among Baguio contemporary artists, scholars, writers and poets, and communities. They were taught formally and informally; visited Baguio, Bontoc and Sagada; and were embraced in the social milieu and discourse of Baguio and Cordilleran art and culture. The culmination of the process of collaboration took the form of art events and exhibitions across the site of the Baguio Public Market. They included artist talks, spoken-word readings, walking tours, and film screenings, with the activities interspersed and integrated with the stalls and shops around them. Artworks were bartered for and presented to the public.

The project engaged with Baguio's history as a "Little America" and colonial hill station and the ongoing echoes of that legacy, and the foundation of Baguio on stolen indigenous land. It explored issues connected to differing models of commerce and the ways different forms of social relations are expressed through them and looked at the potential for deeply rooted cultural spaces, such as public markets, to act as a nexus for oppositional currents to hegemonic forces in the era of globalization.

Kawayan de Guia's work *Liberating a Fall*, an ironic 10-meter-tall mimicry of the Statue of Liberty, was erected on an empty rooftop looking out from the market hilltop towards the SM supermall at the top of Session Road. Next to the sellers of strawberry jam, gin bottles of honey, and wooden tchotchke's, at a stall named Oblika, local writers and artists bartered zines, photographs and paintings for vegetables and craft goods. Elsewhere, on a street known for its second-hand shoe stores, contemporary visual artists set up a temporary gallery under the name Nikimalika.

As with previous AX(iS) projects the heart of the activity was one of joyous outreach, cross-disciplinary collaboration, and an urgent insistence for art to break out of the rarefied spaces which it is at times sequestered to.

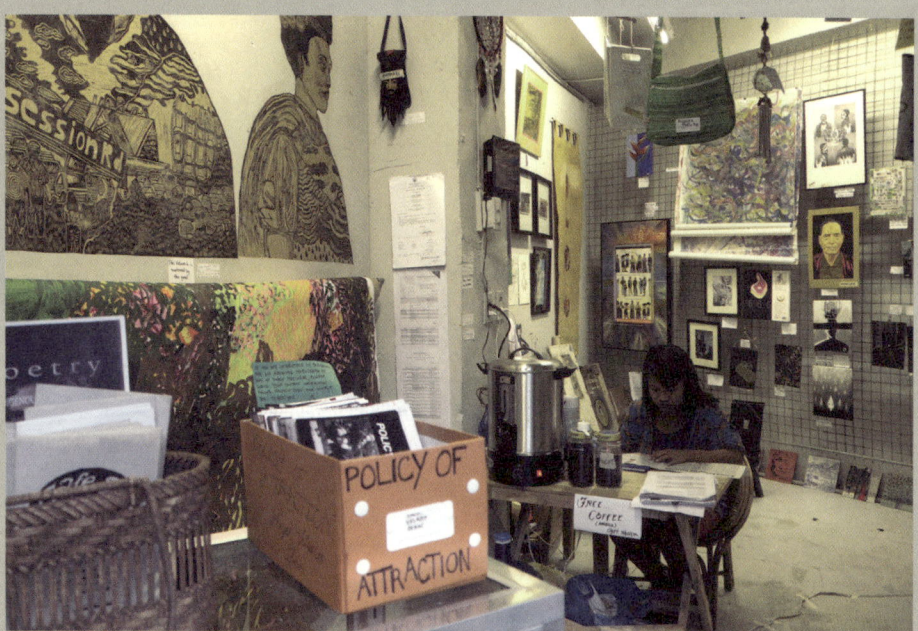

Photograph of one of *Markets of Resistance's* barter stalls at the Baguio City public market. Courtesy Angel Velasco Shaw.

MARKETS OF RESISTANCE

A Visual and Interdisciplinary Trade - Barter Exhibition
Baguio Market Art Stalls. Exhibitions. Music. Performances. Films. Installations

25 October - 9 November 2014

A multi-disciplinary collaborative art and cultural project between the Institute for Heritage, Culture and the Arts in the School of Fine Art and Design at Philippines Women's University and AX(iS) Art Project, spearheaded by Angel Velasco Shaw, Institute director, media artist, teacher, and cultural activist. Seventy plus SFAD students, Baguio and Manila artists, poets, scholars, and cultural community workers will launch a unique two-week exhibition in Baguio City market stalls — painting, photography, media installations, mixed media works, Zines, performances and a spoken word event.

The artworks will not be for sale in the traditional form of a monetary exchange. Instead, an interested buyer must negotiate with the artist about what she/he deems to be the equivalent value in terms of goods—the artists' needs in daily life (e.g. sack/s of rice, poultry, meat, coffee, pre-paid phone cards, houseware, children's necessities, clothing, etc.), which the customer must purchase themselves and then give it to the artist in exchange for hers/his artwork.

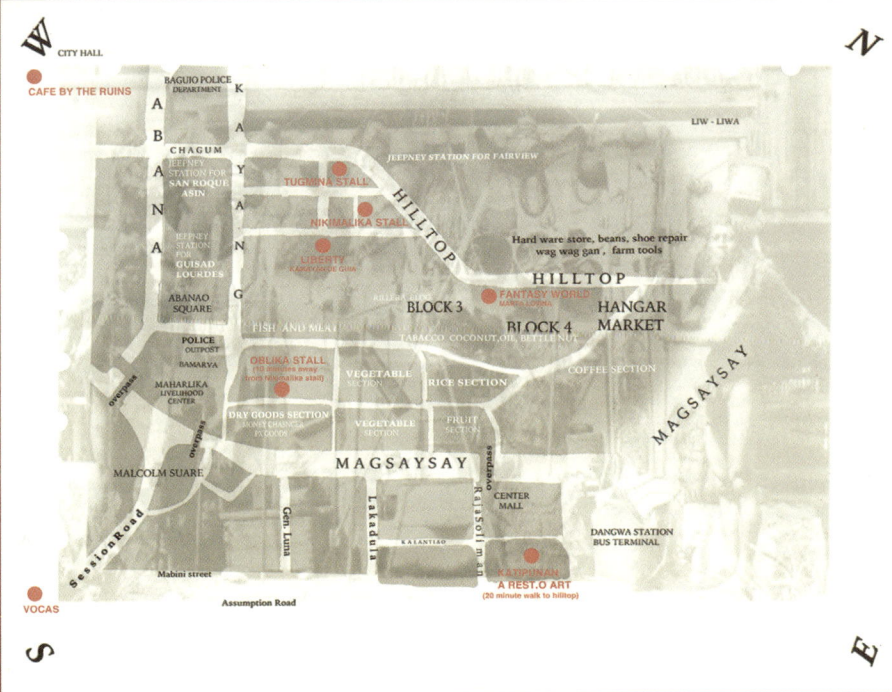

For more information contact
Project Manager: Rocky Cajigan:
Angel Velasco Shaw:
Facebook page: "Markets of Resistance"

Appendix C:

KABILBILIGAN (RE-IMAGINED): THE RESTORATION AND RE-IMAGINATION OF SANTIAGO BOSE'S MURAL

Saint Mary's School
Sagada, Mountain Province, Philippines

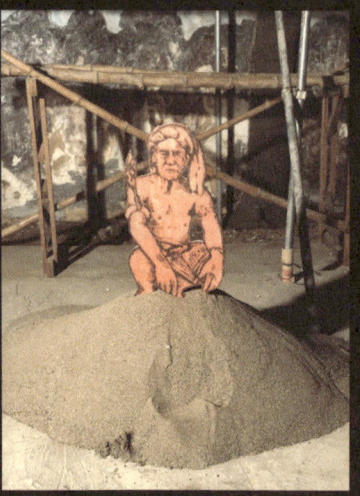

Created by Santiago Bose in the 1980s, **Kabilbiligan** is a mural spanning almost 50 feet in width on the ground floor façade of the Saint Mary's School quadrangle. The heavily-detailed work that took Bose three months to finish features mountain landscapes, indigenous locals, ritual activities, and collages of photographs and newspaper and magazine clippings emblematic of the social circumstances at the time of its creation. During the mural's completion, there was disagreement by Sagada locals over its inclusion of a portrait of the protest leader Macli-ing Dulag. Gulliermo (2010) says:

> "The mural, however, stirred controversy among the conservative sectors of the community. This was due to the inclusion of the well-loved pangat Macliing-Dulag who was killed by the military for leading the community's opposition to the building of Chico Dam, which would submerge their ancestral lands forever. When the conservatives effaced the portrait, activist youth sneaked in to restore it, this happening several times. Thus the mural became a symbolic site of the intense political struggle that was taking place in the region. (p. 75)"

This restoration/re-imagination project considers these historical details and responds to what Sagada represents today as a tourist town and in a postcolony within and beyond the breadth that Bose has depicted the Cordillera and its indigenous locals. Guillermo (2010) adds, "... [Bose] always nourished the hope that the people of the community would give it new life by copying it and adding their stories" (p.75).

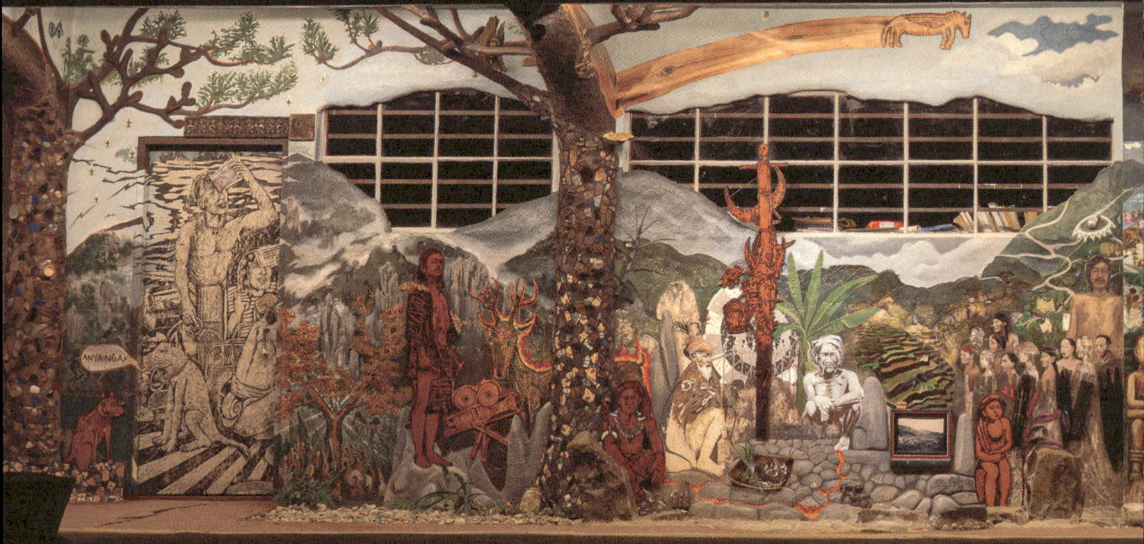

Prior to its restoration and re-imagination, the mural was in a crumbling state with many of the details unrecognizable and in many sections painted over through the years (including a previous restoration attempt). The process of establishing how much of the mural ought to be restored resulted in more re-imagining than strict restoration. In the spirit and fervor of the old Baguio Arts Guild that Bose co-founded, the mural involved the addition of work by many artists working in different media that, in many ways, mirror Bose's plethora of symbols found in his body of work. The re-imagined mural maintains Bose's dioramic composition but with works by artists who were close friends with Bose, including Tommy Hafalla, Leonard Aguinaldo, Jordan Mang-osan, John Frank Sabado, and younger Cordillera-based artists.

The project is a brainchild of Boy Yuchengco, who is a close friend of Santiago Bose and many Baguio artists, and whose family was responsible for the reconstruction of the Saint Mary's School's main building after it burned down in 1975. The restoration/re-imagination was spearheaded by Kawayan de Guia, a mentee to Bose, and documented by veteran journalist Rica Concepcion, a dear friend to Bose.

The re-imagined mural stands as a survey of the local history that Bose depicted and how that history has subverted, cradled, and re-imagined what the Cordillera indigenous is in relation to the world.

RAC, March 2020

Guillermo, A. (2010). History Writ Large. Pananaw, 7, 62-79.

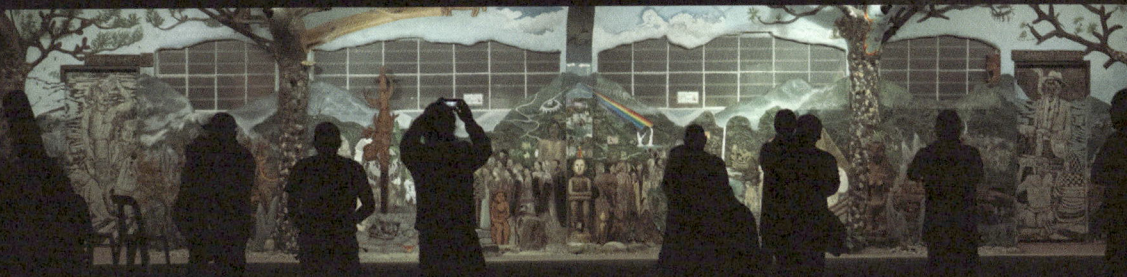

BOYU • AGGIE VILLARIN • BONG SANCHEZ • JOHN FRANK SABADO • SAGADA POTTERY AND TRAINING CENTER • KIGAO ROSIMO
ARSENIO HIMMIWAT • TOMMY HAFALLA • ISIDRO GAYO • NONA GARCIA • JAMES GAONGEN • DAPLI GAONGEN • JANET EASON
HIMALAYA NAVARRO • JORDAN MANG-OSAN • PERRY MAMARIL • GEMMA MALLILLIN • MARTA LOVINA • JOEY HIMMIWAT
GAWANI DOMOGO • KAWAYAN DE GUIA • RICA CONCEPCION • MARY CARLING • ROCKY CAJIGAN • RANDY BULAYO
SIEGRID BANGYAY • TESSIE BALDO • AKLAY • LEONARD AGUINALDO • CHAVI ROMAWAC • THOMAS KILLIP
SANTIAGO BOSE • WALLY BERNARDINO • ROMMEL BELTRAN • SANTOS BAYUCCA • ERNESTO BAUTISTA

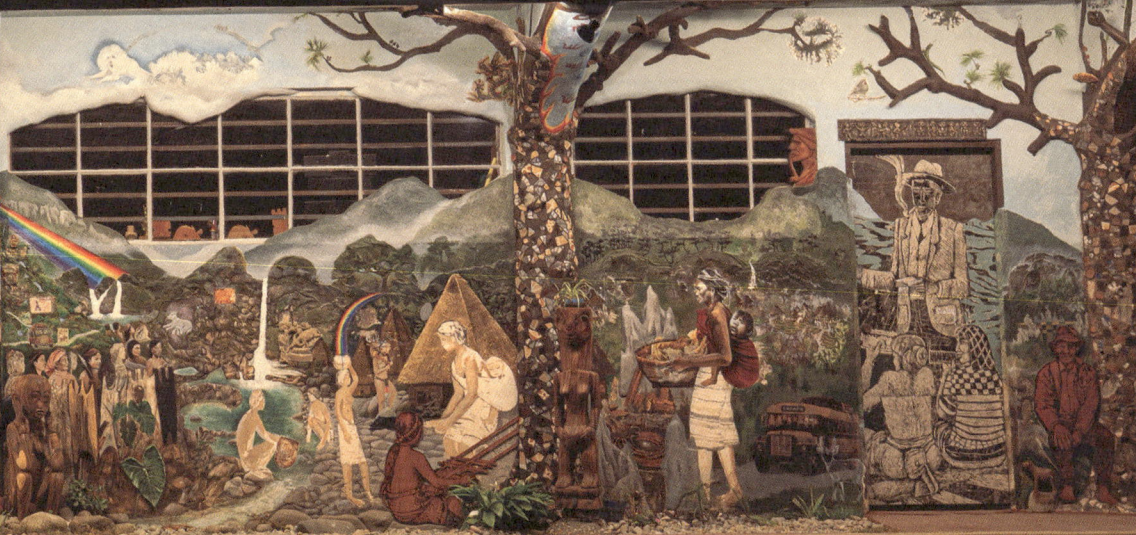

Top and bottom: Photographs of the newly restored *Kabilbiligan* Mural, 2020. Photographs by Kimberly dela Cruz.

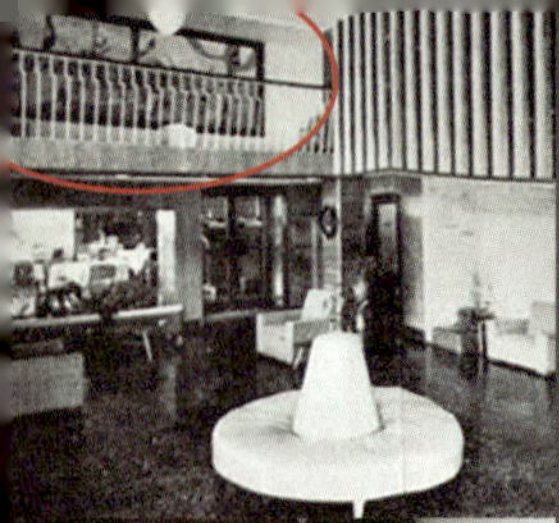

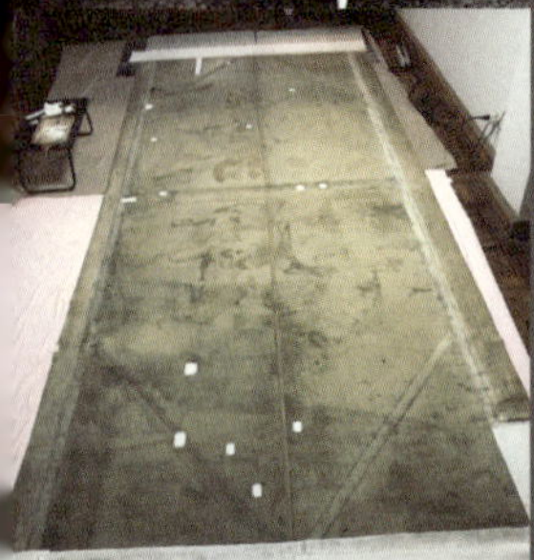

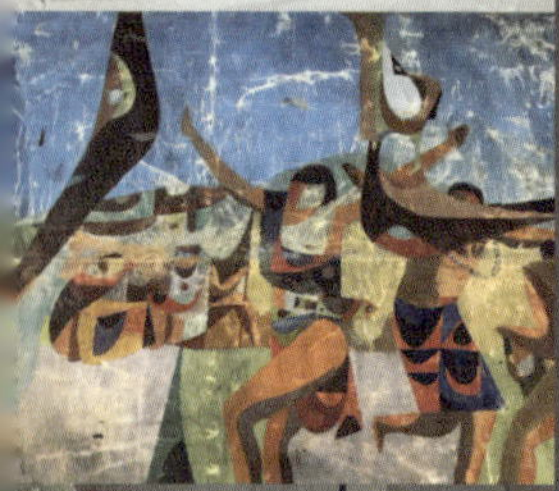

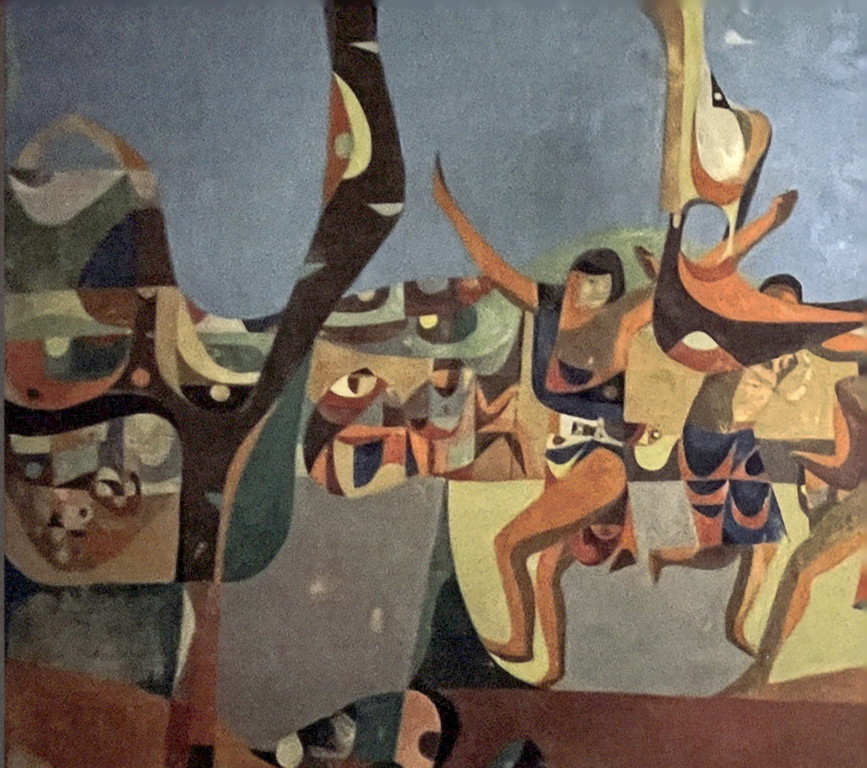

Photograph of the newly restored *Apo Kabunyan Cañao* Mural, 2021. Photograph by Mia Fokno.

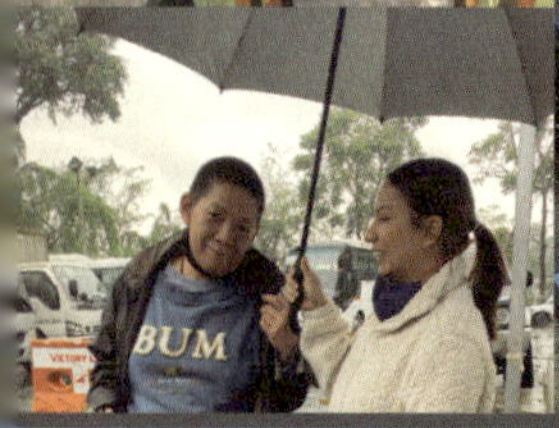

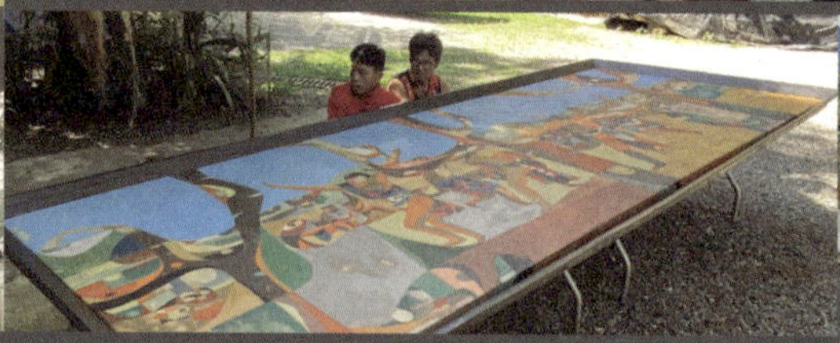

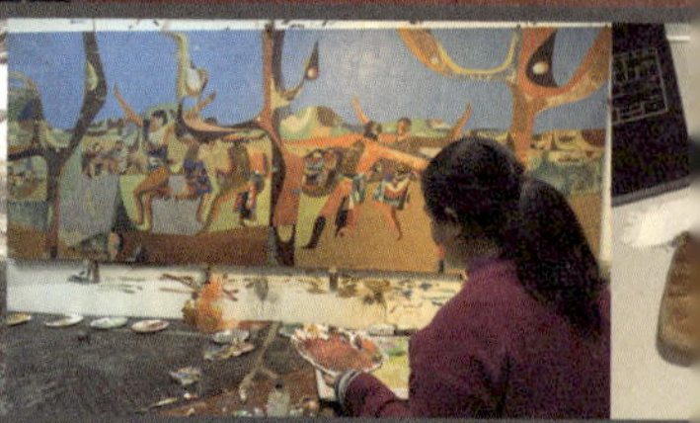

Appendix D:

FORGOTTEN MODERNISM

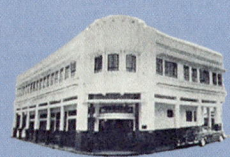

Once upon a time there was a place called "Sayote" Hotel. It was located inside the Bayanihan building, now the wagwagan epicenter of used clothes and assorted bric-a-brac. Over a hundred stalls crowd this beautiful art deco building across Burnham Park. Inside the building slept a modern masterpiece, a mural that, over time, was vandalized, cut, punched, spat on— name it and I'm sure this mural has experienced it.

During the days of intense pandemic lockdown, our good friend Ellen Lao approached Gail Vicente to look into restoring this painting that had been hanging on the stairwell of the Bayanihan for decades. Gail had just come back from New York City on an Asian Cultural Council grant to study archiving and art conservation. No one including Ellen knew who created the work. All we knew was that it was beat up and pretty much forgotten. Our hope was that once the work was cleaned, we would find clues.

Months go by and Gail was able to carefully wash off decades of grime. What was revealead to us was an image of a cañao, a feast with dancing figures in their loincloths playing gongs. At first, I really didn't think much of it. For me it looked generic for the type of work done in that era, which we presumed was the 50s. But as it lay in my studio, the work grew on me. Nona Garcia and I took to work on the painting, attempting to capture and apply the right shades of color where they had faded.

This painting was part of Victor Oteyza's era. He was part of the 13 Moderns, a band of artists that included Cesar Legaspi and HR Ocampo. This band broke away from the classically trained approach to art-making.

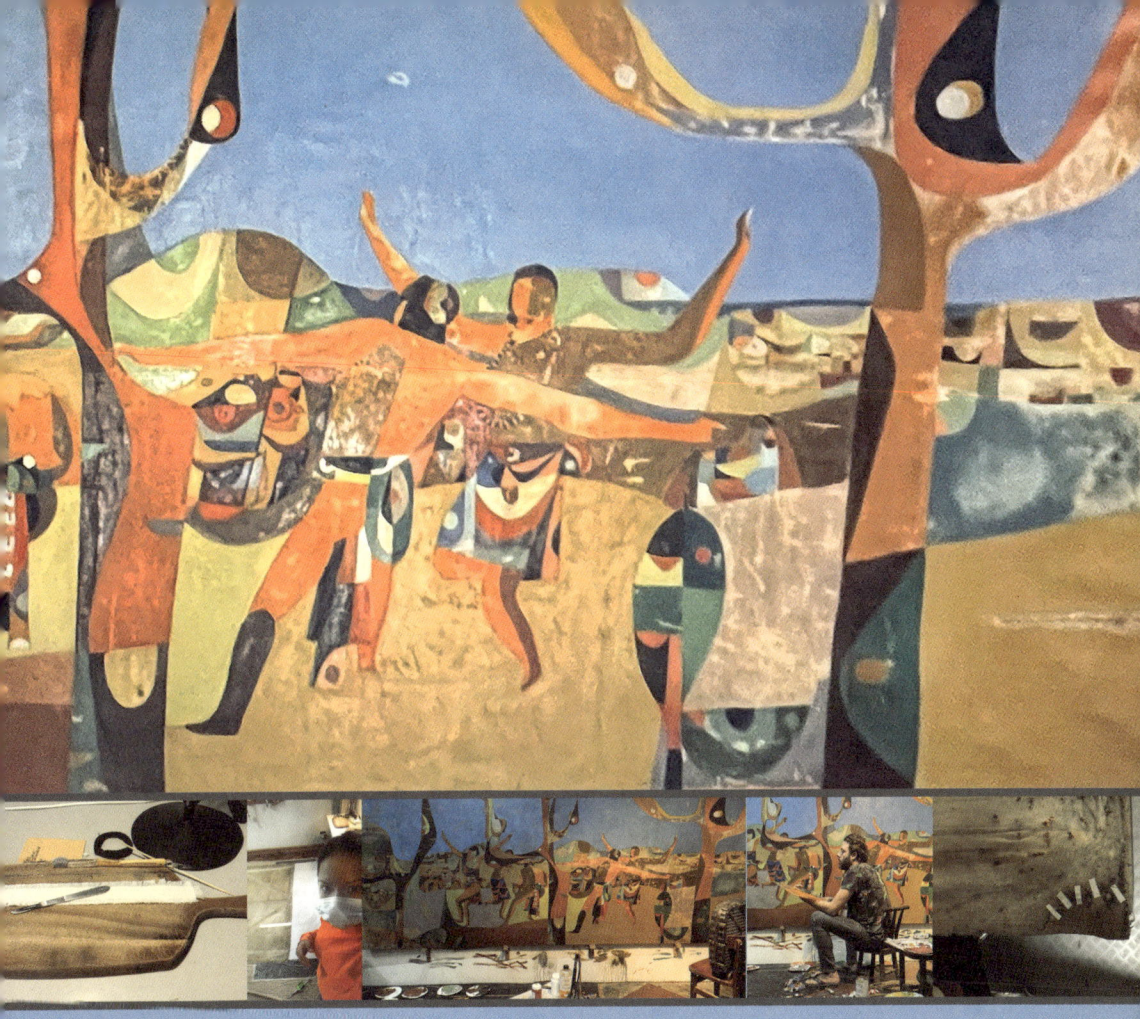

It was the late 40s. Everyone smoked cigarettes. Jazz played loud and the land lay in post-war ruin. This was the world they saw, that of the abstract. And so they depicted a reality born of a long and painful war. The lines they painted were bold, raw, and fearless, the colors extremely bright and loud, as if screaming with frantic life and emotion.

Looking at this newly re-surfaced mural, we felt the same cry—that of the proud, uncolonized people of the Cordilleras, captured in feast, in celebration. Could this be the work of Hugo Yonzon, who painted the mural on 500 Years of Philippine History for the Manila International Fair in 1953 and ten years later designed murals for the New York World Fair? The expert on Philippine art during the post-war years, Dr. Patrick Flores, thinks it highly probable. He pointed out several things to us during a brief video chat. First, that Yonzon was a muralist and that not everyone painted big at the time. Second, he saw the resemblance in the signature, which is almost impossible to make out on painting. Third, and to me the most striking, Yonzon's trademark raindrop-like drips or lines that he secretly placed throughout his works. I only noticed these once I started painting on the work. I wondered whether the blue drips were accidental remnants of a messy paint job at the Bayanihan building.

After getting in touch with the family of the late Hugo Yonzon, his son was quite sure it wasn't his dad's because of the way the limbs were painted. He suggested that it may be Elmer Abustan's work. Elmer was his father's friend, a painter but more known as a Komiks cartoonist in the 40s and 50s.

What happened here with the mural, which we will now call *Apo Kabunyan Cañao*, is not a restoration job. The process for a proper restoration job would be all too sophisticated. Rather, this was an intervention by Gail Vicente, Nona Garcia, and myself to save and enhance a beautiful work of art and bring it back to its former glory. It matters not whether the artist is known. Today in front of us is a sublime testament to the land and people of the Cordilleras. Like the culture which inspired it, this mural will survive these changing times.

KDG, Baguio City, December 7, 2021

Appendix E:
"SAVE THE BAGUIO MARKET" EXHIBITION

People's Park, Baguio City, Philippines

In February 2021, as the COVID-19 pandemic crisis remained unmitigated, the city government of Baguio was caught in a public uproar as plans to develop the Baguio City Public Market revealed a strong possibility of offering the project to two mall chains. One was especially favored after its unsolicited proposal was granted an original proponent status, the first steps in a public-private partnership.

The process disregarded the city government and its public collaborators—its residents, the ability to develop community-based programs in helping rehabilitate its much beloved market. In many political

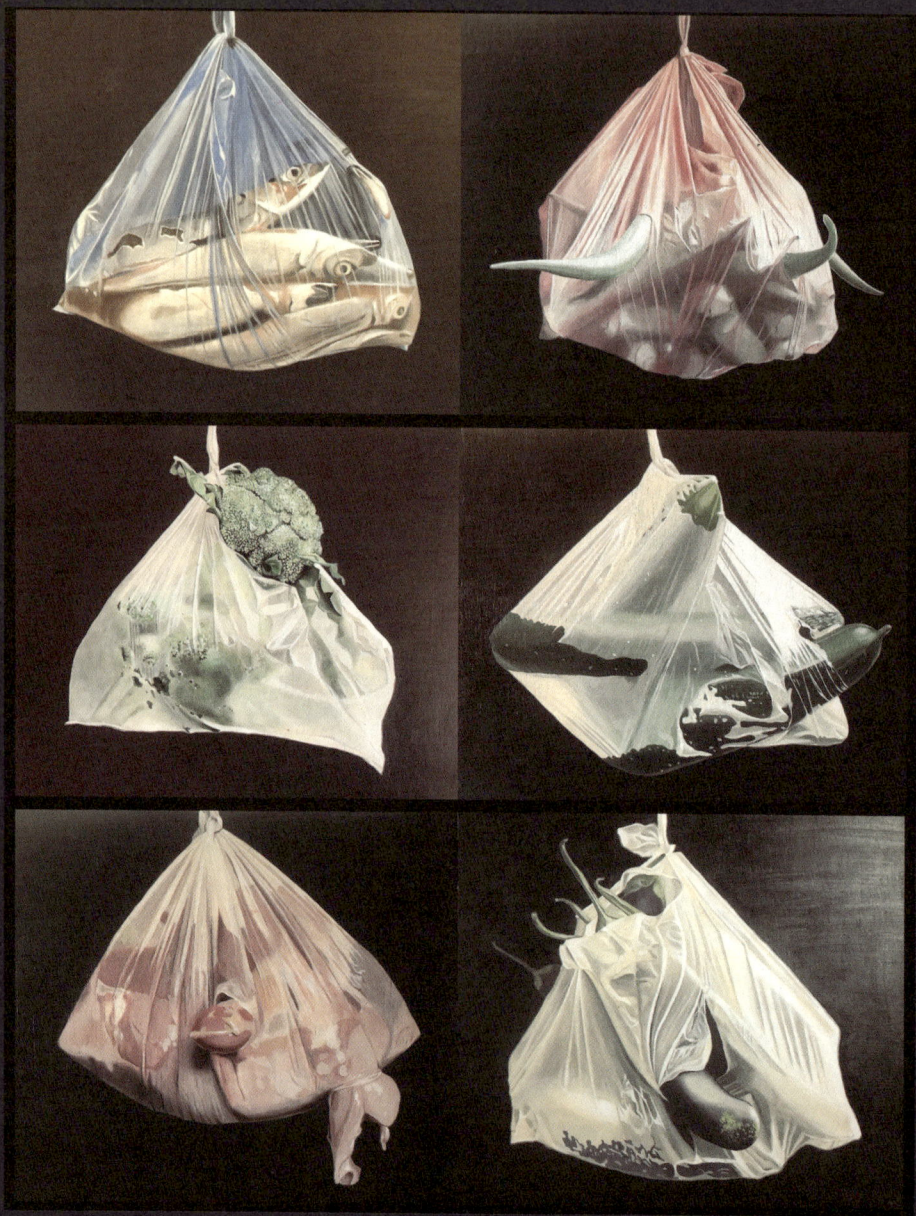

Ration Series by Rocky Cajigan, acrylic on plywood, 2020. Courtesy Rocky Cajigan.

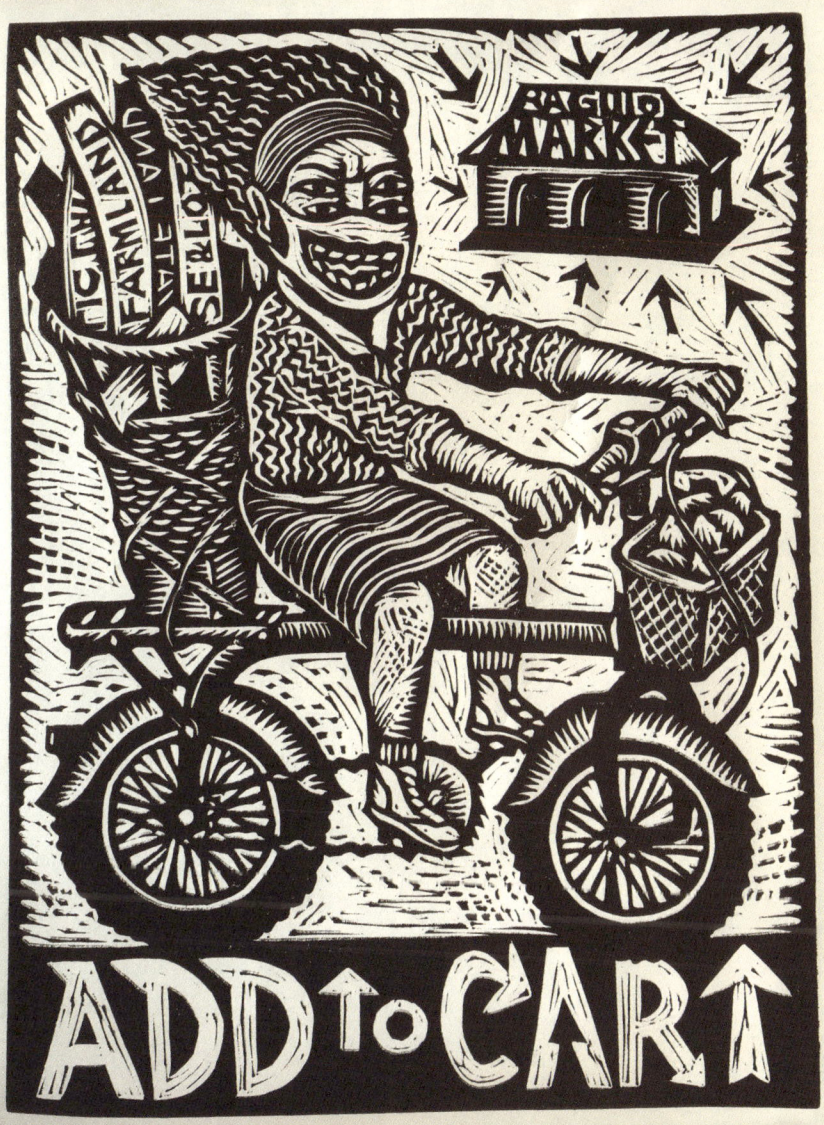

Artwork by Leonard Aguinaldo, 2021.

calendars, a public-private partnership for developing public spaces is often favored. It easily ticks a politician's checklist of 'legacy' projects. It also favors big business much like a catch and kill. It catches cooperatives from gaining access to big capital, and it kills all possibility of a free and thriving local business community which, to many families, migrants, traders, workers, students, teachers, doctors, lawyers, nuns, nurses, engineers, storytellers, elders, arists, and many who belong to this piece of mountain land, is the heart of Baguio City.

The exhibition was put up strategically at the People's Park since a public gathering was not possible due to the pandemic. Apart from this and until today, the authoritarian political climate also ensures a protest rights crisis through militaristic and repressive programs.

In recognition of the continuing efforts of the many who stand against tyranny, the *"Save the Baguio Market" Exhibition* honors the freedoms the market historically and presently represents. RAC.

We are the Mercator

The word 'market' is derived from the Latin word 'Mercatus' which means to trade, merchandise, or a place where business is transacted.

Maybe 'mercator' also shares the same root. Mercator, being a map where the meridians meet. While we are grappling with the pandemic, the city is rushing the sale of our 100-year-old market to a mall which already failed in its promise for a green mall—and all those lies.

We spent our lives in the Baguio City Market.
In fact, we don't even regard the market in the etymological root above.

We don't just do trade or business there.
We pass by there, meet there, eat there, date there, fight there, fall in love there, sell there.

As Gertrude Stein said, there's no there there. We are all 'naderder.'

When the market needed us, we were there. When it was carpet-bombed, we revived it.

When it was gutted by fire a couple of times, we killed the fire and revived the market.

When the market was sold, we prayed and the souls of those who sold it are now there at the gates of Hell. God knows what God will do to those who are doing the same again.

So now we're back here again, fighting for our stinky market.
No matter, this is better than a perfumed nightmare.

We will stand by it and hold our stories and art like ungainly guns to hold the fort.

FYC, Baguio City, March 12, 2021

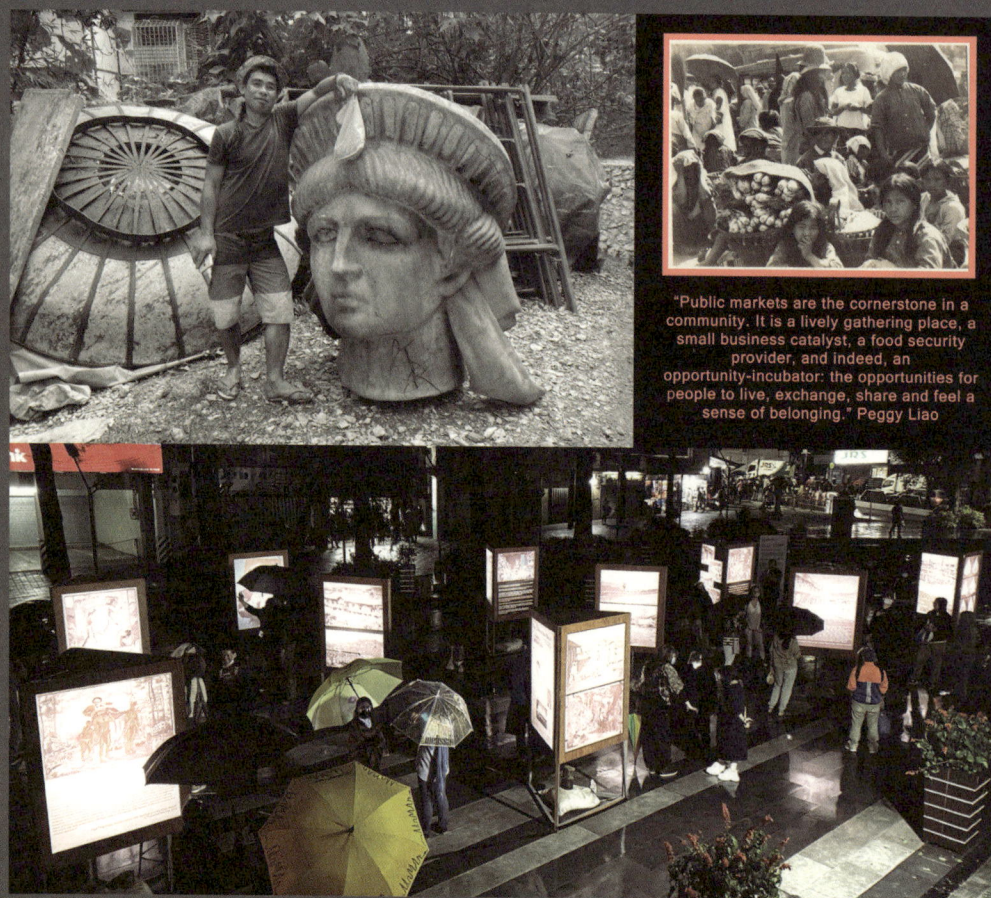

"Public markets are the cornerstone in a community. It is a lively gathering place, a small business catalyst, a food security provider, and indeed, an opportunity-incubator: the opportunities for people to live, exchange, share and feel a sense of belonging." Peggy Liao

Top left: Photograph of parts of Kawayan de Guia's *Liberating a Fall* previously installed at the Baguio City Public Market for *Markets of Resistance* in 2014. Courtesy Kawayan de Guia.
Top right: One of the the posters included in a series of lightboxes for the *Save the Baguio Market* art exhibition in 2021.
Bottom: Installation view of the *Save the Baguio Market* art exhibition in 2021. Courtesy Kawayan de Guia.

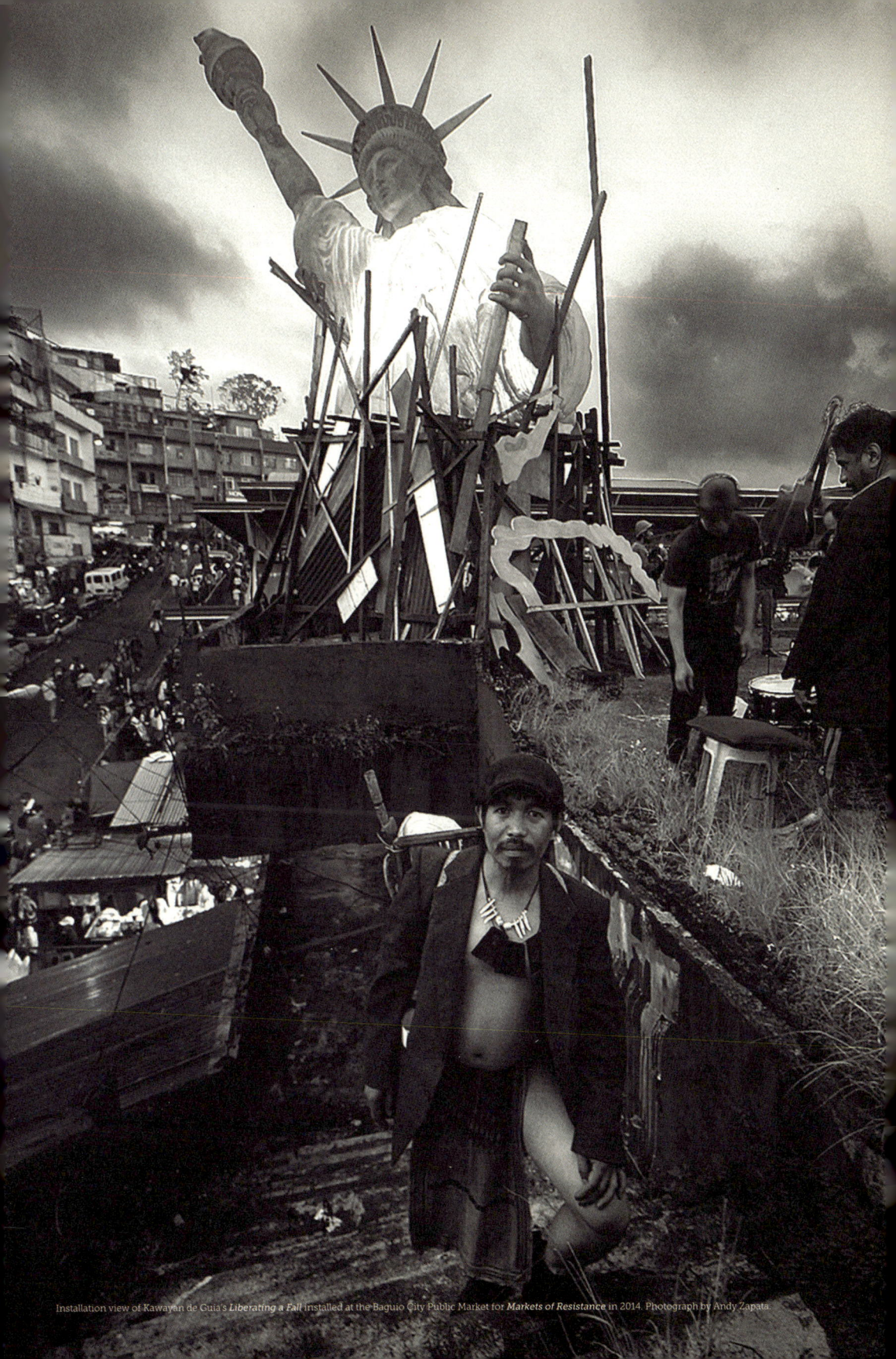

Installation view of Kawayan de Guia's *Liberating a Fall* installed at the Baguio City Public Market for *Markets of Resistance* in 2014. Photograph by Andy Zapata.

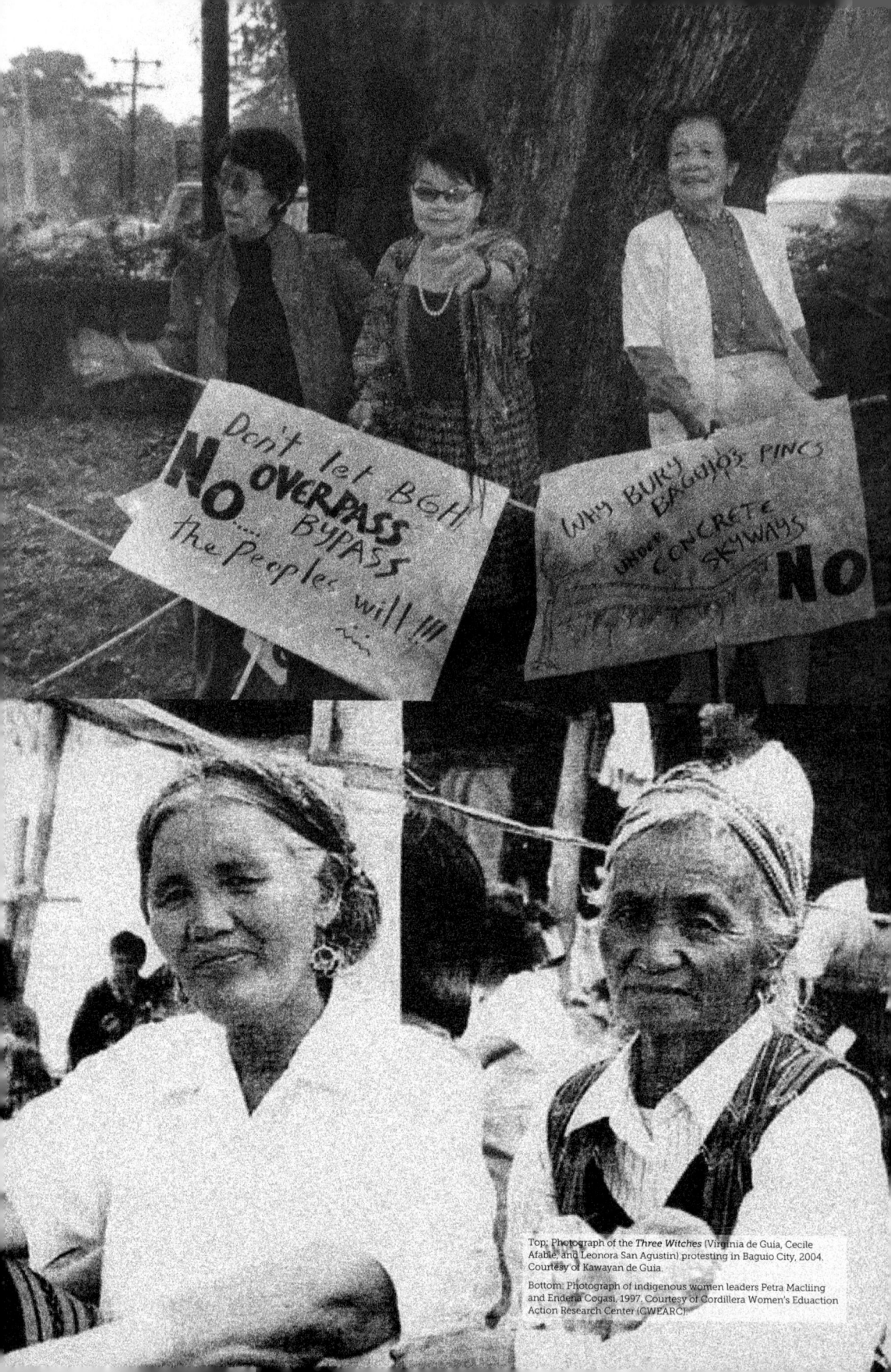

Top: Photograph of the *Three Witches* (Virginia de Guia, Cecile Afable, and Leonora San Agustin) protesting in Baguio City, 2004. Courtesy of Kawayan de Guia.

Bottom: Photograph of indigenous women leaders Petra Macliing and Enderia Cogasi, 1997. Courtesy of Cordillera Women's Eduaction Action Research Center (CWEARC).

MATCHBOXES

Come through my window, ocean of breaths
that hangs above the city, exhaled
from a matchbox stacked with a hundred
thousand other matchboxes of breath
on the moonlit knuckles of the mountain,
each one lonely.
                      Nonetheless the sky
is shared, above Poliwes, up through
San Vincente, the night is breathed out
piece by piece from all our other lungs,
flesh-touched, and patchworked, fractals from tree ferns,
which breathe, uncurl and curl, tight inside
each of our animal chests.
                      I ache,
to need this, backwashed murmur of life,
the window aches for every other light-
bulb-glowing window's mouth, the room
in echoed air exists with every room
collected through my life, where I've been
lonely, which I cannot leave, have never
left, only carried each one with me
and nested it inside the next.
                      Houses
of sediments and silted hours,
always, in corners between these walls,
the work spreads on the floor, the remains
of flowers, food-scrap plates beside torn
paper, regretted drafts, and unhung
towels still wet from the shower, all
stale, all samely, all unfinished things
which forget ourselves.
                      Far off, over, through
the matchbox roads and the bent bamboo,
Baguio is smudged by dreaming lamps
until the pastel times of morning.
The washed out electric slowly blooms,
becoming drowned in dawn, it swallows,
and moves, it bleeds through the parking ranks,
the rice depot, the manure trucks,
the spaces of time when each penciled
building discloses a quiet life
of private light like a cracked fridge door
across the gap.
                      Across the distance.

                                                      ALC, September 2022

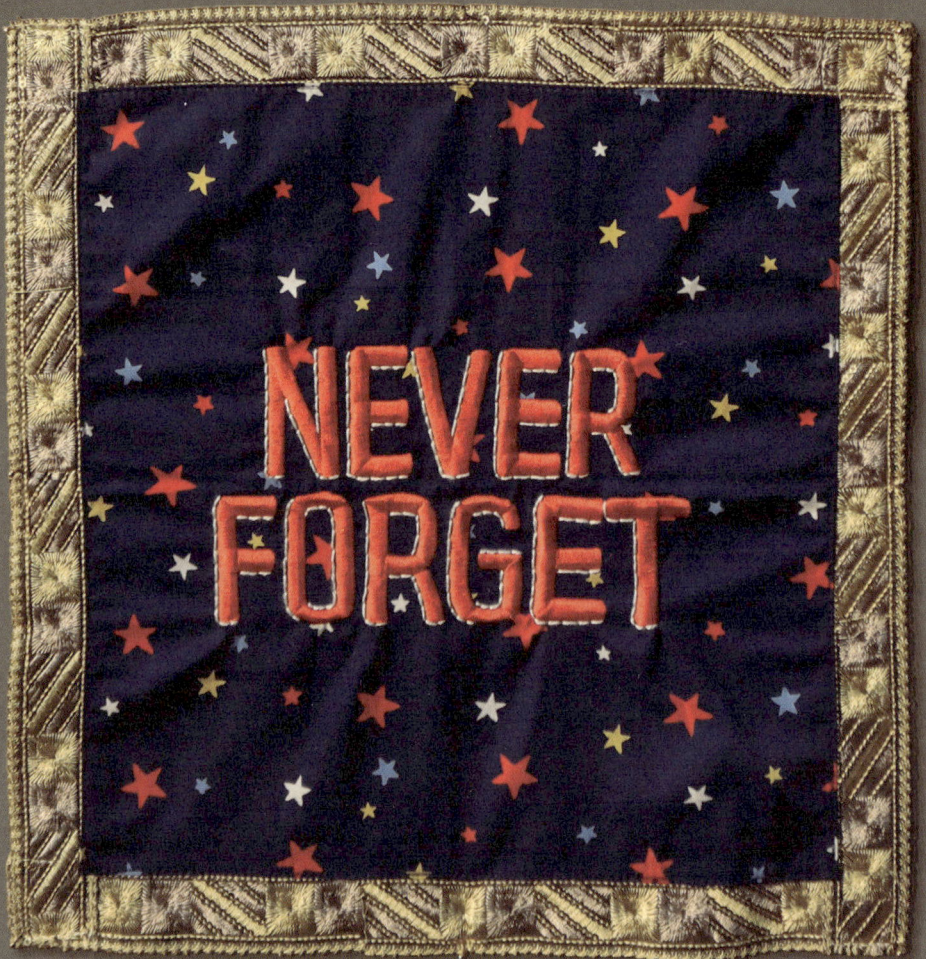

Mad Banner 1: Never Forget by Gail Vicente, mixed media, 2021. Courtesy Gail Vicente.